THE EASTER RISING

M ICHAEL T. F OY & B RIAN B ARTON

The History Press

The authors would like to dedicate this book to the memories of Beatrice Foy and Ivy Barton.

First published 1999
This edition published 2011

The History Press
The Mill, Brimscombe Port
Stroud, Gloucestershire, GL5 2QG
www.thehistorypress.co.uk

© Michael T. Foy & Brian Barton, 1999, 2000, 2004, 2011

British Library Cataloguing in Publication Data.
A catalogue record for this book is available from the British Library.

ISBN 978 0 7524 5703 1

Typesetting and origination by The History Press
Printed in Great Britain

Contents

Authors' Note

The first edition of this book was based on an exhaustive and unrivalled range of primary sources such as letters, diaries and accounts by participants and spectators, many of them hitherto unused. The key development since, which has made this new edition necessary, has been the release in 2004 by the Bureau of Military History of almost 2,000 witness statements written by participants in the events of 1912–21. Closed for roughly sixty years, they are a treasure trove of information and full of dramatic incident. They provide stunningly graphic accounts of a capital city at war, depict vividly the personalities and actions of the leaders on both sides and of the rank and file, and resolve many previously unanswered questions about the Rising. This new edition draws heavily on many hundreds of the most significant of these witness statements. It also draws on, and integrates this with, a considerable range of other, hitherto neglected, primary sources which have recently come to light and are located in the Irish National Library, the Irish National Archives and the Allen Library, Dublin. The consequence is that the text takes the reader closer to the events than was possible previously. Its content is genuinely encapsulated by its title: *The Easter Rising*.

In 1916 the main thoroughfare of Dublin was officially called Sackville Street. However, many inhabitants knew it as O'Connell Street, a name to which it was eventually changed. It is referred to as O'Connell Street throughout this book.

Acknowledgements

We again owe a deep debt of gratitude to Walter Grey with whom we worked closely on the first edition of this book; he was also responsible for drawing the maps. During the writing of this major revision, Walter once more made readily available to us his unsurpassed knowledge of Dublin, directed us to a number of important sources, read the manuscript with meticulous care and suggested many important revisions. As before, his imperturbable good humour, constant encouragement and unrivalled erudition enlivened many discussions during the writing of the text. We also thank Stewart Roulston of the History Department at Methodist College, Dr Timothy Bowman of the History Department at the University of Kent and Michelle Brown for reading and commenting on the text.

In particular, Brian would like to express gratitude to his wife, Valerie, who proof-read and commented on every chapter, and to Ray Bateson who provided invaluable information regarding insurgent fatalities resulting from the Rising.

In addition, we both wish to thank the trustees, archivists and staff at the many archive centres which we visited when conducting our research for their generous advice and assistance. Most notably, the staff of the Military Archives, Cathal Brugha Barracks, Dublin, were heroic in providing us with many copies of Bureau of Military History witness statements, often at short notice. They are Commandant Victor Laing (Officer in Charge), Captain Stephen MacEoin (Second-in-Command), Mr Hugh Beckett (Archivist), Mrs Lisa Dolan (Archivist), Ms Noelle Grothier (Archivist), Private Alan Manning (Archive Assistant) and Private Adrian Short (Archive Assistant).

We are also deeply indebted to the staff at the National Library of Ireland, Dublin; the National Archives of Ireland, Dublin; the Allen Library, North Richmond Street, Dublin; the Archives Department, University College, Dublin; the Manuscripts Department, Trinity College, Dublin; the Public Record Office, London; and the Bodleian Library, Oxford. Every effort has been made to trace the copyright holders of the various primary sources used; in the instances where this search has been unsuccessful, we offer our most sincere apologies.

We owe a profound debt of gratitude to our publishers, The History Press, especially to Simon Hamlet who commissioned this new edition of the book, to our editors Abbie Wood and Christine McMorris and to our proofreader Lindsey Smith.

Finally, we are extremely grateful to Helen Litton, who compiled the index so professionally, to Edmund Ross, Grafton Street, Dublin, who expertly reproduced the photographs used to illustrate the text, and Risteard Mulcahy for copies of the tape recordings made by his father Richard Mulcahy.

Michael T. Foy and Brian Barton
2011

Michael T. Foy is a former Head of History at Methodist College, Belfast, and Tutor in Irish History, Queen's University, Belfast. He has written *Michael Collins's Intelligence War: The Struggle between the British and the IRA 1919–1921*, published both in hardback and paperback by The History Press.

Brian Barton was a Senior Research Fellow in Irish History and Politics at Queen's University Belfast, and is now a tutor in History at the Open University. He has written *The Secret Court Martial Records of the Easter Rising*, a new edition of which was published by the History Press in April 2010.

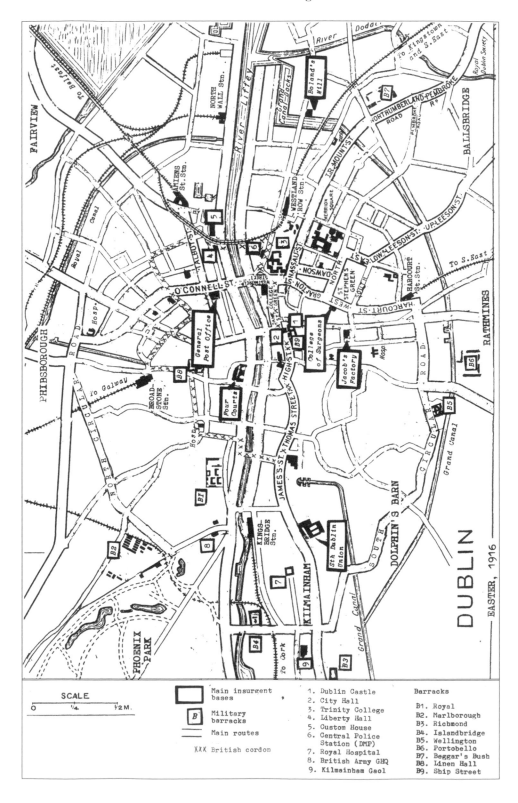

SCALE

0   ¼   ½ M.

☐ Main insurgent bases

B Military barracks

— Main routes

XXX British cordon

1. Dublin Castle
2. City Hall
3. Trinity College
4. Liberty Hall
5. Custom House
6. Central Police Station (DMP)
7. Royal Hospital
8. British Army GHQ
9. Kilmainham Gaol

Barracks

B1. Royal
B2. Marlborough
B3. Richmond
B4. Islandbridge
B5. Wellington
B6. Portobello
B7. Beggar's Bush
B8. Linen Hall
B9. Ship Street

DUBLIN
— EASTER, 1916 —

The Planning of the Easter Rising: Part One

The Easter Rising of 1916 was planned and carried out by a secret revolutionary organisation, the Irish Republican Brotherhood (IRB) and, in particular, a small Military Council of its leaders: Tom Clarke, Sean MacDermott, Patrick Pearse, Eamonn Ceannt, Joseph Plunkett and Thomas MacDonagh. In January 1916 they also formed an alliance with the radical socialist James Connolly who had established an Irish Citizen Army dedicated to a workers' republic but ultimately made common cause with this group of conservative nationalists in order to overthrow British rule in Ireland.

Serious IRB preparations for a rising began only with the outbreak of the First World War but, in one sense, a rebellion had been in the making ever since the organisation was founded in 1858. There had been previous revolutionary attempts to establish an Irish republic, all of them unsuccessful. The Rising of 1798, inspired by Wolfe Tone's Society of United Irishmen, had assumed serious proportions in various places, including Ulster. Those of 1803 and 1848 were miserable failures and while initially the IRB's extensive 'Fenian Conspiracy' in 1867 had seemed dangerous, it too failed ignominiously. But they all left behind potent symbols and memories and the republican revolutionary tradition was never completely eradicated.

With no realistic prospect of revolution during the next decades, the IRB supported Charles Stewart Parnell's Home Rule movement as the best available strategy for undermining British authority. However, even that limited ambition collapsed with Parnell's fall in 1891 and the defeat two years later of a Home Rule Bill for Ireland. During the early 1880s the IRB's sister organisation in America, Clan na Gael, concentrated on a dynamiting campaign in England that had Londoners living under daily threat as bombs exploded at the Tower of London, London Bridge, left-luggage rooms and tunnels in the underground railway system. Eventually Special Branch arrests ended the bombings.

In the early twentieth century the IRB began rejuvenating alongside a cultural and intellectual renaissance in Irish nationalism as many younger nationalists diverted their energies into the Gaelic League and Gaelic Athletic Association, which in turn became IRB recruiting grounds. This new dynamism originated in Belfast where it was driven by Denis McCullough and Bulmer Hobson.[1] They seemed most unlikely

political allies. McCullough was the son of a veteran republican and a Catholic educated by the Christian Brothers, while Hobson came from a middle-class Quaker
family and had attended Friends' School Lisburn, where his study of Irish history
had converted him into a disciple of Wolfe Tone. Despite an austere, intellectual and
rather priggish personality, Hobson soon revealed himself to be a formidable organiser and a prolific journalist and propagandist. He was also a talented platform speaker,
capable of popularising ideas and supporting his arguments with a multitude of facts
and figures assembled through what his biographer has called a 'voracious appetite
for researching topics'.[2] Drawing lessons from Irish history, Hobson was constantly
seeking 'a line of action which was neither abject surrender nor futile insurrection'.[3]
Once he settled on that line Hobson pursued it with great single-mindedness and a
self-righteousness and inflexibility that were always likely to aggravate his IRB colleagues. In March 1908 Hobson moved to Dublin where, by the eve of the First World
War, he had had become arguably the most important – and certainly widest known
– republican leader. With seemingly boundless energy Hobson was 'at the apex of his
IRB career'[4] as chairman of its Dublin Centres Board, editor of the organisation's
journal, *Irish Freedom*, and member of the Supreme Council. In the capital Hobson
worked closely with two allies, Tom Clarke and Sean MacDermott, and the story of
Irish republicanism up to the Easter Rising was largely shaped by their fluctuating
relationships; an association that began harmoniously but ultimately imploded into
mutual loathing and an enmity that knew no cease.

Clarke was born in 1857 in the British military barracks on the Isle of Wight, the
son of an English army sergeant married to a woman from Tipperary.[5] The family
eventually settled in Dungannon, Co. Tyrone, where Tom became involved in various
nationalist societies and was sworn into the IRB by John Daly, a prominent republican. In search of employment, Clarke emigrated to New York where he met John
Devoy, leader of the Clan na Gael. Soon the organisation sent him to England on a
bombing mission which British agents infiltrated from the very start; Clarke's arrest
was inevitable. At the Old Bailey in May 1883 he conducted his own defence, but after
deliberating for just over an hour the jury found him and three fellow defendants
guilty of treason. When the judge sentenced them to penal servitude for life Clarke
shouted to him: 'Goodbye! We shall meet in heaven.' He remembered being 'hustled
out of the dock into the prison van, surrounded by a troop of mounted police, and
driven at a furious pace through the howling mob that thronged the streets from the
Courthouse to Millbank Prison. London was panic-stricken at the time'.[6]

Like all other Irish 'Special Men', Clarke was soon transferred to Chatham Prison,
the British equivalent of Devil's Island. Usually there was no hope of release for twenty
years and he endured a Calvary of 'relentless savagery' that involved physical hardship,
perpetual silence, intellectual starvation and mental and emotional desolation. This
regime was specifically designed to crush a prisoner's body and spirit, something in
which it normally succeeded well. Two fellow defendants went mad and the third
was only released because of a serious heart condition. During three months of one
cold winter Clarke spent forty days of punishment in the so-called Arctic cell, recall-
ing later that 'the horrors of those nights and days will never leave my memory'.[7] He
avoided insanity through his 'unconquerable will',[8] endlessly practising mathematical
calculation by counting the number of bricks in cells, bolts on doors and arrows

and buttons on inmates' clothes. Clarke's salvation came suddenly in 1898 through a government amnesty. He re-emerged as a terribly damaged man, physically wizened, prematurely aged, socially inept, paralysingly shy and filled with hatred for British politicians and British rule in Ireland which he blamed for robbing him of the best years of his life. Yet at the same time he was also now a man 'steeled and hardened, the embodiment of Fenianism, an impregnable rock',[9] convinced that he had survived for a purpose. Now more than ever committed to revolution, Clarke simply decided that he would start all over again.

Initially, Clarke didn't envisage himself as the actual leader of a movement, and making his way to the summit of republicanism involved him in a long and somewhat twisted journey. Returning to Ireland in 1899, he fell in love with Kathleen Daly, the 21-year-old niece of his old friend John Daly. By marrying her Clarke was really joining a political clan and in Kathleen he had found a perfect soulmate whose ferocious political commitment matched his own, who worshipped him and gave him the support that sustained him for the rest of his life. In a later age she would have sat in her own right on the IRB's Supreme Council. In 1900 Clarke emigrated once again from Ireland, partly to get a job but also because of his disappointment at the republican movement's failure to strike a blow during England's entanglement in the Boer War. By 1901 he was working in a New York pump room while serving his political apprenticeship under John Devoy, who was still the Clan leader. Devoy proved to be an excellent mentor who taught Clarke much about leadership and together they established a republican newspaper, the *Gaelic American*, with Tom as its general manager. By now Clarke was developing into an increasingly self-confident operator, a skilled organiser, manipulator and propagandist. However, by 1907 Kathleen's temporary ill health had forced him to resign from the *Gaelic American* and move his family to a farm. When American newspapers began speculating about a coming Anglo-German war Tom decided to return home to be ready for such an opportunity. Although Kathleen would have happily stayed she knew that for her husband 'everything began and ended with Ireland and her freedom'.[10] The birth of the first of their three sons was a double delight for Tom because 'having a son to follow him to carry on the fight for Ireland's freedom was almost too good to be true'.[11] The Clarke who landed at Cork in November 1907 was very different from the naïve young man of a quarter of a century earlier. Now more rounded and experienced, with Devoy's endorsement, he brought with him a vision of rejuvenating the Irish Republican Brotherhood by recruiting men of action and setting it on a course to revolution.

Clarke was soon co-opted on to the Supreme Council, and he carried on his political activities discreetly from a tobacconist's shop that he set up at 75a Parnell Street. This apparently humdrum public front for his subterranean activities suited him very well because as a 'ticket-of-leave' man he could be returned to jail instantly if he too blatantly violated the terms of his amnesty. Clarke's charisma and implacable purpose rapidly made him an iconic figure, someone whose sacrifices and triumphant survival were inspirational; a towering personality whose shop became almost a shrine to republicans from all over Ireland.

The store was of a size that did not permit more than half a dozen men to stand in front of the counter at a time. There was just about enough space between the counter and the wall for two men to walk in together. Along the wall were arranged all of the important Dublin and Irish newspapers, weekly and monthly periodicals, and so forth. Behind the short and narrow counter was a large assortment of brands of tobacco, cigars, pipes and cigarettes, with a sideline of stationery. The window was occupied mainly by a cardboard representation of an Irish round tower, advertising the Banba brand of Irish tobacco. Both the window and the store itself were brilliantly lighted, and the whole place suggested care and attention and spotless cleanliness.

But the store and its attractiveness were forgotten after the first glance at the man who stood behind the counter. Of medium height, with grey hair thinning away from the temples, dark blue eyes deeply sunken under shaggy brows and high cheekbones standing up in startling prominence from thin, sunken cheeks, the general appearance of the man was keenness personified. Seemingly nearing his seventies, he was, nevertheless, possessed of a force and vigour that might well have been envied by men in their early thirties. The truth was that the man was in the prime of life. Brutality and confinement, however, had left on his features a mark that death alone could remove, but had been powerless to subdue the fire that glowed within and animated every thought and action of his life.[12]

Another visitor recalled Clarke's piercing eyes and the assiduous manner in which he collected information: 'He knew what was taking place in all Irish organisations as the IRB had members in all, but to the stranger he knew nothing outside the news in the press.'[13]

It took a few years for Clarke to winkle out those leaders who had presided over the IRB's decline, but in that time he protected and advanced talented younger protégés. Clarke also revived the pilgrimage to Wolfe Tone's grave at Bodenstown, organised an annual commemoration of Robert Emmet's birth and in 1911 inspired the founding of *Irish Freedom*, a journal whose influence far exceeded its circulation. By then his drive and vision had brought him to the top of the republican movement.

With Sean MacDermott he also established the political friendship of his life, a somewhat unlikely partnership that more than any other inspired the Easter Rising.[14] MacDermott was born the son of a farmer in 1884 in Co. Leitrim, and after leaving home at 15 he had worked successively in Glasgow and then Belfast as a gardener, tram-conductor and barman. Politically he began as a Home Ruler but graduated to revolutionary conspiracy and made a single-minded, lifelong commitment to Irish independence. After joining the IRB in 1906 MacDermott was soon demonstrating formidable energy, drive and self-discipline, as well as a talent for organisation and manipulation. A gregarious nature and considerable charm made everyone around him feel at home although he never for a moment relaxed his own rigid self-control. Even MacDermott's girlfriend, Min Ryan, recognised his caginess; an inability to lower his guard even among people he trusted completely: 'Secrecy was his watchword; he never talked of the business he did with others. I feel certain he has gone to his grave with more of the secrets of how the whole plan was developed than any other leader.'[15] MacDermott exuded charisma, a handsome man with jet black hair, a high forehead and a firm jaw that suggested determination and power. A highly effective, often passionate public speaker; his whole frame would shake with emotion as he denounced British imperialism, and although he wasn't particularly well read MacDermott did know his Irish history, enabling him to weave into his speeches and journalism references to Tone and Emmet and books like John Mitchel's *Jail Journal*.

In early 1908 MacDermott moved from Belfast to Dublin where Tom Clarke recruited him as a national organiser for the IRB. Superficially they seemed very different, separated in age by more than a quarter of a century and with dissimilar personalities; one suspicious, introverted and virtually tongue-tied, the other sparkling, fluent and physically dynamic. But they complemented each other perfectly and established an unshakeable bond in which Clarke treated MacDermott with almost paternal affection while facilitating his protégé's rise within the IRB. Soon MacDermott was on the Supreme Council and later became editor of *Irish Freedom*. Between 1908 and 1912 this secretive, manipulative and relentless pair (co-operating closely with Bulmer Hobson) revitalised the IRB, shaping its policies and promoting talented, like-minded individuals. And yet a suspicion lingers that MacDermott was also using Clarke; that with his nose for power and the icy calculation beneath his smile he realised that through the older man lay his road straight to the heart of republicanism. In 1911, however, he suffered a temporary setback when his extensive travelling throughout Ireland for the IRB left him physically and emotionally drained and possibly vulnerable to the polio virus that he now contracted. From this MacDermott emerged looking somewhat aged, frail and lame in his right leg, dependent thereafter on a walking stick.

By 1911 a revitalised IRB could still only muster about 2,000 members, but these were talented and committed men waiting to act if the Irish political situation changed. The breakthrough came with the Ulster Unionist campaign against the Third Home Rule Bill of 1912 which included establishing an Ulster Volunteer Force (UVF) of 100,000 members. For a long time the Home Ruler leader John Redmond dismissed the UVF as a bluff, but by the autumn of 1913 nationalist Ireland was becoming increasingly uneasy that it might defeat Home Rule. Hobson realised that the IRB could exploit this disquiet to begin organising Irish nationalists militarily, but he knew it had to disguise its involvement so that the new enterprise would have the broadest popular appeal.[16] A nationalist military organisation could particularly maximise its appeal by having an eminently respectable leader as its public face and Hobson had just the person in mind for the role. This was Eoin MacNeill, a fellow Ulsterman and Professor of Early and Medieval History at University College, Dublin. At first sight MacNeill was an unlikely choice, being primarily a scholar who, in the words of one historian, 'might have been expected to fade quietly away among the book-stacks of the Royal Irish Academy, never more to be heard of except by a few professors and then only when he published an occasional and erudite study on an obscure manuscript'.[17]

Born in 1867 to a farming family living in the Glens of Antrim, he was superbly endowed intellectually with a penetrating mind. MacNeill had performed outstandingly at St Malachy's College, Belfast and later in the Royal University of Ireland; becoming knowledgeable in Latin, Greek, ancient history and modern languages before finally graduating in economics, jurisprudence and constitutional history. MacNeill then spent twenty years in the Accountant General's office at the Four Courts, where he combined his civil service career with a burgeoning interest in Irish history and the Irish language. In 1893 MacNeill and a group of friends invited Douglas Hyde to establish the Gaelic League, with MacNeill acting as secretary and editor of its journal. However an unrelenting workload eventually led to a nervous breakdown in 1899, and though excellent medical care brought him through, the illness' legacy was a crippling inability to deal with immediately pressing tasks even such as writing letters. MacNeill was also afflicted intermittently with serious headaches and he never fully recovered his former zest, a condition that led to accusations of lassitude and indolence.

In November 1913 MacNeill's article 'The North Began' created a political sensation by advocating a military organisation to protect Home Rule and nationalist interests generally. Hobson recognised the appeal of MacNeill's impressive academic credentials, a social standing certified by Woodtown Park, Ballyboden, his residence on the outskirts of Rathfarnham, and his reputation for integrity and moderation. Furthermore, although MacNeill's own sympathies probably lay with Redmond and the Home Rulers, he wasn't identified narrowly with any party and so appealed widely across the political spectrum. After successfully urging MacNeill's publisher, Michael O'Rahilly, to encourage him to begin forming an Irish Volunteer Force, Hobson organised a Provisional Committee that launched the new organisation at a large gathering at the Rotunda in Dublin on 25 November – supposedly on a broad non-party basis. But from the very start there was built into the Irish Volunteers a misunderstanding between the IRB, which had selected MacNeill as its public face, and the man himself. As one of his friends acknowledged, republican leaders had 'sought only an ornament'[18] and a politically inexperienced MacNeill seemed made for the role: a tall, gaunt imposing figure, articulate and eloquent, someone of unimpeachable integrity. To Clarke and MacDermott though, MacNeill was a dilettante who had strayed from the common room into what they regarded as literally matters of life and death. Assuming correctly that Hobson was from the IRB, MacNeill was aware from the start that he was being manipulated by republicans. Though quite prepared to let the organisation play its part in a broad nationalist movement, he wasn't going to be its puppet. In a sense MacNeill on one hand and Clarke and MacDermott on the other were in perfect agreement: each believed they had created the Volunteers and weren't going to let the other take it away from them. It was a perfect recipe for gridlock: creating suspicion and hostility, poisoning relationships among Volunteer leaders and plunging a dysfunctional organisation into a constant state of turbulence. It also inflicted years of frustration on the professional revolutionaries, complicating their plans and ultimately and momentously affecting the Rising to which they had dedicated their lives.

During the first half of 1914 the Irish Volunteers mushroomed to over 150,000 members. Such rapid growth of an organisation outside his control alarmed Redmond, who on 9 June demanded that the Provisional Committee co-opt twenty-five of his nominees or he would establish his own Volunteers. The IRB's Supreme Council ordered members to resist Redmond's demands, but Hobson was always his own man and determined to do what he considered right. He and other influential Provisional Committee members like MacNeill and Sir Roger Casement were initially inclined to resign rather than submit, but Hobson quickly came to believe that resistance to Redmond would result in a civil war within the Volunteers when the organisation was still experiencing teething problems: 'To me the one vitally important thing was to keep the Volunteer movement united.'[19] Arguing with immense persuasiveness that 'this is a bitter pill but one we must swallow if we are to save the Volunteer organisation',[20] Hobson persuaded MacNeill and a majority – including other IRB members – to accept Redmond's ultimatum, although a minority of seven, including MacDermott, dissented.

Somewhat dubiously, Hobson claimed that events had moved so rapidly that he hadn't been able to consult other IRB leaders, but more probably it was because he already knew what their answer would have been. He didn't have to wait long to find out. A friend recalled Clarke's explosive reaction:

> To say he was astounded is understating it. I never saw him so moved. He regarded it from the beginning as cold-blooded and contemplated treachery likely to bring about the destruction of the only movement in a century which brought promise of the fulfilment of all his hopes. During his life he had many, very many grievous disappointments but this one was the worst and the bitterness of it was increased by the fact that it was brought about by a trusted friend.[21]

Sean McGarry hero-worshipped Clarke as someone 'slow to condemn, always ready to hear the other side and was perhaps rather over-tolerant to his friends'.[22] But when thwarted or crossed Clarke could be venomous and at a meeting soon afterwards he and MacDermott ambushed Hobson like two attack dogs. Hobson recalled a 'storm of hysterical abuse'[23] during which Clarke suddenly demanded to know how much the Castle was paying him.

It was the most serious accusation that could be levelled against an Irish republican and created an irreparable rift. A physically and emotionally exhausted Hobson resigned every IRB office that brought him into contact with Clarke and MacDermott, including his seat on the Supreme Council, and he never spoke to Clarke again. Although Hobson and MacDermott did sit together on the Volunteers' Provisional Committee their exchanges were formal and tinged with an unpleasant personal malice. Hobson attributed MacDermott's hostility to a polio victim's jealousy of his immense energy. However, Hobson had sworn MacDermott into the IRB and it must have been galling to see this novice being fast-tracked to the top and manipulating Hobson's difficulties to dislodge him from Clarke's favour. Not for the last time Hobson folded and threw in the towel, displaying a middle-class intellectual's fastidiousness by refusing to get down into the gutter and slug it out with what he saw as two political bruisers who punched below the belt. Hobson claimed later that he was worn down through overwork and that was undoubtedly true. Nevertheless, there was also a strain of self-pity; a perception that he alone was struggling valiantly without his colleagues' support; a victim and martyr who could take no more outrageous vilification. Hobson also claimed that he had acted to avoid splitting both the Volunteers and IRB. But whereas he believed that accepting Redmond's ultimatum was for the Volunteers' long-term good, by not taking on Clarke and MacDermott head-to-head he was abdicating control of the IRB to men and policies that he regarded as dangerously irresponsible.

Although ostensibly the triumvirate had collapsed over a single issue, both sides were really divided by two very different visions of how the IRB should influence political developments in Ireland. Hobson was convinced that England's tremendous military and economic resources doomed any Irish rising involving untrained men and inexperienced leaders. Only by strengthening the IRB organisationally, building up its membership and constructing a broad nationalist movement could British rule be eventually overthrown in a campaign of guerrilla warfare. Besides, the IRB's own constitution specifically forbade its Supreme Council from initiating a rebellion without the support of a majority of the Irish people. Hobson's vision then reflected the man himself: patient, logical, sober, responsible, bureaucratic and evolutionary. By contrast, Clarke and MacDermott were daring, impatient romantic gamblers driven by a great fear that Home Rule would lead to Redmond accommodating Ireland permanently and comfortably within the United Kingdom. They were convinced that unless decisive action was taken soon a distinct sense of Irish identity would disappear and its people become effectively west Britons. Both men regarded Hobson as defeatist, someone who preferred postponing revolution indefinitely and fundamentally lacking an appetite for war. They were also elitists who deemed that they knew the national interest best; they were unwilling to share power, compulsively needing to control any organisation within their orbit and drive out anyone opposing their course of action. Believing that they were the creators and sole owners of the Irish Volunteers they had been sceptical of Hobson's more pluralistic outlook even before the rift of June 1914. He in turn regarded them as 'narrow partisans, inclined to distrust anybody who was not a member of our small organisation. They were very suspicious of my co-operation with men like MacNeill ... who belonged intellectually and socially to a different world.'[24]

It was a permanent estrangement with reconciliation impossible. Disagreements so deep and poisonous didn't heal and indeed having put Hobson under siege Clarke and MacDermott next tried to starve him out of Dublin. They even engineered his dismissal as Irish correspondent of the *Gaelic American,* his sole source of regular income, but Hobson wouldn't give them the satisfaction of disappearing, particularly as he retained a power base as head of the IRB's Dublin Centres Board and secretary of the Irish Volunteers. Fittingly, as an advocate of guerrilla warfare, he decided from these offices to do battle with his conquerors in an unrelenting campaign of obstruction and sabotage designed to madden them and frustrate their ambitions. If vengeance is a dish best served cold then Hobson was determined that eventually he would dine at high table. So an incessant struggle began within the Volunteers between Hobson's determination to keep the organisation a broad national movement, and Clarke and MacDermott's resolve to forge it into a sword for the IRB to smite England. But after being outvoted within the Volunteers on the issue of Redmond's ultimatum, Clarke and MacDermott would never again risk an open showdown with their former ally. Instead, over the next two years they infiltrated their protégés into leadership positions in the Volunteers in what amounted to a silent coup; they slowly stripped MacNeill of effective control and intended to leave him as titular leader while IRB loyalists acquired operational control of the organisation. Hobson, for his part, was watching for incriminating evidence against his enemies and became a brooding nemesis over Clarke and MacDermott, forcing them and their allies to be perpetually on guard. When challenged about their activities they adopted a facade of evasion, pained indignation or simply lied. The split of June 1914, then, lit one of the slowest burning fuses in Irish history, but one that when it eventually detonated in April 1916 just before the Rising, was to do so spectacularly.

Despite his split with Hobson in the summer of 1914 Clarke believed his strategy was succeeding because overhauling the IRB had populated it with highly motivated men who shared his revolutionary goal and were infiltrating the leadership of the Irish Volunteers. Clarke now longed for an opportunity to strike at England and, like all Irish republicans, he thought that would most likely occur when it became involved in a great military conflict. It was partly the IRB's failure to do so during the Boer War that had driven Clarke away to America and it was the prospect of an Anglo-German war that induced him to return. Thereafter he had spent years, metaphorically, scouring the horizon and waiting for that particular ship to come in. Finally it arrived. On 29 June Gearoid O'Sullivan bought an evening newspaper and told Sean MacDermott that its headlines only concerned some old duke who had been shot in the Balkans:

'Give me that' said Sean excitedly. As he read the few lines his piercing eyes seemed to dart from their sockets. Holding the paper in his left hand, staring at me intently he smacked the paper with the upturned right hand (this was the usual method of emphasis for him) and addressed me 'Look out, Geroid this is no joke for us. We're in for it now. Austria will move against those fellows (I didn't know who the fellows were) Russia will back those fellows up, Germany and Italy will back Austria, France will take on Germany. You'll have a European war. England will join and that will be our time to strike.'[25]

The First World War was a seminal event in Irish history. It involved more combatants and casualties than all subsequent conflicts in Ireland combined and it utterly changed the country's political situation. Initially, people appeared gripped by pro-war sentiment as patriotic crowds in Dublin waved Union Jacks, wrecked shops owned by German immigrants and wildly cheered soldiers departing for the Western Front. By the end of 1915, encouraged to join by press campaigns, good wages and separation allowances, 86,000 men had been recruited. Irish soldiers had won seventeen Victoria Crosses. But the war quickly crystallised differences between the two nationalist traditions. Redmond saw the conflict in broad and generous terms, as an opportunity to unite Protestants and Catholics in a common cause. He hoped that Ireland's participation in the war effort would create a national consensus and eradicate pre-war political differences, leading after the war to the implementation of Home Rule. On the other hand militant separatists could only see the Irish race sleepwalking to extinction. Observing the wave of pro-war hysteria sweeping the country, one Volunteer officer was convinced, apocalyptically:

that the final end of the Irish race was at hand. For centuries England had held Ireland materially. But now it seemed she held her in a new and utterly complete way. Our national identity was obliterated not only politically but in our own minds. The Irish people had recognised themselves as part of England.[26]

Such differing outlooks increased tensions within the Irish Volunteers and these were heightened on 3 August 1914 by Redmond's speech to a cheering House of Commons, pledging the Volunteers to Ireland's defence while urging the British government to concentrate on the war against Germany. Many Provisional Committee members were, of course, opposed to any support for the British war effort.

Patrick Pearse wrote that 'it seems either madness or treachery on Redmond's part. A supreme moment for Ireland may be at hand. We shall go down to our graves beaten and disgraced men if we are not ready for it.'[27] The militants' patience finally cracked on 20 September when Redmond, speaking at Woodenbridge, Co. Wicklow, urged Volunteers to go 'wherever the firing line extends'. The uneasy truce within the Volunteer leadership since Redmond's takeover in June now collapsed and on 24 September Redmond's nominees were expelled from the organisation. Redmond retaliated by establishing the rival National Volunteers, to which over 90 per cent of the 180,000 Irish Volunteers immediately defected. Although MacNeill retained most officers and the Dublin rank and file, his 11,000 supporters were a geographical rump, restricted outside the capital to a sporadic presence in the south and west. But the smaller Irish Volunteers were stronger than they appeared because Dublin was now the power centre of Irish politics, a city in which the political agenda was set, great public rallies took place and headline events were made.

Clarke and MacDermott were overjoyed at a schism that ended the threat of Redmond emasculating the Irish Volunteers. While only a small minority of members had stayed loyal they were the most committed and determined, and in their view, the only ones worth having. The Irish Volunteers now adopted a new structure with MacNeill as president and chairman of an Executive on which sat, among others, Hobson, MacDermott and Pearse. In December 1914 a Headquarters Staff was also created with MacNeill as chief of staff. Previously the Volunteers had been perceived largely as a political weapon to pressurise the British government into enacting the Third Home Rule Bill. The organisation lacked weapons, experienced officers, training facilities, instructors and equipment of all kinds; many Volunteers didn't even possess a full uniform and made do with caps, belts and puttees. The new Headquarters Staff began creating a credible military organisation, something indispensable to Clarke and MacDermott's vision of a revolutionary sword. IRB members were quickly infiltrated into key posts, including Patrick Pearse as Director of Organisation, Joseph Plunkett, Director of Military Operations, Eamonn Ceannt, Director of Communications and Thomas MacDonagh, who became Director of Training.[28]

Initially, mainstream nationalist support of the war was derived from sympathy for Catholic Belgium, the prosperity that it brought to rural Ireland and a general expectation of a short conflict. During 1915 this enthusiasm declined gradually in the face of a seemingly endless war of attrition in which casualties mounted incessantly and the wounded became a common sight in Dublin. Fear of conscription rose, especially after its partial introduction in Great Britain, while Sir Edward Carson's inclusion in the coalition government that Asquith formed in May 1915 also outraged many nationalists. So did the War Office's insensitive rejection of Redmond's advice to create Irish brigades with officers chosen from his National Volunteers. All the time the IRB was shrewdly manipulating anti-recruiting and anti-conscription campaigns in the press and at public meetings. As Redmond's National Volunteers lapsed into terminal decline, the Irish Volunteers came to the forefront of public consciousness, widening the organisation's popular base through its drive and an uncompromising hostility to the war effort. The Royal Irish Constabulary (RIC) reported that 'a spirit of disloyalty and pro-Germanism, which had hitherto been confined to a small number, was spreading'.

IRB preparations for a rising that required military plans, weapons and men had already begun in mid-August 1914 when its Supreme Council decided, in principle, to revolt before the end of the war. It had then devolved organisational responsibility to its Executive which effectively consisted of Clarke and MacDermott. Initially they relied on a shadowy advisory committee comprised of Irish Volunteer commandants and vice-commandants who were also IRB members, but although it produced plans for a Dublin insurrection, Clarke wasn't happy with either its report or the committee's unwieldy size. He allowed the committee to lapse but passed its recommendations on to be refined by a smaller successor group consisting of Ceannt, Plunkett and Pearse. Although the last two were new IRB recruits they held important positions on both the Volunteer Executive and Headquarters Staff, as well as being students of military affairs. Furthermore, their membership of the new planning group bound them closely to Clarke and MacDermott while its small size facilitated both men's control of its deliberations and proposals. Clarke and MacDermott had talent-spotted the trio, earmarking them for increasingly important roles in their revolutionary conspiracy. Indeed the three men's lives appear to have brought them inevitably to this moment. *204. 671*

Eamonn Ceannt was born in September 1881 at the police barracks of a small Galway village where his father was the local constable. Christened Edmund Kent – a name that he retained during his childhood and youth – he was a shy, socially awkward and rather lonely young boy who exhibited an unusual stoic calmness.[29] Even his brother Michael thought him 'always a little oddity'.[30] At school Ceannt imbibed an intense Roman Catholicism and a love of Irish history, culture and music as well as mastering French and German as spoken languages. After his father retired in 1892 the family moved to Dublin where Ceannt attended the Christian Brothers School in North Richmond Street, a veritable revolutionary seminary. Classmates regarded him as a distant, guarded youth bottling up his emotions. In 1895 he stood in his mother's death chamber without uttering a single word or shedding a tear.[31] Later, after his father passed away, an adult Ceannt remained alone with the body for a long time and when his brother Michael entered the room Eamonn looked him up and down silently and impassively: 'There was no outward exhibition of feeling.'[32]

After leaving school Ceannt joined Dublin Corporation's finance department where he found the work humdrum and intellectually arid. Colleagues respected his thoroughness, but disliked his sullen and abrupt manner, with one sensing Ceannt's yearning 'for some outlet that would move him from the drudgery of the desk, and give him free scope to be the master of his own destiny'.[33] By now a friend regarded him as 'a single-minded ascetic' who shunned tobacco and alcohol while devoting his energies increasingly to the Irish language, having joined the Gaelic League in 1900 and ceasing to use the name Kent. Five years later he married Aine O'Brennan, a fellow language enthusiast, in a wedding ceremony that he insisted on being conducted in Irish, with French rather than English coins used for the silver. When their only son Ronan was born a year later the child was baptised and registered in Irish.

Ceannt's avid reading of Irish history strengthened his commitment to physical force republicanism and in December 1912 Sean MacDermott swore him into the IRB, urging him to become involved immediately with the Irish Volunteers. MacDermott had discerned in Ceannt useful middle-ranking leadership abilities.

A spare erect figure at 6ft tall with chiselled features, brown hair and hazel eyes, he could impose discipline on subordinates and guarantee organisational efficiency.Yet at the same time Ceannt relied more on drive and determination than natural flair and was willing to defer to more talented superiors. MacDermott also knew that someone who revealed so little of his innermost self even to those closest to him could be entrusted absolutely with the most valuable secrets of a revolutionary conspiracy.

Joseph Plunkett was born in Dublin in November 1887, the son of Count George Noble Plunkett, a papal knight who lived on an estate in the Dublin suburb of Kimmage. Thin, pale and short-sighted, Plunkett was plagued by ill health, and repeated surgery to remove tubercular glands from his neck had left him with appalling scars. One Dubliner thought he looked 'as emaciated as the Spanish saint in his prison cell at Toledo.'[34] His education in Irish and English schools and the National University of Ireland was constantly interrupted by spells in hospitals and nursing homes. Precociously intelligent and knowledgeable in philosophy, literature, the sciences and military strategy, Plunkett enjoyed good food and wine and was witty and convivial company.

Devoutly Catholic and a romantic nationalist, Plunkett gravitated over time towards supporting an insurrection. Imbued with considerable literary talent, he blended mysticism and nationalism in poems that centred on the idea of sacrifice. A contemporary described Plunkett as 'hard as nails ... prepared to die for his beliefs and see others die for them'.[35] Terminally ill with tuberculosis and ambitious for a historic role in reviving the national spirit of Ireland, he sought a more heroic end. Plunkett joined the Irish Volunteer Force at the very start and was elected to its Provisional Committee, putting his journal, *Irish Review*, at the organisation's disposal. Although he voted to accept Redmond's ultimatum in June 1914, Plunkett opposed the Woodenbridge speech, arguing that the purpose of the Irish Volunteers was to secure Irish freedom, not serve England and her empire. Having joined the IRB in August 1914 he was delighted with the ensuing Volunteer split.

Patrick Pearse was born in 1879, the son of an English monumental sculptor who had immigrated to Ireland.[36] At school he developed a love of Irish history and the Irish language in which he immersed himself even after studying law at university. He only tried one case as a lawyer before concentrating on the Gaelic League, of whose journal he became editor in 1903. As the number of Irish speakers plunged Pearse became obsessed with combating an English educational system that predominated in Ireland and which, he believed, was destroying Ireland's separate identity and way of life. As a gesture of defiance he established St Enda's, a school that thrived until 1908 when he overreached himself. Ignoring the warnings of friends, he shifted to a new location on the outskirts of Rathfarnham in a large house with splendid gardens. Here Pearse was headmaster of a boarding school with under a hundred boys, gentlemen's sons taught in classes of seven to ten pupils, whom he hoped would go into farming and business as educated people.

The school in which his brother Willie taught art was part of the Irish renaissance, a prototype for the educational system that Pearse hoped people would receive in an independent Ireland. The teaching emphasised not just the externals of dress and sport but a specifically Irish way of thought and life. Pearse, a poet and dramatist himself, organised visits to the Abbey Theatre and brought in guest speakers, including W.B. Yeats. Pearse was a gentle and popular headmaster and a pupil described the school atmosphere as 'socially and intellectually an exciting and stimulating life'.[37] However, St Enda's was a money pit, expensive to run, with too few pupils and competing against great boarding schools like Castleknock and Blackrock. According to Douglas Hyde, who had known Pearse since he was a boy, it was:

> as everyone had foreseen that he was soon landed in financial difficulties. Nor was he a man of a practical turn of mind who could face them and pull through by sheer application to his business. On the contrary he was an idealist who kept writing poems for magazines and plays and doing things of the like nature when most other people would have been overwhelmed with the dread of debt and impending ruin.[38]

As a result, an educational vision which had considerable appeal in Ireland and the USA was kept afloat only by generous individual contributions, a public appeal and a fundraising American tour by Pearse himself. A friend, Maeve McGarry, who contributed money, recalled how 'Pearse used to come to the house when he got into difficulties with the school. I saw him cry one day on account of his financial distress.'[39]

Distant, driven, seemingly unable to unwind or indulge in small talk and with an ascetic lifestyle that eschewed tobacco and alcohol, Pearse's personal circumstances were forcing him in a radically different direction. According to his biographer Ruth Dudley Edwards, he felt trapped as the headmaster of a minor school perpetually in financial difficulty and yearned increasingly for a public stage commensurate with a man of his perceived abilities. Pearse steeped himself in the writings of Irish revolutionaries like Wolfe Tone, another disenchanted barrister and frustrated man of ambition. In Dudley Edward's judgment 'a craving for action came to dominate Pearse's thinking, and combined with his literary and oratorical gifts it made him an object of interest to revolutionary groups'.[40] Hyde saw it, too: 'Let us do something was Pearse's ambition.'[41]

Pearse's journey to physical force republicanism was slow and rather tortuous because despite being a convinced separatist he still appeared on a Home Rule platform in 1912, arguing that devolution was the best available stepping stone to independence. It was MacDermott who talent-spotted Pearse and persuaded Clarke to give him a chance as orator at an important republican commemoration. Clarke was impressed and said, 'I never thought there was such stuff in Pearse'. By the end of 1913 Pearse was excited by the formation of the Irish Volunteers and in December Bulmer Hobson swore him into the IRB. Despite coming late to republican politics ('at the ninth hour'[42]) it was the start of a rapid rise that within two and a half years was to bring him to the pinnacle as President of the Irish Republic and commander-in-chief. Notwithstanding an evident lack of administrative ability and military skills, Pearse was a valuable recruit to the IRB. He looked a leader, dignified and handsome with a strong jaw and dark hair always sleeked down and never out of place. Rather stocky for someone just over medium height, his dark hair, grey eyes and pale complexion made a strong impression on people, especially when he wore his green Volunteer uniform. An admirer noted, this 'was perfectly tailored, his slouch hat with the brim bound to the crown was always firm and straight on his head, never rakish. It made him look very intent and serious.'[43] Educated, a poet and dramatist, fluent in both Irish and English, a middle-class intellectual filled with self-belief and a longing to change the world, Pearse projected an uplifting vision to an audience in short staccato sentences. Nobody has described Pearse better than Professor F.X. Martin:

> He was dignified and reserved, an educationalist and a teacher, a poet, playwright and journalist in both English and Irish, an orator who spoke with measured burning phrases, drawing from the past and pronouncing with messianic certainty on the future. He had no lust for women or for gold. He was no man's man but was wedded to his own vision of what Ireland had been and what Ireland should be. Out of his reading and meditation he moulded a new ideal, the Irish Hero, a man who exemplified the virtues of Cu Chulainn and the mythological heroes of ancient Gaelic Ireland who was modelled on the Christ of abnegation, suffering, death and ultimate victory who had the verve and unending determination of Wolfe Tone, John Mitchel and Thomas Davis who was identified with the Fenians and the common people of Ireland long suffering under the harrow of English domination.[44]

On the face of it, Clarke and the other conspirators were an extremely diverse group. They included a headmaster, a university lecturer, a corporation official and a former barman. They ranged from sophisticated cosmopolitans who wrote poems and plays, one the son of a count, to proletarians with an elementary education; men who seemed not so much from different generations as from different worlds. Their personalities also differed greatly. The gregarious MacDermott who oozed charm couldn't have been more different from a dour loner like Ceannt. But much more important were those qualities binding them all together: energy, determination, cunning, ruthlessness and a fanatical commitment to the separatist ideal. They also possessed a blinkered belief in the righteousness of their cause and actions that banished all self-doubt. Supremely indifferent to their own lives, in their own different ways they were men of daring imagination, impatient to change the course of history. Finally as gamblers planning a rebellion they were all, in a sense, ready to stake everything they had, including their lives, on one roll of the dice, going for the jackpot.

At the end of May 1915, while MacDermott was serving a short prison sentence for anti-war activities, Clarke upgraded the planning group of Pearse, Plunkett and Ceannt into a formal military committee. Its existence, though never its activities, was only revealed later to the Supreme Council while the committee's small size and completely trustworthy membership satisfied an autocratic Clarke's craving for secrecy and total control. When MacDermott was released in September 1915, he and Clarke joined Pearse, Plunkett and Ceannt on what had now become a Military Council, and personally involved themselves in the planning for a rising.[45] By now, the conspirators were paying particular attention to weapons acquisition. Already in the autumn of 1914, John Devoy had requested the German ambassador in America to have his government send an arms shipment to Ireland. Even before a reply came, the IRB was scouting for possible landing places in remote areas of the south and west, including Kinsale harbour and Tralee Bay.

However, the Military Council realised that the Germans needed to be convinced face to face of its seriousness. For six months the task of strengthening ties between Germany and Irish revolutionaries had been carried out by Sir Roger Casement, a former member of the British Foreign Service who had gained an international reputation for exposing European colonial exploitation in Africa and South America. Highly strung, temperamentally unstable, naïve and completely lacking in political judgment, Casement's impeccable establishment background hadn't prevented him becoming actively involved in nationalist politics, and as a member of the Volunteers Provisional Committee he became increasingly attracted to the idea of a German-Irish alliance liberating Ireland.[46]

When war broke out Casement went to Berlin and in November 1914 persuaded the Germans to announce their support for Irish independence. But this was as good as it got. Soon afterwards the German General Staff ruled out a naval invasion of Ireland and Casement's pet project of an Irish Brigade of Irish prisoners of war reached its peak in June 1915, having only recruited fifty-six men. Casement's minimal progress and deteriorating relations with the Germans, his pessimistic reports back to Ireland and Clarke's suspicions of this former British diplomat, all convinced the Military Council that it needed to send an emissary to kick-start the stalled negotiations. Plunkett's need to convalesce was an ideal cover for continental travel and he was dispatched on a clandestine mission that lasted from April to July 1915. Travelling in disguise with a moustache and beard he went to Spain, Italy and Switzerland before making a twenty-three-hour rail journey to Berlin where he was brought together with Casement. Sharing broadly the same political beliefs – an Irish rebellion with German assistance - they co-operated during Plunkett's stay to produce a thirty-two-page memorandum for submission to the German government.[47] This document, which became known as the Ireland Report, described the contemporary Irish situation, various Irish nationalist organisations, the Irish Volunteers' structure and activities, political attitudes in Ireland and the strength of British military and police forces. It also analysed French intervention in the 1798 rebellion in Ireland and the lessons to be derived from that episode, and how Germany could most effectively assist a future Rising. The Ireland Report reveals the Military Council's intentions and how much it wanted, not just German support. It dispels a long-held belief that Plunkett was engaged simply in an arms procurement mission; he wanted a large expeditionary force sent to Ireland whose arrival would coincide with the start of an insurrection to launch a joint German-Irish military campaign. Foreign help was essential because the Volunteers alone in their 'unarmed, unequipped, partly trained' state were incapable of achieving victory in the capital, let alone the entire country.

Plunkett and Casement estimated that any insurrection would have to overcome a British garrison of 37,000 troops with 5,000 stationed permanently in Dublin and the rest scattered throughout Ireland in camps such as the Curragh, about 20 miles from Dublin, Fermoy in Co. Cork and an artillery depot in Athlone. The British could also rely on 12,000 armed members of the Royal Irish Constabulary. Optimistically they asserted that British forces were not 'equipped for the occupation of the country much less to resist invasion. Those units that are intended for immediate service receive their equipment, munitions and stores in England when they leave Ireland on their way to the front.'

They argued that because of these enemy weaknesses a military campaign could completely destroy British political and military power in Ireland, after which the Military Council clearly envisaged itself as the new ruler of an independent Irish

Republic. Plunkett and Casement conceived a rising as a three-pronged but integrated military operation consisting of an Irish Volunteer seizure of Dublin; a German naval invasion landing a military expeditionary force in the west of Ireland; and a rebellion there by Volunteers and untrained local sympathisers whom the Germans would arm and lead. The Military Council would destroy British transport facilities at selected railway bridges, canals and viaducts then seize and occupy Dublin, arrest British officials and military officers, station guards at banks and British commercial interests and possibly appoint a military governor in the capital.

However, the key to success was a German expeditionary force of 12,000 soldiers landing in the west of Ireland, seizing Limerick and distributing 40,000 rifles to the Volunteers. This would electrify the whole of Ireland and initiate a nationwide revolt by provoking a serious rising in the west that would be a signal for the Military Council to seize the capital. In the west a German-Irish force would combine professional military expertise with the Volunteers' numbers, enthusiasm and geographical knowledge, enabling it to occupy territory and towns, defeat British military forces and divert pressure from the rebels in Dublin – towards which it was ultimately marching. Military operations would commence once the Germans had converted Limerick into a base 'as impregnable as the Dardanelles', and then with their Irish allies started to penetrate the rest of the country.

After capturing a lightly-defended Athlone with its vital bridge over the Shannon, the force would advance on Sligo and gain control of the whole of Connaught, its resources, population and well-protected harbours. At a time when the Germans had initiated a campaign of unrestricted U-boat warfare against Allied shipping, Plunkett and Casement offered an enticing inducement that would make the submarine campaign even more effective. In return for a German expeditionary force to Ireland, the new rulers of an independent Ireland would help sever England's Atlantic lifeline by allowing German U-boats to operate from Valentia harbour, Bantry Bay, Dingle Bay, Ventry harbour, the Blasket Islands and Killary harbour, where 'the biggest battleships in the world can ride at anchor'. The German navy could also have the British naval base at Lough Swilly.

In relation to the land campaign, Plunkett and Casement envisaged a 50km advance by the German-Irish force from Athlone on Mullingar to take control of the midlands before an easy 70km march towards Dublin. They predicted that a British counteroffensive would be ineffective because their forces were top-heavy with cavalry and virtually bereft of artillery; Volunteers would have sabotaged their transport facilities and troops would be moving through a countryside 'eminently suited to a kind of guerrilla or irregular warfare', 'in which the individual rifleman in cover could be of great value' and whose walls, hedges and ditches made cavalry mostly redundant.

Casement and Plunkett also presented a detailed analysis of a previous naval expedition to the west of Ireland that an enemy of England had undertaken during a major European war. This was General Humbert's French invasion fleet which landed at Killala Bay in Co. Mayo in 1798. Even though the main rebellion in Wexford and Wicklow in the south-east of Ireland had already been crushed and although Humbert had only 1,200 troops, four pieces of artillery and no weapons for any Irish rebels who joined them, Humbert's Franco-Irish force descended on Castlebar, the capital of Mayo, and defeated the British garrison. It then advanced rapidly across the

River Shannon and reached Co. Longford before it was finally surrounded and over-whelmed by the British commander-in-chief, General Lake. Despite very inadequate resources and no definite plan of operations, Humbert had still advanced well over a hundred miles through enemy-occupied country. The Ireland Report argued that:

> Had Humbert come with 12,000 men instead of 1,200 and with a supply of arms and ammunition for the hardy and brave men that were so ready to risk their lives and homes by joining him, he could unquestionably have held the greater part of the island and established a provisional national government with a headquarters that would have attracted all that was best in Ireland.

Plunkett's memorandum provides a unique insight into the attitudes, intentions and aspirations of the Military Council. It also casts doubt on the 'Blood Sacrifice' theory of the Easter Rising which postulates a heroic but doomed protest which the leaders knew would end in defeat, but that their executions would achieve a posthumous victory when the nation recognised their sacrifices and retrospectively approved of their actions. To this end, it is argued, they choreographed their own deaths after a creditable military performance to rouse the Irish people's slumbering conscious-ness. In religious terms, a rising timed for Easter with its leaders' deaths supposedly crafted as a political crucifixion would ensure Ireland's resurrection. According to this theory, a short-term defeat would eventually be turned into a long-term tri-umph when a renewed and irresistible campaign of resistance would finally achieve national independence.

There is no doubt that a 'Blood Sacrifice' cast of mind was represented on the Military Council by Pearse, Plunkett and, later on, Thomas MacDonagh. Religious symbolism certainly infused these literary men's writings but it was Clarke and MacDermott above all who drove the revolutionary enterprise. These two practi-cal men were the IRB's senior directors while the other three were junior partners operating under their control and accepting the disciplines of an organisation in which rank and position were all-important. Clearly Clarke and MacDermott were able to contain their subordinates' restless and somewhat excitable energies, focus-ing them on this world rather than the next. Indisputably the Ireland Report reveals the Military Council's plans as optimistic, coherent in relation to land warfare and directed to achieving a military victory by overwhelming the British forces in Ireland. Its campaign was designed to culminate in a victory parade down O'Connell Street by Irish Volunteers and Prussian grenadiers, with crowds cheering and throwing flowers as bands played *A Nation Once Again* and *Deutschland Uber Alles*. Victorious soldiers passing the General Post Office (GPO) would salute a Military Council that by then would have reconstituted itself as the new government of an independent Irish republic. The Ireland Report's wealth of hard detail and its analysis of how a rapid victory over British forces in Ireland was attainable explain why the Military Council held Plunkett's military expertise in such high regard. Above all, there is a striking boldness and daring about the whole scheme and the lengths to which IRB leaders were prepared to go to realise their vision. The radical step which Clarke and the others were prepared to take was, in effect, to join Turkey and Bulgaria in aligning an independent Ireland with the Central Powers in their war against the Allies.

The Ireland Report went to the German General Staff which, had it taken the document at face value, would have seriously considered an invasion of Ireland. Disappointingly for Plunkett and Casement, it reacted instead with extreme caution. The Germans knew nothing about Plunkett and they were losing faith in his co-author's Irish Brigade. Besides, they understood, even if the Military Council did not, the enormous changes that had occurred in naval warfare and that the Royal Navy would make an amphibious expedition to Ireland extremely hazardous and potentially disastrous. The catastrophic Dardanelles expedition later in 1915 can only have vindicated their decision to reject the Ireland Report. When Plunkett left Germany in late June 1915 he did so without any concrete promises of German support. It is often claimed that while he was in Berlin Plunkett secured the Chancellor Bethmann Hollweg's promise to send an arms shipment to the west of Ireland. But there is no evidence that Plunkett ever met Bethmann Hollweg, and every indication that the German army and naval authorities had vetoed military assistance to the Irish revolutionaries. Almost a year was to pass before their scepticism was overcome and a definitive decision was taken to risk sending German personnel on an arms mission to Ireland. In October 1915, when Devoy asked for 'a small quantity of arms' to be delivered to the west of Ireland, an unenthusiastic German Admiralty pigeonholed his request.

Although Plunkett returned to Ireland without definite promises of German support – leaving behind a deeply depressed Casement – his mission hadn't been a complete failure. Unknown to an increasingly marginalised Casement, Plunkett had been conducting parallel negotiations with the General Staff and the Foreign Office, having seen for himself the dire relations between the Germans and Casement and their scepticism about any proposal that he submitted. Plunkett's secret contacts were sufficiently encouraging to allow him to conclude that in the right circumstances the Germans would be interested in helping the Military Council. But that would entail the IRB proving that its revolutionary enterprise was serious and that Plunkett wasn't simply another of the fantasists turning up in Berlin and promising to bring down the British Empire. Above all, convincing the Germans would involve fixing a definite date for an Irish rising. The Germans had clearly decided to steer a course between promising immediate material assistance and definitive rejection. Whatever their reservations about the unknown Plunkett, it was sensible to keep him in play just in case the IRB's plans proved to be serious. In that event minimal German assistance in the form of an arms shipment mission might have an immense impact on the political situation in Ireland. Even if the projected Irish rising failed it would distract the British government's attention from the war in France, force it to divert troops to Ireland to put down the rebellion, undermine the unity of the British state and the Allies' claim to be defending the rights of small nations. Plunkett returned to Ireland, not with definite German promises, but Berlin's commitment that things would change in the months ahead if the Military Council proved that it was worth taking seriously. This can only have emboldened the conspirators to press ahead even more urgently with their planning, particularly by scouting harbours in the west of Ireland where a German arms shipment might land.

Moderates on the Volunteer Executive knew about Plunkett's prolonged absence, but he returned to Ireland with a cover story of frustration and disappointment. Sean Fitzgibbon, the Director of Recruiting, wrote:

I had always regarded Plunkett as rash and unbalanced. He came back from Germany in 1915. Bulmer Hobson told me what Plunkett was saying; that he had conferred with Germans of staff rank. The Germans told him they were not interested in Ireland. Plunkett said that all the German talk of will to win was bluff; that in reality they were trying to arrange a compromise peace with Britain. He gave the impression that his visit abroad had made him sane. I want to stress that he was not sent to Germany either by the Volunteer Executive or with the aid of its funds. I am now of the opinion that his moderation was a pose assumed to deceive.[48]

Germany's encouragement prompted the Military Council to begin detailed examination about possible landing places for an arms shipment. In September 1915, Pearse sent Diarmuid Lynch, secretary of the Supreme Council's Executive, to the south-west of Ireland to scout Tralee. There local Volunteer leaders unanimously recommended Fenit harbour in Tralee Bay, where a light railway could speedily transfer rifles to Tralee.[49] German weapons were vitally necessary because of the Irish Volunteers' limited arsenal, the organisation's shortage of money having allowed only two gun-running operations at Howth and Kilcoole in July and August 1914. More weapons were accumulated after the ban on arms importation was temporarily lifted in August 1914 and an American loan secured another 10,000 Martini Enfield rifles. The Irish Volunteers retained a small proportion of these after the split with Redmond in September 1914 and defectors from the increasingly moribund National Volunteers brought over more. Weapons were bought or stolen from soldiers while thefts were organised from the British Army ordnance stores in Dublin. There was also occasional smuggling. Michael O'Rahilly, Director of Arms, also popularised the use of single-barrelled shotguns loaded with buckshot, a weapon that proved its power and effectiveness during Easter Week.[50] Ammunition and explosives were stolen from the Arklow munitions factory in Co. Wicklow and from railway wagons and colliery magazines in Scotland. Despite all these efforts, the Irish Volunteers in January 1916 still possessed only about 3,730 weapons, including rifles, shotguns and revolvers.[51]

In addition to military plans and weapons, the Military Council needed fighters and this made control of the Irish Volunteers indispensable. By 1915 Pearse, Plunkett and Ceannt were members of the Military Council, the Volunteer Executive and the Volunteers Headquarters Staff. The Military Council also controlled the four Dublin Volunteer battalions through their IRB commandants, Ned Daly, Thomas MacDonagh, Eamon de Valera and Eamonn Ceannt. Its supporters had also become Volunteer commandants in Cork, Kerry, Limerick and Galway and most provincial organisers were also IRB members. MacNeill suspected almost nothing about the extent to which he was being undermined, while Hobson was constrained by his IRB oath of secrecy.

The Military Council took enormous care to shroud its activities in 'almost impenetrable secrecy'.[52] But though no written records of its deliberations were kept and every member was subsequently executed, we can still reconstruct much of its planning for the Easter Rising. The council was small and tightly knit, expanding from three to five during 1915 and then to only seven by the time of the Rising. Operating on the basis of absolute trust and confidentiality, it was designed to eliminate the laxness, betrayal and enemy infiltration that had crippled previous Irish rebellions. Even Denis McCullough, President of the IRB's Supreme Council, was excluded from knowledge of its deliberations and activities. James Connolly, who became a member in January 1916, displayed its obsessive secretiveness when one of his Citizen Army who was stealing gelignite required an operation for appendicitis; he would only approve surgery after receiving a doctor's assurance that any dangerous revelations by the patient would be dismissed as delirious rambling. The council met only in discreet locations where guards and scouts protected it from police surveillance and raids; this was most frequently in the backroom of Houlihan's, a basket-maker's shop in Amiens Street.[53] However it also convened at Clontarf Town Hall, whose librarian was an old associate of Clarke; at a closed restaurant in Henry Street; in private houses such as Ceannt's and, most famously and finally; at Liberty Hall on Easter Sunday, 23 April 1916.[54] As well as general planning sessions, individual council members were assigned specific tasks. MacDermott, for instance, was made responsible for obtaining information on Dublin's telephone and telegraph manhole system. He used IRB members employed by the General Post Office who as clerks and outdoor servicemen surveyed and sketched every manhole in the city.[55]

Paddy Daly, an IRB member, has provided a fascinating description of the Military Council developing a project for the Rising.[56] In 1916 he was a Volunteer in MacDonagh's 2nd Battalion and employed as a carpenter at the Magazine Fort in Phoenix Park, the British army's main weapons armoury in the capital. MacDermott had recruited Daly as a spy to provide intelligence on its layout, its garrison strength and the location of keys, tools and equipment. By Palm Sunday, 16 April 1916, the council had decided that one of the Rising's first dramatic acts would be an attack on the fort. On that day most council members met at Clontarf Town Hall to commence detailed planning of the operation, and over the course of an hour they questioned Daly about such matters as the number of men who would be required and how they would best surprise and capture the guards. Tom Clarke was particularly interested in knowing the relative merits of attacking in daylight or in darkness. A debate then occurred over whether the Volunteers should seize the fort's armaments for use in the Rising or demolish the whole complex in a great explosion. Thomas MacDonagh, who had recently joined the Military Council, favoured seizure but Clarke and MacDermott successfully argued for detonation, with Clarke demonstrating that the passage of time had not dimmed his youthful knowledge of dynamiting techniques. Daly then provided information on the fort's ammunition, oil and tool stores and about the keys that were kept in a glasshouse in the guardroom. He also came up with a stratagem for gaining entry to the fort as he knew that on Sundays footballers often passed its gates and the unsuspecting guards: he suggested that Volunteers posing as a soccer team could get close enough to surprise and overpower the defenders. Clarke was delighted with the idea and the council instructed Daly to assemble a team as well as approving his proposal to use officers from the Fianna, the republican boy scout organisation. MacDonagh, Daly's commandant, then promoted him to lieutenant, a post senior enough to enable him to recruit for the operation. Next day, on MacDermott's orders, Daly took a plan of the fort to Liberty Hall – where Connolly was concerned that the Fianna members needed extra muscle – and added some hefty men to the team. On Wednesday 19 April MacDonagh told Daly to convene a team meeting at which the leadership passed on its final sanction for the operation and a rendezvous point on Easter Sunday was arranged for Daly's men.

Daly's account confirms that while, out of necessity, outsiders were given some information, only the council was ever allowed to see the whole picture or know the innermost secrets. Others to whom the council doled out information were the provincial leaders in Kerry – who were told about the proposed German arms shipment – and Volunteer commandants in the south and west – whom Pearse secretly informed in January 1916 of their military dispositions once a rising had begun. Even McCullough and the Supreme Council were treated as bystanders. When, in either late December 1915 or early January 1916, the Military Council fixed the Rising for Easter 1916[57] it didn't reveal this at the Supreme Council's last meeting in Clontarf Town Hall. At this session on 16 January 1916 MacDermott blandly proposed reaffirming the decision of August 1914 to rise 'at the earliest possible date'. The Military Council had originally chosen Good Friday, 21 April, to begin the Rising but delayed it by a couple of days to Easter Sunday after realising that mobilising large numbers of Volunteers, many of them civil servants, on a Friday might cause the British authorities to suspect that something more than routine manoeuvres was in progress.[58]

While the Military Council refined the general plan it had battalion commandants carry out reconnaissance of important locations in their designated garrison areas. Ned Daly got his assistant quartermaster, who worked at Broadstone railway station, to show him and Vice-Commandant Beaslai around and explain the railway's network of bridges, sidings, points and signal boxes.[59] Ceannt's intended battalion headquarters was the South Dublin Union, a large poorhouse that he visited on the pretext of collecting a toy gramophone for his son. A union official gave him a guided tour during which Ceannt keenly examined from windows the view of its sprawling grounds.[60] At Guinness' Brewery Ceannt also made the observation that its barrels would make excellent barricades. When Eamonn de Valera became 3rd Battalion commandant, he meticulously reconnoitred the district surrounding Boland's mills and had his officers identify garages, stables and factories as well as food, clothing and medical stores.[61] Later, when the Citizen Army came on board, Connolly's deputy Michael Mallin believed that he would be commanding at Jacob's, whose adjacent buildings overlooked Dublin Castle while snipers could operate from nearby houses. Mallin was also impressed by Jacob's height and its ample stores of food. When the Military Council assigned him to the Stephen's Green area later, Mallin examined positions around the park and listed high buildings while noting various park entrances, the fresh water supply, adjoining hotels such as the Shelbourne that would have food and beds and the nearby St Vincent's Hospital. Stephen's Green also had ample space for cars, lorries, stores and holding prisoners.[62] Around September 1915 the Military Council devolved gathering intelligence about British military barracks on to battalion commandants and Ceannt asked Michael Staines to find out all he could about Islandbridge Barracks. Helped by a sympathetic soldier, Staines got inside and sketched every important building. Volunteer employees also smuggled Ceannt into the Curragh army camp, where he made notes and drew maps.

Battalion commandants were also to prepare their men psychologically and militarily for urban warfare with night classes on street-fighting techniques such as constructing barricades; cutting passages through buildings; loop-holing walls; sandbagging windows and firing from rooftops. In the weeks before the Rising the tempo of activity was to increase as commandants conducted a final recruitment drive and attempted to secure more arms. During Holy Week rifles were moved into Dublin or removed from storage places in the city and transferred to dumps prepared for use by Volunteers at the start of the Rising. These included one cache that had been hidden among hundreds of coffins in a church vault.[63]

On 1 August 1915 there occurred an event of enormous symbolic importance, one that inspired revolutionary republicanism and in a subtle way helped condition Volunteers to think and act in a more offensive mode. This was the funeral of a venerable Fenian, O'Donovan Rossa, who had died in America and whose body was brought back to Ireland for a burial that Tom Clarke effectively stage managed and for which he had selected Pearse as the main speaker. Some time before MacDermott had recommended Pearse's oratory to Clarke by commenting that 'if you give him the lines he will dress it up in beautiful language'.[64] A huge crowd followed the funeral cortege and its Volunteer escort to Glasnevin cemetery where a lone bugler played *The Last Post* and Volunteer riflemen fired a salute. For months past Pearse's writings and speeches had been infusing the Volunteers with an increasingly warlike spirit and his graveside oration marked a significant advance in that direction. Delivered with his hands resting on his sword hilt, his address was directed not just at his listeners and assembled Volunteers, but beyond them to the nation. It was effectively a call to arms expressed with great eloquence and in a most impassioned manner as Pearse associated the new republican leaders with the dead Rossa's uncompleted mission: 'I may be taken as speaking on behalf of a new generation that has been re-baptised in the Fenian faith, and that has accepted the responsibility of carrying out the Fenian programme.' He and others would see that responsibility through to the end, come what may and however strong the enemy: 'They think they have foreseen everything, think they have provided against everything; but the fools, the fools, the fools! – they have left us our Fenian dead, and while Ireland holds these graves, Ireland unfree shall never be at peace.'

2

The Planning of the Easter Rising: Part Two

In many respects the Military Council's plans were progressing satisfactorily at the end of 1915 and in early 1916, especially as the general European context seemed favourable. There was a real possibility that the Allies would lose the war because Germany held the military initiative. Its armies occupied large swathes of territory; Belgium, north-east France and a considerable portion of European Russia. In the Atlantic German submarines threatened England's lifeline and the first unrestricted U-boat campaign of 1915 had inflicted considerable damage on Allied shipping. The Dardanelles expedition – designed to knock out Turkey and open up a southern front against Austria-Hungary – was descending into yet another stalemate like that on the Western Front. There the German chief of staff, Falkenhayn, launched a great battle in February 1916 at the fortress of Verdun in an attempt to literally bleed the French army to death. At this time a frequent visitor to the *Irish Freedom* offices in D Ólier Street noticed Clarke, MacDermott and others following the Verdun battle with intense interest. They were absolutely convinced of a 'coming German victory' and 'nearly all the people there were strongly pro-German. They used very frequently to have maps following the movements at Verdun and various places.'[1]

At Clontarf Town Hall in January 1916 Denis McCullough, as president, convened what was to be the last meeting of the IRB's Supreme Council before the Rising.[2] Ten or all eleven members attended and, according to Diarmuid Lynch, everyone accepted Clarke and MacDermott as leaders while Pearse said virtually nothing during the session. The two men kept quiet about their secret planning and came under no pressure from those not in the know to reveal anything. The council also gave them complete freedom in relation to the timing of any rebellion by endorsing a resolution 'that we fight at the earliest date possible.' That was Clarke's intention because three factors were motivating him to drive the revolutionary project on. Unlike most people, he actually feared the war ending soon and a peace conference convening without Irish representation. He was also concerned that the Irish people were 'never at lower ebb',[3] seduced by British rule into a national slumber from which nothing could rouse them 'except the spilling of blood'. Furthermore it seemed to Clarke that perpetual inaction was demoralising the Volunteers – especially when millions of soldiers were engaged in great battles. The rank and file were becoming tired of drills, route marches and manoeuvres that appeared to be going nowhere, especially as they were being mocked and catcalled in public about being toy soldiers.

At the start of 1916 the Military Council was also apprehensive that it might be outflanked by James Connolly, a trade union organiser and socialist revolutionary who, through his speeches, calls to arms and parades, was making an impact far beyond the actual resources of his 200-strong Citizen Army.[3] Connolly had been born in June 1868 to poor Irish parents living in an Edinburgh slum and had an early life that left him with an enduring hatred of poverty. He first saw Ireland briefly in the 1880s while serving in the British army, though after his marriage to Lillie Reynolds in 1890 he settled again in Edinburgh. Working for the Corporation, Connolly was largely self-educated and his reading, especially of Marx, led to him becoming immersed in socialism and nationalism. In 1896 Connolly became a paid organiser for the Dublin Socialist Society and spent the next seven years as an activist and journalist living in the city's slums, honing his ideas and fusing together his socialist and nationalist principles. However, despite his formidable political talents, immense written and verbal powers of persuasion and intellectual clarity, Connolly's advanced views made little headway. Disillusioned by slum dwellers' unresponsiveness and with a growing family to support, he immigrated to the United States in 1903, 'the greatest mistake of my life'. He returned in 1910, determined never to go 'into the Dublin slums again to live; one experience of that is enough for a lifetime. My children are now growing up and it is part of my creed that when I have climbed any part of the ladder towards social comfort I must never descend it again.'[4]

Connolly became a union organiser, helped found the Irish Labour Party, and rose to prominence during the 1913 Dublin Lock-out (which ended in crippling defeat). Afterwards he became General secretary of the Irish Transport and General Workers Union and commander of the Irish Citizen Army, a small force of 200 men established to protect workers during clashes with the police. Both organisations had their headquarters in Liberty Hall which now became Connolly's power base. After the outbreak of war he increasingly envisaged the Citizen Army as a revolutionary weapon and as he became committed to fomenting insurrection, his writings and speeches become more strident and impatient. At the same time the Citizen Army intensified its military preparations through training, route marches and accumulating weapons.

After socialist internationalism had failed to prevent the outbreak of the First World War, Connolly's disillusion became more apparent, particularly as his movement had reached the limits of its growth in the south of Ireland – a conservative society with a small industrial working class and a powerful Catholic Church bitterly opposed to socialism. Increasingly he turned to contemplating a national uprising against British rule in Ireland and by the end of 1915 Connolly was demanding action, threatening that if nobody else took the lead he would strike alone with his tiny Citizen Army. Like Clarke, he too feared a sudden British victory in the war leaving the revolutionary movement high and dry; Connolly, of course, didn't know about the Military Council's secret preparations for rebellion and indeed he directed much of his anger at Volunteer leaders whom he denounced as spineless. His strategy was to appeal over their heads to the rank and file in the hope that if the Citizen Army rose then ordinary Volunteers would support it and drag the Volunteer Executive and Headquarters Staff into the struggle. By the end of 1915 the Military Council felt that Connolly was breathing down its neck and almost physically stalking some of its members, attempting to shame them into action. At a John Mitchel centenary commemoration in November 1915, just as Pearse was arguing that Irish risings of the past had all come too late rather than early, Connolly, from the audience, immediately interjected: 'Will the next one be too late?'[5]

Republican attitudes to Connolly were ambivalent. Many regarded him as 'impatient, irritable and petulant. The slightest upset annoyed him and he, I almost said, sulked.'[6] However the same person also paid tribute to Connolly's 'massive intellect' and his 'great resource and courage' and many people admired his determination, drive and organisational ability. Nonetheless, the Military Council's primary concern was that his independence and impatience threatened their own ambitions and that his violent public exhortations to revolution might cause the British government to suppress both the Citizen Army and the Volunteers simultaneously. Connolly was very dismissive of secret societies or conspiracy, telling a friend that while he acknowledged the present generation of republicans' determination 'in his earlier years in Ireland many IRB men of this time did not mean business but just jogged along and talked physical force and he had no use for that sort of thing'.[7] While Connolly accepted that keeping plans for revolution secret was necessary he also believed that rousing popular support meant publicly proclaiming an intention to act. The distinction alarmed a Military Council that suspected Connolly was spiralling out of control. Diarmuid Lynch said of Connolly's public calls for a rising:

> It was sheer madness – expressed, it is true, in complete ignorance of the decisions and plans conducted through the Military Council. It cannot be gainsaid that it was chiefly the mercy of Providence that blinded the British authorities to even an approximate sensing of the situation and kept them [in the first place] from pouncing on Connolly and his I.C.A. of 200 men – who could have been nabbed outside the precincts of Liberty Hall in the early months of 1916. Had they [the British] attacked the I.C.A., the Irish Volunteers were bound to become involved in some haphazard fashion. Incidentally, the leaders of the IRB as well as those of the Irish Volunteers [as such] might have been caught off their guard and arrested by the British. One shudders to think of the possible result![8]

Hobson too recognised how perilous Connolly's strategy was and persuaded MacNeill to confront him at Volunteer headquarters on Sunday 16 January 1916. At the meeting – which Pearse also attended – everyone was appalled by Connolly's candid admission that he was prepared to use the Citizen Army to ignite a nationwide chain reaction. They warned Connolly that they would never allow him to drag them into such a venture. According to MacNeill, 'Pearse remained with me after Connolly left and he told me that he agreed with my attitude. He added that he was confident that he would himself persuade Connolly to abandon his project. Very shortly afterwards he assured me that he had succeeded with Connolly.'[9] In his own way Pearse was speaking the truth. He was dismayed by Connolly's strategy and he did set out to persuade him to desist, but in so doing Pearse was acting on behalf of and in the interests of the Military Council, not those of MacNeill and the Volunteer moderates. Immediately after the meeting Pearse warned his fellow conspirators that Connolly was risking massive British repression before their own plans had been completed and that they had to neutralise him quickly. Despite being angry at Connolly's irresponsibility and no doubt tempted to act against him, the plotters finally accomplished their goal in a most imaginative and even generous manner by reeling him into their own conspirators. MacDermott had a great ability to read others and they realised that behind his mask of inflexibility Connolly could bend and be tempted if something enticing was dangled before him. Three days after the meeting at Volunteer headquarters Connolly vanished, apparently voluntarily, from Liberty Hall in the company of two IRB members, who brought him to a brickworks in Dolphin's Barn. During three days of negotiations with Pearse, MacDermott and Plunkett he learnt about the Military Council's existence and its plans for a German arms shipment and a rising. In return for abandoning his own insurrectionary plans Connolly was offered an alliance between the Irish Volunteers and the Citizen Army, and a place on the Military Council. He accepted eagerly because in exchange for a few months' delay he had been promised certain action by a far larger number of men than he could ever hope to put in the field. The Military Council, for its part, was delighted to eliminate the constant concern about a premature strike by the Citizen Army whose support it had now acquired. Its members could now concentrate absolutely on refining its plans for a rising, utilising Connolly's military expertise in its own deliberations, as well using him to educate and lecture to Volunteer officers and members.

By the end of January 1916 the Military Council's plans were well advanced, being essentially a modified version of Plunkett's memorandum to the Germans. The centrepiece remained the Irish Volunteers seizing Dublin and inspiring the rest of the country to rise, thus transforming the insurrection into a truly national affair. The provincial rising would still be initiated in the west, where the Volunteers were relatively strong, and precipitated by the anticipated arrival of a large German arms vessel. The original destination of this shipment, which the Germans had not yet finally approved, had been Limerick, but about the end of January 1916 the Military Council changed it to Fenit, which the western Volunteer leaders had always favoured. Plunkett had believed that at most Limerick contained only a small British army garrison but in 1916 one Kerry Volunteer estimated there were 1,000 troops.[10]

Dublin's central importance to the Easter Rising is obvious. The rebellion was planned there and the headquarters of the Irish Volunteers and the Citizen Army were located in it, as were the homes of the members of the Military Council. The Rising would begin in the capital, an Irish Republic would be declared there and a provisional government would be based in the city. The general outline of the insurrection in Dublin had been decided by the time Connolly joined the Military Council. For months past Volunteers had switched their training to handling explosives, bomb throwing and classes on street-fighting, though Connolly's assiduous study of urban warfare in European cities provided useful advice. He especially stressed the importance of highly motivated men of initiative employing unorthodox methods against an enemy superior in numbers and firepower. He also rejected the traditional use of barricades with static defenders firing at oncoming troops and cavalry, arguing that the British would annihilate them. Instead Connolly proposed using unmanned barricades to frustrate cavalry charges and slow up advancing troops, allowing concealed Volunteers to decimate them. These defenders should loophole buildings and knock down parts of walls so that they could slip from building to building and rain rifle fire down on an enemy trapped in the open. This method would give Volunteers a vital fluidity, whereas with a static defence the British would be able to pin defenders down and eventually overrun them. Connolly stressed that urban warfare was a lethal battle of wits in which, for instance, an insurgent occupying a house who was unwary enough to answer a telephone would probably be cut down by rifle fire directed by the caller on the other end of the line.

In Dublin the four Volunteer battalions were to seize a series of strongholds in the city centre sufficiently close to one another to form an inner defensive cordon. These garrisons would also threaten rail and road communications along which would head British reinforcements for the city centre. The Provisional Government would seize the GPO in O'Connell Street. Ned Daly's 1st Battalion would occupy the Four Courts, a large classical building that lay on the direct route of troops coming into the city centre from the Royal Barracks, a short distance further up the Liffey. Daly's seizure of North King Street to the rear would also neutralise the route of troops coming from Marlborough Cavalry Barracks on the north-western edge of the city. MacDonagh's 2nd Battalion was to occupy Jacob's biscuit factory, which was less than three-quarters of a mile from both Portobello and Richmond Barracks on the southern rim of the central city area. De Valera's 3rd Battalion would take Boland's bakery close to Beggar's Bush Barracks and cover the road and rail routes to Kingstown, a port through which the British would almost certainly rush troops from England. Ceannt's 4th Battalion's occupation of the South Dublin Union was designed to threaten Richmond and Islandbridge Barracks. In addition the Military Council intended seizing railway stations such as Kingsbridge, the terminus of the line from Cork and the south; Broadstone, from Athlone, Galway and the west; and Amiens Street which connected with Belfast and the north. It also intended taking control of the capital's telegraph and telephone system.

That the Military Council did not plan to seize either Dublin Castle or Trinity College has caused endless debate. The Castle was the nerve centre of British rule in Ireland and Connolly had conducted Citizen Army manoeuvres in its vicinity during the winter of 1915/16. It is often argued that the council missed a wonderful opportunity on the first morning of the Rising when the small number of guards at the Castle was revealed, but the council was concerned with occupation over seizure. The conspirators decided, no doubt with some reluctance, that the complex of buildings was too extensive to be held for the duration of a rising. Furthermore, the Castle contained a military hospital and protecting and feeding the sick and injured as well as guarding many prisoners would have over-stretched resources. Trinity College was not seized but there are indications that it was originally a target because it features on a list of strongholds to be occupied by de Valera's 3rd Battalion, only to be excised, suggesting a late abandonment.[11]

The Dublin Rising is often depicted as a siege in which encircled defenders endured as long as possible an onslaught by attackers who, after being initially surprised, always held the initiative. Yet enough is known of the Military Council's plans to indicate that its strategy was considerably more imaginative, aggressive and optimistic. Having seen the consequences of submarine warfare in the sinking of the *Lusitania* off the coast of Ireland on 7 May 1915, it clearly hoped that the German navy would be able to prevent troop reinforcements arriving from Britain. Attacked by a U-boat, the liner went down with the loss of over 1,000 lives, and the Military Council clearly envisaged similar attacks on British troopships during the Rising. In April 1916 the conspirators were to demand the dispatch of a U-boat to Dublin Bay when the Rising began.[12] This submarine, which existed only in the council's imagination, appears to have assumed an almost talismanic significance during Easter Week, particularly in the General Post Office where Pearse mystified some of the garrison by his constant assurances that the U-boat would soon appear. If the U-boat failed, then Volunteers would attack reinforcements when they disembarked, as de Valera's 3rd Battalion planned to do at the port of Kingstown. If the British garrison in Dublin could be isolated, then Volunteers in North County Dublin and surrounding counties might be able to exert pressure on it before being joined by mobile relief columns coming from the west. In this scenario, then, the inner city cordon can be seen as a trap, designed to lure the British on until they were squeezed between the rebel strongholds in the city centre and the large numbers of provincial Volunteers on the outskirts who would exert increasing pressure as they pushed forward to relieve the inner cordon. In that event, the Rising was envisaged as ending with the capitulation of the British army leadership, not that of the provisional government.

As Plunkett had envisaged, the Rising in the west was to be co-ordinated with that in Dublin and the Military Council had to hope that the German arms landing would incite a popular uprising in which large numbers of enthusiastic civilians would join the Irish Volunteers. German rejection of an expeditionary force vexed the Military Council, which was reluctant to abandon its dream of being supported by the best army in Europe. It tried, unsuccessfully, in April 1916 to bounce the Germans into supplying at least a token force by insisting that it required officers to accompany the arms shipment. It anticipated that even a small number of experienced and well-trained men would provide leadership to Volunteers in the west and give shape and direction to the rebellion there. Undoubtedly it would also electrify the country as a whole.[13]

The western Rising was planned to erupt suddenly. Triggered by the seizure of Dublin and the arms ship arriving at Fenit, Volunteers would surprise and overwhelm police and soldiers.[14] As soon as the German vessel landed, news was to be transmitted to Tralee, where Austin Stack, the Kerry commandant, would mobilise his men, occupy the General Post Office and take control of telephone and telegraphic communications. At the same time roadblocks would isolate the town from the outside world to prevent pro-British sympathisers alerting Cork and Limerick. Once Tralee was under full control Stack was to dispatch a goods train to Fenit to receive the German arms. Simultaneously, other Volunteer units in places like Listowel, Castleisland and Killarney would prevent British forces disrupting the Fenit landing by capturing police and troops in the open, isolating their barracks with sniper fire or destroying them with fire and explosives. If, as was likely, the British authorities in Cork and Limerick discovered that communications with Tralee had been severed and sent out reconnaissance units, the Volunteers in Cork and South Kerry were to intercept them on the main roads or sabotage the railway lines with explosives. The German weapons were for use by the Volunteers in Kerry, Cork, Limerick, Clare and

Galway and they were to be distributed quickly throughout the west. When the train carrying them from Fenit arrived at Tralee, some would be removed for the Cork and Kerry Volunteers, while the rest went to Limerick, then across the Shannon by boat and on by rail to Clare and Athenry in Galway. Once mobilised, the Volunteers in the western counties would eventually link up with each other to occupy a line running from the Shannon through Limerick and east Kerry to Macroom in Co. Cork.

Ulster was to play no part in the Rising because the Military Council feared a sectarian war in the province. Denis McCullough, the President of the Supreme Council of the IRB, was to be told by Pearse and Connolly in March 1916 to assemble his men in Dungannon and march to join up with Liam Mellows and the Galway Volunteers. He was sceptical about the prospects of u
150 miles during which he was ordered not
route passed a strong British garrison in En

The Military Council clearly hoped that
the provisional government established effe
defeat any attempt to re-conquer Ireland.
Plunkett's offer to make Ireland a partner in the German war effort; by making its ports available for naval operations in the Atlantic the Irish Sea would become a new theatre of war, with a potentially crippling impact on Britain. If Ireland were able to hold out until the end of the war she would then be an independent nation, but if the Rising developed less favourably then the western Volunteers might at least be able to hold the line of the Shannon to receive the provisional government and those men who had broken out of Dublin. In those circumstances the joint force might be able to conduct a campaign of guerrilla warfare.

Both Connolly and the conspirators concealed their new relationship from moderate Volunteer leaders. MacNeill reported getting:

> firm assurances in conversations that no plans of insurrection was adopted. I cannot say now from what persons I got these assurances but they included Pearse, Joe Plunket [sic] and T. MacDonough [sic]. Within the following weeks I observed various indications that a plan of insurrection was meditated, and one day walking home from University College with MacDonough I told him what I thought I observed. MacDonough assured me that I was mistaken, and reproached for not believing the assurances I had already got.[16]

Although MacDonagh wasn't yet a Military Council member his close friendship with Pearse and Plunkett must have given him a good idea of the way things were going. Sean Fitzgibbon was mightily sceptical at the next Volunteer Executive meeting when:

> Pearse, obviously in great stress of emotion, and speaking very tensely, said that he and MacDermott had induced Connolly to take no action without the aid of the Volunteers. I asked Pearse if he had given any promise or had pledged the Volunteers. Pearse said 'No.' His right knee kept quivering as he spoke. He kept raising his right foot slightly, tapping the ground with it, like a horse pawing as he answered my questions. He was lying, for at that time the date of the Rising had been decided upon.[17]

Hobson, for his part, didn't believe a word of the entire charade. During the next three months an increasingly desperate power struggle took place at the top of the Volunteers between him and members of the Military Council. It was a battle waged behind closed doors, away from the gaze of the rank and file and the general public who had no inkling that serious policy differences existed within the Volunteer leadership. Although Hobson had allies such as J.J. O'Connell, the Chief of Inspection, he often felt that he was carrying an intolerable burden. He was also frustrated by his inability to secure certain proof of his opponents' activities and they consistently outmanoeuvred the moderates by their unity of purpose, energy and unscrupulousness. Nor was it easy to propel MacNeill into decisive action; Hobson often found it easier to convince him 'that nothing could be done than it was to spur him into positive action'.[18] For example, in February 1916 MacNeill agreed to summon a special Volunteer convention to lay down policy. He then changed his mind, opting for a private meeting at which Pearse, Plunkett and MacDonagh reacted with hurt innocence and provided unqualified assurances about their loyalty. Their ability to subvert the Volunteers from within was greatly assisted by MacNeill's frequent absences from headquarters where an overworked Hobson despaired about a regime of organisational indiscipline. In early April 1916, when Hobson demanded that all important orders should be signed by MacNeill, Pearse and his associates simply voted for the motion and blithely continued as before.[19]

As chief of staff MacNeill displayed a remarkable capacity for ignoring incriminating evidence. While visiting Limerick in late 1915 he learnt accidentally that Pearse, on his own initiative, had issued important orders to Volunteer officers and had even instructed Michael Colivet, the Limerick commandant, to 'hold the line of the Shannon in the event of actual hostilities'.[20] MacNeill regarded this revelation as 'incredible' but declined to investigate the matter further. Later, when an American correspondent warned him about a planned Irish rising, he lamely told MacDermott and wrote about the revelation in *Irish Volunteer*, expecting the publicity to frustrate any such venture.[21]

The conspirators' freedom of manoeuvre on the Volunteer Executive was due largely to MacNeill's negligence. Perhaps haunted by memories of a nervous breakdown precipitated by overwork, he avoided burdening himself with Executive meetings and Volunteer administration so that he could concentrate on his historical studies. MacNeill's great gift, and flaw, was his talent for capturing the zeitgeist – the spirit of the times – by enunciating a big idea in well argued and persuasive detail and creating a public mood of excitement and intellectual ferment. He did this three times in his life: first with the Gaelic League, then by revolutionising Irish historical scholarship, and finally through an article that began the Irish Volunteers. Following through with the hard grind was a very different matter. MacNeill's fatal weakness as a politician was that he lacked a real appetite for politics, a field that he had entered from a sense of public duty and from whose frustrations, demands and unpleasantness he increasingly shrank, but for which others like Clarke and MacDermott felt only unbounded passion. Increasingly MacNeill took flight to the comfort of dusty documents that never answered back or contradicted and defied his interpretation, unlike so many people he met in real life. A friend observed how MacNeill:

had more and more frequently tended to absent himself from executive meetings to step back into the tenth century and the Book of the Dun Cow and to leave the chairmanship of the weekly meetings to Pearse; that therefore he had mostly lost the right to be offended when he suddenly came back to modern times and found that things had been done unknown to him.[22]

MacNeill's inept performance helps explain one of the Rising's greatest mysteries: how, against all odds, such a small group of men got away with it, outmanoeuvring Irish and British opponents to realise their seemingly outlandish ambitions. However, they also excelled in their conspiratorial skill, mendacity, drive, ruthlessness and clarity of vision. Furthermore, they possessed a unity of purpose and absolute dedication that wasn't remotely matched by opponents like Hobson, Fitzgibbon, The O'Rahilly and Seamus O'Connor, who might have comprised an executive majority but were never in complete ideological agreement. Leadership was another crucial factor, with a gulf separating MacNeill and Clarke in terms of personality, willpower and commitment. Ultimately the conspirators lost all respect for MacNeill and Pearse was really speaking for every one of them by describing him as 'weak, hopelessly weak. I knew that all along'.[23] An exasperated MacDonagh saw only vacillation as 'MacNeill would leave their meeting agreeing to their policy and, at the next meeting would have changed his mind due, as he said, to some outside influence'.[24]

Although MacNeill must have often been tempted to walk away from it all, he held back, probably fearing being accused of desertion, a lack of patriotism even, and of disheartening members during a great war when conscription was a real possibility. Perhaps he also believed that only he could hold together the warring factions within the Volunteers and prevent a split. Nor did he trust those Executive members who might take over to keep the organisation on the right course. However, almost certainly, he just couldn't bear to let go of his creation and the prominence and excitement that came with leading the Volunteers. As so often is the case with the academic involved in politics, MacNeill appears to have succumbed to the aphrodisiac of power, the thrill of not just writing about history but actually making it.

Drift and indecisiveness at Volunteer headquarters in the early months of 1916 suited the Military Council very well. So also did a developing anxiety – which it helped generate – that the British government intended to provoke and then disarm or suppress the Irish Volunteers. In the face of this atmosphere of crisis and apparent threat, the need for Volunteer unity became paramount. This, in turn, enabled the radicals to explain away any activities that looked suspiciously like preparations for a rebellion as purely precautionary and defensive measures, designed to protect the organisation from attack. This indeed was invariably the line taken by Pearse when he was challenged at Executive meetings.[25]

The Military Council never doubted that for the higher good it had the moral right to deceive Executive moderates, rank-and-file Volunteers and even IRB members. Nevertheless, it understood that future generations would debate the morality of manipulating into battle men who had not explicitly given their consent. The conspirators no doubt justified their behaviour by the impossibility of seeking open approval for rebellion. Also they believed that every Irish Volunteer by 1916 accepted that, in certain circumstances, he would engage in conflict with British forces and that the overwhelming majority had also come to accept its inevitability. In such circumstances it seemed to the Military Council that the issue of rebellion had been reduced to a matter of timing rather than principle between 'extremists' and 'moderates'. Furthermore, some moderates like The O'Rahilly were in practice just as radical as the extremists.[26] Michael O'Rahilly, universally known (at his insistence) as The O'Rahilly, had been born in 1875, the scion of a prosperous Kerry family who became manager of the Gaelic League's journal. Somewhat melodramatic, his open and ebullient personality appealed even to political opponents who recognised his generosity of spirit and tenacious loyalty. In August 1914 he had advocated seizing Dublin Castle, proclaiming Home Rule and inviting Redmond to become President of Ireland, so although The O'Rahilly refused to join the IRB, there was clearly no inflexible line separating him from Pearse, whom he in fact eventually joined in the GPO during the Rising. Similarly MacNeill, in the crucial days before the Rising, was to conclude a short-lived alliance with representatives of the Military Council and even after it broke down was only just dissuaded from donning his Volunteer uniform and joining the rebellion.

The Military Council went as far as it dared in psychologically conditioning the Volunteer rank and file to the inevitability of revolution by having Pearse deliver a series of brilliantly ambiguous speeches. When lecturing a Dublin Volunteer Company in February 1916, Pearse deftly walked a tightrope by hinting at possible eventualities while at the same time taking care not to alert the British authorities.[27] He galvanised his audience by openly advocating separatism and talking about 'being called into action', yet he also cautiously stressed that it would be wrong of him to tell Volunteers 'that they might soon be called into action'. His speech then 'succeeded in conveying the desired idea to those who were ready to be impressed by it but at the same time in minimising the full and immediate purport of his remarks to others'. By constant repetition, Pearse gradually effected an almost unconscious transformation in the outlook of many Volunteers away from a defensive cast of mind to an offensive one. One Volunteer officer recalled that 'At no time was it stated at any of our meetings that we were to engage in an insurrection, with or without assistance, but very definitely an atmosphere was cultivated which pointed towards the uprising'.[28] Another officer, Oscar Traynor, has described a meeting of Dublin Brigade officers shortly before the Rising at which the heightened sense of anticipation was almost tangible:

> Patrick Pearse was wearing his greatcoat of volunteer green and a slouch hat when he entered the room. His brother helped him to take these off. Pearse then approached the head of the table and, after a short time, was introduced to the Volunteer officers who had already spoken. Patrick Pearse rose amidst dead silence, stared over the heads of the Volunteers assembled in the room, and paused for almost one minute before he spoke. The first words he uttered sent a thrill through all present. The words were somewhat as follows: 'I know that you have been preparing your bodies for the great struggle that lies before us, but have you also been preparing your souls?' These words made such a deep impression on all present that there was complete silence for a considerable period. Following this, Pearse went on to urge the Volunteers to do everything possible to prepare themselves for the

great struggle ahead. Most of us left that meeting convinced that in a short time we would find ourselves in action.[29]

The Military Council also cunningly manipulated its opponents' self-deception, they exploited the anxiety of the British government and Executive moderates to cling to any hope that Ireland would remain peaceful and reasonably stable. As a result of this desperate optimism they failed to recognise the many small changes that had cumulatively altered the political situation in Ireland. Connolly encouraged his opponents' wishful thinking by his strategy of 'wolf, wolf, wolf'.[30] He had the Citizen Army conduct endless exercises in the vicinity of Dublin Castle and Wellington Barracks and even advertised them in advance on a blackboard outside Liberty Hall. Eventually the authorities became bored and lost interest. For his part, Pearse sought to lull the Irish administration into a false sense of security by toning down public displays of extremism by the Irish Volunteers. He prohibited the tricolour and insisted on a flag with a plain gold harp on a green background, a design that was identified with conservative nationalism.[31] He also arranged a clever deception of the ever-suspicious Hobson by planting Liam Mellows, an Irish Volunteer organiser, to pose as Hobson's eyes and ears in the provinces and apparently an enthusiastic supporter of his gradualist policy. Whenever Mellows came to Volunteer headquarters he cultivated Hobson, who came to believe that he could trust Mellows to warn him of any dangerous developments outside the capital. Hobson never suspected until it was too late that he had been comprehensively duped and that Mellows had already been chosen by the Military Council to lead the Rising in Galway.[32]

By March 1916 the radicals had succeeded in presenting British policy towards the Irish Volunteers as aggressive and provocative, with Executive moderates and extremists alike incensed at an apparently systematic harassment of their organisation. There was the arrest of Volunteers under the Defence of the Realm Act, constant police surveillance, closure of militant newspapers, imprisonment and deportation of organisers like Mellows and government pressure on employers not to recruit extremists. Tension was ratcheted up even further by a violent confrontation in the town of Tullamore, King's County, on 20 March 1916. Fighting between pro- and anti-war nationalists ended with supporters of 'separation women' (wives of men enlisted in the Bristish army) attacking the Irish Volunteer Hall in the town, and as the crowd stampeded up the stairs, a Volunteer, Peadar Bracken, fired over their heads.[33] When the police arrived and threatened to search for arms there was a scuffle in which Bracken fired at an inspector and wounded a sergeant in the ensuing mêlée before he fought his way down the stairs and escaped. Thirteen Volunteers were subsequently arrested and charged with attempted murder, though they were eventually released on a legal technicality.

The shots at Tullamore were, in a sense, the first shots of the Easter Rising. Although the affair had not been deliberately engineered, its timing and manner were wonderfully helpful to the Military Council; outraged moderates on the Volunteer Executive now endorsed resistance measures by declaring that government raids would be met by 'resistance and bloodshed'. MacNeill warned that Volunteers would 'defend our arms with our lives'. Events and propaganda had created a perception among nationalists of a coherent and aggressive British policy that was completely at variance with reality. Augustine Birrell, Chief Secretary for Ireland, was a cultured and civilised politician who got on well with mainstream nationalist politicians, but his reputation for indolence was well deserved and he was frequently absent in London. The day-to-day administration of Ireland was the responsibility of his undersecretary, Sir Matthew Nathan, a highly intelligent, hospitable, prodigiously hard-working public official. But his sense of loyalty and obedience to his political masters made Nathan reluctant to pressurise Birrell.

Birrell and Nathan were also constrained by a political sea change that happened in August 1914. For the first seven months of that year Ireland was not just the main issue in British politics, it was effectively the only one that mattered. The Ulster Unionist campaign of resistance to Home Rule and political negotiations about a compromise solution consumed the Cabinet and parliament. The major crises, such as the Curragh Mutiny, the Larne gunrunning and Howth and Bachelor's Walk, were all connected to Ireland whose affairs dominated press coverage and obsessed public attention. The British prime minister, Asquith, arguably the most important politician in the world, devoted much time to Irish affairs to the extent of knowing the names of many small towns in Fermanagh and Tyrone and census returns for both counties which might have to be partitioned. By the end of July 1914 many people feared that the United Kingdom stood on the edge of a precipice and because of Ireland was about to tip over into civil war. The outbreak of war with Germany in August 1914 changed everything almost overnight. Thereafter for the British government it became a case of don't mention anything but the war, and Dublin Castle's mandate became one of keeping Ireland quiescent so that the Cabinet could concentrate absolutely on mobilising resources for a conflict that was developing into a total war.

The policy of Birrell and the Irish administration then consisted of crisis avoidance and shying away from confrontations with the Volunteers that might destabilise the country. It was a policy of containment that the chief secretary's critics soon began denouncing as appeasement. Even in that limited ambition Birrell and Nathan constantly discovered the narrow limits of their apparently sweeping emergency powers. At a conference in Dublin Castle on 17 March 1916, for instance, Nathan, Major-General Sir Lovick Friend the army GOC, Ivon Price the British Intelligence Officer in Ireland, the Irish attorney-general and police representatives examined proposals to frustrate the Volunteers.[34] They worked through a list of options but, because of political expediency or legal complexity they rejected internment; action against organising instructors; Tom Clarke's re-incarceration under his old sentence; and even the banning of night manoeuvres. After weighing 'the comparative disadvantages of a suppression of the movement with the risk of some bad collisions and of allowing it to continue and possibly grow stronger', Nathan was more impressed with 'the difficulties of the former course' but he took comfort in his belief that the Irish Volunteers were still being restrained, though he was giving them 'a good deal of rope'.[35]

This complacency which embraced most, though not all, of the British authorities in Ireland in the eighteen months before the Rising was reinforced by Redmond's advice to allow the Irish Volunteers to wither away. When Field-Marshal French, commander of Home Forces, mentioned that information had been 'received that certain parts of Ireland are in a very disturbed way – an insurrection had even been suggested in the public press', Nathan replied, reassuringly, that, 'though the Irish Volunteer element has been active of late, especially in Dublin, I do not believe that its leaders mean insurrection or that the Volunteers have sufficient arms to make it formidable if the leaders do mean it. The bulk of the people are not disaffected.'[36] On 13 April an upbeat Nathan informed Birrell that 'Things are getting better for the moment. We are at last getting some information as to what is going on here – for the first time since I have been in place.'[37]

Sir Neville Chamberlain, the RIC's inspector-general, didn't share such optimism. He repeatedly warned Birrell and Nathan about the Irish Volunteers and whether an armed organisation 'so hostile to British interests, can be permitted to increase its strength and remain any longer in possession of arms without grave danger to the State'.[38] He urged them to consider arresting Volunteer leaders, who were a pro-German 'pack of rebels who would revolt and proclaim their independence in the event of any favourable opportunity'. Chamberlain went on to warn that:

> If the speeches of Irish Volunteer leaders and articles in Sinn Fein journals have any meaning it must be that the force is being organised with a view to insurrec-tion, and in the event of the enemy being able to effect a landing in Ireland the Volunteers could no doubt delay the dispatch of troops to the scene by blowing up the railways and bridges, provided the organisers were at liberty to plan and direct the operations.

Chamberlain's detectives had planted among the Irish Volunteers two spies, code-named Granite and Chalk, who provided mixed signals about the organisation's intentions. On 27 March 1916 Granite reported no present danger of a rising because 'Standing alone, they are not prepared for any prolonged encounter with the forces of the Crown and the majority of them are practically untrained'.[39] Instead, he believed they were concentrating on stockpiling explosives and this was 'the real danger' – apparently a warning about a possible renewal of the 1880s dynamite campaign. Alarmingly, Chalk believed that 'the young men of the Irish Volunteers are very anx-ious to start "business" at once, and they are being backed up strongly by Connolly and the Citizen Army and things look as if they were coming to a crisis'. While 'The heads of the Irish Volunteers are against a "rising" at present … the rank and file say that if they wait until the war is over they will all be shot'.[40]

With exquisite guile, the Military Council solved the problem of commencing the Rising by bringing numbers of Irish Volunteers on to the streets of Dublin unop-posed. Their strategy was to present the organisation's Easter manoeuvres as training exercises which Pearse, in his capacity of Director of Organisation, announced pub-licly and well in advance on 8 April. He even had them approved by MacNeill and the entire Volunteer Executive. Similar exercises had taken place at the same time the previous year so those of 1916 could be presented convincingly as a rou-tine operation. Also their stated purpose, 'to test mobilisation with equipment' was reassuringly anodyne. Furthermore, as another masterly piece of camouflage, each battalion commander was ordered to submit to Pearse before 1 May a detailed report on the manoeuvres carried out by his unit. This implied a peaceful exercise that the Headquarters Staff would review subsequently at leisure.

By the middle of April 1916, Hobson was convinced that the radicals were planning a confrontation between the Volunteers and the British government. Having failed to neutralise them within the organisation he decided to go public with his concerns on Palm Sunday evening, 16 April, when he attended a Volunteer fundraising concert in Parnell Square. Sean MacDermott's girlfriend Min Ryan had organised the event knowing almost nothing about MacDermott's political activities or the mutual hatred between him and Hobson. However, initially, her concert couldn't have suited MacDermott better as it gave credence to the Military Council's fiction that everything was winding down to the Easter holidays. Things changed when a performer failed to appear and Ryan invited Hobson to fill in by addressing a hall crowded with Volunteers and other militant nationalists: 'On the spur of the moment I made a speech in very guarded language so as not to excite the suspicions of the authorities and yet sufficiently definite to be intelligible to the many Volunteers who were in the hall.'[41] Hobson had finally crossed the line. He might claim that his coded warning against any precipitate action that might ruin the Volunteers was spontaneous and not designed to alert Dublin Castle but to the conspirators it seemed premeditated treachery, a deliberate attempt to torpedo their plans for a rising. One audience member recalled a frisson of concern gliding around the auditorium:

> One could feel that he was treading on dangerous ground. There was a certain breathlessness in the hall. One could see glances passing between those who were probably aware of what decisions had already been taken. When it was all over there were groups talking earnestly, some denouncing him and others praising his speech. On the following days that speech was a general subject of conversation. Opinions differed, from those who thought that it was a timely word of caution, to those who thought that it was black treachery. It was quite clear that those who knew most about the plans regarded it as disastrous.[42]

Hobson believed that a majority in the hall was on his side but even if that were true such public frankness was extraordinarily risky – especially for someone in the IRB. Denis McCullough, President of the Supreme Council, had only just been told by Clarke about the Rising starting on Easter Sunday and he became increasingly alarmed as he listened to someone to whom he had once been so close but whose intervention seemed potentially ruinous: 'To me it sounded like bedlam. I feared that divided councils would be fatal to any attempt at an armed Rising.' Afterwards he 'met Sean MacDermott limping in. I told him what Hobson was saying inside and with a good round oath Sean said that we would "damned soon deal with that fellow"'.[43] Min Ryan's friend, Nancy Wyse Power, believed that 'on that night Hobson's life was in danger of being taken and that it might have been saved by the fact that he was with a group'.[44] But a reckoning had only been postponed because Clarke and MacDermott's loathing of Hobson was infecting the entire Military Council. By now they all hated the very sight of him, his endless obstructionism and the influence that he wielded over MacNeill and Volunteer organisers like Ginger O'Connell and Eimar Duffy. They longed only to banish the baleful presence from their midst of someone whom Clarke had begun describing as the devil incarnate. Connolly denounced Hobson as 'the villain of the piece' a person who was publicly 'preaching red revolution at the secret councils of the nation he does everything to retard those who are working for the day that we all so much desire'.[45] MacDonagh told Ceannt that Hobson was 'the evil genius of the Volunteers and if we could separate John MacNeill from his influence all would be well'.[46] A day after Hobson's speech the Military Council decided to terminate his interference but only nearer the Rising.

Its meeting on Monday 17 April, however, was mostly devoted to approving a draft of the Proclamation of the Irish Republic which was to be announced on the first day of the Rising. It also ratified the provisional government, whose members would sign the Proclamation and who coincidentally were also the council's seven members. Finally, the Military Council approved the circulation of a so-called Castle Document, an exercise in disinformation apparently devised by Plunkett, which purported to reveal a British plan of mass arrests, including the entire Irish Volunteer Executive, and supposedly named strategic locations to be seized, including Volunteer headquarters in Dawson Street. Later that day, according to MacNeill, the document was planted on him and he was told 'through I.V. sources' that British forces were engaged in movements preparatory to an offensive against the Volunteers was outlined in the document.

According to MacNeill 'this document served the purpose of creating great excitement and apprehension of the Volunteers being suppressed – an event which we were all bound to resist'.[47] On Tuesday and Wednesday he convened emergency meetings of the Volunteer Executive which took place well away from headquarters to avoid making it easy for the British authorities to arrest them all. MacNeill recalled that 'there was great tension at these meetings' as they discussed the Castle Document and he toned down more radical suggestions for responding to apparent British plans for aggression. Instead, he drafted a general order to Volunteers declaring a state of alert and warning them to prepare to resist. However, before MacNeill issued it the Castle Document became public knowledge. After government censors denied its publication in the newspapers the Military Council passed it on to Alderman Tom Kelly – a MacNeill associate – who read it out on Wednesday 19 April 1916 at a meeting of Dublin Corporation. The government then backed down and allowed publication, though denouncing the document as a fabrication. Denying the Castle Document's authenticity didn't prevent next day's newspapers electrifying the political atmosphere in Dublin however. Soon after MacNeill's order appeared, Volunteer headquarters resembled a fortress frantically preparing for an enemy onslaught. Desmond Fitzgerald, a Volunteer officer remembered that:

> what seemed to be an enormous amount of surgical dressings were brought into one of the offices, and members of the women's organisation were called in to arrange for the making of field dressings and this work was treated as of immediate urgency. Members of the inner circle came in and out, and when there they retired into a room to hold secret conferences. Bundles of a leaflet which purported to be a secret order of the British that had been decoded were brought in and were being sent through the country for distribution.[48]

By stimulating a war fever the Military Council was psychologically readying Volunteers as well as creating a most convenient smokescreen for its intentions and activities during the final countdown to a rising. At Liberty Hall a Citizen Army officer remembered that:

during the weeks immediately preceding the Rising armed men could be seen, on guard, at the entrance, on the stairs and landings or in the corridors, some in the dark green uniform, some in their ordinary working clothes, some in their Sunday best complete with collar and tie, but however they were dressed did not seem to matter much. They were all fully armed and the building resembled a military barracks in all but name.[49]

For many months the Military Council members had guarded their secrets obsessively, determined to conceal until the last possible moment the fact that the insurrection would commence on Easter Sunday. They always knew that eventually they would have to share this information with senior officers of the Irish Volunteers and Citizen Army, but delayed as long as they could in order to prevent a leak reaching either Executive moderates or Dublin Castle. Only on Spy Wednesday evening, 19 April, when news of the Castle Document began distracting public attention, did commandants learn that the Rising would commence in Dublin at 6.30 p.m. on Easter Sunday, 23 April and half an hour later in the provinces. At the same time individual Volunteers received instructions about specific acts of sabotage that they were to carry out on that day. Pearse dispatched couriers with coded messages to inform some senior officers, such as de Valera. Others were told in person. Tom Clarke informed his brother-in-law Ned Daly while MacDermott broke the news to Diarmuid Lynch over lunch in an O'Connell Street restaurant. Connolly, however, preferred to brief his Citizen Army commanders personally at Liberty Hall where he detailed their roles, revealed the existence of a German arms shipment on its way to Ireland and warned them about the vital necessity of maintaining absolute secrecy until Sunday. One of Connolly's senior officers had a recollection that afterwards they tried to dance in the corridor. Two days later MacDermott gave maps of the garrison areas to battalion commandants, passing them to Daly at the Red Barn restaurant, MacDonagh at the Princess restaurant in Grafton Street, Ceannt at his corporation office and to de Valera who was at home. Connolly had retained the maps for the Stephen's Green and City Hall areas and he distributed them at Liberty Hall. The circle of knowledge widened further as battalion commandants briefed their senior officers. De Valera met his 3rd Dublin Battalion staff on Good Friday evening, 21 April, and outlined the positions they were to occupy at the start of the Rising and the stores that would be waiting for them. He also tightened security by assigning them armed Volunteers as bodyguards to accompany them night and day.[50] The Military Council didn't believe it could risk telling the rank and file, aware as it was of the consequences of doing so for the Fenian Rising in 1867 when, as Ceannt said to his wife, 'as soon as the men were told they thronged the churches for confession and the authorities suspected that something was going to happen and immediately took action'.[51]

Interestingly, Ceannt himself had kept the news about Easter Sunday from Aine until the previous evening, breaking it to her almost as an afterthought. Whether Ceannt was motivated by a highly developed sense of security or a desire to shield his wife from anxiety for as long as possible, even he was an inveterate gossip compared to MacDermott. His fiancée, Min Ryan, knew virtually nothing about MacDermott's activities except that he was an extremely busy man:

He had tremendous vitality in spite of his delicacy and executed a wonderful amount of work. For the last year his office was always crowded with callers about business in connection with the Volunteers. People came from all parts of the country to consult him on important matters. He seemed to be a general secretary of several unnamed societies.[52]

GALWAY COUNTY LIBRARIES

Unsurprisingly, given the length and intensity of their relationship, Clarke treated Kathleen differently. She had long been deeply involved in his political activities and as an assistant and confidante had done work for the IRB since 1909 and was completely trusted. Even so, Tom didn't tell her much about the serious planning for a rising until late 1915 when he revealed that the conspirators had developed a back-up plan in the event of the British arresting them. It required 'some person whose discretion, silence and capability they could rely upon; one who would be fully acquainted with all of their decisions'.[53] They had chosen her as custodian of their decisions and plans and to ensure a framework for continued resistance Clarke gave her:

> the names of the first, second and in some cases the key men all over the country, with whom I could connect should necessity arise; these names I had to memorise. From that time on, after each meeting I was made acquainted with any decisions, changes or anything of importance it was thought I should know.[54]

Tom said that Devoy in America had been told about her new role and that if anything happened to the Supreme Council he was to communicate directly with her, something Devoy in fact did after the Rising. Tom warned Kathleen not to do anything to attract special attention from G-men, Dublin's plainclothes political police, who were already watching her. He also showed her the detailed plans for the Rising well in advance and on Monday of Holy Week, 'wild with excitement', Clarke revealed that his was the first signature on the Proclamation.[55]

Yet even now the British authorities didn't make any intelligence breakthrough about the Military Council's plans. While it is true that those people who were told on 19 April were carefully vetted and sworn to secrecy, many ordinary Volunteers sensed that momentous events were coming. It is amazing that a British intelligence system that had infiltrated and broken previous Irish rebellions – and whose legendary efficiency aroused paranoia among Irish revolutionaries – failed so dismally over such an extended period. Even after Spy Wednesday only one clue reached Dublin Castle before Easter Monday morning, and it came from a most unlikely source: a member of the Military Council itself, Thomas MacDonagh.[56]

Born in Co. Tipperary in 1878, after seven years' teaching experience MacDonagh joined Pearse at St Enda's and went on to become a lecturer in English at University College, Dublin. An ardent cultural nationalist, MacDonagh – poet and dramatist – cut a distinctive figure with his curling brown hair, large nose, cleft chin and grey eyes; but he craved action and joined the Irish Volunteers at its inception. Quickly he rose to a seat on the Executive, became commandant of the 2nd Dublin Battalion and eventually Dublin brigadier. But he lacked the natural revolutionary's steely purpose, being at heart an insecure, gloomy, solitary young man whose temperamental instability manifested itself in erratic and melodramatic behaviour. While lecturing

in the spring of 1916 he startled students by producing a large revolver from his
pocket, laying it on the desk and remarking, as if to himself, that 'Ireland can only win
freedom by force'.[57] When, as late as the second week in April 1916, he was recruited
to the Military Council it was to use him as a linkman between the council and
MacNeill, his UCD colleague.[58] The chief of staff himself recognised that the younger
man was used 'to some extent as an intermediary between that section [the IRB in
the Volunteer Movement] and myself'.[59]

MacDonagh's friends knew his engaging, idealistic side. But his brittle character
and mood swings made him a loose cannon and by Holy Week MacDonagh's heightened emotional state and a penchant for whipping up an audience posed a serious
danger to the conspiracy. On the Sunday 16 April Volunteer HQ sent MacDonagh
and Michael Staines, brigade quartermaster, to settle a dispute within the Fingal
Brigade. Staines couldn't believe it when:

> Tom MacDonagh addressed them and without telling them in so many words made
> it clear that the Rising was coming off on Sunday. This was so pointed that on the
> return journey I said to MacDonagh that we had got instructions not to let them
> know that the Rising was coming off on Sunday, that he had practically told them
> but on the other hand if I was asked to prove it I could not point to any words of his
> to do so. MacDonagh said 'It takes a professor to say a lot without saying anything.'[60]

Pleased with his own verbal dexterity MacDonagh just couldn't stop himself and
in one audience a police spy was listening to him. Subsequently Chalk reported to
Dublin Castle that 'Professor MacDonagh on issuing the Orders on Wednesday night
last said: "We are not going out on Friday, but we are going out on Sunday. Boys,
some of us may never come back – Mobilisation orders to be issued in due course".'[61]
Chalk didn't describe the exact circumstances in which MacDonagh had spoken but
on Wednesday 19 April, as noted, the Military Council revealed its plans to senior
commandants and if MacDonagh, as seems probable, spoke to Volunteers who were
not absolutely trustworthy then it was a remarkable indiscretion. Fortunately for the
Military Council his words didn't alert the Irish Administration: Chalk's report of 22
April lacked explicit detail and it was still working its way through the bureaucracy
when the Rising began. Nevertheless, MacDonagh's behaviour was sufficiently reckless to make one wonder what might have happened had he been a Military Council
member from the start: Chalk's report was a solitary glimmer of light in the black
hole that British intelligence in Ireland had become by 1916. It is hard to disagree
with Leon O'Broin's assessment that:

> Of all the divisions in the Volunteer Executive, of all the moves and counterma-
> noeuvres, the Government knew absolutely nothing and this is all the more
> extraordinary because so many people, including some on the fringe of things, knew
> that a revolt was due to take place … The British intelligence system in Ireland had
> failed hopelessly.[62]

While the British government was ignorant of the imminent danger, Executive
moderates finally discovered something about the conspirators' intentions. The proc-

ess was begun, ironically, by the Military Council itself after it decided to involve in its plans J.J. O'Connell, the Volunteer Chief of Inspection and Sean Fitzgibbon, Director of Recruiting – both moderates and allies of MacNeill and Hobson. For the conspirators to take them, even partially, into their confidence seems inexplicable but it wanted their services because O'Connell's was the best military mind in the Volunteers and Fitzgibbon had successfully organised the Kilcoole gunrunning in August 1914. It also suited them to have the two men out of the capital just before the insurrection as that would increase MacNeill's isolation and remove Fitzgibbon from his post as vice-commandant of de Valera's 3rd Battalion. The deception was skilfully done. Fitzgibbon recalled that:

> On Saturday before Palm Sunday, Kent [Ceannt] called on me as I was having break-fast. He was an official in the City Treasurer's Office. He said he had taken a day off and would walk in with me. If a man was asked to do a job in the Volunteers he invariably agreed. Kent asked me if I would go down the country to handle a job. I agreed and asked what it was. He said it was to land guns from Germany in Limerick and Kerry. I had landed guns successfully at Kilcoole, the week after the Howth gun-running. He wheeled his bicycle and we walked in to work. On the way I asked, 'Does MacNeill know?' 'No,' replied Kent, 'but he will be told by Pearse tomorrow. You are to go to Pearse in St Enda's tomorrow night and he will give you funds.'
> Late on Sunday night I went to St Enda's and well remember the dark walk up to the house – a horrible place. I saw Pearse and said to him, 'Have you told MacNeill?' 'Yes,' replied Pearse: 'He fully agrees.' 'Without any arriere pensee?,' asked I: 'Without any arriere pensee,' replied Pearse. This statement was a lie.[63]

The conspirators' mendacious skill was impressive because they gave Fitzgibbon only a certain amount of information about an arms shipment arriving in the west of Ireland – something to which he had no objection having already organised one at Kilcoole. What they didn't tell him was that it was an integral part of a rising intended to coincide with the weapons landing. O'Connell, for his part, was ordered to lead the Volunteers in south-east Leinster, allegedly with MacNeill's authority. Perhaps surprisingly, Fitzgibbon didn't check with MacNeill that Ceannt and Pearse were telling him the truth. The deception was an audacious gamble by the Military Council but in the frenzied atmosphere created by the Castle Document and MacNeill's bellicose response, Pearse's assurances to both men carried considerable credibility. Besides, the Military Council were all gamblers; if the gunrunning was a gamble then so, of course, was the Rising itself. Every previous gamble had paid off and they seemed to be on a roll, making one more well worth the risk. And it almost succeeded, because Fitzgibbon headed west to liaise with the commandants in Kerry and Limerick.

On Thursday 20 April, however, a dubious O'Connell decided to check with Volunteer headquarters, alerting Hobson that something unusual was happening.[64] That evening Hobson attended a Dublin Centres Board meeting at which an IRB member told him about receiving instructions to sabotage a railway line on Easter Sunday.[65] At last, very late in the day, Hobson had found his smoking gun, even though it was only a small part of the Military Council's overall plan. Abruptly terminating the meeting he went to Volunteer headquarters where O'Connell confirmed his suspicions. Determined to act while there was still time, both men drove out to Woodtown Park at 11 p.m., roused MacNeill in his pyjamas and detailed what they knew. The chief of staff grasped that a serious crisis was in the making and after midnight the group drove a couple of miles to St Enda's, where they roused Pearse from bed and confronted him in a 'long and stormy interview'.[66] MacNeill told Pearse that he knew about his secret orders which 'showed the intention of an immediate Rising', an ambush that led Pearse to be more frank and dismissive than usual with Executive moderates. Increasingly incensed by Pearse's nonchalance, MacNeill listened as:

> for the first time I learned by Pearse's admission that the rising was intended. I told him that I would use every means in my power except informing the govt to prevent the rising. He said that I was powerless to do so, and that my countermand would only create confusion. I said that the responsibility in that case was not mine, but his.[67]

Pearse airily brushed MacNeill aside, claiming that the IRB had created the Volunteers and only used him, they were now, in effect, dispensing with his services like an aged retainer surplus to requirements. Rebuffing Hobson's incandescent interventions, Pearse radiated only indifference and condescension like a man who believed himself far beyond his opponents' timid considerations.

Engaged in a race against time, MacNeill's party returned to Woodtown Park intent on reasserting control over the Volunteers. At 4 a.m. MacNeill began organising a counter-coup by drafting three important orders, the first of which nullified Pearse's secret military instructions and warned Volunteers in future to obey only those issued by MacNeill. Secondly, he gave Hobson authority to issue instructions in his name and finally he dispatched O'Connell to Cork by early morning train to assume command over Volunteers in Munster. Early on Friday morning Hobson went to Volunteer headquarters to begin duplicating the order quashing Pearse's arrangements for Easter Sunday – copies of which he intended to dispatch throughout the country. Then he decided to wait until nightfall so that the messages didn't arrive until Saturday, when it would be too late for Pearse to countermand them. Hobson and Claire Gregan, his secretary and fiancée, then started burning incriminating documents in case Dublin Castle became aware of the developing crisis and began conducting raids and arrests.[68]

After MacNeill left St Enda's, Pearse decided on reflection to alert MacDermott about the chief of staff's threats and at around eight o'clock on Friday morning MacDermott arrived at Woodtown Park.[69] MacNeill had just awakened after his long night's exertions and was sitting up in bed when his visitor was shown into the room. That it was MacDermott alone who came for a summit meeting with the chief of staff reveals his new ascendancy as the chief conspirator. Besides political ability and Clarke's friendship, MacDermott had become crucial in organising the Rising because – apart from a seriously ill Plunkett – he was the only Military Council member unburdened by a full-time job. Free to meet local Volunteer and IRB leaders, he travelled around Ireland more than the rest of the council combined; creating an organisation for an intended nationwide uprising was largely MacDermott's achievement, and he was determined now that nothing would now stand in his way. A great Irish historian has asserted that MacDermott's:

genius for intrigue gathered the strings of power into his own hands, and by the eve of the Rising he was the controlling destiny of the IRB. He revealed his full mind to no man, not even Tom Clarke, and there is evidence that he manoeuvred Clarke, as he did everyone else. It would be going too far to describe 1916 as a one-man rebellion but if any single person is to be given credit for acting as stage manager of the drama enacted in Easter Week 1916 it is Sean MacDermott.[70]

With the Volunteer Executive and Headquarters Staff now split, an ordinary member like Clarke would have had no standing to resolve the crisis; like Pearse after his previous night's display he also lacked the temperament and ability necessary to win over MacNeill. This was a task requiring MacDermott's negotiating skills, self-control and his silky talent for dissimulation. Furthermore, having for years been MacNeill's colleague on the Volunteer Executive, he knew his man and how to play him. At this supreme moment of crisis only MacDermott's legendary persuasiveness could smooth over an apparently irreparable rift and actually manipulate the chief of staff into supporting a rebellion in whose planning he had played no part, and about which he had still only the most fragmentary knowledge. From MacNeill's own rather uncertain account he appears to have spoken about his orders to Hobson and O'Connell, a revelation that MacDermott countered by asserting that Volunteers wouldn't obey them. MacDermott didn't respect or trust MacNeill and certainly he wasn't going to tell him everything as he had told Connolly four months earlier. Later he told the rest of the Military Council that he had laid all his cards out for MacNeill, but he lied to them about this as well as another important matter. In fact, MacDermott could hardly have kept his cards closer to his chest, his strategy being to dole out only a little more information than Pearse had given earlier and even then to shape it in order to confuse the chief of staff. He had a considerable advantage in that MacNeill still knew very little about what was really intended to happen on Easter Sunday. Historians have almost universally assumed that either at the start or end of the meeting he knew that on Sunday buildings in Dublin would be seized, a republic proclaimed and an uprising initiated against British rule in Ireland. However, Pearse hadn't actually told him that, Hobson didn't know for sure and MacDermott's subsequent assertion that he informed MacNeill is completely unreliable. And MacNeill himself never made the claim in his various accounts, referring instead much more ambiguously to 'an immediate rising'.[71]

Much of MacNeill's action and behaviour during Holy Week can be explained by his belief that the Castle Document was genuine and a fear that the British would soon descend on his poorly armed Volunteers before instituting a military dictatorship and imposing conscription. Far from revealing the Military Council's long-term ambitions, MacDermott could play on this fear by continuing to peddle the fiction about an imminent British strike and 'that hostilities were inevitable'. In this context Pearse's secret instructions could be sold as a desperate attempt to resist imminent enemy aggression but that it should indeed have been cleared with the chief of staff. Nevertheless, Pearse's oversight and any resentment that MacNeill felt over this and past deceptions couldn't be allowed to destroy Volunteer unity at such a critical moment. If the Volunteers – and Ireland – were to have a fighting chance, then

MacDermott could spin it as MacNeill's patriotic duty to heal the rift and in so doing guarantee his place in history.

Since MacNeill had always acknowledged that resistance to British aggression was justified and that arming the Volunteers was an important priority, MacDermott had just the rabbit to pull out of a hat that would win him over. Only a month earlier, knowing about the coming arms shipment, MacDermott had trapped MacNeill at a Headquarters Staff conference by asking in all apparent innocence whether he would fight if the Volunteers got a large supply of weapons. MacNeill had immediately replied 'Yes'. Now MacDermott revealed that a German cargo of arms would soon arrive, something he knew would have a powerful impact on MacNeill who conceded later that:

> in a previous conversation I had said to him that the importation of arms for the Volunteers was the one thing of importance. This part of the scheme coincided with my view. It was of course evident to me that in the circumstances a landing of arms from Germany meant an immediate challenge to the English government and I said to MacDermott, 'Very well, if that is the state of the case, I'm in it with you'.[72]

How did MacNeill then expect events to play out? It is entirely possible that he believed that Sunday's parades were only significant as something that would distract the British government's attention from the arms landing in the west of Ireland – just as in July 1914 a Volunteer route march had been intended to deceive Dublin Castle about the Howth gunrunning. If the arms landed peacefully then either the Volunteers would be better able to resist British aggression when it came – in a war in which Ireland would be regarded as a victim – or the better armed Volunteers might even force the British to call off what he believed was their intended onslaught on the Volunteers. Alternatively, if the British interfered with the gunrunning, causing casualties and deaths, then (as at Bachelor's Walk) they would unite nationalist Ireland in opposition, giving the Volunteers a *casus belli*. From this perspective MacNeill's focus would have been on the west of Ireland and not Dublin.

Indeed, in their 'don't ask, don't tell' conversation MacNeill – whose reputation as a historian rested on meticulous research – was remarkably unquestioning as MacDermott reeled him in. It was entirely possible that within days a war would erupt in which MacNeill would presumably be commander-in-chief of the Irish forces and yet he failed to press MacDermott for details about how Volunteer forces would conduct the campaign. Nor, despite his later claims, would MacDermott have revealed the plans to seize buildings in Dublin on Sunday because that would have indicated long-term and detailed planning and made him liable to questioning about who had been doing the planning. Not for another year did MacNeill learn about the existence of a Military Council. The result was that MacNeill ended up with less knowledge than the Volunteer battalion commandants or even captains, and it is his lack of inquisitiveness, his failure to explore in detail what was likely to unfold and the absence of any real attempt to pin MacDermott down that make him appear so staggeringly negligent and irresponsible. Afterwards when MacDermott told his fellow conspirators that MacNeill had abdicated as chief of staff he was telling a complete lie but also, in a sense, the absolute truth.

After MacNeill and MacDermott had finished talking they went downstairs and breakfasted with Pearse and MacDonagh who had arrived separately at Woodtown Park. With the chief of staff apparently mollified and co-operative the Military Council seemed to have regained control of events and eliminated any danger of a disastrous split within the Volunteers. MacDermott's discussion with MacNeill marked his ascent to the pinnacle of the IRB and ratified his new position as chief conspirator and the motor of the revolution. From Friday morning onwards every line of communication ran through MacDermott alone and only he among the conspirators had a complete overall view of the progress of events. If knowledge is power then he more than any other member of the Military Council was in charge.

After leaving Woodtown Park MacDermott sent dispatches to Munster ordering Volunteer commandants to proceed with the Rising and ignore any instructions that O'Connell brought. MacNeill, for his part, had to deal with Hobson whom he must have known would never perform the same political somersault that he had just executed. Still, he sent Hobson instructions to put the countermanding orders on hold because he now believed that a rising was inevitable – though he failed to mention meeting MacDermott, Pearse and MacDonagh. This was the moment when Hobson finally gave up on MacNeill and accepted that all the months of imploring, chivvying and cajoling him had been in vain. Exhausted and depressed, he acquiesced and waited for a personal explanation from MacNeill that never came.[73] Hobson decided to leave Volunteer headquarters, having 'realised by this vacillation on MacNeill's part it was impossible to take further definite action and at any rate events by then had got completely out of control'.[74] Eventually, however, MacNeill did turn up to find people destroying papers in anticipation of an imminent British raid. One of them, Kitty O'Doherty, Quartermaster of the Cumann na mBan, recalled a disconcerted chief of staff: 'His face was a study to me. He was always very sallow. He now had two huge pink spots.'[75] Shouting 'Hobson is out joy-riding', MacNeill thrust his personal papers into O'Doherty's hands and ordered her to keep them safe until he could retrieve them later.

More than ever determined to isolate the notoriously irresolute MacNeill from Hobson's influence, the Military Council arranged on Friday evening for Hobson to be summoned to a supposedly hastily arranged IRB meeting at the home of Martin Conlon in 76 Cabra Park. Hobson rightly suspected that this sudden invitation was a ruse to keep him away from Volunteer headquarters and out of contact with other moderate leaders. Still he went along, partly from a fatalistic desire to see whether his suspicions were correct, but also to end an unbearable strain that had left him feeling angry and defeated. Hobson's 'principal feeling was one of relief. I had been working under great pressure for a long time and I was very tired. Now events were out of my hand.'[76] Just as he had done in July 1914, when his dispute with Clarke and MacDermott left him feeling overwhelmed, Hobson had now come to believe that he had no alternative but, in a sense, to flee from his troubles. At Conlon's residence three armed IRB men were waiting. Two of them were from Hobson's own IRB circle, a ploy that the Military Council no doubt intended to emphasise his own isolation and helplessness. But it could have been even worse for Hobson, because Pearse and MacDermott had vetoed Connolly's proposal to lure him to the Plunketts' Kimmage estate and chloroform him through the Rising.[77]

Provided he kept the location secret, Hobson was allowed to send a message to MacNeill telling of his arrest and that it was up to him to prevent an insurrection. MacNeill exclaimed, 'I've been lied to and misled. They've kidnapped Hobson.' 'They may kidnap you,' said someone: 'If they do they'll get this,' replied MacNeill, taking a revolver from his pocket.[78] However, he didn't go as far as to break off his pact with MacDermott and Pearse, nor did he intercede with the kidnappers to secure his chief lieutenant's release. Presumably MacNeill believed that at this critical moment Volunteer unity was more important than the fate of any single individual. Hobson had told his fiancée Claire Gregan about the meeting and she turned up at Conlon's after he disappeared. A Volunteer who answered the door denied, unconvincingly, that Hobson was inside: 'Bulmer told me afterwards he heard me and made a move to come to the door and that another Volunteer who was guarding him pointed a gun at him. I went away and Bulmer saw me going down to the gate. He was in the front room.'[79]

When the Military Council convened on Friday afternoon at Houlihan's shop in Amiens Street for a final overview session everything appeared to be back on track. With MacNeill squared, Hobson in captivity and Dublin Castle winding down for the Easter holidays, every obstacle had seemingly been removed. On Friday afternoon the Ceannts went to church and later in the evening strolled through Phoenix Park where a stream of lorries was emptying the Magazine Fort of ammunition. Knowing that the Rising was intended to begin with a huge explosion at the fort, 'Eamonn was rather silent; the only remark I remember him making was "You can almost over-organise things".'[80] But every previous problem was trivial compared to those that erupted on Saturday and Sunday 22 and 23 April and which brought the conspirators' plans to 'the verge of irretrievable disaster'.[81] Things began unravelling in Kerry, the German arms shipment's destination. Having declined to provide such assistance in the spring of 1915 during Plunkett's visit to Berlin, the Germans changed their mind after the Military Council set the Rising for Easter 1916. The council transmitted this decision through the Clan to the German Embassy in Washington which then passed it on to Berlin along with Devoy's proposal that 25,000 to 50,000 rifles, some machine guns, field artillery and senior officers would guarantee a successful Irish rebellion as well as tying down 500,000 British troops. The Supreme Army Command's support of an arms shipment brought the German navy into line and on 17 March 1916 it decided to send one vessel to the west of Ireland carrying 20,000 captured Russian rifles, a million rounds of ammunition and a consignment of explosives.

By now Casement's relations with the Germans were very bad and he only learnt accidentally about an imminent rising and Germany's limited assistance to it from Robert Monteith, an Irish Volunteer organiser who had come to Germany to join Casement's Irish Brigade. Having always opposed any Irish revolt that didn't have considerable foreign help, Casement now believed the Germans were duping him and only using Ireland for their own selfish ends. Deciding to prevent the Rising, he pretended that he needed to return home to prepare for the arms shipment's arrival and the Germans provided a submarine for himself, Monteith and Julian Beverley, another Irish Brigade member. Just after noon on Good Friday, 21 April, the U-boat reached a pre-arranged rendezvous point off the coast of Kerry. But its captain didn't see either an arms ship called the *Aud*, its pilot boat from Fenit or the Volunteer reception party on the shore. Actually the *Aud* had reached the Kerry coast safely, but its captain had weighed anchor several miles away from and out of sight of the submarine. The Kerry Volunteers hadn't expected either vessel before 23 April and had made no contingency plans for an earlier arrival. A few hours after the submarine arrived the three men clambered into a small boat and made their way ashore. There local police soon captured Casement and Beverley, though Monteith managed to escape. The arms ship remained free but only for a little while longer.

In fact the *Aud*'s chances of reaching Fenit, certainly of discharging its cargo, had been almost non-existent from the very start. British naval intelligence had broken German codes and had known about the plan since March 1916. However, naval intelligence only told a small military circle that included Kitchener, the Secretary of State for War; Field Marshal French, commander of British Home Forces; Major-General Friend, the Irish GOC; and Admiral Bayly and General Stafford, both of whom were based at Queenstown in Co. Cork and had responsibility for preventing the importation of arms into Ireland. Surprisingly it didn't warn Birrell or Nathan, possibly because it didn't trust politicians to keep a secret. Bayly intended intercepting the *Aud* by having armed trawlers, a light cruiser and a destroyer patrol the west coast of Ireland from the Aran Islands to Tralee. Stafford had alerted the police in Limerick, Clare and Kerry to be ready and arranged for troops to move rapidly if the ship reached shore and was met by Irish Volunteers intent on discharging its cargo.[82] This intense British surveillance had eliminated the element of surprise on which the Military Council were counting.

The Germans had disguised the *Aud* as a 1,200-ton Norwegian merchantman on an apparently innocent voyage along the west coast of Ireland on its way to the Mediterranean. After embarking on 9 April its captain, Karl Spindler, had followed a route between Norway and the British blockade line about 60 miles east of Shetland and by noon on Thursday 20 April the vessel was 45 miles from Fenit. Spindler's crew was preparing for a successful end to their perilous voyage, unaware that fatal misunderstandings had arisen between the Military Council and the German government. Communications between both parties had been seriously flawed because direct contact by wireless didn't exist and face-to-face meetings were very rare indeed; they relied on exchanging messages through American proxies – German diplomats and Clan representatives in Washington. Originally it had been intended for the *Aud* to arrive at Fenit some time between 20 and 23 April, a sensible flexibility given the problems of navigating in a war zone. But late in the day the Military Council had attempted, ineptly, to impose unilateral changes on the incredulous Germans by demanding that German officers accompany the arms shipment and a submarine be sent into Dublin Bay once the Rising had begun.[83] The German navy rejected the submarine while the general staff wouldn't send any officers to lead an Irish Volunteer force about which it knew almost nothing. This entirely predictable response was never conveyed to the Military Council, which naïvely assumed that merely dispatching its requirements guaranteed German compliance with them.

The Military Council then compounded its problems by attempting to change the date on which the arms vessel was supposed to arrive. Originally the ship was to reach Ireland sometime between 20 and 23 April, dates that the conspirators had chosen when they had intended beginning the Rising on Friday 21 April. When they delayed the start of the Rising to Sunday 23 April this risked the arms vessel arriving possibly

days early and alerting the British authorities to the possibility of an imminent insurrection. The Military Council decided that the arrival of the arms shipment would
have to be delayed also to much nearer the 23rd. It sent Plunkett's sister, Philomena,
to New York to have the Clan tell the Germans that the ship now had no leeway: it
had to enter Fenit on the evening of Sunday 23 April as the Rising was beginning.[84]
The message was absurd and demonstrated the conspirators' complete lack of reality
in demanding that the *Aud* maintain clockwork timing over large distances without
taking into account the many factors that could delay a ship navigating in a war zone.
Not that any of this ultimately mattered, because the *Aud* had already left Germany
and wasn't equipped with a wireless, meaning that even if the Germans had wanted
they couldn't have told Spindler about the Military Council's new arrangements.

British naval intelligence had tracked the *Aud* all the way from Germany but
allowed the vessel to approach the Irish coast, a trap intended to draw into the open
everyone involved in the smuggling operation and prove to the British authorities' satisfaction the Volunteers' pro-German sympathies and treasonous activities.
However, as the vessel approached Fenit on the night of Thursday 20 April there was
no reception party waiting for Spindler because the Kerry Volunteers had assumed
that the Germans had accepted the new date. So did the Military Council which had
made no alternative arrangements for an earlier arrival. Furthermore, MacDermott
had vetoed a local proposal to have armed Volunteers patrolling the area, fearing that
such activity would risk arousing British suspicions. A local Volunteer, Mortimer
O'Leary, had been chosen to pilot the *Aud* into Fenit. He expected a vessel of about
150 tons – a fraction of the *Aud*'s size – to arrive on Easter Sunday night and wasn't
unduly concerned on Thursday night when he saw a large vessel in Tralee Bay: 'I
watched the boat until dawn on Good Friday morning but did not see her make any
signal during that period.'[85]

By Friday morning Spindler was increasingly nervous about his failure to make
contact with his Irish counterparts. At the same time the British waited for the *Aud*
to land its weapons so that they could spring their trap. But soon after 1 p.m. Spindler
spotted an armed British trawler and weighed anchor, forcing Bayly to order the
Aud's capture. During the afternoon two British sloops shadowed Spindler as he
headed into the Atlantic where he intended to begin a new mission by attacking
enemy merchant ships. They eventually cornered him in the early evening and were
soon leading the *Aud* back towards the Irish coast, but as it approached Queenstown
in Co. Cork on Saturday morning Spindler scuttled his vessel within sight of harbour.

As news of Casement's arrest spread in the area, the Kerry Volunteer leadership
dispatched a messenger to Dublin to inform the leading conspirators about this setback. He arrived in the capital at dawn and reported to Liberty Hall where Connolly
immediately began summoning the rest of the Military Council. MacDermott and
a group of republicans were staying in a Mountjoy Square boarding house and they
all drew revolvers on hearing a loud knocking on the front door.[86] Even though
it turned out to be only Connolly's messenger summoning him to Liberty Hall
MacDermott realised that only an important development would necessitate such an
early morning conference. Sensing a gathering crisis he sent a taxi full of Volunteers
to collect Pearse as well as posting a relay of cycle scouts from the vicinity of the
vice-regal lodge to Liberty Hall to watch for any unusual British movements. At its

meeting the Military Council clearly decided to hide from MacNeill the news about Casement and indeed later that morning they sent Plunkett to Woodtown Park in an attempt to suck the chief of staff even deeper into their preparations. Plunkett tried to persuade him to sign the Proclamation but MacNeill hedged, saying he wouldn't put his name to any document without knowing its terms and Plunkett dropped the matter.[87] This wariness saved MacNeill's life, because if his name had appeared along with the other seven signatories on the Proclamation it would have committed him completely, guaranteeing – like all the signatories – a firing squad at the end.

By early Saturday afternoon the Military Council had also learned about the loss of the *Aud*, a calamity that was to transform the Rising from a planned national insurrection into a predominantly Dublin affair. Even so, when a Limerick emissary arrived at MacDermott's new safe house in Hardwicke Street, he found MacDermott exuding a surface bonhomie and insisting there was no going back now. With scant regard for the truth, he even claimed that more German arms shipments were on their way.[88] Clearly by now MacDermott was prepared to lie to anyone and everyone, even his Military Council colleagues, to prevent the Rising being derailed at the very last moment. Everything – including the truth – was subservient to MacDermott's credo that 'the only failure in Ireland is the failure to act'.[89] But a few hours later, when another Limerick Volunteer arrived and suggested postponing the Rising MacDermott's composure disintegrated completely. He became physically sick and began shouting that delay was out of the question: the Volunteers would fight even if they only had sticks and stones.[90]

In case the British government decided on a last-minute swoop to arrest them, the leaders stayed on Saturday night at safe houses, guarded around the clock by squads of young Volunteers who had orders to resist to the death any British attempts to arrest the Military Council. Clarke had introduced this measure after realising that he had come under intensified surveillance by detectives.[91] Clarke himself decided to stay at Fleming's Hotel in Gardiner Place. Pearse and his brother Willie had been living all week at Sean T. O'Kelly's house on Mespil Road and remained there – though Patrick shuttled constantly between it and St Enda's. Plunkett had been in a Mountjoy Square nursing home but now shifted to the Metropole Hotel in O'Connell Street. MacDonagh and his brother John had been staying at the Clarence Hotel but switched to the home in Lower Gardiner Street of brothers John and Tom Meldon, both Volunteers in MacDonagh's own battalion. Having finally told Aine about the Rising at teatime on Saturday evening, Ceannt left home at ten o'clock for the home of John Doherty, a friend who lived nearby in James's Terrace. Connolly remained in Liberty Hall, an armed fortress where he was the safest of them all. After the early morning scare at his Mountjoy Square boarding house, MacDermott shifted to the Hardwicke Street, home of Mrs Kissane, a member of the Cumann na mBan's Central Branch.[92]

The leaders now hoped to recuperate from a hectic few days and ready themselves for battle. Soon after going into hiding a more relaxed MacDermott wrote to Min Ryan from 'somewhere in Dublin'. Shedding the burden of a double life and years of planning, he was clearly looking forward to soon realising his dreams:

> I suppose you and all my friends think I am very rude lately. I realise fully that for
> several months past I have been very irritable. My attempts at being light-hearted

once in a while have been a poor attempt at acting – though I enjoyed myself again
in those attempts. Soon I hope to be my natural self again then, I suppose my friends
will realise to some extent the reason why I have been so morose lately. I cannot see
you tonight though I had hoped to and I cannot promise for tomorrow night but
I hope to see you early in the week for a certainty.

But MacDermott was acutely aware that nothing was ever really certain and for the
first time he ended a letter to Min – his last letter – with the farewell, 'Good bye'.[93]

At much the same time and unknown to MacDermott, MacNeill began slipping
the Military Council's leash. This proved to be the catalyst for two days that convulsed
the Irish Volunteers, broke its chief of staff's new alliance with the conspirators and
threatened their years of planning. On Saturday morning MacNeill was still committed to his alliance with the plotters and indeed passed de Valera on the stairs with the
greeting, 'God speed the good work tomorrow'.[94] The crisis began later on Saturday
afternoon and was precipitated by Sean Fitzgibbon. He had spent most of Holy Week
in Kerry preparing for the *Aud*'s arrival, a mission that the Military Council had
misled him to believe had been authorised by MacNeill. On Easter Sunday morning
Fitzgibbon met Colm O'Loughlin, Dr Jim Ryan and Liam Lynch who had been
dispatched on similar missions and learnt from Lynch about Casement's arrest and the
sinking of the *Aud*. Fitzgibbon decided to return immediately to Dublin along with
O'Loughlin, a Volunteer Executive member and a captain on Plunkett's staff – but like
Fitzgibbon a MacNeill loyalist whom the conspirators had manipulated.

In the capital both men went straight to Volunteer headquarters where they discovered Plunkett burning piles of papers and unwilling to give a straight answer to any
of their questions. So they went to The O'Rahilly's house: 'He opened the door and
the first thing he said was "I've got to tell you that there's to be an insurrection in
Dublin tomorrow." He then told me that Hobson had been captured by the war party.
"Pearse speaks as if he thought he was the Almighty," said O'Rahilly.'[95] The trio then
drove to Woodtown Park at six o'clock in the evening. Poking the fire with an old
bayonet, MacNeill listened to Fitzgibbon describing how the conspirators had misused
MacNeill's name to get him out of the way. Fitzgibbon also revealed that Plunkett had
fabricated the Castle Document, a fraud on whose veracity MacNeill had staked just
about everything. The chief of staff was appalled, not just by the plotters' past deceptions but at Fitzgibbon's final revelation that the *Aud* had sunk with all its weapons.
By withholding such crucial information from him, despite the previous day's accord
and a promise to keep him informed, MacNeill now realised that with these men co-
operation was solely a one-way street. Clearly they regarded him simply as a useful front
man whose position and influence they could exploit but with whom they would on
no account share power – and that they would never change their attitude or behaviour.

However, MacNeill had never been prepared to accept a purely decorative
status and he no longer felt bound by an alliance that he was convinced had been
negotiated in bad faith. Furthermore, he believed that the *Aud*'s disappearance had
transformed the political and military situation in Ireland. Dublin Castle's failure
to respond forcefully to the arrival of both Casement and the arms shipment had
vindicated Fitzgibbon's claim that the Castle Document was fraudulent. If ever the
British government had wanted an excuse to crush the Volunteers then these events

had provided it, yet Dublin Castle hadn't moved. That a group of his own Executive officers had engineered such a deception of himself, Executive moderates and indeed Irish nationalists as a whole jolted MacNeill into recognising that he was really dealing with a mutiny. Moreover, he had gone along with the conspirators not simply because he believed that a British offensive against the Volunteers was imminent but because the arms shipment would enable the organisation to resist with some chance of success. Now a clash between the Volunteers and the British army would result in a catastrophic defeat and a military regime characterised by mass arrests, possibly executions and conscription.

MacNeill now calculated that if he acted speedily he had a narrow window of opportunity in which to defuse an immense crisis. If he neutered the conspirators and prevented their Sunday military parades going ahead he could prove to the Castle that the Volunteers were not bent on militarily challenging British rule in Ireland. Patriotic duty and saving the Volunteers from oblivion were now his only concerns. By engineering what was, in effect, a counter-coup MacNeill was on solid constitutional ground because he still enjoyed majority support on the Volunteer Executive and could also rely on The O'Rahilly and Fitzgibbon, who had both replaced Hobson as his emotional crutch. Two days earlier MacNeill had instructed Hobson to initiate what was in effect a first countermand only to back off; but this time there would be no retreat. He told Fitzgibbon and The O'Rahilly that he intended convening an eight o'clock meeting at the house of a friend and fellow Ulsterman, Seamus O'Kelly, at which he would 'stop all this damned nonsense'. But first the quartet drove to St Enda's where, according to Fitzgibbon, 'Pearse met us on the steps. "It's terrible, all this deception," said he. "It was all done for the best." When he spoke he was perfectly cool, as if what he had done was of no importance. Nevertheless he gave me the feeling that he was sorry he had deceived me'[96] Later, O'Loughlin saw MacNeill and Pearse talking for a while in the hallway before they 'came out to the steps of the house and it was there I heard Pearse say to MacNeill, "We have used you and your name and influence for what it was worth. You can issue what orders you like now, our men won't obey you".'[97] MacNeill retorted that he would do whatever his conscience and common sense dictated and that if Pearse had anything more to say he could do so later that evening at O'Kelly's. Just in case the conspirators considered detaining any more opponents O'Rahilly warned that he wasn't going to be another Hobson: 'Whoever comes to kidnap me, Pearse, will have to be first on the draw.'[98]

MacNeill had twenty-four hours to abort a rising that had been years in the planning but at O'Kelly's residence on Rathgar Road he, for once, rose superbly to the occasion.[99] This command centre was closer to the city centre than Woodtown Park and more easily reached for the many people MacNeill needed to carry out his orders. In the front room he was joined by Volunteer Executive loyalists such as The O'Rahilly and Fitzgibbon, as well as associates like Arthur Griffith, Sean T. O'Kelly, Liam Ó Briain and Eimar O'Duffy, while their friends arrived by car, cab and bicycle and awaited instructions. Even MacDermott's fiancée Min Ryan attended. She thought that Seamus O'Kelly:

was like a man awaiting news of the birth of a baby – in and out, fussing and in an awful state. We were all waiting and getting into an awful state. Then after a long,

long time and very late into the night I remember someone coming into us and handing to each of us a piece of paper. I remember MacNeill's handwriting on it.[100]

It was a dispatch cancelling Sunday's Volunteer parades. Griffith had helped MacNeill write out the countermand orders, an action that had it subsequently become widely known might have ruined him. Griffith had brought along Sinn Fein's secretary, Padraig O'Keefe, a Volunteer and IRB member who saw the way things were going and slipped out to summon Ceannt's vice-commandant Cathal Brugha who lived nearby. Brugha was incandescent at what was going on and on reaching O'Kelly's house he and others argued unsuccessfully against disseminating MacNeill's countermand orders. Afterwards he remarked that 'MacNeill had better mind himself for he'll be shot'.[101] Having been tipped off by Pearse, MacDonagh arrived by taxi, intent on charming an angry chief of staff into backing off once again. Just two days earlier a remarkably prescient MacDonagh had warned his battalion, 'One thing I want you to sink into your minds and that is; order, counter-order, disorder: that always happens'.[102] But his persuasiveness no longer worked with MacNeill, who recalled that 'from what MacDonagh said it was plain that the plan of an immediate rising was still being pushed. I gave my reasons against it, and they evidently impressed him but his reply in the last resort always was "I must act under the authority of my council".'[103] John MacDonagh remembered his brother leaving, 'rather agitated. He said that MacNeill greeted him, "We will be very glad to have you in consultation" or words to that effect. Tom told me that he replied, as he looked around the table. "I am sorry, but there is nobody here I can consult with."'[104]

By around midnight most messengers were heading into the counties: James Ryan to Cork in MacNeill's brother James' car; Colm O'Loughlin to Dundalk and Coalisland; Sean Fitzgibbon to Waterford. Min Ryan took the early morning train to Wexford. Besides sending personal dispatches to provincial Volunteer leaders, MacNeill intended going over the conspirators' heads with a public message appealing directly to the rank-and-file Volunteer members' instinctive loyalty to him. By demonstrating his pacific intentions this would simultaneously offer an olive branch to Dublin Castle. Having sent Padraig O'Keefe ahead to the *Sunday Independent* offices in Middle Abbey Street with information that the President of the Irish Volunteers would be coming in personally with a message that the newspaper had to carry, MacNeill started out for the city at about 1 a.m.[105] When he arrived at the newspaper he handed a written countermand order to the acting editor who also told MacNeill that he had time to put up headline placards across the city and suburbs, though not in the countryside. The order read: 'Owing to the very critical situation, all orders given to the Irish Volunteers for tomorrow, Easter Sunday, are hereby rescinded and no parades, marches or other movements of Irish Volunteers will take place. Each individual Volunteer will obey this order strictly in every particular.'

MacNeill had drafted the order very skilfully. While his reference to 'the very critical situation' was bound to puzzle many ordinary Volunteers, MacNeill's mention of 'other movements' was a coded message to those in the know that there was a deeper purpose behind Sunday's mobilisation and he wanted nothing to do with it. Moreover, there was every chance that the rank and file, who knew nothing about policy differences at the top of the Volunteers, would obey their chief of staff's orders.

At the same time The O'Rahilly was carrying to officers in the west of Ireland a more explicit message that the chief of staff had been completely deceived and all the secret orders that they had received from Pearse and his associates were null and void.[106] Suffering from a heavy cold, The O'Rahilly was unwilling to drive through the night and didn't want to be seen behind the wheel of a car at all. A government exclusion order had banned him from entering the south-west. Instead, he had slipped into the back of a closed taxi cab and set off into the darkness, a motorised Paul Revere travelling in reverse gear with the news that the British weren't coming after all and that the revolution had been cancelled. Four hours later he arrived in Limerick city and after a brief rest made his way through the counties of Limerick, Kerry, Cork and Tipperary showing MacNeill's instruction to Volunteer officers and explaining its background to these very confused men. They had assumed that the Volunteer Executive was a united body. This mistaken belief, combined with an ingrained tendency to obey their superiors' orders explains behaviour that is otherwise inexplicable. Only the day before, Sean MacDermott had sent James Ryan to Cork with final instructions for Commandant MacCurtain about the Rising in Munster. However, twenty-four hours later when Ryan returned to Dublin MacNeill reprogrammed him to deliver orders that totally contradicted MacDermott's, but which Ryan unhesitatingly obeyed. Perhaps even more surprising was Min Ryan's participation, but despite being Sean MacDermott's girlfriend she knew nothing about an intended rising or her boyfriend's deep involvement in it.

For someone who had long suffered from a crippling reluctance to deal with immediate crises and who usually made Hamlet look the embodiment of ruthless decision, MacNeill had acted with astonishing energy and guile in blindsiding the Military Council. Furthermore, by taking his deliberations at Rathgar Road right to the wire and sending his emissaries across Ireland throughout the night he had picked the worst time for the conspirators to react. And by just making the *Sunday Independent*'s deadline in time he had ensured they couldn't prevent the paper publishing his countermand order. Ironically, MacNeill was greatly helped by the Military Council's own security arrangements which now worked against them. Their dispersal to safe houses made it very difficult for them to contact each other during the night of 22/23 April and respond speedily and in a co-ordinated manner to any sudden emergency. When MacDonagh left O'Kelly's he began attempting to locate other Military Council members. Brugha eventually tracked Ceannt to Doherty's house whereupon Ceannt left hurriedly for Hardwicke Street. There he found MacDonagh already briefing MacDermott, who was 'shocked beyond measure'.[107] At around midnight Kathleen Clarke also turned up carrying an urgent message from a northern republican. Admitted by a man with a torch, she was shown into a completely darkened room where by another torch she recognised MacDermott and by degrees MacDonagh, Pearse, Plunkett and Diarmuid Lynch. They were all holding flashlights, fearful that a lit-up house might attract police attention. Although MacDermott fobbed off her inquiry about the Kerry arrests she knew from his face that a setback had occurred and challenged him about Tom's absence from their meeting. She thought that MacDermott's assertion that her husband badly needed rest was disingenuous and replied that Tom would react very badly on discovering what they had done. Clearly something very important had occurred to bring them together at such an hour. After leaving the house Mrs Clarke considered going to see Tom but feared that detectives might follow her to Fleming's Hotel or see her trying to get into the premises at so late an hour.[108]

Clarke's absence from this crisis meeting was indeed remarkable but clearly MacDermott – and the others – feared how he would react to MacNeill's actions. At this critical juncture the fate of the revolution was even more important to MacDermott than the greatest friendship of his life. As the group dispersed Ceannt returned home at 2.30 a.m. telling his wife, 'MacNeill has ruined us – he has stopped the Rising. The countermanding order is already in the hands of the paper. I am off to see if anything can be done.'[109] But he was out of luck. The armed guards at Liberty Hall refused to wake Connolly, and Ceannt returned home at 5 a.m. He went to bed but slept only fitfully. MacDonagh and Plunkett set out for Rathgar Road to make a final appeal to MacNeill. Seamus O'Kelly was in bed and was awakened by a knock at the door where he told both men that MacNeill had already gone home: '"Shall we go out to him?" asked Tom. "Indeed we shan't" said the other man. "God help the poor man!" said Tom kindly and sympathetically and they both went away. It was daybreak by this time.'[110]

MacNeill's change of mind was now sending a tremor reverberating through the Military Council. If it had been able to assemble and been so inclined it might just have been possible to dispatch couriers to frustrate MacNeill's countermand and proceed with the Rising as originally planned. Instead, when MacDonagh managed to get into Liberty Hall he found Connolly seething after learning that county commandants had received MacNeill's countermanding orders. Connolly now dispatched messengers summoning an emergency meeting of the Military Council later that morning at Liberty Hall. The dispatch reached Ceannt's house by 7 a.m. but Aine Ceannt put it beside her sleeping husband whom she only woke at 8.30 a.m. Eamon then rushed away on his bicycle without taking breakfast or putting on a collar and tie.[111]

Having slept little, the Military Council found MacNeill's countermand order disagreeable early morning reading. Like Claudius in *Hamlet* they were now discovering that sorrows came not singly but in battalions: to the bafflement and rage of these professional conspirators an unworldly academic – whom they had repeatedly ignored, undermined and deceived – had completely blindsided them. By using the press MacNeill had gone over their heads directly to the Volunteer rank and file, successfully bypassing regular channels that they had long ago subverted. Over eighteen months of planning were now imperilled, causing Clarke to denounce MacNeill's action as 'the blackest and greatest treachery'.[112] Learning of the countermand made MacDermott almost demented, weeping with frustration as he ripped his pyjama top to pieces.[113] Fionan Lynch remembered that when he actually showed MacDermott Sunday's newspaper 'it was the first and only time I ever saw Sean really angry and upset'.[114]

A Citizen Army officer described Easter Sunday at Liberty Hall as a day of 'confusion, excitement and disappointment'.[115] A visitor 'found the place in a commotion' with hallway, passages and stairs crowded with people coming and going, everyone emotionally denouncing the countermand as either a betrayal by MacNeill or a British hoax.[116] Sean Connolly, a Citizen Army captain, wept while James Connolly's bodyguard, Henry Walpole, volunteered to shoot MacNeill.[117] Two women wandered around the building that morning, both searching for Bulmer Hobson though with diametrically opposite intentions concerning his well-being. One was his fiancée, Claire Gregan, who says that she 'walked up the stairs and there was a boy at the door on duty with a bayonet in his hand which he pointed at me'.[118] Although the guard refused her admittance to the conference room he relented when she broke down in tears and allowed a message to be sent inside. Eventually Connolly emerged, surly and taciturn, and listened to Gregan's plaintive inquiries. After initially giving her the run-around, he finally admitted that Hobson had been detained, though Pearse appeared to reassure her that he wouldn't be physically harmed. MacDermott:

> was very sympathetic and assured me Bulmer was safe and that I need not worry. He caught me affectionately by the arm and said very emphatically that of course they knew Bulmer was a man of integrity and sincerity. He could not tell me where he was but that he was quite safe. I remember he took my hand and told me not to worry but Bulmer would be released the following night. He shook hands with me and that was the last I saw of Sean MacDermott.[119]

Gregan wasn't completely convinced by MacDermott's comforting words: she had long regarded him as 'deadly sly'. Countess Markievicz was also hunting for Hobson, not to rescue but to annihilate him; their former friendship now counting for nothing against what she denounced as his treason. Waving a small automatic pistol, she rampaged throughout Liberty Hall in her Citizen Army uniform, bursting into one room and demanding to know Hobson's whereabouts because 'I want to shoot him'. When nobody could help her she forced her way past a sentry into the leaders' conference room only for Connolly to sternly order her out again.[120]

Before the leaders' crucial session began at 9 a.m. some council members ate a breakfast of bacon and eggs that Connolly's daughter Nora had cooked for them. Emotionally drained and angry they were also wracked by sleeplessness and anxiety; despite all their precautions MacNeill had ultimately eluded their control. Now a fear haunted them that at the very last moment all their hopes and dreams would be dashed. Despite all the turmoil the Military Council methodically examined its options. For the first time a body that hitherto had been Clarke and MacDermott's instrument now became a genuine War Cabinet, a forum of argument and dissent in which members like Ceannt and MacDonagh at last found their own independent voices as they negotiated a way out of the blind alley into which MacNeill appeared to have driven them.

During the course of the next four hours they wrestled with the central problem of overcoming MacNeill's countermand. Abandonment or even lengthy postponement of the Rising wasn't an option for men who were utterly committed to an insurrection. There were also practical reasons for pressing ahead because everyone believed that British suppression of the Volunteers was both inevitable and imminent. Even if, by some chance, this was avoided, MacNeill would almost certainly purge them from a power base they had spent years establishing. In a mood of now-or-never they focused on steadying their followers and re-scheduling the arrangements for a rising. Only Tom Clarke opposed any delay.[121] He had arrived at Liberty Hall knowing least about overnight developments, and whatever the other members' justification for ignoring him on Saturday night they had diminished his authority. Terrified that everything he had worked for was about to evaporate, Clarke opposed any delay and argued fiercely in favour of sticking to the original plan. He insisted that once the Rising began Volunteers would assume either that MacNeill's cancellation was a hoax or that events had overtaken it. But to Clarke's shock he stood alone at this critical juncture while men whom he had groomed and promoted rejected his advice. Even Sean MacDermott deserted him. Reluctantly Clarke fell into line and agreed to postponing the Rising until noon the following day, Easter Monday, 24 April, a delay that gave the conspirators a day to devise and implement their new arrangements.

The Military Council now turned to finalising a Proclamation of an Irish Republic that the President of the Provisional Government would read out on Easter Monday in O'Connell Street. There in the GPO most of the council would be operating in a dual capacity as members of the Provisional Government and of the Headquarters Staff of the Army of the Republic. They apparently offered the post of president first to Clarke out of respect for him personally as well as for his service to the republican cause. But Clarke had spent a lifetime shunning the limelight and he declined the offer, though his pre-eminence was recognised by his signature's pride of place on the Proclamation. The post went instead to Pearse, who had both the presence and the oratorical ability to make the historic address. Pearse was also appointed Commandant-General of the Army of the Irish Republic, an amalgamation of the Volunteers and the Irish Citizen Army. Connolly became vice-president and commandant-general of the army's Dublin division, meaning that he would effectively be in military command of the rebel forces in the capital during the Rising.

Having re-ordered its timetable, the Military Council now had to reassert its control over people and events for just another twenty-four hours, during which time their interests actually coincided with MacNeill's, ensuring that Sunday's parades were abandoned. Publicly, Pearse sent messages to local commandants confirming the chief of staff's cancellation order, but behind this smokescreen he immediately began secretly drafting, for later distribution, fresh orders confirming that the Rising would proceed.[122] Meanwhile, the conspirators had to make sure that firebrands didn't defy MacNeill's instructions and start premature local revolts. In Dublin three out of four battalion commandants – Ceannt, MacDonagh and Clarke's brother-in-law Ned Daly – could guarantee complete adherence to the new instructions, but the conspirators feared de Valera's 3rd Battalion going it alone anyway. To keep de Valera in line they dispatched Michael Staines, Dublin Brigade quartermaster, and Sean Heuston, a 1st Battalion officer, to tell him that MacDonagh, O/C Dublin Brigade, had approved cancelling the mobilisation.

Initially de Valera was having none of it because he was suspicious that a huge deception was being perpetrated on the Volunteers. Many of his officers also opposed abandoning the parades and his closest confidant Joseph O'Connor successfully urged de Valera to push ahead. Staines remembered that a suspicious 'de Valera said he thought he should make me a prisoner, presumably because I brought him that order'.[123] Staines retorted that if he went ahead his would be the only battalion in the field, but 'de Valera gave me no indication whether or not he was prepared to obey the order. Heuston was very indignant and told me afterwards he was almost on the point of drawing his gun.' But after hearing about this encounter MacDonagh still seemed confident that de Valera would obey and indeed eventually he did, though only just in time. O'Connor was about to set out from Earlsfort Terrace when he received de Valera's message cancelling his parade. O'Connor told his commandant that the battalion would take six months to recover. Whereas 120 of his men turned out that day he believed that only about twenty would answer another call to arms. At 3 p.m. on Sunday afternoon one of de Valera's company commandants, Liam Tannam, had mobilised almost all his sixty-three men and was about to set out when a Rathfarnham priest brought him MacNeill's confirmation of his countermand: 'This is to authenticate my statement in this morning's Sunday Independent every word of which is true. Great influence is needed immediately and in all directions to ensure complete obedience to the order and so to avert a frightful catastrophe.'[124] Tannam wasn't prepared to accept a message from someone he didn't know and was about to press on when he received both MacDonagh's countermand and de Valera's written confirmation. Just to make sure, Patrick and Willie Pearse and MacDonagh suddenly came up the road and instructed Tannam to send his men home, though to stand ready for a sudden mobilisation.[125]

After the Military Council's meeting word filtered throughout Liberty Hall that there was still hope and at 4 p.m. Connolly took the Citizen Army out on a final, short practice route march that was virtually a dress rehearsal for Easter Monday. Connolly led his men straight to Stephen's Green, and on the return journey passed so close to Dublin Castle that its guards hurriedly closed the gates. Afterwards, in front of Liberty Hall, Connolly gave what proved to be his last public speech, telling his followers that they were not to lay down their arms until they had struck a blow for Ireland.[126] Afterward, officers and section leaders received their final instructions and made arrangements to reassemble next morning. Most Citizen Army members remained in the building overnight, but some were granted passes to return home. A heavy guard was maintained throughout that night both at Liberty Hall and in the street outside.

Clarke had left Liberty Hall a devastated man, after MacNeill's 'betrayal', MacDermott's abandonment and an unwanted delay that seemingly risked his entire life's work. Sean McGarry thought that 'for the first time since I knew him he seemed crushed. He was weary and seemed crestfallen. I accompanied him home that evening. He was very silent.'[127] Another bodyguard recalled how Clarke:

> spoke bitterly of the confusion caused by MacNeill's countermanding order. He spoke with unusual emotion: 'We had got over so many difficulties,' he added 'and all seemed working well. Our plans were laid in the most thorough and efficient manner. We had a great opportunity. Now in a way we could never have foreseen all is spoiled. I feel as if I would like to go away somewhere and cry.'[128]

Kathleen Clarke was at home in Richmond Avenue waiting for the Rising to commence when suddenly Tom turned the corner, looking 'old and bent, and his walk, which was usually very quick and military, was slow. He looked very ill, and seemed scarcely able to speak. He did not eat anything up to the time he left the house next morning.'[129] Clarke raged at MacNeill's failure to discuss his doubts with the conspirators before abruptly changing his mind and endangering the Rising.

MacNeill and Fitzgibbon spent Sunday gauging reaction to the countermand and ensuring compliance with it because otherwise they feared that the country might soon be in flames. They hoped that Volunteers' instinctive loyalty to their chief of staff and the chain of command would carry the day, creating disarray in the conspirators' ranks and forcing them to back off. If the Military Council were gamblers willing to play for the highest stakes in this political poker game, then so now was MacNeill. While waiting for provincial messengers to return he had dispatched men across Dublin urging battalion officers to obey his instructions. He also sent intermediaries to Liberty Hall to establish whether Pearse and the others intended to respect his authority and abandon their plans. But he avoided a face-to-face meeting with them that would inevitably have been tempestuous and possibly dangerous. In addition, MacNeill met provincial Volunteers gathered in Dublin for a Gaelic Athletic Association convention and persuaded a group of them to go to Liberty Hall and plead for observance of his countermand.[130] After all that had happened the Military Council would probably have liked nothing better than to reacquaint MacNeill with the incarcerated Hobson, but kidnapping the President of the Irish Volunteers was too dangerous a step, even for angry and desperate men who felt as if they were standing with their backs to the wall. MacNeill also persuaded one of Pearse's pupils who was attending morning Mass in Rathfarnham to carry a message to his headmaster, as well as urging Father Eugene Nevin, a Mount Argus priest, 'to secure faithful obedience to that order throughout the country and avert a very great catastrophe'.[131]

Seeking to sway officers and rank-and-file members, Nevin visited Volunteer meeting places. At Count Plunkett's residence, 'Larkfield', Kimmage Road, George Plunkett promised him that the countermand would be obeyed and there would be no parade. However, Nevin was somewhat disconcerted that 'at the same time I noticed a war kit complete, piled in the centre of the drawing room with an officer's broad sword laid atop. As far as I recollect George was in uniform so likely the kit I saw was Joseph's.'[132] Nevin then moved on to Dolphin's Barn; Ceannt wasn't home but his battalion officers gave repeated assurances that they would comply with MacNeill's instructions. The chief of staff also used John Keegan, another Rathfarnham churchgoer, to carry written confirmation of the cancellation to city centre addresses where he might find Clarke, Pearse, MacDonagh and Plunkett. After being repeatedly stonewalled Keegan eventually ended up at Liberty Hall, where he saw the four men and Sean MacDermott as well. As Pearse accepted the dispatch all of them probably hoped for another MacNeill somersault: 'Before he read it he asked me did I want an answer to it. To which I replied I didn't think it required an answer. It is as far as I know the commands of the chief of staff. He then read the dispatch and said, "Tell him it shall be so".'[133] At his crowded residence, Woodtown Park, MacNeill listened anxiously to Keegan relaying Pearse's assurance before exclaiming 'Thank God'. For MacNeill the worst appeared to be over and soon it just got better and better. In the late afternoon he received a dispatch stating 'I have ordered demobilisation. The Dublin Brigade has been demobilised. E de Valera. 3.20 p.m.'[134] The Military Council also arranged one final, exquisite deception designed to convince MacNeill that his appeals had won them over. During the afternoon Pearse sent MacNeill a letter that, while tinged with condescension, seemed to represent unconditional surrender: 'Commandant MacDonagh is to call on you this afternoon. He countermanded the Dublin parade

today with my authority. I confirmed your countermand to the country as the leading men would not have obeyed it without my confirmation.'[135]

When MacDonagh arrived, he knew that this would almost certainly be his last
meeting with MacNeill and that his difficult assignment was to perpetuate Pearse's
fraudulent assurances. But he concealed whatever qualms he might have felt and the
deception of MacNeill was achieved with practised ease. Sean Fitzgibbon, who was
also present, recorded that:

> He, MacNeill and I walked around the grounds and talked. He was most friendly
> and assured us that everything was off. He was quite optimistic and said that all that
> had been intended was to occupy certain buildings as barracks and that the British
> would then come to terms with us.[136]

Later in Rathgar Road the returning provincial emissaries brought more good news.
An exhausted O'Rahilly, who had gone without sleep for two days, arrived covered in grime but elated at having delivering his countermand order just in time. By
evening a contented MacNeill was surrounded by colleagues and friends as he basked
in triumph at what was effectively a victory rally. With a catastrophe apparently
averted, his pre-eminence as head of the Volunteers reasserted and the conspirators
seemingly chastened, the following day appeared destined to pass uneventfully. The
Dublin battalions had complied with his countermand, even de Valera had fallen into
line and reports from Cork, Kerry and Limerick indicated that it was all quiet. Later
he insisted 'on the evening of Easter Sunday I believed with full assurance that the
efforts had completely succeeded'.[137] That night MacNeill went to bed as the hap-
piest man in the world. It could be argued, of course, that he had been in dreamland
for years and that by accepting Pearse and MacDonagh's bland assurances he made
himself look as gullible as ever. Even after the Rising he told his court martial that:

> I believe that the decision [to suppress the Volunteers] was the cause of the
> Insurrection on Easter Monday. I have no doubt about it. Nothing else could
> explain it. The men who told me that I had compelled them to act as I wished
> them to act [to agree to countermand the rising] – those men I knew well. I will
> answer for them. They were men of honour. They were truthful and honoura-
> ble men. They gave me that assurance on the evening of Easter Sunday. I have no
> reason to doubt it.[138]

But on that Sunday, 23 April, MacNeill must have been convinced that this time it
really would be different and the conspirators would keep their promises to him.
Now he simply didn't believe that they had any alternative. In his estimation the loss
of the arms shipment and his own countermand order had torpedoed their plans and
on any rational calculation they would have to fall into line. What MacNeill failed
to comprehend was that men like Pearse and MacDermott marched to a different
drummer. MacDonagh's own brother saw this clearly enough:

> They were men exalted by their mission to strike once more with arms as had been
> done in every generation against the British oppressor, and this purpose was so all

embracing that it completely dominated their lives and no consideration such as family or strict adherence to any formal procedure, could be allowed to interfere with their accepted destiny, to which they gladly dedicated their lives.[139]

To them retreat was tantamount to death: they couldn't go back now. However, with almost two years of detailed planning in ruins, any rising was bound to be a leap in the dark. All they could hope for now was that against all odds they could still land on their feet.

The O'Rahilly shared MacNeill's optimism and this even survived a chance encounter with Desmond Fitzgerald, a Volunteer friend who 'told him what I had heard at Liberty Hall, from which I gathered that the Rising was not abandoned, but he did not take it seriously. He felt that a disaster had been effectively prevented.'[140] But across the city couriers, protected by armed guards, were assembling at the Gaelic League offices in North Frederick Street. At 8 p.m. Pearse arrived with dispatches which the couriers were to take to local Volunteer commandants throughout the country. The messages read: 'We start operations at noon today, Monday. Carry out your instructions. P.H. Pearse.' Some of the messengers left Dublin that night, others not until Monday morning.

Like MacNeill, Pearse now went to bed, but with totally different expectations of what the next day would bring. In churches across the city men who knew what was intended were attending Mass to 'clean the slate'. Two members of the Military Council felt sufficiently secure to spend the last night before the Rising in their own beds. Ceannt had returned from Liberty Hall to find his house besieged by agitated Volunteers who had read the morning newspaper, bicycles stacked four deep in the front garden and a drawing room packed with officers. To pass the time until Ceannt's return Captain Douglas ffrench-Mullen, an accomplished pianist, had entertained them with a succession of airs, including *The Dead March*. After instructing them to remain in the city and stay available to be contacted at short notice, Ceannt lunched with his wife Aine. Afterwards they went out to Howth: 'I remember him standing silently staring at the pier where two years previously the famous gunrunning had taken place.' Later Ceannt apologised for not having mentioned that the Rising would take place next day: 'Eamonn slept at home that night, remarking "I may thank John MacNeill that I can sleep in my own house – the cancelling of the manoeuvres will lead the British to believe that everything is all right."'[141] Before retiring the Clarkes agreed that they and Tom's two bodyguards would resist any police or army raid and 'were to fire at each man as he came in, and it was to be a fight to the finish'. But a knock on the door turned out to be only an agitated old man: 'It took Tom a long time to quieten him down and persuade him to go home, but he finally went, still protesting. I slept in my husband's arms for the last time that night and slept soundly.'[142]

The day before, Saturday 22 April, the Irish authorities were confident that the danger had passed. General Friend, the Irish GOC, who knew much more than Birrell or Nathan, had gone to London on leave as soon as he knew of the *Aud*'s capture. To his considerable embarrassment and the detriment of his army career he was still there on Easter Monday when the Rising broke out. Also in London, to the ruination of his political career, was Chief Secretary Birrell, who had attended Cabinet and decided to remain until after Easter. The governance of Ireland then had been left in the hands of Under-Secretary Nathan who, on Saturday, was in an upbeat mood. Writing to Birrell about the Kerry arrests and the *Aud*'s sinking, he said that 'The Irish Volunteers are to have a "mobilisation" and march out from Dublin tomorrow but I see no indications of a "rising"'.[143] Next day, before he had learnt of the MacNeill cancellation, Birrell replied cheerily in reference to Casement's capture, 'All this (particularly if RC is <u>the Prisoner</u>) is most encouraging. The march of the Irish Volunteers will not be conducted in high spirits.'[144]

On Saturday evening Nathan met the Viceroy, Lord Wimborne, to discuss responding to recent events.[145] They were convinced that the government now held the initiative because of an erroneous belief that Casement was the prime mover in the conspiracy. Nor could they imagine that, after the loss of the *Aud*, any other plotters would persist with plans for a rising. Wimborne argued for the arrest and internment of Volunteer leaders, but Nathan did not commit himself at that stage. Early next morning Nathan was faced with conflicting signals. On the one hand he learnt that one of Casement's companions had spoken of a rising planned for that day, but on the other MacNeill's countermand seemed to indicate that the crisis was subsiding with the Irish Volunteers apparently in disarray and retreat. When he was informed that a large quantity of stolen explosives had been smuggled into Liberty Hall, Nathan proposed raiding the building that night. But Wimborne pressed for more radical action, such as the arrest of the Volunteer leaders and to this Nathan finally gave his support, providing Birrell approved. A telegram to this effect was sent to the chief secretary in London but did not reach Birrell until the following day. At 6 p.m. Nathan collected Colonel H.V. Cowan and Major O. Lewis, the most senior of Friend's staff officers, and they accompanied him to a meeting with Wimborne.[146] Cowan urged caution over the proposed raid on Liberty Hall which he thought might provoke strong resistance.

To allow Cowan time to consult army and police officers about the wisdom of the operation, another conference was fixed for 10 p.m. at the Vice-Regal Lodge. At this meeting – which was also attended by Edgeworth-Johnstone, the Chief Commissioner of the Dublin Metropolitan Police (DMP); Price the military intelligence officer; and Colonel Cowan – Wimborne supported Cowan's reservations about a raid on Liberty Hall and pressed forcefully for the immediate arrest of the Volunteer and Citizen Army leaders. But Nathan demurred because he wanted any arrests to be legally watertight and he had still not received Birrell's approval for such a dramatic step. By the time the meeting broke up at 11.30 p.m. it had been decided to await the chief secretary's verdict and meanwhile prepare lists of those to be apprehended in any government swoop. The strains of recent days had told on Nathan and one close friend noted how grave and preoccupied he had become and how hard it was to raise his spirits.[147]

On this Sunday, Percy Bick, a soldier based at Richmond Barracks, wrote one of the last letters to leave Dublin before the Rising. He wrote that 'Things are pretty quiet in spite of periodical alarms', but warned that if the Volunteers 'start any trouble, it will be a serious matter and there will be bloodshed. I do not understand why they are allowed to go on spreading sedition. They should have been suppressed at their inception or at any rate at the outbreak of the war.'[148]

3

The First Morning of the Rising and St Stephen's Green

Easter Monday morning, 24 April, was brilliantly sunny as a sombre Under-Secretary Nathan walked from his residence in Phoenix Park to the nearby Vice-Regal Lodge. After briefly meeting Wimborne he travelled to an almost deserted Dublin Castle for a discussion about the political situation with Major Ivon Price, the military intelligence officer.[1] At the same time Chief Secretary Birrell's authorisation to arrest and intern Volunteer leaders was being dispatched from London. However, Nathan was still anxious to avoid acting precipitately, fearing the impact of police and army raids on a city thronged with holidaymakers. He believed that the government could afford to wait a while now that a rising had apparently been averted. Little did Nathan know that from the early hours Irish Volunteers and Citizen Army members had been arriving at Liberty Hall along with all but one member of the Military Council.

Accompanied by his two armed bodyguards Clarke had left home after breakfast, promising Kathleen that whatever happened he would never surrender. Like Clarke, Sean MacDermott also walked to Liberty Hall. Having apparently slept in their uniforms, Patrick and Willie Pearse ate a hearty breakfast before, according to Margaret O'Kelly, 'they took their bicycles which were in the hall, wheeled them down the four steps and turned to wave at me. I can see them still. They rode down along Upper Rutland Street in the direction of Liberty Hall.' The terminally ill Plunkett who had recently undergone a serious operation on his glandular neck was driven from his apartment in the Metropole Hotel. As a battalion commander, MacDonagh had been designated to occupy Jacob's factory, but he intended on spending the final hours before the Rising with his fellow conspirators. Connolly was already in Liberty Hall. The only absentee was Eamonn Ceannt who was at home preparing to lead out his men to the South Dublin Union.[2]

Unlike the nearby docks, silent on this public holiday, Liberty Hall was very busy. Most of the Citizen Army had stayed overnight in the building while those with overnight passes were now coming back. Every couple of minutes Irish Volunteers in their grey-green uniform cycled away with dispatches; inside the building engineers were assembling a stockpile of bombs from a large supply of stolen gelignite and still trying to finish a machine gun on which they had been working for some weeks. As a precaution against a last-minute government swoop, Connolly sent scouts to observe army barracks and verify that no unusual troop movements were taking place.[3] He also proudly displayed one of the first copies of the Proclamation. But soon afterwards the uniformed Connolly solemnly presented a pistol to his daughter Nora who was leaving for the family home in Belfast. He then embraced her and saluted.[4] At 11 a.m. The O'Rahilly suddenly appeared in a car laden with rifles. Having been tipped off that the Rising was definitely on, he reasoned that 'If men are determined to have a rising, nothing will stop them'. He was more hurt than angry at the Military Council for deceiving him and with typical generosity decided to join his erstwhile adversaries. They greeted him warmly but his resentful sister Anna didn't reciprocate, pinching Pearse on the arm and hissing, 'This is all your fault'. The O'Rahilly, however, was already warming to the task ahead, remarking to Countess Markievicz, 'It is madness, but it is glorious madness'. He didn't expect the Rising to last very long and wanted to be involved from start to finish.[5]

At 11.45 a.m. bugler William Oman of the Citizen Army sounded the fall-in at Beresford Place outside Liberty Hall and every man collected two grenades encased in condensed milk cans as they surged out of the building.[6] James Connolly issued final orders to his officers and shook hands with Sean Connolly, whom he had recently promoted to captain and chosen to lead the Citizen Army occupation of the City Hall. After James Connolly shouted, 'Good luck, Sean! We won't meet again', the column of thirty men set off along with a dozen women who had slipped in at the last moment.[7] As they crossed Butt Bridge and marched along Tara Street, College Street and Dame Street, mocking civilians shouted 'pop guns'. Sean Connolly's orders were to neutralise Dublin Castle and Ship Street Barracks next to it by occupying high buildings overlooking them and prevent incoming and outgoing troop movements.[8] These places included the City Hall, the *Evening Mail* offices, the Corporation rates building, a public house and Henry and James tailor's shop at the corner of Parliament Street. Sean Connolly knew the City Hall well – he worked in the motor tax office – and the surrounding area, one reason no doubt why Connolly put him in command.

As the Citizen Army approached the City Hall at noon, sections peeled away to occupy designated buildings but Connolly's continued towards the Upper Yard entrance to the Castle. The policeman on duty, Constable O'Brien, signalled for them to pass on and went to close the gate but Connolly shot him dead. An armed sentry nearby made as if to return fire but thought better of it and ran to the guardroom. As Connolly shouted 'get in, get in' fifteen Citizen Army members followed, overpowering and disarming all the soldiers on duty before tying them up with their own puttees. In his office about 25 yards from the gate Nathan was meeting Major Ivon Price and A.H. Norway, head of the Irish Post Office, to arrange restricting to military personnel the telephone and telegraph services throughout much of southern Ireland. Suddenly shots were fired just below their first-floor window. According to Norway: 'I looked up. "What's that?" I asked. "Oh, that's probably the long predicted attack on the Castle," cried Nathan, jumping up, and leaving the room.' Price ran outside, saw O'Brien's body and fired his revolver to chase off half a dozen Citizen Army members.[9] After a few minutes Norway went downstairs and 'found all the messengers huddled together in a frightened crowd. They had just seen the policeman at the gate shot through the heart. They were badly shaken.'[10] Nevertheless they had shut the gates of the Lower and Upper Yards. Norway then located Nathan in the armoury where he was intent on arming the few DMP constables who guarded the Castle. But the few revolvers had no cartridges. Nathan next alerted British military headquarters in Phoenix Park and the Vice-Regal Lodge about the attack and telegraphed Birrell in London.

Ever afterwards there has been controversy about Sean Connolly's intentions at the Castle gate and especially his killing of an unarmed policeman. It remains uncertain how closely he adhered to the Military Council's instructions and how independently or spontaneously he acted on the day. Only he knew, having told his column nothing about the coming operation even after it left Liberty Hall. Connolly cannot have planned to seize and hold the Castle – most of his men had already been diverted to occupy other buildings. It is possible, though very unlikely, that he misinterpreted O'Brien's gesture as threatening or that, excitable as he certainly was, Connolly simply lost his head and ambushed someone who was, after all, in an enemy uniform. Perhaps the bigger plan was for the Citizen Army to commence the Rising with a dramatic act just like the simultaneous Volunteer and Fianna attack on the Magazine Fort. Connolly's shouted orders do seem to imply an incursion into the Castle grounds. Perhaps his mission was to shoot the place up or capture prominent figures like Nathan and Price. Possibly he intended a situation where British troops rushed to the Castle on a relief mission, giving his men in overlooking buildings an opportunity to decimate them or at least prevent the enemy from getting into a position to attack Citizen Army units as they occupied the City Hall and other buildings. Any lengthy blunting of a British counter-attack was impossible because of the limited resources at Sean Connolly's disposal. The men occupying the guardroom stayed until the early evening and evaded a British assault by slipping away surreptitiously through a door and passage leading into Castle Street.[11]

With the Castle gates now shut Connolly's force headed off to occupy the City Hall beside it. As this was shut for the Easter holidays they entered by Exchange Court, a small cul-de-sac on the east side. Getting in through the basement they reached the ground floor from where they ascended stairs to the roof. From here Connolly was able to shout instructions to Citizen Army members on the parapets of other occupied buildings. At 12.30 p.m. he observed a troop of twenty lancers moving easily along Ormond quay – a tempting target, but one that he left to Daly's men in the Four Courts. Soon afterwards Connolly's 15-year-old brother Matthew heard firing and 'some of the Lancers, less than half their original number came galloping back along the quays, their horses hooves knocking sparks off the cobblestones'.[12] As the tempo of shooting increased it crept towards the Castle and City Hall. On the roof an exhilarated Connolly was scampering about and ignoring his own warnings about keeping one's head down. Unsurprisingly an enemy sniper soon wounded him. Matthew noticed that:

> his tunic was rolled up to near the elbow of one arm. He had what appeared to be a red handkerchief bound round his forearm. When asked what it was he held it out and said, 'Look at the blood I'm shedding for Ireland.' I offered to dress the wound properly as I had a first-aid kit on my belt but he made light of it and said 'not to trouble' and moved away to another part of the building.[13]

At 1.30 p.m. Connolly sent Helena Moloney of the Citizen Army to the GPO for reinforcements and later James Connolly did send some men to the City Hall. Having escaped with only a flesh wound, Sean Connolly couldn't resist pushing his luck and Dr Kathleen Lynn, a captain in the Citizen Army of which she was chief medical officer, noticed him 'coming towards us, walking upright, although we had been advised to crouch and take cover as much as possible. He suddenly fell mortally wounded by a sniper's bullet. First-aid was useless. He died almost immediately.'[14] Moloney, an Abbey Theatre actress and Connolly's girlfriend, watched Lynn attending him until she gave up, remarking, 'I'm afraid he is gone. He was bleeding very much from the stomach. I said the Act of Contrition in his ear. We had no priest. We were very distressed at Sean Connolly's death.'[15] Ironically, he had inflicted the first fatality on the British before becoming the first rebel to die in the Rising. As Matt Connolly cried bitterly other snipers silenced the British marksman who was operating from the Castle's Bedford Tower. Sean Connolly's irresponsibility had rendered his garrison leaderless and demoralised, as well as distracting it from neutralising enemy movements near the Castle. Moloney recalled a garrison suddenly drained of confidence and enthusiasm; one that felt 'there was nothing to do, only sit. They fired desultory shots all day at anything they saw.'[16]

Inside the Castle, Nathan and Norway were acutely aware of their vulnerability and spent the afternoon waiting for military reinforcements as well as debating how such a dire situation had come to pass. Norway just happened to be holding an intelligence report from Nathan that had evaluated the IRB as dormant – an assessment that now applied more accurately to the under-secretary's job prospects. Norway had long regarded the government's Irish policy as vacillating and appeasing and he couldn't resist putting his finger on the passage and passing the document back to Nathan with the comment, '"It seems the I.R.B. is not so dormant after all." Sir Matthew smiled uncomfortably but said nothing.'[17] Finally, at dusk, a battalion of soldiers from the Curragh entered the Castle completely unimpeded and at about 9 p.m. they began attacking the City Hall. Standing in the Lower Yard, Norway listened as:

> the rifle volleys came in crashes, mingled with the tapping of machine guns and the shattering bursts of bombs, so near that they seemed close beside us. The Yard was lit by torches and crowded with men and soldiers, among who from time to time was carried in a woman, caught in the act of carrying ammunition to the rebels and fighting like trapped cats. It was a strange and awful scene.[18]

A female sentry on the City Hall's ground floor recalled the British concentrating on a large window at the rear of the building and bombing and blasting it with machine-gun fire: 'The din was terrific: the effect nerve-shattering.'[19] Kathleen Lynn remembered an intense, unrelenting assault during which 'bullets fell like rain. The firing came from all sides and continued till after darkness. There was no way of escape although we discussed all possibilities.'[20] Earlier, Lynn had given Matt Connolly two tablets and ordered him to take a meal and then go to bed for a rest, having gone without sleep for three days: 'When I awoke, it must have been some hours later, the building seemed to shudder and vibrate with explosions and machine-gun fire. The room was quite dark. Glass crashed, doors and woodwork were being shattered and

somewhere in a distant part of the building women screamed.'[21] Connolly returned
to a roof that was now completely deserted. Puzzled, he pulled two hand grenades
from his pockets, laid them down on a ledge and sat down on a slope of the roof
trying to work out where everyone had gone. In fact they had fled earlier under
heavy enemy fire, jumping a wall on to a Castle building where they were pinned
down again before eventually surrendering on Tuesday morning. Standing beside his
brother Sean's body and peering:

> through the stone railing of the balustrade opposite the Evening Mail office, I could
> see the bluish light of the street arc lamps shining down on the wet cobblestone
> while, above, the upper part of the buildings took on a dark, almost black appear-
> ance. The lanyard on the flag pole shook in the wind, rattling against the pole every
> now and then.[22]

Soon afterwards he heard voices on the street below and the sound of wheels before a
Verey light or a rocket shot skyward, briefly illuminating the entire district.

The British had smashed their way through into the City Hall and troops with fixed
bayonets began pouring inside. Using torches they first captured those people – mostly
women – occupying the ground floor. Lynn made the surrender. Over the course of
the next three to four hours soldiers worked their way upstairs to the kitchen and
top floor, opening doors and firing into the rooms as they went. When the rest of the
garrison finally gave up the British initially just couldn't comprehend that the women
were actually female members of the Citizen Army. To Helena Moloney's annoyance
'the British officers thought the girls had been taken prisoner by the rebels. They asked
them, "Did they do anything to you?"'[23] The attackers then turned their attention to
the *Evening Mail* offices but when they entered it after a heavy machine gun assault its
four defenders had already vanished over the roofs of adjacent houses. In all, Citizen
Army casualties amounted to four men dead and three wounded.

Another group that left Liberty Hall at much the same time as Sean Connolly's was
a combined unit of Volunteers and Fianna led by Patrick Daly. The Military Council
had designated it to blow up the Magazine Fort in Phoenix Park.[24] Cycling in twos
and threes along the quays they stopped at a shop to buy a football. At the park they
strolled towards the gate posing as a football team, throwing the ball back and forth.
Arriving at the fort, Daly distracted a sentry by inquiring about the location of a
soccer pitch whereupon Paddy Boland jumped on the soldier and seized his rifle.
Daly and two Volunteers then dashed through the archway into the guardroom, forcing other soldiers to raise their hands and face the wall. Daly then kicked in the glass
door of a cabinet and grabbed a bundle of keys. By now Paddy Boland had wrestled
his prisoner into the guardroom where armed Volunteers were also watching Mrs
Playfair, the commandant's wife, and her two sons who lived in an adjoining house.
Daly now made his way to the ammunition, paraffin, oil and tool stores which he
opened before dispatching another Volunteer with the keys to the guncotton store.

Daly and his team now commenced smashing the ammunition store with sledgehammers and hatchets while paraffin oil drums were wheeled in to saturate the
premises. After tin-can bombs had been distributed among the ammunition boxes
most of the team cleared out leaving Daly and others to light fuses to the paraffin-

covered boxes. They left the door half open to let in air and locked the outer iron gate, though to Daly's chagrin the man sent to the guncotton store couldn't get in and that part of the operation was abandoned. Daly now went to the guardroom and released Mrs Playfair and her two boys, telling them to leave the fort immediately as it was about to blow up. He also freed the soldiers with a warning that they would be shot if they went towards Islandbridge Barracks. Daly's team got away safely, leaving the park, as previously arranged, either individually or in small groups. A Fianna, Eamon Martin, and four others jumped into a horse-drawn hackney cab that had been held in readiness. When it reached the main gate they heard the first of the disappointingly dull explosions that destroyed the firearms and ammunition. There were no high explosives in the fort. Just as Aine Ceannt had suspected on the previous Saturday, the British army had removed them for use in France. As Martin's group drove out on to the main road they noticed one of the Playfair boys running towards his home nearby, one that Martin knew contained a telephone:

> As we had yet to make our way back to the city, and realising that we were behind time – that the insurrection would have already begun – we could not afford to take any chances with this boy. Accordingly one of our party who was cycling alongside our hackney car speeded up and shot – to wound – the boy, just as he was entering the door of this house. The boy died of his wound.[25]

Stephen's Green

Stephen's Green, the oldest and largest of Dublin's residential squares, comprised 22 acres of open space and was over a quarter of a mile long on its north and south sides. Prominent at its centre was an equestrian statue of George II. With the passing of time, hotels, clubs, institutions and churches had come to mingle with or replace its impressive eighteenth-century town houses. In 1880 the Green had been opened as a public park for the recreation, health and enjoyment of Dubliners, and a bandstand and ornamental lake had been added. On the west side stood the substantial classical edifice of the Royal College of Surgeons in Ireland, a building that was to feature prominently in the Rising.

The insurgents chosen to occupy Stephen's Green were mostly from the Citizen Army and their commander was 42-year-old Michael Mallin, Connolly's second-in-command and, like his boss, a former soldier in the British army. He was the eldest surviving son of a family of nine, four of whom had died by the time of the Rising. An accomplished flautist, Mallin had enlisted in 1889 as a band boy in the Royal Scottish Fusiliers and during the next twelve years he served mainly in India and South Africa – though not in the Boer War. He finally left the army filled with resentment, judging that his political beliefs had blighted his promotion prospects: as a devout Catholic he had refused to contribute to a memorial for Queen Victoria because she was head of the Church of England. On returning to Ireland in 1902 Mallin became a qualified silk weaver and eventually secretary of the silk weavers' union. A year later he married Agnes Richey whose father was a former Fenian who had participated in the 1867

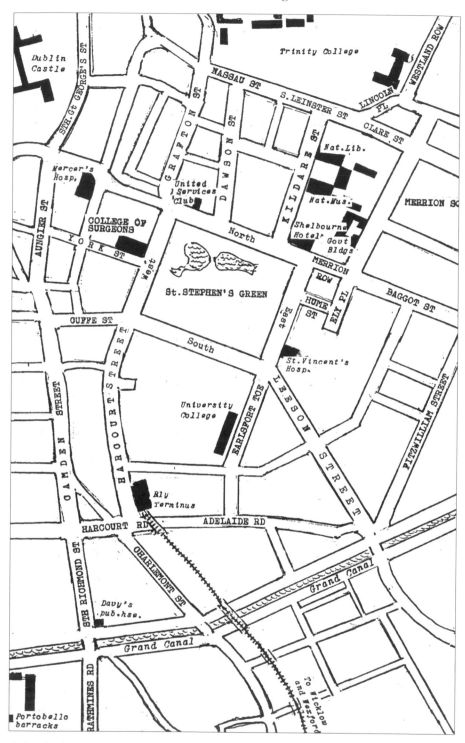

St Stephen's Green

Rising. By 1916 they had four children and the family was still growing because Mrs Mallin was pregnant again, though that wasn't her only concern. On the Sunday night before the Rising Sergeant Jimmy O'Shea of the Citizen Army met Agnes outside Liberty Hall when:

> she appeared as if the weight of the world was on her. And so it was. She was pale and very shaken but I admired her courage. She was going to see Mallin, probably for the last time. She knew all. I was sorry for the kids, so young and not knowing what was on.[26]

Mallin returned his wife's devotion and a few weeks earlier this former weaver had brought a loom into Liberty Hall to weave some poplin in his spare time, hoping to sell it for £10 which he hoped would tide his family over until the end of the fighting.[27]

Partly through his union activities, Mallin joined the Citizen army at its inception in 1913 and within a year had been promoted to chief of staff. His relations with Connolly though were more formal than friendly and Mallin, who suffered from periodic recurrences of malaria that made him appear tipsy, had been extremely hurt when his chief accused him once of being drunk.[28] During the months before the Rising Mallin had actively accumulated weapons by organising members to steal or buy arms, ammunition and equipment from British soldiers home on leave. Eventually the losses became so serious that troops were ordered to leave their rifles at Holyhead before travelling to Ireland. Mallin also got some weapons himself because his house actually backed on to Richmond Barracks, under whose walls he would wait for friendly soldiers to hand over material.[29] Standing only 5ft 7in tall with thick black hair, a moustache and a body that seemed to taper from his broad shoulders, Mallin wasn't the most physically imposing rebel commandant of Easter Week. But he had earned his promotion through military experience, organising ability and dedication. Despite a rudimentary education and rather dour personality, Mallin's subordinates trusted him as a calm, capable and methodical leader. Indeed, Connolly and he had been mainly responsible for transforming the Citizen Army from its somewhat lax beginnings. In the early days Connolly had remarked sardonically that 'I can always guarantee that the Irish Citizen Army will fight, but I cannot guarantee that they will be in time for such fight when it takes place'.[30] Soon however, according to Frank Robbins, 'With the help of Michael Mallin all this laxity disappeared, as did a number of the then members of the Citizen Army'.[31] O'Shea was filled with pride that this strict regime turned them into 'real soldiers' bound together so tight that 'home or nothing else mattered'. By 1916 Connolly estimated he had 300 members, all fully armed. About two-thirds of them (220) turned out in Easter Week and almost half (104 men and 14 women) were to fight at Stephen's Green. Proportionately, this was much higher than the Irish Volunteers managed and reflected the Citizen Army's more unified leadership, higher levels of cohesion and discipline and its greater militancy.

As Mallin's column was about to set off from Beresford Place O'Shea was approached by a tall old man with a flowing beard and carrying a stick, whom he deduced was an old Fenian. Emotionally he gripped O'Shea's hand and wished him luck in the terrible task that lay ahead before turning away and departing with tears falling down his face.[32] Mallin left with only thirty-six men and supporting units of women and Fianna, some of whom were in uniform and carrying rifles and shotguns while others could only be distinguished by their bandoliers. Originally Mallin was supposed to have more than twice as many people at his disposal. One member, Margaret Skinnider, had cycled ahead to scout for British troop movements, but because of the bank holiday the streets were quiet and she only encountered a single bored policeman on duty at the Green.[33] The column marched across Butt Bridge and up Grafton Street in a mood of uncompromising determination. At the top, according to Robbins, they encountered a young police recruit who, 'annoyed by our singing of "The Peeler and the Goat", foolishly lost his temper and intervened. He was lucky not to lose his life for our lads were certainly not in the mood for interference from that quarter.'[34] However a British army officer holidaying in Dublin sensed immediately that something serious was happening. Captain E. Gerrard went straight home, picked up his uniform and reported to Beggar's Bush Barracks.[35]

Jimmy O'Shea recalled that as the Citizen Army entered the Green 'the poor gardener on duty thought the world had ended when we demanded the keys'.[36] The insurgents then began closing and locking the gates, posting guards and expelling the public from a park teeming with mothers and children enjoying the sunny bank holiday weather. Some indignantly threatened to summon the police and rebels fired shots into the ground to hurry them along. Some civilians were simply bemused. O'Shea recalled 'an old priest – a Canon – who was sitting on a seat. I told him what I wanted and he asked me the reason. When I told him the fight for the republic had started, he shook. I was terribly sorry for him as I escorted him to the gate.'[37] However, almost immediately O'Shea brought him back to give conditional absolution to a worried young rebel: 'He also asked me to kneel and gave me absolution. I thought it was a very brave action for an old man in such a nervous state.'[38]

Shortly after noon a young unarmed police constable, Michael Lahiff of College Street station, was shot dead at Stephen's Green for supposedly 'refusing to leave his post'.[39] Lahiff's death is one of the most controversial of the Rising and it had a powerful impact on contemporaries. St John Ervine, an Ulster Unionist visitor lodging at the United Arts Club, passed the scene later and saw 'a pool of congealed blood. I almost sickened at the sight.'[40] It is impossible to know for certain whether Lahiff was indeed killed for resisting orders from Citizen Army members. With remarkable charity St John Ervine attributed the shooting to an attack of nerves but it is undoubtedly true that Connolly's men and women had never forgotten or forgiven the DMP for its role in the Dublin Lockout. As revolutionary socialists they regarded this bitter industrial dispute as having proved that the police were the enthusiastic servants of capitalism and at least some of the Citizen Army at Stephen's Green welcomed Easter Monday as their long-awaited day of revenge. Moreover, their hostility can only have been enhanced when Connolly met his senior officers in the middle of Holy Week to reveal the date of the Rising. Connolly told them then that he was leaving the treatment of policemen to their discretion but he gave a very broad hint by suggesting they should remember the Lockout and 'how they treated you in 1913'.[41] In stark contrast, Connolly advised them to urge Irishmen serving in the British army to come over to the side of the rebels. The identity of the person or persons who killed Lahiff remains unresolved almost a hundred years later, but Geraldine Fitzgerald, a nurse who witnessed the incident, claimed that soon afterwards she saw

Countess Markievicz running triumphantly into the Green shouting "I got him" and some of the rebels shook her hand and seemed to congratulate her'.[42]

Mallin had just appointed Markievicz as his second-in-command. She was one of the most colourful figures of the Rising in her green puttees, tunic, riding breeches and slouch hat with ostrich feather, invariably carrying a weapon. Markicvicz's idio syncratic appearance and behaviour added to her notoriety because a woman dressing in trousers and smoking cigarettes in public was widely regarded then as most unusual and somewhat shocking behaviour. Despite her foreign name, this exotic creature had actually been born in 1868 as Constance Gore-Booth on the family estate in Sligo. For the first forty years her lifestyle and attitudes were those of her ascendancy class and like many other young privileged women she was presented at court as a debutante. She later married a Pole, Count Casimir Markievicz, but as the marriage disintegrated Constance immersed herself in politics. By now a rebellious streak had caused her to shed almost every aspect of her former life except her courtesy title and a refined upper-class accent. Becoming a nationalist, republican, socialist, revolutionary and finally a Roman Catholic, she involved herself in a plethora of militant organisations. In 1910 she and Hobson founded the Fianna, a republican boy scouts group intended to give young men a military training. She also played a formative part in the establishment in 1914 of the Cumann na mBan organisation for republican women and by 1915 she was helping to organise and train the Citizen Army. Beneath her aristocratic hauteur and a capacity for embroidering her own exploits, Markievicz possessed courage and flair, and certainly craved military action.

While unreservedly acknowledging Markievicz's courage and knowing that once the fighting began she would be in the thick of things, Tom Clarke distrusted her talkativeness that might threaten the secret planning for a rising.[43] Certainly Markievicz hardly conformed to Clarke's ideal image of Irish womanhood and it is impossible to imagine her cooking in Volunteer kitchens or delivering messages during the fighting. Only the Citizen Army offered her a starring role in the great drama of Easter Week because of its acceptance of gender equality and Connolly's emphasis on propaganda and public display. These factors attracted members who were actors and actresses in civilian life. Liberty Hall staged frequent plays and concerts. Connolly regarded theatrical people like Markievicz as revolutionary assets: Clarke would have liked nothing better than for him to have shut her mouth. When she arrived at the Green carrying a rifle, Markievicz had just delivered medical supplies to Sean Connolly's Citizen Army garrison at the City Hall. Although originally earmarked to liaise between Stephen's Green and the GPO, Mallin insisted he needed her to stay because of a shortage of followers and promoted her to be his second-in-command. At the Green, Markievicz had a friend and kindred spirit in Margaret Skinnider, a Scot of Irish descent who had developed powerful nationalist sympathies and whom the countess had summoned to Dublin a few days before the Rising.[44]

The commotion around the Green had begun to attract the attention of civilians, including Douglas Hyde, founder of the Gaelic League and later the first President of Ireland. He had just cycled from his home nearby to purchase cigarettes and had initially dismissed the gunfire as car tyres being punctured, but his unease deepened when he saw gates closed at the Green and gardeners leaving early. Hyde believed that Mallin's force might have been clearing the park for a military review until a vicious, shabbily dressed Fianna shouted an angry warning and pointed a gun directly at him. The youth was watched admiringly by a young girl with a bandolier whom Hyde thought 'looked as if she would have liked to kill' him. Eventually he departed, still mystified and unaware that he had witnessed the first minutes of an Irish revolution.[45]

Throughout Monday afternoon Mallin's garrison laboured to make the park secure by digging deep pits or trenches at many points, placing armed guards at railings or in shrubbery along the entire north side. They also moved bystanders on to prevent crowds gathering. Trenches were dug at the four main entrances whose gates were blocked with park benches, wheelbarrows, lorries, cabs and motorcars. The rebels also erected barricades in adjacent streets. Republican women established a kitchen and a first aid centre in the summerhouse while shotguns, grenades and ammunition were distributed to the garrison from a handcart. A park kiosk was improvised as Mallin's headquarters. During Monday the garrison was augmented by other Citizen Army units that had initially been deployed elsewhere and with up to twenty people who were keen to participate in the Rising. The Green was a convenient place to reach for anyone who had earlier missed their own battalion's mobilisation or had initially obeyed MacNeill's countermand. It was central, accessible and word soon spread that it had been occupied; it was short of manpower and welcomed any new recruit. At least three people who joined up with Mallin's garrison that afternoon – Nora O'Daly, Bridget Murtagh and May Moore – were Cumann na mBan members. They were anxious to get involved and gratefully accepted Markievicz's invitation to stay.[46]

After leaving MacNeill, Liam Ó Briain had been making his way past the Green on his way to join his Volunteer company when he accepted a challenge to 'come in and fight for Ireland'.[47] Although handed a shotgun, Ó Briain spent the first after-noon digging trenches and dealing with frequent inquiries from mothers searching for their missing sons and daughters. Mallin and Markievicz, meanwhile, circulated around the Green reassuring the garrison that everything was going well. Once the Green had been secured Mallin concentrated on establishing and fortifying outposts in houses and business premises in surrounding streets and then manning them with sharpshooters. Because of the public holiday many of these buildings were unoc-cupied, including the Bank of Ireland branch in Stephen's Green East and the Winter Palace, a public house on the west side of the park. Most important, though, was the Royal College of Surgeons on the west side facing the park, and Mallin's immediate purpose in ordering its occupation in mid-afternoon was to seize its Officer Training Corps rifles. Frank Robbins, who led the raiding party, just managed to prevent the caretaker slamming the doors shut and 'the gentle persuasion of a revolver at his throat managed the rest'.[48] While the caretaker and his family were locked in a room, the insurgents searched the building but, infuriatingly, couldn't locate any weapons. Mallin then sent messengers with a supply of bombs and orders for Robbins to hold the building and take up positions on the roof, where he ran up a tricolour.

A critical and surprising tactical blunder was the failure to occupy Dublin's pre-mier hotel, the Shelbourne. This was a relatively high building from which could be seen most of the park and which Connolly had identified before the Rising as a potential garrison because of ample stocks of beds, food and barricading materials. On Easter Monday the hotel was full to capacity with Irish and English race-goers, war-time officers on leave (many with their wives and families) and theatrical types.

Most residents, however, had gone to watch the Irish Grand National at Fairyhouse, where by the last race word was spreading among the military present that a rebellion had broken out in Dublin. When the hotel's head porter peeked out nervously he saw rebels constructing a barricade across the street, just outside the main entrance.[49] Mallin was anxious to provide additional defensive cover against an expected British assault and similar obstructions were going up on every side of the Green. During the afternoon Markievicz was in command on the west side as cars and wagons were commandeered. Sometimes the seizures were done with impressive diplomacy, as when three armed and apologetic insurgents saluted when they requested the occupants of a motor to step out on to the sidewalk while they directed the chauffeur to drive the vehicle to a barricade.[50] At other times some insurgents were considerably less courteous. From the College of Surgeons' roof, Frank Robbins witnessed clashes between rebels and recalcitrant bystanders. The latter:

> presumably wives or relatives of Irishmen in the British army, were bent on making trouble for our men by prevailing on motorists and drivers of other vehicles to go by alternative routes. They also obstructed comrades who were detaining the vehicles. They lived in the vicinity and were aggressively pro-British.[51]

Not every motorist meekly complied with rebel orders, such as the driver who attempted to recover his car from a barricade at the Shelbourne and was warned off at gunpoint. Unco-operative tram drivers also risked their lives, including the man who immobilised his vehicle by throwing away the control handle and was chased and fired on by the rebels.[52] Robbins related another incident:

> The driver proved to be an enterprising chap. He whipped off the control handle of the tram and changed to the other end, while the conductor reversed the trolley. It was the quickest bit of work on the part of two tramway employees I have ever seen. Detecting their intention, I as the officer in charge, gave the order to fire. We planned to frighten the tram crew, but not to kill and our widely aimed volley had no effect whatever. The driver and his mate were not to be frightened and undauntedly stuck to their post and drove the tram out of danger. We were furious at the loss of our potential barricade but we could not but admire the crew's adroit manoeuvre and their coolness in danger.[53]

Poor barricade construction made confrontations more probable because it tempted motorists to drive around or even through the barriers. Mallin's garrison does not appear to have received clear instructions as to how to respond to this situation. Undoubtedly differences in social class and political attitudes between vehicle owners and those manning the barricades must have given a sharper, rawer edge to their disputes. Furthermore, many rebels were young, inexperienced and undisciplined but very keen to assert their authority. One boy who looked about 12 was seen 'strutting the centre of the road with a large revolver in his fist'.[54] They blew open tyres to immobilise vehicles they had halted and warned off the owners at gunpoint. On Monday evening one visitor to the city saw a cab passing the United Arts Club and being challenged at an adjacent park gate. When the driver defied repeated warnings to stop some insurgents opened fire and downed the horse while the driver leapt out and ran away up Merrion Street. By Tuesday morning the horse had been dragged out of the way on to the pavement where throughout Easter Week it became perhaps the most distressing sight around Stephen's Green. Only after the surrender was its rotting carcass collected by Dublin Zoo where food stocks had run low.[55]

Inevitably civilians were seriously injured or killed at Stephen's Green. They included Michael Cavanagh, an elderly guest whom rebels shot dead in front of the Shelbourne on Easter Monday afternoon. Although his vehicle of theatrical effects had been commandeered, he had been given permission to remove some luggage, but when he gripped the shafts to remove the lorry armed men appeared at the railings and told him to desist. Cavanagh appears not to have grasped the danger he was in or else he possessed a commendable but excessive dedication to the maxim that the show must go on, because he ignored increasingly vehement threats. When three warning shots were fired he dropped the shafts but then made the lethal mistake of approaching a group of ten armed men with a raised finger. A voice shouted repeatedly, 'Go and put back that lorry or you are a dead man. Go before I count four. One, two, three, four …' Rifle fire then fatally wounded Cavanagh in the forehead. A watching crowd was ordered to leave but several angry men carried Cavanagh over to the kerb and shouted, 'We'll be` back for you, damn you'.[56] A St John's Ambulance volunteer witness wrote of the effect on the crowd of bystanders: 'Women began to shriek and cry and kneel down to pray in the street, and the vivandieres with the rebels began crying and swearing and wringing their hands to be told by the rebels to go home and several of them were sent off.'[57] Cavanagh was the most notorious and widely reported civilian casualty at the Green.

But a list of people 'killed by rebels' that Dublin Castle compiled after the Rising from police and hospital reports gives numerous examples of people shot 'for refusing to erect a barricade', 'for not getting off the street' or for failing to stop a vehicle when ordered.[58] The Shelbourne's assistant manager reported various incidents to the police, including a guest who was wounded as he went through the revolving door, another shot in the leg as he sat down for lunch and another hit in the jaw by a bullet fired through the large sitting room window. On Tuesday, when Dr Wheeler, Surgeon to the Forces in Ireland, was called to treat the three casualties at the hotel, a boy was shot as the doctor approached the entrance.[59] During the first day of the Rising the Stephen's Green area acquired some of the characteristics of a battlefield, though most casualties were non-combatants. Mercer's Hospital nearby recorded sixteen dead and 278 injured civilians during Easter Week, as well as four dead and five wounded soldiers. Hospital capacity in the area was quickly overwhelmed, prompting the St John's Ambulance organisation to provide temporary casualty services at converted premises in Merrion Square and Harcourt Street.[60]

Prisoners were also taken at the Green on Easter Monday, including up to seven British servicemen. The rebels speedily released most because of a shortage of guards and suitable accommodation, though a small number of civilians were imprisoned for much longer. These included Lawrence Kettle, chief of the Dublin Corporation electricity department, whose car had been seized at a barricade on Monday afternoon. Kettle was detained until the surrender as a suspected British informer because he had been seen entering a military barracks, though he had probably only been visiting his brother, Tom, a Home Rule MP who was serving as an officer in an Irish regiment. Others were detained, first in the park bandstand and later in a greenhouse adjacent to the College of Surgeons. One policeman, Sergeant Hughes, was kept overnight on Easter Monday but shot after he was told he could leave. He lay unattended on the pavement for almost five hours before some students carried him to hospital. A British Red Cross worker was also detained because his medical skills were useful to the insurgents.[61]

On Monday afternoon Captain Richard McCormick led a Citizen Army company of twenty-five men into the Green. Earlier they had not stopped at the park but continued on, intending to establish a small number of strategically valuable outposts a short distance further south that would prevent, or at least delay, a British military advance north towards the Green or central Dublin. When McCormick's men entered Harcourt Street railway station they ordered the public to assemble on the platform, a situation which then threatened to get out of hand when women and children among the day-trippers panicked. Also a group of men had locked themselves inside the ticket office and had to be forced out by a revolver shot through the door. Suddenly Robbins, who appears to have spent Monday permanently on the brink of shooting someone, saw:

> a uniformed staff officer of the British army, obviously on holiday, looking out from the restaurant. My first impulse was to shoot. But seeing no visible side arms I called on him to surrender. He very foolishly ran behind the door, banging it shut. The upper portion of the door was smoked glass. This helped to save his life, for on reaching the door I kicked it open, called on him again to surrender, while at the same time watching his figure as he flattened himself against the wall behind the door. He had no fight left. When he surrendered I handed him over to Captain McCormick.[62]

In another incident at the station an old man, who intervened to dissuade an Irish soldier from discarding his uniform and joining the rebels, had his top hat blown off by rifle fire.[63] Then an attempt to block the railway line by overturning an engine had to be abandoned when a signalman blocked the points and there was neither time nor manpower to undo the sabotage. Instead, some men scattered along the line and briefly took up position on two railway bridges from which they could attack any British troops advancing across Portobello Bridge on the Grand Canal. Another group of seven men had been sent to occupy Davy's, a public house on the corner of South Richmond Street, and Charlemont Mall, about half a mile from the Green. These premises were strategically important because they overlooked the entrance to Portobello Barracks as well as commanding both Portobello Bridge and the Rathmines Road. British troops from the barracks immediately launched a strong counter-attack by wheeling out a Maxim machine gun and after less than an hour they had forced the garrison in Davy's to retreat through a rear entrance.[64]

By the time McCormick returned to the Green Mallin's meagre force was well entrenched. Outlying streets were covered and the British army still couldn't mount an effective counter-attack. Later, Liam Ó Briain was in a squad of rebels which occupied and barricaded houses in Leeson Street before posting snipers on the roofs to guard the nearby bridge over the Grand Canal. Well before dusk the crowds of curious onlookers had melted away and traffic around the Green and adjacent thoroughfares had all but disappeared. Towards evening, Mallin went among the garrison with more assurances that the Rising was going well and the whole country had risen in support. There was little shelter in the Green on that first cold, damp night and most insurgents lay on the open ground in the constant rain, though some women bedded down in the summerhouse and Markievicz retired to the car of Dr Lynn, the Citizen Army's medical director. Despite the discomfort, morale was high, no doubt in part because of Mallin's upbeat military assessments and the entertainment provided by a young comedienne loudly complaining about British snipers disturbing her sleep. Skinnider recalled: 'We were all happy that night as we camped ... Despite the handicaps we were under with the lack of men, almost everything was going our way.'[65] But outside observers were much less sanguine and Douglas Hyde was convinced that the park would be evacuated during the hours of darkness. He thought the Green would be impossible to defend for any length of time; the trenches were too vulnerable to machine gun and rifle fire from the tops of surrounding houses.[66]

Even so, most of the hours until dawn passed fairly uneventfully. There was some shooting at what might have been British troop movements, but the most serious incident occurred just before 2 a.m. when a column of shadowy figures was spotted moving along Leeson Street. The park sentries were tempted to fire, but couldn't be certain that the targets were not in fact fellow rebels – a wise restraint because they were indeed thirty Volunteers from the 4th Battalion marching to the GPO. These men, unknowingly, were doubly lucky because they also just missed decimation by British machine gunners who arrived soon afterwards to occupy the Shelbourne and the Hibernian United Services Club in Stephen's Green North. The troops had made their way from Dublin Castle to Trinity College and then moved as a 'noiseless column' along Kildare Street, undetected by the garrison in the Green, barely 30 yards away.[67] They had then crept into the hotel from the rear and posted guards at its entrance and snipers at every window. They also hauled a machine gun up to the roof and from there and the United Services Club they dominated the Green.

Mallin does not seem to have anticipated the threat on his northern flank and within an hour British firepower from these newly established positions had exposed his garrison's vulnerability. At a stroke it had undermined the viability of occupying the Green and nullified an entire day's effort by the Citizen Army. From four o'clock on Easter Tuesday morning British guns raked the whole area along with supporting fire from troops stationed behind sandbags in Merrion Row. Women in the park's summerhouse scattered for shelter behind an embankment while men in the trenches fled into shrubbery. Although casualties occurred throughout the Green, a disproportionate number of the garrison had been concentrated opposite the Shelbourne.[68] For civilians living in nearby streets the gunfire was terrifying. At his home in Fitzwilliam Street the poet James Stephens was kept awake until almost five o'clock in the morning: 'I went to bed convinced that the Green had been rushed by the military and captured, and that the rising was at an end.'[69] A female guest of the Royal Hibernian Hotel in Dawson Street described it as 'awful and I lay and quaked'.[70] A visitor from Ulster staying at the United Services Club had looked out of a window at four o'clock and seen 'a huddled heap lying in front of the gate where the sentries had been a few hours before'. He then heard shots and low moans and when he looked out again a few hours later he saw in the better light that the huddled heap was in fact a dead rebel's body. Nearby, just off the pavement:

> lay the body of an old man, a labourer evidently, who had been stumping to his work. I suppose he had not realised the rebellion was a serious one and had started off on the usual routine of his life. I think It was between eight and nine o'clock that the ambulance came and took away the two dead men.[71]

Other civilians died from wounds they had sustained during the night.

Having survived Monday's tumultuous events at Dublin Castle, Arthur Norway went to the Green on Tuesday morning to observe the results of the British assault. He saw a group of men peering through a side gate at a man lying full length on a barricade of garden seats, bleeding profusely and with his lower jaw blown away. According to his wife, Norway climbed the railings:

> and found that the man was still living; he then turned and fairly cursed the men who were looking on, and asked if there was not one man enough to come over and help him. Whereupon three men climbed over and together they lifted down the seat with the poor creature on it, dragged away the other seat, when they were able to open the gate, and then brought out the seat and the man on it and carried him to the nearest hospital, where he died in about five minutes.

Norway assumed that the deceased was one of the prisoners that the rebels had captured on Easter Monday who had either been attempting to flee the gunfire or had taken the opportunity to escape from his captors. He had then either been cut down by British bullets or Mallin's garrison had shot him dead 'while trying to escape'.[72] The British officer commanding at the Shelbourne estimated that eleven rebels had been killed during the barrage, whilst Margaret Skinnider stated that the garrison lost just one man, and the Citizen Army's historian R.M. Fox insisted that only a 'few casualties' were sustained.[73] But almost certainly four of the insurgents died.

Initially the unremitting machine gun barrage forced the rebels to flee the gates and railings on the northern side of the Green, but by 8 a.m. Mallin had accepted the hopelessness of his position. He now initiated a retreat to the extreme southwest corner of the park, as far away as possible from the Shelbourne. Although this area also had protective tree cover it only offered a temporary respite and Mallin soon ordered a general transfer to the College of Surgeons. Women went first with bullets 'flying everywhere and sending the gravel up in showers off the path', while wounded Volunteers were forced to take a circuitous route through the shrubs and bushes.[74] Throughout the evacuation Mallin provided strong leadership and considerable courage and wouldn't leave the Green until he was sure that everyone had been accounted for. Earlier he had dashed out of a gateway to drag a wounded man to safety in the face of machine-gun fire from the Shelbourne, taking a bullet through his hat but coolly remarking to Frank Robbins, 'Wasn't that a close shave?'[75] Not every insurgent evacuated the Green: at noon on Easter Tuesday British snipers in the Shelbourne were still firing at men in the trenches, some of whom continued to operate covertly and sporadically throughout much of Easter Week. They also held prisoners in a glasshouse where the park superintendent brought them food. Nevertheless, as time went on the British penetrated the Green in increasing numbers and brought it more fully under military control. On Easter Tuesday the OC Shelbourne dispatched a search party to recover bombs, rifles, revolvers and ammunition. Another party on Friday located and released a prisoner.[76] Within hours word of the evacuation reached the GPO and depressed Connolly, who told a friend that the Citizen Army 'had done badly in Stephen's Green, and that a large number of them were killed … mainly through a machine gun sited on the roof of the Shelbourne Hotel'.[77] His mind was put at ease, however, when Chris Caffrey, who delivered dispatches every day, saw him at the GPO and 'told him who there were of us. "Thank God for that", was his reply.'[78]

But the pressure was not all one way and Mallin's snipers shattered many of the Shelbourne's windows as well as frightening its residents. The hotel's entrance doors were now locked and barricaded and the lower windows shuttered, with mattresses placed behind them. Social life was transferred to smaller, less opulent back rooms where guests endured a claustrophobic existence of card-playing and fitful conversation while machine-gun fire overhead caused chandeliers to tremble on every floor. Many eventually slept in corridors or passed the time by covering for staff, whom the rebels had warned to stay away. During the Rising the Shelbourne became a metaphor for an ascendancy class and a way of life that had been in retreat for decades, but now, suddenly, found itself in deadly peril. For a week its residents came to regard themselves as an oasis of civilisation in a violent land whose restless natives had finally slipped the leash. Surrounded though they were, the residents maintained a determinedly stiff upper lip and put on a good show until they were relieved.[79] Meanwhile, the hotel's twenty military residents had departed after a telephone call from Dublin Castle on Tuesday morning requesting every officer staying there to report for duty.[80]

Robbins later conceded that the decision to seize and entrench the Green without simultaneously occupying the large surrounding buildings was widely regarded as an 'act of suicide'.[81] A female garrison member believed that even to a military amateur the place 'looked a regular death trap'.[82] Mallin's strategy has created doubts about whether the Military Council ever intended occupying the Green. Kathleen Clarke claimed later that it had formed no part of the council's plans and that when Mallin dispatched a messenger to the GPO about the occupation he was ordered to evacuate immediately.[83] But the smooth and co-ordinated manner in which the park was cleared, guarded, barricaded and entrenched, without hesitation by any insurgent, suggests careful advance planning. One of Connolly's confidants, William O'Brien, remembered interrupting a meeting at Liberty Hall on Good Friday morning between Connolly, Markievicz, Mallin and his own brother Dan, who told him later that they had been making an in-depth study of occupying Stephen's Green.[84]

The operation showed a limited understanding of the nature of urban warfare, but in Mallin's defence he was functioning with an unforeseen and acute lack of manpower. Robbins was emphatic that 'there were insufficient men available to seize and secure' the Shelbourne, but that the Citizen Army had originally intended occupying the hotel.[85] Had the Green and surrounding buildings been securely held, they might have fulfilled a more significant military role – as a centrally located rebel base, a potential barrier to British military penetration of the city from the south, a communications and transport centre and a source of fresh water.

While retreating to the College of Surgeons, Mallin's garrison gained a clearer insight into public attitudes towards them. Skinnider claimed later that she found onlookers friendly and anxious to advise her if the coast was clear, but Liam Ó Briain encountered abuse from a group of hysterical, fainting women.[86] On Tuesday afternoon St John Ervine saw a dead rebel lying face down in a hole in the ground just inside a side gate at the Green. When another onlooker suggested getting the body and burying it:

> there were three women from the slums standing by and one of them when she heard what he said rushed at him and beat him with her fists and swore at him horribly: 'No, you'll not get him out,' she yelled: 'Let him lie there and rot like the poor soldiers!'[87]

Robbins was attacked outside the college by a crowd, some of them armed with crowbars and a hatchet. He recognised the female ringleader as someone who had been unremittingly hostile to the rebels throughout Monday. By now Robbins had had enough:

> With my mind finally made up I ran into the centre of the roadway, dropped on one knee with the feeling that this woman would be a good riddance. Lieutenant Kelly who was now almost at the door, guessed my intention and shouted 'Frank, don't shoot' while at the same time he ran out into the roadway and grabbed my arm. I felt sore over it and wondered what would the consideration have been shown by the opposing forces if they were to be obstructed in the same way.[88]

Robbins estimated that about 125 men had transferred from the park, of whom roughly 100 belonged to the Citizen Army, most of the rest being Irish Volunteers and Fianna.[89]

The college was solidly built and made an ideal stronghold. On the ground floor were lecture rooms and a museum, upstairs there were classrooms, laboratories and a library, while the caretaker's rooms and a kitchen were situated on the top floor. According to Skinnider the British 'peppered' the 'impregnable' building for the next five days but with so little impact that they might as well have been firing dried peas.[90] However, the college was also cold and uncongenial. Its large, draughty rooms were filled with cases containing the students' specimens, including jars with human body parts preserved in liquid. The air reeked with formaldehyde. There was also virtually no food. Mallin's priority now was to secure the building and its main entrance and he had the front windows barricaded with desks, park benches and library books, while sentries were posted at every doorway. A lecture hall on the ground floor was converted into a dining room, recreation area and dormitory, and rugs and carpets were brought in for bedding. When food was available, cooking was done in a small kitchen in the caretaker's quarters on the third floor. A sick bay was immediately improvised in an area at the end of a lecture theatre and placed out of bounds to all but the wounded and first aid assistants. Stretcher beds and mattresses were brought in from the Turkish baths a few doors away.[91] Finally, a mortuary chapel was devised using seats from the examination theatre and the anatomy room; the dead were laid out on slabs, a tall dark cross was located and a rough altar constructed from coffin plates.[92]

Mallin made his headquarters in a central room on the first floor and placed his best marksmen on the roof where spotters equipped with field-glasses assisted them. For at least the early part of the week he continued operating the barricade nearest the college; it crossed the road to a point where the trees in the park were tall enough to obscure the view of British machine-gunners in the Shelbourne and the United Services Club. A garrison member, Harry Nicholls, describes how on Tuesday night they had to shoot at 'those trying to remove cars' from it.[93] But it became more vulnerable as the military acquired further positions, and appears to have been abandoned by Wednesday. Despite their continuing presence on the streets, the rebels were on the defensive, attacked by machine-gun fire from a growing number of British positions.

Attempting to relieve this pressure, Mallin decided to counter-attack by setting up new outposts and sniper positions. He hoped these would forestall their occupation by British forces as well as, possibly, finding additional food stocks. These included the Turkish baths and Kapp and Petersons – both on the same side of the Green as the college. On Wednesday, bystanders also reported rebel snipers in the houses between Kildare Street and Grafton Street, on the north side, with soldiers firing in an attempt to dislodge them. By Easter Thursday, the OC Shelbourne estimated that the rebels held about a dozen premises around the Green, mostly on its western side. Robbins describes a party of rebels trying to turn their positions into traps for the enemy:

> Robert de Coeur and a small party of our men had taken over a number of houses on the west side of the Green, south of York Street. They put into effect a very novel defence measure, one which hitherto we had not adopted in our area. Instead of barricading, as was done in almost every other place, the bottom portion of the house was left as if nothing unusual had taken place. The idea was to invite the opposing forces to regard the house as an easy position to occupy. The stairway had, however, been carefully sawn through, with sufficient left intact to bear only its own weight. However, the exercise was in vain for the British did not attack. The men who had expended so much labour and ingenuity to bait the trap must have been disappointed. Such are the fortunes of war.[94]

Mallin also considered sending parties to knock out or force the abandonment of key British machine-gun posts, including those at the Shelbourne and the United Services Club. On Tuesday night he planned to launch an intense fusillade against the Shelbourne and the United Services Club as cover for two parties of rebels to set fire to houses at the corner of Grafton Street and the Green. However, according to Robbins the mission was cancelled at the last minute. O'Shea suggests that the covering fire commenced too soon and exhausted the supply of ammunition.[95] Instead, Mallin decided to approach and, hopefully, burn out the British positions on the north side by having men bore through from house to house from the Turkish baths towards the junction of King Street South and Grafton Street, in the extreme north-west corner of the Green. Once there, they would ignite a bookshop and houses on the north side at Grafton Street corner.

When about twenty rebels managed to force their way into the Alexandra College past pupils' club they terrified two servant girls until one of them saw rosary beads on a man's wrist and cried in relief, 'Look! They're Catholics!'[96] As soon as the British realised their presence in the club they directed intense machine-gun fire at the building, forcing insurgents to lie prostrate on the floor for an hour. But thereafter, until the surrender, little happened and on Friday men were still boring through the final houses. Ultimately the whole enterprise proved abortive and arguably had been unrealistic from the very start because the British presence was burgeoning all the time in the Shelbourne and the United Services Club and soldiers had far superior weaponry. Furthermore, over fifty properties between the College of Surgeons and the Shelbourne would have had to be burnt out or bored through before an assault could have been launched. And Mallin's men lacked adequate manpower, sufficient time and all but the most basic equipment.

With some reluctance Mallin approved one further stratagem. On Easter Wednesday Skinnider and Joe Connolly pressurised him into letting them lead a small group to lob a bomb through the Shelbourne's front windows. However, he insisted on a practice run against property in Harcourt Street, where they would start a fire that was intended to spread into the British-occupied Hotel Russell. Unfortunately British snipers spotted the party and killed a young Citizen Army member and critically wounded Skinnider three times in the back and shoulder. Not expected to live, she was carried back to the college where Mallin immediately cancelled the proposed bombing raid on the Shelbourne. It was fortunate that he did so because the British OC in the hotel had received prior intelligence from local sympathisers that his position was to be attacked that evening; his men were ready with a maxim gun commanding the main entrance and every soldier was on duty throughout the night. One morale booster for Mallin was the discovery of the OTC's arms cache in the college basement – eighty-nine rifles in perfect condition, with bayonets and 24,000 rounds of ammunition.[97]

After Skinnider returned to the college, she discovered an agitated Mallin blaming himself for putting her in such a dangerous situation but she tartly reminded him that women had the same right as men to risk their lives and that the Proclamation guaranteed their equality. Citizen Army women generally participated much more actively in the actual fighting than those attached to the Volunteers, though most of its male members' perception of their proper role tended to be a highly traditional one, despite Connolly's reminders about gender equality. Robbins asserted that it was only because of the shortage of men that Mallin nominated some of the women's section to guard the gates and chase civilians out of the Green. A number of men remained defiantly unreconstructed about the women's section, regarding it as an encumbrance during the fighting.[98]

Mallin now tried to solve his shortage of food and men. Throughout the week women from the garrison had managed to buy or commandeer some supplies, but even so Markievicz later recalled being 'absolutely starved' on Tuesday and Wednesday,[99] by which time some of the garrison were 'fainting at their posts for want of nourishment'.[100] Milk and bread carts had long since disappeared from the streets and little that was edible was found in the outposts. A thorough search of the college produced just two eggs and some tea. On Wednesday evening Mallin sent a female dispatch carrier, Chris Caffrey, to Jacob's urgently requesting food and the transfer to the college of any Citizen Army members. MacDonagh responded by sending flour, sacks of cakes and some reinforcements who were extremely impressed by Mallin's strict regime. This was a considerable contrast to Jacob's where Douglas Hyde was amazed to hear that 'Volunteers were passing in and out of it freely. He says they were dancing inside and taking it by turns to fight. As one goes out in order to go home and sleep he takes off his bandolier, and hands it along with his rifle to another man coming in.'[101] This may have been an exaggeration, but one of the new arrivals, William Oman, noted the quiet atmosphere in the college where reveille was sounded each morning, beds were neatly made and every available man recited the rosary in the evening.[102] No doubt this harsher discipline was rooted in Mallin's and other senior officers' experience in the British army, and the commandant displayed a ruthless intolerance of any infraction. He strongly reprimanded several younger men who slashed a portrait of Queen Victoria with their bayonets and he threatened to shoot anyone else who damaged a work of art. But not even Mallin's threats were effective in matters of the heart in wartime. One young Volunteer on guard duty in a York Street outpost had been smitten by one of the girls in the college and after locating some hair oil had deserted his post and slipped over to the headquarters to conduct an assignation. When discovered he was given a mock court-martial by his lieutenant, Bob de Coeur, and a solemn reminder of the penalty for deserting a post on active service.

As the week progressed the constant barrage and a growing expectation of an all-out British attack created considerable emotional strain, sleeplessness and fatigue within the college. During a brief visit there from his outpost Liam Ó Briain noticed the grimmer atmosphere. Grenades were located on the main balustrade and other strategic places ready for a British assault while in the sick bay three first aid assistants nursed gravely wounded patients. Men on the roof and at windows were returning fire as best they could against concentrated British shooting from buildings north of the Green.[103] To J. Smith, a St John's Ambulance volunteer, the situation seemed like 'a dreadful nightmare, which was only made a frightful reality by the dead, dying and wounded which began to stream in. I can never forget the dreadful wounds we had to look after, for as night fell, more and more wounded poured in on every hand; the fighting got fiercer.'[104]

According to James Stephens, on Thursday night, 'the sound of artillery, of rifles, machine guns, grenades, did not cease even for a moment'.[105] At his home near Leeson Street Bridge, half a mile away, Douglas Hyde spent much of Friday afternoon sitting in the garden. Its peace was constantly shattered by the sounds of battle nearby with 'bullets whistling in the air, striking the slates on our house' and as he listened, it seemed evident that the College of Surgeons had become 'the principal storm centre in this part of the city'.[106] But in fact this was probably not the case. From his lodgings in St Stephen's Green East, St John Ervine noted that by Thursday the rebels in the college 'were keeping very still. Now and then the soldiers in the Shelbourne fired.'[107] O'Shea claimed that nothing happened in the college from Wednesday onwards except occasional sniping from the Shelbourne and elsewhere.[108] Likewise, Robbins stated that 'later on during the week things were very much easier. We had plenty of time on our hands.'[109] To the garrison's surprise and bewilderment, the British persisted with their strategy of containment, steadily increasing the number of troops in the Green area and occupying a growing number of strategic positions from which they fired intermittently at the college. It was enough to pin down Mallin's battalion but at no point were more aggressive tactics deployed. It sustained just two fatalities – one self-inflicted – after the retreat from the Green.

Mallin's garrison had also become increasingly isolated from other rebel commands, in particular the General Post Office (GPO), as the military cordon tightened around O'Connell Street. Another factor hampering the movement of Mallin's dispatch carriers was the active hostility of some civilians. Until Easter Wednesday, Chris Caffrey had operated successfully as a courier disguised as a grieving war widow, draped in black and wearing a red, white and blue emblem. However, some onlookers had become suspicious of her and when angry 'separation women' barred her entry to the GPO she was forced to fire her revolver into the ground to make them back away. Then on Easter Thursday morning, she was spotted leaving the college and shadowed by hostile civilians who denounced her as a spy to a party of British soldiers. Caffrey was escorted to Trinity College where she decided to bluff her way out. As they passed through the college gates she put the message in her mouth and started chewing. When challenged by a soldier who had seen her action she coolly replied that she was eating a sweet and offered him one from a bag in her pocket. After being searched and then questioned for two hours she was released when no incriminating material was found on her person.

The decline in dispatch-carrying considerably diminished Mallin's appreciation of the overall situation in the city; not that he had ever divulged information to the rank and file, who were fed bland assurances that everything was proceeding smoothly. Increasingly, however, the true position could not be concealed. James Stephens found pieces of burnt paper on the gravel paths near his home and concluded that they 'must have been blown remarkably high to have crossed all the roofs … From my window I saw a red flare that crept to the sky … the smoke rose from the ground to the clouds'.[110] Liam Ó Briain remembered that as he looked out 'the fires on the north side of the city seemed to be enormous and widespread. There was a continuous dull roar which I imagined to be artillery.'[111] Those like Stephens, who witnessed the artillery bombardment in O'Connell Street at first hand, doubted that the fighting could last much longer. In anticipation of an imminent British assault, the wounded were transferred from the college on Friday to nearby hospitals. Mallin's staff also debated pre-empting a British attack by fighting through the enemy cordon and conducting guerrilla warfare in the Dublin hills. During the discussion Ó Briain heard an animated Markievicz longing for a bayonet or 'some stabbing instrument for action at close quarters', which elicited Mallin's amused but admiring comment: 'You are very blood-thirsty.'[112] Despite the countess' bravura some men had begun to collapse from mental and physical strain and others had contracted pneumonia from exposure to the rain.

Deserted neighbouring streets heightened an all-pervasive sense of eeriness, isolation and claustrophobia inside the college. After Monday, public and private transport had collapsed and from Tuesday the military had closed most bridges to civilian traffic. On Wednesday, bills proclaiming martial law were posted on the railings of St Stephen's Green, warning citizens to remain indoors between the hours of 7.30 p.m.

and 5.30 a.m. Increasingly, at all hours, citizens were being hemmed into their own neighbourhoods and confined to their homes and by Friday one Dubliner wrote that 'the streets were as silent as a tomb; firing was so frequent, no-one would venture out except at great risk'.[113] Hotels, offices and clubs predominated around the Green, so at least the members of Mallin's garrison were largely spared the scenes of looting which so distressed their comrades at the GPO and elsewhere. Nonetheless on Wednesday and Thursday some minor outbreaks occurred in Grafton Street, though undoubtedly these were related to the deepening food crisis. On Sunday, a Red Cross driver reported about a thousand people gathered at a bakery in Ballsbridge almost 2 miles east of the Green.[114]

Throughout Friday night and Saturday morning there was heavy firing in and around the college, but then it tapered off for reasons that were not yet known to the garrison. It had not yet learnt of Pearse's surrender or Connolly's subsequent confirmation that it applied to the men 'under my command in the Moore Street District, and for the men in the Stephen's Green Command'.[115] Gradually, however, a highly confused version of recent events trickled through to the Green, where Robbins first heard rumours from civilians shouting up to his post from the pavement below. The result was to renew speculation of a possible break-out to conduct guerrilla warfare in the countryside.[116] On Sunday morning an uneasy college garrison tried to conduct business as usual, whether on sentry duty, on the roof, at the windows, in the kitchen or in the sick bay, but by mid-morning the British authorities had already begun the process of conveying Pearse's surrender to every rebel stronghold. The news was brought to the college by a British army officer, Major de Courcy Wheeler, and Pearse's messenger, Nurse Elizabeth O'Farrell, after Wheeler had first arranged for troops in Trinity College to be ready to escort Mallin's followers to Richmond Barracks. When their car reached the top of Grafton Street O'Farrell continued on foot under the protection of a white flag to the college. Bullets were still ricocheting around the Green as she approached the building. When she was eventually admitted at the York Street entrance Mallin was asleep and Markievicz was first to see the surrender order. When he was awakened the commandant said nothing to O'Farrell, who then retraced her steps to the car, where Wheeler was annoyed that she had not got Mallin to indicate whether he intended surrendering.[117] A Citizen Army member, Rose Hackett, remembered sensing that something was wrong:

> I found Madame one time, sitting on the stairs with her head in her hands. She was very worried but did not say anything. I just passed in as usual, and she only looked at me, but I knew that there was something wrong. Mr Mallin went round, shaking hands with all of us. I was coming down the stairs when I met him. He took my hand and did not speak. He was terribly pale. I thought his face 'was drawn and haggard. The worry was there. This was after Mallin and Markievicz had received news of the surrender.[118]

At around 11 a.m. Mallin convened a half-hour officers' conference at which many favoured escaping into the countryside and forming a flying column. When Robbins suggested that the surrender order was a hoax he saw a momentary flicker of hope in Mallin's eyes but it was quickly snuffed out when another senior officer was adamant that they should trust the messenger.[119] That being so, Mallin was greatly influenced by Connolly's endorsement of the surrender and, like a good staff officer, was determined to obey his superior's order. O'Shea recalled that he tried to persuade Mallin to go to the hills:

> We argued for a long time. There was a burst of machine-gun fire and I pushed him out of the way. He said 'Let it be now rather than later, as I and many of our friends will not live long.' He rejected my plan and said 'As soldiers we came into this fight obeying orders. We will now obey this order by James Connolly to surrender.'[120]

Mallin now summoned the entire garrison to the college lecture hall where Robbins was struck by 'the atmosphere of awful gloom that had settled over the place. Men and women who had been gay and light-hearted were now crying.'[121] Mallin confirmed Pearse and Connolly's surrender order was genuine and insisted that as soldiers they had to obey. One person present remembered how pale and slight Mallin appeared and how he had to repeat the surrender order three times.[122] Predicting that he and other senior officers (though not Markievicz) would be executed, he had just started to pay tribute to their courage when his composure left him and he broke down. Though other senior officers spoke in support of his appeal, murmurs of dissent developed. Once officer recollected 'poor Joseph Connolly nearly went mad. He said he would not surrender.'[123] As murmurs of dissent grew Markievicz, whom Skinnider had heard urging Mallin to fight on, moved through the ranks repeating 'I trust Connolly, I trust Connolly'.[124] However, Ó Briain confessed that 'a certain feeling of relief came over me. There was no more need for work and vigilance. We could relax, one was alive.'[125] Mallin had stated that he would not think the less of anyone who slipped away and some left, including a Londoner whose accent enabled him to pose as an Englishman trapped in Dublin while on holiday. Most, however, stayed and a total of 121 insurgents (110 men and 11 women) surrendered.[126]

Whilst the garrison was preparing to surrender, Mallin noticed that the officers were standing out in their habitual positions in front of their men as they paraded inside the building. According to one of his officers Mallin at once ordered them 'to get back to the ranks saying that the British knew himself and Countess Markievicz but there was no use in any of the others, as he put it, sacrificing themselves'.[127] At noon Mallin ordered that weapons be discarded and, under sniper fire, he and some others ran down the tricolour flying over the college and replaced it with a white flag. The British OC at the Shelbourne Hotel then advised Dublin Castle by telephone to dispatch troops to take Mallin's surrender and Wheeler returned to the College of Surgeons with a troop escort. There, initially, Wheeler received no answer at the barricaded main entrance door but after some time a civilian advised him to go to York Street, where he saw a white flag hanging out of the side door. It was now between 12.30 p.m. and 1.00 p.m. and inside most of the garrison was in tears and a restless and impatient Mallin was relieved to learn of Wheeler's arrival. Accompanied by Markievicz, Mallin saluted the British officer, said he wished to surrender and presented him with a walking stick as a memento. Markievicz was dressed in her now familiar green puttees, riding breeches, tunic, slouch hat with ostrich feather and an officer's Sam Browne ammunition belt. When she was asked to disarm, she kissed her revolver before handing it over. This simple, defiant but calculated gesture was to become one of the most celebrated of the entire Rising. When the military escort arrived the pent-up emotion of the assembled men threatened to erupt. Joe Connolly reached for his automatic but was overpowered before he could shoot Wheeler. Unperturbed and accompanied by Mallin and Markievicz, Wheeler inspected the garrison, ascertaining that it had been disarmed before he examined the arms cache. He later described 'an indescribable state of confusion and destruction – furniture, books, etc., being piled up in barricades – food, clothes, arms, mineral water, surgical dressings were mixed up and lying about in all directions. The portrait of Queen Victoria torn.'[128] But other reports, including that of hostage Lawrence Kettle, complimented the rebels' respect for property and he said afterwards that they 'even took care not to drop ash on the carpet'.[129] Afterwards some college staff reported little or no damage when they again took possession of the building.[130]

Wheeler now ordered Mallin to assemble his men at the front of the college where a generally hostile crowd had gathered. He offered to let Markievicz – to whom he was actually related – travel by car for her personal protection, but she insisted, as Mallin's second-in-command, on sharing the fate of the men and women. So she and Mallin marched at the head of the column between a double line of British troops, one of whom whispered to Ó Briain in a pure Dublin accent: 'Why in the name of — didn't yiz wait till the war'd be over? We'd ha' been all with yiz. I fired over your heads the whole week.'[131] Many onlookers were far less sympathetic and when the prisoners were escorted along Stephen's Green West and York Street there was 'a great demonstration by the crowd, which surged in on all sides'.[132] The mood became steadily more threatening and after some attacks on the prisoners soldiers threatened to open fire, though later in the march some troops were heard muttering that they were 'goin' to biyenet 'em [the rebels] like the rest [sic]'.[133] When the insurgents eventually reached the apparent sanctuary of the lower castle yard, at about 1.45 p.m., they passed a freshly dug pit which some of them feared contained quicklime graves prepared for their interment.[134]

After a short delay they proceeded via the Ship Street gate to Richmond Barracks, Inchicore, where Robbins remembered the crowds cheering, waving their hats and Union Jacks and applauding the men of the Staffordshire Regiment as they marched in. There were also cries of 'Shoot the traitors' and 'Bayonet the bastards' and Robbins had no doubt that 'were the British army to have withdrawn at that moment, there would have been no need for court-martials or prisons as the mob would have relieved them of such niceties'.[135]

Markievicz later claimed that as they walked along she discussed with Mallin whether they would be shot or hanged; indeed, shortly before leaving the college, she had made a will that was smuggled out in the lining of Skinnider's coat when she was transferred to hospital. Whether or not this was merely bravura on the countess' part, it was her exploits above everyone else's in the garrison that had most caught the public imagination. There were few places where she had not allegedly been sighted during Easter Week, either lying dead on the steps of the City Hall, dressed in men's clothing or arrested at bayonet point in George's Street. The many alleged reports on her activities derive to some extent from the fact that Markievicz had been very active throughout Easter Week in a fighting capacity. It was widely believed at the time and has been authoritatively asserted since that on several occasions she shot at and may have killed members of the Crown forces, though in fact no definite confirmation has ever been established.[136] Clearly the countess' aggressively defiant attitude persisted after the surrender. A.A. Dickson, a soldier based at Richmond Barracks, recalled her transfer to Kilmainham shortly after her arrival:

> While I was there I had to escort two important lady prisoners – Countess Plunkett and the celebrated Countess Markievicz – to another prison. There was confusion as to how they were to be taken there; apparently they refused to go in a cab with any soldiers, and the army would not risk them in a cab unaccompanied for fear of escape or rescue. Eventually they agreed to walk under escort. Accordingly very early one morning, while curfew was still on under martial law, these two dignified and determined ladies were committed to my charge and set out, walking stoically along the middle of the dingy streets, with half a dozen soldiers in file keeping level with them on each pavement, others under NCOs ahead and behind, and myself half a pace behind them on their left; their stately deliberate pace was slow march for us, but my enquiries as to whether this rate of progress suited them were acknowledged only by a silent bow of the head. No incidents interrupted us and they were formally handed over to their fresh custodians.[137]

Even after Mallin's garrison at the college had surrendered, the sound of gunfire continued to be heard near Stephen's Green, but normality gradually returned. On Monday morning the last British troops in the Shelbourne transferred to Trinity College and by Tuesday the barricade near the hotel entrance had been removed. But the Green remained closed, and elsewhere in the city lurid rumours were circulating about the rebels who had been there. One Dubliner recorded in her diary:

> I believe … it was pitiable to see the number of dead lying in the park, also on top of the spike railings, etc., where they have been shot by the military on top of the different clubs and houses in the vicinity. It is stated not one of the rebels escaped and all are buried in the park, which will have the effect of closing this beautiful place.[138]

If such a grotesquely distorted account was indeed widely accepted, it was bound to colour popular responses to the Rising.

4

Boland's Bakery

The story of 3rd Battalion during Easter Week is always associated with Eamonn de Valera, then in his mid-thirties and at the start of a career that was to make him the most influential and controversial politician of twentieth-century Ireland.[1] An intellectually gifted student at Blackrock and Rockwell colleges he became a mathematics teacher at Blackrock and later at a number of Dublin schools, including Belvedere College. An Irish language enthusiast, he joined the Gaelic League in 1908 where he met his future wife with whom he had five sons and two daughters. Joining the Irish Volunteers at the start, he participated in the Howth gunrunning and rose rapidly through the ranks because of his high intelligence, commanding physical presence and meticulous organising ability. In March 1915 Pearse appointed him battalion commandant after he promised to obey his superiors' orders in the event of a rising. Soon afterwards MacDonagh, now Dublin brigadier, made de Valera his adjutant and he was persuaded somewhat reluctantly to join the IRB. After being told that in a rising his battalion would be assigned the Boland's area, de Valera began studying it. Apparently strolling innocently with his eldest son Vivion, he reconnoitred the stretch along the canal from Baggot Street to Grand Canal Street. He also travelled by train from Lansdowne Road on the important Kingstown line that crossed his area; this was to decide how best to immobilise the railway.[2]

Even though de Valera is almost always described as occupying Boland's mills it was actually the firm's bakery some distance away in Grand Canal Street that became his headquarters on Easter Monday. While the mills were occupied, de Valera never once set foot inside them during the entire Rising.

During Holy Week de Valera had virtually taken up residence at his battalion headquarters in Great Brunswick Street (now Pearse Street), where armed guards watched over a store of weapons and ammunition that Volunteers would soon use in earnest. For some time his officers had also been accumulating haversacks, kit bags, ground sheets, blankets and belts. Nearby and under constant Volunteer surveillance was Dublin Metropolitan Police's headquarters, whose famous or notorious 'G' detective division would lead any last-minute swoop that the British government still might order. One Volunteer captain remembered that 'the whole atmosphere about the week before Easter was one of highly-strung nervous activity'.[3] Such intense

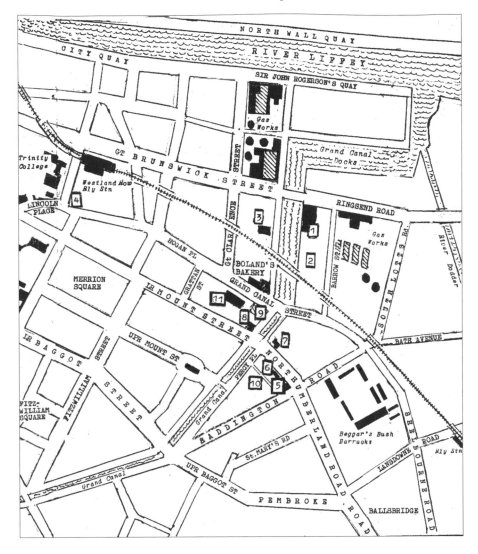

Boland's bakery and Mount Street Bridge

1.   Flour mills
2.   Locomotive works
3.   Former distillery
4.   Oriel House
5.   No 25
6.   Parochial Hall
7.   School
8.   Clanwilliam House
9.   Roberts' Yard
10.   Percy Lane
11.   Sir Patrick Dun's Hospital

pressure had strongly affected de Valera himself; he had had to carry an even heavier burden during Holy Week after the Military Council got his vice-commandant, Sean Fitzgibbon – a leading MacNeill supporter – out of the capital by sending him on a mission to the west of Ireland. De Valera was actually glad to see him go after they clashed over Fitzgibbon's assumption that, as an Executive member, he enjoyed a superior military status. De Valera had wanted to replace him with Joseph O'Connor, but this talented captain preferred staying with his company at such a crucial time so de Valera reluctantly took on battalion adjutant Begley, an unfortunate choice that he would soon have cause to regret.[4] At a battalion council meeting on Friday 21 April de Valera carefully allocated to company captains their positions and responsibilities during the rising as well as detailing the equipment that would be at their disposal, right down to where they could find alternative water supplies and tools for loop-holing the walls of buildings.

Having geared themselves up for a fight on Easter Sunday, de Valera and most of his officers only grudgingly complied with MacNeill's countermand order. Captain Simon Donnelly estimated that only thirty-five to forty of his 120 men would respond to another mobilisation,[5] a prediction that was rapidly vindicated at 9.30 a.m. on Easter Monday, after de Valera ordered another mobilisation within two hours at Earlsfort Terrace, beside University College. Turn-out was dismal. After the previous day's confusion an incredulous O'Connor 'asked him were they mad. His reply was, "I am a soldier and I know you are a soldier also." I saluted and retired. Before leaving the room he shook hands and said: "We may never meet again".'[6] By 11.30 a.m. only thirty-four out of C Company's 120 men were present, not including the captain whose place Donnelly had to assume at the very last moment. A Company's captain was another no-show, along with all but eighteen of his 120 Volunteers; fourteen Ringsend Volunteers did turn out but seven of them were to desert on the first day, along with a large supply of food. D Company's captain was another absentee, but most embarrassing of all was that Vice-Commandant Begley was a no-show. Eighty men from B Company comprised over half the total that mobilised on Easter Monday and even though others trickled in later only 173 Volunteers served in the Boland's area. De Valera had hoped for a minimum of 500 men, while O'Connor had estimated that between 800 and 1,000 Volunteers were needed to hold every designated target.[7] Furthermore, de Valera had no adjutant or quartermaster. Lieutenant Charles Murphy did what adjutant's work he could, as did Volunteer Michael Tannam with the quartermaster's job, but neither had been trained for these tasks.

De Valera envisaged C Company seizing Boland's bakery, an adjoining poor law dispensary, Robert's building yard at the canal, four outposts near Mount Street Bridge over the canal and three more bridges at Upper Mount Street, Baggot Street and Leeson Street. A Company was intended to dominate Beggar's Bush Barracks, occupy railway workshops in Upper Grand Canal Street and take the railway line that ran between Grand Canal quay and Kingstown (Dun Laoghaire), 7 miles away from where British forces could be expected to arrive by road and rail. B Company would occupy Westland Row station and link up with A Company on the railway line. D Company had been ordered to capture Boland's mills, the adjoining Dublin City distillery, the gasworks and the granaries on the northern side of the canal basin. They would also have to guard the lock gates connecting the basin with the Liffey and defend the main body of Volunteers from any British attack that might come via Ringsend Road and Brunswick Street, or from the direction of the river. E Company would be away, having been designated as part of the headquarters battalion in the GPO garrison, while F Company was to link up with A Company and control the railway line and the landing pier at Kingstown harbour.

At 11.50 a.m. on Easter Monday 3rd Battalion moved off from Earlsfort Terrace. At Upper Mount Street Lieutenant Michael Malone broke away with fourteen men and headed along the canal to Mount Street Bridge while the main column continued on to Boland's bakery, 1¼ miles south-east of the GPO and situated within a generally poor district that bordered on the Liffey docks. De Valera's headquarters in the bakery were strategically positioned between the mills and Malone's Mount Street Bridge outposts, a well chosen location containing low-lying sheds surrounded by higher buildings from the top of which Volunteer snipers could target the enemy.

As Volunteers entered the bakery they ordered out its staff. Some mistook this for another routine manoeuvre and were initially reluctant to leave until the insurgents threatened them with rifles (though the bakers were allowed to remain until they had taken bread out of the ovens).[8] Anticipating that the British might counter-attack before Boland's was in a state of readiness, Donnelly established four small defence groups while Volunteers fortified and loop-holed the building and manned its low-lying walls. The bakery also had a canteen and sleeping quarters for de Valera's men, but he established his personal quarters in the dispensary, with a hole being punched in the wall separating both buildings. With sword drawn, de Valera had led his men into the dispensary intending to drive out its occupants only to find it empty except for Mrs Healy, the doctor's wife. She became hysterical and fled upstairs when given five minutes to pack up and leave. De Valera then discovered other pressing responsibilities and left Lieutenant Joseph O'Byrne to resolve the problem. When Mr Healy arrived soon afterwards he too refused to leave. An officer, George Lyons, recalled that:

> The doctor asked what would happen if his property was destroyed: 'The Irish Republic', said O'Byrne, 'will compensate you when it is established.' The doctor proceeded solemnly to take an inventory of all the appurtenances. This done, he asked for a receipt for all the articles: 'I will give you no receipt for anything as I am taking nothing from you,' said O'Byrne: 'We are only in temporary custody here and may be elsewhere tomorrow.'[9]

Although the Healys eventually agreed to go he left an inventory that strangely over-looked six gold sovereigns which Volunteers found lying loose around the premises. The doctor retrieved them after the Rising.

D Company's small turn-out was only sufficient for it to occupy Boland's mills on the Ringsend Road and even then they couldn't sandbag or loop-hole the building. If the British had captured an adjacent distillery they would have dominated the entire battalion area. Captain McMahon's B Company did manage to clear, barricade and lock Westland Row station which meant that British reinforcements landing at Kingstown would have to march to Dublin and, crucially, come within firing range of Malone's outposts at Mount Street Bridge. McMahon also sabotaged part of the railway line and entrenched some men about 300 yards away from the station.

O'Connor's company had already stopped and emptied a train, in the process capturing a British army officer who was kept prisoner in the bakery for the entire Rising.[10]

When Volunteers entered the railway workshops they barricaded the front, broke all
the glass inside and constructed a balcony for snipers to dominate Grand Canal Street
and Grand Canal Street Bridge. Marksmen were positioned on the roof between two
reserve water tanks that overlooked the canal bridges and which later came under
heavy enemy attack: 'I remember visiting the tank position and whilst I was talking
to one of the men, the rifle which he had been using stuck to his hand and we had
to pull his hand from the rifle leaving the skin thereon.'[11] O'Connor established his
company headquarters in the workshops, which had to be held because if the British
had captured them they would have controlled the entire area. When British forces
entered the yard on Monday and tried to entrench themselves O'Connor organised a
bayonet charge that forced the soldiers to flee and leave some of their rifles behind.[12]

Holding the railway line to Kingstown was also vitally important because losing
it would have cut de Valera's command area in two. He assigned McMahon and
O'Connor, two of his best officers, to its defence and they arranged for small units and
even single Volunteers to snipe and engage in running battles from Monday onwards,
when they repelled soldiers from Beggar's Bush Barracks and killed a sergeant major.[13]
The railway line was carried on nine stone archways between Westland Row and
Ringsend and their walls protected Volunteer marksmen as they attacked British
troops on Great Brunswick Street, Grand Canal Street and the square in Beggar's
Bush Barracks. Volunteers also briefly seized gasworks on the city side of the canal
and removed vital pieces of equipment, resulting in darkness across much of the city.
According to O'Connor, 'Very soon the firing had penetrated the gasometers which
were very close to our positions and as the evening fell the smell of gas was stifling'.[14]

De Valera's resources were stretched even further when he decided to leave
a Cumann na mBan party behind. This was partly because of his notorious diffi-
dence with women, but also because he wanted to spare them the horrors of urban
warfare.[15] De Valera didn't send a promised courier to their mobilisation point in
Merrion Square, causing some to go home while others made their way to join
MacDonagh's garrison in Jacob's factory. These women could have given medical
aid in the dispensary or worked in the bakery kitchens but instead Boland's operated
with only one Red Cross man, Lieutenant O'Byrne, who was eventually forced to
send seriously wounded men to the regular hospitals. Volunteers also had to cook
meals while one man cared full time for thirty bakery horses until their food ran
out and they were released into the streets.[16] The garrison's weaponry proved to be
pathetically inadequate during Easter Week, with only fifty rifles of varying manufacture and ammunition of a different make forcing men in the middle of battle to
stop firing and change the bullets. The battalion's heavy hand-made grenades were
completely unreliable and couldn't be used: they were more dangerous to Volunteers
than the enemy. The shotguns were just as unstable though, ingeniously, it was discovered that by inserting them into metal rain pipes and pulling the triggers with
string the Volunteers could manufacture loud explosions that seemed to intimidate
the enemy.[17]

Originally de Valera had planned to seize the railway station and landing area
at Kingstown to repel enemy reinforcements coming from England, but the few

Volunteers who turned out there made their way instead to Boland's. At midnight on Easter Monday he ordered an unenthusiastic Donnelly to attack any enemy troops moving through Blackrock and Ballsbridge towards the capital: 'I didn't altogether like the job as I knew it was rather ticklish and the men fairly nervy, however, orders were orders and we were just about to start off when the Commandant changed his mind, much to the relief of those going on the expedition.'[18]

Nevertheless, Malone's men at Mount Street Bridge and in Northumberland Road provided a last line of defence against British reinforcements marching from the south. The district's large houses epitomised prosperous middle- and upper-class Dublin, its residents being mainly Unionist and politically moderate Roman Catholics. About two-thirds of the way along, going towards the city, Northumberland Road intersected with Haddington Road, at which point it turned slightly left and ran straight on to the bridge, after which it became Lower Mount Street. Lieutenant Malone's Volunteer outposts had to be defended at all costs. O'Connor 'knew that Clanwilliam House was a keep which meant that the garrison was to maintain their post to the very last and that there was to be no evacuation of the building. This was agreed to on Friday as the position was of such vital importance.'[19]

Malone, a 28-year-old carpenter with a reputation as a crack rifleman, had arrived on Easter Monday morning with four groups – each of which was to occupy an outpost – and Joe Nugent, a young Fianna cyclist who had carried their ammunition from Earlsfort Terrace. Malone's men were among 3rd Battalion's toughest and most determined Volunteers. George Reynolds had turned out despite recently suffering from blood poisoning, and only discarded his arm sling when he set off for Northumberland Road. There, Reynolds' five-man unit went to the rear of Clanwilliam House, a three-storey building at the corner of Lower Mount Street where it faced across the bridge. When a maid answered a knock on the door Reynolds ordered his men to take their bikes inside; the baffled maid could only laugh.[20] James Doyle, Willie Ronan, Daniel Maher and Daniel Byrne quickly set about fortifying the residence, locking the hall door, placing vessels filled with water in an upstairs room and shifting furniture to the ground floor windows – though without arousing the curiosity of passers-by. Reynolds meanwhile confined the owner, Mrs Wilson, her daughter and two maids in a downstairs room to prevent news spreading about the take-over. He and Doyle also exited through a trapdoor on to the roof where they identified the valley as a potential escape route by which their unit could leap on to the tops of neighbouring houses.[21]

Adjutant Denis O'Donoghue's group, consisting of James Kavanagh, Robert Cooper and James Doyle, occupied the schoolhouse on Northumberland Road, a building that was situated just a few yards down from the canal.[22] They filled sacks with coal and slack and barricaded every door and window before realising that it was a poor choice for an ambush, located too far from the road and with a tall hedge that restricted any sniper's view. Almost directly opposite Padraig O'Dubhghaill led William Christian, John McGrath, Joe Clarke and Paddy Doyle into the parochial hall.[23] Built in a recess of a line of houses, this suited marksmen much better because they could see everything and everybody on the road while remaining hidden from enemy fire. Malone located himself, James Grace, Michael Rowe and Paddy Byrne in No 25, the corner house at Haddington Road, from which they could see the front gate of Beggar's Bush Barracks. They would also be first to catch sight of any British soldiers from Kingstown heading straight towards Mount Street Bridge, the parochial hall, the schoolhouse and Clanwilliam House. Malone had cleverly created a killing field in which his Volunteers could attack the British from front and rear while being supported from a distance by marksmen situated on Grand Canal Street Bridge, the railway embankment at the dock, in Robert's builders and others who were perched high on top of the railway workshops.

But before facing regular British troops Malone's men were in action against the Dublin battalion of the Volunteer Training Corps. This military reserve was comprised mostly of professional gentlemen, many of them past their prime and whom local wags had dubbed the 'Gorgeous Wrecks' on account of their armlets being inscribed 'Georgius Rex'. They were returning to their base in Beggar's Bush Barracks from manoeuvres in the Dublin hills when Malone's men ambushed them, as such it is often depicted as a massacre of ordinary citizens, with many republicans even believing that Malone had mistaken the corps for British infantry. However, the corps had learnt about the Rising during lunch at its field day and quickly became involved when its commander, Lord Moloney, ordered them back to base before telephoning Nathan at Dublin Castle and offering his men's services. It was subsequently admitted that 'it was not then anticipated that they would be attacked on the way back but it is clear they came back with the intention of assisting the military authorities and that the latter were aware of their purpose'.[24]

Soon after three o'clock in the afternoon, as they started to return to Dublin, locals warned the officer in charge, Major Harris, that Volunteers had seized the GPO and Stephen's Green though not yet Beggar's Bush Barracks. Deciding to head for the barracks, he split his men into two sections and led the first down Shelbourne Road before halting when told that rebels had occupied houses in the Haddington Road area. Harris then dispatched a motorbike rider to Beggar's Bush, whose commanding officer had closed the front gate and refused to come to the corps' aid: they would have to make their own way to the barracks walls.[25] Harris led the first section, losing a wounded corporal on the way, before most managed to scramble up ladders and ropes to safety inside Beggar's Bush. From there they could hear Malone's men shooting at the rest of their column as it marched into Northumberland Road, wounding seven, four of whom died later. The others fled into nearby houses and hid until darkness when they managed to escaped, disguised in civilian clothes and women's garments and leaving their weapons and uniforms behind.

Soon afterwards Malone visited the schoolhouse and described the encounter to its garrison, they told him that while they had heard the shooting they could see nothing. Convinced now that continued occupation of the schoolhouse served no military purpose, Malone ordered O'Donoghue and his men back to the bakery. Under cover of darkness they evacuated at four o'clock on Tuesday morning and although they left sandbags and barricades in place the schoolhouse was never reoccupied.[26]

Malone's men now barricaded No 25's doors and high windows with bicycles and furniture, though he deliberately avoided loop-holing the walls. He had vowed to do as little damage as possible to civilian property, a gesture typical of this quietly impressive man who seemed concerned only about others. By deliberately locating himself in the first outpost that would engage British reinforcements Malone demonstrated, in the clearest way possible, that he believed in literally leading from the front. However, while accepting that his was effectively a suicide mission, Malone couldn't bring himself to demand a similar sacrifice from others. He dismissed Rowe and Byrne, telling them that they were too young to die: the older Grace was under no illusions about his and Malone's likely fate. As darkness fell Volunteers in the Mount Street Bridge outposts waited, watched or tried to snatch some sleep. But overnight Reynolds lost two men before they fired a single shot when Maher cracked under the strain and Reynolds ordered him to don a civilian overcoat, go home and return when he felt better. Maher left his rifle and equipment behind but he didn't come back to use them. Then by dawn Reynolds realised that Daniel Byrne had vanished from Clanwilliam House.[27] Both Maher and Byrne had discovered, as many other combatants were to do during Easter Week, that it was the waiting and anticipating that really frayed a person's nerves. In the parochial hall Christian couldn't sleep on that Monday night: 'A nervous excitement was eating me up and I longed to be doing something definite instead of just lying there in bed. The suspense in waiting for the fight to begin was far worse than the actual battle.'[28]

At dawn on Tuesday Malone cut the electric tram wires briefly, illuminating the entire district as they fell sparkling to the ground. Reynolds experienced another set-back at lunchtime when he sent Doyle to the schoolhouse for more ammunition only to learn that it had been evacuated. Reynolds urgently requested reinforcements from Boland's and Simon Donnelly squeezed out four Volunteers – Paddy Doyle, Richard Murphy and two brothers, Tom and James Walsh – who reached Clanwilliam House at 3 p.m. carrying extra ammunition and food parcels.[29] Soon afterwards Malone arrived and told Reynolds about his concern for the detained residents and how 'it would be terrible if any of them got killed'.[30] Shortly afterwards Reynolds let the civilians go. His new recruits were puzzled that he hadn't smashed and fully barricaded windows, but Reynolds too had promised to hand back the house undamaged. He did, however, approve placing mattresses at the windows along with torn sheets as bandages and siphon bottles for drinking water. On Tuesday evening, after two days of almost complete isolation, a passer-by gave Reynolds a copy of the *Irish Times* that carried a British government proclamation warning people to stay indoors. At a complete loss, he told James Doyle that 'if our men hold the city it is curious that paper can appear'.[31]

During Tuesday a trickle of Volunteer reinforcements arrived at Boland's, including some who were also bakery employees, and proceeded to make bread for the local population. Although by the weekend enemy fire made production and distribution too dangerous, civilians appreciated the thoughtfulness. De Valera also worried about civilian safety, dashing through gunfire to Grand Canal Street Bridge to warn spectators to get off the roads.[32] By now British snipers were surrounding Boland's and as Volunteer casualties rose an enemy attack from Westland Row and Lansdowne Road became ever more likely. Excited and nervous, Volunteers manned the trenches but handled with remarkable clumsiness American shotguns that tended to go off spontaneously. Some Volunteers were also rushed along the railway to repel Royal Irish Rifles soldiers who had slipped out through the rear gate of Beggar's Bush Barracks. After a short but fierce encounter the British troops were forced to retreat. During the afternoon de Valera also selected a detachment to relieve the pressure on Mallin and the Citizen Army in Stephen's Green. According to George Lyons:

De Valera carefully inspected us and commanded us to cast off our knapsacks and packs for the sake of greater mobility, warning us we would have tough work to do. As we got the word to go one of the men rushed back through the gates with the extraordinary complaint that he 'had no hat': 'Here's a hat, — you!' cried de Valera pitching the man his own headgear. The fellow clapped it on his head and rejoined the rank.[33]

However, de Valera cancelled the operation after learning that Mallin's garrison had abandoned the Green.

The garrison's morale remained high partly because de Valera's officers deliberately shielded their men from unpalatable reality. Donnelly didn't want any unsettling rumours circulating and ordered that any outsiders carrying demoralising news should report directly to him.[34] O'Connor even circulated optimistic bulletins about Volunteers seizing the ports and how the rest of Ireland had risen even though privately he was fairly certain that the Rising was confined to Dublin. Indeed, by Tuesday evening he believed that the insurgents were in trouble after learning about the *Daily Mail* being on sale in the capital. If its port was indeed open and 'the British were able to get their newspapers in there was certainly nothing to prevent them landing troops'.[35]

In the early hours of Wednesday morning O'Connor's fears were confirmed by reports of enormous British reinforcements arriving at Kingstown. Shortly afterwards, scouts told Malone about thousands of Sherwood Foresters marching towards the city. Christian's father then arrived to warn him that their chances were poor: 'With a father's natural anxiety for his son he begged me to come home with him but having taken up my post nothing but death would make me desert it.'[36] One British column travelled through Blackrock and Donnybrook and reached Dublin completely unscathed. However, another 2,000 troops took the main road through Blackrock and Ballsbridge towards Mount Street Bridge, where Malone and his garrison were waiting. Their commander, Brigadier Ernest Maconchy, fully expected opposition on the way into Dublin because an officer from Irish Command had briefed him that rebels controlled the route from Ballsbridge into Dublin and 'the houses and points held were detailed to me'. Although he also received warnings from local inhabitants along the route, Maconchy wasn't overly concerned since fighting, after all, was the reason he and his men had been sent to Ireland. He was more worried about being expected to attack and carry houses 'three storeys high, occupied by riflemen behind sandbags, without artillery and bombs'. Maconchy's heavy weaponry had been delayed in Liverpool and his men were only equipped with rifles and bayonets. During the march towards Dublin he acquired additional officers, soldiers on leave and 500 grenades from a bombing school. At Ballsbridge he commandeered the town hall for his brigade headquarters and established telephonic communications with Irish Command, which had transferred to the Royal Hospital at Kilmainham.[37]

Shortly after midday the Sherwood Foresters entered Northumberland Road, preceded by a line of flankers with fixed bayonets who moved carefully in single file along both sides of the road. Malone, in No 25, allowed the advance guard to pass before he and Grace opened fire, scattering soldiers in all directions. British officers rallied their troops who began returning fire with rifles and machine guns, though they also came under long-range attack from Reynolds' unit in Clanwilliam House, 300 yards away at the bridge. Realising that they had stumbled into a deadly trap, the soldiers scattered in search of cover before regrouping to assault No 25 with showers of hand grenades. By 5 p.m. Malone and Grace stood dazed as the house shook and glass and woodwork shattered all around them. One grenade thrown through a back window ignited a pile of ammunition and wrecked the room just after they vacated it. Both men now recognised that the end was near and fixed their bayonets for a last stand at the head of the stairs, but were separated when a British storming party broke into the house. Malone was driven to the top of the building where a volley of rifle fire cut him down, but Grace managed to hide in the basement from searching troops before escaping under the cover of shrubbery and dense clouds of smoke into the back garden, eventually making his way into an outhouse in Haddington Road. The owner promised to deliver a note to Grace's family, only to return with a party of soldiers who arrested him.[38]

With one point of resistance eliminated, the Sherwoods now concentrated on Clanwilliam House. But repeated charges down Northumberland Road disinte- grated in the face of devastatingly rapid and precise fire that caused officers to fall with their swords flashing in the sunlight. Supporting fire also came from the paro- chial hall, which the British had not identified as rebel-held, as well as from four marksmen positioned at a wall of Robert's builders' yard on the city side of the canal. Inside Clanwilliam House Tom Walsh was impressed by the courage of soldiers who stepped forward to take their fallen comrades' places, creating the impression of a giant khaki-coloured caterpillar.[39] Knapsacks and guns lay scattered among the dead and dying while the wounded, some of whom had tripped over their fallen comrades, lay still on the ground and waited for an opportunity to dash for cover. According to one local resident, Mrs Ismena Rohde, 'The poor fellows fell in rows without being able to return a shot. It was ghastly for those who saw it.'[40] Another observer suddenly saw a trooper fall and:

> a woman came out into the open with what looked like a blue enamel jug. She ran down the canal bank into the firing zone and disappeared from view. Then a poor girl ran out on to the bridge while yet the bullets from rifles and revolvers were flying thickly from both sides. She put up both her hands, and almost instantly the firing ceased. Again the woman turned up, and she and the girl picked up the sol- dier, others then going out from the crowd to help bring him in. He was taken into Sir Patrick Dun's Hospital.
>
> It was a throbbing incident that brought tears to the eyes, and the crowd cheered the little heroine. Several more soldiers were hit, and again the little girl ran out and brought them in time after time. I saw about eight soldiers taken into that hospi- tal wounded, and I helped one in myself along with others of the crowd. The man I helped with was reached by a little girl before we got him in, and she pushed an apron down his trousers to staunch the blood. He was shot in the small of the back and in the thigh. He was a Sherwood Forester, and the little girl was crying over him.[41]

Already angry at being expected to take fortified houses without heavy guns, Maconchy was becoming alarmed at the heavy casualties his men were taking. He now ordered one of his two senior officers, Colonel Oates, to detach a company and attempt turning the enemy position from the direction of Beggar's Bush Barracks. Oates' men had hardly set off before General Lowe, who had taken over command of the army in Dublin, overrode Maconchy and insisted on pressing home a frontal assault. To Lowe, who wasn't on the spot, it must have appeared absurd that large numbers of troops from an army that Field-Marshal Kitchener was moulding into a war-winning instrument should seek to evade direct battle with a small number of untrained and badly armed Irish amateurs. In addition to professional pride, Lowe probably believed that he was requiring no more of the Sherwoods than Haig was asking of the British Expeditionary Force in France every day against the Germans. Although the bulk of Oates' men returned, a section actually reached Beggar's Bush where they were detained by the OC to assist in defending the barracks. Not knowing what had happened, Maconchy had the men posted as missing.

Maconchy now convened a conference at which he instructed his other senior officer, Colonel Fane, to storm Clanwilliam House, after which Oates' troops would pass through to Trinity College. When Fane launched his attack he was assisted by the bombing school officers, but the Sherwoods suffered heavy casualties, including Fane himself, though he continued in command. The co-ordinated Volunteer rifle fire was deadly and even when troops managed to get close the defenders switched to emptying their revolvers on them. Reynolds also put a coat on a dressmaker's model and placed it at a window where it was riddled with bullets, drawing considerable pressure away from the human occupants. When a small settee caught fire Jim Walsh grabbed a soda-water siphon to extinguish the flames, took a swig from it and was handing it to his brother when it was smashed by a bullet. As the ceilings and walls shook, plaster fell on a grand piano creating weird background music, and parts of a chandelier descended on the smouldering chairs which were giving off choking fumes.[42]

Maconchy had become very concerned about the situation:

> I then returned to Ballsbridge (not a very nice walk) to the telephone and asked Irish Command if the situation was sufficiently serious to demand the taking of the position 'at all costs' saying that I could take it with another battalion but that we should lose heavily. The reply was to 'come through at all costs'.[43]

At 4.40 p.m. Maconchy summoned Oates and revealed the terrible pounding taken by Fane, most of whose officers were now wounded. After Oates was ordered to storm the enemy positions 'at all costs', he summoned his officers and, under Maconchy's silent gaze, outlined their mission. A battalion now formed up at intervals on Northumberland Road and on Maconchy's signal Oates led his men forward. They captured the schoolhouse by 7.30 p.m. only to discover it empty, while an initial attempt to storm Clanwilliam House cost the life of the officer in charge. Oates now called up a reserve battalion for whom it had become a matter of honour to avenge their fallen comrades; Clanwilliam House had to be taken. To minimise casualties that were already reaching alarming proportions the troops switched from frontal attack to concentrated sniping; firing from concealed positions in captured houses by the canal, along whose banks others wriggled, partly protected by iron railings and their stone bases: 'The soldiers crawled on their faces under cover of this stone, and seeming, in the distance, like a long yellow boa-constrictor creeping under cover of the wall.'[44] From a distance, Volunteers watched the snake-like progress with fascination and opened fire whenever a knapsack appeared or someone rose with his rifle aimed: 'About 200 yards off, the stone parapet had a break of about three feet at a gate. Several soldiers were caught by the oblique rifle fire of the marksmen in Clanwilliam House while creeping past this exposed spot, which proved a veritable death trap.'[45]

Nevertheless, throughout the evening soldiers worked their way ever closer to houses on the same side of the canal as Clanwilliam House. From them they poured devastating gunfire:

> Clanwilliam House had now become a perfect inferno. The glass, sashes, window frames and side shutters had been carried away by rifle fire. The curtains and hangings were torn to ribbons; pictures from the walls, glass mirrors, chandeliers, lay on the floor shattered into pieces, the plaster had fallen from the ceiling and almost every square foot of the walls inside was studded with bullets. The repeated ping of a bullet as it pierced through the woodwork and struck the strings of an upright piano could be heard, or the bell-like sound as it struck the hollow electric posts in the street. Any article of furniture drawn towards the window for cover was immediately carried away in splinters, whenever exposed, and the water pipes had burst, threatening to flood the house. The staircase facing the fanlight of the hall door and the landing windows were also cut into splinters and threatened every moment to collapse under foot. The passage by the stairway from the upper rooms could only be taken by pressing close to the wall, when running up or down, to escape the leaden hail from the windows. The smoke filling the room and the sulphurous smell of burnt powder made breathing difficult; and the wild cries of assault outside, combined with the unceasing rattle of the musketry, made an incredible din. Incendiary bullets seem to have entered the house; some of the beds and the sofa upholstering went on fire and frequently had to be extinguished and the floor carpentry was smouldering in several places.[46]

In the first-floor drawing room as sheets of fire lit up the sky, Reynolds stood behind three Volunteers, directing their shooting, while another three fought on upstairs. The company musketry instructor, Paddy Doyle, was exhilarated, shouting what a great day it was for Ireland. Then Tom Walsh noticed that 'after some time Paddy was not saying anything. Jim spoke to him and got no reply. He pulled him by the coat and he fell over on his arms. He was shot through the head. We told Dick Murphy about him and we three said a prayer for his soul.'[47] Soon afterwards Murphy, a tailor who had intended marrying during Easter Week, became 'very silent and I turned to him and touched him but he was gone to meet his maker'. Eerily, Murphy remained in a kneeling position clutching his rifle as if aiming to fire.

The time had now come to evacuate Clanwilliam House. But Reynolds couldn't resist one last shot and it cost him his life, struck by a bullet in the hip. The remaining defenders knelt, said a prayer and took a final look at Murphy and Doyle. Then, with the building gripped by flames, the four survivors fled, scrambling over barricades and out through a small window. There they flung themselves over the wall of the adjoining house and ran down a lane at the back. When return fire ceased, soldiers rushed through the front garden gate. One who was carrying a bucketful of hand grenades lobbed some into the building, one of which rebounded and wounded a British officer. With Volunteer resistance broken and the slaughter finally ended, the Sherwoods erupted in cheering, singing and hysterical relief that their ordeal was over, although intermittent sniping continued for some hours. The defenders' flight was not without attendant dangers. Jimmy Doyle, who did not know the neighbourhood well, made his way into Lower Mount Street where local people seized him but before they could hand him over to the soldiers he was rescued by other residents and taken to safety. The Walsh brothers and Willie Ronan went to the rear of Clanwilliam House and into a laneway, crossing several garden walls and moving carefully because at the same time wounded soldiers were being carried to Sir Patrick Dun's Hospital close by in Grand Canal Street. When the coast was clear they entered a house with an open front door and asked a young girl to provide them with coats to cover their uniforms. When she told her mother about Volunteers being in the house, her mother ordered them out before they were all shot. As Tom Walsh laconically records: 'We did not trouble them but continued over the walls.'[48]

In a nearby house they entered an open basement and 'discovered a tram driver's overcoat and a lady's coat. Jim donned the lady's coat and Ronan the tram driver's. It was tripping him up, it was so long. But it served our purpose.'[49] Soon afterwards they took shelter in the grounds of a nearby convent and lay low until darkness. As a heavenly contrast to hours of gunfire, explosions and smashing glass, they now luxuriated in the beautiful singing of a girl's choir. Next day they separated and eventually reached safe houses.

The four Volunteers who evacuated the parochial hall by the rear were captured in Percy Lane by angry soldiers who were comforting masses of wounded comrades. When a Sherwood searched Joe Clarke and discovered a revolver he put him against a door with his hands above his head. Clarke sensed that he was about to be shot dead and ducked just before the trigger was pulled; the bullet whizzed just over his head and through the door, narrowly missing a doctor who was attending a wounded man. The doctor quickly intervened to prevent another shot being fired and Clarke was hustled away, his hands tied behind his back. When the burnt shell of Clanwilliam House was searched later for human remains only a leg was found. Whilst at No 25 soldiers had interred Malone's body in the garden, burying him in his uniform, his head and shoulders covered with a canvas cloth. A fortnight afterwards the remains were transferred to Glasnevin cemetery. When it was all over, five Volunteers of C Company were dead, while British losses amounted to four officers killed and fourteen wounded with 216 men of other ranks killed and wounded.[50]

This carnage took place amid sedate Victorian houses: urban warfare had suddenly arisen in Dublin, something unprecedented in a city of the United Kingdom. Ordinary lives found themselves interrupted by extraordinary events. Louisa Nolan gave a drink of water to the wounded and dying on Northumberland Road. In Percy Place Miss Scully and her maid, sitting in a bullet-riddled room, were arrested by soldiers who thought firing was coming from her house. A woman neighbour was shot in the hand – while watching the action through binoculars. And an old man who tried to make a run for his house was caught in the open and cut down in a hail of bullets.

The Sherwoods' heavy casualties were due in large part to the Volunteers' high motivation, especially that of Malone who proved to be an inspired commander, a born leader; courageous and endowed with indomitable willpower. Undoubtedly, they themselves contributed to the slaughter by having the advance guard move down Northumberland Road without checking houses for rebel occupation, while the main body of troops followed too close behind. Once the gap between them was closed and they merged into what was in effect one large mass, the advance guard's reconnaissance function had ceased.

Malone understood both the importance of his mission and its almost inevitable outcome. At the battalion's Good Friday staff conference it had been agreed that Mount Street Bridge garrison would stay to the very end and Malone told O'Connor: 'Well, Joe, it's pretty close to hand. I know you'll come through, but I won't.'[51]

Malone himself had taken the most advanced and dangerous position in No 25 and his dismissal of two very young men demonstrated wisdom as well as humanity. He needed to be certain that nobody in his command would buckle under a heavy attack. Maher and Byrnes' removal from Clanwilliam House before real fighting had begun shed the remaining weak links and left him only with men who were totally committed, a group loyalty strengthened by the Walsh brothers' family bonds. Time and again during the battle the garrison proved determined, patient and disciplined and its co-ordinated, accurate and well-timed rifle fire demonstrated teamwork of a very high quality. Its members also refrained from going for the kill at the first sight, waiting until they received their orders.

Furthermore the choice of outposts was excellent; creating between No 25, Northumberland Road and Clanwilliam House a rectangular killing zone. Troops could be seen well in advance, particularly as Malone's men were equipped with powerful field-glasses, while the side windows of No 25 gave an oblique view of Northumberland Road for a considerable distance. In addition, the landing of the Sherwoods at Kingstown had been observed by Irish Volunteer scouts, as was their march northwards. Lastly, the Volunteers had decent weapons. Malone possessed a state-of-the-art, high-powered automatic Mauser pistol with almost smokeless fire, while Grace had a serviceable Lee-Enfield rifle and the spare rifles left behind by the two young Volunteers. Malone was also an especially good marksman, as was Patrick Doyle, the company musketry instructor.

The battle of Mount Street Bridge is often regarded as the heroic episode of the Easter Rising, an encounter in which the Irish defenders, and indeed the British attackers, displayed enormous courage and self-sacrifice. Malone and his small garrison faced impossible odds, yet battled for hour after hour and exacted a terrible price from the Sherwoods. With forgivable exaggeration, an Irish historian had described the battle as an Irish Thermopylae. Certainly the Volunteers' endurance in the face of almost certain death, the scale of the casualties that they inflicted relative to their own numbers and the legend which subsequently grew up around the garrison all contain echoes of the 300 Spartans. And at the end Malone, like the Spartan king Leonidas, lay, obedient to his orders. Even as the fighting took place a stirring myth was being created. One Dubliner, Miss Lilly Stokes, recorded on Wednesday 26 April: 'They took the corner house in Haddington Road after an obstinate fight – they bombed it. They say there were 36 dead men, women and children in it who had all been fighting.'[52]

When George Lyons returned to the bakery on Wednesday evening from an out-post in Grand Canal Street he told a sceptical de Valera that Clanwilliam House was on fire and unsuccessfully recommended sending a party to escort its garrison to safety. However, as the sky became illuminated it seemed certain that something terrible had occurred, though the garrison didn't discover exactly what until after the Rising. What was undeniable was that British troops had marched along Baggot Street and were beginning to exert pressure on Boland's through Kildare Street and Lincoln Place. Anticipating a night attack, Volunteers were placed behind empty trenches that had been dug facing Westland Row and Lansdowne Road. Hidden by small embankments, the defenders waited, ready to cut down any soldiers who stepped into the trenches. Lyons records that: 'De Valera passed along the lines exhorting the men to remain steady in their positions. He gave thrilling pictures of how we were going to have a glorious victory or a still more glorious death.'[53] The attack, however, never came and that was fortunate because by now many exhausted men were collapsing on duty.

By Thursday every outpost of Boland's had fallen and de Valera's headquarters had also lost touch with the GPO. The British net drew ever tighter. Soldiers had crossed Mount Street Bridge and occupied many tall houses in Lower Mount Street that provided them with excellent sniping positions. From rear windows British marks-men dominated the low-lying bakery and fired continuously, limiting the ability of Volunteers to move around inside and forcing them to crawl on the ground. They also made it frustratingly difficult for de Valera's men to distribute their plentiful sup-plies of bread. De Valera attempted to break the developing British stranglehold by instructing Donnelly to lead a firing party to a tenement house at the corner of Great Clarence Street and Grand Canal Street and dislodge enemy marksmen. Donnelly first dashed across the road with a sledgehammer to smash open the hall door. But it was unlocked and he hurtled through, ending up bruised on the ground. His men then followed and climbed to the top of the house, where British machine guns fired on the first person to put his head through the skylight. As Donnelly's party retreated to the upper rooms enemy snipers tracked them, seriously wounding a Volunteer and firing on the stretcher party carrying him across Great Clarence Street.[54]

De Valera had originally hoped to occupy many high buildings surrounding Boland's, especially Oriel House at the corner of Westland Row, whose capture would have allowed Volunteers to dominate British movements in Merrion Street and Lincoln Place. He was heard muttering continually to himself 'Oriel House, Oriel House, oh, if only we had Oriel House', and repeatedly selected Volunteers to seize it, only for him to conclude time and again that such an expedition was too risky. De Valera then decided to withdraw a few men stationed in the former distillery that was situated beside his headquarters. But while this would have concentrated his forces it also risked a British occupation of this high building. Instead he cleverly lured the enemy into destroying it for him by ordering Captain Michael Cullen to ascend the distillery tower and simulate semaphore messages, creating an impression that it was the Volunteers' headquarters. Cullen soon drew fire from a British naval gun situated on a horse lorry in Percy Place, operated by an officer and half a dozen sailors. The *Helga*, a British naval vessel on the Liffey, also joined in and some of its shells – the first of the Rising – landed in Barrow Street. De Valera gleefully raced up and down the line cheering and shouting 'Hurrah! a rotten shot' but, as Lyons noted, the men did not share his jubilation at the first artillery shells of the Rising:

> They were rather curious to watch the effect of the shell-firing which they had never before experienced. Moreover the enemy marksmanship was not to be scoffed at. The shells hit the tower of the Distillery every time and a racket and din was kept up by the explosion and falling masonry. They were small shells, however, but they practically had demolished the tower.[55]

To everyone's astonishment, when the shelling stopped two dazed young Volunteers whose presence in the distillery had been overlooked stumbled out shouting that they couldn't take any more. Cullen, who had stayed in the distillery during the bombardment, had his nerves shattered and was sent to a secure area to convalesce. A Volunteer recorded that 'one of the shells dropped on the Bakery and struck a bread van on the top of which was a large number of our own grenades but luckily no damage was done and the grenades did not explode.'[56]

Up until Thursday de Valera was completely in command, impressing everyone with his courage, agility, keen eyesight and ability to evade enemy fire. However, he was driving himself to the limit. Even before Monday he had been under enormous strain and his small garrison had suffered many setbacks during Easter Week. He also believed that some of his officers were inefficient and unreliable, an attitude that can only have been strengthened on Thursday by the stunning news that Vice-Commandant Begley – who turned up late on Monday – had now deserted.[57] Even though this time O'Connor accepted an invitation to become his deputy, de Valera now cut a lonely figure who was unable or unwilling to delegate and attempting to do everything himself, almost as if he believed that by sheer force of personality he could overcome his depleted resources. He constantly circulated around the garrison to keep the men alert and issued orders that guards were to shoot dead anyone who failed to identify themselves properly. Some men did indeed shoot and wound their own officers on Thursday night and de Valera himself was almost shot at the dispensary door after giving the previous night's password. With every street light extinguished the complete darkness unsettled many Volunteers. The garrison didn't dare risk a single target for British snipers, and smoking was strictly forbidden at night. Many guards became jumpy: 'Our sentries (as can well be imagined) often imagined suspicious movements at various places within view and fired at the suspected point. This of course roused their slumbering comrades who stood to arms and waited and watched for any development.'[58] By Thursday night many men were flat out exhausted on the bakery floor but one truculent Volunteer talked incessantly despite an order that strict silence be maintained. When an officer, Peadar Macken, reprimanded him, the man went berserk and shot Macken through the heart, only to be cut down himself by a sentry.

George Lyons recalls:

> When Friday dawned it bore the burden of many rumours of the gloomy night before. A new terror crept amongst us in the feeling that one's immediate comrade might go mad, or what was even worse, that you might go mad yourself.

Each man eyed his companion with suspicious glances and a most uncomfortable uneasiness prevailed.[59]

Fatigue, sentry duty, sniping, combat, even cooking and of course a lack of men, made intense demands on a reduced and overstretched garrison. Burying the dead became a low priority: Paddy Whelan was killed on Tuesday and on Thursday his body was still lying under the third-storey window where he had been shot. Finally, according to O'Byrne:

> Early on Friday morning my brother Peter with the help of Volunteer Willie Bruen constructed a rough coffin and we had the body removed to the ground floor and placed in its temporary coffin. We decided to bury the remains under a large heap of clinkers in the yard of the building. I read some prayers, we said the Rosary and performed our sad task about midday on Friday, taking cover as well as possible from the showers of splinters and ricocheting bullets.[60]

Surprisingly, in the bakery hunger became a problem. On Monday the departing bakers had left plenty of food and Volunteers – who had brought provisions – could also use the ovens. However, distributing food and refreshments became difficult, especially when fighting was taking place. O'Connor remembered:

> a 3 gallon bucket of tea having been brought up from the Bakery to the railway repair shop for the garrison. After all the trouble, and there was great trouble and personal danger in bringing the teas that distance, just as the men were bringing their mugs forward a shower of bullets struck the wall against which the teas had been set and it was destroyed.[61]

By Friday the pressure on Boland's steadily intensified as British marksmen inched ever closer. Its garrison became convinced that the enemy was dressing snipers in the blue clothing of military wounded in order to infiltrate and use Sir Patrick Dun's Hospital. An inordinately large number of men with stiff legs were seen in the hospital grounds: Volunteers suspected they had rifles stuffed down their trousers. At this stage the Volunteer officers were increasingly concerned about de Valera's behaviour. Donnelly noted his 'very worn and tired-out appearance.'[62] De Valera's behaviour also worried Sam Erwin, one of his three bodyguards, during Easter Week. Erwin saw a man who lacked training for his command position, was afflicted by chronic indecision and acted 'like a scalded cat.'[63] When he was off duty Erwin wandered around Boland's and on to the railway line, where he saw men placed here and there for no apparent reason or purpose. Communications between the different units were limited and it appeared to Erwin that the men at Mount Street Bridge had been abandoned there to die. He and two other bodyguards had to make their own arrangements in what he regarded 'a Fred Karno affair.'[64]

But de Valera obdurately rejected pleas to rest until finally he was persuaded to retire to his quarters in the dispensary. Donnelly then placed a guard there with instructions to divert every message to him while simultaneously he overrode the commandant's instructions by withdrawing men from the trenches to get some sleep.

Lyons noticed officers 'turning more and more to the imperturbable Donnelly for guidance and advice. It began to be rumoured that the strain was telling severely upon de Valera and that he might not again appear in the field.'[65] But the commandant would not be contained and reappeared within a few hours, only to display the same behaviour patterns that had aroused such concern in the first place. Indeed, Lyons states that at one point he came very close to being removed from command.

De Valera's staff officers were especially concerned at the extent to which on Easter Friday his fixity of purpose appeared to have disintegrated completely. Sam Erwin describes him waking up 'distraught' with 'startled eyes' and oscillating wildly thereafter, issuing a series of dramatic orders only to countermand them soon afterwards. In the early morning he decided to transfer the headquarters to the granary on Grand Canal quay, but the advance party under Donnelly realised its isolated position and returned to the bakery.[66] He then organised a party to 'raise Hell for Leather' on Merrion Square, but then cancelled the mission and instructed the men instead to pack up in readiness for a retreat to the Dublin mountains, a project which he had mentioned as a possibility to O'Connor earlier in the week. De Valera then sent a courier across the canal basin to order the commandant in Boland's mills to set fire to the building and evacuate to the bakery. The officer was appalled at the destruction of an enormous quantity of potential food and disregarded the message, as well as taking the courier prisoner when he attempted to carry out the assignment. Next Erwin heard de Valera shouting for men to be sent to 'burn down Westland Row station.' He ordered Lieutenant Sean Quinn to set it on fire and though he lacked incendiary materials, Quinn finally managed to start a blaze of sorts. In the meantime, two horrified officers persuaded de Valera that he was also jeopardising Westland Row church and he sent Lyons to stop Quinn who despite a 'hurricane of expletives' managed to extinguish the flames.[67]

Despite some piercing criticisms, Lyons respected de Valera's charisma and knowledge but remained concerned after a bizarre encounter on Friday when the commandant's appearance seemed utterly incongruous. Observing de Valera standing hatless with scarlet flannel puttees in glaring contrast to his green Volunteer uniform, Lyons ventured to suggest that he might seek more rest, as the men were rather anxious about officers overworking themselves. He eyed me suspiciously:

> Do you think that I am going insane because I am wearing these?' he queried, as he pointed to the scarlet flannel puttees: 'Sure,' he added, 'this is where I show my sanity.' I walked away rather abashed and depressed. Everyone seemed to be thinking in terms of sanity and insanity.[68]

Late on Friday night de Valera mystified Donnelly by ordering a withdrawal from the bakery to the railway line. Donnelly reluctantly obeyed but the men panicked when they reached a higher elevation and witnessed the fires in the city. Soon afterwards de Valera issued a countermand that told Donnelly to reoccupy the bakery, a risky enterprise because the British in the mean time might have occupied the evacuated headquarters. Fortunately scouts reported that the enemy had not realised that the Volunteers had temporarily abandoned the building.[69]

By Friday night Boland's situation seemed desperate, especially when scouts reported British soldiers crossing the loop line from Amiens Street station. Lyons urged de Valera to destroy the bridges spanning Westland Row and Great Clarence Street but the battalion possessed neither dynamite nor effective hand grenades: 'There was nothing for it but to await the advance of troops along the line. Night closed in and we set ourselves in the trenches once again to meet the onslaught that never was delivered.'[70] De Valera's command was probably saved by the fact that Saturday proved to be remarkably uneventful at Boland's with only intermittent sniping, though the silence across the city seemed to indicate that something significant had occurred.

Early on Sunday morning as Donnelly conducted a weapons inspection he was called to the rear of Boland's; Nurse O'Farrell had arrived with an urgent message for de Valera having been helped in through a window by Sam Erwin. The commandant was shaving but quickly came to meet Pearse's emissary who had brought news of the surrender. In an echo of Staines and Heuston's encounter with the commandant on Easter Sunday, O'Farrell recorded that de Valera, who didn't know her, appeared to regard the whole thing as a hoax and refused to accept the order until it had been countersigned by MacDonagh, his immediate superior as Dublin brigadier. When O'Farrell left to go to Jacob's to see MacDonagh, de Valera began consulting his staff, convening a meeting of officers some of whom knew O'Farrell and were able to confirm her message's authenticity.[71] With the British deadline for surrender drawing closer, de Valera warned them that they could be shot out of hand if found with weapons in their possession, but he had lost his grip on these officers days earlier and overwhelmingly they wanted to fight on. It was his vice-commandant O'Connor who rescued de Valera by insisting that they had come out as soldiers under orders and had to remain loyal to their leaders. O'Connor's support enabled de Valera to state that under a white flag he would personally tell the British that he was surrendering.

De Valera now ordered O'Connor to bring in men from their positions. The situation in Boland's became remarkably tense as British snipers shot one Volunteer in the throat and grazed O'Connor himself on the side of his head. In a foul mood the garrison finally assembled in the bakery where some men accused officers of engineering a betrayal behind their backs, though tempers cooled slightly when they learnt that the surrender order had come from Pearse. Lyons says that 'De Valera suddenly rose with tears in his eyes and declared: "I obeyed the orders of my superiors in coming to this fight. I will obey the orders of my superiors to surrender and I charge you all to observe the same discipline."'[72]

Accompanied by Lieutenant O'Byrne carrying a white flag, de Valera left to contact the British and elicit details about the surrender process. However, despite his appeal for loyalty Lieutenant Sean Guilfoyle began organising a 'Spartan' band to conduct a heroic last stand, a course he only abandoned after realising that the British would be showing de Valera no mercy. An exception to the general despair was Volunteer Joe MacDermott, who had radiated optimism throughout the entire week and now gloriously misinterpreted Pearse's dispatch by running up and down the lines shouting, 'By Heavens we have beaten the Hell out of them and Pearse has ordered an Unconditional Surrender.' When de Valera returned all but one intransigent lined up behind him and marched out into Great Clarence Street (now Macken Street). Nobody was prepared to carry the white flag and it was handed to Lieutenant O'Byrne, the Red Cross officer.[73] Whatever the reaction in other places, the local population was friendly and sympathetic, giving Volunteers an ovation in Grand Canal Street and Hogan Place, where women unsuccessfully begged them to take refuge in the houses and men offered to hide their weapons. De Valera was consumed with regret, saying to himself: 'Ah men, men, if only you had come out to help us, even with knives, you would not behold us like this.'[74] In Grattan Street there was a reception party of British officers and soldiers with grenades in each hand and de Valera brought the column to a halt. His men then flung their rifles down very violently, raised their hands and marched into Lower Mount Street through lines of bayonets. The Volunteers saluted their commandant, some shouted 'God save you, sir' and others ran forward to clasp his hand, causing de Valera to break down in tears.

5

Jacob's Factory and the South Dublin Union

According to plan, MacDonagh's 2nd Battalion assembled at Stephen's Green West at 11.30 a.m. on Easter Monday morning and departed when Mallin's Citizen Army contingent arrived to occupy the park. MacDonagh's second-in-command was Major John MacBride, who over fifteen years earlier had led an Irish Brigade alongside the Boers against the British army in South Africa. Subsequently his celebrity rose even higher when he married Maud Gonne – the most famous beauty of her day, but incompatible temperaments and lifestyles soon drove them apart amidst her accusations of cruelty, infidelity and drunkenness. Obloquy was heaped on MacBride by contemporaries including Yeats, a defeated rival for Maud Gonne's hand, who portrayed him in the poem 'Easter 1916' as:

> A drunken, vainglorious lout.
> He had done most bitter wrong
> To some who are near my heart.

In Ireland he sank into financial hardship, unemployment and alcoholism before finally securing a job as a water bailiff with Dublin Corporation. He also remained active in the IRB, to whose Supreme Council he was elected in 1911, before Clarke quickly eased him out in favour of Sean MacDermott, despite MacBride having been best man at Tom's wedding.

Clarke and MacDermott also excluded MacBride from their revolutionary planning because they didn't trust him to keep a secret. Even so, MacBride remained on good terms with the new republican leaders, they kept in mind that one day MacBride's military knowledge and reputation might come in useful. It has been claimed that on Easter Monday morning MacDermott sent a messenger to MacBride's office, where he often went during holidays to inspect ships arriving overnight in the port of Dublin, but that MacBride wasn't there to receive his mobilisation orders. MacBride himself asserted that only through last-minute chance did he become involved in the Rising when he was on his way to the Wicklow Hotel for lunch with his brother and accepted MacDonagh's offer to become his vice-commandant at Jacob's.[1] Now just over 50 years old, MacBride grabbed this opportunity,

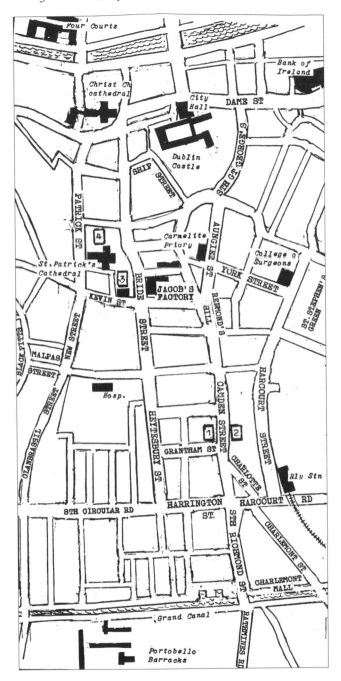

Jacob's factory area

1.   Byrne's stores
2.   Delahunt's stores
3.   Kevin Street police barracks
4.   St Patrick's Park

perhaps his last, to redeem a decade and a half of failure and dissipation. At Jacob's he was to cut a distinctive and rather incongruous figure, dressed in civilian clothes of navy-blue suit and grey hat, carrying a malacca walking cane and smoking a cigar. It had been a great piece of luck for MacDonagh to secure the services of MacBride, whose common sense and unruffled manner provided some ballast to a febrile and sometimes erratic commandant.

The main body of MacDonagh's Volunteers marched a short distance to Bishop Street where Jacob's biscuit factory was, one of the city's few large employers. This huge building was strategically situated more or less on a line: between Dublin Castle a quarter of a mile to the north, and two army barracks, Wellington and Portobello, three-quarters of a mile to the south. Close to a warren of narrow streets, it was an impressive sight: tall and apparently impregnable, with two high towers providing a panoramic view of much of the capital. From here snipers with binoculars and range-finders could command Portobello Bridge (over the Grand Canal), Portobello Barracks, the roof of Ship Street Barracks, Dublin Castle and much of Stephen's Green – where considerable fighting was anticipated. Nearby was the large medieval St Patrick's cathedral where Church of Ireland people from the comfortable suburbs came on Sunday to hear some of the finest church music in the country. Alongside the cathedral, through the Guinness family's beneficence, slums of the most wretched kind had recently been replaced with St Patrick's Park, working-class flats, public baths and a daily free cup of cocoa and bun for every child.

The surrounding area was strongly pro-British and during the war almost 400 Jacob's employees enlisted in the British army. Their wives ('separation women') depended on state allowances and they verbally and physically abused MacDonagh's battalion as it approached the factory. When a Volunteer sledge-hammered open one of Jacob's main gates a large crowd attempted to seize rifles from the waiting column; one woman who threw paraffin over the gate only desisted when a shot was fired over her head.[2] No sooner had the entrance been barricaded than the mob tried to burst the gates open, kicking, barging and banging with no effect before they tried unsuc-cessfully to set it alight. They were finally driven off when MacDonagh ordered a few blank rounds to be fired at them.[3] Hostility was also directed at men establishing out-posts, including in Fumbally Lane where Peadar Kearney, composer of *The Soldier's Song*, helped seize a malt house and erect barricades from shop shutters and old carts. About forty men occupying three premises in Malpas Street and a house opposite Kevin Street police barracks encountered locals singing pro-British tunes and throw-ing stones. One man was shot and bayoneted fatally after attempting to disarm a Volunteer. When Volunteers spotted a man observing their positions and taking notes they ordered him to move on. When he didn't budge one of the best shots in the bat-talion shot him dead.[4] Bill Stapleton recalled that 'this was a very hostile area. We were booed and frequently pelted with various articles throughout the day.'[5] Thomas Pugh said: 'the women were in a terrible state, they were like French Revolution furies and were throwing their arms around the police hugging and kissing them, much to the disgust of the police. I got a few kicks but somebody fired a shot to clear them off and they went away.'[6] When this antagonism persisted until evening MacDonagh decided to abandon these outposts and concentrate the men in Jacob's. As they withdrew the Volunteers brought with them captured policemen, six of whom spent Easter Week in Jacob's with two Dublin Metropolitan Police detectives, peeling potatoes in the cookhouse. They were lucky. MacDonagh's brother John recalled that:

> on entering the building 'a very officious DMP man refused to leave the street when ordered by Tom who warned him that he would be shot if he persisted. I whispered to Tom, advising patience, but he answered that it might be necessary to shoot some of these policemen and detectives to show our men that we were at war.'[7]

The prisoners also included: the caretaker Thomas Orr, whose family were away for the day; a watchman Henry Fitzgerald; a number of fitters and boilermen who had been doing maintenance work; and some sweeps.[8]

As Volunteers streamed into Jacob's through the front gates others scrambled in through a high broken window, one of whom 'let off his shotgun and bored a large hole in the ceiling. John MacBride, who had entered and was assisting others from above pulled some of the powder from his moustache and casually warned the boys to be more careful.'[9] Time and again during Easter Week MacBride was to demonstrate this remarkable sangfroid. Jacob's turned out to be pleasantly warm though dimly lit – even more so when electricity was cut off and the garrison resorted to using a supply of factory candles. Fortifying the building began immediately. MacDonagh established his headquarters in the clerk's office while his men barricaded windows with sacks of flour, removed flammable material, placed barbed wire entanglements in the yard and removed horses from the stables to safety in case of fire. The engine room and boiler house at the base of a big chimney were used as a billet. But the tiled floor there led to widespread sleeplessness and eventually a rest base was established and furnished with blankets, mattresses and pillows brought in by foraging parties. These came back with surgical and chemical supplies for the Red Cross station in a ground-floor office that was supervised by Patrick Cahill, a chemist. A supply store and canteen under the supervision of Henry O'Hanrahan had plenty of clothing, socks, underclothes, boots, tobacco and personal commodities on long benches. Cumann na mBan women who were active in the commissariat department improved an initially repetitive diet of biscuits and sweets with vegetables, meat and some fruit. Although machinery had been covered for the weekend the occupiers were soon covered in dirt, flour and sweat.[10] However, morale soared when MacDonagh addressed the garrison in what one Volunteer remembered was the 'picturesque language of which he was master'.[11] They thrilled as he told them that the country was up and Volunteers were marching to their aid from outlying districts, that allies were landing on the coast and German submarines had formed a cordon around Ireland to repel any British fleet bringing reinforcements. MacDonagh left himself and his men buoyant but unfortunately keeping morale high became an end in itself for the commandant, who specialised in a stream of good news stories about rebel military successes that foretold an inevitable victory. It was self-deluding spin which at the end of Easter Week was bound to collide with unavoidable reality to grisly effect.

The Jacob's garrison eventually consisted of 178 men, most of them Irish Volunteers but with a sprinkling of Citizen Army members, a few Fianna boy scouts and some Cumann na mBan cooks. Biscuit tins were placed on the pavement to give warning of a night attack and barbed wire entanglements put up in the yard to entrap British soldiers.[12] However, the men were disappointed and frustrated that almost their entire military action at Jacob's occurred within the first hour when Volunteers ambushed about thirty British troops at the junction of Bishop Street and Redmond's Hill as they moved tentatively down Camden Street, wounding an officer and six men.[13] MacDonagh's men assumed that this was the precursor to a full-scale British assault, but Jacob's was actually of no great military or political importance to the British. Furthermore, its fortress-like impregnability meant that launching a frontal assault would have involved diverting considerable manpower from other more urgent locations as well as using artillery in a warren of tenement streets which would have inflicted devastation on civilians and property. Instead, General Lowe, the commander of the British forces, decided to contain Jacob's garrison and wear it down psychologically by low-intensity pressure until he was ready to deal with MacDonagh. Lowe preferred employing sleep deprivation on the defenders and using snipers to unnerve them while armoured cars sped noisily past the factory during the night. The cumulative effect wore down many insurgents, one of whom recalled how:

> the ear-splitting crash of all sorts of arms gave the impression that the building was being attacked front and rear. All this meant that nerves were as taut as a violin at pitch, in addition to which physical exhaustion and lack of sleep had the men in such a condition that rows of houses marching solemnly away was a usual occurrence.[14]

To another it seemed that 'the days were all mixed up because we had got very little sleep and we did not know one day from another'.[15]

Lowe's refusal to take the bait robbed MacDonagh of the initiative and he never regained it. Instead, his Volunteers concentrated on constant sniping, especially from one of the factory towers:'This continued day and night, a slight lull in the dark hours before dawn, broken by occasional interchange between alert snipers, to increase in intensity at dawn when we were always 'standing to' against attack.'[16] Guided by the glint of enemy bayonets and buckles, the best rebel marksmen pinned down British soldiers on Portobello Bridge a considerable distance away. MacDonagh also sent out small groups to forage, reconnoitre, conduct ambushes and attempt to establish a defensive screen. At 2 a.m. on Easter Tuesday morning he dispatched about fifteen Volunteers to Byrne's stores at the corner of Grantham Street and another half-dozen to occupy Delahunt's pub directly opposite to serve as outposts guarding the Portobello approaches to Jacob's. Shortly afterwards other outposts were established in Camden Street but nearer the factory. The British attacked them next day with fourteen soldiers acting as an advance guard for a much larger party that moved down Charlotte Street; they surrounded Byrne's and began firing repeated volleys into the building. They also attacked Delahunt's and forced an entry but captured only the rifle, shotgun and pistol left behind by the fleeing defenders.

Inside Jacob's, effective leadership gradually passed from MacDonagh to the dynamic and decisive MacBride. Throughout Easter Week MacDonagh seemed to ooze supreme confidence during his tours of inspection and he certainly looked the part in a Volunteer commandant's full uniform, cloak and cap. Underneath, however, there was a complete lack of realism and his leadership proved to be mediocre at best. Over-promoted, separated from the Military Council's collective strength and wisdom and lacking Plunkett's comforting presence, MacDonagh surrendered completely to wishful thinking. His delusions were compounded by the fragmentary but overwhelmingly positive information brought by couriers like his own sister-in-law Nellie Gifford: telling of Volunteer successes at Mount Street Bridge and Ashbourne, heroism at the Mendicity and fierce fighting in North King Street. These grossly distorted military reality but, when recycled by MacDonagh, these bulletins aroused enormous enthusiasm among the Jacob's garrison. This situation was made worse when the dispatch system began disintegrating and one rank-and-file Volunteer at Jacob's recalled that 'we were not aware of the growing superiority of the enemy' and another that 'we of the rank and file had only a dim idea as to what was happening elsewhere in Dublin and none at all of the position outside it'.[17] When defeat eventually compelled MacDonagh to return to the real world it would be a crash landing.

This shy, sensitive academic lacked ruthlessness and drive and now the pressures of command found him out. At Jacob's MacDonagh's lacklustre approach led to a lax regime in which Volunteers experienced long periods of inactivity and boredom that they tried to overcome by tinkling an upstairs piano while others raided the library and debated quotations from Julius Caesar in a study circle that met during fatigue hours: 'It reminded one of a school rather than a war camp.'[18] In addition, MacDonagh's man-management was poor: his attempts to assert himself and act decisively only causing exasperation or resentment. On one occasion he awakened a group of Volunteers who had just bedded down, ordering them to take food supplies to the College of Surgeons and return with rifles. After completing their mission MacDonagh complimented them but then asked the officer in charge what had happened to the bayonets:

> The officer replied that he had heard nothing about them. MacDonagh then said that there were bayonets in the College of Surgeons to fit the rifles and that they would have to be brought over. He then told the officer that as the men present knew the way he had better take them back and get them! That was nearly the last straw.[19]

On another occasion, when Mallin asked MacDonagh to send Citizen Army members from Jacob's to the College of Surgeons, MacDonagh told one of them, William Oman: '"I'm not letting you go. I am keeping you beside myself." Then he asked me what I thought of that arrangement. "Well," I said, "you are in command, sir." However, just as the party was about to depart, he changed his mind and released me to go with them.'[20]

Ballast to the febrile MacDonagh was provided by the older, calmer and infinitely more experienced MacBride who was enjoying a re-run of his glory days and a renewed sense of purpose after years of dissipation. His presence lulled the garrison's anxieties as on one occasion an officer recalled an over-excited Volunteer rushing into the headquarters room 'where I was sitting with McBride and announced that thousands of British troops were advancing up the street. McBride calmly replied "That's all right." David Cutter went away satisfied there was nothing to be alarmed about.'[21] Like many others at Jacob's MacBride also drew religious strength from Capuchin priests who visited it throughout Easter Week to hear confession. Over time his faith had lapsed but now, as one Volunteer recalled, 'MacBride was telling me what satisfaction he derived from Confession, as he had been away from the Sacraments for some years'.[22]

For many of its defenders their presence in Jacob's was an eerie and, at times, surreal experience. The building's size (especially in relation to the small number of defenders), its gloom and creaking floorboards became extremely oppressive. Some incidents had an almost hallucinatory quality as when one man woke to the sight of armed Volunteers escorting a blindfolded lady who was dressed in widow's weeds and wearing a Royal Dublin Fusiliers emblem. She was not, in fact, an illusion but a female dispatch carrier who had passed in disguise through British lines carrying a message from Mallin in the College of Surgeons. Another problem for MacDonagh's men, surprisingly, was an absence of proper food after the superabundance of rich cake soon induced nausea and a craving for ordinary plain bread. An announcement that roast beef and vegetables were to be served resulted in a fevered excitement that instantly evaporated when a meal of a cubic inch of beef and one potato arrived. After this repast one Volunteer commenced a siesta under a long table where he accidentally discharged his shotgun and sent another man's plate flying through the air, narrowly missing taking his brains with it.[23]

On Easter Thursday MacDonagh seized the opportunity for some action when de Valera sent a message from Boland's asking for some arms and ammunition to resist pressure from British soldiers in Merrion Square. MacDonagh set off with fifteen cyclists on a relief mission, travelling by the south side of Stephen's Green and Leeson Street before dismounting at Fitzwilliam Street near Merrion Square. There he and his men shot a lone sentry outside a house and fought a brief encounter with soldiers inside, but broke off after deciding they couldn't force their way through to Boland's. When returning they rode in open formation along the dangerous west side of the Green where one cyclist, John O'Grady, was wounded. Although he managed to reach Jacob's, supported by riders on each side holding him up, O'Grady collapsed shortly afterwards and died.[24]

Besides an absence of real fighting, Jacob's isolation depressed many of its garrison. Volunteers had only a fragmentary knowledge of events in the rest of the city, especially since MacDonagh did not communicate the dispatch carriers' news to the rank and file, and the absence of hard news caused rumours to swirl through the factory. One of them recalled:

We heard that German troops had landed at Wexford and were striking inland in thousands, routing British garrisons as they drove towards Dublin in support of the Rising; it was said that the Volunteers were fighting bitterly along the coastline to Cork where the city was supposed to be out like Dublin; British troops were being rushed from the Curragh camp and reinforcements were pouring into Dublin along the Naas road; Dublin Castle was on fire; the British were using explosive bullets and shooting prisoners; buildings all over the city were being burned indiscriminately; Dublin was almost in ruins. Each rumour was more fantastic than the last, one contradicted the other. Everyone was confused, nobody knew the true state of affairs.[25]

What was certainly real and visible were the fires beginning to grip the city centre and on Easter Friday a female cook, Maire Nic Shiubhlaigh, ascended one of Jacob's towers to gaze on the inferno.

> Over in the north the GPO was blazing fiercely; it seemed as though the flames had spread the length of O'Connell Street. There were huge columns of smoke. Around us, in the turret, the Volunteers were still keeping up a steady fire on British outposts nearby. In the distance sudden little flashes accompanied the crackle of gunfire. All around, through the darkness, bombed out buildings burned. From where we stood, the whole city seemed to be on fire. The noise of artillery, machine-gun and rifle fire was deafening.[26]

By Saturday Jacob's defenders knew in their hearts that the end was in sight, though they avoided using the word 'surrender'. The British now occupied St Patrick's Park and had ordered civilians to evacuate houses around the factory. Expecting an artillery and incendiary attack at any moment, the garrison prepared for a last stand, intending to inflict massive casualties on enemy attackers. But they did so with mixed emotions. Notwithstanding all the defences they had constructed:

> it was clear that a few well directed shells would have made Jacob's a death trap for the garrison. On the other hand suppose an attempt was made to take the place by assault – what carnage might have occurred around the machines on the ground floor. The fighting would have been of a desperate nature. A few of the squad toyed with the grindstones in the machine shop, sharpened bayonets and pen knives for the twofold purpose of shearing the enemy and rations.[27]

On Saturday, while Pearse was arranging surrender elsewhere, they were actually strengthening Jacob's defences and firing on British troops in the area.

However, on Sunday 30 April MacDonagh's world fell apart with dramatic speed. One Volunteer could sense what was coming: 'The sound of heavy guns, machine gun staccato and the crack of the rifles had gradually died down the previous day and Saturday night had been unnaturally quiet. It was obvious that the struggle in Dublin was finished.'[28] During the morning the British began conveying Nurse Elizabeth O'Farrell and Pearse's surrender order to various city garrisons and during the morning she eventually arrived at Jacob's. With her eyes covered she was taken to MacDonagh and when the blindfold was removed O'Farrell delivered the order before describing the GPO's evacuation and subsequent events in Moore Street. MacDonagh refused to accept instructions from a prisoner and declared that as Dublin brigadier and next in seniority to Pearse he wouldn't commit himself. He was also visited by two priest mediators, Fathers Augustine and Aloysius, whom Lowe had warned that he intended demolishing Jacob's if he couldn't establish contact with MacDonagh. It was a deadly threat because there was a considerable amount of glass at the top of the factory.[29] Still the priests couldn't get this message through to MacDonagh. Donning the mantle of de facto commander-in-chief he declared that he would only negotiate with the British GOC. Detached from reality, MacDonagh talked like a man holding all the cards, claiming his garrison was well supplied and that the conflict was about to change to the insurgents' advantage. If Jacob's could only hold out Ireland would be guaranteed representation at a peace conference. With time slipping away, Augustine and Aloysius returned to Lowe who offered to meet MacDonagh at St Patrick's Park at lunchtime. During this meeting, which began on the footpath and concluded in the general's car, Lowe began the painful process of reconnecting MacDonagh to the real world. After Lowe described the overall military situation and the hurricane that was about to engulf Jacob's, MacDonagh informed Augustine and Aloysius that he intended advising his men to surrender. He had secured from Lowe a truce lasting until 3 p.m. to allow him to return to the factory and then communicate directly with Ceannt at the South Dublin Union.[30] Lowe's warning had not been an empty threat. The North Staffordshire Regiment's war diary records an order at 1 p.m: 'to move to Dublin Castle, preparatory to an attack on any rebels in Jacob's who had not surrendered'.

MacDonagh's men knew that he had gone to meet Lowe and wanted to hear what he had to say, resisting Father Monahan's attempts to persuade them to go home. Maire Nic Shiubhlaigh remembered them waiting apprehensively for the commandant's return, an agony made worse by 'the almost uncanny silence which had hung over Dublin since the last shell was fired during the bombardment of the GPO', which 'made everyone uncertain. Everybody waited for MacDonagh to come back.'[31] From his post on top of Jacob's, Sean Murphy suddenly saw a car drive up to the back entrance carrying a Franciscan friar and MacDonagh who hurried inside. Upstairs in his headquarters, the commandant was met by silent and apprehensive officers with whom he now began a lengthy meeting.[32] Standing at a table alongside a composed MacBride, MacDonagh read out Pearse's surrender order and announced that he had been driven around various garrisons and was satisfied that it was a genuine capitulation.[33]

MacDonagh then asked for their advice since they were not bound by a prisoner's command. According to Bill Stapleton, officers at first couldn't quite believe what they were hearing.[34] MacDonagh's own brother admitted that 'there were loud cries of dissent amongst the men against surrender. Many were crying fiercely and shouting 'Fight it out. Fight it out. We will fight it out.'[35] Sean Hughes argued passionately that they would be offering up their leaders to execution and that it would be better instead to die with rifles in their hands.[36] Eamon Price, however, declared that continued resistance would result in British artillery destroying everything, the factory, civilian lives and their houses.[37] Speaking slowly and in measured tones, Henry O'Hanrahan also advised surrender. After listening carefully, 'MacDonagh began summing up in a shaking voice but as tears welled up he broke down, crying "Boys, we must give in. We must leave some to carry on the struggle".'[38]

MacDonagh was shattered and couldn't bring himself to tell the women about surrendering and instead summoned Maire Nic Shiubhlaigh:

> When I went in, he was standing behind his desk, beside Major MacBride. He said, very simply, 'We are going to surrender.' He seemed the same business-like person we had always known, until he spoke; his voice was quiet, and he seemed very disillusioned. He said, 'I want you to thank all the girls for what they have done. Tell them I am issuing an order that they are to go home. I'll see that you are all safely

conducted out of the building.' I started to protest, but he turned away. One could never imagine him looking so sad.[39]

Nic Shiubhlaigh fainted at the news, especially after MacDonagh's continual reassurances to her about the Rising's great success, even after she had seen the fires in O'Connell Street. She had been accompanied by Min Ryan and a friend, Louise Gavan Duffy, who had come to see Jacob's situation for themselves. Speaking with brutal frankness to MacDonagh, Duffy told him it was all over, that the Rising should never have happened, was wrong and couldn't have succeeded. The commandant retorted angrily, 'Don't talk to my men if that is the way you are feeling. I don't want anything to be putting their spirits down.'[40] Since they weren't on his staff he told them to go and both women left, taking a virtually hysterical Nic Shiubhlaigh home and putting her to bed.[41]

Neither did MacDonagh inform rank and file Volunteers who had been assembled on the ground floor. Instead he delegated responsibility to Tom Hunter, a puzzling choice given his strident opposition to any surrender. Weeping as he descended the stairs, Hunter drew his sword and smashed the blade in two before delivering the news in a manner that hardly amounted to a ringing endorsement of his commandant.[42] Eamon Price recorded 'a scene of incredible pandemonium and confusion'.[43] Some Volunteers wept hysterically while others collapsed in disbelief or hurled rifles through the air. Many suspected betrayal, a deal done behind their backs and an ugly mood gripped a garrison that was on the verge of anarchy. The men moved upstairs to confront a listless and careworn MacDonagh, who stood on a table to announce that they were surrendering within the hour. He disowned personal responsibility for a surrender not of his making; he was only carrying out Pearse's orders. Before breaking down in tears, MacDonagh concluded sadly: 'We have to give in. Those of you, who are in civilian clothes, go home. Those in uniform stay on. You cannot leave if you are in uniform.'[44] After arguing with little basis in fact that they had succeeded in establishing the Irish Republic according to international law by holding out for a week, he assured them that while he would be shot they would be treated as prisoners.[45]

Far from restoring discipline this lacklustre farewell precipitated virtual mutiny. An emotional Hunter was having none of it, shouting, 'All I say is, any of you who go home now ought to be ashamed of yourselves! Stand your ground like men!' Others cried: 'We won't be shot like dogs.' MacDonagh's response was hardly reassuring: 'They might shoot some of us. They can't shoot all of us.'[46] Father Augustine interjected that anyone firing another shot would bear a terrible responsibility, at which point MacDonagh could stand no more and fled the room.[47] With some support Peadar Kearney advocated a mass breakout while others denounced them as deserters[48] and, as his garrison stood on the brink of imploding, MacBride entered the room, the epitome of sartorial elegance, puffing on a cheroot. His appearance and serene demeanour contrasting dramatically with a dishevelled, unshaven MacDonagh, he urged anyone considering escape to go: 'I'd do so myself, but my liberty days are over. Good luck, boys. Many of you may live to fight some other day. Take my advice, never allow yourselves to be cooped up inside the walls of a building again.'[49]

With MacBride's approval Kearney and many others now slipped away, procuring fresh clothes at the Carmelite priory and taking their chances in the streets. Others delayed leaving until the Volunteers eventually marched out of the factory and then they simply melted into surrounding crowds during a half-mile march to the surrender point.[50]

Meeting Lowe again at St Patrick's Park at 3 p.m. on Sunday afternoon, MacDonagh announced he was going to surrender. His garrison had assembled in the basement ready for evacuation and at this very last moment Mick McDonnell vainly implored MacBride to disappear:

> He replied by saying 'Mac, every G man in Dublin knows me.' And I said, 'I have been upstairs looking out the window and there is not a G man in sight and there is no chance of you escaping if you remain here and my advice is to get out.' He slightly bowed his head and replied, 'Oh Mac! I wouldn't leave the boys.'[51]

Then, Fathers Aloysius and Monahan 'heard a loud crash and sounds that seemed like bombs exploding'[52] as looters broke into Jacob's. They had climbed up ropes left hanging from windows by which visitors and late arrivals could enter the factory.[53] Having been freed, the caretaker Thomas Orr was relieved to discover that Volunteers hadn't vented their rage on the factory machinery but now he feared that a rampaging mob just might. Grabbing rifles left lying around he and some other employees temporarily stopped the looters. MacBride then showed Orr a supply of bombs and grenades that he instructed him to guard until the military could deal with them. The last thing MacBride wanted during the evacuation was a huge explosion massacring civilians. MacBride had hardly done when soldiers appeared and, seeing them with rifles shot at Orr's group, piercing the main sprinkler. They also threw one of the bombs out of a window into the street before Orr identified himself.[54] Then Fathers Aloysius and Monahan arrived and told the officer in charge that the Castle had agreed that troops wouldn't enter Jacob's before six o'clock that evening. When the troops left the looting resumed, overwhelming Orr's protests and only desisting when Aloysius waded through 8in of water to berate the looters and urge them to go home. To his delight 'before doing so, several gave up the articles they had pilfered – which included rounds of ammunition, revolvers and articles of clothing'.[55]

As they walked the half-mile to St Patrick's Park a solitary Volunteer sniper in the tower continued firing; the garrison had forgotten to tell him about the capitulation. The pace of events had taken an enormous physical and emotional toll on MacDonagh and at the park the sudden collapse of his hopes, the certainty of British retribution, the chaos of the final hours and the looting all coalesced in his mind. His tenuous emotional control disintegrated entirely as a looters' rampage became a murderous enemy assault. Major de Courcy Wheeler, the British officer taking the surrender, listened, bemused, as MacDonagh raged that:

> although his men had laid down their arms in order to surrender the soldiers had opened fire on them, were throwing bombs and that the military had broken into the factory and were killing his men and that he had seen one of our soldiers taking up a position in the factory and was using his bayonet.[56]

MacDonagh remained impervious to contradiction until Aloysius and Monahan told him what had really happened in the factory.

The South Dublin Union

After Ceannt rose early on Easter Monday morning he was soon dealing with a stream of couriers, sitting, as his sister-in-law Lily Brennan could see:

> at the round table in the front room the door of which was half open. I noticed his large haversack on a chair, beside which was his gun. His cap was on the table. All his equipment seemed handy by him and he was taking notes, his face pale and serious looking.[57]

Shortly beforehand, one of his most senior officers, William O'Brien, had backed out of the Rising and hurried away, though a shaken Ceannt magnanimously conceded that 'at least he had the courage to come and tell me'.[58] However, O'Brien had retained important papers and maps, something that partially explains the organisational confusion that affected 4th Battalion during Easter Week. By mid-morning, as mobilisation drew near, Aine Ceannt recalled that her husband:

> proceeded to collect his equipment. He had a lot to carry – a large bag full of ammunition, an overcoat and a bicycle. I helped him to get on his Sam Browne belt and then adjusted his knapsack, which was exceptionally large and protruded out beyond his shoulders. While dressing I asked him how long he expected the fight to continue and he replied, 'If we last a month then they – the British – will come to terms'.[59]

After embracing Aine, Ceannt bade farewell to their son Ronan who last saw his father 'walking up the road from 2 Dolphin Terrace where we lived towards Rialto direction pushing his bicycle. He was wearing an ordinary Volunteer uniform but had instead of a cap an Australian bush ranger's hat at one side. I remember that.'[60]

When Ceannt arrived at Emerald Square, in a working-class area half a mile south of the union, only about a hundred Volunteers had assembled, most of them still unaware that a rising was imminent. It was a thin turn-out, especially as they would have to occupy not just the South Dublin Union but a defensive screen of three outposts – two of them distilleries and one a brewery. Surprisingly William O'Brien was also present, attempting at the last minute to justify defecting only to leave after Ceannt brushed him angrily aside.[61] Ceannt was now even more reliant on his muscular vice-commandant, Cathal Brugha, the embodiment of militarism who:

> knew nothing of fear and had little sympathy for anyone who did. He spoke little of his political views, but one gathered he regarded the gun as the only effective sound in Irish politics. If one could not or would not take a gun one simply did not exist as far as he was concerned.[62]

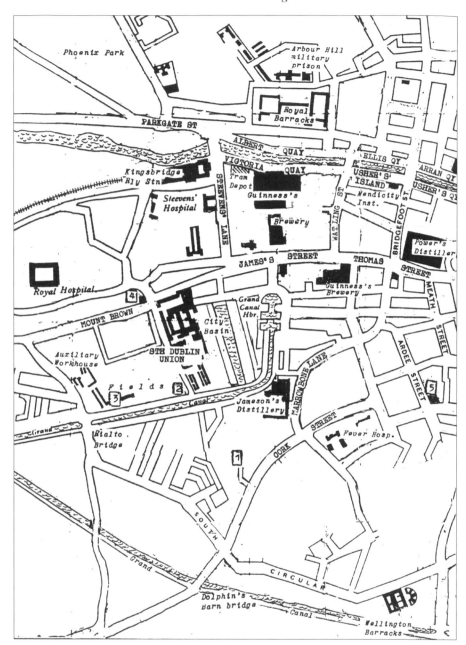

South Dublin Union area

1.   Emerald Square
2.   Rear Gate, SD Union
3.   Sheds
4.   Roe's malt house
5.   Watkins' brewery

Surveillance of nearby Wellington Barracks had revealed no unusual military activity and at 11.30 a.m. Ceannt led out the 4th Battalion. His main contingent separated at the South Dublin Union, leaving the remaining column to continue on to Watkins' brewery (Ardee Street), Jameson's distillery (Marrowbone Lane) and Roe's distillery in Mount Brown.

Situated in James's Street, at the western edge of Dublin, the South Dublin Union was home to thousands of the capital's destitute, infirm and insane, the largest poor-house in Ireland and possibly the world. Its large complex of buildings and grounds covered 50 acres and included an administration block, dormitories for over 3,000 inmates, residences for officials, a nurses' home, churches, sheds, workshops and fields. There were also three hospitals including one for the mentally ill. At the main entrance there was a block of houses running parallel with the road but facing inwards while to the right was the South Dublin Rural District Council Office, immediately over which was situated the boardroom. The remainder of the block was laid out in wards. At the end of the row was a paint shop and running at right angles was the night nurses' home with a Protestant church opposite its entrance. Slightly to the right was the inmates' dining hall. The South Dublin Union was more like a small town, with its southern wall following a full half-mile of the Grand Canal.[63]

Ceannt and Brugha's main party of thirty men approached on the rear side by travelling along the canal bank to Rialto Bridge, where they cut telephone wires, entered the union grounds through a small back door and seized keys from an unco-operative porter. Standing in acres of fields used for market gardening and dotted with sheds, Ceannt posted ten guards in a galvanised building near the Rialto gate and sent other men to the main gate half a mile away in James's Street. By the time Ceannt arrived at the front more Volunteers had entered there as well as a horse-driven lorry laden with hand grenades, barbed wire, tools and implements. Initially union officials didn't realise this was the start of a rebellion and one, Dr McNamara, tried to raise the alarm by phoning from the front gate office, ignoring an order by Volunteer James Coughlan to desist:

> I repeated it in a louder and more menacing tone, at the same time giving him a light prod of the bayonet in the shoulder. He then turned to me and said: 'I'll get your name and give it to …' He left the sentence unfinished as, by this time I had been joined by some other Volunteers who dismantled the 'phone while I kept him covered.[64]

The union administration decided not to evacuate inmates, transferring them instead to buildings draped with Red Cross flags. Initially some inhabitants didn't understand the tumult breaking out all around them, including a nun who mistook an armed Volunteer at her door for someone wanting to read her gas meter. In the following days, both Volunteers and the British tried hard to minimise the inconvenience and danger to non-combatants and permitted free access for provisions, but even so some residents perished in the ensuing gun battles and were hurriedly buried in the union grounds until after the Rising.

When the Angelus bells rang out at noon Ceannt told his men: 'We should hear an explosion any minute', but an expected detonation at the Magazine Fort never came.

He was amused though by the sounds of a military band wafting through the air from nearby Richmond Barracks, remarking, 'They do not know yet'. However, a sudden silence indicated that news of the Rising had just reached Richmond's garrison. Because of the union's size and strategic importance, a rapid British attack was inevitable. As the largest outlying group of buildings in the west of the city, it was close to Kingsbridge railway station, the terminus of the line from Cork. Across the Liffey lay the Royal Barracks, while on a low rise to the north stood the Royal Hospital, Kilmainham, the residence of the British commander-in-chief. The dramatic challenge that its occupation presented to the British army was symbolised by a large tricolour flag that Ceannt had placed at the top of the west wing and which came under fire all day from a machine gun situated on the roof of the Royal Hospital.

The Volunteers now hurried to ready their defences, barricading the main gate, windows and passages and evacuating non-combatants from some buildings, including the night nurses' home. At first Ceannt dispatched Liam Murray's unit to fortify the boardroom situated over the front entrance, while he located his headquarters about 200 yards away on the left hand side in a wooden hut that some union staff used as their quarters. Peadar Doyle was in the hut watching Ceannt and Brugha conferring and writing dispatches to the officers commanding at Marrowbone Lane and Jacob's as bullets came in through the windows, fired by a group of about ten British soldiers who had mounted the canal wall opposite about 200 yards away. But Ceannt quickly realised this building's vulnerability to heavy enemy fire and transferred his headquarters to the night nurses' home. He and Brugha also posted sentries at strategic points throughout the union. One was continually on duty at a small side door that wasn't barricaded so that the garrison could communicate with Roe's distillery. Other guards were located at the back of one of the hospitals, where Dan McCarthy remembered his unit leader Captain Douglas ffrench-Mullen's determination to run a tight ship:

> 'Don't fire without my orders, you hear?' With that a British major, who was trying to get over the wall, showed himself at the top, and immediately the Volunteer group fired at him. He fell back over the wall. He was killed. Mullen then said, 'Although I did not give the order to fire, it was damn good shooting.'[65]

Ceannt's force was stretched dangerously thin; never at any time had he more than sixty-five men at his disposal, and he could only allocate fourteen Volunteers to the buildings and sheds dotting the large fields near the canal and on the canal wall itself. Here they were exposed to British sniper fire from the other side of the canal and, more distantly, from the Royal Hospital. Despite covering fire from the main union buildings, it was impossible for these Volunteers to maintain satisfactory communications with Ceannt while the mattresses with which they had barricaded shed windows offered minimal protection to any of the crouching defenders.

On Monday the Volunteers were quickly attacked by a column of a soldiers marching down James's Street on its way into the city. Ceannt led a group of men into the fields and the fight was on. Soon afterwards Captain Edward Warmington and Lieutenant Alan Ramsay led British troops to the Rialto side of the union where they launched a heavy bombardment of the main gate as Volunteers in the sheds returned fire. Unable to get in, the soldiers switched their attention 50 yards along to a smaller gate that they successfully forced, despite rebel sniper fire from Jameson's distillery. As Ramsay led the charge inside the grounds he was shot in the head and killed; so was Warmington when he led another charge. As the British poured in reinforcements, Volunteers also fired on soldiers climbing the southern wall, fatally wounding a soldier who was perched on a telegraph pole.[66] Under sustained firing and considerably outnumbered, the defenders retreated across the fields towards the front entrance. Some raced into a hospital, only to be captured when a soldier used a lawnmower to break through a door. Very quickly Ceannt's garrison became concentrated in the main group of buildings at the James's Street entrance. Here British soldiers almost captured Ceannt as he reconnoitred the Protestant infirmary and suddenly encountered a Volunteer who was being chased by troops. When both of them fled into a blind alley and couldn't force a wooden gate, they stood with their weapons at the ready and prepared for a last a stand. However, the British soldiers had already broken off their pursuit and Ceannt was able to make it to safety in the Catholic hospital through a gate that was opened by a nun.[67]

Other inhabitants of the union became actively involved in the struggle. Ceannt instructed his orderly, Peadar Doyle, to requisition a group of inmates to carry boxes of ammunition into the night nurses' home. But Doyle felt uncomfortable about coercing them and instead set a price for the job which they completed enthusiastically in under ten minutes.[68] Other residents, however, didn't have to be bribed and willingly assisted the Volunteers. Mr Tallon, a union employee who knew Brugha's deputy, William Cosgrave, helped the garrison maintain communications with the outside world by passing messages – and food – over the garden wall that ran between his home and the rear gate of the nurses' home. Another worker, Martin Ennis, wanted to fight with the Volunteers but Ceannt regarded him as more valuable providing details about British positions and troop movements. Nurse Margaretta Keogh told Ceannt and his Red Cross staff 'that she was with them heart and soul and was glad to get an opportunity of serving her country'.[69] The night nurses had been asleep when the occupation began, but unlike her colleagues who were hurriedly escorted away to a safe building where they spent the week, Keogh was given a Red Cross armband and stayed to tend the wounded.

Within hours Keogh was dead. Dan McCarthy was on guard duty with Jim Kenny in one of the hospitals when:

> to our surprise a British military party appeared in the corridor and we opened fire on them. Since there were only the two of us in it, having fired on the military party we decided to get out of the building. Kenny went one way – to the right – and I went to the left. Kenny was fortunate to reach the Nurses' Home where the defence was but I was wounded. Evidently the British party was taken by surprise when we fired on them and they seemed to panic, lost their head momentarily because a nurse in full uniform opened the door and came down the stairs. They fired at her and killed her.[70]

During a follow-up search in the hospital soldiers also shot dead an inmate in the kitchen. Later, hearing noises, they climbed up to the window of a room in which eight inmates were clustered around a fireplace and hurled a grenade. The devastating explosion killed one man outright and severely injured most of the rest.[71]

On Monday evening Ceannt called in the men stationed in the fields and concentrated his force in two buildings, his new headquarters in the night nurses' home, and the boardroom. In these almost adjacent locations the fighting became almost hand-to-hand, with Volunteers forcing the British to battle for every foot. Nervous and frightened combatants thought it was like walking through a shooting gallery as they moved cautiously and quietly along many long intersecting corridors and past numerous hiding places, never knowing if they were about to be shot at point-blank range. Often only a wall separated both sides, and the slightest sound would produce a fusillade of bullets. For tired and stressed men the daytime was bad enough, but night fighting was a terrifying experience. The cunning removed their boots before creeping along the corridors and listened through thin partitions for voices or even the sound of breathing. Some fired first and asked questions later, others wilted and opted out entirely. One British soldier hid in the carpenter's shop until he saw union officials placing the body of a soldier on a hearse, whereupon he surreptitiously slid into an empty coffin beside the corpse. After an eerie journey out of union, he emerged to the consternation of civilian onlookers and legged it to safety.[72] The strain was great because the battle was so uncompromising: on Monday evening the British rejected Ceannt's offer of an hour's truce to remove the wounded and bury the dead: 'We shall give you no terms, you have killed our major', was the reply.[73]

In such ferocious and unfamiliar conditions rank-and-file Volunteers depended on high-calibre leadership and Ceannt and Brugha delivered it in full measure. Both men were alike in terms of character, courage, energy, resilience, daring and their uncompromising political philosophy. ('Brugha was a hard hater of everything British.'[74]) Time and again they risked their own lives and somehow survived. Ceannt moved about 'as if he had an enchanted life'[75] while another Volunteer thought Brugha indestructible, 'possessed of a charmed life; bullets almost touching him yet leaving him unscathed'.[76] Moving panther-like, Brugha would suddenly materialise to check a sentry's alertness, inspiring not so much simple admiration as an adulation that coursed through the entire garrison. Many Volunteers also felt pride in risking their lives: 'I followed ffrench-Mullen and noticed as we reached the hall that he limped slightly. He leaned on my shoulder and said, "Do you know, I believe I've been hit. I feel very hot about the leg" and he smiled as if he were happy.'[77]

Ceannt and Brugha also cared for their men's spiritual and material needs by arranging for a priest, Father Gerhard, to hear confessions almost every day. In the union there was none of the food shortage and hunger that affected the garrisons in Marrowbone Lane and Watkin's brewery because the storekeeper provided food to both Volunteers and British soldiers, while its bakers supplied bread to combatants, staff, inmates and the local population. Civilians reciprocated by hurling small parcels of cooked food over the union walls, accompanied by supportive messages.[78] Meals in the ground-floor kitchen bonded the Volunteers as 'officers and other ranks dined together and Ceannt chatted informally on these occasions. Cathal Brugha spoke (when he did) quietly and always appeared composed and contented. Eamonn Ceannt was always cool and cheerful.'[79] Ceannt and Brugha also held daily conferences with officers and men to inform them about developments.

At 5 a.m. on Tuesday heavy British sniping front and rear awakened Ceannt's men in the nurses' home, where Frank Burke – Cosgrave's safety-conscious half-brother – warned Volunteers to be careful as they moved about. Within half an hour he was dead. Burke was on sentry duty at a window along with Volunteer T.G. Fogarty when he leaned across to light his cigarette from Fogarty's pipe, making an easy target for a British sniper in a hospital across the roadway. As Burke fell with a bullet in his neck a Volunteer lieutenant shouted at Fogarty: 'You are responsible for that man's death.' Shortly afterwards Coughlan:

> saw Burke's body lying in the pool of blood where he died. From the instant of Burke's death until some weeks later Fogarty was mentally deranged and during the remainder of Easter Week with us he was kept disarmed and a Volunteer – Jim Kenny – was detailed to keep him company and out of harm's way.[80]

Despite this fatality, the routine work of fortifying the nurses' home went on in the absence of any fighting and indeed not a single British soldier was seen all day. British sniping though was sufficiently heavy to cut communications between the board-room and the nurses' home. Ceannt ordered the nurse's home entrance barricaded: the front door was secured, boards were nailed across the framework of the porch doors and the space between the boards and doors filled with rubble. This effec-tively made a second barricade, almost a wall, a couple of yards behind the front entrance. The entrance's very large windows made the staircase particularly vulner-able to enemy snipers and so these were laboriously sandbagged. This work went on into Wednesday when the military appeared to have withdrawn completely, allowing Volunteers to stroll around the interior courtyard. Ceannt also led men in boring through walls to allow free movement between the nurses' home and Liam Murray's unit in the boardroom.

But the lull was only temporary as the British built up their reserves for a massive attack. By Thursday Sherwood Foresters had arrived from England, supplemented by troops from the Curragh, Belfast and Athlone, and a number of RIC officers. In the morning Patrick Smith, the union wardmaster:

> was outside the kitchen when a British soldier came through the dining hall and was talking to some inmates when he was shot. I had him carried into the hospital and sent for Father Gerhard who came along immediately but the soldier said, 'I don't belong to your church, leave me alone. I am dying for my King and Country.' He died shortly afterwards.[81]

While Ceannt spent until late afternoon boring the final stretch towards the board-room, he left Brugha in command of the nurses' home. Among Ceannt's men was Sean McGlynn, who made the final breakthrough into the boardroom and recalled that because Volunteers were boring towards him from the opposite direction:

> each section thought that either was the enemy. I was the first to put my head through the hole which I had cautiously made and my reception on the other side was the point of a big six chamber revolver in the hands of Jim Foran and only that

he being an old soldier and had used an old soldier's judgement I would have been 'minus my head' today.'[82]

Just after lunch, heavy and well-directed British sniper fire riddled the back windows: 'Many of the bullets split diagonally and, coming from many angles prevented us from replying to the fire. In a short while the interior of our building had a dense cloud of dust.'[83] Sensing an imminent all-out attack, Coughlan and four other Volunteers crouched behind sandbags on the entrance landing, aiming their weapons at the front door windows. About 3 p.m. the British launched a co-ordinated offensive against the night nurses' home with a bombardment by rifle, machine gun and grenade: 'The noise and din were terrific.'[84] Hundreds of troops now fanned out from the Rialto side under heavy attack from Volunteers in Marrowbone Lane. Firing continuously, the soldiers moved in sections on Ceannt's headquarters. From an adjoining building they bored into the nurses' home and finally broke through by using high explosives to blow in the gable end. For the next five hours there was incessant firing, deafening noise and exploding grenades as Volunteers put up fanatical resistance. Crouching behind a dustbin, Coughlan heard a British officer calling for more bombs:

> 'A grenade, quick,' I whispered to ffrench-Mullen. He obtained one (canister pattern) and I watched him as he lighted the fuse and leaned over the balustrade. I cursed him inwardly as he counted 'One-two-three' loudly (as I felt that he was giving the enemy warning) before he threw his grenade. Uncertain of his aim I ducked behind the dustbin and the grenade exploded – on which side of the barricade I was not sure.[85]

Another defender grabbed a grenade with its pin intact and threw it back.

After forty minutes a British hand grenade blasted Brugha, causing him frightful injuries. Lying among dust clouds in the hall between the kitchen door and porch barricade, he shouted: 'I'm done boys, retreat into the next building.' Cosgrave now assumed command, ordering everyone to evacuate the nurses' home and make their way to the boardroom: 'Seamus Kenny asked what about bringing Brugha? Cosgrave answered that a soldier's duty was to obey and pointed the way with a .45 revolver swinging on his finger.'[86] Exiting by the nurses' home yard, they made their way through the paint shop into a large dormitory where they halted because British troops occupied the next room. Sitting on a barrelled-shaped stove was an old man, an inmate whom Coughlan put down on a mattress and blankets well out of the range of fire: 'Although he appeared to be in an advanced state of senility he obviously understood my intentions and thanked me with prayers.'[87] Anticipating a British attack, Cosgrave ordered the room hurriedly fortified with mattresses and pillows. After half an hour Ceannt joined them. On his way back from the boardroom Ceannt's men had wounded a British major and, from behind a wall, he could hear officers accusing Dr McNamara of having led them into a trap and threatening to shoot him. Ceannt, who knew better, vowed vengeance on the irreconcilable doctor for acting as an enemy guide, telling Volunteers afterwards 'that if any of our men saw Dr McNamara they were to arrest him. He would then be tried and if found guilty of treason he would be hanged and hanged by our men.'[88]

From the dormitory the Volunteers heard Brugha shouting: 'Come on, you curs, till I get one shot before I die. I am only a wounded man. Eamonn Ceannt, come here and sing God save Ireland before I die.' Since Brugha's survival meant the British were not in occupation, Ceannt led his men back into the night nurses' home where his vice-commandant was sitting with his back against the wall and his 'Peter the Painter' revolver ready for any enemy soldier. Then poignantly, both men, hitherto the epitome of belligerence, embraced with an emotional Ceannt down on one knee. For about a minute they conversed quietly in Irish before Ceannt regained control and rose. He ordered Brugha shifted to the kitchen because as fighting began again in the hallway, all-pervasive gunfire prevented his wounds being treated immediately. The fighting was intense. A British grenade actually rolled into the kitchen where a Volunteer stamped on it before pitching it back to the hallway where it exploded. Ceannt shot dead a policeman who was wearing RIC trousers and a khaki tunic: the only member of the Provisional Government who killed someone during the Rising. Coughlan 'heard him refer to it afterwards with obvious satisfaction'.[89] 'The bottom of the stairs was now blown away by enemy grenades, the hall, floors, walls etc were riddled and shattered. Some of the barricades were blown from behind the hall door. Still that building could not be captured.'[90]

At 8 p.m. a bugle sounded ceasefire and the British finally called off their attack, allowing the wounded to be treated. Tending Brugha lasted until 1 a.m. but despite intense pain he never once complained. Except for sentries the entire garrison surrounded Brugha, everyone convinced that they were mounting a vigil over a dying man:

> In some of the more serious wounds the clothes were embedded into the flesh and had to be torn away. In others they were cut away – in no place were they taken off. Throughout he was entirely conscious but did not utter a murmur. He seemed to be sinking fast. Only a few times did his lips twitch. After his wounds were dressed he suffered a raging thirst and continually asked for a drink of cold water. He was given hot coffee in small sips. In the early morning he became delirious and remained so until his removal to the Union Hospital on Friday morning. The First Aid man who dressed the wounds officially reported to Ceannt that there were 25 wounds – 5 dangerous, 9 serious and 11 slight and that one of the dangerous wounds had an artery out. His left foot, hip and leg were practically one mass of wounds.[91]

After the surrender Brugha was treated for months in Dublin Castle's hospital and made a remarkable recovery, though he never fully regained the use of his limbs.[92]

On Friday British snipers operated from dawn to dusk but there was no other fighting and Volunteers could see that every nearby building had been cleared. At about 10 a.m. Father Gerhard came in to hear confession and he then arranged for a feverish Brugha to be carried on a stretcher to the union hospital. The entire week had been very stressful for Ceannt and Brugha's removal left him ever more alone, but with only occasional lapses his mask of leadership held well:

> About 3 o'clock the Red Cross man wanted to ask him about T. Fogarty who was inclined to get violent about this time. He found Ceannt in a small room by himself, his rosary beads in his hands, and big tears rolling down his cheeks and face. The

Red Cross man saw him, paused to go back but was seen by Ceannt. Ceannt called
him in, buried his face in his handkerchief, and after about half a minute was again
the leader. He advised great care to be taken of Fogarty. No lethal weapon or grenade was to be left near him. In fact anyone going into the kitchen or room where
he was, was only to go there if unarmed.[93]

Volunteers who saw fires raging in the city centre and heard big guns booming suspected the British retreat from the union was simply clearing the way for a massive
bombardment of them and Ceannt showed his men where they could dig trenches if
the enemy began using artillery.

Saturday was quiet; again there was sniping from dawn to dusk but little or no
fighting. While Ceannt moved about checking barricades the garrison cleaned and
oiled its weapons, checked food supplies, counted ammunition and grenades and
took in water. Sunday was much the same though now the big guns had gone silent
and only occasionally was the crack of a rifle heard. Now and then defenders fired on
soldiers who were sauntering about in the distance. Ceannt called the men together
for a recital of prayers. His last news on Friday hadn't been reassuring. The provinces
were quiet and British artillery was systematically bombarding Dublin city centre.

At about noon on Sunday Volunteers in the boardroom saw two cars pulling up
outside containing MacDonagh, Fathers Aloysius and Augustine and three British
officers.[94] Aloysius waved a white flag and MacDonagh kicked the gate. Both were
admitted to the boardroom and cagily deflected a barrage of questions until Ceannt
appeared. He and the visitors then talked for half an hour, discussing Pearse's unconditional surrender order. Ceannt said that if he did surrender he wanted to march his
men to Marrowbone Lane, pick up its garrison and proceed to a surrender location.
The senior British officer was nervous about his soldiers marching prisoners to a
place he didn't know and where they might be attacked, but they eventually compro-
mised on two British staff officers, MacDonagh and both priests going to Jameson's
distillery to prepare its garrison for surrender.

After MacDonagh had gone Ceannt summoned a garrison conference in a dormitory underneath the boardroom. His gut instinct was to battle on; afterwards 'he
expressed his personal view that the surrender was a mistake and that he would have
preferred to continue the fight'.[95] But Ceannt was also a member of the Provisional
Government and bound by collective responsibility, something that made him very
ambivalent about capitulation. Struggling with these conflicting emotions, Ceannt
stood before his men and read out Pearse's surrender order, unconditional so as to
save Dubliners' lives from artillery and incendiary shells. They were not bound by it
but Connolly, Pearse and Tom Clarke had all surrendered. Thus they too could honourably surrender. But if his men refused Ceannt would lead them. If the big British
guns blasted them they could always find somewhere else to fall back on or get away
to the mountains. He couldn't order them to capitulate and any men who wanted to
get away could go; but he believed that, having behaved as soldiers from the start, they
should do so to the end. Ceannt then puzzled many of the garrison by remarking
enigmatically that 'You men will get a double journey but we leaders will get a single
journey'.[96] After he asked them to decide they placed the onus back on him by saying
they would agree to whatever he suggested. Ceannt then recommended surrender,

adding that no man was to escape or desert his post and that they were to disperse and collect their weapons. Even so several men did break away.[97]

At about 3 p.m. Ceannt asked the union wardmaster to open the front gates because he was about to surrender:

> I admitted a priest and a British officer. The priest was covered with flour. Commandant Ceannt was inside in the office at the gate. He came out to the British officer and on meeting him the British officer put out his hand to shake hands with him but Ceannt remained rigid. Then the British officer said 'You had a fine position here'. Ceannt replied 'Yes and made full use of it. Not alone did we hold your army for six days but shook it to its foundations'.[98]

After dispersing at the end of their meeting, most Volunteers had something to eat. Forty minutes later Ceannt sounded his whistle for everyone but the wounded to fall in while Father Gerhard collected messages from Volunteers to their families. When Captain Rotheram came in:

> Ceannt made a grab at his Peter the Painter, pulled it about an inch in the holster, paused for about a second, shoved his revolver back to its place again and brought his hands to his side. Here the officer stepped over to Ceannt, placed his hand on Ceannt's revolver, but walked away again without saying or doing any more.[99]

After a Red Cross ambulance collected the wounded, Ceannt ordered the men to move off, leading them out the main gate with the British officer stepping alongside him. Almost immediately afterwards a civilian mob poured into the grounds on a looting rampage, ransacking the nurses' home and stealing personal belongings, furniture and mementoes.[100]

Climbing over four barricades on the way, the column went down James's Street, up Thomas's Court and along Marrowbone Lane. Throughout the journey local civilians cheered on the Volunteers right up to the distillery where they halted.

The Outposts of the South Dublin Union

1 Roe's Distillery

At an officers' conference two weeks before the Rising, Ceannt told Captain Tommy McCarthy that his company would occupy Roe's distillery in Mount Brown. He was puzzled that he wasn't informed 'what military advantage was to be gained by occupying it – just to take the building and hold it – and with just respect to the dead, I could not see the military justice at all'.[101] As McCarthy's men mustered at Emerald Square on Easter Monday he suffered the first of many setbacks when one officer, Patrick Dalton – whom he had recently discovered selling British army rifles to the company – insisted on returning home to change his clothes. McCarthy was baffled because Dalton was already in Volunteer uniform. Only four of two dozen men turned up in uniform bringing just four modern rifles, three revolvers, a single shotgun, a few bayonets and swords and one pike. In James's Street they separated from Ceannt's main column and carried on to Roe's, near the north-west corner of the South Dublin Union. The distillery kept grain at the front, though it was washed, dried and roasted in a three-storey building on the west side. The manager's detached house adjoined a wall of the South Dublin Union while the upper and lower yards at the rear were overlooked by the Royal Hospital, a home for the British army's old Irish soldiers.[102]

Discovering Roe's front door locked, McCarthy's men marched to one at the back, arriving just after the manager had bolted it. Volunteers attacked this door with trenching tools until other men scaled the broken glass-topped wall and opened it from inside. The distillery was located at the rough end of a poor neighbourhood and McCarthy recalled a hostile crowd gathering: 'We were practically attacked by the rabble in Bow Lane and I will never forget it as long as I live. "Leave down your .rifles" they shouted "and we'll beat the — out of you." They were most menacing to our lads.'[103] Cornering the recalcitrant manager, McCarthy demanded every key for the building: 'He was a bit hesitant at first but I said "If you don't deliver the keys I'll have to take them off your corpse."' After the manager complied, McCarthy's men set about consolidating their defences, placing sacks of corn at windows and positioning Volunteers throughout the building, including two lookouts on the side going down to Bow Lane. McCarthy also removed window bars from the manager's house in case his men were driven out or had to evacuate the distillery quickly.

Roe's teemed with dust and loose barley that irritated throats and induced cough-ing fits. They were also potentially fatal. McCarthy's deputy, Lieutenant Patrick Egan, recalled one Volunteer dashing in from the side building to report:

> that the grain was ready to burst into flames. The Captain and I ran over and found the men with their coats off, shovelling the grain for all they were worth. The place was reeking with the smell of roasting barley. It appears that the men near the boil-ers, like all of us, were longing for a cup of tea. They started up the fires and put on fresh coal, unaware of what was happening above. After the fires were extinguished and the barley turned and turned we sat down exhausted.[104]

Furthermore, like Watkin's brewery and Marrowbone Lane distillery, Roe's experi-enced long periods of military inactivity and isolation from the main garrison at the South Dublin Union. McCarthy hadn't anticipated this three days earlier when he confidently predicted, 'Well boys, it looks as if it won't be long before we'll be having a crack at the Sassenach'.[105] A complete absence of heroic opportunities wasn't improved by McCarthy's own lacklustre performance. Cosgrave regarded him as industrious and efficient but most effective when directed by a superior officer. However, McCarthy's uninspired leadership doesn't completely explain his com-pany's dismal performance. Extraordinarily, McCarthy still had been given no idea why Roe's was being occupied; Egan could only surmise that it was to ambush troops from Kilmainham on their way to attack the South Dublin Union. Furthermore, British soldiers concentrated almost exclusively on winkling out Ceannt's garrison;

marginalising not just Roe's but Marrowbone Lane and Watkin's in Ardee Street as well. Roe's only military activity consisted of brief sniping and machine-gun fire twenty minutes after the occupation began. Face-to-face combat with the British never materialised at all. The nearest to it occurred on Monday afternoon when Egan ordered Volunteers not to open fire on a small party of unarmed British troops wearing Red Cross armbands as they marched past. He did this again shortly afterwards when a horse-drawn Red Cross ambulance with three soldiers came down a nearby hill. Egan learnt later that the vehicle contained British troops who had been ambushed at the foot of Mount Brown. McCarthy confessed to seeing 'only one British Red Cross officer in Bow Lane. I never saw an armed soldier during our stay there.'[106] His confidence diminished further on Monday evening when he solved the mystery of Dalton's absence. From a window McCarthy saw him sauntering down the street, having changed out of his Volunteer uniform into an immaculate navy suit.[107] He had doubted Dalton from the moment he caught him profiteering; now he knew for sure.

Roe's isolation frustrated McCarthy, especially as he had received no guidance about reporting to Ceannt in the South Dublin Union: 'As a matter of fact I had no instructions where we should evacuate to or even instructions to keep in touch with the Union. We tried to but could not. A fly could not get into them never mind us.'[108] Short of using homing pigeons he tried just about everything to establish contact. About noon on Tuesday his men spotted a figure at a window in the union and shouted, whistled and waved handkerchiefs, but all to no avail. Then:

> Mick McCabe who was probably the youngest member of the post and who had been a signaller in the Fianna and able to semaphore volunteered to signal from the roof. He was hoisted up through the skylight and no sooner had he started to wave his handkerchief when the machine guns burst open on him. He was dragged in immediately.[109]

Eventually McCarthy dispatched three messengers – one of them camouflaged as a Dublin gentleman wearing chamois gloves – but despite kicking and hammering on the union gates nobody inside responded.[110]

During Tuesday lassitude and uncertainty gripped McCarthy, who was further unnerved after discovering that both lookouts had disappeared from the side building; they had slipped out through the evacuation exit McCarthy had created in the manager's house, leaving behind their rifles, haversacks and ammunition.[111] His faltering resolve began crumbling completely in the late afternoon, by which time the entire mission seemed jinxed and continued occupation futile, especially with food supplies dwindling. Some hours later Colbert at Watkin's was to reach the same conclusion but decided then to continue fighting and even marched his men to Marrowbone Lane in their stocking feet to avoid alerting the British. By contrast, McCarthy displayed a crippling lack of initiative, telling Egan that he intended evacuating the garrison either singly or in pairs to avoid attracting the attention of British spotters.[112] While Egan agreed with abandoning Roe's, he argued strongly for preserving company unity and continuing the fighting by marching en bloc to the South Dublin Union where their numbers stood a better chance of being seen by Ceannt's defenders.[113] Perhaps McCarthy feared that British snipers would easily pick off such a large body of men even under cover of darkness. In any event he stunned Egan by replying that it was too late and he had already ordered the side building's evacuation. When Egan checked it was indeed empty. On his return there were only nine men left.[114] McCarthy's vision of a skilled tactical withdrawal had rapidly descended into an undignified scramble for the exit; Lawrence O'Brien was one of a section abandoned on a top floor. They only noticed that something was amiss when 'an uneasy quiet seemed to settle over the distillery buildings'.[115] According to one Volunteer 'After our withdrawal it was a case of every man for himself'.[116] The evacuees' fate differed widely; some went home, some were captured. O'Brien's group, however, reached Marrowbone Lane where a shocked Captain Murphy couldn't believe what they told him, though Colbert did.

Throughout Wednesday Ceannt became increasingly puzzled by Roe's stillness and in the darkness decided to investigate personally. After climbing an adjacent wall and wandering through the distillery like a bemused seafarer stumbling upon the *Marie Celeste*, he found it completely deserted. Upon returning he didn't try to hide this disheartening development from his men.[117]

2 Marrowbone Lane

On Easter Monday about fifty Volunteers and twenty Cumann na mBan from Captain Seamus Murphy's A Company occupied Jameson's distillery in Marrowbone Lane. The premises commanded both sides of a canal that ran along the back of the South Dublin Union as far as Dolphin's Barn Bridge. When they arrived at the distillery Murphy shouted twice – in the name of the Irish Republic – before the caretaker opened a little wicket gate. Once inside Murphy detained him and his wife to prevent them alerting the authorities before ordering his men to fortify the building by barricading exits, collecting water and distributing ammunition. Because of the disappointingly small turn-out he also adopted the *beau geste* defence of putting caps and hats on brush handles and positioning them at the windows hoping to convince the British that he had a much larger garrison.[118]

British snipers were soon firing from the direction of the canal and Murphy ordered the women to crawl along the walls and ascend ladders to the upper storey. Ceannt's sister-in-law Lily Brennan was shaken by her first taste of war: 'The reality of it all was now upon me. My mind was a perfect blank by this. All my preconceived ideas had left it. How very far away from the truth I had been.'[119] The women were stationed in a very large room from which they could peer down on the courtyard and main gates. The floor was strewn with sacks of grain that they covered with coats and on which they slept. There was also a small window nicknamed the Crow's Nest that commanded the canal and Dolphin's Barn Bridge and from which snipers could target British troops gathering at the back door of the South Dublin Union. Because of its importance, the crow's nest was sandbagged and guarded day and night.[120]

On Monday afternoon and Tuesday British troops engaged in desultory firing from the direction of Rialto Bridge on the far side of the canal bank. Initially slow to recognise the rebellion's seriousness, they exposed themselves to sniper fire and suffered casualties. However, the Volunteers found their own Howth rifles almost as dangerous:

It was a bad weapon for street fighting. Flame about three feet long came out through the top of the barrel when it was fired and a shower of soot and smoke came back in one's face. After three shots were fired from it, it would have to be thrown away to let it get cool and the concussion [sic] of it was so severe that it drove me back along the floor several feet.[121]

On Tuesday afternoon there was a fierce two-hour gun battle in which Murphy's men inflicted serious losses on the British attackers, one of whom was dragged away by his horse with a foot caught in the stirrup.[122] Eventually troops were withdrawn from the surrounding area and as darkness fell Volunteers collected the fallen soldiers' weapons. Holland remembered crawling across a field until he 'picked out the first dead soldier. I cut off his web equipment and one of the others took his rifle. In this manner we stripped quite a lot of dead soldiers. In all we got five rifles.'[123]

Returning from no-man's-land, Holland witnessed the lethal consequences of making one false move or sound. Jack Saul:

told me that whilst I was away he thought he heard someone digging at the Canal double gate right under us. He knew I had crossed the wall to the left of us but he could not account for this noise. I listened and heard this noise, like chains rattling. Something very hard was being moved about. Saul shouted out 'Halt' but the movement still went on. I shouted 'Halt or I fire!' and we both shouted that we had it covered. We then decided to fire at the gate. Both of us fired and then a lot of confusion and noise ensued. A few minutes later Sergeant Kerrigan came up and shouted that someone in our wing had shot and killed 'Mock' Keogh's horse. The horse had been rambling around the yard, nibbling the grass and throwing the collar up around his head.'[124]

During the night of Easter Tuesday, Con Colbert evacuated Watkin's brewery in Ardee Street. The building was too large for his small garrison and its occupation contributed nothing to the overall battalion effort. Colbert now transferred his men to Marrowbone Lane where he soon became de facto commandant.[125] On Wednesday Mick Liston, 4th Battalion's best shot, was grazed in the head while stationed in the crow's nest. Holland recalled:

We all had a great affection for him and his wounding brought the first bit of bitterness in us. We all set our teeth to get revenge. Mick was no sooner up in position when he was down again with another head wound, this time more serious. As he passed me I saw blood running down his face. He said he was all right but I got a chilly feeling in my stomach. He was about twenty years of age. Our hearts sank ... as they brought him down.[126]

As the battle raged, Holland became puzzled by the increasing intensity and accuracy of British sniper fire pouring in from all sides. On the previous day he had noticed a woman leaning out of a window at the gable end of a house opposite and now, scanning the roofs of James's Street Christian Brothers' school and houses in Basin Street and Basin Lane, he saw her again:

She had a hat, blouse and apron on her and I got suspicious. I told Mick O'Callaghan that I was going to have a shot at her. He said 'No.' I said it was a queer place for a woman to be and that it was queer she should have a hat on her, as she must have seen the bullets flying around but took no notice of them. I made up my mind. She was only 35 or 40 yards away from me and I fired at her. She sagged half way out of the window. The hat and small little shawl fell off her and I saw what I took to be a woman was a man in his shirt sleeves.[127]

Holland also spotted the tops of rifle barrels behind tree trunks that were situated under the window. However, by now super-sniper Liston was back in action:

A few shots came from the hidden soldiers, but the soldiers did not show themselves. After another few minutes, another fusillade was fired at us, during which one of them made a mistake and showed himself. Liston potted him. The soldiers then broke cover and ran along the wall towards the South Dublin Union and Rialto Bridge. They had to run about three-quarters of a mile, during which they were under our fire. There were twelve in all and every one of them was hit. From that time on we were very careful and kept a look-out for snipers.[128]

Liston felt invincible. After identifying a British sniper sitting on a branch about 200 yards away on the Dolphin's Barn side of the canal, one shot left the soldier hanging out of the tree for the remainder of the day. These small victories boosted the garrison's morale:

We had no one killed and only two wounded and these were back in the fight again. If all the garrisons were like ours, and we had no doubt that they were, we were doing very well indeed. We must win and none of us thought otherwise. Failure was the last thing that I or the rest of us thought of. After reading and thinking over our history of the short, quick battles, we could not lose now. We were more than two days and a half fighting and that was longer than four previous rebellions put together.[129]

From Wednesday onwards Murphy's situation at Marrowbone Lane became increasingly difficult. His garrison numbers had swollen to 145 men after Colbert's garrison arrived en masse from Watkin's and individual Volunteers drifted in from Roe's distillery. Murphy's outpost now had three times as many men as Ceannt's main garrison in the South Dublin Union. There was insufficient action for so many men because despite the heavy sniping the British never attempted a serious assault on Marrowbone Lane, let alone using artillery. Murphy's limited food supply began to run out and by the weekend hunger had become a major problem. There was also a growing sense of isolation. Until Wednesday direct contact between Marrowbone Lane and the South Dublin Union was maintained by runners, one of whom carried Murphy's messages written on the inside of his collar.[130] Thereafter it became increasingly difficult as the messengers failed to get through and flag signalling proved ineffective. Furthermore, distressing news from home reached some men: Holland's brother Watty reported crowds attacking and looting Volunteers' homes which had also been raided by soldiers and policemen, one of whom had promised their mother to manure Marrowbone Lane with rebel bodies.[131] The quartermaster Seamus Kenny also remembered that 'during the week some of the fellows began to cry when they heard shots because they were a long time from confession'.[132] Murphy requested priests from Mount Argus to hear confession, though one of them, Father Barry, was keener on urging surrender: Colbert tersely replied, 'What about asking them to come down here and surrender to us?'[133]

By Friday Murphy's senior officers had become disillusioned with his leadership, especially Con Colbert and Joseph McGrath. The small, stocky Colbert had once been Fianna chief scout and actually outranked Murphy. He didn't smoke or drink, an ascetic lifestyle derived from studying Irish history: 'All his lectures centred around the subject of "Why we failed." His answer to this question was always "Drink and want of discipline and loose talk."'[134] Colbert now became de facto commandant after an officers' conference decided that on Sunday, failing orders to the contrary, the entire garrison would march to the South Dublin Union. On Saturday morning all British troops were withdrawn out of range of Volunteers' weapons and only a few shots were exchanged. On Sunday the British weren't seen at all and at noon the garrison assembled in the courtyard in an atmosphere of almost religious euphoria. Men cheered and cried 'Yes' when Colbert asked if they were ready to fight to the last, even if the enemy tried to starve them out. From her window Lily Brennan saw Murphy read out Ceannt's message that his Volunteers had driven the British out of the South Dublin Union and were full of fight: 'We too may have hard fighting yet our captain said "and we may have to go on half rations, quarter rations or no rations. Are you ready?" A ringing cheer greeted Captain O Murscada [Murphy] and the men quickly returned to their posts.'[135] GALWAY COUNTY LIBRARIES

Within four hours it was all over. Brennan suddenly saw Murphy in deep conversation with MacDonagh and Father Augustine and wondered why the commandant was so far away from his post in Jacob's. One Volunteer noticed that MacDonagh was 'hatless and unarmed and looked old, weary and ill and something in his general appearance told me the worst had happened'.[136] Then at about 6.30 p.m. after MacDonagh had departed in tears, Lily Brennan suddenly realised that Murphy was talking with Ceannt who had suddenly appeared 'as if he had fallen from the sky'.[137] Annie O'Brien thought that Ceannt 'was like a wild man; his tunic was open, his hair was standing on end and he looked awful. He evidently hated that task of asking the garrison to surrender. He put two hands on the barricade, with his head bent and he presented a miserable appearance.'[138] Brennan then saw that 'A restlessness was stirring on the courtyard. Men were gathered together and as if wirelessed like a flash the news was revealed. Some of the men wept but we girls were dumbfounded.'[139] Amid emotional scenes a Volunteer got down on one knee and was about to shoot Captain Rotheram when someone grabbed his weapon away from him.[140] Brennan approached her brother-in-law who stood capless 'on this the most calamitous day of his life',[141] his uniform torn, hair tousled and face strained . She inquired what was wrong but Ceannt simply handed her a purse, saying 'Go home and give this to Aine'. Murphy and Ceannt then resumed their conversation, after which the captain confirmed the surrender. Murphy told the women to go home but they would have none of it, shouting, 'We came out with you. We surrender with you.'[142] So Marrowbone Lane became the only Cumann na mBan contingent to participate in the surrender. Harry Murray recollected that 'the members of the Marrowbone Lane distillery garrison in particular were deeply humiliated. They could not understand the necessity of surrender.'[143] Holland noticed that 'Colbert could hardly speak as he stood in the yard for a moment or two. He was completely stunned. The tears rolled down his cheeks. I glanced at Captain Murphy and he had turned a sickly yellow. Harry Murray bowed his head.'[144] The garrison hadn't been under any real pressure nor had it seen much action, barely using arms that had been acquired at so much personal sacrifice. The capitulation pole-axed Colbert. All he had ever wanted to do during Easter Week was fight the enemy. Denied this at Watkin's, he enjoyed only marginally more satisfaction at Marrowbone Lane. Sunday's proposed shift to the South Dublin Union created an emotional high as his speech thrilled the entire garrison, but now Colbert psychologically collapsed. Holland:

> asked him what the excitement was and had anything serious happened. He said
> – 'Bobby, I do not know what to say or think but if what I think comes true our
> cause is postponed to a future generation. We are to surrender unconditionally and
> I cannot forecast what that will mean. We must have been let down very badly as we
> have not had the support of our people that we had expected.'[145]

Colbert also spoke to Annie O'Brien, whom he had proposed as a Cumann na mBan member and tentatively dated just before the Rising. She had been smitten by him but Colbert's absolute commitment to the Volunteers put their budding relationship on hold. After giving O'Brien two photographs of himself he 'said, rather significantly, "Would you mind very much if anything happened to me in this fight that is coming" and I said "I would indeed, why do you ask?" He answered, "I might just be the one to be killed."' During the occupation she had darned a pair of his socks, aware of how much Colbert abominated holes in them. When the Marrowbone garrison surrendered she 'asked Con what was going to happen to himself. He said he did not know, whatever the British authorities liked to do with him; but if he came through he would come back to our house.'[146]

Disconsolately, Colbert blew his whistle and assembled the garrison in the yard where he announced an unconditional surrender. Anyone wishing to escape could do so. Immediately Joe McGrath shouted 'Toor-a-loo, boys, I'm off' and jumped the wall.[147] Others followed. Then, with Colbert at the head, the remainder marched out through the front entrance and fell in behind the South Dublin Union column.[148] There was chaos as crowds outside jostled the emerging Cumann na mBan and poured in looking for food, especially three dead calves dressed and hanging in the courtyard.

A large crowd had gathered outside and Ceannt remarked bitterly, 'Where were you men when you were wanted?' They marched in military fashion by Marrowbone Lane, Cork Street, Patrick Street and Bride Street. Despite the all-pervasive melancholy, the journey was not without its lighter side. Holland recalled that:

> When we were almost at the Coombe Maternity Hospital, two drunken men
> insisted on falling in with us. They were ejected from our ranks several times on the
> route but eventually must have got into the ranks in my rear, for about two months
> later I saw these two men taking their exercise in Knutsford Prison.[149]

However, as they marched into Bride Street, soldiers with fixed bayonets were formed up two deep on each side of the road while machine guns were also trained on the prisoners. There a British officer ordered them to lay down their weapons, which were then collected and thrown into a lorry. A few shots were discharged inside the vehicle because Volunteers had forgotten to extract cartridges. Here Annie O'Brien approached a forlorn Con Colbert:

> to see whether there was anything he wanted me to do for him and also to get some souvenir in case I should never see him again. He was standing in rank with the other Volunteers with one sock in one hand and a piece of my mother's brown bread in the other. I asked him for a souvenir: 'Here' he said, 'these are all I have.' He had like all the others been stripped of all his accoutrements. I did not take either of the articles he offered to me, as I thought he might need the brown bread and the sock.[150]

After a meticulous search of every man the column marched back to Patrick Street, then on to James's Street, Mount Brown and Kilmainham. For most of the journey there were few people on the streets but when they arrived at Kilmainham Cross at about 8 p.m. in the gathering dusk an angry, jeering crowd had assembled and Holland remembered 'men, women and children cursing loudly'.[151]

6

The Four Courts and the Mendicity Institution

General Maxwell thought that except for Mount Street Bridge the fighting around the Four Courts was 'by far the worst that occurred in the whole of Dublin'.[1] In the narrow surrounding streets Ned Daly's 1st Battalion engaged soldiers in what one military historian has described as a 'miniature Stalingrad'.[2]

The Volunteers who fought there came from an area north of the Liffey that stretched from Phoenix Park to O'Connell Street and contained some of the poorest parts of the capital. Former British soldiers had trained them regularly in street-fighting techniques at battalion headquarters in Parnell Square or in the Gaelic hall in Blackhall Street. By Easter 1916 Daly's officers had identified buildings around the Four Courts to be occupied, vantage points for sharp-shooters, manholes covering subterranean wires and properties which contained food, bedding, clothing and medical supplies.[3] Daly's reconnaissance had been particularly thorough and included an overnight stay at the Four Courts Hotel, which he expected to seize and occupy.

Daly himself was a spare, self-contained but forceful 25-year-old whom one officer described as:

> a fine figure of a man with a rather serious looking face and sad dark eyes. In his well-tailored green uniform he looked every inch a soldier. The combination of the soldierly figure with the pale complexion and the dark moustache created havoc among the ladies, while his smart military bearing inspired great respect in the minds of the rank and file of the Battalion.[4]

Daly's family was steeped in republicanism, his father having participated in the 1867 Fenian Rising while his uncle John had been imprisoned along with Tom Clarke – who subsequently married Daly's sister Kathleen. Such connections undoubtedly assisted Daly's rapid rise in the Volunteers, and in January 1915 he was made commandant of 1st Battalion, a post to which he brought considerable dedication and fervour. One Volunteer remembered Daly telling him that when the Republic was proclaimed every man would be expected to defend it with his life and while some leaders would fall others would carry on against overwhelming odds. Daly's eyes 'appeared to shine and I saw that he was dead in earnest in every word he spoke.'[5] Although some people

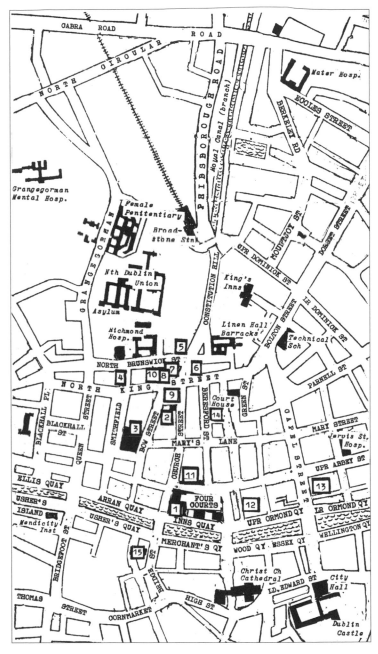

Four Courts and North King Street area

1.	Four Courts Hotel	8.	'Reilly's Fort'
2.	Father Mathew Hall	9.	Blanchardstown mills
3.	Jameson's distillery	10.	St John's Convent
4.	Red Cow Lane	11.	The Bridewell
5.	Moore's coach factory	12.	Charles Street
6.	Monks' bakery	13.	Strand Street
7.	Clarke's dairy	14.	Malt house
		15.	Brazen Head

regarded him as withdrawn and taciturn, Daly was to provide highly effective and humane leadership throughout Easter Week, when he proved himself probably the most tactically shrewd rebel commandant.

Fewer than a third of the battalion mustered in Blackhall Street on Easter Monday when towards noon Daly ordered them to fall in and disclosed that this was 'the day': very soon their leaders would proclaim an Irish Republic that he expected them to defend with their lives. His announcement surprised many but although Daly gave everyone an opportunity to go home with honour, only two men withdrew while the rest cheered loudly. When some Volunteers requested a priest Father Augustine from the Capuchin friary in Church Street took Holy Communion and heard confession.[6] However, the low turn-out was to inhibit Daly's tactics and operations throughout Easter Week and forced him constantly to improvise because the Four Courts area was both extensive and of great strategic significance. It stretched from the Mendicity Institution and the Liffey quays in the south, initially as far north as the Cabra and North Circular roads, east towards the Bolton Street approach to North King Street, and west to North Brunswick Street as far as Red Cow Lane. Daly's original intention was to hold a line that extended from the Four Courts to Cabra, occupying Broadstone station (a possible headquarters), the North Dublin Union poorhouse, the Four Courts and the area in between. He even envisaged linking up with Thomas Ashe's Fingal battalion in North County Dublin.[7] Daly's primary military objective was preventing troops deploying eastwards from the Royal Barracks about ten minutes away, from Marlborough Barracks on the north-west fringe of the city and from Kingsbridge station, the terminus for troop reinforcements from the Curragh. His main column marched south along Queen Street and then by Arran quay to the Four Courts, Dublin's seat of justice and an imposing eighteenth-century edifice of classical design facing the Liffey. Other units that were to occupy outposts struck eastwards through Queen Street, Smithfield, Bow Street and Mary's Lane to Church Street, an area intersected by the narrow, though more substantial, North King Street. To the north-west, behind the parallel North Brunswick Street, was an area dominated by hospitals and grim nineteenth-century institutions including two asylums, a female prison and the North Dublin Union. On rising ground half a mile due north lay Broadstone station, the terminus of a railway line running from Galway and the British army's artillery base at Athlone. Broadstone was crucially important because if it fell into enemy hands the military could launch a counter-attack from the station.

Because court sittings had been suspended for the Easter vacation Daly's column discovered the Four Courts virtually deserted. After some hesitation the solitary policeman on guard duty opened the gate and handed over his keys before being made prisoner. A caretaker discovered in the basement was allowed to leave. Volunteers were soon systematically radiating throughout the complex while others cut telegraph and telephone wires on the roof, or occupied the adjoining Four Courts Hotel and houses in nearby streets. Simultaneously, a group of sixty-five Volunteers had marched from Blackhall Street to North Brunswick Street and halted in front of St John's Convent to an enthusiastic reception from the nuns. Daly established his battalion headquarters in a room in the convent's entrance hall but transferred next day to the Father Mathew Hall in Church Street, whose central location gave him greater control over his command area. The building, which belonged to the local Capuchin priory, could also serve as a prison and first aid station. Not until Easter Friday, and only then in the face of mounting British pressure, did Daly again shift his headquarters to the Four Courts, where the largest concentration of his Volunteers was based during the Rising.[8] While the Four Courts was being occupied other Volunteers erected barricades along the quays and established outposts in nearby buildings, while some units on the northern fringe of Daly's command area tried unsuccessfully to demolish three railway bridges with inadequate supplies of ammunition.

One of Daly's most important outposts was the Mendicity Institution on Usher's Island, whose capture was assigned to Sean Heuston, a 25-year-old railway clerk. He couldn't have looked more different from the immaculately uniformed Daly, with his thick-soled boots and brown tweed suit incongruously combined with a Sam Browne belt and a green Fianna hat that was a size too small for his head. It could have made him look ridiculous but Heuston's constantly calm exterior concealed considerable depths of strength and passion and none of the men doubted his commitment, reliability and competence. Originally the Military Council seems to have envisaged him as commandant of a new headquarters battalion based in the GPO and Connolly's decision to deploy him to the Mendicity seems to have been a last-minute improvisation brought about by the original Mendicity leader's failure to show up on Easter Monday morning.[9] The building itself became Daly's responsibility, although it didn't appear in his pre-Rising plans, as it was located south of the Liffey and outside his battalion's normal recruitment area and field of operations. Throughout the Rising Heuston was to report much more frequently to Connolly than his own commandant. It all gave a semi-detached air to Heuston's mission.

When Heuston's unit left Liberty Hall his dozen men didn't know their destination, let alone that this wasn't yet another route march ending up back at battalion headquarters. No doubt with barely concealed excitement, Heuston led them over Butt Bridge and right along the quays. Patrick Stephenson recalled:

> silence in the ranks as Sean led us along the south quays but there was a tremendous amount of speculation going on in our minds about our destination. We had passed over Parliament Street and were abreast of Adam and Eve's before anyone spoke. We had been watching the back of the silent marching figure at our head since we left Beresford Place for some sign and listening as we approached each corner for the order to turn left or right. But none came. We began to question each other as we marched. We were getting very near Battalion Headquarters now, and someone said, 'This is all a bloody cod, the damn thing is off again.'[10]

Disappointment percolated through the ranks as they pushed on, yet Heuston appeared serenely oblivious to an audible muttering behind. He gave no indication of his ultimate intentions except to his much-trusted lieutenant, Sean McLoughlin, a precocious 18-year old who was beginning one of the great adventures of Easter Week. At last the column reached Usher's Island and halted in front of the Mendicity and as the angelus bell rang:

> Sean turned right about, faced us and shouted, 'Company left wheel, seize this building and hold it in the name of the Irish Republic.' At once our pent up feelings

of bewilderment and frustration sought relief in yells and shrieks and with a wild
rush we went in through the open gates, up the stone steps and in the front door.[11]

The Mendicity Institution was located in the much-altered shell of Moira House,
once a sumptuous and beautiful town mansion where the elite of eighteenth-century Dublin socialised; the city's destitute could now get two free meals there every
day.[12] Its once beautiful garden replaced by a barren courtyard, it was pervaded by an
atmosphere of poverty and decay. But it occupied a commanding site for the only
insurgent position that could prevent, or at least delay, a British advance from the
Royal Barracks towards the GPO and the Four Courts, as well as hindering troop
reinforcements moving from Kingsbridge station into the city centre. Heuston's
insurmountable problem was that with such a small garrison command he couldn't
even fully secure the building itself and had to restrict the occupation to that part
facing the Liffey and covering the back windows with blankets. Stephenson recalled a
miniature riot breaking out in the front room as:

> furniture was manhandled into the windows, the glass was smashed out of the
> frames, the curtains were ripped down and stuffed in between the sashes and the
> furniture as a substitute for sandbags. The china ornaments, vases, and a glass case
> of stuffed birds were broken in the fireplace to reduce the chance of wounds from
> flying glass. A bucket of water was provided in case of fire. Everything in the nature
> of cloth in the room was stuffed into the barricades at the windows, and anything
> likely to burn was jammed into the fireplace. In the midst of all this shoving and
> pushing a woman's voice screamed inside the house while from the back came
> hoarse cries and angry shouts as the unfortunate down and outs denied their chance
> of their midday meal, were being hustled out of the basement dining hall across the
> courtyard at the back and into Island Street.[13]

Connolly didn't expect the Mendicity to hold out for more than a couple of hours
before British troops overwhelmed it, but he hoped that Heuston could buy sufficient time to let Volunteers occupy other positions in the city centre.[14]

Daly's battalion was in action almost immediately because of fifty lancers from
Marlborough Barracks riding westwards along the northern quays, escorting
two horse-drawn wagons full of cases of ammunition from the North Wall docks.
Commanded by Lieutenant Sheppard, they were going to the Magazine Fort in
Phoenix Park and Volunteers had actually allowed them to pass unhindered at Liberty
Hall and the top of O'Connell Street while Sean Connolly's City Hall garrison on
the other side of the river left them to the Four Courts garrison. Alerted by shooting
from the direction of Jacob's and the GPO, Sheppard became increasingly uneasy
and sent ahead a scout who spotted armed men on the roofs of houses near the
end of Ormond quay. But he was shot dead riding back to warn the main column
which then came under fire from Volunteers at a barricade on Church Street Bridge
about 50 yards away.[15] Three riders who fell wounded off their horses were captured
and taken inside the Four Courts but most lancers charged wildly up Charles Street
searching for cover. As Volunteers continued firing and terrified horses reared and
plunged trying to escape from danger, Sheppard got his dazed men and the ammu-

nition into an empty house that he protected by overturning the wagons. A local shopkeeper, John Clarke, observed the lancers not offering a single shot in reply to continuous rebel volleys; this was because they only had five rounds each and their rifle grenades were useless without detonators or cartridges. Anyone attempting to escape through the north end of Charles Street was forced back by heavy fire from the rear of the Four Courts, though some managed to reach the Bridewell police station in Chancery Street. Later, when Volunteers entered and searched this building they found four saddles and bridles, four dead horses lying in the courtyard and two lancers hiding in a cell.[16]

With every escape route blocked the lancers remained cooped up in Charles Street until they were relieved on Friday morning. Although they were relatively secure their conditions were harrowing, particularly as 'the horses, after a few days, became maddened by hunger and several had to be destroyed by the soldiers. Eventually the rest were cut loose and ran wild about the locality, the clattering sound of their hoofs in the darkness occasionally raising false alarms at Volunteer barricades.'[17] Daly's men celebrated their victory by placing a captured lance surmounted by a tricolour in a barrel of sand at the junction of Church Street and North King Street and firing a volley of revolver shots.[18] Their ambush of the lancers and the sound of battle from the Mendicity galvanised the Four Courts' 100-strong garrison into making their position secure; they were vulnerable to attack from all sides. To the north, Broadstone station was soon in military hands; in the west lay the Royal Barracks, Marlborough Barracks and Kingsbridge station where troops were soon arriving from the Curragh; to the south, army units from Dublin Castle were by mid-week fanning out along the quays and building up positions in the Capel Street area east of the Four Courts. The Four Courts gates were closed, windows smashed and barricaded with books, furniture and sandbags, guards posted at the various entrances and snipers stationed on the roof. The Lord Chancellor's office was converted into a first-aid post furnished with beds that had been commandeered from neighbouring hotels. Throughout Easter Week the Four Courts was to prove a secure base from which Volunteers could be dispatched to various outposts and in the Rising's final stages it became Daly's headquarters and a relatively safe haven for retreating rebels.[19]

From Monday onwards reinforcements arrived at the Four Courts, bringing Daly's resources to almost 300 men. The new arrivals included Volunteers who had initially obeyed MacNeill's countermand while others were returning from missions such as the attempt to blow up the Magazine Fort. Nonetheless, garrison strength never came near the levels that Daly had anticipated. Nor initially did he have a first-aid post in his command area. On Tuesday Cumann na mBan members responded to an urgent appeal, some collecting medical supplies at the GPO and others acquiring dressings for prospective patients from local houses and 'stimulants' (whiskey and brandy) from a public house. A dozen women stayed at Daly's HQ in Father Mathew Hall while others went to the Four Courts. There they were kept well away from the fighting, working in a kitchen at the rear, preparing food, washing up and filling vessels with water. Because windows had been sandbagged they worked always by candlelight though they could at least luxuriate by sleeping wrapped up in judges' ermine robes. They actually did little first aid work because casualty levels were much lower than expected and indeed most wounded men were treated in nearby hospitals.[20]

Within half an hour of arrival Heuston's Volunteers in the Mendicity were also fighting, in their case against a considerable force of British troops on their way from the Royal Barracks to strengthen Dublin Castle's defences. Stephenson watched fascinated as 'they erupted suddenly on the quays and continued to pour out in khaki bulk like a sausage coming from a machine', marching four-deep along the northern quays with their rifles at their slope and headed by an officer carrying a drawn sword. He thought that:

> the brass band alone was missing as the column came still nearer to us, and to add to the air of festivity a tram came running along the tracks from the Park. The Tommies had reached half way between Ellis Street and Blackhall Place, when possibly the strain becoming too much, someone fired. At that the reaction of the rest was instantaneous and we all let go.[21]

Firing mostly from the Mendicity's upper storey, with their view unobstructed by walls and railings, Volunteers poured several volleys into the soldiers' ranks, wounding nine and killing the commanding officer, Lieutenant Neilan.[22] The rest scattered panic-stricken, crouching behind the quay wall, hiding in abandoned tram cars or running into houses in side streets. Eventually they recovered and began returning fire across the Liffey. Soon afterwards another group of soldiers wheeled around the corner of Blackhall Place equipped, bizarrely, not with rifles but with picks and shovels, still apparently unaware of the recent fighting. When Heuston's men resumed firing these soldiers fled into Blackhall Place. Within a short time and out of sight of the Mendicity, British forces began concentrating in Queen Street and started firing at the building from a concealed machine-gun post:

> We were down under the cover of a window-sill in a flash, and for a while lay there stunned by the appalling din as the machine-gun continued to rake the front of the building without ceasing. It seemed as if some giant steel whip was lashing the stonework with a tremendous vindictiveness. Heuston shouted to us to hold our fire, but in truth all we could do was to lie watching the back walls of the room being riddled with bullet-holes and the plaster float around the room in a fine grey mist.[23]

One of the epic sieges of Easter Week had begun.

Yet it almost had a very different outcome; the Mendicity came close to falling or being abandoned on the very first day of the Rising. Under cover of the machine-gun fire soldiers began crossing Queen Street bridge and heading towards the Mendicity where they crouched under coping at the front of the building. Watching from a window, a lit candle in one hand and a bomb in the other, Stephenson watched the moving tip of a bayonet until the lead soldier reached the gateway and then, inexplicably:

> jumped across the opening like a rabbit and was gone to Watling Street. He was followed by his comrades. How many of these rabbits hopped across that opening I could not tell. They seemed to be innumerable. At last there were no more hopping Tommies and incredible as it seems even now, nothing happened, and quiet settled down again on the area. The expected assault had not materialised.[24]

All the soldiers had to do was blow open the gateway, rush into the courtyard and overwhelm the Mendicity's dozen defenders by sheer weight of numbers; instead, inexplicably, they returned to barracks. The garrison realised they had had a miraculous escape and Heuston became increasingly uncertain about again tempting fate. He dispatched Sean McLoughlin to the GPO with a request for more ammunition and Connolly grimly warned him that British reinforcements arriving at Kingsbridge railway station would soon probably attack the Mendicity. Towards evening Heuston became increasingly puzzled by McLoughlin's prolonged absence as well as Dublin's apparent normality. From his vantage point he couldn't hear any gunfire from the city centre, pedestrian traffic was still flowing and a tram that had been abandoned nearby since early morning suddenly sprang back into life and moved away. Fearing that the rebel leadership had been driven out of the GPO and that the Rising was destined to be a one-day wonder, Heuston decided to evacuate the Mendicity and his men were actually cleaning up the building and about to go home when McLoughlin suddenly returned with news that the GPO had been occupied, the Proclamation read out, a Provisional Government established and numerous buildings seized across the city. Overjoyed, the garrison 'yelled with delight and danced around in an excess of joy. We were now thinking in terms of how long it would take to establish the Republic over the whole of Ireland.'[25]

Meanwhile, Volunteers had blocked Church Street bridge, positioned units on the North Circular and Cabra roads, and erected eight large barricades in North King Street, four in Church Street, five in North Brunswick Street and others across the quays. One barricade in North Brunswick Street was over 14ft high. The materials for these obstructions had been requisitioned from local business premises, including a coach factory, a builder's yard, a foundry, a large bakery and a distillery, as well as furniture from private houses, bricks from a building site and vehicles wherever they could be commandeered. The barricades were often ramshackle but they proved cumulatively effective in an area 'penetrated by infinite passages and alleys and more nearly resembling a rabbit warren than a battle field. In such mean and compact streets the barricade system of the rebels was indeed formidable.'[26]

Many 1st Battalion's outposts were situated in business premises including Reilly's public house ('Reilly's Fort'), situated at the corner of North King Street and Church Street, which became of great strategic significance because of its clear view up North King Street as far as Bolton Street. Another important sniping post was Jameson's malt house in Beresford Street, while other units were located in Moore's coach works, Monks' bakery and Clarke's dairy in North Brunswick Street. These were Daly's most northerly positions and provided an open field of vision north towards Broadstone station which, as yet, Daly's limited resources had prevented him occupying. Other properties were held only briefly. Daly had vacated St John's Convent 'to avoid disturbing the nuns' and the North Dublin Union where shooting endangered the inmates as well as a growing number of local inhabitants seeking sanctuary behind its massive walls, including the entire male ward from Richmond Hospital.[27] Even in the union they weren't immune to danger because on Easter Friday morning, a 17-year-old boy and his father, who had mounted its clock tower to view the fires then raging nearby, were shot dead by a British military sniper in Broadstone station.[28] Once the Four Courts and its outposts were occupied Daly's men began combing the battalion area for supplies, commandeering weapons from a gunsmith, provisions from local hotels, shops and stores, and large stocks of flour, meal and cereals from Blanchardstown mills. They also seized Monks' bakery and forced its staff to maintain production for as long as flour supplies lasted. The battalion appears to have had plenty of food throughout Easter Week. In the North King Street area Volunteers supplemented fresh bread from Monks' bakery with supplies of tea, sugar, bacon, ham, tinned meats, cheese and milk. Local sympathisers also chipped in, including the Master of the North Dublin Union who provided 10-gallon cans of soup nightly while nuns from St John's Convent distributed meals to barricades and private houses. At the Four Courts a man went out every day to fetch bread, milk and meat, sides of bacon and mutton were prepared, a live sheep was brought in and cases of apples were stored in the basement.[29]

After attacking the lancers, Daly's men near the Four Courts had direct contact with Crown forces until Thursday. Fighting consisted of sporadic and inconclusive engagements and sniping from elevated positions, such as 'Reilly's Fort'. When John Clarke reconnoitred the neighbourhood on Easter Monday afternoon he discovered that 'It was safe at this time to move about as there were neither police nor soldiers to be seen'.[30] By Monday evening throngs of anxious and confused holidaymakers were arriving back in the Four Courts area, where they had to negotiate a way home through the barricades. At some they were initially allowed through individually or in small groups but later as their numbers grew they were escorted in a convoy system.[31] Volunteers expected an enemy attack and assumed that the British were preparing one inside their barracks; a mood of nervous anticipation descended on them, accentuated by the debilitating effects of sleep deprivation. Stationed on a roof in North Brunswick Street, Paddy Holloman imagined that 'every chimney pot was a soldier and I was shooting at them during the night. The nerves of everyone were at their tensest awaiting the expected attack.'[32] Stress increased even more because the area surrounding the Four Courts had been plunged into darkness, while inside the building officers wouldn't allow lights to be turned on.

Volunteer edginess was understandable because soon British snipers in the North King Street area had forced rebels down from the roofs of outposts such as 'Reilly's Fort' and the malt house. Other enemy marksmen using field glasses fired intermittently into the Four Courts. Volunteers manning barricades on or near the quays were especially vulnerable to enemy sniping. They sustained their first casualties on Tuesday in Lower Church Street when one man was killed and another two wounded. They responded with a steady, if indiscriminate, barrage along both sides of the river. However, the battalion's strategic position had already significantly deteriorated as the most northerly outposts fell rapidly to British soldiers from Marlborough Barracks. They then completed a military cordon along the north side of the city by employing intense rifle and machine-gun fire to force Volunteers off bridges on the North Circular and Cabra roads.[33] Cut off from the battalion command area, some men strove to join Connolly's force at the GPO and a number arrived there in the early hours of Tuesday. Others scattered northwards towards Glasnevin cemetery. On Wednesday Daly was still unaware that the bridges had been lost.[34]

Significantly, the Volunteers on the bridges had been attacked from Broadstone station which they had assumed was unoccupied, but then a scout sent by Daly soon reported it 'full of military'.[35] To reconnoitre and possibly seize the station Daly organised a party of fifteen men whom a priest blessed in front of St John's Convent while nuns recited prayers for their safe return. Cautiously approaching the station, they realised that the British were too firmly entrenched and retreated after a brief fight.[36] It was the last rebel attempt to capture the Broadstone, although throughout the week Daly's North Brunswick Street outposts constantly exchanged fire with its British occupiers.

The Mendicity was by far the most exposed position in Daly's command area. Soon after daybreak on Tuesday Heuston began assessing his garrison's situation, inspecting the building, checking side gates and the backs of houses in Thomas Street that dominated about half the courtyard of the Mendicity and its upper half. He also asked Dick Balfe about using clay from the small garden to make sandbags for the windows and questioned Stephenson about the best way of retreating up to Thomas Street if they were driven out.[37] By now, however, Heuston was infused with a new sense of purpose and only considered retreat to be a last resort. He intended holding out as long as possible and for the Mendicity Volunteers to play an important role in the Rising, not in a suicide mission, but through buying time for other garrisons in the city and giving them a fighting chance. After wavering on the previous day, Heuston had been given another opportunity and this time he grabbed it.

Just after nine o'clock he announced his decision to the men and sent McLoughlin to the GPO to get the reinforcements and supplies that he needed to defend the Mendicity. Heuston's men realised their vulnerability. Because of a dearth of suitable material they hadn't been able to barricade a large double wooden gate that led into Island Street, through which a British storming party could cross the courtyard. Furthermore, although the Mendicity was completely detached from adjacent houses, its side passages' high walls would provide perfect cover for enemy soldiers. Heuston didn't have enough men to occupy these houses and if the British did it would only be a question of time before they punched holes in the walls and came within 15ft of firing at the second floor of the Mendicity. But the garrison respected Heuston's dedication and leadership and their morale was high as they began preparing for an inevitable British onslaught. Already they could see the enemy erecting a barricade at the Watling Street end of Island Street and hear hammering from Watling Street itself as soldiers began boring their way through unoccupied houses.[38] In fact, these tactics suited Heuston's men because by eschewing a direct route the British were wasting time and allowing McLoughlin to secure more Volunteers. At the GPO Connolly was astonished and impressed to learn that the Mendicity was still holding out and allocated a dozen of twenty men that he had summoned from the Fingal battalion in North County Dublin. Under their captain, Richard Coleman, they had walked all the way in to O'Connell Street and were just recovering from exhaustion when McLoughlin began leading them to the Mendicity. On the way they discovered a British soldier hiding under a cart in a back garden and brought him to the Mendicity as a prisoner, ignoring his protestations that he was a deserter who wanted to join the rebels. Inside the Mendicity the Fingal Volunteers were greeted by loud cheering and applause from a garrison that had now expanded to twenty-six men. After allowing Coleman's unit some time to sleep and recover, Heuston placed the entire garrison on high alert overnight. The Mendicity came under sustained enemy sniping and there were never less than half the men on a two-hour watch at any one time, eating their food while positioned beside inadequately protected windows.[39]

Daly's battalion captured many prisoners, especially in the early days, including a group of soldiers seized at noon on Easter Monday while on their way to Fairyhouse racecourse. Others were detained along the quays, such as the poet peer Lord Dunsany who was in the uniform of a British officer when Volunteers ambushed his car at the Church Street barricade.[40] Close to the rear of the Four Courts on Easter Wednesday Volunteers captured the Bridewell police barracks in whose cellars they discovered twenty-five fatigued and hungry policemen whom they then marched to the Four Courts. There, Brigid Thornton was initially exhilarated by the sight of men 'wearing these capes and helmets with chinstraps and spikes on top. They looked to me like Germans and my first thought was that the Germans had arrived at last. But of course they were just policemen … and they did not know what to do with them.'[41] On Wednesday morning Daly's men also captured the isolated Linenhall Barracks in Yarnhall Street which housed the Army Pay Department. Initially they had surrounded and twice unsuccessfully attempted to set the building on fire before breaching the outer wall with gelignite, using sledgehammers to smash open a gate. Thirty-two beleaguered and unarmed clerks then emerged under a white flag accompanied by a single policeman. All of them were escorted to Father Mathew Hall where Daly put them to work filling sandbags for rebel barricades.[42] Volunteers bombed the complex to prevent its reoccupation but accidentally started a fire that spread with alarming speed to threaten adjacent tenements and houses. By Easter Thursday afternoon it had enveloped a local wholesale druggist's and detonated a huge store of flammable chemicals. To one onlooker the conflagration was:

> like a rearing furnace, really spectacular as barrels of oil were projected high in the air and exploded loudly. A stifling smoke cloud shrouded the district. On Thursday night, it was as bright as day. A pin could be picked up by the glare overspreading the surrounding streets. By Friday, it had subsided, though occasionally the dying flames flickered before it finally extinguished.[43]

The blaze was visible a quarter of a mile away in the Four Courts where a Volunteer watched an 'awesome spectacle' as the whole area lit up 'brighter than daylight'. It was Daly's greatest triumph and raised not just his own men's morale but that of Volunteers throughout the city. In the GPO Connolly praised 'Commandant Daly's splendid exploit'.[44]

Daly's prisoners appear to have been humanely treated. Some were released, while at the Four Courts British officers were given separate accommodation and received meals and bedding. One of them recalled 'the curious hardship of subsisting for the best part of a week on sherry, champagne, port, claret and Benedictine for food was very scarce and the cellars were well stocked'.[45] Another prisoner, Captain Brereton, praised his captors as 'not out for massacre, burning or loot. They were out for war, observing all the rules of war and fighting men. They fought like gentlemen … They treated the prisoners with the utmost courtesy and consideration.'[46] On Easter Friday, when fighting became intense, the prisoners were transferred to safer locations and Daly even struck up a relationship with one British officer whom he took into his confidence.[47]

As in other garrisons, morale in the Four Courts was temporarily sustained by rumours that Cork and Limerick were up and that 10,000 Germans had landed in Kerry, reached Kildare and were marching along the Naas Road towards the capital.[48] Despite Wednesday's successes, Volunteers realised even then that the British military net was relentlessly tightening around them, especially with a burgeoning military presence south of the quays. On the previous day a messenger had been able to carry ten dispatches to Connolly in the GPO but soldiers were now picketing road crossings and bridges and bringing Volunteer outposts under sustained sniper fire from the roofs of Christ Church cathedral, Power's distillery and Jervis Street Hospital – though the malt house garrison in Beresford Street used a powerful field-glass to locate and eliminate British machine-gunners at the hospital.[49] A scout had reported to Daly the danger of the lancers in Charles Street being reinforced and becoming a serious threat to the Four Courts, and so a message was sent to the GPO. Connolly agreed to mount a joint GPO/1st Battalion attack on the lancers' position at eight o'clock that evening, but it never materialised. A British advance from the City Hall towards Capel Street soon severed communications between the Four Courts and the General Post Office. Daly considered attacking enemy forces in Capel Street but didn't have enough men and even those he had would have been easy targets because of the brightness of the fires around the Linenhall Barracks. One Volunteer officer thought Daly was 'beginning to look very tired and haggard. His tunic was torn at the sleeve. I believe that he had not closed his eyes since the outbreak on Monday.'[50] Depressingly, there was little he could do to arrest his garrison's deteriorating strategic position, though on Wednesday night Volunteers trying to relieve the enemy pressure managed to ignite properties on the south quays that threatened their Church Street Bridge barricade. The flames engulfed seven houses before stopping just short of the historic Brazen Head Hotel.

In the west British forces based in Smithfield were threatening Volunteer positions. Soldiers had entered Blackhall Street soon after midday on Easter Monday and by Wednesday the whole surrounding area was 'black with Tommies'.[51] In an attempt to disrupt further enemy advances, Daly ordered men to destroy a footbridge spanning Bow Street whose seizure would have exposed the rear of his headquarters in Father Mathew Hall. Volunteers carried a large canister bomb on to the roof of a building and dropped it on the footbridge, but it failed to explode.[52] On Wednesday morning rebels also attempted to burn down the medical mission in Charles Street close to the side of the Four Courts but men dashing across the road to set the building alight were driven back by enemy fire.[53] At midnight, snipers in the Four Courts foiled an attempt by an ambulance crew to recover the body of a lancer officer.[54]

On Wednesday morning Heuston was shaken to discover that two men had deserted: Lieutenant Liam Murnane and a Volunteer named Byrne. Murnane had complained that 'it's murder to stay here' and simply went home after Heuston sent him with a dispatch to the GPO.[55] Murnane's defection devastated Heuston, who later told his brother that 'I would never have expected it from him. I trusted him more than the rest. He left his uniform behind and went away.'[56] Disappointed and angry, Heuston instructed his men to shoot Murnane if they ever saw him again – which indeed they did later at Frongoch interment camp in Wales after the surrender. They settled for just refusing to speak to him or acknowledge him in any way. Murnane and Byrne had got out just in time because on Wednesday morning the British cordon began closing rapidly and inextricably around the Mendicity. About 300–400 soldiers had flooded surrounding streets and ordered occupants out of their houses, at the same time they mounted machine guns on the roof of the Phoenix Picture Palace and on a bridge to the north. Across the river they placed snipers in houses and under the quay wall, and soldiers moved into the lane behind the Mendicity to block off Heuston's line of retreat.[57] As his small garrison got ready Heuston once again dispatched McLoughlin along with Stephenson to the GPO to tell Connolly about his beleaguered situation and extract whatever reinforcements they could from him. Connolly was euphoric that the Mendicity still hadn't fallen and summoned Clarke, MacDermott, and Pearse to hear the news as well as dictating a glowing message of praise to Heuston and his men. But that was all he could send because another British military cordon was tightening around the General Post Office itself. The Mendicity was on its own.[58]

James Brennan recalled how:

> the British opened an attack from all sides; close quarter encounters were frequent; I remember firing at a soldier only twenty feet away. Machine gun fire and rifle fire kept up a constant battering on our position. Heuston constantly visited the posts to cheer up the men. But he knew the position was hopeless.[59]

Unlike on Monday, these soldiers were good shots and at around noon they crept along the quay until they reached the protection of a wall in front of the Mendicity. They began hurling hand grenades into the building through its shattered and unshuttered windows. This change of tactics proved decisive because although Heuston's men tried catching the bombs and throwing them back, two Volunteers, Liam Staines and Richard Balfe, were seriously wounded. According to Brennan 'The small garrison had reached the end of its endurance. We were weary, without food and short of ammunition. We were hopelessly outnumbered and trapped.'[60]

Heuston faced the certainty of soon being overrun and admitted later that 'they were bringing the place down on us and we had to surrender'.[61] After consulting his men Heuston decided that it was his duty to save the wounded and indeed his entire garrison by capitulating. He threw out a white sheet but soldiers continued firing. He then sent out his soldier prisoner, but the British made him return with a message that they would only deal with a Volunteer. So Heuston came to the door, showed a white flag and surrendered with his twenty-three men. The Mendicity became the first rebel garrison to capitulate.[62] Led by a Volunteer waving a white flag, they left through the back gate into Island Street where a British sniper shot dead a Fingal man, Peter Wilson. Why this happened is still unclear. Perhaps the sniper wasn't aware of the surrender. Another Fingal man, James Crenigan, thought Wilson was trying to escape. Perhaps the soldier was just angry, as many of his comrades had been ever since the ambush at the quays on Easter Monday. Outside, the Volunteers were escorted past a formidable group of soldiers, some lying prone with their rifles cocked. Brennan and the others 'were compelled to march to the Royal Barracks with our hands raised, held behind our heads. The British were infuriated when they saw the pigmy force of twenty-three men who had given them such a stiff battle and caused them so many casualties.'[63]

The battle of the Mendicity was an extraordinary and indeed unique event in the Rising because at no other location did the British employ so much firepower and expend so many bullets to so little effect. Not only did they fail to kill a single defender before the surrender, they didn't even manage a scratch on one – the two serious casualties were really self-inflicted by men lifting grenades to hurl them back. Only one round did any damage to the defenders and that occurred after they had given up. The Mendicity's collapse also happened with remarkable speed. On their way back from the GPO McLoughlin and Stephenson went into an occupied confectioner's shop in Church Street to scout the final stretch to the Mendicity:

> To our amazement there was a Tommy on sentry-go in the front. Our excited enquiries of the men on the barricade elicited no information. No one had seen or heard any signs of attack on the Mendicity, as so far as they knew Heuston still held the post. But there was something wrong, that was obvious. We knew that when Heuston had sent us out that morning he had intended to hold out as long as he was able so he would not have evacuated voluntarily. There was only one alternative – the garrison must have been driven out in some way or another and were now prisoners, or perhaps all had been wiped out.[64]

Mystified, McLoughlin got as close as he could to the Mendicity and signalled without response or indeed getting any sign of life whatsoever from inside the building. None the wiser, he returned to Stephenson. Soon afterwards he went back again and met a lady employee who had been evicted on Easter Monday and she confirmed the Mendicity had fallen to the British and that Heuston's garrison were on their way to the Royal Barracks as prisoners. In Queen Street McLoughlin saw crowds of residents giving bread, butter and tea to soldiers and fled just as one person made to point him out as a rebel. He and Stephenson then made their way disconsolately to the Four Courts, but in fact McLoughlin's rising had really only just begun.[65]

As time went on normal civilian life around the Four Courts disintegrated. Transport and mail services collapsed, shops shut, newspapers became unavailable and the absence of gas forced residents to rely on candles. But Daly's battalion successfully discouraged looting. They also arranged for bread to be given out to queues of local inhabitants and conveyed supplies to local institutions such as St John's Convent. Movement in the area became increasingly dangerous as two early casualties in Father Mathew Hall discovered after they had been 'fired on and wounded on refusing to halt their motor car when called on by the Volunteers'.[66] Residents in North King Street were progressively evacuated, especially after the fire at the Linenhall Barracks. Some sought refuge at the municipal technical school in Bolton Street, but most fled to the North Dublin Union which eventually housed 400 refugees, most of them women and children.[67] John Clarke, who lived on the fringe of Daly's command area, didn't vacate his home but he became increasingly apprehensive. When strolling on Easter Wednesday a fellow shopkeeper on Ormond quay warned him that he was 'walking into death'. Shortly afterwards two men were wounded nearby and a young man was shot inside the porch that Clarke and his friend had just vacated. They carried the casualty to Jervis Street Hospital and 'the moment the doctor saw him, he ordered a priest'. That night the danger of breaking the curfew, which extended from 7.30 p.m. to 5 a.m., was brought home forcefully to Clarke:

> In early or dark hours, it seems there was a poor man walking through … Charles Street and the soldiers in the Medical Mission [who had been attacked on Wednesday morning] shot him dead. There he lay on the street outside Doyle's until Friday evening, when four brave fellows walked up carrying a white flag and stretcher.

Next day, Clarke roamed the neighbouring streets for a last time and was standing in Strand Street when heavy firing commenced: 'The earth shook. I lost all nerve. How was I to get home? I darted out on the quays, got in safely and shook hands with myself. Not out since.'[68] Mounting casualties had begun to stretch the resources of local hospitals. By Easter Friday morning there were about thirty bodies in Jervis Street Hospital, which also treated many civilians who were wounded while searching for food.[69] Before the street-fighting became intense, Volunteers passed freely in and out of Richmond Hospital bringing their most severely injured, but less serious cases were treated at their own first aid station in Father Mathew Hall. Several doctors from the Richmond helped out as well as a dozen Cumann na mBan women who, at great personal risk, also prepared and delivered meals to the barricades and outposts.[70]

The Mendicity's fall – which Daly had watched from the quays – had left his battalion more exposed by allowing the British to advance further along the quays.[71] On Thursday morning Volunteers repelled twenty soldiers on Usher's quay but the British assault from across the river intensified and defenders retreated from the bridge soon afterwards. The Four Courts garrison became increasingly vulnerable. Volunteers feared a frontal assault by the enemy and redeployed to the side facing the quays, but the attack never came. Sniper fire was an all-pervasive danger to completely exhausted Volunteers pitiably exposed at inadequately barricaded windows. At one upper-floor window on the west side of the building a bullet hit Sean O'Carroll on the tip of an elbow while beside him Thomas Allen was also struck, fatally, when a round pierced his left lung. Because of the incessant gunfire, Father Augustine was forced to crawl on his hands and knees to reach Allen and lie beside the body in order to anoint him.[72] The most terrifying moment of the Rising for the Four Courts men came when the British positioned artillery on the south side of the quays and immediately fired a round into the building. When another three hit the south-east corner the women were ordered to shelter under the stairs. Con O'Donovan recalled: 'a shattering explosion. The room trembled. For more than a minute I think we didn't realise whether we were dead or alive amidst the debris, dust and smoke. We made our way to the ground floor where we found out comrades praying for us as if we were dead.'[73]

As the likelihood of an all-out military assault grew by the hour, Daly spent Wednesday and Thursday preparing for a last stand by strengthening barricades and strategically placed outposts. In North King, North Brunswick and Church streets glass was removed from shop windows and the frontages blocked with corrugated iron while Volunteers were also positioned at upstairs windows behind bags of meal and sawdust and ordered to scrutinise every movement carefully. The first significant British manoeuvre occurred on Thursday evening when General Lowe ordered the Sherwood Foresters to move out of Dublin Castle and occupy Capel Street and Parnell Street. After forcing their way across Capel Street Bridge the soldiers moved towards the quays despite heavy fire from the Four Courts in which bullets struck parapets and tramlines causing sparks as they ricocheted. After securing a city map from a newspaper office, they erected barricades along both sides of Capel Street, driving a wedge that completely cut off Daly's command area from the GPO, allowing the British to saturate the entire area with troops.[74] When the Capuchin priests, Fathers Augustine and Albert, heard confessions in the Four Courts and one of the Volunteers raised the possibility of the garrison fighting its way out into open country, Captain Frank Fahy 'smiled and said that it was impossible, as they were being gradually surrounded'.[75] Concerned at his battalion's growing isolation, Daly summoned an officers' conference at midnight on an open space in front of 'Reilly's Fort'.[76] Illuminated by the glow from the burning Linenhall Barracks, they discussed sending a party to force a way through to the General Post Office, but the flames' intense light made such an operation foolhardy because Volunteers would have been an easy target for enemy snipers.[77]

That the tide of battle was running irreversibly against the rebels became clear on Friday when the first British armoured cars arrived in Charles Street. Their immediate task was rescuing the trapped lancers and removing Lieutenant Sheppard's body from Collier's dispensary across the way from the medical mission. Then, reinforced by the South Staffordshires operating from their base in Trinity College, the British launched their assault in the afternoon. Soldiers began by placing around the Four Courts a cordon that passed from Bridgefoot Street and Queen Street in the west, along North King Street to Bolton Street and Capel Street on the east side, believing, mistakenly, that it lay outside the rebel area.[78] The main British thrust was westwards along North King Street from where they intended driving south into Church Street and finally on to the Four Courts. This surprised the Volunteers who had assumed that the main enemy attack would come from the west – from the Royal and Marlborough Barracks and Kingsbridge station, but troops there made no attempt to advance, content with sniping at rebel posts and barricades. Daly's men also thought wrongly that the British would launch a frontal assault on the Four Courts, but the building saw little action and after the first artillery shells landed the enemy ceased its bombardment. Even so the mood inside on Friday was apprehensive as defenders lay low and preserved their ammunition.[79]

The worst fighting by far occurred in the North King Street area to which Daly dispatched men to reinforce units struggling to resist the main British attack. Lieutenant-Colonel Taylor, the South Staffs OC, said later that the North King Street operations were 'conducted under circumstances of the greatest difficulty and danger for the troops engaged who were subjected to severe fire not only from behind several rebel barricades but [in some sections] from practically every house'.[80] The South Staffs official history described how:

> the successful storming of a barricade achieved no more than to drive its defenders into the houses, and having emerged by back doors, they were able to repeat their resistance further along the street. [Their strength was because] they reinforced or

were reinforced by sniping posts in the houses of the street. [They] delayed the troops and made them a steady target. [The snipers were mostly] isolated rifle-men, shooting from sandbagged windows ... They had so situated themselves as to be able to inflict maximum casualties on the English troops with minimum loss to themselves.[81]

Frontal attacks risked repeating the battle at Mount Street Bridge in which the Sherwoods had suffered grievously, and so armoured cars containing up to twenty men were employed to approach rebel strongholds at high speed. Half the party would suddenly erupt from the vehicle and, under covering fire from those inside, they would storm the nearest buildings and take up positions at top windows. Meanwhile, the rest would be dropped at the corner opposite to repeat the manoeuvre.[82]

The first attacks were sudden and dramatic when at daybreak on Friday, an armoured car accelerated along Bolton Street and screeched to a halt outside the municipal technical school. After the building was stormed it served as the headquar-ters of the commanding officer, Lieutenant-Colonel Taylor. A barricade was then put across the street, snipers positioned on the roof and residents questioned to gather intelligence about Volunteer numbers and dispositions. Taylor's men quickly captured corner houses at the junction of North King Street and Bolton Street which became a useful first base of operations on the fringes of the rebel stronghold. It was over the next 150 yards that the real battle was to be fought. As troops attempted to push through North King Street and on to Church Street, a ferocious fight occurred at the first rebel barricade outside 27 North King Street. Although only a few Volunteers manned this house they received supporting fire from successive barricades behind them, as well as outposts such as 'Reilly's Fort'.[83] One account describes how:

> Whilst advancing in the darkness the military fired into practically every house in the line of advance, and the few terrified inhabitants who had had the temerity to remain throughout the terrible night took refuge in the cellars or by lying flat, face downwards on the floor, sought to escape the continuous fusillades, whilst the flying bullets shattered everything around. In storming the houses several soldiers were shot down. During the conflict a soldier bursting in a door accidentally killed a comrade beside him through the premature explosion of the gun.[84]

Repeated British assaults were hurled back and, as night fell, the attack ground to a standstill amidst steadily mounting casualties. However, soldiers had occupied houses commanding the first barricade and by Saturday daybreak its defenders had retreated to avoid certain annihilation. Troops could now advance under cover towards Church Street by boring through terraced houses that ran along the south side of North King Street and consequently Volunteers and soldiers on opposite sides of lower North King Street were soon firing at each other from almost point-blank range. Defenders crouched in the shadows or beneath splintering window sills whose protective bags of meal had been sliced to pieces. In this small area the fighting was of concentrated ferocity and the pressure on combatants was increased by intense and all-pervasive noise from gunfire, shouted commands, screeching armoured cars and the crash of artillery shells. The darkness was also pierced by the flash of rifles and machine guns and the glow of burning buildings as nervous combatants were only too aware that, unseen but close by, were men seeking to kill them. A couple of Volunteers from 'Reilly's Fort' crept into a disused house in Beresford Street carrying hand grenades with which to attack passing armoured cars, but just as one man carefully opened an upstairs window and lit a match to ignite a grenade the momentary gleam was spotted by a British sniper, whose bullet passed clean through the Volunteer's hat.

While the battle raged anyone stepping into the open was inviting disaster but John Shouldice, who manned barricades at the Church Street/North King Street crossing, recorded troops making at least one open attack at dawn on Saturday on his barricade facing Bolton Street while his unit gave 'a hot reception' to about fifteen soldiers rushing into Beresford Street about 50 yards up North King Street. This was 'a veritable death trap' because the attackers were vulnerable to fire from Volunteer snipers in cottages backing on to Beresford Street and the malt house. According to Shouldice the soldiers were 'practically wiped out' and after the survivors retreated Volunteers collected about a dozen rifles, shattered and useless: 'This finished the open attacking by the military who continued their tactics of breaking through house to house to reach our positions'[85] – just as they had done at the Mendicity. Capturing the first barricade at No 27 North King Street had cost the British thirteen dead and wounded, and after breaking through they avoided frontal assaults and even more heavy casualties by advancing under cover, boring through walls and moving forward yard by yard, house by house. Nevertheless the inexorable advance of troops and their intense machine gun and rifle fire – from North King Street, Capel Street, the back of Monks' bakery and Smithfield – progressively forced insurgents to abandon the barricades in North King Street; most retreated into houses but a few joined the unit in 'Reilly's Fort'. There, ammunition supplies had been running ominously low since before dawn on Saturday and, at 4 a.m., the officers held a conference at which they agreed that, despite the risks involved in crossing North King Street, two Volunteers should be dispatched to Father Matthew Hall to obtain additional supplies. On their return one of them, Patrick O'Flanagan, was caught up in machine-gun fire directed from North King Street at the corner of the public house. He was attended by Father Albert and a doctor from Richmond Hospital, where he was taken but died of his wounds.[86]

Because Father Mathew Hall had become increasingly vulnerable to the British advance, as well as being congested with wounded Volunteers and civilians, Daly transferred his headquarters, arms and ammunition on Friday to the Four Courts. The Army Pay Corps prisoners were escorted to the Bridewell, 'under heavy fire, the bullets spattering the walls around the party who stumbled in the dark over obstacles strewn between the barricades'.[87] Inside they were confined in three large cells on the ground floor but were treated well and men who had served on the Western Front even regaled their guards with a running commentary about how to distinguish between the different sounds of shotguns, rifles and machine guns. At one point they faced great danger when a large water main burst and threatened to drown them, but the leak was repaired. At this time a heavy artillery bombardment was under way and, presumably unaware that the Bridewell was in rebel hands, Dublin Castle notified it by telephone on Friday morning that the military were about to shell the Four Courts and advised them to take shelter in the cellars. Meanwhile, the twenty-four policemen from Bridewell station, held since Wednesday, were released.[88]

Inside Father Mathew Hall, Bridget Thornton recalled 'the enemy closing in. The fighting was intensifying, the firing deafening'.[89] The hall's windows were riddled by sniper fire from Smithfield and beds in the first-aid post had to be rearranged to protect the wounded. About a dozen Cumann na mBan members continued preparing food and, accompanied by Father Augustine, they risked gunfire to distribute it to Volunteers at posts and barricades in Church Street. Further heavy casualties were suffered as soldiers reduced more rebel barricades and outposts and by daybreak on Saturday, troops held strong positions on both sides of lower North King Street. At 6.30 a.m. on Friday Lowe was informed that the cordon around the Four Courts had been completed. By 9.00 a.m. Volunteers had abandoned a barricade in Beresford Street and also 'Reilly's Fort' and were retreating on a broad line south into Church Street in the general direction of the Four Courts. Nonetheless, intense fighting persisted in this area with insurgents still active in the upper part. Volunteers attacked troops advancing up Church Street. Furthermore, strong outposts in North Brunswick Street, such as Monks' bakery, Clarke's dairy and Moore's coach works, lay outside the military cordon. By the time the last volley was fired, late on Saturday afternoon, the operation had cost the South Staffordshires sixteen dead and thirty-one wounded. Treating the wounded Volunteers had exhausted the supplies of drugs and dressings in Father Mathew Hall and transferring them to Richmond Hospital became impossible once the military cordon on North King Street had been completed. A British officer later claimed that 'the men in the Four Courts had been nearly off their heads with strain' and certainly the records describe symptoms such as 'shock and fatigue', 'shock and fainting fits' and 'shock and loss of nerve later in night'.[90] One Volunteer went mad and had to be handcuffed to a bed.

By this time Daly had concluded that his garrison's parlous situation necessitated him considering desperate measures and he even sounded out a British prisoner, Lieutenant Lindsay, who told him his position was hopeless and that he should surrender.[91] Insisting that he couldn't do so without orders from his superior, Daly convened an officers' conference just after midday. This decided to launch a counter-attack that evening to regain lost positions and relieve enemy pressure on the Four Courts. Daly's officers also hoped to re-establish contact with leaders whom they believed were still occupying the GPO. Beaslai recalled that 'we were only too well aware of the fires that had been raging in O'Connell Street which lit up all Church Street and made night as bright as day but we were not aware that the GPO had been evacuated and was now a smoking ruin'.[92] The conference intended sending a Volunteer to the General Post Office to consult Connolly, but if no reply was received by nightfall they would launch a counter-attack. But even as they debated one officer pointed out that an unusual calm had descended on the city.[93] Beaslai had noticed it too because:

> For many hours, day and night, our ears had been deafened by the incessant noise of bullets from every part of the city – our own Howth rifles. All this had now ceased. There was certainly a lull but it seemed to us it must only be temporary and the enemy was preparing for an attack on all the positions.[94]

Exhausted, Beaslai went to bed and was asleep at four o'clock in the afternoon when Pearse's emissary, Nurse Elizabeth O'Farrell, and Father Augustine arrived with a copy of Pearse's surrender order: 'He was very much cut up about it but accepted his orders as a soldier should.'[95] At the back of the Four Courts Daly told Eamonn Duggan, the battalion adjutant, before going out to meet a British officer who had been allowed in through a barricade. Meanwhile, Duggan was violently shaking Beaslai awake, shouting 'Connolly has surrendered unconditionally'.[96] Beaslai was stunned because he knew Connolly well and had never dreamt that a general surrender was a possibility, always assuming that every garrison and post would fight to the very end. Michael O'Flanagan recalled how a dumbfounded Beaslai 'scoffed at the idea, pointing out that the post was impregnable, and could be held for a month'.[97] However, by the time Beaslai reached the back railings he saw Daly saying 'very well, it is the fortune of war' and exchanging salutes with the British officer before handing over his sword. As Daly returned he beckoned Beaslai and:

> he led me indoors and to the private room of the battalion staff. We sat down and he handed me a small typed document with Pearse's signature. It was the order to surrender. I looked up. His head was buried in his hands. He was weeping. I was still in a degree unable to assess the situation.[98]

Having surrendered without even consulting his officers, Daly made his way to the hall where garrison members had gathered after Duggan told them about the surrender. One Volunteer remembered how 'the news spread like wildfire', with angry men vowing never to give up their weapons.[99] Daly didn't flinch, confronting a good friend who was waving an automatic pistol and telling him, 'If you fire a shot you must fire at me. I have my orders from the Commander-in-Chief. I have given my sword and my word to the British officer and nobody shall go back on it.'[100] At this point Father Augustine intervened by insisting that the garrison had to surrender or be wiped out – hardly an appealing argument to the many men who preferred making a last stand. According to Beaslai, 'Daly interrupted him. "We don't give a damn about that, Father," and he said "We must surrender because we have the order from our Commander in Chief."'[101] It was saving the lives of civilians and especially women and children that Daly stressed and, while he admitted with surprising candour having been beaten by a superior force, he reassured the garrison that they had done their duty and could carry themselves with pride after redeeming Ireland's name. The Volunteers were then instructed to hand their rifles through railings to British soldiers outside.[102] Aware of his battalion's grave situation Daly must have been relieved that the Rising had ended without further loss of life. Ten Volunteers were dead and an indeterminate number wounded, though British casualties were greater. Civilian losses were impossible to gauge but by Friday there were already thirty bodies in Jervis Street Hospital and on Sunday 30 April local people were trying to identify dead bodies lying in a market near the Four Courts.[103]

Volunteers sleeping in the Four Courts were awakened and told about Pearse's surrender order as messengers summoned men in from the outposts. In the courtyard Bridget Thornton witnessed 'a terrible, shattering, chaotic moment. They cried, and they wept and they protested and they did their best to destroy their guns. I could see them hacking away at them.'[104] Beaslai was seriously irritated by a nervous British officer who 'affected an air of breezy familiarity as though he were about to conduct us in an excursion' in an attempt to jolly them along.[105] Eventually, after the garrison's rifles had been stacked inside British army lorries, the men fell in and a column of prisoners set off with Daly at the front and Beaslai and Duggan just behind. Marching through streets swarming with armed British soldiers and armoured cars, they left Chancery Place and proceeded along the quays. To Beaslai 'the sight of the familiar streets under these conditions was like something seen in a dream'.[106] Behind him a couple of young men were in tears while others were defiantly shouting 'We will rise again' at soldiers plodding silently alongside. Finally at around 8 p.m. the prisoners reached the foot of O'Connell Street and marched to the northern end, where Beaslai gazed at the shells of the outer walls of buildings on the east side that were still standing. When they stopped a British officer inquired who was in charge. Daly replied 'I am. At all events, I was', a remark that Beaslai considered he must have known would be his death warrant.[107] Daly was said to be quiet, calm and self-possessed throughout. By contrast Beaslai was in a foul mood, refusing to hand over his sword and breaking it over his knee instead, shouting 'Long Live the Irish Republic'. He was especially annoyed when a tall British officer waved his revolver and announced that prisoners' names would be taken and anyone giving a false one would pay for it:

> A fat little officer came to me with a notebook and asked me for my name and address. I told him. He asked me to repeat it. My nerves were on edge and this irritated me. I answered him sharply in an angry voice: 'You swine, don't speak to me like that or I'll smash your face', he said. The tall officer overheard him. He rushed over and levelled his pistol at my head: 'You don't realise your position,' he said: 'You are only a prisoner – and a rebel to boot.' Then turning to the fat little man he said, 'Put a special mark against that man's name.' Somebody behind me whispered, 'Keep quiet. Don't say anything. They only want an excuse to shoot us all'.[108]

Daly's men were marched to the grassy plot inside the railings at the front of the Rotunda Hospital where they remained overnight in the open.

Incredibly, even when the main column left for Richmond Barracks on Sunday morning, one of Daly's units had not yet surrendered. Still holding out were sixty Volunteers in North Brunswick Street, who had lost contact with the Four Courts after the closure of the military cordon in North King Street on Saturday morning. They conducted a fierce gun battle until late Saturday afternoon when news of the surrender was brought by Father Albert, a Capuchin priest. But their young commanding officer, Paddy Holohan, wasn't prepared to countenance unofficial instructions and told Albert that he and his men would hold out until the end. He remained intransigent even when the British broke off the attack and an officer under a white flag confirmed that Pearse had indeed surrendered. Holohan was adamant that he would only capitulate to a direct order from his commander-in-chief, so an overnight truce was arranged. But the truce seems to have been honoured more in the breach because Volunteers claimed that the British manoeuvred to gain territorial advantage while Lieutenant Taylor insisted that for some hours rebels continued firing, wounding his men and preventing the removal of wounded soldiers. Early on Sunday morning Father Columbus, another Capuchin priest, travelled to Arbour Hill Barracks where Pearse wrote, signed and dated an order of surrender. This was presented to Holohan at 9.30 a.m. and shortly afterwards the final surrender from the 1st Battalion took place outside Monks' bakery. It occurred under the gaze of the sisters from St John's Convent, one of whom stuffed a Volunteer's revolver up her sleeve. After Holohan briefly addressed his men they proceeded to Richmond Barracks and the last resistance inside Daly's command had come to an end.[109]

For the next ten days the South Staffordshire Regiment combed the Four Courts area and claimed to have found pistols, shotguns and dum-dum bullets. Even so, a number of rebels evaded capture. They included all the insurgent casualties in the Father Mathew Hall, who were evacuated on Saturday evening during the truce. The seriously wounded were carried on stretchers to Richmond Hospital, while those with minor injuries were smuggled into safe houses. By 11.30 p.m. on Saturday evening the hall was deserted, apart from the Cumann na mBan members who had helped organise the evacuation and destroy incriminating papers. The women were allowed by Father Augustine to sleep overnight in a small room in the church. On Sunday they attended early Mass and then slipped away with some Volunteers who were also in the congregation. Their escape was made easier by the crowds which had gathered outside the church searching for relatives.[110]

The Irish military historian Pat Hally has argued that throughout the Rising the Four Courts area was well held, well defended and well led. He considered that Daly had displayed fine military skills, concentrating his unexpectedly small force, establishing strong outposts, impeding the movement of British troops from the Royal Barracks, tying them down and delaying their attack, and then finally marching his garrison into O'Connell Street 'in perfect order'.[111]

7

The General Post Office

On Easter Monday morning it was evident that MacNeill's countermand had deterred many Irish Volunteers from mobilising. Only about 150 Volunteers and Citizen Army members assembled at Liberty Hall for duty with the Headquarters Battalion that was responsible for occupying the General Post Office (GPO). The Volunteers present consisted of companies drawn from the four city battalions as well as about seventy-five men from the 'Kimmage garrison' – Irishmen who had fled conscription in Britain or were on the run in Ireland. Based in a mill on Count Plunkett's Kimmage estate, they manufactured pikes, bayonets and most of the buckshot that was used in the Rising. In his capacity as Commandant-General of the Dublin Division, Connolly was to lead the Headquarters Battalion. As it prepared itself Mary Brigid Pearse pleaded in vain with her brother Patrick to return home and leave all such nonsense behind.[1] Just before the column departed at about 11.50 a.m. a Post Office employee in overalls set off to disconnect the telegraph and telephone wires in streets adjacent to the General Post Office.[2]

Connolly led the column with Pearse and Plunkett (swinging a sword cane) close beside him. In deference to age and ill health, Clarke and MacDermott had travelled ahead by motorcar and would be waiting for them at the Prince's Street corner of the GPO. Winifred Carney, Connolly's devoted political secretary, was the only woman to make the journey. One Volunteer officer has described how 'As the order "By the left, quick march" was given a rousing cheer rang out from the rather imposing crowd who had by then gathered in front of Liberty Hall. We had, for good or ill, set out on a great adventure.'[3] To remain as inconspicuous as possible, only a single cab full of ammunition and explosives was brought initially to the GPO while the chosen route avoided the main thoroughfares until the last moment by marching along Eden quay, turning into Lower Abbey Street and then wheeling right on O'Connell Street. From there it moved northwards, passing the Metropole Hotel where British officers on the pavement outside grinned and chortled. When the column reached the General Post Office at noon an order was given, 'Left Wheel! – The GPO! – Charge!'[4] The main entrance was invaded and a specially selected squad entering the side in Henry Street raced to occupy the roof. Downstairs, public customers and staff were hustled out and a number of British soldiers who had been in the GPO on private business

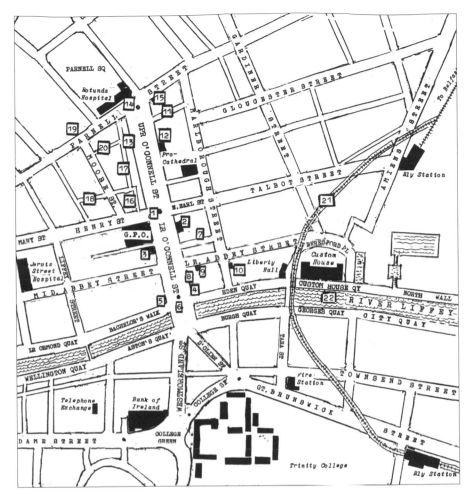

The General Post Office and O'Connell (Sackville) Street area

1.	Nelson Pillar	12.	Gresham Hotel
2.	Imperial Hotel	13.	YMCA
3.	Metropole Hotel	14.	Parnell monument
4.	Hopkins & Hopkins	15.	Tom Clarke's shop
5.	Kelly's gunpowder store	16.	Henry Place
6.	O'Connell monument	17.	Moore Lane
7.	Sackville Place	18.	Sampson's Lane
8.	Dublin Bread Co.	19.	Williams & Woods
9.	Wynn's Hotel	20.	Sackville Lane
10.	Abbey Theatre	21.	Loopline (elevated)
11.	Findlater's Place	22.	The *Helga*

were taken captive. The garrison then set about fortifying the building, which had the advantages of being situated in Dublin's main street, containing a vital telegraph office and providing roof snipers with a commanding view of the surrounding area.

From the start it was understood that Connolly was, in the words of Pearse, 'the guiding brain of our resistance'. However, it was not because Connolly cut an impressive military figure: many thought him a glaring contrast to the magnificently attired Plunkett with his immaculate uniform, riding boots, spurs and pince-nez. Slightly pot-bellied with bandy legs and an unkempt moustache, Connolly appeared a drab figure, but from the moment he entered the General Post Office nobody doubted that, while Pearse was titular commander-in-chief, it was Connolly who was in charge of military operations. His performance during Easter Week established indisputably that he was a born leader of men. It was a role for which, in a sense, he had been preparing himself for years, gradually shedding his earlier persona as a trade union organiser and agitator in favour of that of a charismatic military boss and theorist. By 1916 he was no longer referred to as Mr Connolly but routinely addressed as 'commandant', and an aura of remote authority surrounded him.

Since opening in 1819, the General Post Office had been the most impressive structure in O'Connell Street. Adjacent to it in the centre of the street the city's best known landmark, Nelson's Pillar, stood where the street's upper and lower sections met. This thoroughfare – popularly claimed to be one of the widest in Europe – originally provided residences for Dublin's aristocracy and professional classes, but during the nineteenth century it had become predominantly commercial in character. In 1916 it was lined with shops, offices, restaurants, a cinema and a number of large hotels including the Gresham and Imperial. Just beside the GPO was the Coliseum, a 3,000-seat theatre which, coincidentally, had opened on Easter Monday 1915; by Easter Saturday 1916 it was to be a smouldering ruin, never to be rebuilt. The General Post Office was situated on the western side of Lower O'Connell Street which ran from Henry Street to O'Connell Bridge, where a right turn took one westwards along the Liffey quays and past the Four Courts. Other important buildings in this section were the Hotel Metropole and Eason's stationers. On the opposite side Lower O'Connell Street ran from North Earl Street to the bridge where a left turn took one down Eden quay to Butt Bridge and Liberty Hall. Its most prominent buildings were the Dublin Bread Company, which was actually a large restaurant, the Imperial Hotel and Clery's department store.

The GPO was well over 200ft wide and 150ft long, and its three storeys stood 50ft high to the top of its cornice. Dick Humphries, a Volunteer and The O'Rahilly's nephew, observed that 'The building seems immense. The number of separate rooms in the place is unbelievable.'[5] While its interior was functional, the General Post Office was one of the major edifices of Dublin's eighteenth- and early nineteenth-century classical architecture. It was built from mountain granite except for a 50ft-long portico of Portland stone that included a pediment surmounted by three statues of Hibernia, Fidelity and Mercury and a tympanum decorated with the royal coat of arms. Above the cornice was a balustrade which ran round the entire building and completed its elegant exterior. The heart of the recently renovated building was the main sorting hall which extended to Henry Street and around this ran a block of offices whose windows looked out on to the street. A door and a glass partition separated this hall from the public office at the front. On the upper floors were a telegraphic office and a restaurant for staff.

Accompanied by a loud noise of breaking glass and hammering, the Volunteers now set about putting the GPO into a state of defence, knocking out windows, barricading them with furniture and posting guards. The door and glass partition were also smashed and screens were used to create a hospital, an armoury and a kit store that was stocked with boots, trousers, shirts and overcoats. The sorting tables were employed as beds and a secluded corner was soon set aside for Father Flanagan of the nearby pro-cathedral to hear confessions. Almost immediately news of the occupation began percolating through to the upper floors, where the most important room in the building, a communications centre, was situated at the very top. At the outbreak of war Arthur Norway, the secretary of the Irish Post Office whose own office was within the building, had insisted that an army sergeant and half a dozen Connaught Rangers should guard it, not against Irish rebels but against any German agent attempting to throw a bomb inside.[6] Inexplicably, and without Norway's knowledge or consent, ammunition eventually ceased being issued for the guards' rifles. Norway only discovered this after the Rising because at 11.45 a.m. Under-Secretary Nathan had suddenly called him to the Castle for an urgent meeting. Had he been inside the GPO when it was occupied he and the colt automatic that he kept in his desk would have provided the only resistance. Soon the chief technical officer alerted Post Office employees in the communications room that most lines – including the cross-Channel wires – had been severed. Then, at 12.30 p.m. the sergeant shouted a warning that rebels were ascending stairs to the northern entrance. With only unloaded rifles available he hastily organised a barricade of chairs and paper boxes to block the 10-yard long corridor from the top of the stairs to the communications room. After the guards retreated inside, the Volunteers led by Michael Staines fired their revolvers through the door, grazing the sergeant's head.[7] The noise in such a confined space terrified the female employees, who were ordered out of the southern end and into their retiring room, where they changed into civilian clothes preparatory to evacuation. The O'Rahilly's Volunteer unit had climbed the steps at this end and demanded that the superintendent and male clerks also surrender. Rebuffed, he ordered his men to force their way inside where they captured the soldiers. Staines was astonished to discover that they really didn't have a round of ammunition between them. The six Connaught Rangers also surprised Staines by asking for their rifles back so that they could fight with the rebels, only to be disappointed when he set them to work in the kitchen cooking meals for the garrison.

The shock and humiliation inflicted on the sergeant appeared to unhinge him; he adamantly refused to go to hospital because he was on duty until six o'clock that evening. Staines allocated four Volunteers to escort the sergeant to Jervis Street Hospital from which after his wound was treated they all returned to the GPO.[8] Subsequently he displayed increasingly delusional behaviour. Seeing a priest in O'Connell Street who was attempting to disperse a crowd he mistakenly concluded that the cleric was obstructing an outraged populace clamouring for his release. He screamed, 'I'm no religion no more! [sic] Look at the people of Dublin coming to rescue me and the priest is pushing them back!'

With the exception of a female supervisor who refused to leave, all remaining civilian staff were escorted off the premises. Afterwards they acknowledged The

O'Rahilly's chivalrous behaviour towards them. Initially suspicious or hostile because he had sided with MacNeill, the Volunteers quickly came to admire The O'Rahilly's generosity, courage and inspirational qualities as well as his energy and efficiency. He intended an honourable occupation of the GPO with no indiscipline, looting or criminality and almost immediately organised men to gather money from tills and deposit it in a safe. He was also responsible for the safety of prisoners – British soldiers, a Dublin Metropolitan policeman and later on, looters – whom he insisted on being treated humanely. It was a wise precaution because not every Volunteer shared his gracious attitude: 'One Cork man – Tom Walsh – had taken off the police-man's helmet and filled it with .303 bullets, saying he would like to put one of them through his head.'[9] Finally The O'Rahilly took command of the top floor and roof of the GPO, a post that assumed critical importance later in the week when British shells and incendiaries started a conflagration and he led firefighters attempting to dowse it. By the end of Easter Week The O'Rahilly had risen in the garrison's eyes to almost co-equal status with the leaders of the Rising.

The female supervisor stayed until late afternoon sending out telegrams about births and deaths, though Staines suspected her of trying to transmit information to the military authorities. Eventually he ordered her out of the GPO and assigned Volunteer J.J. Walsh, a trained operator, to continue sending out the messages. Later, however, Walsh contacted Cork, Galway, Athlone and Wexford and created consterna-tion inside the GPO by revealing to some men that these counties hadn't risen. When Staines reported this morale-threatening behaviour to Pearse he was told to have Walsh shot if he didn't desist – though Staines didn't take this seriously.[10]

Within half an hour of the occupation a tricolour had been run up at the Henry Street corner and a green banner with the inscription 'IRISH REPUBLIC' was hoisted on the Prince's Street side. Then at 12.45 p.m. Tom Clarke locked the doors and handed the Proclamation of the Irish Republic to Pearse who, accompanied by an armed guard, went outside. Standing on the step he read out the Proclamation and announced the establishment of a Provisional Government, of which he was president and commander-in-chief. This was a document that in time was to prove momentous: 'In the name of God and the dead generations ... Ireland, through us ... strikes for her freedom.' The right to freedom was fundamental; long usurpation by a foreign people could not extinguish it. Six times in the past 300 years the Irish people had asserted that right in arms: 'Having organised her manhood ... she strikes in full confidence of victory.' The Republic it now proclaimed guaranteed religious and civil liberty to all its citizens; 'cherishing all the children of the nation equally', it disregarded the differences 'carefully fostered by an alien government which have divided a minority from the majority'. The signatories invoked the blessing of the Most High God on the cause of the Republic and prayed that no one who served that cause would dishonour it by 'cowardice, inhu-manity and rapine'. In this supreme hour the Irish nation must by valour, discipline and readiness to sacrifice for the common good 'prove itself worthy of the august destiny to which it is called'. Clarke, the prison veteran who had dedicated his life to reaching this day, headed the seven who had put their name to this Proclamation. MacDermott, Pearse, Connolly, MacDonagh, Ceannt and Plunkett followed.

The Proclamation was the paced composition of an orator such as Pearse, who prob-ably wrote most of it. The sometimes overblown language and inflated sentiments only reflected the passion behind it. If it was stronger in rhetoric than historical and other realities of a deeply divided country, its understanding of 'the nation' was inclusive and generous. The dogmatic claim that through this group of revolutionaries Ireland was summoned to her flag, sprang from a conviction that they spoke from the country's deepest self and that freedom was essential for Ireland's well-being as a nation. For this, in the wider political spectrum, they would be classed as 'extremists'.[11]

There was a distinctly muted response from the crowd and only a few cheers before Pearse withdrew inside, after which hundreds of copies of the Proclamation were posted up around the city centre or taken to other garrisons. The Provisional Government was also keen to announce its Rising to the world and hoped to bypass British censorship by sending three Volunteers, including an ex-British army signaller, to occupy the Atlantic School of Wireless in Reiss's Chambers at the junction of Lower Abbey Street and O'Connell Street. They managed to reassemble its transmitter which had been dismantled as a wartime precaution and their messages were picked up in parts of Europe and on ships which brought the news to America. But this remained unknown to them and the leadership in the GPO because it proved impossible to get the receiver working before Reiss's was burnt out on Easter Wednesday.[12]

Two small but crucially important garrisons were also established early on Monday in Kelly's gunpowder store on the corner of Bachelor's Walk and Lower O'Connell Street, and in Hopkins & Hopkins, a closed and shuttered jewellery shop on the opposite corner.[13] These two positions fronted O'Connell Bridge and the Liffey quays and looked down towards College Green and Trinity College, from which direction a British counter-attack against the GPO was likely to come. The defence of both locations had been entrusted to Kimmage men, Hopkins to Seamus Robinson and Kelly's to Peadar Bracken, who had been in hiding at Kimmage since firing the shots at Tullamore in March 1916.[14] As Robinson's party attempted to force a way into Hopkins a party of lancers, escorting an ammunition train, came along Eden quay, having got so far because the guards protecting the ammunition stocks in Liberty Hall were only permitted to respond to a British attack. Even at O'Connell Street, where they sneered at the Volunteers, they did not grasp what was occurring, and they moved on, only to be cut down shortly afterwards at the Four Courts. Hopkins was finally entered through a hall door on Eden quay and after the building was fortified the garrison commenced tunnelling through adjacent premises. On the other side of the street Bracken had barricaded the ground floor of Kelly's and placed men at windows on the first storey, protected by large piles of books and ledgers. One Volunteer made bombs by filling kettles and saucepans with the shop's store of gunpowder and when the entire block down to Middle Abbey Street had been tunnelled every available vessel was filled with water in case the British cut off the supply.

Half an hour after Pearse had read the Proclamation the General Post Office garrison was in action in what is often described inaccurately as the 'Charge of the Lancers' down O'Connell Street. The cavalry had in fact been dispatched from Marlborough Barracks to investigate reported disturbances in O'Connell Street and were simply trotting down from the northern end, completely unaware of the danger ahead. When they reached Nelson's Pillar the waiting Volunteers in the General Post Office opened fire, killing three soldiers and fatally wounding another. One horse was also killed and its putrefying body lay in O'Connell Street till the end of the Rising.

About the same time, Liam Ó Briain encountered Eoin MacNeill and his son and Sean Fitzgibbon cycling along the Rathgar Road. After they adjourned to a nearby house, MacNeill said that although he was investigating rumours of Volunteer movements he still believed that only harmless route marches would occur. Fitzgibbon went off to gather more information but after returning he threw himself down on a sofa and shouted, 'They have started'. Although actual fighting hadn't yet commenced, Fitzgibbon knew, as a Headquarters Staff member, that the Volunteer dispositions he had seen must mean that hostilities were about to start. MacNeill still could not bring himself to accept this, but after a cycle tour Ó Briain stunned the chief of staff by reporting that the Citizen Army was in action at Portobello Bridge. MacNeill raged at the conspirators: 'I have been fooled, tricked and betrayed' he told Ó Briain:

> He sat down and stared at the floor for five minutes, not saying a word. I'd never seen a man so deep in thought. Then he lifted his head: 'I'll go home and put on my Volunteer uniform and I'll go out.' 'You'll go out,' I said, greatly surprised, 'after all that's happened?' 'I will,' he said quietly: 'People are fighting and dying. I will go with them.' Those words went through me like a knife.'[15]

Soon afterwards they were joined by councillor Tom Kelly and Father Nevin who found everyone 'in a state of utter consternation; John MacNeill and Tom Kelly chiefly stunned and bordering on desperation, because there was a rebellion on and they weren't in it'.[16] MacNeill was already anticipating the abuse that would soon be heaped upon him for ruining the Rising's chances of success. Nevin could see 'the mental torture he was enduring' and the 'anguished thoughts that were plainly written on his face'. But MacNeill literally couldn't make a move because of the fighting and his fear of arrest. However, when darkness fell MacNeill was determined to return home even though that involved passing two police stations. To Nevin 'he seemed dazed and reckless as to consequences' and the priest almost tried to restrain him physically as he mounted his bicycle. MacNeill only alarmed him even more by grasping something in his overcoat pocket and warning that 'if they attempt to arrest me they won't have it all their own way'. Nevin watched as MacNeill rode away, the last time he was to see him for fifteen months. When MacNeill finally arrived back at Woodtown and met his wife 'he threw himself on his knees on the floor with his head on her lap, and it was the only time in their long life together that she remembered him to have broken down and wept. "Everything is ruined," he said.'[17]

When order was finally restored in the General Post Office after the attack on the lancers, Tom Clarke and Diarmuid Lynch discovered reports in the RIC's pigeon-holes on the Irish Volunteers' strength and activities and 'chuckled at the fact that all their spying was in vain, and that neither the police nor their superiors realised the imminence of the climax'.[18] Clarke and MacDermott were now in their element; both men were physically and emotionally revived after the strain of recent days that had seemed to age the younger man. Lynch was delighted to see them sitting on the edge of the mails platform, beaming satisfaction and expressing congratulations amidst the frenetic activity in the central hall. It was:

full of uniformed Volunteers, boxes of ammunition, revolvers and automatic pistols lying on tables and chairs, knapsacks, blankets and tents. The middle of the hall had been allocated for use by the leadership, some of whom like Pearse and Clarke chatted while a sombre and tired Connolly was dictating notes to his secretary Miss Kearney [sic] who was typing furiously by his side. Plunkett and The O'Rahilly, who had just returned from a tour of inspecting the building's defences, were in jovial mood and laughing heartily.[19]

Outside, a few angry soldiers' wives attempted to force their way in but friends in the crowd dragged them away. In the late afternoon Frank Thornton of the Citizen Army transferred Liberty Hall's munitions stores in fifteen commandeered lorries and cabs under armed guard to the GPO. The last vehicle trundled into O'Connell Street just as the angelus bell rang. Liberty Hall was now empty except for a caretaker and another civilian but Thornton had left it barricaded and flying a Starry Plough, the Citizen Army's flag. He wasn't surprised when later in the week the British bombarded the building believing it was still occupied.[20] As brigade quartermaster, Michael Staines had all munitions taken to the sorting office at the back of the main hall where he used pigeonholes to segregate the different types of rifle and revolver ammunition.[21] The O'Rahilly's car stationed in the GPO yard was used frequently to bring in more ammunition from other locations while civilians also handed in bullets that they possessed or had found.

Thornton also brought with him a considerable number of latecomers who had arrived at Liberty Hall after the Headquarters Battalion's departure, and during Monday other reinforcements trickled into the General Post Office. These included the Hibernian Rifles (an organisation of Irish-American exiles), a group of older republicans who had been waiting for the call in a house in Parnell Square and individual Volunteers who made their way to O'Connell Street. Some had been delayed arriving at Liberty Hall; others were unable to reach one or other of the four battalion locations or had initially complied with MacNeill's order and then changed their minds. The GPO also became a magnet for civilians wanting to participate in an exciting adventure. On Easter Monday Liam Tannam was called to a window where two foreign sailors, a Swede and a Finn whose ship was in town, were appealing to be allowed to fight England, an ally of their detested enemy Russia. When the Swede said he could use a weapon Tannam decided to let them in, giving the Swede a rifle and the less-experienced Finn a shotgun, and put them on guard duty at the windows. Despite both men's enthusiasm Tannam had to supervise them closely, especially later in the week when:

> there was another alarm and again we moved to the windows but it was a false alarm. Everyone cocked his piece, including the Finn. When the alarm passed he stepped down off the barricade, banged the shotgun against the Terrazzo floor and off it went and down came a shower of plaster over six or seven of us.[22]

Not everyone demanding entry to the GPO was politically motivated. On Easter Wednesday Eamon Bulfin heard a voice shouting:

'I'm a Dublin Volunteer. I don't give a damn about anyone.' He staggered out to the middle of O'Connell Street where he was riddled with machine-gun fire. One of our men with a white flag, went over to where he lay, knelt down, said a prayer and dragged him to the side.[23]

The reinforcements eventually doubled the strength of the headquarters garrison. Winifred Carney was also joined by other women from the Cumann na mBan and the Citizen Army who arrived in the late afternoon. Connolly allocated them to the nursing and kitchen staff or appointed them dispatch carriers.

Feeding hundreds of men and women was a considerable undertaking but meals were served round the clock in the upstairs restaurant, allowing Volunteers to eat whenever they were relieved of their duties. Pearse, Connolly and other members of the Headquarters Staff took their meals in this canteen along with the rank and file, and even a captured British officer. Pearse, who did not consider him a fighting man, placed Desmond Fitzgerald in charge of the commissariat with the six captured Connaught Rangers and some Cumann na mBan women responsible for cooking and serving the meals. There was plenty of food since bread, groceries, meat and even chocolates had been brought in from nearby shops and a Kennedy bakery van had been commandeered. Staines also seized a large supply of milk cans from dairy engineering in Bachelor's Walk to store water in case the British severed the water supply – though it never came to this.[24] Despite the ample provisions Fitzgerald, who seemed to believe the occupation would last for months, made himself decidedly unpopular by doling out rather miserly portions.

One distressing development for the insurgents on Monday in O'Connell Street was having to watch civilians from nearby tenements engaging in looting and sporadic arson. Sean T. O'Kelly was sent out to stop them but he couldn't cope and on his return Connolly angrily rebuked him: 'Shooting over their heads is useless. Unless a few of them are shot you won't stop them. I'll have to send someone over there who'll deal with these looters.'[25] Clearly, however, Connolly never did get round to acting in such a ruthless manner. In Kelly's, Peadar Bracken held up several looters with his rifle and forced them to abandon their booty. One of his men, Joe Good, threatened to open fire and forced a group to place their jars of sweets on the pavement, but when he turned his head momentarily both the looters and the jars had disappeared. Good was later offered a new motorbike by a young boy who complained bitterly that he couldn't get the bloody thing started. A 21-year-old Londoner and the son of Irish parents, Good was another Kimmage man who had fled to Ireland in February 1916 to escape conscription.[26] On the other side of O'Connell Street, Brennan-Whitmore, who commanded the North Earl Street garrison, was followed into the first house he occupied by a crowd of looters whom he then had to eject.[27] Ultimately, all attempts either to intimidate or reason with the looters proved futile and the GPO garrison settled for an uneasy truce with them.

During Monday afternoon and evening more outposts were established close to the GPO, in houses in Henry Street and the block opposite the General Post Office. At the same time Volunteers erected barricades that were:

models of ingenuity. In a carpet and linoleum warehouse, the linoleum and carpets were arranged so that the unwary pursuer could be buried under an avalanche.

Another barricade stretched across Upper Abbey Street was made with the entire stock of a bicycle warehouse: thousands of bicycles, piled eight or ten feet high, jammed into each other. Fire had little effect on it. To cross it on foot was impossible. The most delightful of all was a barricade of clocks. At last I saw a use for those horrible marble clocks, like the ones inside the entrance to a bank. I had seen them in many homes, rarely keeping the correct time.[28]

On Monday afternoon The O'Rahilly persuaded MacDermott and Clarke to authorise Bulmer Hobson's release from detention. It didn't come a minute too soon for either captive or captors. Conlon had been landed with an intermittently obstreperous Hobson and guards who wanted to join the fighting:

They felt so keenly on this point as seriously to contemplate drastic action to rid themselves of the prisoner. They were even suggesting he should be executed and dumped on the railway line which runs at the back of my place but, possibly they were not really in earnest about this.[29]

In the unlikely event that they were, Conlon drew his revolver and indicated that it would, literally, only happen over his dead body. When Sean T. O'Kelly arrived at Martin Conlon's house with the release order he was shown into the parlour where he found Hobson sitting in an armchair holding a book, watched over by a guard holding a gun: 'I announced I had an order for the release of Bulmer Hobson and immediately relief was visible on all faces.'[30]

O'Kelly claimed, improbably, that when they left Hobson agreed to come to the GPO but only after he went home for his rifle. Any such promise, if given, can only have been intended to ensure a safe getaway. Instead Hobson remained at home until Tuesday morning when he went to stay with MacNeill at Rathfarnham, where he found an agitated chief of staff still craving to join the Rising. On Easter Wednesday MacNeill actually donned his Volunteer uniform, and was only dissuaded from setting out for the GPO by Hobson's protest that if he did so he would put those Volunteers who had obeyed his countermand in an impossible position.[31]

On Easter Tuesday, 25 April, Dick Humphries noted that:

The sun rose at 4 a.m. on a beautiful summer like day with a slight breeze coming in through the GPO's many glassless windows. O'Connell Street was eerie, silent, empty of people and with its cobbles snow-white with sheets of paper. Not a living thing is in sight. Even the birds shun the district.[32]

Some Dubliners still found it difficult to grasp the upheaval that had occurred in their city. A group of postmen gathered outside Hopkins the jewellers and debated whether to enter the GPO, but departed when a fellow worker reported that he had been threatened with a bayonet and warned that there would be no mail deliveries for some time to come. In the early morning Connolly ordered barbed wire to be placed across O'Connell Street to keep out civilians. Overhead tram wires were to be blown down and used as well. Inside the GPO a calmer regime now existed, with breakfast being served in the restaurant, guards on security duty and the hospital (which was filled with beds from the Metropole Hotel) fully functioning under Jim Ryan, a UCD medical student. All the ammunition, rifles and revolvers were now stored in one central department in the general sorting office and another room had been allocated for grenades.

During the morning lull Volunteers commandeered a car and went to Parnell Square, the headquarters of Redmond's National Volunteers, where they appropriated the armoury of rifles and ammunition.[33] Members of the Cumann na mBan brought in more rifles from dumps across the city and Quartermaster Jim O'Neill of the Citizen Army dispatched these weapons to various parts of the building. O'Neill also issued bombs (tin cans filled with explosive, each with a long fuse covered with red sulphur). His instructions were short and to the point: 'Strike a match, touch the fuse, count three, throw the bomb and the job is done.'[34] Although there were large supplies of bombs in the General Post Office, additional stocks were being continually manufactured and shotgun cartridges were filled with buckshot. Fire extinguishers were also distributed throughout the building. In the yards men filled sandbags. Basic telephonic communications had been installed throughout the GPO, including a line to the roof to enable Connolly to contact the sniper posts. Large rolls of newsprint were seized in a printing store in Lower Abbey Street and trundled across O'Connell Street to reinforce the defences of the General Post Office. Cumann dispatch carriers were in contact with other garrisons and provided headquarters with reports of the progress of the Rising in the rest of the city.

The mood of the General Post Office garrison was relaxed and in the yard younger Volunteers passed the time doing trick-riding on the bicycles of the telegraph boys.[35] But discipline was strict, especially in the matter of alcohol. When looters pillaged a public house in Henry Street, alongside the GPO, and a woman staggered across to offer bottles of stout all but one Volunteer rebuffed her. However, just as he put a bottle to his lips an officer appeared, smashed it to pieces and warned that the next man found taking drink would be shot without warning.[36] The garrison's high morale on Easter Tuesday was reflected in the Provisional Government's public utterances, bulletins and published statements. At 9.30 a.m. a statement by Pearse claimed that there had been 'heavy and continuous fighting' in which the British had suffered far heavier losses, that the whole of the city centre was in the hands of the Republic and that the people of Dublin were overwhelmingly on its side. The same message was propagated in the first and only issue of *Irish War News*, a four-page paper costing a penny. In the afternoon Pearse stood on top of a table in O'Connell Street and, in his dual capacity of president and commander-in-chief, read a manifesto to the citizens of Dublin which asserted that republican forces were holding the line everywhere and that the country was rising in support, and which then outlined ways in which the civilian population could assist the revolution.

Nevertheless, despite the insurgents' euphoria and optimism, the initiative was passing inexorably to the British army. An early harbinger of things to come was a British armoured car that got as close as O'Connell Bridge and from time to time sprayed the street with machine-gun fire at any sign of movement. The Military Council's original plan had been to sandwich the enemy forces in the city between the garrisons in the centre and Volunteers moving on Dublin from the countryside, but that had failed. By Tuesday, despite Pearse's claim that, 'the country is rising' a nationwide revolt had not materialised and Connolly hurriedly began to fashion a new strategy. He now set about preparing for a siege in which the British army, no longer liable to attack from the rear, would launch a frontal assault by infantry on the General Post Office. As a revolutionary socialist Connolly believed that the capitalist class would never permit an artillery bombardment that would certainly cause widespread destruction of property. Envisaging close, even hand-to-hand, fighting, Connolly decided to garrison buildings in the immediate vicinity that commanded those routes along which British soldiers might attack the GPO. The block opposite the General Post Office containing the Imperial Hotel and Clery's department store was occupied around noon, with Frank Thornton commanding its garrison of seven Citizen Army men and one woman as well as some Volunteers. For Connolly it was spectacular revenge for his union's defeat in 1913 during the Dublin Lock-out at the hands of William Martin Murphy, the hotel's owner and leader of the capital's employers. It was Connolly who ordered Thornton to fly the Starry Plough over the building, which was to be a charred ruin when Murphy eventually regained possession. Connolly had told Thornton that 'The British must not occupy these buildings'. Shortly after the Imperial was occupied by the insurgents the British attempted to shell the GPO from an 18-pounder located at the Parnell monument at the north end of O'Connell Street, but the gun crew was sniped at so effectively while trying to get the gun into position that they were all badly wounded or killed. British reinforcements managed to load and fire the gun but the shell missed the GPO and hit the YMCA in Upper O'Connell Street which British troops were occupying. Assuming this was a rebel attack, they immediately evacuated the YMCA, whereupon they were really attacked, suffering heavy casualties.[37]

Another strategically vital location occupied was the Metropole Hotel next to the General Post Office.[38] Indeed, the whole block of buildings from Prince's Street to Mansfield's boot shop at the corner of Middle Abbey Street guarded the western side of O'Connell Street and commanded three lines of approach to the GPO via Middle Abbey Street, Lower Abbey Street and Sackville Place. To secure sufficient men to occupy the hotel in strength, Connolly dispatched couriers to Fairview to order units of the Irish Volunteers and Citizen Army there under the command of Captain Frank Henderson to withdraw to the GPO. Sixty-six insurgents and half a dozen British prisoners in full khaki then marched into the city centre where, as they crossed in single file to the General Post Office, they came under fire from the garrison in the Imperial Hotel. In the ensuing gun battle some of Henderson's men were wounded and the shooting stopped only when Connolly dashed out into O'Connell Street, shouting and waving his hands over his head. As they assembled outside the GPO a chagrined Connolly apologised, 'It's all a mistake'. In the GPO's new public office at the entrance Pearse addressed the Fairview men. One of them, the 30-year-old Oscar Traynor, noticed a pile of saddlery and sabres that had been collected from the lancers on Easter Monday.

Connolly now divided them into three groups, sending Henderson and twenty men to occupy outposts in Henry Street, another twenty to reinforce the Imperial garrison and the remainder under Traynor to occupy the Metropole Hotel and adjoining premises.[39] Connolly had promoted Traynor to lieutenant over the head of one of his own Citizen Army officers, Captain Poole, a turbulent character who Traynor correctly sensed could make trouble. When Traynor raised his invidious position with an irritated Connolly, Poole shouted, 'Did I say that I would not obey you?' Poole was now spoiling for a fight and not necessarily just with the British. No sooner was he through the Metropole's swing doors than he picked on Harry Boland, a Volunteer who had joined up with Henderson's men in Fairview, and whom Poole accused of being a deserter. Poole continued to rant, ignored Traynor's exasperated explanation that a deserter would hardly be fighting alongside them, and threatened the hapless Boland with a rifle butt. Traynor managed to separate them and got Poole out of the way by ordering him to verify that the guests had vacated their apartments. However, a triumphant Poole was soon back with a civilian captive whom he had discovered in the smoke room and in a surreal scene he charged the man with being a British officer and a spy. As he explained to an incredulous Traynor, the man had given himself away by stepping off with his left foot when ordered to quick march; irrefutable proof of military training! But Traynor soon established that he was simply a teacher from Enniskillen and he was quickly escorted from the premises. Traynor could now turn his attention to fortifying the hotel, arranging for his men to bore through on the first floor into Eason's next door and on to Mansfield's Corner. Every available receptacle, from bath to jug, was filled with water. To their delight the garrison discovered that the hotel was a gastronomic paradise, stuffed with food, biscuits and rich cake, as well as cigars and cigarettes. However, the drinks cabinets remained untouched except for a particularly expensive brand of tonic water. The Metropole defenders saw very little action during Easter Week because the British shrank from taking the hotel by storm, preferring to shell it instead. On Tuesday night darkness fell on O'Connell Street after a day of comparative quiet and most of the General Post Office garrison managed to get a good night's sleep.

After Connolly sent a messenger to Commandant Thomas Ashe of the North County Dublin battalion pleading for reinforcements twenty Volunteers marched into the city on Tuesday morning. But they didn't remain long at the General Post Office. The young Fianna scout Sean McLoughlin, who was attached to Ned Daly's 1st Battalion and serving as Sean Heuston's dispatch carrier, had arrived seeking reinforcements at the Mendicity which was still holding out. McLoughlin's youth belied considerable strength of character, boldness and energy and nor was he intimidated by rank and experience. Connolly liked the young man's decisiveness and willingness to speak out, as well as his courage and comprehensive knowledge of the city as shown when McLoughlin volunteered to guide Ashe's men to the Mendicity and brought them safely to Heuston. On Easter Wednesday morning McLoughlin was to report once again to the GPO and astonish Connolly with the news that the Mendicity was still holding out though it fell before he got back. Subsequently McLoughlin joined the GPO garrison.[40]

Whereas Monday and Tuesday had been devoted to occupation, fortification and preparation, Wednesday was dominated by military activity at an increasingly relentless tempo. Shooting began early when the Imperial garrison hoisted the Starry Plough and British snipers retaliated. Movement in and out of this building now became very dangerous and a cord was tied across O'Connell Street so that messages in cans could be sent across to the GPO. At 8 a.m. the garrison in Hopkins heard explosions and initially assumed that they were being shelled. But when a Volunteer raised his improvised periscope – a mirror attached to a broom handle – he was shocked to see a British naval vessel, the *Helga*, attacking Liberty Hall. From Kelly's, Peadar Bracken was able to shoot at crewmen on the deck, forcing them to take cover, and he continued firing until the ship pulled up at the Custom House. Despite the considerable noise and the psychological impact on the insurgents, the *Helga's* bombardment was mostly ineffective because of the angle of fire. However, heavy guns situated near Trinity College were soon scoring direct hits on Liberty Hall, reducing the deserted building to a charred ruin.[41]

The British were not yet able to target the General Post Office, but as the morning went on Volunteer roof snipers were in action against British troops operating at Amiens Street station, Parnell Street and Findlater's Place. The British increased pressure on O'Connell Street from across the Liffey and for half an hour Hopkins came under heavy but ineffective machine-gun fire from the tower of Tara Street fire station. Frustratingly, the defenders in both Hopkins and Kelly's could see troops marching into Trinity College, out of range of their shotguns. Only Peadar Bracken had a rifle. Just before noon he spotted British soldiers about 300 yards away in D'Olier Street, standing in the open and preparing to shoot across the river, confident that they couldn't be hit by enemy fire. But Bracken had a surprise for them:

One exposed himself a little at a side door whom I pointed out to my comrades. I told them not to move a trigger until he came outside and to leave him to me. He came out on the path and I dropped him. Another showed up and I allowed him to pull in the casualty. In a few seconds he reached out with his rifle to 'fish in' the rifle on the path. While doing so he exposed his arm and side and I let him have one which caused his cap to bound out on the street.[42]

But British machine guns on top of Trinity College were soon sweeping O'Connell Street, turning it into a no-man's-land. In the afternoon intermittent sniper duels also developed between Volunteers on the roof of the GPO and British marksmen at the Custom House, Westmoreland Street and the Rotunda. Inside the General Post Office the defences were strengthened by building a 7ft-high wall made of notebooks and sacks of water-drenched coal. Then, according to Dick Humphries, at:

About 2 o'clock a gigantic boom shakes the edifice to its foundations and everyone looks up with startled eyes. From all sides come questioning words. Some say that a bomb has exploded in a lower room. Others that it is a dynamite explosion but a second and third in quick succession prove the correctness of those who proclaim it heavy artillery. The detonations are truly tremendous and were we not absolutely certain that the gun was situated on the opposite side of the river, one could have sworn that it must be in Abbey Street.[43]

The big guns at Trinity College had begun to shell 'Kelly's Fort', as it was now called, displacing plaster everywhere and starting a blaze on the top floor. Bracken failed to eliminate the British gunners crouching behind their weapons' shields and at about 2.30 p.m. Connolly ordered him to evacuate his garrison to the General Post Office. Three hours later Hopkins was also abandoned along with the Dublin Bread Company whose fragile tower was too thin to withstand even sniper bullets.

The Hopkins garrison now reinforced Traynor's men in the Metropole block, which stretched from Middle Abbey Street to Prince's Street. On late Wednesday afternoon this was extended to Eason's in Middle Abbey Street, thus achieving Connolly's goal of dominating Sackville Place, the Lower Abbey Street approach and the whole of Lower O'Connell Street. A British frontal attack on the General Post Office now risked suffering formidable casualties. Still, when Connolly inspected the work he rather ungraciously remarked, 'I wouldn't like to be getting through that hole if the enemy was following me with bayonets'. However, he had the good grace to smile broadly when Traynor retorted that the tunnelling had been carried out in accordance with his own lectures on the subject. Traynor recorded:

Although at this time heavy firing was taking place, Connolly insisted on walking out into Abbey Street and giving me instructions as to where I should place a barricade. While he was giving these instructions he was standing at the edge of the path and the bullets were actually striking the pavement around us. I pointed this out to him and said that I thought it was a grave risk to be taking, and that these instructions could be given inside. He came back to Eason's with me, absolutely unperturbed, and while we were standing in the portico of Eason's a shell struck a building opposite – I think it was the Catholic Boys' Home – and a gaping hole appeared in the front of the building. Connolly jokingly remarked 'They don't appear to be satisfied with firing bullets at us, they are firing shells at us now.'[44]

Late on Wednesday night the British fired shrapnel shells into O'Connell Street, some hitting the Metropole Hotel and collapsing its chimney stack. Traynor noted that:

The amazing thing was that instead of bullets coming in, it was molten lead, actually molten, which streamed about on the ground when it fell. I was told that the shell was filled with molten wax, the bullets were embedded in wax, and the velocity of the shell through the barrel and then through the air caused the mould to melt. As the first of these shells hit the building the Volunteers informed me of the fact. I rushed up to the third floor, which had been hit, and found an oldish Volunteer crawling about on his hands and knees gathering up the stuff as it hardened. I asked him what he was doing, and what he intended to do with the stuff. He answered 'Souvenirs'. That was all he said.[45]

A British machine gun on Tara Street fire station attacked the Imperial Hotel while another at Trinity College sent up clouds of mortar from the front of the Dublin Bread Company. Snipers on the roof of the GPO retaliated against both positions. Towards six o'clock fighting subsided and quiet reigned for a few hours, but inside the General Post Office the defenders could hardly relax in comfort. Dick Humphries noticed that:

When an off-duty turn arrives we hunt around for a reasonably quiet place where we might snatch a short sleep. But despite its huge size the GPO seems to possess no amenities of this kind. At the best most us can do is to bed down under a table or desk with a top cover thrown over us in lieu of the normal sheet or blanket. Needless to say, no one gets much sleep. The short intervals of silence outside are

even more ominous in their eerie intensity than the shots, explosions, strange whistling sounds, odd bursts of patriotic songs which punctuate the night.[46]

At dusk Joe Sweeney, on top of the GPO, saw a British armoured vehicle moving
slowly down O'Connell Street. After locating a slit at the front through binoculars he
shot and brought it to a halt. He and the rest of his unit kept firing to prevent its being
evacuated by its occupants, but another vehicle came along and towed it away. Even
more satisfying for the garrison was the news brought in by dispatch carriers about
the fighting at Mount Street Bridge and the large casualties inflicted on the British
reinforcements there. It was a good way to end what must, on balance, have appeared
to the garrison to have been a good day. Michael Staines recalled that 'Wednesday
night was immensely calm. Scarcely a sound was to be heard outside the garrison. It
was indeed the calm before the storm.'[47]

By now the expectations of the GPO garrison had begun to change when it
became clear that the country had not risen in support of the Rising and that British
reinforcements were pouring into Ireland. Pearse, however, continued to radiate
supreme optimism and assured a sceptical Desmond Fitzgerald that a German submarine would soon appear in Dublin Bay. But among his men there was a growing
conviction that their struggle would culminate in a massed British infantry assault
and even hand-to-hand fighting in the building. A heroic last stand would be a fitting
end that would echo through the ages. Jim Ryan, the GPO's medical officer, recalled:

In spite of that optimism we all seemed to take it for granted we would finally be
crushed. By common consent it was to be a fight to a finish. It was thought that the
enemy would rush our position with superior forces and would take it with enormous losses. None of us expected mercy but we felt we would sell our lives dearly.
There was no feeling of despondency. The atmosphere was one of subdued excitement and determination – desperation maybe – for we appreciated only too well
the odds against us. We talked confidently of holding out for two or three weeks, of
being able to make enough noise to draw the attention of the world to this small
nation. We would hold our post until the last man's rifle was silenced.[48]

These expectations as to how the Rising would end were not confined to the rank
and file alone. Whatever the personal inclinations of individuals such as Pearse and
Plunkett, the words and actions of the collective leadership during Easter Week do
not endorse the blood sacrifice theory: that they had carefully planned to survive the
Rising and end their lives in front of British firing squads to redeem the nation and
inspire it to future freedom. The leaders did not talk and act like men who intended
to die in such a manner. Tom Clarke, for instance, clearly did not expect to survive the
General Post Office. Jim Ryan has recorded that:

On Wednesday Tom Clarke came to the hospital and sitting down quietly beside me
began to talk … I was now Red Cross and so he said I might possibly be spared by
the enemy in the final bayonet charge which was evidently expected by him as well
as by the rest of us. If therefore I should survive he hoped I now understood and
would make known the motives of those who signed the Proclamation.[49]

Clarke later took Desmond Fitzgerald out to a yard and pointed to a concrete shelter into which he wanted him to herd all the women when the final moments came. He held out little hope for Fitzgerald and thought he would perish in the final British assault or be executed soon after.[50] The actions of some of the Provisional Government are also hardly consistent with that of men who were bent on the preservation of their persons at all costs for future execution. Connolly, for example, risked death on a number of occasions. He might well have been killed on Easter Tuesday night when he dashed out of the GPO to stop the garrison in the Imperial firing on Frank Henderson's men. His two subsequent wounds inflicted by British snipers came as he exposed himself to them in the open air and they could as easily have been fatal.

On Easter Thursday, 27 April, the GPO garrison awakened early to another glorious cloudless day. Although heavy firing could be heard in the distance morale was still high and as yet the full weight of the British counter-attack had not been brought to bear. Ryan's hospital staff had not been busy and had treated only three or four men for minor wounds. But everyone sensed that this day would be different because a well-equipped enemy cordon had been tightened around the GPO and its adjacent outposts.[51] Many garrison members sensed increasingly that their occupation of the building was nearer its end than its beginning. The O'Rahilly told Desmond Fitzgerald that 'we should have lasted only thirty-six hours. It is against the rules of warfare that we are still here. But don't worry, it will not be long now',[52] and to cheer up the men he led them in community singing. The British were now concentrated in strength in College Street, Trinity College, the Custom House, Liberty Hall and Amiens Street, and from Parnell Street to Findlater's Place. At the same time, The O'Rahilly was supervising teams strengthening the window barricades. In the subsequent defence of the GPO, its roof snipers played a crucially important role, being responsible for locating enemy machine-gun posts and snipers and putting them out of action. They also had to monitor and counteract British troop movements in the surrounding streets, which usually consisted of sudden dashes, allowing only a second or two to react. A measure of their importance was the fact of Pearse's frequent visits to the roof, though he also wanted to see the St Enda's boys who were positioned there.

Shortly after dawn British machine-gun fire from Abbey Street was countered from the General Post Office and adjoining outposts, and the fight was fully on. One defender recalled that 'Every machine gun within range began to pour in a fierce fire upon the area and every soldier, including the British snipers, joined in with rapid rifle fire. The torrent of bullets on and around our Field Headquarters could only be compared to a violent hailstorm.'[53]

The British tried repeatedly to advance from the junction of Marlborough and Abbey streets, but Traynor's men and especially Harry Boland were outstanding in repelling them, even when their rifles became over-heated and had to be cooled by oil extracted from tins of sardines. Towards noon a tremendous explosion startled the General Post Office garrison, who saw an incendiary ignite the offices of the *Freeman's Journal* in Prince's Street. Intensive bombardment of outposts such as Hopkins, the Dublin Bread Company and the Imperial had resumed and heavy sniping was also directed against the GPO, where a shell damaged the figures over the porch, though a direct hit had still not been registered on the building. In the Imperial an incident took place which might have come from a Hollywood disaster epic. Some of Frank

Thornton's men were resting in an annex at the back of the hotel when a large over-head tank was hit by a shell and sent down a huge cascade of water, washing the men out of it and along the main passage.[54]

During Thursday Connolly inspected the Metropole and allocated an additional twenty men to its garrison. Shells did hit the hotel whose ceiling collapsed, sending bricks tumbling down the chimney and acrid yellow flames leaping in through the windows. Nevertheless, under one window two men disdainfully reclined on mattresses beneath a window, calmly smoking their pipes. But the hurricane was unremitting and Traynor ordered his men to descend two storeys, except for a young Cockney member of the Citizen Army called Neale. He had ruined his shoes and stockings on Easter Monday and replaced them in the Metropole with a guest's boots and a pair of girl's stockings which he pulled up to his knees. He now made a bizarre spectacle acting as lookout during the bombardment, sitting right out on the parapet on the top floor and scanning O'Connell Street with a pair of field-glasses.[55] But lighter moments like this did not alter the seriousness of the situation. When a man came up to the GPO and asked to be allowed to join, Joe Good of the Kimmage garrison overheard Connolly tell him: 'Go home while you can, man, we thank you. Too late now, man; it's a hopeless case.'[56]

About 3 p.m. a report of an imminent British attack on the General Post Office from the north-west side brought every available man scurrying from the eastern to the western windows. As they braced themselves a false alarm that an armoured car was driving up Henry Street caused many Volunteers, dangerously, to stand up and look out the windows. Shortly afterwards the shooting ceased abruptly. During the subsequent lull Pearse made a morale-boosting speech in which he claimed that all the principal targets had been taken and the Linenhall Barracks captured and set on fire, the country was still rising and a large band of Volunteers was marching from Dundalk to Dublin. In addition they had successfully held out as a republic for three full days and under international law were entitled to send a delegation to the peace conference which would immediately follow the end of the war. When he finished the men's spirits had revived and a deafening cheer spread throughout the entire building.

The first serious casualty among the GPO garrison occurred on Thursday when a Volunteer was wounded in the neck by a bullet which came out under his eye. Much more serious in its implications was the injury to Connolly's left leg inflicted by a British sniper. This was, in fact, his second wound. He had already received a flesh wound in the arm but had managed to conceal it from the garrison by having Ryan treat him behind a folding screen and swearing him to secrecy.[57] The new wound, which was much more grim and could not be hidden, happened as Connolly returned from establishing two outposts in Liffey Street, though he managed to drag himself to Prince's Street where he was collected by a stretcher party. In the GPO Connolly was treated by a captured British army doctor and chloroform had to be used as anaesthetic. The bullet had shattered almost 2 inches of Connolly's shin bone and the leg was dressed and set in splints with a wastepaper basket cut in two to make a large cage for it.[58] Thereafter Connolly survived on frequent injections of morphine and for the rest of Thursday was removed from the action.

Connolly's incapacitation led to The O'Rahilly assuming the most prominent military role in the General Post Office but, in terms of overall control, it also led to the growing assertiveness of Clarke and MacDermott. Pearse, who was unable to sleep throughout the Rising, was clearly suffering the effects of sleep deprivation. As was obvious to the whole garrison, Plunkett was seriously ill after the operation on his glandular neck but accounts which depict him lying helplessly and ineffectually for the entire Rising are wide of the mark. There are enough sightings of Plunkett in the GPO, animated and in good humour, to confirm that he enjoyed periods of remission. His emotional health, however, can only be guessed at; on Easter Thursday, as fires swept the east side of O'Connell Street, he was exulting that 'It's the first time this has happened since Moscow! The first time a capital city has burned since 1812!'[59] Although both Clarke and MacDermott were in civilian clothing their increasingly open authority was accepted without question by the garrison. Those Volunteers who were members of the IRB knew the importance of the pair, now publicly proclaimed by their membership of the Provisional Government and the respect and deference displayed to them in the GPO by Pearse, Connolly and Plunkett. Neither Clarke nor MacDermott had any formal military rank but they now intervened to issue promotions, give instructions on the movement of munitions and prisoners, and command Volunteer parties who fought the fires that swept the General Post Office on Friday.

At 3.45 p.m. British howitzers began dropping shrapnel shells over the roof of the GPO where also three men were wounded by British snipers. Their unit was then hastily evacuated and tumbled down into the telegraph room through safety manholes – spaces torn in the slates from which a rope stretched down to the floor inside. Dick Humphries watched as 'Some of the men in their hurry fail to catch the rope altogether and take the eighteen foot drop as though it were an everyday occurrence. The wounded are lowered safely by means of two ropes.'[60] The bombardment continued for two and a half hours but the shells failed to inflict any serious damage to the GPO. British snipers on top of the Gresham Hotel poured bullets through the windows of the General Post Office where the defenders crouched as low as possible. On the roof Humphries and his comrades determined to eliminate this threat: 'We allow them to continue firing until, mystified at our silence, they grow bolder, and incautiously show themselves over the top of the parapet. Immediately a single volley rings out. There is no more sniping that evening from the Gresham.'[61] The British were clearly increasing the pressure, especially at the rear of the GPO, and Connolly transferred men to Henry Street and Liffey Street to guard the approaches. Also by now the dispatch system had completely collapsed and this strongly reinforced the GPO garrison's increasing isolation; they were now on their own and as they listened to the big guns they realised that the other garrisons were similarly isolated. On Thursday evening a rumour swept the building that a British gas attack was imminent and the defenders were issued with cans whose liquid was to be dipped in handkerchiefs and placed over their mouths. When the false alarm was over the tins of magic fluid were stored in a corner, close to a thirsty Dublin raconteur nicknamed 'The Cuban'. When he imbibed the contents of one he developed pains all over his body and was rushed to the General Post Office hospital, though he recovered and returned to duty.[62]

At 7.30 p.m., after the battle had subsided, the reinforcements were transferred back to their positions in the eastern rooms. There Dick Humphries spent a nerve-shattering evening when the British launched intense sniper attacks against the roof of the GPO, a tremendous bombardment of the Metropole block and dropped incendiary shells on the Imperial Hotel. An inferno now developed along the opposite side of O'Connell Street and soon Hopkins, the Dublin Bread Company and indeed the entire block as far as Lower Abbey Street were well ablaze. The fires gradually worked their way round the corner and soon ignited Wynn's Hotel, the Royal Hibernian Academy and nearby buildings, their progress helped by flames travelling along the barricades.

Humphries saw that:

> Hopkins is just beginning to blaze, while somewhere down in Abbey Street smoke is rising into the still evening air. Not realising that this is the commencement of the large conflagration which is to devastate O'Connell Street we watch the leaping flames while gradually night darkens over the city. On returning to our post after tea we are appalled at the stupendous increase that the fire has made. The interior of our room is as bright as day with the lurid glow of the flames. Reiss's jewellery shop is a mass of leaping, scarlet tongues of light.[63]

Often spectators could watch the fires develop gradually from the first impact of the incendiary shell but at other times they grew rapidly. One spectacular detonation occurred at Hoyte's, the City of Dublin Drug Hall, which combined a pharmaceutical chemist with a glass and oil warehouse in Lower O'Connell Street, four doors from the Imperial. Here an incendiary created a blaze both frightening and beautiful, as graphically described by Humphries:

> Suddenly some oil works near Abbey Street is singed by the conflagration, and immediately a solid sheet of blinding death white flame rushes hundreds of feet into the air with a thunderous explosion which shakes the walls. It is followed by a heavy bombardment as hundreds of drums of oil explode. The intense light compels one to close the eyes. Even here the heat is so terrible that it strikes one like a solid thing as blast and scorching air come in through the glassless windows. Millions of sparks are floating in masses for hundreds of yards around O'Connell Street and as a precaution we are ordered to drench the barricades with water again. The whole thing seems too terrible to be real. Crimson-tinged men moved around dazedly. Above it all the sharp crack of rifle fire predominates, while the deadly rattle of the machine gun sounds like the coughing laughter of jeering spirits.[64]

From a different vantage point in the Metropole, Charles Saurin was awed by the sight:

> When Hoyte's first caught fire it was a terrific spectacle, as it burst into one huge flame the moment it was hit. It was a roaring inferno in less than a minute. Stored as it was with chemicals of all sorts and with oils and colours it spouted rockets and stars of every hue and was the most wonderful fireworks show I ever saw.[65]

To one Volunteer the noise of the inferno was 'like the song of a great dynamo'.[66] In the Metropole Saurin dashed through the front rooms from second floor to the top pulling down all flammables and cutting away curtains and blinds. As the fire spread to Clery's and the Imperial Hotel, Traynor's men sent urgent but unavailing semaphore warnings and soon the huge plate-glass windows of Clery's were running molten from the tremendous heat.[67]

The fires had now reached such terrifying proportions that Humphries felt that he was:

> situated in the midst of a circle of flame. Inside the central telegraph room which runs along the entire length of the GPO the men stand silently at their posts, black and bronze statues against the terrible glow of the sky. Unawed and undaunted, their gaze ever-fixed on the glistening cobbles and the shadowed lanes whence all attacks must be directed, they wait expectantly. Now and again the flames beat upwards in a flash of light that reveals every detail behind the barriers. Then they subside as suddenly and lines of black shadow, rays of darkness, as it were, creep over us. Fortunately the wind is blowing seawards, the myriads of blazing fragments are carried away from the GPO. Glowing sparks however now begin to shower down with a pattering sound like soft rain and threaten to set everything on fire.[68]

Michael Staines wrote:

> The heat from the burning block opposite the GPO was beyond belief. Despite the great width of O'Connell Street the sacks, etc. in the windows began to scorch and show signs of smouldering. Batches of men had to be hastily formed to continually drench the window fortifications with water. Dense volumes of acrid smoke, myriads of sparks and splinters of falling debris were being blown to the GPO by a strong north-east wind. Lurid flames leapt skywards and the spectacle in the gathering darkness could only be likened to Dante's Inferno. The intensity of the heat grew steadily worse and the water being poured from buckets and hoses was converted into steam as it touched the fortifications. There had to be a withdrawal from the front of the building of all save those who were combating the risk of a conflagration in the Post Office itself. Our struggle with this new danger seemed to go on for interminable hours. The men were soot-stained, steam-scalded and fire-scorched, sweating, weary and parched.[69]

In the Imperial Frank Thornton was determined to hold out as long as possible but he knew that the end was near. The hotel had been riddled with gunfire from the dome of the Custom House, Amiens Street station tower, the Bank of Ireland, Trinity College and the YMCA in O'Connell Street. This had been followed by the explosion in Hoyte's when many barrels of methylated spirits and turps had been blown into the sky and exploded when they landed on the roof of the Imperial. Quite a few of Thornton's men had been wounded as a result of this 'cauldron of flames' and he now started to concentrate his men in one area.[70] At last the terrific heat in O'Connell Street died down, the smoke lessened and, although the fires were to smoulder for days, the immediate danger had passed. The rest of the night was peaceful as the big guns were silent and, except for an occasional sniper shot, the riflemen and machine-gunners appeared to have gone to sleep. At about 12.30 a.m. Patrick and Willie Pearse and The O'Rahilly appeared satisfied after a tour of the General Post Office defences.

In the light of day on Easter Friday, 28 April, the General Post Office garrison could witness for itself the spectacular impact of the British blitzkrieg on the eastern side of O'Connell Street. Humphries saw that:

> On the opposite side of O'Connell Street nothing is left of the buildings except the bare walls. Clouds of grey smoke are racing in and around everywhere and it is difficult to see as far as the Bridge. Occasionally some side wall or roof falls in with a terrific bang. The heat is stupefying, a heavy odour of burning cloth permeates the air.[71]

Sean MacEntee was stunned:

> Directly opposite me was the Imperial Hotel, or what had been the Imperial Hotel, for only the façade of the building remained The rest, windows, floor and roof had become a prey to the fire, so that now without any substantial background, with its gaping window-sockets and the flames that licked around them, the façade itself was like a huge stage-set prepared for some spectacular drama. There was no sign of the enemy.[72]

Thursday night's hurricane of fire and the fact that British infantry were not massing for an assault on the General Post Office meant that a last stand was now very unlikely. The British were not prepared to conduct their operations in the way the enemy desired, particularly as the troops who encircled the GPO were the Sherwoods who had suffered so grievously at Mount Street Bridge. Having lost so many men in a frontal attack against a fortified building containing a small number of opponents, they were not prepared to risk an even more bloody repetition in O'Connell Street. Instead, frustratingly and maddeningly for the General Post Office garrison, there were only fleeting and distant glimpses of soldiers dashing across the street or else snipers wriggling across rooftops.

It seemed certain now that the British intended to devastate the western side of O'Connell Street. Aodogán O'Rahilly has speculated convincingly that the rebel leadership must have convened to determine its response. That such meetings took place during Easter Week is not in doubt because Eamon Dore, Sean MacDermott's bodyguard, saw one in progress on Easter Wednesday in a room at the front of the General Post Office with Clarke presiding and MacDermott apparently acting as secretary.[73] A crisis session would almost certainly have been held in the early hours of Friday morning and, in addition to Clarke, MacDermott, Pearse, Connolly and Plunkett, The O'Rahilly probably attended and perhaps Willie Pearse. Almost certainly it was now conditionally agreed that if the British attempted to annihilate them by shelling or to engulf them in flames they would not stay to be incinerated in a Gaelic Masada but would depart. When the British strategy of blasting and burning the rebels out was confirmed on Friday the continued resistance from the GPO and the fire-fighting efforts within it can be only understood as holding operations to allow outposts to congregate in the headquarters and an orderly evacuation to proceed. One major step to prepare for a British bombardment commenced at 1 a.m. when MacDermott ordered Diarmuid Lynch to transfer munitions from the upper floor to a basement room which extended under the Henry Street sidewalk. As this got under way galloping hooves in O'Connell Street sparked fears of a cavalry charge, though in fact they were from terrified, riderless horses which had been released from their stables in Prince's Street. Snipers in the Metropole fired at them and one Volunteer swung a billy-can packed with bolts, nuts and gelignite above his head to gain impetus until the handle parted company and the can flew across the room and hit a wall. Luckily it did not explode.[74]

At daybreak the weather was fine and the guns were silent but many Volunteers in the GPO sensed that the end was near, even though only the inner circle knew for certain. To Sean MacEntee it seemed that 'The air was heavy with premonition, and the brooding calm forebode a storm'.[75] True enough, at daybreak the British launched a bombardment of incendiary shells and continuous bursts of machine-gun fire raked O'Connell Street. Having discovered a winning formula on the previous day, their tactics for Easter Friday were simply more of the same. Initially the shrapnel shells which hit the Metropole inflicted only minor damage to the roof but large numbers of British troops assembled around the Abbey Theatre a short distance away. Traynor warned his men to expect a frontal attack up Sackville Place and those in Mansfield's boot shop attacked the soldiers constantly; they, in turn, were fired on from a new British position at the junction of Westmoreland Street and D'Olier Street. Then shells finally set the top of the Metropole on fire and the hoses and water-filled baths proved useless to combat its spread.[76]

Inside the GPO, where the commissariat still functioned and those not on duty took breakfast, MacDermott instructed the medical officer, Jim Ryan, to prepare the sixteen wounded Volunteers for removal to Jervis Street Hospital.[77] Connolly, apparently cheerful, had insisted on becoming actively involved again and moved among the garrison on his bed, which was on castors. A message which he had dictated to Winifred Carney was read out by The O'Rahilly, declaring that other garrisons were holding out and urged, 'Courage boys – we are winning!' However, the preliminaries to evacuation were already under way. Just before daybreak MacDermott had ordered Diarmuid Lynch to withdraw the outposts in Henry Street and Middle Abbey Street to the General Post Office, though a post in Liffey Street was overlooked and remained in place until after the surrender.[78]

As the men in the General Post Office continued strengthening the defences Connolly sat up joking and laughing as his bed was wheeled among the garrison. After encountering the Fianna scout Sean McLoughlin, whom he had earmarked for greater responsibility, Connolly told MacDermott, 'This is the young man I told you about. He's seen more of Dublin this week than any of us. We had better keep him with us now.'[79] The O'Rahilly now read out eloquently a communiqué that Connolly had earlier dictated to Winifred Carney, a message that Joe Good considered the most amazing thing he had witnessed during the entire week and completely divorced from reality.[80] Certainly the overall picture that it depicted of the state of the rebellion was distorted – something hardly unique in the annals of military history. Connolly claimed that the various outposts were still defeating enemy attempts to dislodge them while everywhere outside the capital the population was rallying to the cause. But of course his primary purpose was to boost morale as well as thank the men and women who had fought for the cause during Easter Week and pay tribute to their

1 The inscrutable Tom Clarke, veteran revolutionary and the driving force behind the Easter Rising.

2 Anticipating his future? Patrick Pearse at 8 years old.

3 James Connolly, founder of the
Irish Citizen Army, signatory to the
Proclamation and commandant of the
Irish forces in Dublin during the Rising.

4 Members of the Citizen Army on
guard on the roof of their headquarters
at Liberty Hall, Dublin.

5 Countess Markievicz (centre, second row), surrounded by boys and young men of the Fianna. Chief Scout Con Colbert, executed after the Rising, is second to the right of her.

6 A well-equipped section of Ceannt's 4th Battalion of the Irish Volunteers in September 1915.

7 Eoin MacNeill, President of
the Irish Volunteers.

8 An imaginative recreation of
the signing of the Proclamation
at Liberty Hall on Easter Sunday,
1916. The members of the
Provisional Government (from
left to right) are Plunkett, Pearse,
Clarke, Ceannt, MacDermott,
Connolly and MacDonagh.

9 General Sir John Grenfall Maxwell, who was appointed commander-in-chief of the British Army in Ireland during the Rising.

10 General Maxwell and his staff pose for a group photograph after the Rising.

11 Brigadier-General W.H.M. Lowe, who directed British army operations in Dublin during the Rising.

12 The main entrance gates to Upper Yard, Dublin Castle. The circle indicates the point where the first fatality of the Rising, Constable O'Brien, was shot.

13 British soldiers manning a barricade.

14 An apparently posed photograph of British soldiers at an improvised barricade of beer barrels on the Dublin quays.

15 British troops on guard against a possible rebel attack at the corner of Parnell Street and Moore Street.

16 A civilian motorcar is stopped and searched by British soldiers at a military cordon.

17 An armoured car with mounted machine gun. This type of vehicle became familiar to the city's population during the Rising.

18 An armoured car of the type used by the British army to get to close quarters with houses occupied by the rebels. Like others it was constructed out of disused boilers by tradesmen at Guinness'.

19 This watercolour by Walter Paget is an imaginative recreation of the scenes inside the General Post Office during the final stages of its occupation. Pearse, Clarke and Plunkett hover over the wounded Connolly. Members of the garrison confirmed that it gave an accurate impression of the situation.

20 Brigadier-General Lowe (centre) and Major de Courcy Wheeler receive Pearse's surrender. The figure standing beside Pearse, almost completely hidden, is Nurse Elizabeth O'Farrell.

21 British troops inspect the ruined interior of the General Post Office at the end of the Rising.

22 Firemen removing a red-hot safe from the ruins after the Rising.

23 The exterior of the gutted General Post Office.

24 Rounding up the rebels. A Volunteer prisoner is escorted by British soldiers to Dublin Castle.

25 Rebel suspects who were detained at Richmond Barracks after the Rising.

26 Rebel prisoners after the Rising being permitted to meet with their families and friends.

27 O'Connell Street on Easter Monday, 24 April 1916.

28 O'Connell Street as it appeared on the Monday after the collapse of the Rising.

29 The structural damage inflicted on the east side of O'Connell Street by British incendiary and artillery shells.

30 The devastation wreaked on O'Connell Street and Eden quay.

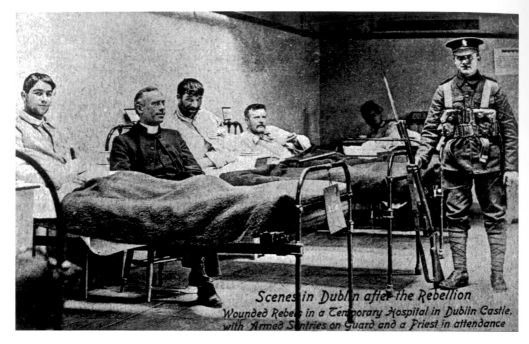

31 Wounded rebels in a temporary hospital in Dublin Castle, with an armed sentry on guard and a priest in attendance.

32 Business as usual after the collapse of the Rising. A newsvendor stands among the ruins.

courage, especially the General Post Office garrison. And there was more than a grain of truth when he referred to the impact of their resistance on enemy commanders:

> The British Army, whose exploits we are for ever having dinned into our ears, which boasts of having stormed the Dardanelles and the German lines on the Marne, behind their artillery and machine-guns are afraid to advance to the attack or storm any positions held by our forces. The slaughter they suffered in the first few days has totally unnerved them and they dare not attempt again an infantry attack on our positions.

About midday a British machine gunner and snipers opened fire on the General Post Office, while howitzers situated in gardens behind the Rotunda Hospital lobbed shells and incendiaries into the building, setting fire to a corner of the roof. The evacuation process commenced soon afterwards when about thirty women assembled in the main hall. When Pearse revealed that they had to leave their anger and tears left him so shaken and confused that MacDermott limped forward and appeared to countermand the order. However, Pearse reasserted control and the women were ushered into Henry Street during a brief lull in the fighting, leaving Winifred Carney and a few nurses as the only females still in the GPO. About 1 p.m., as the fires spread and parts of the roof fell in, Pearse ordered the rooftop snipers to abandon their posts and descend to the next floor. At about 3 p.m. Clarke, MacDermott, Diarmuid Lynch and Sean McGarry had a final meal with Father Flanagan just before he led out the wounded. Connolly was entitled to leave with them but absolutely refused to go. For a last supper the mood was remarkably cheerful. McGarry joked to Flanagan that even if they were damned for eating meat on Friday they were still going to chance it.[81]

Soon afterwards the final British assault began. In the Imperial Thornton's garrison had stuck to their instructions until only six men remained on the first-floor landing as the British worked their way to the rear in Marlborough Street. Only when the ceiling fell in did Thornton order a retreat, and when he and his men failed to reach the GPO they made their way to a building at the corner of Gloucester Street where they remained until the surrender.[82] Inside the General Post Office the first fires had been quickly brought under control, but about 3 p.m. a shell inflicted serious damage over the portico. Having at last got their range, the British intensified the bombardment and serious fires broke out around the building where every hose, fire extinguisher and bucket of water was employed against them. On the ground floor Volunteers continued to pile up higher breastworks. Men scouring the building burst into a room and discovered hundreds of mailbags. Diarmuid Lynch organised squads in the yard to fill them with debris to reinforce the defences. Soon the flames had eaten their way through the roof of the cupola and about 3.30 p.m. a hail of incendiary bullets came from the direction of the Gresham Hotel. Dick Humphries watched, astonished, as the walls where the bullets lodged apparently flashed into flames, though, finding no hold, they soon died out. On the roof the fires had taken a grip on the portico and burnt through to the interior. Humphries wrote:

> Someone discovers that the roof is on fire and immediately commences a perfect babel of shouting, order-giving and talking. The two main lines of hose are quickly

brought to the spot and two streams of water are thrown against the lower part of the roof. Lines of buckets are also organised and after a quarter of an hour's hard work the outbreak seems to be practically under control. Suddenly another part of the roof is set on fire by the incendiary bullets and half the available water supply has to be turned upon it. Heavy firing in the meantime is going on in all directions, and adds to the confusion. Pearse and J Plunkett are holding a short conversation in the doorway. They both appear very excited. Finally a large number of men are selected for extinguishing work and the remainder are ordered to be at the windows. Everyone seems to consider it his duty to give orders at the top of his voice. The noise is terrific. The fire is gaining ground like lightning.

Humphries also discovered that an astonishing situation had developed in the telegraph room:

It presents a most extraordinary spectacle. In one part the fire has eaten right through the roofs and slates of mortar are commencing to fall on the floor. The two hoses are brought to bear on the spot. They are held six feet above the ground (to enable a better head of water to be obtained) by lines of men. Here and there the water spurts out through small holes in the rubber, drenching the men completely. In one place a huge leak from a faulty connection runs down the uniform of an officer. In a few seconds he is wet to the skin but stands as unconcernedly as though on parade. Further above a line of buckets extending down to the second floor is working with incredible rapidity. After a few minutes, however, we see that all is useless. The fire is gaining ground in all directions. Huge masses of the roof commence to fall inwards with terrific noise. The floor on which the men are working threatens to give way with each blow. Clouds of smoke from the burning debris writhe around the corridors and passages. It gets into our eyes and noses and compels fits of coughing. The floors are covered to a depth of three inches with grimy water.[83]

Amid tumultuous scenes at the top of the building men attempted to extinguish the fires. Among them was Plunkett's brother, Jack. Originally when he had seen the holes where the shells had gone through the portico and little specks of smoke appearing, the situation seemed harmless enough. Then he heard the cries of 'Fire' and they discovered that the low pressure was preventing the hoses from bringing water to roof level. The garrison should have prepared for this because the canteen boiler on the top floor had been running short of water. Jack Plunkett and the others were ordered down from the roof to the top floor, where smoke was filtering into the telegraph instrument room at the front of the building. Heavy boxes were thrown frantically in efforts to break the glass of the roof-lights and allow fire extinguishers to be directed out on to the roof, though one bounced off and landed on the head of Jack Plunkett's neighbour. The irony was that there was plenty of water but it could not reach the top of the building, so although the floor was deep in water the roof was blazing away. Jack Plunkett's hair caught fire from a falling spark and pieces of timber fell on his head, but his heavy felt hat saved him from serious injury. Eventually he and the others gave up and soon the only firefighters left were a few men on the ground floor using pitifully inadequate hoses. The sacks of water-drenched coal now caught fire and the atmosphere became one of fire, smoke, burning timber and cascades of melted glass and molten lead. Another problem was the British sniper who was working the roof of the burnt-out Imperial and targeting the firefighters in the General Post Office. Jack Plunkett was ordered back on to an undamaged part of the roof where, despite the dark and smoke, he eventually located the soldier. From behind a chimney stack he fired and the sniper fell so hard that his rifle snapped in two on impact with the ground.[84]

Sean MacEntee, one of the firefighters, found himself in the middle of a nightmare:

> When the water from the fire-hoses impinged on the glass of the canopy, it appeared to explode into hundreds of gleaming stars which reflected lurid rays of flame. Often a jet of water from the hoses, as it flowed across the glass, would seem to sweep the fire before it. And if the mass of water was large, it would go billowing back and forward from end to end of the transparent ceiling; so that the flames went oscillating to and fro on the crystal above us.[85]

MacDermott and Patrick Pearse were actively involved in trying to keep the fires at bay until the wounded had gone and an evacuation proper could get under way. MacDermott supervised Volunteers sweeping up flammable materials and rubbish while Pearse oversaw firefighters, stopping occasionally to peer outside through a loophole. According to one witness, Pearse:

> seldom spoke except when a spark or a fall of burning matter from the roof set some of our defences ablaze. Then he would direct his men in extinguishing the fire. He appeared cool and unmoved. Now and then an orderly would report to him on the progress of the fire, although indeed the progress was only too apparent. From my position at the window I could see the advance of the flames. I was fascinated by the long snaking tongues of fire that went curling and writhing above the glass canopy of the central hall, and I watched them like a boy at his first fireworks display.[86]

Thomas Devine could see how the:

> bombardment had worked havoc in the building especially in the roof and upper storeys which had got the brunt of the shelling. Daylight was visible in many places, twisted girders hung at queer angles, walls, floors and staircases were in a chaotic state. Down on the ground floor many wounded lay, sat or stood by whilst those active went about their tasks.[87]

Eventually the situation became untenable as intense heat melted the glass overhead and every man was ordered to assemble in the general sorting office at the rear. Sean McLoughlin recalled that 'everybody was gloomy and there was a sense of foreboding that the end was near'.[88] There, at about 6 p.m., the wounded and their Volunteer escort were readied for evacuation, except for Connolly who utterly refused to leave. Father Flanagan led them out accompanied by most of the remaining nurses who were carrying Volunteers' farewell messages. Tom Clarke had told one, 'If you see my wife, tell her the men fought …' but then broke down and turned away.[89] Only three women remained now: Connolly's secretary, Winifred Carney, and two nurses, Elizabeth O'Farrell and Julia Grenan.

By 7 p.m. the flames had spread along both sides of the roof. Diarmuid Lynch recorded that:

> Myriads of live sparks fell through the open shaft to the immediate vicinity of the Henry Street basement room in which the stocks of gelignite, powder and bombs had been placed for safety; a possible explosion of these just then might have had serious consequences, not alone in casualties but in blocking the intended exit for retreat.[90]

Sean McLoughlin pointed out this danger to MacDermott but he laughingly replied, 'I have not seen any of them go off yet. I don't think they are the best job in the world.'[91] However, he did order McLoughlin, The O'Rahilly and Diarmuid Lynch to lead twenty men to transfer the munitions along an underground passage around three wings of the GPO and down to a cellar in an outside yard. Lynch had already explored this route and discovered a large protruding tube at which he stationed Volunteers with candles as well as other unlit places. He also made the carriers cover their bombs with water-soaked cloths. Even so, one petrified Volunteer set his grenades down on the stairs and walked away.[92]

On his return The O'Rahilly snatched a hose from MacDermott and began spraying the sparks coming down the elevator and air shafts, through the doorways and every other aperture. Despite this, the lift began to blaze, convincing McLoughlin that nothing could be done to stop the fire spreading. He warned MacDermott that 'It is hopeless, we will have to get out'.[93] Accidents were occurring all around as the garrison prepared for evacuation. As the men collected their provisions Liam Tannam noticed:

> piles of rashers, some ham, I think, cases of eggs, and bread which were hastily divided. I remember one man named Gallagher who was assisting to slice some meat get his hand in the slicer and sliced a piece off his thumb and he immediately passed it on between two pieces of bread as a sandwich.[94]

Eamon Bulfin recalled that 'we got an order to unload weapons and a chap standing beside me was wounded in the foot when his shotgun went off while in the process of being unloaded'.[95]

Pearse now required an advance guard to precede the main garrison and make ready a new headquarters at Williams & Woods, a jam factory in Parnell Street. These premises were full of foodstuffs and close enough, Pearse believed, to British lines to make shelling them a risky enterprise for the enemy. Raised now to almost heroic status, The O'Rahilly was the obvious choice to lead an attempted breakthrough to Williams & Woods. After selecting twenty-five men he brought them to the side entrance at Henry Street. At the last moment he walked over to a priest, took off his hat, knelt down and said, 'I don't suppose, Father, that we will ever meet in this world again. Please give me your blessing.'[96] Next he lined his men up outside the GPO windows. Most lacked the bayonets necessary for storming a barricade. Drawing his sword, The O'Rahilly arranged them into fours, took his place at the front and shouted, 'Quick March – at the double'. After the hectic scenes inside the GPO, Sean MacEntee was startled by the tranquillity until they reached Henry Street. As he put it: 'All was quiet and still. It might have been a lakeshore at the fall of evening.'[97] But upon turning into Moore Street that changed with deadly suddenness. Over 250 yards long with a British barricade near the end, it was an intimidating distance to traverse under fire from soldiers armed with rifles and machine guns. The first British volley scythed through the attackers. Thomas Devine, heard groans and thuds as men fell all around him: 'The wonder is our small force wasn't wiped out there and then. After the first burst myself and six others swerved from the middle to the left –hand side of the street and hugging the shop fronts dashed on at breakneck speed for a distance of about 170 or 180 yards.'[98]

Half a dozen yards ahead on the opposite pavement, Devine saw the 41-year-old O'Rahilly running 'like a deer' to within 30 yards of the barricade before he realised that most of his party lagged far behind and swerved into a doorway. He stood stiffly erect in the narrow framework for protection while Devine's party hurtled into Riddall's Row, an alley on the opposite side of Moore Street. From there they stared across and awaited their leader's signal while fighting raged between soldiers at the barricade and those Volunteers who were stranded more than half way down Moore Street: 'The din was deafening, smashing glass and splintering woodwork adding their quota to the effect.'[99]

When fighting momentarily subsided The O'Rahilly nodded towards Devine, blew twice on his whistle and dashed out into the middle of the street, apparently intending to rejoin his men farther back in Moore Street. However:

> he had covered only a few yards when he was shot from the barricade and he fell forward, his sword clattering in front of him. He lay motionless for a few seconds and we thought him dead. Then with a great effort he raised himself a little on his left arm and with his right made the sign of the cross. Again he lay down and such was the greyness of his face we thought him dead; then minutes, seconds – I can't tell – he stirred and by supreme efforts slowly and painfully dragged himself inch by inch into Sackville Lane, a few yards away where he lay down for the last time.[100]

According to his son Aodogán the injuries in themselves weren't lethal, but the loss of blood was catastrophic, especially with no medical assistance available. The O'Rahilly knew his inevitable fate but still had time to compose a last message to his wife Nancy, which ended: 'I got more than one bullet, I think. Tons and tons of love, dearie, to you & the boys and to Nell and Anna. It was a good fight anyhow. Please deliver this to Nannie O'Rahilly, 40 Herbert Park Dublin. Good-bye Darling.' He became the most famous of nine members of the General Post Office garrison killed in action.[101] Meanwhile, inside the GPO Pearse became increasingly perplexed that no dispatch had arrived from The O'Rahilly announcing the occupation of Williams & Woods. When MacDermott announced that evacuation to the jam factory would soon commence an incredulous McLoughlin, aware that the British had already seized the premises, denounced the move as madness. When Pearse told him that The O'Rahilly had gone there, 'I [McLoughlin] said "My God: he'll be killed: It is certain death." I then asked, "What way have they gone?"' Drawing his revolver, he dashed across the road into Henry Place and ran towards Moore Lane. There, a handful of men who had accompanied The O'Rahilly told him, 'He's gone'.

As darkness fell the top of the Metropole block became a blazing mass and several roofs now collapsed. MacDermott suddenly remembered the Metropole garrison and sent Traynor an order to retreat to the GPO. The Metropole men dashed across Prince's Street, through the big doors and into the sorting office where they lined up with about 300 men of the GPO garrison. Barely 30 yards away a wall of flame extended to the roof, loose ammunition exploded like machine-gun fire and bombs detonated. In the midst of this Wagnerian denouement men with rifles slung or at the slope stood to attention while one grinning Volunteer had even insouciantly plonked a German *pickelhaube* on his head. Just then Traynor's men lost Neale, their Cockney lookout, wounded by either a carelessly discharged shotgun or a stray British sniper bullet exploding an ammunition pouch and ripping his lower torso to shreds. Neale swayed, gasping to a neighbour, 'Can't you stand away and let a fellow lie down'. He was set down on a pile of mail sacks where he told Traynor, 'I'm dying, comrade'; an accurate prognosis because he expired the following day.

Pearse now made his final speech of the Rising to the assembled garrison, paying tribute to their gallantry before they erupted spontaneously into *The Soldier's Song*. The evacuation began at about 8 p.m. from the Henry Street side entrance: 'Shells were screaming and exploding with periodic regularity, the ear was assailed with the roar of machine-guns in full action; the incessant pattering and zipping of bullets; the crash of falling beams and tumbling masonry and a circle of blazing fires menaced them.'[102] Having conditioned himself emotionally for a last stand, Tom Clarke proclaimed that he would never leave the GPO alive. Waving his automatic pistol, he shouted: 'You can all go and leave me here. I'll go down with the building', and only Sean MacDermott could persuade him to change his mind.[103] Uncontrollable panic was never far away. Liam Tannam steadied his men's nerves by lighting a cigar and nonchalantly walking up and down, though inwardly his emotions were churning.[104] The garrison departed in batches, with the devoted Winifred Carney shielding Connolly's stretcher from enemy sniper fire. Pearse stood by the door until the last contingent had passed safely through and then went back into the blazing building to conduct a hasty search through the rooms for anybody left behind. After what seemed an interminable interval he returned, 'begrimed with soot and dust, his face and eyes swollen with the heat', and emerged into Henry Street.[105] The occupation of the GPO was over. Pearse believed, and subsequent accounts assert, that he was the last person to leave the doomed headquarters but he had missed Diarmuid Lynch and Harry Boland. They were still underground making the ammunition safe, unaware of events overhead. When they re-emerged they were astonished to see the hall completely deserted and so it was Lynch who had the distinction of being the last person to depart the General Post Office.[106]

Any evaluation of the performance of the rebel leadership in O'Connell Street during Easter Week must emphasise Connolly's contribution. For years before 1916 he had written and spoken in favour of a rising and, through his Citizen Army, prepared for one. The Citizen Army was entirely his creation: its organisation, officers and men were chosen by him alone and he controlled it autocratically through a leadership style that stressed distance and authority. He demanded efficiency, sobriety, seriousness, ideological commitment and absolute obedience. At times Connolly could be positively brutal even to his inner circle, once unjustifiably accusing Michael Mallin of being drunk. However, it is a measure of the respect and indeed fear which he inspired that his absolute integrity, moral ascendancy and leadership position were never challenged.

Connolly's achievements before the Rising had been impressive because, while the Irish Volunteers numerically dwarfed the minuscule Citizen Army, in almost every other respect Connolly's organisation was superior. Its members were committed ideologically to the single, unambiguous goal of revolution. The Citizen Army's training was directed towards preparing them for urban warfare and its unity of purpose and discipline contrasted starkly with the Irish Volunteers, an organisation riven with ideological disputes and faction-fighting, and whose indecisive chief of staff was being continually and successfully subverted by a determined minority.

The Military Council's eagerness at the start of 1916 to have Connolly on its side then is understandable, but more surprising and impressive was the ease and effectiveness of the subsequent military collaboration between this one-man band and a group of similarly strong-willed men. Behind the stern, humourless, prickly, stubborn exterior there was a greater flexibility in Connolly than is often realised, an ability to react to changing circumstances that he displayed throughout Easter Week. Ratifying his selection as commandant-general of the Dublin forces must have been one of the Military Council's easiest decisions. There simply was no rival. By insisting from the start of the Rising that the only army he now recognised was the Army of the Irish Republic, Connolly ensured an amicable working relationship between his own Citizen Army and the Irish Volunteers. Any lingering hostility was greatly diminished by many Volunteers' admiration for the Citizen Army's professionalism, dedication, bravery and ruthlessness, as well as Connolly's insistence that his only criterion was military effectiveness.

As a leader Connolly emerges as inspirational, brave, decisive and energetic. He also showed a greater ease with the rank and file, softening his usual brusqueness with some rather wooden humour. His willingness to share every danger actually led directly to his fearsome wound. Arguably, as commandant-general he should never have placed himself in such jeopardy at a crucial time, but Connolly reviled those First World War generals who, safely ensconced in châteaux behind the front line, dispatched countless soldiers to their death.

Connolly's ability to read the overall strategic situation was quite impressive. On Easter Tuesday he grasped quickly the implications of the failure of the country to rise in support of the Dublin Volunteers, remodelling his strategy, redeploying his forces in the city and strengthening the GPO's defences in readiness for a British assault. It is often argued, correctly, that Connolly was found out by his insistence that British capitalists would never permit widespread devastation of property – even to suppress a rebellion. However, if Connolly was blinded by Marxist theory many politically different people shared his conviction. Indeed, before Easter 1916 almost everyone would have regarded it as inconceivable that any British government would level much of the centre of one of the largest cities in the United Kingdom. If Connolly had miscalculated then so had many others. In addition, Connolly was prepared to recognise his miscalculation and respond accordingly. Above all he cared about the men under his command and while he certainly expected them to be prepared to die for the cause, they always had to be given a fighting chance. Once the British resorted to blasting and burning the Volunteers out, Connolly wasn't prepared to let them be physically annihilated from a distance without being able to retaliate effectively.

Returning to the GPO after his futile search for The O'Rahilly, Sean McLoughlin was astonished to see the entire garrison running towards him: 'There was terrible confusion – almost panic. No one seemed to have any idea what to do.' Waving his sword McLoughlin cried: 'Come on and fight for Ireland.'[107] Eamon Bulfin thought 'there was no cohesion. Nobody seemed to be in charge once we left the General Post Office. It was every man for himself.'[108] When someone shouted that British snipers were firing from the roof of a mineral water factory McLoughlin detached men and ordered them to force their way inside. There they confronted a second group of Volunteers entering from the opposite side. Both opened fire simultaneously, leaving one man dead and another seriously wounded. When a temporary calm descended McLoughlin encountered the leaders. Pearse stood beside Connolly while MacDermott was shouting: 'My God, we are not going to be caught like rats and killed without a chance to fight.'[109] McLoughlin tried to calm him, insisting that he could get them all out if he were in sole command. A despairing MacDermott replied, 'We have no chance now: this is the end'. McLoughlin went to the head of the column where he told the men they had to get out as quickly as possible:

> The British were now alive to what was taking place and were opening up with all they had. Beyond us the Post Office was an inferno and the only light in the lane was the terrible glow in the skies. The wounded were groaning but we could not attend to them. I realised we had to get past Henry Place.[110]

He ordered a motorcar to be dragged out of a yard and pushed across the end of Moore Lane, screening them from enemy view.

Henry Place was in complete chaos. Someone cried that British snipers were attacking from a whitewashed house and McLoughlin led Traynor, Staines, Saurin and others in storming the building. Saurin:

> could see puffs of white smoke coming from the front of it, which I imagined to be enemy fire from the windows. With the crowd I went charging into the side entrance ready for hand-to-hand encounter. The house was completely empty of enemy and what seemed to be fire directed from it was the flaking and scattering of the white-washed surface by the countless bullets fired down Moore Lane opposite from British machine guns.[111]

In a bizarre incident, Liam Tannam broke into another house where:

> lurid flames from the burning buildings that moment flashed up and disclosed about a dozen heads ranged along the room and apparently without bodies. I put my hand on something hairy and nearly died of fright. I then found it was a workshop belonging to Drago, a Hairdresser and Wigmaker.[112]

Some Volunteers injured their comrades when battering doors with rifles whose safety catches had been left off.

Crossing into Moore Street was extremely dangerous because of British machine-gun fire from the Rotunda Hospital roof. At one point amidst the gunfire Plunkett stood exposed in the middle of the road and drew his sword, dipping it periodically when he judged it safe for men to dash across.[113] All this time Connolly was lying on his back on a stretcher crying out to men around him who eventually lifted him through a window into Cogan's shop on the corner of Moore Street; the Cogans, who lived on the premises, took shelter in the basement.[114] Tom Clarke attempted, unsuccessfully, to blow the lock off a gate in order to get through a building and save his men exposing themselves to British fire.[115] Volunteers started forcing their way into houses in Moore Street, many of whose doors had been closed by frightened residents. One Volunteer blew the lock off just as the owner, Mr McKane, was about to open the door; the bullet passing through his shoulder, killing his 15-year-old daughter Brigit and frightening fourteen screaming children. As Mrs McKane cried, 'My child, oh my child', an agitated MacDermott shouted for the Volunteer's name but she insisted it had been an appalling accident. Joe Good noticed a piece of skull, about the size of half an orange, lying on the floor and he surreptitiously slipped it into his pocket.[116] Believing her husband was dying, Mrs McKane hysterically grabbed a pillow slip, burst her way past Volunteers barring her way and rushed down Moore Lane waving her white 'flag' towards the British barricade – ignoring warnings shouted by astounded soldiers. Eventually she returned to her house with a young Dominican priest who broke down and wept when he saw what had happened.[117]

Meanwhile Connolly was being manhandled up the stairs but the house was so cramped that he was carried almost perpendicularly over the banister. Despite his agony he never complained, though like all the wounded he had a dreadful thirst, speaking longingly of a cup of tea. When Nurse O'Farrell asked Connolly how he felt, he replied, 'Bad'. Shortly afterwards other leaders joined him and some mattresses were procured for Connolly and many of the seventeen men wounded during the retreat. O'Farrell and others spent the night treating them amid 'the roar of burning buildings, machine guns playing on the houses, and, at intervals, what seemed to be hand grenades'.[118]

By now Connolly's ability to exercise effective command had gone and something extraordinary took place. Sean McLoughlin, the 18-year-old Fianna scout was summoned to meet the leaders with whom he now shared a cup of tea and a meal eaten in silence. MacDermott then told him that 'you are going to get a big job': McLoughlin would replace Connolly as commandant, with sole responsibility for issuing military orders and leading the garrison to safety. MacDermott, who had known McLoughlin for a couple of years, had proposed him and Connolly had ratified the appointment.[119] Both of them excellent judges of men, they recognised McLoughlin's courage, daring, decisiveness and leadership ability – as well, no doubt, the powerful symbolism of handing the torch to a younger generation. And if they expected him to be unsparingly candid in his analysis of their predicament, they weren't disappointed. He told them bluntly that the garrison was in this situation because of their failure to provide a proper line of retreat towards the Four Courts. The British had been building up their strength in this area since Thursday morning when they erected a barricade in Moore Street at the Parnell Street end. Snipers and an 18-pounder gun had then become very active, setting four houses in Moore Street on fire and an officer had warned residents that he intended levelling as many houses as necessary to root out the rebels. Diarmuid Lynch recalled that:

> As the night wore on the fires became more menacing. We deemed it wise to retreat somewhat from them. In one small room we came across two of our men lying fast asleep their heads near the fender, a good fire in the grate and feet almost touching the wall opposite. They were so exhausted that they had to be lifted bodily through the bored walls.[120]

McLoughlin said that it was now a race against time before the British completed their encirclement of the garrison and either shot, blasted or burnt them out. However, any break-out would have to wait until daylight. Moving large numbers of men in darkness was potentially catastrophic because command and co-ordination would be very difficult and they would almost certainly panic if the British heard sounds of movement and opened fire. The first priority was to disperse the garrison as much as possible to present a less inviting target and McLoughlin ordered tunnelling parties to begin work immediately on boring their way through walls so that Volunteers could spread out into the houses of Moore Street. The street consisted almost entirely of traders – victuallers, fishmongers, dairies, fruiterers and others – often with families living over the shop; the tunnellers would have nearly a score of premises to get through before the end.

As almost sixty Volunteers bored from house to house they carried Connolly along in his stretcher. Since British dispositions and intentions were unknown, they carried daggers, hunting knives, rifles, pistols and home-made bombs ready for hand-to-hand fighting with any soldiers coming from the opposite direction. One man's unsheathed knife accidentally stabbed the backside of the person in front; he also used it to bag a ham hanging on a wall.[121] The houses occupied were darkened to prevent enemy sniper fire. Connolly and the other leaders finally came to rest at 15 and 16 Moore Street. There, MacDermott and Jim Ryan slept briefly on a mattress in the kitchen, Patrick and Willie Pearse covered themselves with their coats and lay on top of a table, underneath which snored a weary Volunteer clutching his rifle. The wounded were transferred through the back yard to an open hayshed. Outside, shelling, machine-gun fire and bombing continued until 3 a.m. The GPO munitions dump finally detonated in a massive explosion that caused everyone to jump, and created 'a sparkling volcano which quaked the foundations of the surrounding streets'.[122] Some people resting in the rear yard of Kelly's poultry shop at the corner of Sackville Lane claim that during the night they heard The O'Rahilly calling out for a drink of water. His body was indeed lying outside Kelly's and if he died a lingering death then it was entirely possible. If the Kelly family also heard him they might have thought it was only a drunken man, and going outside to look risked a sniper's bullet. Already a woman at the opposite corner near Riddall's Row had been shot dead stooping by her bedroom window.

Meanwhile, Sean McLoughlin had placed sentinels to protect the tunnellers as they continued to work by the light of burning buildings. Oscar Traynor's party worked all night and eventually made its way through to the end of Moore Street. Saurin recalled that: 'We went on and on for what seemed an interminable journey, a trailing exhausted crowd, dirty and dusty, some wounded and bandaged.'[123] As they went along Volunteers barricaded the houses, throwing every piece of furniture down into the hallways and blocking doors. Eamon Bulfin recalled that 'one shell hit a house which we had evacuated down at the lower part of Moore Street and flattened it absolutely. It went down like a house of cards.'[124]

Traynor witnessed many distressing sights. Covered from head to foot in plaster and brick dust, he broke through into one house, finding a terrified woman, an old white-bearded man and two young children crouching in a corner. In another he crawled out into the street, dragging a semi-conscious and delirious Volunteer into the hallway where he successfully bandaged a leg, the whole calf of which had apparently blown away. By now Traynor thought that he had seen it all, until he looked through a hole and saw a pair of staring eyes:

> It was hard to know if the dog was looking scared or fierce. Some of the men thought it would be safer to shoot it. I thought I would have a try at coaxing it, but all my approaches were met by the same stony stare. I decided to take a chance and go through the hole. I approached very gingerly, and eventually put my hand on his head. At this he seemed to come out of a trance and immediately became friendly. He was probably there on his own for the best part of the week with an inferno raging round him.[125]

In one shop an odour from piles of fish bones almost overcame Saurin. In the back yard Pearse appeared and went up a stepladder into the loft of a big empty barn. Risking a sniper's bullet, he looked up and down the street before descending silently and going on his way. Curious, Saurin ascended too and saw that: 'a very well constructed one [barricade] spanned the lane at the top and in front of this sprawled three dead horses, shot no doubt as they galloped frantically up the lane on being released from their stables the night before.'[126]

At daybreak McLoughlin saw Volunteer bodies lying on the pavement and in the roadway:

> One familiar one I approached and this was O'Rahilly lying on his back, his arms outstretched, blood oozing from his body in a pool under him and flies buzzing about his head. Two or three others lay dead near him. I called Sean MacDermott over and some of the men followed. We knelt for a few moments and said an Act of Contrition. I then took my handkerchief out of my pocket and covered O'Rahilly's face. The same was done for the other three. That was all we could do.[127]

Having promised that he could save the garrison, McLoughlin had used his intimate knowledge of the surrounding area to formulate a plan of brutal clarity that focused entirely on extricating the Volunteers and fighting on from another location. Staying where they were wasn't an option because soon the British would either burn or shell them out. As Connolly and Pearse listened, he proposed using twenty to thirty men gathered in Sackville Lane to rush the enemy barricade at the end of Moore Street. McLoughlin would simultaneously throw a bomb at the British, giving cover for

everyone else to emerge from doorways in Moore Street and dash across the road.
They would reassemble in Little Denmark Street, beside a warehouse that screened
them from soldiers in Parnell Street, and then make their way towards Capel Street,
the markets and then hopefully link up with Daly's battalion in the Four Courts.
His strategy depended entirely on speed of movement and the rapid reactions of
able-bodied men; they had to be unencumbered so everyone else was surplus to
requirement. Other than Connolly, 'we could not be burdened with the prisoners
and wounded'.[128] McLoughlin intended his line of retreat to avoid the thickly populated areas of Little Denmark and Britain Street but even so Pearse feared that '"the
only difficulty with this is that more innocent people would be killed." I said, "I am
sorry. I cannot help that. This is a military operation and I can only make it successful if I don't think about these things."'[129] And they had to move soon. McLoughlin
warned Connolly and Pearse that zero hour was noon, when he believed the British
would launch an attack: 'I then went out and formed the men into the "Death or
Glory Squad."'[130]

McLoughlin assumed that Connolly and Pearse had endorsed his plan for a new
evacuation, but clearly it disturbed both men. Throughout the Rising Connolly
had insisted on sharing every danger with the rank and file and would considered it
unthinkable that he be singled out for special consideration while every other casualty and all the prisoners were abandoned to their fate. This was almost certainly the
moment when he decided that enough was enough: he couldn't impose any more
sacrifice and sorrow on his men. Pearse had also witnessed death and terror being
inflicted on the local civilian population. During the morning he saw British soldiers
shoot at a mostly female group attempting to leave Moore Street. There were other
distressing and fatal incidents in Moore Street. One man fleeing his burning house
died holding a white flag, while a man and his wife lay prone on the roadway beside
their daughter. When the Doyle and MacDonagh families living in one house feared
it was about to catch fire, Mr Doyle attached his wife's apron to an umbrella and led
out seven people only for them to be sprayed with bullets. As Mr Doyle lay dying
in front of his wife she tried to drag him out of danger but was wounded as well.
Eventually a neighbour threw out a rope and pulled both of them inside his shop.[131]
These scenes had a powerful impact on Pearse, concentrating his mind on the necessity of ending civilian suffering.

Unaware of Pearse and Connolly's doubts, McLoughlin selected his suicide squad,
assembled it in a yard in Sackville Lane and gave each man his instructions. Suddenly
he was called back. Pearse was sitting on Connolly's bed, Clarke and MacDermott
occupied chairs and Plunkett was hunkered down on the floor in a corner. Once again
McLoughlin outlined his plan, but this time Pearse told him to put it temporarily on
hold. While McLoughlin left to stand down his men, the Provisional Government
wrestled with the dilemma of whether to go on or not. Six days earlier it had debated
starting the Rising; now – minus Ceannt and MacDonagh – they debated ending it.
Pearse, Connolly, Clarke, MacDermott and Plunkett held their lengthy 'council of
war' alongside Willie Pearse, three wounded Volunteers, a badly injured British army
sergeant and three women, O'Farrell, Grenan and Carney. Also watching over their
deliberations was a uniformed Robert Emmet, his portrait hanging on a wall. Every
fibre of their being would have resisted even contemplating that this moment would

happen, but now it had arrived and a decision – one way or another – was unavoidable. It must have been especially agonising for Tom Clarke, who had promised his wife never to surrender and who as a human being had long been characterised by defiance and a refusal never to give in. But Clarke was also bound by collective responsibility and a need to demonstrate to the enemy – and history – that the leaders remained united to the very end. Even had he wanted to, he could not turn on his comrades if they went against his wishes.

Eventually they resolved to seek terms from the British in order to prevent 'further slaughter of the civil population and to save the lives of as many as possible of our followers'. Once again, as a minute by Pearse confirmed, their decision was by majority vote. Although he didn't identify individuals, it was only the irreconcilable Clarke who opposed surrender, almost as if he believed that by sheer force of will the tide of battle could still be turned. This bestowed an exquisite symmetry on the Rising, because less than a week before, at Liberty Hall, Clarke had stood alone and argued for action that day; now on Easter Saturday he stood alone again. Soon afterwards Joe Good noticed Connolly, Pearse and Plunkett 'talking quietly and occasionally laughing, like men who had made a decision and were passing the time', while Clarke stood silently by himself at a window.[132] Almost twenty years earlier he had been given a second chance to rebuild his life and resume a political career and he had done so with extraordinary single-mindedness. Now the project to which he had dedicated his every moment since release from prison was collapsing all around him.

Soon afterwards, MacDermott told Jim Ryan:

> That the signatories would be shot and the rest of us set free, he thought. I found it hard to believe this at first but later Tom Clarke and Joseph Plunkett used practically the same words when I asked them. Is one to conclude then that these men had agreed amongst themselves before Pearse went to the Castle that they should offer their own lives in an attempt to save those of their followers?[133]

This fascinating speculation puts the blood sacrifice theory into an entirely new light, not as a strategy carefully thought out in advance but one that only emerged as the Rising disintegrated. Probably conceived on Saturday morning at the war council around Connolly's bedside, it was designed not to redeem Ireland but to perform the eminently practical task of saving the lives of their men.

After McLoughlin stood down his men, rumours about surrendering began circulating, provoking a furious reaction. When selected for this probably suicidal attack on the barricade, Traynor had remarked, 'Well, this looks like the end for us', but the indomitable Boland simply replied that 'the only thing that is wrong about this order is that it should have been given a long time ago'.[134] At this point, they were waiting in a butcher's slaughterhouse, eating tins of pears, when McLoughlin postponed the operation. Up until then everything had been subordinated to tunnelling, barricading and preparing for action, now inactivity allowed divisions to surface, creating a potentially difficult situation for the leadership.

At about 12.45 p.m. MacDermott led Elizabeth O'Farrell to the door of No 15. Carrying a stick with a white handkerchief, she stepped outside and walked very slowly up Moore Street. As she did so Tom Clarke wept openly while Connolly reassured an agitated Julia Grenan that the British wouldn't shoot her best friend.[135] O'Farrell took a verbal message from Pearse to the commander of the British forces requesting a discussion about surrender terms. When she reached the barricade at the top of Moore Street a British officer dispatched her initially to a house in Parnell Street where a hostile officer accused her of being a spy and removed the Red Cross insignia from her arm and apron. She was then transferred to meet General Lowe, who, by coincidence, received her in Tom Clarke's shop in Parnell St. He listened to her courteously and then drove her back to the top of Moore Street, instructing her to tell Pearse that unconditional surrender was required within half an hour. He confirmed this in writing. It was now about 2.25 p.m.[136]

On her return journey O'Farrell passed Sackville Lane and saw The O'Rahilly's body with the feet lying against a shop's side entrance and his head resting on the kerbstone. After she delivered Lowe's ultimatum another leadership confer-ence decided to send her back with a note that attempted to bargain, but Lowe was immovable, reiterating his demand for unconditional surrender. If Pearse did not return with O'Farrell within half an hour, followed by Connolly, he would recommence hostilities. The Provisional Government members reluctantly agreed. Kneeling at Connolly's bedside, a weeping Winifred Carney asked, 'Was there no other way?' Connolly quietly reassured her that he was not prepared to see his brave boys burnt to death. Just before Pearse left, a dying British prisoner who was lying on a bed caught Julia Grenan's attention:

> He called to her, and as she bent over him, whispered that he wanted to speak to Pearse who stood close by: 'But that is Pearse!' said Julia, puzzled at the request: 'Yes, I know,' said the soldier: 'I want him.' Pearse, ever gentle and courteous, came to his bedside: 'I want you to put your arms round me and lift me,' gasped the soldier. Pearse did so and, holding the man up, said: 'And now what shall I do?' 'That's all I want!' said the soldier as he closed his eyes.[137]

Wearing his heavy military greatcoat, Pearse shook every Volunteer's hand silently before stepping into Moore Street. With O'Farrell almost trotting by his side, he marched to the British barricade and handed his sword, pistol and ammunition to Lowe. Then he signed a formal document of surrender that was lying on a bench taken from a nearby shop. At both leaders' request O'Farrell agreed to convey the sur-render to Volunteer outposts before Pearse, smiling shyly, shook her hand and stepped into a military car. As the vehicle, with armed soldiers hanging on to its runner boards, disappeared from view at the Parnell Monument, O'Farrell heard a British officer say, 'It would be interesting to know how many marks that fellow has in his pocket'.[138]

When Pearse reached British military headquarters at Parkgate, Maxwell had him sign a formal instrument of surrender stating that:

> In order to prevent the further slaughter of Dublin citizens, and in the hope of saving the lives of our followers now surrounded and hopelessly outnumbered, the members of the Provisional Government at Headquarters have agreed to an uncon-ditional surrender, and the Commandants of the various districts in the City and Country will order their commands to lay down arms.

During Pearse's absence Connolly was made ready for his transfer to Dublin Castle. Dr Jim Ryan, the medical officer in the GPO, treated his leg and renewed the bandages; Julia Grenan combed his matted hair while Winifred Carney tidied his dust-covered Citizen Army uniform, on to which fell her tears. Well away from a barricaded window, three wounded Volunteers and a British soldier huddled on a mattress in the corner. Connolly was a very heavy man and the four stretcher bearers were assisted by three officers, Diarmuid Lynch, Liam Tannam and Michael Staines. Kneeling Volunteers, each holding a rifle in one hand and rosary beads in the other, recited a prayer as they carried him away.[139] Preceding them downstairs, Willie Pearse opened the door and showed a white flag. After a signal from the British barricade, Connolly's stretcher party set off towards Parnell Street. Houses in Parnell Street were crammed with British soldiers while an overflow sprawled out on to the pavements. At the British headquarters in Clarke's shop they were allocated a route to the Castle and surrounded by an escort of fifty men carrying rifles with fixed bayonets. The journey via Capel, Essex and Parliament streets was very demanding but Tannam recalled that:

> Although Connolly was in great pain he took it all smiling and said to our lads 'Boys, you were great'. When we entered the Upper Castle Yard we made a left wheel and halted. Some soldiers who were knocking about the yard assumed a very threatening attitude. One of them belonging to an Irish regiment made an attempt to get at us with a bayonet in his hand; of course he was prevented by the escort.[140]

At the Castle hospital Connolly was brought Pearse's document and endorsed it for the men under his command in the Moore Street district and Stephen's Green area.

Pearse and Connolly's surrender orders were brought to Nurse O'Farrell at the barricade and she took them to the remaining leaders in Moore Street. Breaking the news to the rank and file would be very difficult. Although leadership unity had held there was no guarantee that rank-and-file discipline would do so, especially after enduring so much for the struggle to go on. Yielding now might seem an admission that all their sacrifices since evacuating the General Post Office had been for nothing. They were already emotionally drained. Jack Plunkett remembered Saturday morning as dreadful: 'The absence of activity made it horribly depressing. The lack of news and food and sleep.'[141] At this moment the remaining leaders had to continue to display a rock-like solidarity in the face of whatever dissension the surrender might unleash.

After the cancellation of the bayonet charge, Oscar Traynor had returned to a house in Moore Street and slept on a bare floor until he was awakened with news of a surrender. He and many comrades were dumbfounded. Assuming this meant at least a lengthy prison sentence, they angrily destroyed their weapons. Others demanded that they be granted prisoner-of-war treatment, something that MacDermott promised they would receive:

> As we were leaving the houses to line up in Moore Street I met Sean MacDermott, whom I had met on many occasions, and I said to him, more in sorrow than anger 'Is this what we were brought out for? To spend the rest of our lives in English dungeons?' His reply to that was to wave a piece of paper, about 3" by 6", which he held

in his hand, and which had about half-a-dozen lines of typescript on it, and in addition what I thought were two signatures: 'No! No!,' he said, 'We are surrendering as prisoners of war.' I often wondered what significance the paper had. But though I discussed this incident on many later occasions with my comrades of the fight, we could never arrive at a satisfactory solution as to what it could have been.[142]

Joe Good wrote that 'something close to mutiny'[143] erupted in and around Moore Street, especially among his Kimmage comrades who had fled conscription and now feared being shot as deserters or shipped to the Western Front. As a mood to fight on developed among the rank and file, the leaders stepped forward, one after another, to support their agreed policy. Clarke spoke first and was followed by Plunkett, who dragged himself forward to plead unsuccessfully for unity. It was MacDermott, standing precariously and, for a polio victim, dangerously, on the lid of a dustbin, who managed to quell the mounting disaffection. He urged them to look outside at the dead civilians lying in the streets and imagine how many more there would be if the Rising had been prolonged. He also pointed out the even more terrible destruction which the enemy could inflict on their city: 'You've all seen what happened to the Post Office!' Their duty now was to survive and endure, spend at most some years in jail and then renew the struggle: 'We, who will be shot, will die happy – knowing that there are still plenty of you around who will finish the job.'[144]

The wounded were now carried out in blankets and placed on the pavement, propped against the walls of Hanlon's fish shop where an ambulance collected them later. Willie Pearse and another officer searched the lanes and alleyways, gathering up many scattered Volunteers until finally over 320 men lined up in Moore Street. Sean MacDermott stood out in his navy-blue suit, Willie Pearse waved his white flag victoriously and Plunkett's wobbling sword seemed to unbalance him somewhat. When the garrison was lined up Sean McLoughlin addressed the men. According to Charles Saurin:

> he told us we were to march out into O'Connell Street where we would lay down our arms and then be permitted to go to our homes. Some cheered this announcement, others were bewildered at it and others again were frankly disgusted, for there were determined men in the crowd who did not understand the meaning of the word 'surrender'. He had hardly finished when Joseph Plunkett ran up to him hastily and said something which caused him to correct what he had already said and to tell us we would be prisoners of war. The second statement was received in utter silence.[145]

They were then ordered to slope arms, march down Moore Street and turn left into Henry Place. When they climbed over a barricade there they saw a body: it was The O'Rahilly. One Volunteer officer broke ranks, knelt down, blessed himself and covered the face. In Henry Street a British NCO stood ostentatiously loading a revolver, whilst O'Connell Street was swarming with British soldiers. Leaning on a stick, MacDermott walked calmly on the pavement beside Tom Clarke, hands in pockets and a cap on the back of his head. Eventually the Volunteers stopped near the Gresham Hotel and laid down their rifles, shotguns, revolvers, ammunition, bayonets, bandoliers and belts. But although militarily defeated they exhibited an unbroken spirit and engaged in calculated acts of defiance, such as smashing weapons at their captors' feet, puffing on cigarettes and cigars when ordered to stop smoking and laughing at disrespectful remarks about their conquerors. As darkness descended, military lorries departed with surrendered arms and ammunition while British officers finished gathering the prisoners' names and military rank.

The prisoners were then marched a short distance to a grassy space in front of the Rotunda Hospital at the northern end of O'Connell Street. There they were surrounded by armed soldiers of the Royal Irish Regiment and ordered to lie down. Machine guns on the roofs of the Rotunda and nearby buildings covered the area while angry guards using rifle butts threatened anyone who even dared to stretch their legs on the surrounding pathway. British officers verbally abused and harassed men they regarded as traitors and allies of Germany, who had stabbed England in the back when the war was going badly for the Allies. When one observed to MacDermott, 'You have cripples in your army', the limping polio victim retorted: 'You have your place, Sir, and I have mine and you had better mind your place, sir.' Another officer kicked Plunkett on the soles of his shiny top boots shouting: 'I suppose you looted those boots. You should be shot out of hand for that. You may be later.'[146] The commanding British officer at the Rotunda was Captain Lea Wilson, a 31-year-old Englishman whose military party, Saurin recalled, struck matches and peered in disgust at Volunteers 'as if we were some peculiar type of animal they had never seen before'.[147] When he searched the dying Plunkett and found his will, Lea Wilson proclaimed, 'This bally fellow thinks he's going to be shot', before returning it to Plunkett and remarking: 'keep it, you will be.'[148] Retreating to the roadway, Wilson asked them: 'Men, who are the worst, the Germans or the Sinn Feiners?' As if on cue, they chorused that the rebels were indeed the foulest. Rousing his audience to even greater heights, he then inquired: 'What will we do to the Sinn Feiners?' With one exception they shouted: 'Shoot them, shoot them.'[149] The dissenter had wanted them hanged. Ordinary soldiers of the Royal Irish and the Shropshires were just as unsympathetic; only one crossed the gravel drive to give Saurin and some others a cup of tea.

Saturday night was long and bitterly cold. Prisoners remembered 'a night of horror', with everyone thirsty, 'cold, miserable, hungry and tired and with the canopy of Heaven for a roof'.[150] With no sanitation available many men had to relieve themselves on the grass, despite the presence of a handful of women like Winifred Carney and Julia Grenan. The ground was hard and damp and an area suitable for about 150 men was eventually packed with over 400 prisoners as men from other garrisons arrived, among them Ned Daly's 1st Battalion. Everyone huddled together to generate warmth, many suffering painful cramps, while anyone managing to snatch some sleep was usually awakened by others trying to make themselves more comfortable. British officers and soldiers also roused men, taunting them with mock offers to fetch food and cigarettes. Sean McLoughlin recalled that one British officer 'told us we were covered from all corners and that any man who moved during the night without permission would be shot. There was dead silence. Nobody spoke.'[151] Throughout the night shooting could be heard in the distance. Much closer were the screams and cries for help from inside the Rotunda, the world's first maternity hospital but now one that was also crowded with civilians. Some men thought them calls for a doctor, but to Frank Henderson they seemed 'the shrieks of the patients inside, who appeared to us to have gone out of their minds'.[152]

Eventually a group of uniformed Dublin Metropolitan policemen arrived, all wearing greatcoats and carrying revolvers. To Saurin many seemed ill at ease, unable to look the Volunteers in the eye and apparently ashamed at what they had to do. But the G-men, Dublin's plainclothes political police, were already hunting for the Rising's leaders even before the last shot had been fired. After they identified Clarke as a dangerous subversive Wilson smacked his face, shouting, 'This old bastard has been at it before. He has a shop across the street there. He's an old Fenian.'[153] He then frog-marched Clarke to the Rotunda steps and searched him thoroughly; many Volunteers believed, probably mistakenly, that he also stripped him naked. During an hour's interrogation Clarke was subjected to 'the third degree' before he was returned to his fellow prisoners. According to one of these he:

> told us they had searched him and taken away all he had, and that the record of his whole life had been read out to him. His life in prison, his conduct there, his life in the U.S, even to the cut of clothes he wore there; his life from his return to Ireland up to the present day: 'Everything, they have everything.' he said.[154]

At 9 a.m., after twelve seemingly endless hours, the stiff and sore prisoners were finally allowed to get up and nurses who crowded at the hospital windows saw a cloud of urine steaming up from the grass. By now the guards were from the South Staffordshire Regiment, two lines of whom escorted the column as it set off. Deprived of his walking stick, MacDermott leaned on other prisoners and the brisk pace soon had him covered in sweat. Marching towards the southern end of O'Connell Street, Saurin saw buildings that 'were just empty shells with smouldering fires still burning in them'.[155] Debris littered O'Connell Bridge, exploding gas pipes had blown a large hole in the middle and a dead man lay face down against the parapet. The column's destination was Richmond Barracks, 2 miles away at Inchicore on the western edge of the city; an exhausting journey for men who hadn't washed, shaved, changed their clothes or hardly slept for a week. Swinging right at College Green, they marched along Dame Street and onward, watched by small groups of British soldiers but more often by a single guard at a street corner. One sentry pushed back with his rifle 'a mass of howling women from the back streets who called us filthy names and shrieked curses at us. The mounted officer in charge of us showed faint amusement at all these women's hatred.'[156] In Thomas Street the armed escort prevented Volunteers retaliating against 'separation women' hurling vitriolic abuse; in contrast, officials at Guinness' Brewery in James's Street exhibited a more refined hostility, gazing out with 'superior, contemptuous smiles'.[157] But in the same street people dwelling above shops showed sympathy, causing British officers to warn them to close their windows. Skirting the South Dublin Union the procession passed the Royal Hospital and proceeded down the hill to Kilmainham, before finally entering Richmond Barracks. Far behind came Sean MacDermott who had explained to the officer in charge that he couldn't march in step and was allowed to walk alone at the rear. With an escort he arrived three-quarters of an hour late, completely exhausted from a night's exposure and the rigours of the journey. Plunkett had fainted on arrival and had to be carried in through the prison gates.[158]

8

A City at War

In 1916 Dublin may well have been the Irish capital, but in some respects it wore the appearance of genteel decline. The northern city of Belfast was an industrial power-house at its zenith whereas Dublin reflected a past when it prided itself as the second city of the British Empire. Like an aristocrat fallen on hard times, it still maintained a facade of grandeur as the seat of the viceroy and the centre of British rule in Ireland. The Castle 'season' of receptions and balls and the Royal Dublin Society's horse show were the social highlights of the year. With only light industry, Dublin's functions were primarily administrative, commercial, professional and cultural.

Lack of development had left the city's eighteenth-century heritage of spacious streets and classical public buildings largely unchanged. Despite its social problems, Dublin was considered a beautiful city. Defined on the north and south sides respectively by the Royal and Grand Canals, it was bisected east to west by the River Liffey, with its quays, seven city bridges and two outstanding edifices, the Custom House and the Four Courts. The street pattern related to two main axes, one north–south from O'Connell Street via College Green and Grafton Street to St Stephen's Green, the other east–west from College Green to the oldest part of the city around the cathedrals and the Castle. College Green, with the Bank of Ireland and Trinity College, was the banking and business centre, Grafton Street the fashionable shopping area. St Stephen's Green, the largest of the five Georgian squares, was now a public park. North of the river, O'Connell Street was a broad boulevard whose principal features were the colonnaded General Post Office and the 134ft Nelson Pillar, erected in 1809 and the first such monument to the British victor at Trafalgar. At either end of the street stood Daniel O'Connell 'the Liberator' and the Parnell monolith, with its challenging inscription on behalf of a subject people: 'No man has a right to fix the boundary to the march of a nation.' They symbolised the advance of constitutional nationalism; there was no inkling yet that their tradition, too, with Home Rule now in sight, was in the end to be swept aside by the events about to unfold at the General Post Office.

At the end of the Liffey quays on the western edge of the city lay the Phoenix Park, popularly claimed to be the largest urban park in Europe. Within its wide ter-rain were located the Vice-Regal Lodge (the residence of the lord lieutenant where visiting royalty stayed) and the chief secretary's residence; near the main gates were the headquarters of the British army in Ireland and of the Royal Irish Constabulary. Among its monuments was a towering obelisk to the Duke of Wellington, while the Peninsular War hero, Field Marshal Gough, was a lone bronze horseman on the main avenue that traversed the park for 2 miles. A herd of deer was a reminder of its origins in the seventeenth century as a royal deer-park. Long a favourite resort of Dubliners with its playing fields, band performances and zoological gardens, Phoenix Park, laid out in the grand manner, was also an expression of the imperial state. On the other side of the Liffey, across from the park, lay the Royal Hospital, Kilmainham, opened in 1684 as a home for old soldiers and now as well the residence of the British commander-in-chief. A short distance from its entrance was the gaol soon to acquire a grim significance in the story of Easter 1916.

For many years now Dublin's middle classes had been gradually migrating from the centre to new Victorian suburbs beyond the canals. Here in their leafy avenues the still dominant Unionist businesses and professional elite, and the rising Catholic middle class, enjoyed cleaner air away from the deteriorating central areas. While Merrion and Fitzwilliam squares remained socially prestigious, on the north side the Georgian streets were in decline, with houses often becoming overcrowded tenements. The poor family living in one room under a beautiful plasterwork ceiling became a stock image of the Dublin slum. But that was only one aspect of the widespread poverty. In run-down dwellings, congeries of back lanes and unsanitary courts, 100,000 people – a third of the city's population – lived in conditions that were common in cities at the time, but present in Dublin to an extreme degree. Squalor, malnutrition and rampant disease helped to produce the highest death rate in the British Isles. Dublin was also unusual in that the slums were often adjacent to the principal streets. A few minutes' walk from the hotels and shops of O'Connell Street, for example, deprivation mingled with prostitution in the extensive red-light district. The lowest classes were inured to long-term unemployment or a precarious existence as casual labourers, dockers, coal-heavers and in other occupations with low wages and bad working conditions. But the passive acceptance of their lot was changing. Liberty Hall, the headquarters of the Irish Transport and General Workers Union, was becoming the focus of increasing labour militancy.

For a century after the abortive Emmet Rising of 1803 – a rebellion against the Act of Union – Dublin had been a politically quiescent city. Nineteenth-century violence was concentrated largely in the countryside, but in the years before the First World War the city experienced serious political, social and economic tensions. There was a major and bitter industrial dispute in 1913 between the Irish Transport and General Workers Union, led by Connolly's boss Jim Larkin and the Dublin United Tramways Company of William Martin Murphy, whose business empire also included newspapers, the Imperial Hotel and a department store. It was a violent and protracted struggle which began when Murphy locked out the tramwaymen and retaliated against the subsequent wave of sympathetic strikes by employing strike-breakers. Murphy's trams were stoned and the police were involved in frequent confrontations with Larkin's pickets. On 1 September 1913 Larkin attempted to make a speech in O'Connell Street from the balcony of the Imperial Hotel. Scuffling broke out and the police panicked, baton-charging even the crowds which were coming from Mass in the nearby pro-cathedral. In the subsequent rioting which lasted until the following day, two men were killed and 200 policemen injured along with a far greater number of civilians. The labour dispute dragged on through the winter and into 1914 before the union's resistance collapsed. Nevertheless, Murphy's apparently complete victory engendered resentment in the Dublin slums that surfaced again during the Rising when tenement dwellers took spectacular revenge on those businesses that had supported him. There was another bloody episode on Sunday 26 July 1914, at Bachelor's Walk by the River Liffey. Troops of the King's Own Scottish Borderers, who had been called out in an abortive attempt to frustrate an Irish Volunteer gunrunning operation at Howth, just outside Dublin, were confronted by an angry crowd. Eventually the soldiers opened fire and wounded thirty-eight people, one of whom later died.

In 1916 Dublin was a city involved in a great war. Many citizens were fighting and dying in places as far apart as the Western Front in France and Suvla Bay in Turkey in battles that dominated conversation, political debates and newspaper coverage. Its streets and hospitals contained many disabled and convalescent soldiers while troops on leave mingled with civilians, refugees and recruiting officers. The Defence of the Realm Act had given the government unprecedented powers to regulate social and economic life and sometimes the ruthless face of modern warfare came uncomfortably close, as when hundreds of bodies from the torpedoed liner *Lusitania* were washed up on the southern coast of Ireland. However, in many respects, Dublin was strangely detached from the conflict, hardly burdened by the disciplines of total war. Geographical remoteness removed the fear of falling to enemy attack that was ever-present in Paris and Petrograd, and the city didn't even suffer the Zeppelin raids that occurred in Britain. Nor were Ireland's coastal towns bombarded by German warships or, unlike the south coast of England, afflicted by the sound of the great guns in France. Furthermore, while partial conscription had been introduced into Great Britain in 1915, Ireland continued to rely, with diminishing results, on voluntary recruiting. As a result it had become a refuge to those in Britain fleeing compulsory military service.

During 1915 and 1916 Britain abandoned 'business as usual' and mobilised politically, socially, economically and psychologically for total war. This transformation entailed the sacrifice of many peacetime pleasures and modes of behaviour. By contrast, Ireland became a magnet for those seeking rest and recreation and, for the first time, it experienced the greater traffic of people between the two islands. Soldiers from every part of the empire came on leave and prosperous English couples on motoring tours stayed in Dublin's two finest hotels, the Shelbourne and the Royal Hibernian, frequenting theatres such as the Abbey and the Gaiety. Horse racing continued with meetings which attracted hordes of punters and bookmakers from Britain, visitors who found at their disposal public houses which took a relaxed attitude to opening hours. Soldiers who were based in the city's nine functioning barracks regarded Dublin as an easy posting where they could walk the streets in complete safety, where officers frequented the city's high-class brothels and the rank and file availed themselves of prostitutes in one of the largest red-light districts in Europe. Officers also enjoyed weekend sojourns in the big houses of the Anglo-Irish ascendancy where they socialised, hunted and relaxed. Visitors from Britain travelled to Ireland in complete safety from Holyhead and Liverpool, despite rumours of a

German submarine in the Irish Sea. There were no fatalities until October 1918 when the RMS *Leinster* was sunk just out of Kingstown.

On Easter Monday 1916 Dublin's transformation from normality to deadly urban warfare therfore took its population completely by surprise, and for some hours the city existed in a limbo of unreality. At Stephen's Green, for instance, civilians complained about the disruption caused by 'practice' Citizen Army manoeuvres and threatened to call the 'polis', while one young lady whose British officer boy-friend was arrested insisted that she would wait until the performance was over.[1] At Lansdowne railway station, an amused Volunteer officer, George Lyons, watched the reaction of British officers to the start of the Rising and the premature termination of their Easter leave:

> I turned my attention to some khaki specks I perceived in the motley throng on the departure platform: 'Military men advance to the edge of the platform,' I shouted. I had to repeat the order several times before I could command any attention. There were four British officers in the crowd. They instinctively sought each other and grouped together and looked our way. This was just what I wanted: 'Gentlemen,' I cried, 'you will stand to attention. My men have you covered.' They consulted for a moment, trying to look indifferent and feigning to take the matter as a joke: 'What's the trouble?' enquired one tall cavalry officer, who seemed to be looked upon as a senior: 'No trouble yet,' I answered as I ordered six of my men to keep them covered with their rifles: 'We are in earnest today, however, and there will be heaps of trouble if you break ground without orders,' I added. Some of their fine indifference seemed to fade away to be replaced by perplexion and doubt: 'You will hand over your arms, gentlemen,' I next ordered: 'Oh, we have no arms whatsoever,' declared the senior officer referred to: 'We will take your word as soldiers for that and we will punish you as soldiers if you have lied. Consider yourselves prisoners of war,' I added as I perceived a detachment of my men advancing from the main entrance behind them. These men marched the British officers down to one of the rail offices where they were provided for.[2]

At Boland's bakery one of de Valera's officers recalled how the insurgents:

> started to clear out the staff, but some of them were reluctant to leave until they were shown the business end of our guns – as they were under the impression that we were just on manoeuvres and had carried the joke a bit far. However, our busi-nesslike attitude very soon made them make up their minds.[3]

Douglas Hyde's splendid Easter Week diary shows him spending much of Easter Monday sublimely oblivious to the revolution breaking out all around him and insist-ing to himself that unusual sights and sounds were really part of everyday life.[4] Having gone into central Dublin to visit an art gallery, he was cycling along Stephen's Green when he heard a succession of loud bursts from the front of the Shelbourne Hotel: 'There must be great mortality among tyres today.' Shortly afterwards he noticed the large gate of Stephen's Green shut and thought to himself that it was odd that a park would close on a public holiday. Spotting armed men in the park and two of them digging holes, he mused: 'Are these fools thinking to hide something?' He recorded that he had 'not the slightest idea that there was anything really serious in the air, not even when in the garden half an hour afterwards, I heard a furious outbreak of firing'. What Hyde attributed to Volunteer target practice was in fact a gun battle at Portobello Bridge between the rebels and British soldiers.

A friend of Hyde's, Roderick MacDermott, was outside the General Post Office when Volunteers occupied the building:

They planted a sentry near where he was standing, a raw youth from the west of Ireland armed with something like a rook rifle. An Englishman or some stranger insisted on getting past him to post some letters. The sentry resisted. The man said he must have access to His Majesty's post office. The sentry got more and more irritated and when a second man attempted to pass him he gave him a shove that knocked him over saying 'I didn't come 120 miles to Dublin to go arguing with the likes of ye!'[5]

Although Dublin Castle quickly withdrew the DMP from the streets on Easter Monday some police constables needed time to realise that normal conditions had ceased to exist. Just after Sean Heuston's garrison had finished their initial arrangements to defend the Mendicity a perspiring Patrick Stephenson was lounging in an armchair near a window whose glass had been smashed out:

As I mopped my face I looked out through the window and there with his elbows resting on the coping of the front wall was a tall DMP man. Under the dark blue helmet with its silver facings, there was a big soft face with large eyes like those of an ox. He gazed on the scene with open-mouthed astonishment and you almost heard him say 'What's the world coming to.' After a minute he raised his voice and shouted in a broad country accent: 'Eh, you fellows are going too far at this playing at soldiers. Don't you know you can be arrested for what yez are doing.' The unconscious, ironic humour of this remark struck me as very funny and I burst out laughing. A voice from some other part of the building shouted 'Be off to hell out of that if you don't want a bullet in your thick skull,' but without effect. He stood where he was, seemingly incapable of movement. Just then the small slightly built figure of a boy came running down from the Bridge where he had been helping at the erection of a barricade across the Quay. At the sound of the running feet the DMP man turned and looked down at this pigmy figure with a revolver in its hand. The youngster, Sean MacLoughlin, shouted at the giant in blue, 'you big ejit, why don't you take yourself off while you are alive. Don't you know the Republic has been proclaimed at the GPO and your bloody day is done?' and pointing his revolver in the air, fired off a round. The sound of the shot galvanized the Peeler into action and he fled his post so hastily that he lost his helmet in the flurry.[6]

Even many Volunteers had been caught out by the speed of events. Peadar Healy was a ticket collector at Broadstone railway station and was at work as packed trains departed for Fairyhouse racecourse when he heard rifle fire in the distance. Healy immediately hurried off and entered the combat zone in Church Street near the Four

Courts, dressed in his railway uniform with his ticket-punching machine strapped over his shoulder and a Howth rifle in his hand. Even though news spread quickly by word of mouth or by telephone, some Dubliners still remained ignorant that their world had just changed. Christina Doyle and her family were at Fairyhouse and despite rumours circulating at the course they still hadn't grasped the danger they were in when their car entered O'Connell Street. Doyle's mother became indignant when she saw a dead horse near the General Post Office and began denouncing Dublin Corporation for permitting an animal's corpse to lie unattended on the roadway. Her anger increased when she spotted one of her apprentices walking about armed with a rifle and she warned him that his father would learn about this outrageous behaviour![7] At the GPO a judge whose car had been stopped threatened to summon a policeman but reversed at speed when a Volunteer produced a revolver and warned him that if he didn't co-operate he would be shot.[8]

Many Volunteers mobilised on Easter Monday had only received a few hours' notice and assumed they were going on practice manoeuvres, only to learn the truth at the last moment. Some commandants allowed them an opportunity to withdraw and though only two out of 300 from 1st Battalion backed out it is impossible to know how many with private reservations stayed because of a reluctance to desert their comrades. Other Volunteers had been absent from home when their mobilisation orders arrived on Monday morning. Liam Ó Briain had spent Sunday delivering MacNeill's countermanding order but when he returned to Dublin and saw Volunteers firing at Portobello Bridge he hurried to join his company in North King Street. On the way, however, he was persuaded to join Mallin's Citizen Army garrison at Stephen's Green instead.[9]

The pace of developments also disorientated army reinforcements who had been rushed from England, most of them young recruits untrained for urban warfare. At Portobello Barracks Captain Gerrard recalled that 'the young Sherwoods that I had with me had never fired a service rifle before. They were not even able to load them.'[10] Their emergency mobilisation orders had arrived at teatime on Easter Monday with departure fixed for the early morning hours, precipitating a frantic search for men spending Easter in pubs, cinemas and even on honeymoon. Yet after trains had departed most still didn't have an idea of their destination and assumed that some critical military situation had erupted on the Western Front. During the journey north from St Albans some learned the truth from newspaper posters or the dock authorities at Liverpool, where officers raced into the city centre to scour shops and hotels for guidebooks with maps of Dublin. The soldiers also travelled with few weapons, no bombs and only fifty rounds of ammunition each; their superb Lewis guns were left stranded on Liverpool docks and although large supplies of munitions were rushed to Kingstown these arrived only after the men had disembarked. On the transport ships soldiers were packed together like cattle and an erroneous warning that rebels had taken Kingstown caused officers to fear that units would have to fight their way ashore. Astonishingly, even at this stage many troops still didn't know where they were going and one stunned Irish recruit only realised the truth as his ship sailed into Dublin Bay. Others assumed that they were in France and disembarked shouting '*merci*', while one remarked to his comrade, 'I say, Bill, they've picked up our language pretty quick'.[11] To Douglas Hyde it appeared that many of the soldiers were still in a sense all at sea, apparently convinced that they were in Belgium and amazed that Belgians could speak such good English; some officers entered shops speaking their best French.

The battle that raged in the streets of Dublin during Easter Week was a revealing experience for combatants who learnt much about the realities of urban warfare and its demands on a person's physical, mental and emotional resources. Many of them discovered qualities that they had never suspected they possessed, and in some cases wished they didn't. Irish Volunteers and Citizen Army members at least had an advantage over their opponents in that they had attended classes in street-fighting. But from the first hours of the Rising they realised their limited value and that in urban warfare the expected rarely happened, while the unanticipated frequently did. Joe Good became aware of this uncomfortable fact when he began fortifying occupied premises, knocking holes in walls to facilitate movement between rooms.

> Theoretically, in house-to-house fighting, one bores from house to house, stepping from one room into the next. It does not work out that way, it's a Lewis Carroll looking-glass experience. One bores a hole at a convenient height, and when the hole is enlarged one prepares to step through – only to find oneself at the ceiling-level of the next apartment, and looking down on a dining table. Worse again, after laborious work one gazes down into the well of a staircase and a hall, the stairs perhaps twelve feet distant below one. Sometimes one unexpectedly breaks through such apartments – one may conjecture with humour on what difficulties all of this would present to your pursuers.[12]

Sometimes, frustratingly, little or no military action ensued. At Stephen's Green and then at the College of Surgeons Liam Ó Briain spent most of his time observing and boring holes and he didn't fire a shot until Easter Friday.[13] For others, however, the first sight of blood, a first shot or killing came quickly, and often a senior officer's steadying hand was required to see them through the experience. At the Four Courts shortly after noon on Easter Monday, as Daly's 1st Battalion occupied houses and business premises at the junction of North Brunswick Street and Church Street, a cavalry party appeared escorting munitions lorries. The lancers charged at eight Volunteers who had never fired a shot in anger and Daly took command personally, calming their nerves until he ordered them to fire. A volley from their Howth rifles then fatally wounded the leading officer and sent the others fleeing panic-stricken into North King Street, their horses' hooves knocking sparks off the cobblestones.[14]

The physical act of firing was part of the blooding process in which men became attuned to their weapons. It was often a disconcerting experience as the Howth rifle favoured by Volunteers was an unstable weapon. Tom Walsh learnt this at a window in Clanwilliam House during the battle of Mount Street Bridge:

> I fired for the first time from my Howth gun, and for that matter from any other rifle! I do not know what happened to me or for how long I was unconscious. In the excitement I did not heed the lectures and did not hold the weapon correctly. The result was the butt hit me under the chin and knocked me out. When I came to I discovered that a large piece of the granite window sill had gone ... I had received

a good lesson, and for the remainder of the scrap I remembered it was a Howth rifle I had to deal with.[15]

After the first shots many were relieved, proud but dangerously exhilarated men. The jubilation on Easter Monday of those Volunteers who had attacked the lancers in O'Connell Street was so intense that many suffered a physical reaction. There were chaotic and dangerous scenes inside the General Post Office as rebels who temporarily couldn't fully control their movements accidentally discharged rifles all over the place.[16] Some men revelled in the drama and excitement of war from the very start though many others needed to go through a painful process of adaptation before accepting its reality. Young Matt Walton's confrontation with a howling mob at Jacob's factory left him distinctly queasy:

> There was a big, very big tall woman with something very heavy in her hand and she came across and lifted up her hand to make a bang at me. One of the Volunteers upstairs saw this and fired and I just remember seeing her face and head disappear as she went down like a sack. That was my baptism of fire and I remember my knees going out from under me. I would have sold my mother and father and the Pope just to get out of that bloody place.

However, as in many other cases, Walton's discomfort quickly passed: 'You recover after a few minutes.'[17]

Fighting on the other side was a British officer, Lieutenant Jameson of the Leinster Regiment,[18] who had hurried to Dublin from the Curragh military camp and in letters to his family vividly described his odyssey through its streets. Initially Jameson blanched and lost his appetite at the first sight of death as nurses washed down three dead Volunteers in the Castle Hospital. Soon afterwards he inflicted his first fatality: 'I shot my first man at the top of O'Connell's statue. I felt horrid and as if I wanted to go and apologise and help him!' However, like Matt Walton, Jameson quickly perked up: 'I very soon got over that and was very annoyed when I missed anybody.' Soon he was thoroughly enjoying the Rising, relishing the challenge of command and the excitement of battle. Nevertheless, others were swiftly overwhelmed and crumbled, seeking only to escape from the conflict. These included Begley, de Valera's vice-commandant at Boland's.[19]

Others endured longer but eventually cracked, including two battalion commanders, Thomas MacDonagh and Eamon de Valera. A Volunteer unit at Boland's was also badly affected after having spent most of the week stationed along a low-level, elevated railway line and shielded from the city's skyline. But on Easter Friday they were transferred and suddenly witnessed the inferno raging in the city centre. Captain Simon Donnelly described how the sight 'unnerved a great number of the men. One officer particularly, his nerves completely shattered, lost his head and fired at a Volunteer who was standing near me, inflicting a slight wound. Luckily the revolver used was of small calibre, otherwise the result would have been fatal.'[20]

Another case occurred in the malthouse of Guinness' Brewery, where a British soldier, Sergeant Robert Flood of the Royal Dublin Fusiliers, broke down while on guard in this dark, creaky, rambling edifice and his fevered imagination ran completely out of control. His paranoia focused on Lieutenant Lucas, who had taken over command for the evening and who, tragically, opened a window in direct contravention of a standing order. When Flood saw Lucas smile at John Rice, a civilian nightwatchman, he became convinced that the enemy had infiltrated the complex and were about to attack. He arrested Lucas and Rice, and had them put them up against a wall and shot dead by a firing squad before arresting another lieutenant and nightwatchman and shooting both of them as well. Flood then turned himself in and after the Rising was tried by court martial. Incredibly, he was found not guilty of murder and released.

Lieutenant Jameson's young British recruits dreaded the darkness and required his constant attention. On one occasion he led them fighting down Dame Lane to establish a line of communication to Trinity College before finally getting them bedded down for the night. However, panic broke out soon afterwards:

> At 4 o'clock in the morning they all got an attack of funk – swore they had seen about '20 men stealing by', loosed off any amount of ammunition at nothing and then ran away and collected in a quivering bunch at the end of the street. I had to go and get 'em all back to their places with 12 more of my men to give them confidence and had to report the sergeant next morning for deserting his post. He got it very hot![21]

Officers on the Irish side also fretted about their subordinates' youth and inexperience. Like Matt Walton at Jacob's, Matt Connolly, who fought at the City Hall, was only 15 years old. Fianna scouts acting as dispatch carriers were frequently even younger. One incredulous rebel encountered a cheery 11-year-old with a great head of curls, a cap with a gaping hole and a large cross in his hands standing among flames and bullets in O'Connell Street on Easter Friday.[22] Whilst 12-year-old Tommy Keenan fetched food and medicine for Mallin's garrison in the College of Surgeons, his tiny size deceiving British soldiers who never suspected that the smiling schoolboy was wearing a green Fianna shirt under his jacket. Keenan survived the Rising, unlike 15-year-old John Healy, an apprentice plumber who was shot dead carrying dispatches in the Phibsborough area. Many commandants feared the responsibility of caring for such young lives and ordered them to leave, including the couple Michael Malone sent away before the battle of Mount Street Bridge.[23] Others exerted pressure on them to go home. At Boland's de Valera assembled everyone under 18 on Easter Tuesday morning and persuaded them to leave, all except Richard Pearl who insisted on staying to the end.[24] Sometimes ruses were employed to remove them from the danger. Little Tommy Keenan was induced to return home from the College of Surgeons to reassure his anxious family that he was safe. Other parents endured agonies of uncertainty. Frances Downey had three members of her family involved in the Rising and on Easter Wednesday she recorded that she had:

> been awake since 5 o'clock listening to the heavy firing. Every gun that goes off might as well be going through me for I think to myself, 'that one might have killed Hugh or Frank or Paddy'. Poor Paddy, he is only a kid of sixteen. But he is a real man to go out and fight like this.[25]

Some tried to pluck their sons from danger, though usually without success. Mrs Pearl's journey to Boland's ended with Richard's rebuff that 'This is no place for a woman'. Tommy Keenan was locked in a room on his return and Matt Walton, who on Easter Monday morning had looked in vain for a dentist, returned home to discover that his parents had taken the valves from his bicycle to prevent him going off to join the fighting. However, youth was not to be denied. Keenan escaped through a window to report back to the College of Surgeons, while Walton, after convincing his parents that he had to go to work or he would be sacked, went straight to Jacob's factory.[26] One group of Fianna who were sent home on Easter Monday afternoon simply tried their luck at the GPO and were allowed in to join its garrison. During the Rising, age became relative because many adult combatants were not much older than those sent home: at the Mendicity Institution, apart from a 40-year-old man, every Volunteer was aged between 18 and 25, while their commander Sean Heuston was only 25.

Some parents felt conflicting emotions about their sons' involvement in the Rising, pleading on the one hand for them to abandon the struggle but accepting their rejection with good grace and understanding, with a certain amount of pride – even when fearing the worst. William Christian's father visited him on Easter Wednesday just hours before the battle of Mount Street Bridge and gloomily confirmed what Malone's garrison already knew: that thousands of British troops were marching north from Kingstown.

He felt our chances were poor. With a father's natural anxiety for the safety of his son he begged me to come home with him, but having taken up my post nothing but death would make me desert it. While this grieved him I think he also admired my spirit and wishing me God's blessing and promising to pray for me we parted. I know now that he must have prayed very hard for my safety, even though he confided to my mother when he got home that he had small hope of ever seeing me alive again. Still they prayed – my father and mother and all the neighbours who called on and off inquiring for news and God protected me.[27]

The plight of young men aroused maternal instincts in many Dublin women, though not everyone they sought to comfort appreciated their solicitude. A spontaneous act of kindness towards him after the surrender mortified Andrew MacDonnell as he marched into Mount Street with the rest of Boland's garrison:

I will always remember one woman in that street as we passed along. She was a big woman with a very white apron, or at least so it looked to me not having used soap or water for a week. When I came along she cried out 'Lord look at the child going to be shot.' Stepping out into the road she picked me up in her arms and moved back into the crowd, evidently with the idea of getting me away to safety. This did not enter my mind at the time, my own idea was to go with my comrades and, in particular the Commandant, as by that time I was willing to follow him anywhere. I kicked that good woman good and hard and then ran after the remnants of our army to surrender.[28]

Fourteen-year-old Sean Harling was also annoyed at not being treated as an adult. On Easter Monday he had been standing outside Broadstone railway station selling race cards for Fairyhouse when, on impulse, he attached himself to a 1st Battalion unit. At the surrender a British officer scrutinised the Volunteers:

> I was just standing at the end of the line and he came along and he looks at me, you know, and he gives me a clip on the ear and tells me to get the hell home. I was very annoyed at not being arrested but that's what happened and I watched the others being taken off as prisoners.[29]

The fighting in Dublin at Easter 1916 was multi-faceted, ranging from rifle fire into and out of occupied houses and large buildings, to ambushes and pitched battles. Grenades and bombs were thrown from roofs while snipers operated from windows, barricades, church spires and clock towers and were, in turn, hunted down by individual enemy marksmen or units. Sometimes combat was at close quarters, almost hand-to-hand. At the Mendicity, the British concentrated rifle and machine-gun fire on Heuston's Volunteers and crept along the quayside to the wall in front from where they hurled grenades that rebels attempted to catch and throw back. Both sides also engaged in incendiary warfare. While Volunteer attempts were crude, the British made sophisticated use of shells fired from howitzers. Furthermore, while the insurgents were restricted to pistols, shotguns and rifles, the military possessed machine guns and artillery, with big guns used on land and also by the vessel *Helga* on the River Liffey. The British also made increasing use of armoured motorcars which had been fitted out by engineers at Guinness', who welded engine boilers on to lorries equipped to carry up to fifteen troops. These vehicles had dummy holes painted on them to deceive the snipers who peppered the vehicles whenever they appeared on the streets. Working to a set pattern, they advanced up a street to the house to be stormed, inching as close as possible to the front door before the attacking party emerged with crowbars and sledgehammers to smash down the a door and occupy the house while the rest of the party fought any Volunteers nearby. The car would then return to collect another party of soldiers and another until the whole street had been brought under control.

In the scale of military operations Dublin 1916 was not Flanders, the GPO wasn't Verdun and the Mendicity wasn't the Somme. Furthermore, the casualty figures for Easter Week were dwarfed by those of a single day on the Western Front. Nevertheless, the intensity of combat endured by participants should not be lightly dismissed, especially since most of them had little or no previous military experience and were denied an opportunity to gradually acclimatise before being pitched suddenly into battle. Certainly the sights and sounds of Dublin at Easter 1916 became etched in British Lieutenant Jameson's memory:

> Nobody had any idea how serious matters were. However, we started fighting on Tuesday at midday and never stopped until midday Saturday! It was a very ghastly affair – so many civilians and women and children shot. Everybody who had been in France seemed to think the Dublin fighting was a far worse thing to be in![30]

He vividly recalled the strains of being involved in an armoured car operation that was launched in rebel-held Capel Street on Easter Thursday:

> I was right in front with the driver when the car stopped and had quite a job in making the men get out. When they did they all lost their head and shouted. However, they eventually bashed in the house and bullets were whizzing at us all the time from the barricade in Little Mary Street and the house at the end.[31]

To survive in this battleground men required various mental and physical qualities. Vigilance and extreme caution dramatically reduced the odds of being shot dead and combatants survived by not offering themselves as a target at windows, putting their head through a skylight or even making a shadow. Doing guard duty on the roof of the College of Surgeons, rebel James O'Shea slid down to a balustrade with two small roofs behind it where he and his comrades came under heavy and sustained British sniper fire from the Shelbourne Hotel. As bullets and chips of stonework flew in all directions, preventing them from standing up, a Volunteer crouching beside O'Shea was:

> just putting a new clip of ammunition in the magazine when he touched me and asked me for God's sake to do something with the man behind us. I turned around and saw Mick Doherty sitting eating a sandwich as if he was at a picnic. I stared at him and, before I had the words out of my mouth he got a burst of machine gun bullets all over him. I actually saw the bullets strike him. The side of his face seemed to be gone.[32]

Fighters had to move and speak as quietly as possible, always on guard against enemy traps. At the College of Surgeons on Easter Wednesday Frank Robbins led an occupation of a club for former pupils of Alexandra College, where he almost made a fatal mistake. His Citizen Army unit had been warned that a ringing telephone was always to be regarded as a British ruse, yet a captain still lifted the receiver. When a British officer heard his pronounced Dublin male accent in such a location he had the building raked with machine-gun fire that Robbins and his men only just managed to evade by hurling themselves on the floor.[33] Careful handling of weapons was important. On both sides there were many narrow misses but some fatalities occurred from discharges by men using rifle butts to smash in doors and windows. Others were dangerously lax, causing accidental shootings when clearing a bullet jammed in their weapon. Volunteer Liam Archer was at a barricade in the Four Courts area when a comrade pointed out the stupidity of standing with a rifle barrel lodged in his toecap; when Archer jerked the weapon away he actually shot himself in the foot.[34]

One Volunteer learned this lesson more than once within an hour of the Rising, starting when his unit reported late to the GPO and had to climb in through broken windows. As one comrade jumped down from the sill he let his rifle drop on the ground where it discharged, sending a bullet through his thigh and mortally wounding him. Soon afterwards the Volunteer and some others were sent round to the Prince's Street side of the GPO to bring in a cartful of hand grenades that had just arrived. Like many rebels who saw and used these weapons during Easter Week, they concluded that they were more dangerous to Volunteers than the enemy. Carrying an armful he:

saw Lieutenant Liam Clarke of my own company standing inside clearing some of the grenades from the sill. As he was lifting them, as luck would have it, one slipped from his hand and to my consternation exploded. I expected the whole lot would go off but fortunately they didn't, but Liam Clarke got the full contents in his face and he was soon all covered in blood and had to be removed to the field hospital inside.[35]

Some of the casual handling of bombs and grenades was hair-raising, especially with the primitive concoctions manufactured at Liberty Hall. These cocoa tins filled with explosive had a string attached which had to be lit, pulled and then thrown quickly as far away as possible. In the Metropole Hotel Charles Saurin was terrified as he watched a bomber playing with his lethal hoard:

He put his complement of bombs in a row at his feet with the sulphur-tipped fuses pointing upwards. He was continually lighting his pipe and throwing the ignited matches amongst the bombs, greatly to my terror, for every second I expected to see one catch on a fuse and eventually send himself and myself through the roof.[36]

Circumspection and a cool head were especially important at night, when darkness frayed men's nerves and, as Matt Connolly discovered in the City Hall, played tricks with the imagination:

Prowling about the dark, deserted rooms imagination exaggerated things. For instance, I entered one room and was startled to see an armed man confronting me. I immediately challenged, and receiving no reply, fired. The crash of breaking glass brought me to my senses. I had fired at my own reflection in a wardrobe mirror.[37]

Many Volunteers were reluctant to reveal human frailty or let down their comrades and tried to avoid showing fear, even in the most stressful and dangerous situations. As British shells and incendiaries rained down on the GPO roof on Easter Friday, Liam Tannam and Harry Boland saw an 18-year-old Volunteer standing half in and half out of a trap door operating a heavy hose pipe:

As Boland and I approached I could hear his teeth chatter. I saw him hold up the hose with one hand and take his handkerchief from his pocket and insert it into his mouth and he bit on that while Boland and I passed him so as not to let two officers hear his teeth chatter. I thought that fellow was the bravest man I ever saw.[38]

On another occasion he and Boland:

had just emerged on to the roof when a shell burst upon us. The spot seemed to be suddenly deprived of air and we were left gasping. I saw two spots of blood on Boland's face and I believed he might be dangerously wounded but he pushed me off, wiped the blood off his face with the back of his hand and said, 'Don't mind that. It's only bloody shrapnel' Boland had been in the South African War.[39]

Those combatants who focused completely on the battle, controlling their emotions and filtering out extraneous concerns had a tremendous advantage. This wasn't easy for many, especially those who worried about their families and relations at home or in some cases fighting elsewhere in the city. The Rising indeed was to some extent a family enterprise. The Pearse brothers, for instance, fought in the GPO alongside the Connollys, father and son; the MacDonagh brothers were in Jacob's while the two Walsh brothers fought together at Mount Street Bridge. Sean Connolly had two brothers and a sister alongside him in the City Hall and another brother, Joe, fighting with Mallin at the College of Surgeons. Poignantly, in some families members served with the Volunteers while others served in the British army. The O'Reillys, for instance, had four sons, two of whom, Richard and John, fought with the rebels at the South Dublin Union where Richard was killed on Easter Tuesday. The other two brothers had joined the British army and one of them had been killed fighting in France.[40] Sometimes, however, family members in the British army weren't as far away as the Western Front. Volunteer Joe Sweeney discovered this after surrendering on Easter Saturday when soldiers were processing his unit:

> Officers with notebooks then came along and took down our names. A funny incident happened there. One of the officers just looked at one of our fellows and without asking him anything wrote down his name and then walked off. After he had gone a certain distance, somebody asked this fellow, 'Does that officer know you?' 'That's my brother,' he said.[41]

Home weighed heavily on many insurgents, especially those who hadn't been able to take proper leave of their families on Easter Monday morning. Dispatch carriers sometimes brought them news, but that could be chilling. At the South Dublin Union Frank Holland learned that soldiers and police had been raiding houses in the Inchicore area and threatening parents of Volunteers. A mob of hostile neighbours had also gone on the rampage, wrecking and looting another Volunteer's house.[42]

Physical and mental stamina helped lessen the pressures caused by sleeping fitfully on floors, tables, roofs, pavements or in fields. By the end of Easter Week many combatants ached for the joys of a bath, a wash, a shave or a change of the clothing in which they slept. Those who spent extended periods in cramped tenement houses often suffered from claustrophobia, longing for fresh air and the sight of open blue skies. Others discovered that they had opened a new battlefront against multitudes of fleas. Men in the open were often drenched and risked contracting severe chills and even worse. On 1 May Douglas Hyde recorded that many Volunteers were 'in hospital with pneumonia which they got fighting in heavy rain during Tuesday night. This was the only rain that fell during Easter Week.'[43] Usually the sick and wounded received only rudimentary treatment as at the Mater Hospital which functioned without gas and electricity and whose surgeon, Alexander Blayney, operated by candlelight night and day for an entire week. Seriously wounded patients were brought straight to theatre without removing any clothes except shoes and despite an absence of boiling water to sterilise instruments and dressings there wasn't a single case of sepsis after an operation. Casualties included a schoolboy shot through the skull and a

Fianna member 'whose brain was hanging all over his forehead when he was brought in, died after two days'.[44]

In the City Hall, Dr Kathleen Lynn's facilities for the Citizen Army garrison amounted to a small room for the dispensary, a supply of tablets, some nurses and a treatment room. At the GPO the medical officer was James Ryan, a student who had four assistants and a dozen Cumann na mBan. His hospital consisted of two rooms used as a first-aid post and a recovery station equipped with beds. Ryan treated his most famous patient, James Connolly, without a choice of anaesthetic and had to use chloroform. Thereafter, Connolly only survived with frequent injections of morphine. At Stephen's Green and the College of Surgeons, Nora O'Daly stitched the wounded without any anaesthetic, though to her delight she discovered that she could indeed work miracles: 'Mr. Partridge had received a wound on the top of his head which I dressed and bandaged. He told me the next morning that since the bandage was put on he was free from a headache which he had suffered from for years.'[45]

In the Four Courts area Father Mathew Hall doubled as Ned Daly's headquarters and a hospital in which thirty-two patients were treated during Easter Week, the overwhelming majority of them Volunteers. Minor injuries that were treated included a sprained ankle and broken fingers, but others had been shot in the ear, arm, hip, face, thigh, stomach or lungs. One rebel had been seriously wounded when the grenade he was about to throw exploded in his hand. A Volunteer wounded in the hip and leg bled to death and another died after being shot in the temple – deaths that occurred despite the services of the Red Cross and three doctors from nearby Richmond Hospital. Others were suffering from shock and one had gone 'religiously mad'.[46] Physical and emotional resources were drained by lack of sleep; many men got little or none during Easter Week and in the College of Surgeons Frank Robbins slept only two hours out of sixty on duty. Ultimately men ached physically or longed only to surrender themselves to overwhelming fatigue. At the City Hall Matt Connolly stayed awake for three days and struggled on even after his fellow guards had curled up on the ground snoring. Nevertheless, he finally succumbed just before the British offensive that captured the building:

> I lay down flat in the valley gutter and remained quiet. Some form of helplessness came over me and I felt unable to move. I tried to fight off a drowsy feeling, but failed and passed into a sound sleep. A hand gripped the shoulder of my coat and a voice shouted, 'Get up!' My eyes opened to see a revolver pointed at me. It was in the hand of a British officer who wore a white arm band on which was a red cross. It was now daylight.[47]

In the General Post Office Pearse stayed on his feet for the entire week and even a sleeping draught had no effect on him. Sleeplessness made many men prone to misjudgements, hallucinations and sudden reactions when they were startled, causing them to become more dangerous to themselves and their comrades than the enemy. They also suffered from losing their sense of time, a disorientating condition that was exacerbated by an absence of watches and the disabling of many clocks riddled by bullets during sniper battles. Many combatants and civilians lost track of the day of the week and even whether it was day or night. Stress subsequently brought on nervousness, anxiety, sleeplessness, breathlessness, fatigue, lack of concentration or inability to think clearly. Hands or palms firing rifles became clammy and some men experienced serious chest pains. One Volunteer officer at the Four Courts found his:

> captain Fred Fahy lying on the footpath. I thought he had been killed but he called me over to him and I found that he had got a heart attack and was unable to move. At this time he and my men were under fire from Hammond Lane. With the assistance of some of my section we carried our company captain into the building where we handed him over to the care of the Cumann na mBan.[48]

The psychological moorings of many combatants became loosened by hunger since neither side fought on a full stomach during Easter Week, when most men existed on a monotonous, inadequate and inappropriate diet. During the Rising Liam Ó Briain consumed only a small cake of home-made bread on Easter Monday and a meal consisting of a big pot of tea, plenty of bread and butter and ten boiled eggs that he shared with his unit the following day. After that he received nothing except for a little boiled rice on Easter Friday evening.[49] The GPO garrison had ample supplies, but Desmond Fitzgerald, in charge of the commissariat, doled out only small measures and often seemed to many to be preparing for a medieval siege.[50] At Boland's bakery there was plenty of food with ovens and fuels for cooking, but distribution to the various posts was difficult because of the continual fire from British sniper nests in the surrounding high buildings. The British commissary arrangements broke down under the strain of thousands of soldiers flooding into the city: many of these had to exist half-starved on a diet of bully beef and biscuits.

Luck often decided who lived and died because some men and women seemed to have charmed lives, surviving impossible odds while others perished simply through being in the wrong place at the wrong time. Cathal Brugha survived multiple gunshot wounds at the South Dublin Union. In the College of Surgeons Rose Hackett was ordered to go for a much-needed cup of tea. Just after she left her bed a Volunteer threw himself down on it and was immediately shot in the face by an enemy sniper. He lingered for a week but after the surrender he died in St Vincent's Hospital: 'Had I not got up when told to go for the tea, I would have got it through the brain, judging by the way the bullet hit this man.'[51] Another Volunteer in O'Connell Street demonstrated an amazing ability to dodge the bullets after he:

> appeared at the door of Clery's, the big drapery establishment opposite the GPO. It was the headquarters of the Citizen Army and they had their flag, the Plough and the Stars on top of it. But this fellow came out with a mattress wrapped around him and he ran like the blazes. But when he got to the middle of the street he tripped and fell. We all thought he was a goner because the fire was so desperate. But he discarded the mattress then and ran like the hammers of hell for the GPO and got in safely. I found out afterwards that it was Gearoid O'Sullivan, who later became Adjutant-General of the Free State Army.[52]

Liam Tannam was another Volunteer who chanced running the shooting gallery that O'Connell Street became during Easter Week. Returning to the GPO from the Dublin Bread Company, he sprinted across during a lull in the fighting:

> I was wearing hob nailed boots. When in the middle of O'Connell Street I wanted to change direction suddenly as the machine gun was on me and bullets were striking the roadway at my feet, the nails of the boots then slid on the paving stones as I came a cropper. When I arrived at the GPO I discovered that I had left my haversack containing amongst other things my shaving gear and I decided to return to Reis's for it and successfully negotiated the journey to and fro being all the time under machine-gun fire.[53]

When Oscar Traynor's party evacuated the GPO on Easter Friday they dashed across the roadway. Just as he heard the whiz of ricocheting bullets a tin of cocoa dropped out of his haversack and, against all logic, Traynor turned back to pick it up. A colleague who was following him remarked that it was a dangerous thing to do and then said: 'But maybe it saved you from another bullet': 'As far as I was concerned I did it without thought, and of course it is possible that I might have run into one of the many bullets which were flying around had I not turned back.'[54] At almost exactly the same time a British sniper shot Charles Saurin in the right hand. Saurin:

> was holding one of those billycan bombs which I had carried from the Metropole. Apparently the shock of being struck by a bullet caused me to loosen my grip on the bomb though I still held tight to the rifle. The bomb fell to the ground, made a half circle and came to rest behind me. I had helped to manufacture a number of these bombs and I knew precisely what they contained and wondered what would happen to me if this one went off. They were not self-igniting, however, which was lucky for me and a number of others around.[55]

Sometimes, though, a run of good luck was intoxicating, convincing some combatants that a guardian angel was watching over them. After evacuating the Imperial Hotel on Easter Friday Harry Colley's unit was making its way up Gloucester Street (now Sean MacDermott Street) when a British machine-gun post opened fire on them. Jumping into a doorway, he and another Volunteer:

> came to the conclusion that if we were captured we would be just put up against the wall and shot. We decided that we would make a break for it even if we had to die that way, that it would be preferable. We accordingly set out, me leading, and made a zig-zag run up the street. Immediately very heavy fire, both machine gun and rifle, opened up on us. I came to the conclusion while on that run, that I had a charmed life as bullets seemed to be hopping like rain around me. The only thing I felt was one that hit me above the ankle. Suddenly I saw a barricade about ten yards in front of me with British soldiers firing over it at me. I already had my bayonet fixed. I charged, jumped on the barricade and lunged at the soldier on the other side. As I did I fell on the barricade and found that I was not able to rise. I had been wounded but did not know it until I had occasion to realise it when I put effort into

it. The soldier had also lunged at me with his bayonet and got me in the thigh as I was falling. I then began to feel pain all over and was moaning. Shortly afterwards he caught me by the collar and pulled me to the top of the barricade. Apparently others of our men were making the same effort and the British were firing at them. The soldier put the rifle across my back taking cover behind and kept on firing for some time. I will say in fairness to him that I think he thought I was dead. I was now absolutely helpless and found that I was unable to move whatsoever. Some few minutes later he again caught me by the back of the neck and pulled me over to his side of the barricade and let me fall. My head stuck in the back of a chair that formed part of the barricade and my body fell over. I thought my neck was broken. I must have gone unconscious at this period for the next I knew was that there were some R.A.M.C. men carrying flashlights and a stretcher. A corporal of the R.A.M.C. was stooping over me and he raised himself and said 'Take him gently boys, he appears to be very badly hurt.' I shall always remember the humane and Christian attitude of that R.A.M.C. corporal.[56]

In contrast to Colley's good luck in surviving, another insurgent who had endured everything in the Metropole and managed to reach the GPO as the evacuation was under way was fatally injured when a large haversack of ammunition exploded. He even lingered on until after the surrender when he died in the Castle Hospital from severe loss of blood.[57]

Courage was important and there were many acts of astonishing heroism during the Rising. But the bravery of the hot-headed and impulsive was a dubious commodity, and it was self-discipline and prudence that saved Volunteer Joe Good's life in O'Connell Street on Easter Wednesday. Ordered to leave the GPO and reoccupy a vacated building, he had serious reservations about an operation that initially entailed erecting a barricade across Abbey Street:

> The method was simple enough. Baskets on wheels were loaded and packed tight with newspapers and journals; those were to be run out one after another from a shop to form a barricade across the road – and I was to push out the first hamper. Fortunately, there was an inclined plane leading from the shop into Abbey Street. It was cut to bits by machine-gun fire. We shut and barricaded the door, withdrawing towards the GPO.[58]

Many British soldiers displayed a similar caution, particularly as they were fighting with an inadequate knowledge of the city's topography, very aware that any impulsive movement could lead them straight into a death trap. These considerations clearly influenced soldiers involved in a major operation to clear suburbs on the North Circular Road. A local resident, Austin Clarke, who was sunbathing in his front garden, observed their nervousness as they warily advanced behind a field gun driven by men crouching low behind its shield. Their cautious tactics consisted of firing shells at a barricade a quarter of a mile away, from which Volunteers retreated by skipping over back garden walls and fleeing along a railway embankment. Finally, and seemingly in slow motion, the troops crept gingerly forward through flower beds and then over walls, and to Clarke:

the twenty minutes of advance seemed as slow as an hour. At last, the entire regiment seemed to have vanished. Suddenly there was volley after volley. Then a detachment of the infantry charged past the broken barricade. In a few moments the empty houses had been captured. The Battle of the North Circular Road was over.[59]

People with good faculties prospered during the Rising. Sharp hearing enabled men to heed an enemy creeping up a staircase or the whizzing of a shell. They could also distinguish between the bark of a shotgun, the loud explosion of the Howth rifle and the sharp crack of the Lee Enfield British standard rifle. Clear eyesight and a steady hand made some men crack shots. Michael Mallin, who had served in the British army, proved himself to be such during an early-morning tour of the College of Surgeons when Liam Ó Briain saw that he was carrying his long 'Peter the Painter' revolver in his hand:

He motioned me aside, stood in front of the glassless window, took aim and fired. An answering shot seemed to whisk by his head. He took aim deliberately again and fired: 'Got him,' he said. I looked at him enquiringly: 'A sniper who had come across the Green to the railings opposite,' he said, in his usual quiet tone of voice and went off.[60]

But many combatants on both sides proved to be abysmal marksmen. This is hardly surprising in view of their lack of training and consequently there is a striking contrast between the vast expenditure of ammunition during the Rising and the relatively small number of casualties. There were a few exceptions, such as at Mount Street Bridge, but even there, as one Volunteer marksman admitted, 'A lot of their losses were their own fault. They made sitting ducks for amateur riflemen.'[61]

Many British artillerymen were also incompetent, though the potential consequences of their mistakes were correspondingly greater. One team almost demolished Under-Secretary Nathan's lodge in Phoenix Park by landing a shell in the garden. Two 18-pounder guns outside Trinity College had no directors or ranging instruments of any kind and were placed in the charge of newly recruited gunners who had never before fired a round. Another gunner, James Glen, who had taken refuge in the university, had no experience of such big weapons but only narrowly missed the honour of demolishing a famous O'Connell Street landmark. A brigadier-general:

told me that a lot of coming and going had been reported between the GPO and Clery's across the street, most of it under the shelter of Nelson's Pillar. He was considering whether it was a good plan to demolish the Pillar, using artillery, and he asked me whether I had any good ideas as to the size of gun and the number of rounds that would be needed. This was beyond my limited knowledge of ballistics, but it was plain to anyone that, even if it could be done, there were two serious flaws; the pillar could only be cut through at a level above the base portion, and the resulting debris would provide even better cover than before the operation. And so the Pillar lived to fall another day.[62]

High morale was most important and the rebel leadership used every available technique to sustain it. Volunteers engaged in defiant singing of patriotic tunes such as

The Soldier's Song and *The Bold Fenian Men*, communal cheering and reading out loud the Proclamation and 'war news'. In the General Post Office Pearse read to the men encouraging dispatches from his 'generals'. Seeing a flag flying over a garrison headquarters also inspired many insurgents, though, surprisingly, the Military Council hadn't approved a common pattern. A tricolour and an Irish Republic bannerette flew at the GPO; a tricolour at the Four Courts; a green flag with harp at Marrowbone Lane; a tricolour seems to have been raised at the South Dublin Union and the City Hall; as it certainly did at Jacob's, the College of Surgeons and the Imperial Hotel, where it was joined on Easter Wednesday by the Plough and the Stars. A green flag with harp was also hoisted at Boland's.[63] The British devoted an inordinate amount of time and ammunition trying to blast the flags off their poles and a failure to do so heartened many rebels, such as Joe Sweeney in O'Connell Street: 'Friday dawned on a desolate sight opposite us. All that remained of Clery's and the Imperial Hotel was the front wall of the building on the top of which to Connolly's great delight the flag of the Citizen Army still floated proudly.'[64]

Rebel morale was also temporarily sustained by a welter of rumours swirling throughout the city purporting to reveal that Verdun had fallen to the Germans, that Zeppelins were raiding London and the German North Sea fleet was trying to affect a landing in England. The whole of Ireland was supposedly up in arms with insurgents marching on Dublin, Derry was in flames and Dublin Bay was full of German submarines. On his way to the GPO on Easter Monday Dick Humphries encountered an excited old lady claiming that a 'corpse' of Germans had just landed in Phoenix Park ('whether from warships or Zeppelins is not stated'). Some Volunteer commandants were exponents of a 'good news' philosophy, spinning any favourable information and filtering out adverse reports. At Stephen's Green on Easter Monday Mallin reassured his garrison that the Rising was proceeding successfully, not just in Dublin but throughout the entire country. In contrast Desmond Fitzgerald in the GPO, refused to let men live in a fool's paradise, and after discovering Volunteers telling Cumann na mBan women that the Germans had landed he tried unsuccessfully to kill off such fantasies.[65]

The infectious humour of individual Volunteers was often effective in lightening a mood on even the most sombre occasion. Dublin had many natural comedians and, time and again, men and women were reduced to helpless laughter because of their extrovert comrades' antics. Many tears were shed during the Rising but at least some of them were tears of mirth. The waxworks besides the GPO provided considerable amusement. Patrick Stephenson recalled passing it and seeing that inside 'a figure attired in the robes of the Emperor of Austria stalked around in a parody of Imperial dignity, amusing a few onlookers by sloping and presenting arms with a Howth rifle'.[66] The General Post Office garrison roared when a Volunteer suddenly appeared in an exhibit's postman's trousers, puttees, a magnificent fur-lined blue coat with very high collar and an Australian hat. Even Connolly – never a barrel of laughs – rather awkwardly entered into the spirit by circulating through the building and repeating a joke he had heard: 'Well, boys it's all over. We just bagged three of their generals,' pausing for effect before remarking 'We captured them in the waxworks.'[67]

On the British side, Lieutenant Jameson demonstrated his sense of the ridiculous on Easter Wednesday. Working the roofs of the Tivoli and adjoining houses, he and his men removed slates and smashed holes because of the absence of skylights, but as he attempted to squeeze through his corpulence had comic results:

> It's a horrible thing being so fat! When I got the slates off I was too fat to get thro' the beam, so I got my burberry off and tried again – still too fat. Then I tried with my Sam Browne off – still too fat, so I had to take my tunic off, and just managed to squeeze through with the help of my sergeant who shoved! They were sniping at us from over the river all the time but they were rotten shots and hit nobody! However it cheered us up lots, cos all the men and myself were roaring with laughter![68]

Some people used laughter as a release mechanism. Joe Good employed it to calm the frayed nerves of a group of young Volunteers petrified by the fires sweeping O'Connell Street:

> It was awe-inspiring. The red glare of the burning buildings opposite lighted the rooms. It was no wonder that the lads were depressed, at that height and looking at an inferno all day long, and now night falling without darkness. There were twelve of them, mostly young boys and they lay there quietly at their posts, not talking to each other. I spoke to them one by one and concluded by asking them, 'Do you think you are going to die?' Each of them answered 'I suppose so, Sir.' I told them all to fall in, in the corridor outside the room. One of our flags was flying at our corner of the Post Office. I got them in line facing and gave the 'Present Arms.' Then I said, 'Lads, you have done that in accordance with tradition. You're now free to go back and die – but I'm damned if I'm going to do so.' There was a roar of laughter from the young fellows; they had been left too long looking at that holocaust. I took care not to look at it at all.[69]

Even in the midst of absolute despair some people managed a laugh, as did vice-commandant Beaslai in the Four Courts just after Ned Daly told his men that the garrison was surrendering: 'There was one laughable incident that stays in my memory. A tall man carrying a rifle walked into the hall and up to Captain Fahy. "Are we to surrender?" he asked. "Yes" said Frank, "We have the order." "Well" said he bitterly, "I've lost my job over this."'[70] Others took a guilty pleasure in the misfortunes of others. Douglas Hyde had felt embarrassed in Earlsfort Terrace on Easter Tuesday when machine-gun fire 8ft over his head raked the window and rain-pipe of a disused house. Instinctively he wanted to jump but fear of looking ridiculous won out over a fear of being shot. Hyde made up for it later in the week when he thought it:

> most comical to see the people flying down the road when shots are fired near them. I saw five men today waiting in the lane at the corner of our house all in a group, when a shot went off a few yards from them. The whole group sprang into the air and then retreated farther down the lane.[71]

However, because of their temperament and the environment in which they found themselves some Volunteers found it difficult to stay cheerful. Liam Ó Briain actually contracted a depression that afflicted him intermittently for the rest of his life, an illness triggered by physical and mental strain as well as a habit of meditating on his personal responsibility for the destruction and suffering all around him. He also had the misfortune to be teamed up with an elderly, deranged obsessive from Tralee called Sullivan. He had jumped the railings at Stephen's Green along with Ó Briain who was only fighting the British army and empire. Sullivan had set his ambitions much higher as the nemesis of an academic who had offended him in the dim and distant past but whose villainy he would now avenge. His malice infected everyone:

> The men were all in very good heart but Sullivan was beginning to worry us. The inaction was getting on his nerves. Had it come to real fighting he would probably have been the best and coolest of us. As it was, he began and kept up for the next three days an extraordinary muttering of hate against his fellow-Traleeman, Doctor Denis Coffey, president of University College, Dublin, demanding to know why we did not go over there and kill him. He usually accompanied his demand with an odd, malevolent glance at me, as if he suspected me of being contaminated by contact with Doctor Coffey in U.C.D. I became more and more convinced as the days went by that he might be demented and violent and, with so many weapons lying about, dangerous. I was prepared to shoot him if it really became necessary.[71]

Cunning and a willingness to innovate were useful qualities. At Boland's, de Valera didn't have enough men to occupy a distillery that dominated the area, but he still managed not just to eliminate the threat the building posed, but also to trick the British into doing it for him. His ruse entailed flying a green flag on top of the distillery to convince the enemy that it was rebel-occupied, an impression which he reinforced by transmitting misleading messages for the British to intercept. As a result they launched a severe artillery bombardment that badly damaged the building.[72] Cunning allied with patience was another effective combination in the sniper duels of Easter Week. Some daring snipers deliberately presented themselves as targets in order to draw fire from enemy nests that their comrades could then eliminate. Often the sniper engagements developed into a protracted battle of wits, a duel between two individuals or groups manoeuvring to outwit each other. Sometimes these contests became distinctly personal. On Easter Monday a Volunteer unit that included Cormac Turner occupied Hopkins & Hopkins, the jeweller's shop on the corner of O'Connell Street at the bridge. Next day, as Turner came back from delivering a message to the GPO, he was targeted by a British sniper operating from McBirney's, a general store at Aston's quay on the southern side of the bridge and diagonally opposite to Hopkins. But instead of downing Turner, the sniper shot dead a civilian passer-by and a young girl, and although the British marksman stopped as night fell he resumed on Wednesday morning, concentrating initially and unsuccessfully on Hopkins before turning his attention to the large crowds of civilians which had gathered at the O'Connell monument. These fled across the bridge, but not before a blind man had been wounded along with a St John's Ambulance member who tried to help him. Until then Turner's unit hadn't been able to locate the sniper's exact position and they were also hindered by girls standing at the windows of McBirney's. While they had only one rifle and a limited supply of ammunition, Turner was determined to deal with the sniper once and for all and by using a pair of binoculars found in Hopkins, he managed to pinpoint the shooter at a top window. He and his unit now co-ordinated a stalking operation with the Volunteer garrison in Kelly's gunpowder store on the opposite corner of O'Connell Street. While one Volunteer in Hopkins waited with the single rifle, Turner scoured McBirney's through this binoculars and when the sniper reappeared Turner directed his men's aim and cried, 'Fire'. Simultaneous volleys from Hopkins and Kelly's eliminated the enemy marksman.[73]

The problems that Volunteers encountered when occupying private residences differed in size, complexity and danger from factories like Boland's and Jacob's or government buildings like the GPO and the Four Courts. Jacob's was a health hazard in many different ways. There was a constant risk that gases and sulphur could be ignited accidentally and its caretaker Thomas Orr persuaded MacDonagh to ban Volunteers from smoking inside during Easter Week. Even so fumes either sickened or ruined the sleep of many Volunteers. Jacob's sprinkler system imperilled vast quantities of flour and late on Tuesday night a garrison member set off the fire alarm controlling it. Fortunately another Volunteer, a plumber in civilian life, managed to turn the water off.[74] The factory's machinery and equipment also caused problems. Seamus Pounch's unit had a narrow escape when exploring a cold storage compartment with a self-closing door that could only be opened from outside. It started swinging closed while they were inside and only swift action by one man sticking his rifle in the door joint prevented them from possibly freezing to death.[75] Even the chance of accidental death preyed on minds: 'There was something uncomfortably threatening about that big chimney shaft. "Suppose", said Pat Callan "a shell struck it and the damn thing crashed." It was most improbable at this stage it would occur but the thought was disconcerting.'[76] At Roe's distillery dust and loose barley irritated throats and induced coughing fits while roasting barley produced a pungent smell. And there was almost an explosion when Volunteers on a lower level started up the boilers to make cups of tea, almost igniting the grain upstairs.[77] The Boland's garrison worried that British sniper fire or artillery might set fire to nearby gasometers and incinerate them, though enemy bullets that penetrated the tanks only produced stifling fumes. Andrew MacDonnell was more concerned about being posted at the top of a very high ladder from which he watched troop movements in Ringsend Basin. His greatest fear was falling asleep and plunging to his death from a great height.[78]

The Rising's military conduct is often compared favourably with subsequent and more squalid conflicts and is depicted as a clean, chivalrous fight – civilised warfare at its best. Even Under-Secretary Nathan conceded that 'Undoubtedly many of the rebels behaved in a manner to which exception would not have been taken had they been belligerents'.[79] For its part, the Military Council was very conscious that future generations and historians would scrutinise the rebellion and through orders to followers it sought to prevent conduct that would leave the rebels open to accusations of barbarism. Unarmed British soldiers promenading on the streets of Dublin at the start of the Rising were not to be fired on while military and police personnel captives were to be treated as prisoners of war. Many captives were seized on Easter Monday in parks, on streets, in railway stations, hotels and business premises. One British officer was on a train that was stopped passing Boland's and he was taken to the bakery for the duration of the Rising. Others were taken when their cars were stopped at barricades, including Lord Dunsany and Lieutenant Lindsay, two high-ranking officers from the Inniskilling Fusiliers who were ambushed by Daly's Volunteers from the Four Courts. Dunsany and Lindsay had been on leave in Londonderry but on hearing about the Rising on Easter Tuesday they hurried to Dublin and were assigned to Amiens Street. But they were not provided with directions through an unfamiliar city and were fired on and stopped near the Four Courts. Both men were wounded along with their chauffeur and all three were taken prisoner.[80]

Policemen were opportunistically seized in the vicinity of rebel garrisons, while off-duty colleagues were often recognised on the streets or in shops and pubs. Others on plainclothes assignments were captured during the week after the unarmed Dublin Metropolitan Police were withdrawn from the streets entirely on Easter Monday. More soldiers and police were seized later when their barracks were surrounded. At the isolated Linenhall Barracks thirty-two unarmed clerks of the Army Pay Department resisted Daly for four days and managed to douse two fires, but capitulated when gelignite was employed against them and the barracks door was smashed open with sledgehammers. The Volunteers then successfully attacked the Bridewell and captured in the cellars a group of policemen who were transferred to Daly's headquarters in Father Mathew Hall.[81] But an attempt to capture forty policemen pinned down in Moore Street Barracks failed.

In most cases prisoners were treated reasonably well. Nobody acted with more generosity of spirit or magnanimity than The O'Rahilly did in the GPO. Given overall responsibility for prisoners, an innate humanity made their safety his paramount consideration. Min Ryan recognised this as she witnessed him briskly admonishing the captives' guards:

> Now these prisoners are in our charge and we are honour bound to see that they are treated as prisoners of war. If it's the last bit of food in the place it must be shared with the prisoners and if any man does not follow my instructions he will get this – and he pulled out a gun.[82]

That was a typically theatrical gesture meant only for effect. When he later discovered that his charges hadn't been fed The O'Rahilly simply returned with trays of food and tea which he and two women proceeded to serve to them. He also dispatched Ryan and others with reassuring messages to deliver to the wives of captured British officers. Unsurprisingly their response was hostile: 'I always remember the look on the women's faces. They looked at us as if we were awful women.'[83] Even on Easter Friday, as the GPO began literally collapsing around him, The O'Rahilly didn't forget his obligation to the prisoners. One later recalled him telling them:

> men this place is now in the zone of danger and I'll have to bring you back to your old room, but you'll be quite safe there. We thanked him again and he said, 'That's all right. I'll give you my word that you'll escape with your lives. Again we thanked him and many of us said a prayer for him.'[84]

On Easter Tuesday Ned Daly released a policeman and fourteen soldiers who were stripped of their uniforms and weapons and provided with safe-conduct passes. Later he led the Bridewell policemen outside where, frightened, they believed they were about to be shot. Instead, after warning them to forget everything they had seen, he had two bespectacled and rather small Volunteers escort them to Richmond Hospital where they were handed over to doctor Sir Thomas Myles.[85] The wounded Lord Dunsany was also sent to recuperate in Jervis Street Hospital and was full of praise for his captors who apologised for wounding him.[86] Dunsany returned the compliment at the end of the Rising by lending some Volunteers a razor to shave off moustaches and beards to evade military policemen checking the wounded.[87] Daly used the captured army pay clerks in his headquarters, Father Mathew Hall, to fill sandbags. British officers in the GPO were guarded in a room at the top of the building and ordinary soldiers served in the Volunteer commissariat.

There were also instances of Volunteers having an enemy in their sights and exercising considerable restraint in not pulling their rifle trigger. In the GPO a sniper pointed out to The O'Rahilly that a British officer standing at a top window across O'Connell Street was scanning Volunteer positions through a pair of field glasses. When the marksman requested permission to shoot him – entirely legitimate under the rules of war – The O'Rahilly understood well that by such decisions did a man discover the kind of person that he really was. According to his son, Aodogán:

> this British officer was also a human being and, possibly with a wife and family. To kill him for no better reason than the colour of the cloth he was wearing was different from that worn by the Volunteers was something that does not come easily to any civilised person. O'Rahilly had not yet arrived at that stage of dehumanisation at which a soldier thinks no more of killing a man than he does of shooting a rabbit. He said to the Volunteer, 'Don't shoot, you would only give away our position. In any case, you would probably miss.'[88]

Similarly, in Northumberland Road on Easter Wednesday morning Volunteer William Christian was sipping a cup of tea when he saw:

> a young man in khaki uniform who was entering a house on the opposite side of the road. While waiting to be admitted he stood facing us with his arms well away from his body indicating that he was not armed. This put Pat Doyle into a bit of a fix as he had him covered from the time he came into view, and of course, he could not fire on an unarmed man. Had this stranger not given this sign Pat would certainly have pressed his trigger finger.[89]

When Patrick Kelly was manning a barricade near the Four Courts he saw a policeman and 'took steady aim at him and was about to pull the trigger when Captain Laffan knocked up my rifle and asked what I was doing. I pointed to the policeman and said I was going to shoot him. He said, "You can't do a thing like that, the man is unarmed."'[90]

But Nathan also accused the insurgents of conduct in which 'the lapses from fair conduct were both numerous and grave' and 'made hideous by cold-blooded murder and arson'.[91] One of his most serious allegations was that, whatever the Military Council may have stipulated, many unarmed soldiers were shot on sight and wounded or killed. There are many verified accounts of such incidents.[92] Peter Ennis, an unarmed private in the Scots Guards, was killed on the canal bank on Easter Monday morning by de Valera's Volunteers, who were then believed to have climbed on to the roof of Sir Patrick Dun's Hospital and fired on convalescent soldiers. Doctors intending to examine Ennis were warned by onlookers that Volunteers were shooting at anyone approaching him. Eventually a civilian rescued the body under fire and doctors were able to confirm that he had been shot though the heart and died instantly. At about the same time Captain Humphries, a British officer returning from furlough, was fatally wounded by a shot through the head in Westmoreland Street. At Stephen's Green a captured policeman was released on Easter Tuesday but shot in the back as he walked away, lying on the ground critically wounded for five hours before being rescued. A motley crew of vacationing Irish, Australian and South African soldiers came under fire in O'Connell Street and took refuge in Trinity College. Others who received sanctuary in private houses in some cases managed to reach nearby barracks disguised in clerical or female clothing.

Outside Dublin, Lieutenant Dunville of the Grenadier Guards, in uniform but unarmed, had his car stopped at Castlebellingham by Volunteers from Dundalk. He and three captive policemen were placed against railings and guarded with rifles and revolvers for about five minutes before, without warning, fire was opened on them. Dunville was shot in the chest and though he recovered in hospital one of the policemen was killed. Nevertheless, it should be acknowledged that some British soldiers during the Rising displayed a careless disregard for their own safety. On Easter Wednesday, a priest in Parnell Street noticed 'soldiers home on leave, standing about hallways with their friends. Though in khaki, and well within the danger zone, they did not seem to fear being shot at by the Volunteers.'[93] It should also be pointed out that members of the Royal Army Medical Corps wore khaki with only a small badge on the arm to distinguish them from the regular army. Since the badge was almost impossible to see at even 50 yards it is hardly surprising that many people wearing it became targets of Volunteer snipers during the Rising.

Some prisoners of the Volunteers had frightening experiences. At Boland's, a terrified detective who was accused of spying was paraded from post to post by a delighted de Valera, though he wasn't physically harmed.[94] Soldiers in the GPO were put up against a wall on Easter Friday and mistakenly feared the worst was about to happen. Later that day, in a most controversial incident, one of them, Lieutenant Chalmers, alleged that they were locked in the basement to 'die like rats' but were then taken out at the time of evacuation to be offered a choice of leading the way and being shot at, or staying to be shelled and incinerated. Chalmers said that they decided to take their chances outside – where the dead body of one who took a chance was later seen in Moore Street. However, Chalmers' allegations were strongly contested by Diarmuid Lynch, the senior officer at whose court martial Chalmers testified. Lynch had been in charge of the General Post Office prisoners and was ever after indignant at what he regarded as Chalmers' dishonourable behaviour. He was adamant that, far from the prisoners being deliberately placed in danger, everything was done to protect them. The transfer to the basement of which Chalmers complained had been made because the room at the top of the building where they had been lodged was endangered by fire. Even then it was only a temporary measure prior to evacuation. Lynch despised Chalmers for failing to acknowledge this 'honourable act' and regarded him as scared witless and incapable of rendering any coherent account of the final hours in the GPO. Lynch's assertions are substantially corroborated by Volunteer Joe Good who, near the end, discussed the prisoners with The O'Rahilly and suggested that they be let go to take their chances. The O'Rahilly initially misinterpreted this as using them for cover and was so incensed that Good thought he was about to be struck before The O'Rahilly recognised his true intention and apologised. Good says that The O'Rahilly let them go, but most likely this means that they were informed that they were to be released. Certainly they were still in the GPO when The O'Rahilly left with his advance party at 8.10 p.m. on Easter Friday. They were still under Lynch's command then and he categorically states that twenty minutes later the prisoners were given the choice of staying with the insurgents or advancing towards the British lines. All of them decided to take the second option except three members of Irish regiments, two of whom enthusiastically threw in their lot with the rebels.[95]

There were no independent witnesses to these events but Lynch's arguments are persuasive, especially given the emphasis on accuracy in his writings about the Rising. Furthermore, it is impossible to believe that members of the Provisional Government, so concerned with ensuring their Rising's legitimacy, would ever have condoned an action that would have besmirched their historical reputations.

Another of Nathan's allegations was that insurgents used dum-dum ammunition – split-nosed, soft-nosed and flat-nosed bullets that inflicted terrible wounds. His claims were supported by post-mortems on Volunteer Training Corps members killed on Easter Monday near Beggar's Bush Barracks. While these accusations have often been dismissed as British propaganda, it is beyond doubt that Volunteers employed dum-dum bullets. A bag of such ammunition was left behind by a Volunteer unit in a house in Lansdowne Road. Also, while standing at Nelson's Pillar after the surrender, Volunteer Patrick Rankin dropped dum-dum bullets at his feet and then realised an inspecting British officer was looking at them:

> I stared at him but never answered for fear he would call me a coward. None of my comrades spoke up for me. The officer eventually moved on while his aides were filling their pockets with small arms etc, for souvenirs. I was saying my prayers as never before as he moved away.[96]

Many British soldiers decided that the rebels were employing dishonourable tactics with the connivance of at least part of the civilian population. On Easter Wednesday, when Brigadier Maconchy was leading troop reinforcements into Dublin he was given a glass of water by an old lady, only for fire to be opened from surrounding houses and garden walls the moment she returned to her cottage.[97] At Trinity College British officers regaled the provost's daughter, Miss Mahaffy, with stories about the enemy's 'dirty tricks', including a trap that they had supposedly set in Middle Gardiner Street where Volunteer snipers had been positioned on a roof:

> Our soldiers wondered greatly at seeing the civilians in the street suddenly all lie down, faces downwards on the pavements but at this moment bombs began hurtling down. The throwers had evidently instructed their sympathising friends what to do when this crucial moment came. Here also for the first time the aged beldames from

the tenements brought hot cups of tea to the tired soldier boys; which proved to be poisoned and from the results of which three soldiers died.[98]

The poisoning seems apocryphal and it is impossible to know whether this is an embellished account of a real incident. What is not in doubt is that such stories circulated on the military grapevine and strengthened a belief that the friendliness of many civilians was a mask for treachery. Lieutenant Jameson believed that he had seen the rules of warfare violated:

> The brutes always took either a woman or child with them whenever they crossed the street so it was hard to get a shot at them, but we got a good few. They had a house with a small Red Cross flag hung out and I told my men not to fire at it. But one of my men fired just as a Red Cross ambulance drew up there; and I asked him what he fired at. He said he saw a man firing behind the van. I was just beginning to curse him hard when about 15 armed rebels ran out of the Red Cross house round the corner. We blazed away like fury but only winged a couple as they had only a few feet to cross.[99]

Mrs Norway, wife of the secretary of the General Post Office, heard from her army contacts that troops had been tricked by Volunteers pretending to capitulate behind a white flag only for officers stepping forward to take the surrender to be allegedly gunned down by snipers hidden in nearby houses. An order was then issued to soldiers that white flags were not to be recognised and rebels who surrendered did so at their own risk.[100]

Dublin's civilian population suffered more deaths and casualties than the British and Irish combatants combined – a degree of suffering that the Provisional Government had never intended. Although seemingly it never considered evacuating the capital, the rebel leaders were anxious to minimise the inconvenience and danger that the population would have to endure. Previous rebellions had degenerated into undisciplined, drunken rampages and the Proclamation warned against dishonouring the Rising by 'cowardice, inhumanity or rapine'. Volunteers were admonished not to consume alcohol and ordered to destroy any stocks in private houses, open taps in pubs and pour the content of bottles down a sink. Commandant Daly's first action in the Four Courts was to empty every bottle of spirits and barrel of beer into the sewers. When Catherine Byrne discovered a small bar containing beer and minerals in the GPO she asked a Volunteer for a bottle of lemonade just as Tom Clarke appeared. After pouring out a bottle he left them to finish the job, but typically, wasn't going to taking any chances – either with them or the rest of the garrison: 'Later on Tom Clarke came up and examined all the crates to make sure that all the stout was gone. He said he did not want the men to be tempted.'[101] The Volunteers' almost universal abstemiousness made a favourable impression on the general public. One of Hyde's friends praised Volunteers who had occupied a public house in Leeson Street for two days but only consumed a bottle of lemonade: 'Everyone agrees there was no drinking going on among them.'[102] Nevertheless, despite the leadership's aspirations it was never going to be a completely teetotal rebellion. Just before setting off for Jacob's Peadar Kearney, composer of *The Soldier's Song*, encountered a fellow member of

MacDonagh's battalion who 'announced that he was going over to the Grafton Bar to get a plebeian pint. He was immediately reminded that an order had been issued that any Volunteer found taking intoxicating liquor was liable to be shot. The incorrigible one simply grinned and said, "The way things are looking you'll be all shot, order or no order before the night is out". He crossed the road and called for the usual.'[103] When Dick Stephenson found a bottle of Guinness in the Mendicity 'in an excess of priggishness my first impulse was to empty the stout down the sink'.[104] As a student of Irish rebellions he was haunted by the drunkenness that had brought about defeat at the battle of Ross in 1798 and was determined that this time there would be no repetition. Yet for some reason that he couldn't explain even to himself, Stephenson hid the bottle behind a dresser instead of getting rid of it. Then amidst the garrison's elation on Easter Monday evening he decided to give the drink to Volunteer Tom Kelly, who was on sentry duty and whom he knew liked stout:

> Down I went with it, feeling my way carefully in the darkness, for fear I should trip and break the bottle on the staircase. I found Tom sitting beside Jimmy Brennan behind the barricade of furniture at the foot of the stairs. I whispered to him in the dark: 'Would you like a bottle of stout Tom?' His reaction was instantaneous, 'Oh the blessings of God on you,' he said, 'This is like manna from Heaven,' was his remark as he took the bottle from my hand in the darkness.[105]

Winning the hearts and minds of civilians involved treating the residents of occupied houses courteously, even if they were politically suspect. Shortly after midnight on Easter Monday a Volunteer unit seized a house on prosperous Lansdowne Road that belonged to a judge whose son, Denis Johnston, later became an important Irish dramatist. He marvelled at the rebels' courtesy and almost forgot that his family being hostages coerced them into sharing potentially lethal danger:

> There we were in the middle of the night, with four men in our house, preparing to turn the place into a fortress from which to fight the British Empire, and extremely apologetic about it all. That is the thing that remains most firmly in my memory – how polite and reasonable it all seemed. They were sorry to disturb us, and would do no more damage than was absolutely necessary. And any damage that they were forced to do would all be repaired by the Irish Republic. So we weren't to worry. They would take over the upper part and we could have the rest. And would we please not leave because these were their orders, and it would be dangerous anyway. Meanwhile if we required any food from the shops on the following day, they would be glad to go and get it for us.[106]

There were many such stories. After the Rising Douglas Hyde was told that Jacob's had been handed back so undamaged that it could have resumed production immediately. Dr Frank Purser, a friend of Hyde, insisted that:

> the Volunteers never disarranged anything nor did any mischief whatever in the College of Surgeons. They might easily have wrecked thousands of pounds worth of instruments in it. He said they never fired on the Red Cross and that during the

first days of the fighting it was sufficient for a doctor to hold up the hand and firing would cease when he went to attend the wounded.[107]

At the Metropole in O'Connell Street, Charles Saurin, a Volunteer officer, gently escorted the manager and his wife from their beloved hotel and they thanked him when he kept them well away from any Volunteers in order not to put them in danger from British snipers.[108] At Mount Street Bridge, George Reynolds displayed extraordinary solicitude in Clanwilliam House by promising to return it to the owners untouched. He refused to allow his unit to barricade the building, break windows or smash walls to provide an escape route. At the end of the subsequent battle against the Sherwoods one of Reynolds' men ruefully recalled this self-denying ordinance as he stood in the devastated and burning shell and water poured all over him from the shattered pipes.[109] Even many who were politically hostile to the Rising paid tribute to the insurgents' behaviour; Denis Johnston's mother described them as 'very nice civil boys'. Diarmuid Coffey heard widespread praise of their attempts to prevent looting and how Mallin's garrison in the College of Surgeons hadn't even left a drop of cigarette ash on the carpets.[110]

In regard to looting the valuables of civilians many Dubliners contrasted Volunteer behaviour favourably with that of British soldiers. When occupying buildings or private houses insurgents often made arrangements to protect the owner's money, jewellery and other prized possessions. In the GPO The O'Rahilly filled sacks with postal orders, money, stamps and everything else of value from drawers and placed them in a guarded upstairs room. As often happened, he went the extra mile after discovering a need for candles and instead of commandeering them he sent out a female garrison member with his own cash to purchase a supply.[111] In the Mendicity Patrick Stephenson discovered a lady's wristlet watch and some other jewellery during a search and secreted them inside a china teapot sitting on a dresser, intending to return them after 'a victorious peace was declared'.[112] By contrast British soldiers were often accused of looting and stealing just about anything they could get their hands on, especially money, jewellery and bracelets, but also anything ranging from cigars to binoculars. Douglas Hyde heard about the Gaelic League's offices being raided and its funds going missing as well as a soldier on a train pulling down his collar proudly showing a necklace underneath. A friend told him that:

> in many of the streets especially the poorer streets every house was searched by patrols of three soldiers one of them being generally a captain. They entered normally to search for arms but really to carry away anything that was of value. They used to compare notes openly and shamelessly in the street saying 'That house was no good at all. There was nothing in it,' meaning nothing to lift.[113]

Stephenson's good intentions came to nothing with the fall of the Mendicity but after being released from internment he was stunned to hear that the valuables' owner, the caretaker's wife, was accusing Volunteers of stealing her property. He was mystified because she was a Gaelic League member and was ignoring the most likely explanation that it had disappeared into the pockets of troops who had combed the Mendicity after Heuston's surrender.[114]

Many Dubliners felt as if they had been made prisoners in their own houses during the Rising. A large number remained indoors throughout Easter Week and even then they weren't entirely safe because people standing at their front window or going upstairs were often mistaken for snipers. Douglas Hyde recorded many people being shot in their beds or on the landing and stairs. On Easter Wednesday friends of his, the Coffeys, had their house riddled, collateral damage for an attack on the next-door house that had the bust of a man on display which soldiers mistook for a real person, blowing its head away.[115] Continuous confinement could be claustrophobic. On Sunday 30 April Mrs Salkey who lived in Merrion Square complained that 'it is now a week since we began to live under a reign of terror', and that the constant firing was very wearing and getting on the nerves of herself and her husband Richard. Because the front rooms weren't safe they had been forced to live in the bedroom at the back of the house. A lack of fresh air took its toll on many people and Mrs Salkey was delighted that on 30 April, a sunny day, she and Richard could at last get half an hour in their tiny garden, though her husband was exhausted: 'My poor Richard, it is tiring for him being always anxious and shut up so much.' He wasn't any better next day with sniping still going on:

> I don't like to leave R as he was so unhappy and upset so I stayed with him and just as we were going to get a little fresh air in the garden. What an extraordinary experience it is to be isolated from the whole world – not to be able to get the slightest information as to what is going on, not to know what has happened in the street within a few hundred yards, and to listen for two days to the firing without being able to ascertain where it has taken place or what has been the result.[116]

Especially for the many Dubliners like the Salkeys who felt that they were virtually under house arrest, time was passed playing a game of spot the weapon by listening to the sound of gunfire and identifying the weapon. Combatants were armed with a considerable variety in the Rising, including double-barrelled shot guns, Winchester repeaters, the latest pattern Lee Enfield British service magazine rifle and the powerful Howth rifle, as well as small arms from the .32 to a German parabellum. Douglas Hyde noticed that:

> when shots come singly, as they mostly do, it is quite easy to recognise which side has fired. The Army service rifles make a loud explosion. It sounds like bang-g-g, while the rifles of the Volunteers make a short sharp sound like the crack of a whip, a bang without any gs at the end of it.[117]

Matthew Connolly of the Citizen Army remembered that at the City Hall he quickly got used to differentiating the sounds of weapons, from the shotgun with its distinctive bark, through the German Mauser that created a loud explosion and an echo all of its own, to the sharp crack of the Lee Enfield 'with a ring to it as if one could hear the bullet whistling through the air'.[118] At Boland's Joseph O'Connor was less interested in rifles and small arms than the:

> curious effect the artillery fire had on me, my officers and men. Needless to say none of us had experience of being under artillery fire or in fact any danger at

all up to this week but I know myself that I enjoyed the artillery fire and took a pleasure in counting the interval between the flash and the noise of the explosion. The bursting of grenades and the continuous machine-gun and rifle fire was quite another matter.[119]

However, sometimes the noise of battle and the shouts, cries and commands of combatants was interrupted by a sound like a songbird making itself heard in the midst of bedlam. At the Four Courts Sean Kennedy recalls a fierce engagement being suddenly halted:

> While manning the barricade at Church Street bridge, and while the attack on the Mendicity Institution by the British was at its height, a street musician came along and from secure cover close to the Mendicity itself, commenced to play an Irish tune. The effect was so extraordinary upon all of us that with the exception of the fight going on at the Mendicity action in our vicinity almost ceased.[120]

However, the sound that some Dubliners recalled best was that of silence. One was a civil servant living in North Great George's Street who looked outside and was struck by an eerie quietness:

> The appearance of the street as viewed from this house has been quite extraordinary. A constant flow of people, largely women and young girls going and coming without the slightest appearance of excitement – more than double as many as one would see in the streets on any ordinary day, the only thing remarkable being their absolute silence. No one speaks. In the interval between the outbursts of firing there is an almost eerie silence; you could hear a pin drop. Then a few scattered shots, then a furious fusillade, then again silence, and occasional shrieks and shouts in the distance.[121]

British soldiers detained many innocent civilians and confined them in the Custom House along with republican sympathisers and suspected Volunteers. One civilian was a friend of Hyde's, Mr Kavanagh, Keeper of the Hibernian Academy, who had stayed at his post to the last and only just escaped the fires. Fleeing a hail of bullets in Abbey Street he ran straight into a group of soldiers who took him prisoner. In the Custom House captured Volunteers were kept in the yard but civilians were in rooms whose daytime conditions, despite overcrowding, weren't too unpleasant. Most guards were elderly reservists and quite friendly. Because of a food shortage they smashed down doors and grabbed anything available, including tins of currants, biscuits and bags of tea that they shared with prisoners.[122] Soon, however, according to the trade unionist William O'Brien, it was party time:

> Some drink was discovered and each prisoner was offered a drink of whiskey. Things became very noisy. Songs were sung in the inner room where the bulk of the guards were congregated. I did not fully realise at first what the position was but, apparently a number of the troops were under the influence of drink.[123]

As word seeped out about this state of affairs senior officers decided to bring down the curtain on the two men held responsible: 'The corporal and the old trooper were led out as prisoners. The old trooper was hardly able to walk and the corporal was arrested, presumably, for permitting that state of affairs.'[124] Nights were different. Kavanagh recalled prisoners sleeping on the floor 'like herrings in a barrel'. He told Hyde how during the night in pitch darkness when they were told:

> they were not allowed to light even a match, one of their number went mad and with awful screams went tumbling over their faces and bodies. Everyone cried out and tried to defend himself but nobody could see anything. It would have been bad enough in daylight but the horror of the darkness made it appalling.[125]

Another of Hyde's friends confined in the Custom House 'was made to sleep on the floor with I don't know how many people around him. Thinking that his head was lying on something dirty he struck a match to try and find out. Immediately the shout rang out "Put out that light or I fire."'[126]

And yet many civilians still suffered during the Rising at the hands of Volunteers and soldiers, resulting in injury or death. The elderly were extremely vulnerable because declining faculties made them slow to comprehend and react, causing many unfortunate incidents. After Joe Sweeney's unit evacuated the GPO on Easter Friday its members reached Moore Street and ordered that a house door be opened. When it remained closed they shouted for the occupants to stand away and blew open the lock only to find the dead body of an old man lying on the floor.[127] Austin Clarke's sister witnessed the last moments of an old lady:

> One night on her way home she was stopped with several others at Binn's Bridge by a party of British soldiers. An elderly woman went on, although a young sentry called on her several times to stop. Before anyone could rush forward to drag her back he raised his rifle, fired and she fell dead. Afterwards a girl who had known her told my sister that the old woman had been stone deaf for many years.[128]

Senior citizens who ventured out during fighting were often simply too slow to reach cover when bullets started flying. British soldiers mistook some people dressed in green as rebels and cut them down. Civilians clambering on to roofs to get a better view of the fighting were often assumed to be snipers and fired on. Some people came too close to the action because, extraordinarily, many Dubliners regarded the Rising as almost a spectacle laid on for their enjoyment and they competed for the best view. From the GPO Dick Humphries marvelled at an 'ever-inquisitive crowd' standing in D'Olier Street and at O'Connell Bridge, quite unconcerned, as firing went on: 'Indeed, one would think from their appearance that the whole thing was merely a sham battle got up for their amusement.'[129] Across the city during the battle of Mount Street Bridge a British soldier noticed maids coming out of the houses in Northumberland Road to watch the fighting and then throwing their aprons over their heads and running away whenever a bullet came too close. A Dubliner watching the same battle noticed how reluctant spectators were to drag themselves away, despite the danger and a large number of civilian casualties. Even when they fled into neighbouring streets 'they could not resist the temptation to creep back again and join the crowd of stalwarts who shadowed the advancing soldiers'. Later he cycled to near O'Connell Bridge, where he secured 'a ring seat view' of a British attack on a music shop. Observing the crowd of spectators, he discovered why they were acting in such a manner:

> Even the booming of the guns of the gunboat Helga down the river near the Custom House did not terrify them, and they paid no more attention to the bullets whistling over their heads than if they had been a drove of starlings. Their foolhardiness and disregard of danger was due, I believe to insatiable curiosity plus a good deal of fatalism. Dublin, even in normal times, is an inquisitive city. Any little incident that occurs – the break-down of a car, a fight between husband and wife, a dog fight – collects a crowd of interested onlookers quicker than in any other capital in the world.[130]

Some civilians who felt obliged to risk such danger were members of voluntary organisations such as the St John's Ambulance Brigade. During the battle at Mount Street Bridge a house in Northumberland Road was occupied as a dressing station and during Easter Wednesday afternoon and evening a Red Cross ambulance with a Mrs Chaytor sitting beside the driver drove continuously under heavy fire to remove wounded from it to the hospitals.[131] One British soldier marvelled at the bravery of such people:

> No one who saw it will ever forget the spectacle – the blazing house in the background, with the spurts of fire coming from the rifles of the Rebels concealed on the neighbouring housetops and behind the street windows, the answering shots from the troops, and the grandest sight of all – four white-robed Red Cross nurses calmly walking down the centre of the street between the combatants, their leader holding her right hand above her head, demanding that their errand of mercy should be undisturbed. Largely owing to the courage of these devoted women, assisted nobly by loyal inhabitants, the wounded were speedily dragged into the neighbouring houses and received whatever attention was possible on the spot.[132]

In some places such as Mount Street Bridge, short, informal truces took place to allow the wounded to be removed but elsewhere the firing continued without interruption. A St John's Ambulance member was shot dead by Volunteers in Baggot Street on Easter Wednesday as he attempted to treat a wounded man, while a driver was hit in the lungs whilst carrying wounded passengers past the Four Courts. On Easter Thursday W. Smith, a St John's Ambulance man, witnessed the carnage inflicted on civilians who were being ferried from Mount Street Bridge ('a regular death trap for its inhabitants') to Sir Patrick Dun's Hospital. The nurses' home brimmed with wounded who were lying on the floor, in the passages, on sofas and even two in a single bed. Smith watched one old man who had gone out for a loaf of bread die from gunshot wounds and saw the body of a servant girl who had been shot dead at her bedroom window.[133] In a Red Cross hospital in Merrion Square Mrs Augustine Henry, a VAD, was shocked by the ghastly scenes she encountered: 'The packing room is turned into an extempore theatre with operating tables. There are about twenty cases upstairs. One boy is shot through the lungs and dying. A woman leading a child has come out crying as we went in. It is awful.'[134]

Not every civilian casualty was an accidental victim. Captain Gerrard, a British officer stationed in Beggar's Bush during the Rising, later described being approached on Easter Tuesday evening by an edgy sentry who had swallowed rumours about Volunteers disguising themselves as women:

> I beg your pardon, Sir, I have just shot two girls.' I said 'What on earth did you do that for? He said, 'I thought they were rebels. I was told they dressed in all classes of clothes. At a range of about two hundred yards I saw two girls – about twenty – lying dead.'[135]

Others civilians were clearly the intended target even when no fighting was in progress. A large number of such cases occurred at Stephen's Green. Liam Ó Briain attributed civilian casualties there to poor barricade organisation, which allowed cars to filter through, and to the absence of a clear policy for dealing with such vehicles. However, the casual violence of some rebels also demonstrated arrogance, insensitivity and a determination to chasten those deemed insufficiently respectful or obedient. This is hardly surprising, since some clearly lacked discipline and were having the time of their lives. Douglas Hyde noticed that:

> Among these were some who were only infants – one boy seemed about twelve years of age. He was strutting the centre of the road with a large revolver in his small fist. A motor car came by him containing three men, and in the shortest of time he had the car lodged in his barricade, and dismissed its stupefied occupants with a wave of his armed hand.[136]

Some cars had harrowing experiences at Stephen's Green, such as the chauffeur-driven vehicle of Lord Donaghmore on Easter Tuesday afternoon. He later complained bitterly that he and his companions had travelled from Naas without any sign of military or police activity and had been allowed to drive straight into a trap. Only when they were 200 yards from the Green did a pedestrian warn them that every motor was being seized by rebels who were firing indiscriminately on passers-by. When his driver started to reverse a bullet shattered the hood and ricocheted around the interior, wounding all three passengers.[137] In O'Connell Street on Easter Monday, Professor Pope of Trinity College suddenly saw a man in green uniform open the door of the General Post Office and fire a revolver at the crowd, fatally wounding a young woman of about 17 in the left breast.[138] The police files on such incidents are replete with phrases such as 'bayoneted by a rebel as he looked like a policeman', 'shot by a rebel when he refused to go away', 'bayoneted by rebel at New Street, whilst walking along the thoroughfare', 'shot by rebels for refusing to erect barricades when requested by them to do so', 'shot by rebel, it is said because he refused to join them when requested' and 'shot by rebels for not getting off the streets'.[139] It was also noted that the information on such cases came from people who, almost without exception, refused to give their names because they were afraid of their businesses being attacked or their lives endangered.

Tram drivers and passengers who didn't comply with Volunteer orders placed themselves in danger. Near Boland's Andrew MacDonnell was:

> ordered to hold up a tram, my first taste of active service. I stood in the street with my six-foot pike 'to the ready' as the tram approached. Not an inch did I move as the tram came closer but to my great relief it stopped and I ordered the passengers out. I have considered since what would have happened had the driver rung the bell and kept coming.[140]

Another Volunteer who stopped a tram on Easter Monday near Stephen's Green had no such crisis of conscience. David Fitzgerald recorded how a friend called MacLaughlin was standing at the corner of Kildare Street talking to an acquaintance when a tram passed by:

> A man rushed out brandishing a rifle and ordering it to stop. The driver went on whereupon the man pulled out a revolver and threatened the driver who stopped and got off the car. The passengers were ordered to alight. A powerful civilian rushed at the man and pinned him from behind. He did not catch him low enough down and he was able to fire 3 shots over his left shoulder at the civilian (without effect). The civilian then dropped him and ran behind the car the Volunteer firing 1 shot at him with his rifle. He then came up to McLaughlin brandishing the revolver in his face and asked him what he did there. Mac said what have I done to you? Said he had a great mind to shoot him too. He was not drunk but in a state of wild excitement, like a native 'run amok'.[141]

Many Dubliners didn't believe that British troops behaved much better during the Easter Rising. Arthur Mitchell, a volunteer ambulance driver, was convinced that he witnessed soldiers deliberately and callously allowing a Volunteer to bleed out. Mitchell had four orderlies and an army sergeant to help collect bodies from hospitals and morgues for transport to Dean's Grange cemetery. He recorded driving through Moore Street, near the end of the Rising, where a man in a green uniform was lying in a gutter in nearby Moore Lane. Mitchell's party approached the man, who seemed to be still alive, only for a young English officer to refuse them permission to lift him. The sergeant told Mitchell that 'he must be someone of importance and the bastards are leaving him there to die of his wounds – it is the easiest way to get rid of him'.[142] Returning that evening, a different officer adamantly refused to allow them to lift the body which several people later told Mitchell was that of The O'Rahilly. They were almost certainly mistaken, because if it was Easter Saturday afternoon when Mitchell first entered Moore Street and the man was still alive it couldn't have been The O'Rahilly; by then he was already dead.

Another Dubliner described the Staffordshires as 'demons' and another complained that:

> The English soldiers are showing no mercy. A young lad of fifteen riding on his bicycle was shot stone dead for not answering when challenged crossing Portobello Bridge and a young girl was wounded in the leg. There has been slaughter in the town. The soldiers are shooting anybody and everybody.[143]

Nathan rejected all allegations of slaughter and wrote that:

> considerable numbers of troops were required to cope with the insurgents, and on
> the whole the troops behaved unexceptionally. There may have been a case here
> and there where soldiers dealt out a summary justice, but it is remarkable in view
> of the nature of the struggle that these instances were not the rule. The soldiers
> found a great majority of the citizens sympathetic to them and a small but violent
> minority hostile and treacherous. Cakes and drinks were offered them at one
> house, bullets were fired at them from the next. In every large city are strong ele-
> ments of lawlessness, and these elements in Dublin responded when the moment
> was opportune.[144]

His concession that summary justice might have occurred was wise, because some
rebels were clearly killed when they posed no danger. A Volunteer who surrendered
at the Mendicity was shot dead by a British sniper, despite the fact that his unit had
walked into the open behind a white flag.[145] Many other soldiers took no chances,
especially after an order issued on Easter Wednesday that they were to fire immediately on any armed man in uniform or in plain clothes whom they believed to be
a rebel but who did not surrender.[146] British soldiers clearly shot at civilians, sometimes in the mistaken belief that they were insurgents but in other cases certainly
not. When a milkman's cart was stopped by troops on Leeson Street Bridge it was
searched despite the driver's pass and when the soldiers discovered ammunition they
shot the driver as he attempted to escape.[147] At the General Post Office, Joe Sweeney
watched a drunk stagger along O'Connell Street and though the man was abusing
the rebels he was cut down by British snipers. Volunteers with Red Cross armlets
who tried to rescue the victim were also shot at.[148] Early on Easter Wednesday a theatre critic, Joseph Holloway, saw British soldiers firing on anyone crossing O'Connell
Street at the Parnell Monument, bringing down a woman at the foot of the statue
and a man near the pavement. Both bodies were eventually allowed to be removed
by ambulance, the incident, bizarrely, being recorded by a man with a camera.[149] One
factor which led to Pearse's decision to surrender on Easter Saturday was seeing three
civilians being shot dead by British snipers, despite carrying a white flag. Lieutenant
Jameson, who had been so indignant at the behaviour of Volunteers, was nevertheless
delighted in Marlborough Street when:

> My corporal saw a civilian walking where a whole lot of Sinn Feiners were so he
> said he didn't know whether he was a Sinn Feiner or not, but anyhow he oughn't to
> be there so he'd 'just shoot him in the foot'. So he up with his rifle and fired, and the
> man hopped down the street on one leg!

Jameson was also prepared to coerce civilians to risk their lives, even those with military passes:

> At that time I had three men lying in the street, so I took the passes of the first few
> civilians who came by, and made them go down Little Mary Street and take the
> men into the nearest houses to be looked after, and wouldn't give them back their

passes till they had done so, 'cos I didn't like to see them wriggling. I thought it was
rather a good idea![150]

By Easter Thursday British troops obviously regarded certain areas as free-fire zones
in which anybody who had remained was deemed a rebel liable to be shot dead. On
Thursday afternoon, for instance, military parties in Amiens Street, Store Street and
Beresford Place and from Talbot Street to Gardiner Street ordered everyone off the
streets. Those who did not comply were fired on and several seriously injured men
were taken away in an ambulance.[151]

Sometimes in the free-fire zones armoured cars raked entire streets with machine-
gun fire, such as occurred in North King Street where fifteen soldiers fired into every
house and the few remaining civilians threw themselves on the floor. In five houses
in North King Street, between 6 p.m. on Friday and 10 a.m. on Saturday 28–29 April,
thirteen men died in extremely controversial circumstances. Locals alleged that troops
of the Staffordshires, supervised by officers, had systematically murdered them, not in
the heat of battle but in some cases hours after any danger had passed. One resident,
Miss Anne Fennel, described the death of a fellow tenant, George Ennis, who worked
as a carriage-maker in a local factory. She claimed that early on Easter Saturday about
thirty soldiers and two officers burst into the house, shouting furiously:

> I nearly fell on the ground and clasped the officer's hand in terror, but he flung me
> off. As poor Mrs Ennis saw her husband being led upstairs she clung to him and
> refused to be parted from him, and said, 'I must go up with my husband.' One of the
> soldiers pulled her off and put a bayonet to her ear and uttered the foulest language.
> She said, 'You would not kill a woman, would you?' He shouted, 'Keep quiet, you
> bloody bitch.' After a long time, it must have been a couple of hours, we heard a
> noise at the parlour door, and to our horror poor Mr Ennis crawled in. I will never
> forget. He was dying, bleeding to death, and when the military left the house he had
> crept down the stairs, to see his wife for the last time. He was covered with blood
> and his eyes were rolling in his head. He said to his wife, 'O Kate, they have killed
> me.' She said, 'O my God! for what?' He said, 'For nothing.'[152]

At a subsequent inquest, Lieutenant-Colonel Taylor, the commanding officer, denied
every allegation and stated that 'only those houses were entered by the military which
the exigencies of the case rendered actually necessary, and no persons were attacked
by the troops other than those who were assisting the rebels, and found with arms in
their possession'.[153] However, the allegations were so serious that the army instituted a
court of inquiry which, perhaps surprisingly, wasn't a whitewash. But despite exhaustive efforts it couldn't establish for certain what had happened in North King Street.
The inquiry examined, in particular, the deaths of four men in No 27 but without
locating any witnesses. It did turn up a next-door neighbour who said he had spoken
to the men through a grating in his cellar and thought that later he heard some crying
but not any shooting. He was also present later when the bodies that were hurriedly
buried in a garden on Saturday were dug up and noticed that one had the top of his
head blown away and another his throat and chin. The court confessed bluntly that it
could 'get no evidence as to how these men were killed'. No soldier admitted being

inside the house or seeing anyone entering and it noted their lack of co-operation. Neither had the inquiry been helped by the chaotic situation existing after the Rising when army companies had become mixed up, making it difficult to trace participants and reconstruct which soldiers had been in any particular house at a given time. The court concluded, tentatively, that marks in the room where the men were found indicated that if they were shot there one of them must have been lying on the floor with his head against the wall at the time – an unlikely scenario. There were no other bullet marks showing where the others could have been shot. The court praised the Staffordshires ('a quiet and very respectable set of men'), whose behaviour had been praised by many civilian witnesses, and concluded that it was 'very unlikely that any persons were shot or killed, unless the men had reason to think that they had been fired on, whether they were mistaken or not'.[154]

The report complimented the women who had appeared before it as 'very respectable people who gave their evidence clearly and showed no animosity to the soldiers'. The Staffordshires, however, were less gracious after 2,000 of them were forced into one of the largest identity parades in history. After making a 20-mile taxi journey to this mass line-up the women couldn't pick out the alleged perpetrators, an episode that is laced with vitriol in the regimental history: 'One lady, arrayed in a fur coat evidently looted during the burning of O'Connell Street, wished [for] whiskey before she started, and shouted for it when passing public houses. When passing along the ranks she remarked: "Sure, I feel just like Queen Victoria reviewing the troops."'[155]

In late May 1916 Sir Edward Troup, permanent secretary at the Home Office, produced a detailed, persuasive analysis of the episode, citing as 'the root of the mischief' an order of Brigadier-General William Lowe, who was in overall command of military operations at the time. This stated that rebels 'had placed themselves outside the law, and that they were not to be made prisoners'. Troup believed that as a result soldiers didn't 'distinguish between refusing to make prisoners and shooting immediately prisoners whom they had made' and that it should have been made clear that the order 'did not mean that an unarmed rebel might be shot after he had been taken prisoner, still less could it mean that a person taken on mere suspicion could be shot without trial'.[156] Certainly residents of North King Street and nationalist Ireland generally regarded the episode as a 'cold-blooded calculated atrocity' in which innocent bystanders were murdered by British soldiers, sometimes after the immediate danger had passed.

General Maxwell assured Prime Minister Asquith that demands for public inquiries into civilian deaths were manufactured to discredit the military. He acknowledged publicly that it was 'perfectly possible' that 'some innocent' persons were killed, that perhaps the troops in the heat of battle 'saw red', and that 'some unfortunate incidents which we should regret now may have occurred', but he suggested that such occasions were rare. However, he admitted privately to his wife about being 'bothered to death with these cases where soldiers are accused of having murdered innocent civilians in cold blood. I fear there have been some cases of this.'[157] He told Kitchener that 'It must be borne in mind in these cases that there was a lot of house-to-house fighting going on, wild rumours in circulation and owing to darkness, conflagrations, etc, apparently a good deal of "jumpiness". With young soldiers and under the circumstances I wonder there was not more.'[158]

The most notorious such incident involved the murder of Francis Sheehy-Skeffington, a well-known, loved and somewhat eccentric Dublin character dressed in a knickerbocker suit who was actively involved in every worthy cause, such as pacifism, socialism, vegetarianism, alcohol abstinence and votes for women. He had become an object of resentment in military circles because of his opposition to the war, which the authorities believed hindered recruiting. In one speech in May 1915 he had blamed the Allies for provoking the war and declared that if there were any power that should be smashed in the conflict it should be England.[159] He had been arrested, gone on hunger strike and been released on health grounds. When the Rising broke out Sheehy-Skeffington was moved by the suffering of the civilian population and on Easter Tuesday he convened a poorly attended public meeting to co-ordinate relief measures. Walking back to his suburban home he was arrested at a British army checkpoint and taken to the nearby Portobello Barracks; there his rather outlandish appearance, which included a votes for women badge, convinced Captain J.C. Bowen-Colthurst that a radical subversive had been apprehended. Bowen-Colthurst had already rounded up two completely innocent journalists and he seems to have decided that he was in charge of a group of extremely dangerous men. During the night he took the three prisoners out on a raiding party during which he shot dead an innocent youth. On Easter Wednesday morning he had them taken out into the barrack yard and shot dead by a firing party.

When Bowen-Colthurst submitted a report on the events to his superior officer, Major Rosborough, later on Easter Wednesday he stated that a study of documents found on the three men had led him to conclude that they 'were all very dangerous characters'. He had sent for an armed guard of six men to escort them to a small courtyard close by where he could conduct an interrogation. Unfortunately, he added, he did not have them handcuffed and when they arrived in the yard he discovered that it was a place from which an escape could be easily accomplished. When he realised this, and aware of the risks the prisoners posed, he ordered the guard to fire, shooting them dead.[160]

It might be thought that even this sanitised version would have raised questions. Far from it. As it worked its way up through the system it reached Major-General Sandbach, commanding troops in the Dublin area on 3 May, and he noted that 'Capt Bowen-Colthurst seems to have carried out his duties with discretion'.[161] On the very same day Bowen-Colthurst was arrested, largely as the result of the indefatigable efforts of another officer in Portobello Barracks, Major Sir Francis Vane. His determination to expose the crime led to his professional ruination at the hands of a military establishment that was hardly grief-stricken at Sheehy-Skeffington's death; General Maxwell wrote of 'a certain Sheehy Skeffington, a very poisonous person. But he was shot in a very unceremonious way.'[162] As Bowen-Colthurst's culpability became clear his fellow soldiers in Portobello raced to dissociate themselves from him and his actions. On 16 May Sandbach withdrew his previous commendation saying: 'I never imagined for one moment that the men could actually have been killed by design. But having since read the evidence of Sergt. J Aldridge the act appears to me in quite a different light and if this latter statement is true, then the officer in question used no discretion.' Sergeant Aldridge who had commanded the guard revealed that 'He [the Captain] told the prisoners to stand up against the wall and then ordered the guard to load, present, fire. The prisoners were shot dead.'[163]

Bowen-Colthurst's statement to a court of inquiry at Victoria Barracks in Belfast on 10 May 1916, while obviously self-serving, does plausibly convey the picture of a stressed man who, like others in the city, had been tipped right over the edge. As Portobello Barracks swarmed with terrified women and wounded soldiers he was overwhelmed by fears of an imminent attack by a rebel army marching on Dublin:

> I knew of the sedition which had been preached in Ireland for years past and I was credibly informed that unarmed soldiers had been shot down in the streets of Dublin by the rebels; on the Wednesday morning (26th) all this was in my mind; I was very much exhausted and unstrung after a practically sleepless night. I took the gravest view of the situation and I did not think it possible that troops would arrive from England in time to prevent a general massacre. I was convinced that prompt action was necessary to ensure that these men should not escape and further spread disaffection. It was impossible for men to move the prisoners to a more secure place of confinement owing to the armed rebels having possession of the streets all around the barracks; believing that I had the power under martial law, I felt under the circumstances that it was clearly my duty to order these men to be shot.[164]

There was a general consensus in army circles that Colthurst had had a complete breakdown. Maxwell told his wife that 'his history points to madness but he refuses to plead insanity'. Major Vane, likewise, was in no doubt that he had been 'temporarily insane' at the time of the shootings. There was no high-level attempt to protect or save Bowen-Colthurst; he was as expendable as Sheehy-Skeffington. His superiors regarded his behaviour as indefensible, the actions of a deranged man. But there was a cover-up – an exercise in concealment which was designed to protect the reputation of the British army, whose elite was alarmed at the affair's ramifications. Maxwell regarded it as 'a bad case and [it] excites much interest in army circles'.[165] The fact that Sheehy-Skeffington had been a completely innocent victim was irrelevant and indeed British military intelligence even considered a desperate, ludicrous scheme to smear him as the leader of a Volunteer bombing unit in O'Connell Street. The strategy which was finally adopted was to attempt to bury the scandal as deeply as Sheehy-Skeffington himself. Nevertheless, keeping the case well away from public and press scrutiny did not prove easy. On 16 May Deputy Judge Advocate Marshall decided that Bowen-Colthurst should be charged with murder, with an alternative charge of manslaughter. To the horror of the legal and military establishment he also concluded that the Army Act forbade a trial by court martial if the offence was committed in the United Kingdom, even if the accused was on active service at the time. Unless martial law was still in operation when the case was heard Bowen-Colthurst would have to be tried by a civil court. This opened up the alarming and unacceptable prospect of testimony in open court and while the Irish law officers agreed with Marshall's interpretation they warned him that a civil trial with widespread coverage would lead to 'turbulence and disorder'.[166]

The machinery to circumvent such an eventuality cranked into action immediately and the conspiracy went right to the top. The lawyers recognised that the route out of this judicial swamp lay in a new DORA regulation overriding Section 41 of the

Army Act and ordering a military tribunal. To facilitate this, the Lord Chief Justice of England, Lord Reading, was brought in and he convened a meeting in his office at the Law Courts in London on 18 May 1916. The conference was attended by the English Solicitor-General, the Director of Public Prosecutions, the Irish attorney-general and Brigadier-General Byrne, Deputy Inspector-General of the RIC. In the course of three hours' deliberations they mulled over the opinions of Marshall and the Irish law officers and concurred that a Special Defence of the Realm regulation should be framed to allow civil offences to be tried by court martial. Work began immediately and on 22 May 1916 the DPP forwarded the new regulation to Byrne in Dublin with the comment that 'In this case there has been much to do and comparatively short time to do it in, but I hope that everything may be in order'.[167]

All that was required now was to close one final bolthole. It was learnt that the nationalist MP Tim Healy was to call on the attorney-general in parliament to examine a provision in the Army Act, 'from which we were somewhat concerned to learn that a trial by court martial would not be a bar to a second trial in a civil court. In the particular case to leave such a contingency even remotely possible was not, in the L[aw] O[fficers'] opinion to be thought of.'[168] Accordingly, the new regulation had been framed to exclude the possibility of a civil trial. Bowen-Colthurst was finally convicted of murder and ordered to be confined to a hospital for the criminally insane. After some years he was released and emigrated to Canada where he lived for the rest of his life.

Fear, anxiety and suspicion all whipped up a spy paranoia in Dublin during Easter Week, a variant of the war psychosis created by the First World War in which civilians with German names had to be spying for the kaiser and dachshunds were stoned in the streets. Nothing was what it seemed. Undoubtedly, especially on the British side, intelligence gathering about the enemy's strength and dispositions occurred and during the Rising, for various reasons, men disguised themselves, sometimes in women's clothes. However, almost everyone accused of being a spy was innocent, simply caught in the wrong place at the wrong time. On the canal near Marrowbone Lane on Easter Saturday the garrison captured someone they thought was a female spy and brought her inside the distillery to be interrogated by Cumann Na mBan members. According to Rose MacNamara:

> We were afraid that the person might be a man in women's clothes, so we had to be careful as she was a very masculine looking woman. We each of us had our knives in case of a fight but she was harmless. We did not find anything on her so she was let go with a warning.[169]

At Stephen's Green Volunteer James O'Shea was berated by a man seemingly under the influence and cursing cowards who should be fighting for king and country. O'Shea claimed that he thought the man was a spy only pretending to be drunk and when he continued to ignore warnings to leave, O'Shea picked up his rifle and shot him dead.[170] On the British side many soldiers believed the welter of rumours that a German expeditionary force had landed in Ireland, elements of which had probably already reached the capital. Believing they were now engaged in a new battlefront with the Hun, troops were on the look-out for anyone of Germanic appearance and late in Easter Week at the back of houses near O'Connell Street they believed they had bagged a real enemy agent. The Volunteer recalled how the British soldiers:

> thought I was a German spy. The officer questioned me in German but all the German I knew was 'Ich' which I did not say. He then put me up against a wall to shoot me. The shooting party was actually formed up. My hair which was very fair had grown long and had fallen over my forehead and nose so I asked if I might brush it back: 'Yes go on then.' he said, 'and I will brush it back for you.' He countermanded the order to shoot and he put me in an armoured car. I think it was that request that saved my life.[171]

The Rising came as an unexpected and shocking experience to the civilian population of Dublin. One inhabitant, Ismena Rohde, wrote after the Rising about how 'that fortnight of shot and shell, fierce fighting all around and death and destruction was like a lifetime. We thought Ireland was the only safe place to live in at present, so remote from battle. And then this storm burst over our heads.'[172] Many were initially confused as to the Rising's character and purpose. Mrs Nellie O'Brien, who lived near Trinity College, believed at first that it was simply a demonstration against conscription.[173] But the reality of rebellion and urban warfare soon began to make a tangible impact on the fabric of Dublin life, especially as essential services such as transport and gas began to shut down. By Easter Monday afternoon trams had been withdrawn to their depots, taxis had ceased to ply for trade and the number of private cars had declined dramatically. The railway stations closed down or were occupied. The gas system was also closed down by de Valera's battalion at Boland's; this was vital to prevent explosions in any buildings occupied by Volunteers and attacked by the British. The loss of the gas supply had a major impact on domestic and industrial life, except on those firms which had their own supplies. Street lighting was also run on gas and the nights of fearful darkness had begun. Cinemas and theatres also closed.

The first real intimation that the theatre critic and inveterate first-nighter Joseph Holloway had that something serious was happening came on Easter Monday when the matinee performance at the Empire was cancelled and a group of agitated actresses stood on a street corner. The public houses also closed temporarily on Easter Monday, partly on their own initiative and partly because the authorities had instructed plainclothes policemen to advise owners to shut their doors. One gleeful Dubliner observed the incredulity of thirsty race-goers just back from Fairyhouse: 'They looked up at the windows, in through the keyholes and couldn't believe the evidence of their own senses.'[174]

There was an increasing dearth of accurate information partly caused by the severance of communications between Dublin and the outside world and within the city itself. The telegraph connection to England was broken at 12.20 p.m. on Easter Monday, but the telephone system continued working despite the Military Council's intention to seize the telephone exchange in Crown Alley near Dublin Castle, or at least cut wires from both the exchange and the Castle. It has been claimed that the plan failed because Volunteer members of a joint team with the Citizen Army didn't turn up. Crucially, the twenty female telephone operators remained on duty along with the manager and male staff when the Rising started: 'They wept but carried on

the work notwithstanding the fact the switchboard and ceiling were scarred with bullets.'[175] A party of Royal Irish Rifles only arrived at Crown Alley at 5 p.m. on Easter
Monday, barricading the building with stationery presses, pads of tickets and sand
from fire buckets. Initially the telephonists returned home at the end of their shift but
by Wednesday conditions were so dangerous that everyone remained permanently
at Crown Alley, sleeping in the cellar with boards protecting them from snipers' bullets. Even so, throughout the week civilians could only receive calls and not initiate
them.[176] The newspapers were also seriously disrupted. Of the Dublin papers, only
the Unionist publication the *Irish Times* managed to keep going for the first half of
the week, though copies of English papers such as the *Mail* and *Sketch* were brought
in and sold for a shilling each. As a result the city swam with all sorts of wild rumours
during the Rising. Much of the city's distribution network broke down, including
deliveries of bread, milk and coal. Many shops closed along with much of the commercial and administrative system, such as post offices, banks, offices, civil service
departments and Dublin Corporation. No mail was collected or delivered. Funeral
parlours and cemeteries ceased to operate.

Dublin's unarmed police force, the Dublin Metropolitan Police, was also quickly
taken off the streets on Easter Monday. News of this spread rapidly and droves of
residents emerged from the slum districts on free shopping expeditions to premises
whose owners had already locked up and departed. Some of the looting which
occurred directly opposite the General Post Office shocked the more idealistic or
naïve rebels. It also embarrassed Pearse, who in his valedictory address of 28 April
attributed the phenomenon to 'supporters of the British government and hangers-on
of the British army'. Many accounts of the Rising describe the comic and even carnival aspects of the looting. There are numerous stories, including that of the old lady
whose swag had been stolen chasing the perpetrator and bawling: 'Stop thief, stop
thief. I've been robbed.' In another, a woman in O'Connell Street whose bundle of
looted shoes had vanished raged that the police could not even 'protect the property
of a poor old woman'. Thomas Johnson, a trade union leader, saw boys in silk hats
mimicking Charlie Chaplin, old ladies in rags sitting on the pavement trying on fancy
shoes, a paper-seller with a gold watch on his wrist and young boys with toy guns and
helmets in uniforms taken from the fancy goods stores, playing 'shoot the German'.[177]

Much of the looting verged on the pathological and the looters, many of them
women and children, displayed an extraordinary rapacity. One onlooker in O'Connell
Street on Easter Monday night followed a woman and her small daughter who was
pushing a pram. The mother emerged from one shop with an armful of ladies' shoes
and deposited them in the pram. They moved on to an already pillaged confectioner's,
where she 'slowly and obstinately butted her way through the looters like a Whippet
tank at the front', emerging with a large jar of lollipops and boxes of chocolates. There
then followed an assault on a clothes shop, which they left with the girl in a red-rid-
ing-hood cloak and the woman dressed in a fur coat and large feathered hat. Sated at
last, they journeyed to the pro-cathedral, sacred ground being regarded as sufficiently
safe to hide their booty from thieves. The looters were brazen and, despite the fact
that hundreds were arrested, they continued like locusts right up to the collapse of
the Rising. Both soldiers and rebels fired over their heads and some were shot dead
but nothing seemed to deter them. One old biddy waddled past a military checkpoint

openly carrying a huge box of soap, receiving only an insult from a soldier that she looked dirty enough to need it all. In Dorset Street on Friday 28 April, a looting expedition broke into a row of shops in full view of soldiers stationed at nearby corners:

> Suddenly a shot is heard, then a series of shots striking the bricks and raising a cloud of dust like smoke which makes many onlookers think snipers are firing on the houses. But it is the military sending warning shots to frighten the looters. Suddenly as though one shot has gone through a window and taken effect a panicky rush is seen from one shop door – a full score of women and children with parcels and bundles rush out of the doorway and into the lane leading to the back street and for a few minutes there is no one to be seen in that quarter. But only for a few minutes. In less than ten out they come again one by one, then more openly in couples and threes and start the game again.[178]

One witness to the 'macabre and fearless' looters was reminded of Goya's paintings of the Witches' Sabbath. Another watched from her hotel as a mob in Grafton Street stripped fruit shops:

> It was an amazing sight, and nothing daunted these people. Higher up at another shop we were told a woman was hanging out a window dropping down loot to a friend, when she was shot through the head by a sniper, probably our man; the body dropped into the street and the mob cleared. In a few minutes a hand-cart appeared and gathered up the body, and instantly all the mob swarmed back to continue the joyful proceedings.[179]

The looters also displayed considerable self-righteousness, taunting the Volunteers that they were only following their example in smashing windows and appropriating the contents. They gleefully set up stalls opposite rebel garrisons to sell their plunder and even sidled up to offer bargains to the insurgents. The mobs were extremely vicious, brooking no opposition: a civilian who attempted to remonstrate with them on Easter Tuesday was shot dead. Some looters were also arsonists. They ignited Lawrence's toy shop with fireworks and set off explosions over O'Connell Street from showers of sky rockets, star-bursts, Catherine wheels and Roman candles. Even the old displayed infinite malice, as Volunteer Joe Good discovered when he returned to the GPO from an outpost with a sword he had found:

> On my way I found a pavement littered with stiff starch collars the looters had no use for; it's hard to march through a street carpeted with stiff collars, and it was a strain on my dignity as I walked along carrying my shotgun and sword. An old lady, one of the looters still as busy as termites in the streets, perhaps sensed my embarrassment, struck me in the face with a rotten red cabbage. She was about to follow up her attack. If I'd threatened her with my gun, it would not have stopped her. I drew the sword and slashed – intending to clear her head. She fell on her knees – and to my horror something rolled on the pavement. It was her high toque. She begged for mercy and showered silver napkin rings on the pavement from her apron. I marched on – as shaken as she was.[180]

When looters struck even in very poor districts neighbourly solidarity went rapidly south. After a mob in Moore Street ransacked the McGrane family's butcher's shop it had its booty confiscated by another resident waving a toy gun – who then kept it for himself. Earlier in the week looters, dressed in grotesque regalia stolen from drapery shops, turned the Home & Colonial Stores upside down using handcarts taken from Tommy Keely's stores – which normally loaned them out at a shilling a day. Soon the carts were overflowing while tattered, barefoot children gorged on sweets, pelted one another with packets of tea and kicked tins of preserves into the roadway in 'a boisterous carnival of destruction.'[181] However, not all looters came from the slums. A civil servant living in North Great George's Street observed on Easter Tuesday that:

> all yesterday and again this morning a steady stream of women, girls, and young children have passed up this street, laden with loot, clothes, boots, boxes of sweets etc, etc. It is horrible to see some well-dressed, respectable-looking girls laden with loot. Just now a woman passed with a baby's perambulator piled with boots.[182]

The Volunteers had anticipated rampaging mobs and before the Rising had manufactured batons for a republican police force – but on Easter Monday every man was needed for other duties. Sometimes the looters posed more threat to the Volunteers than the military. On Easter Tuesday children set off large numbers of rockets and Catherine wheels in O'Connell Street, alarming garrison members guarding bombs and grenades on the top of the GPO. One, Eamon Bulfin, remembered that 'We got no sleep on Tuesday night'.[183]

The strain of urban warfare on civilians was intense, often producing fainting fits and hysteria, and harmless occurrences were suddenly interpreted in the most sinister light. Dorothy Stopford, a guest in Nathan's lodge in Phoenix Park:

> Saw a Volunteer clothed all in green with something in his hand, advancing across the field about 300 yards away. Every now and again he knelt down taking cover then got up ran a few paces and dropped down again. I watched petrified for a few moments thinking that at any moment he was going to snipe.

However, with the aid of opera-glasses she could see that the deadly menace was in reality only 'a child in a green frock picking cowslips'. Later, when Stopford ventured out she suffered palpitations as 'to our horror we saw five men come across the road signalling with a white flag. I started to go round and climb in a back way over the fence to the lodge.' Again her glasses saved the day when through them she saw that, 'instead our five Sinn Feiners were aged road makers wielding their tools, spades and picks and talking to a young lady holding a white jersey'.[184] The situation was also ideal for Dublin wags and practical jokers who had a field day, causing panic by shouting supposed warnings of gunfire and chortling at the resulting stampedes.

Those civilians whose houses were occupied by either the rebels or the army were sometimes forced to leave but others stayed, partly because they were too old or infirm to flee. On Easter Monday a unit of Volunteers arrived in Leeson Street to commandeer the home of an aged, bed-ridden judge. His feeble protests that 'You are not my guests' were ignored by insurgents who took over the top floor, leaving him to fend for himself. He managed to survive on supplies brought by a minister every day until the end of the Rising when he was rescued by relatives.[185] However, some senior citizens put up very spirited resistance. One 80-year-old lady who was forced to admit a Volunteer unit on Easter Monday warned it that 'I am an old woman and I can't do anything against four armed men but if you come in I will make it as uncomfortable as I can for you'. She was as good as her word and climbed the stairs frequently to bang her dinner gong and shout: 'As long as you're in my house, I'll take care that you don't get any sleep.' Next day, to their immense relief, the Volunteers were withdrawn.[186]

Dubliners experienced a serious food shortage during Easter Week, with bread especially in short supply. The situation had been created because of the collapse of the distribution system, the closure of many grocery and butcher shops, the commandeering of meat supplies by the military to feed troop reinforcements, seizures by the rebels and also because of panic hoarding by civilians. The bread crisis worsened when flour and meal sold out early on and greatly diminished home baking. Furthermore, while some bakeries kept going, Boland's, a main supplier, was occupied by the Volunteers. When de Valera's battalion arrived at Boland's on Easter Monday a batch of bread was actually being baked in the ovens and the employees' offer to stay until it was ready was accepted. The loaves were made available to the garrison and local residents but not to the wider population.[187] Because of abnormal demand the prices for eggs, butter and milk doubled and then trebled. Vegetables were virtually impossible to obtain in Dublin during the first part of the week. Then news of the prices available brought in supplies from outlying areas, where, incidentally, gangs of hungry poor were scavenging for cabbages and cauliflowers in the fields of large market gardens.

In the hunt for food many wealthier people who normally had their supplies delivered had to swallow their pride and go foraging: 'It was a novel sight to see well-known clergymen, professional and commercial men passing along, struggling with bunches of cauliflowers, cabbages, meat, biscuits, bread and a hundred and one other articles which in ordinary times would be sent home in receptacles more imposing than a wrapping of old newspapers.'[188]

Queues formed very early at those bakeries and shops which continued to function. Some people travelled to suburbs such as Rathmines and Terenure or farther afield to Bray and Kingstown, though even in such districts they experienced difficulties. In Rathmines, for instance, a committee of traders and prominent residents was established to deal with the food crisis and though it secured an offer by the authorities to get supplies to the town hall for distribution to shopkeepers, these did not arrive until Tuesday 2 May. In Bray stocks gave out and shopkeepers sent a ship to Liverpool for supplies, while one Dublin priest obtained 1,000 loaves in Belfast and brought them to the city on Easter Saturday. On Easter Friday the Local Government Board had been requested to arrange for a supply of food for the poor of the city to be brought to Kingsbridge and the North Wall channelled through depots established by the St Vincent de Paul organisation. By Easter Saturday supplies were being distributed from thirty-one depots.[189]

Certain groups of civilians and organisations were heavily involved in the events of the Rising. Holden Stodart, the Dublin superintendent of the St John's Ambulance

Brigade, provided orderlies for the RAMC at Portobello Barracks and the hospital at Dublin Castle, and also established an ambulance service. Brigade volunteers were also allocated a room at the City of Dublin Hospital in Baggot Street from which they ventured out to Northumberland Road to deal with military and civilian casualties from the battle at Mount Street Bridge. It was here that Stodart was shot dead as he accompanied a stretcher party to relieve a wounded soldier. Particularly vulnerable were those St John's volunteers who staffed the motor ambulance service provided by the Irish Automobile Club. This undoubtedly saved many lives during the Rising because without it many wounded would have been unable to reach hospitals, either because of the distance involved or the risks from the fighting. One St John's Ambulance man graphically described the conditions they endured:

> Day by day these cars ran the gauntlet of bullet-swept streets, frequently struck by shots whilst on their journeys to and fro; the dangers always present by day increased a hundred fold by night, when streets shrouded in Cimmerian darkness and encumbered with obstacles had to be negotiated without the aid of lights.

A brigade officer attached to Dublin Castle Hospital described his own experiences:

> The north side of the quays just over Capel Street Bridge had always to be rushed at as high a speed as possible, it being constantly swept by fire from the Four Courts and our wonderful driver just gloried in the pace he got out of the very fast ambulance. On several occasions elsewhere we were very thankful indeed it was so fast, and wonderfully driven. While not saying we were deliberately fired on, the fact remains we cannot recall a single journey on which we did not get a bullet through somewhere. Picture the conditions – no traffic, of course, but glass everywhere around, tram wires coiled in big loops lying about, and once we had to stop, much against our will, at the top of Capel Street and remove yards of telephone wire coiled round our wheels, making progress impossible: houses partly down everywhere, military barricades, etc. all to be noted and remembered in the daytime for it was necessary to remember them when out at night. No street lamp lighting, no houses lighted, no head lamps on the ambulance, nothing but Stygian darkness, so if obstacles were not remembered the consequences might be awkward. Yet our driver never made a mistake; he drove carefully but very skilfully and brought us home safe.[190]

On Easter Saturday evening he was dispatched in an ambulance to Church Street to collect two members of the Staffordshires who had been wounded in the operation to clear North King Street. Because the insurgents were shooting in breach of a ceasefire entered into several hours earlier, they were ordered to transfer with their stretchers to an armoured motorcar which proceeded at a snail's pace to Church Street:

> The armoured car turned so as to interpose its bulk, as far as possible, between the snipers and ourselves, and we opened the door, threw out the stretchers, and, acting on instructions, jumped out ourselves, lay down in the street and crawled, dragging the stretchers after us, into the house. The shop was small, a wooden counter in front, no plate glass windows, six or seven soldiers (two dead), two RAMC men,

five of our squad, and the sergeant in charge of the soldiers all lying down. One of us lifted his head to see where the wounded lay, and was told more forcibly than politely to keep his head down unless we had a spare stretcher. It was not easy, in any case, to load a man on to a stretcher, but lying down yourself in the dark and under fire does not make matters more easy. However, we got the men on the stretchers and loaded into the armoured car safely. Two bearers had very narrow escapes, bullets passing through their clothing; one stretcher handle had a splinter knocked out of the extreme end. Two stretchers loaded take up a great deal of room, and having seen all safely away our Superintendent had to remain behind, the armoured car promising to return later on and take him and the soldiers away. The snipers were very busy when the armoured car went off, several bullets striking the floor a short distance from the bulkhead behind which the soldiers were lying.[191]

The St John's Ambulance Nursing Division set up a temporary hospital in a house in Merrion Square in three hours, with beds acquired from neighbouring houses. VADs, doctors and nurses all gave their services and by early evening on Easter Monday an amputation was taking place in an improvised operating theatre. Auxiliary hospitals were also established at Litton Hall in Leeson Park, in the high school in Harcourt Street and in private houses in Fitzwilliam Square and Busby Park Road, Rathgar. St John's Volunteers also helped house women and children refugees, assisted at RAMC dressing stations, carried bales of dressings on stretchers through the firing lines to the various general hospitals, fed the poor and gave first aid to numerous civilians.

Priests were deeply involved in the events of the Rising. Many were hostile to the rebellion either on theological grounds or because they feared its destructive impact on the city and its inhabitants. While the Volunteers were religiously devout, some rejected clerical strictures in uncompromising terms. The subtle and complex relationship between the Church and the rebels is illustrated by an incident at Lansdowne Road station after George Lyons had bagged his brace of British officers:

By some means the front gates leading to the street had been opened and a number of priests from St Andrew's Church were advancing up the sloping passage towards our point of occupation. Shouting through the iron rails which still divided us, I commanded the reverend gentlemen to turn about and depart. They paid no heed whatever to this but continued to advance: 'Reverend Sirs,' I said, 'you must return and those gates must be closed and barricaded. You are endangering your own lives and ours. An enemy force is expected from the street and you will be in the line of cross-fire.' Still the priests approached and some of them, looking extremely excited, tried to climb over the railings onto the platform: 'Retire,' I cried: 'Soldiers, prepare to fire.' Only two of my men raised their guns. Discipline seemed to be on the verge of dissolution. I trembled for the consequences: 'May I speak a word to you,' enquired the priest whom I was personally threatening with my weapon: 'You may give us your blessing, father,' I answered: 'What are you here for?' asked the priest: 'We are out to fight for Ireland, father. We love our country and we are going to die for her,' I cried bringing my rifle butt to the pavement with emphasis: 'Do you refuse me your blessing?' I challenged as I removed my cap, an example which was followed by the men nearest me: 'Wait a moment. Tell me who is in charge here,' demanded the priest: 'I am in charge for the present,' I answered: 'Are you going to start a war here and have all our people killed?' he enquired: 'Every man is fighting for his own country now, father, and we are going to fight for ours. Better that than we should fight for an enemy land,' I answered: 'But,' replied the priest, 'you will have all our people slaughtered and our country made desolate.' 'We hope to set our country free, father.' 'But will you cease fighting, if you see you cannot win or will you fight to the last man? You are morally bound,' he added, 'to yield to superior odds and save useless sacrifice.' 'I will promise you to retire if we cannot hold our ground,' I answered: 'There is no disgrace in defeat.'

Just then one of my men rushed forward and knelt at the feet of the priests and started his confession. The other priests demanded that they be allowed to minister to the spiritual needs of the men. I consented to open the gates and let them pass through the lines on the strict understanding that they would regard us as soldiers under orders from our superiors and that they would not seek to advise the men to go home or otherwise interfere with the military situation. Receiving this information, I caused the gates to be opened and I passed the priests down the line with a small escort.

The incident was witnessed by one of the British officers whom we had captured and he afterwards described it in the public press as a shocking display of 'irreligious savagery'. I presume the same officer was really disappointed to find we are not as priest-ridden as we are supposed to be.[192]

Another futile attempt to dissuade the rebels was made at Jacob's factory where Father McCabe, the prior of the nearby Carmelite Priory, warned MacDonagh's garrison that the Rising was an insane enterprise. He singularly failed to make any impression during a heated argument, in the course of which a Volunteer perched on an upper landing dropped a bag of flour on him. A disconsolate McCabe left the building white as a sheet from head to foot.[193]

Many priests attempted to sustain a semblance of normality by keeping their churches open and celebrating Mass. They also offered a refuge to distressed parishioners who had been forced to leave their houses either because these had been seized by the combatants or because of the shooting and fires. Many Dubliners who stayed still prepared for a sudden evacuation by packing their money, life insurance policies, post office savings books and food into pillow cases. Priests, sometimes under fire, entered rebel garrisons such as the GPO, Jacob's and Boland's to hear confession or give the last rites to the dying. Others were attached to hospitals such as Jervis Street, Mercer's and Sir Patrick Dun's, where they gave religious comfort to the wounded. They also intervened at great personal risk during fighting to comfort or rescue wounded civilians and belligerents, and minister to the dying and the dead. At Mount Street Bridge Father John McMahon of Haddington Road tended British soldiers who had fallen during the attack on Clanwilliam House and here also Father Watters, the President of the Catholic University School in Leeson Street, was fatally wounded. One of the most haunting incidents which involved a priest occurred in O'Connell Street on Easter Wednesday evening. An old man with a walking stick hobbled past Hopkins the jewellers, one of the most dangerous locations in the city, when firing was in progress. As bullets sent sparks shooting around his feet he jumped in the air before embarking on a feeble attempt to cross O'Connell Bridge as bullets whistled around him. Finally he collapsed mortally wounded on the spot where his body lay for the rest of the Rising. It was not until Saturday evening after the surrender that the first non-combatant, Father Brendan O'Brien, was allowed to enter O'Connell Street. O'Brien went up to the body and, as his military escort stood with bare heads, he was finally able to give the last rites to the old man.[194]

Some priests witnessed enough drama during Easter Week to last a dozen lifetimes. Capuchin Father Aloysius, whose church was near North King Street, had been concentrating on a fete at Father Mathew Hall and, though he saw the Pearse brothers cycling past as he went to Mass on Easter Monday morning, he believed that they only intended to conduct the cancelled Volunteer manoeuvres. At lunchtime his world changed for ever when he heard rifle fire and soon afterwards a small wounded boy was brought into the friary, followed by a group of frightened children seeking shelter.[195] By 1.30 p.m., as the fete continued, Volunteers had erected barricades in Church Street and Aloysius ordered the participating children to hide under the stage. They were later sent home. On Tuesday morning Aloysius sent priests to the Richmond Hospital, where the wounded were already pouring in, and allocated others to take up residence in Father Mathew Hall which Daly's battalion had appropriated as a hospital. On Friday, as the Staffordshires tightened the net around North King Street and the Cumann na mBan girls tending the wounded became hysterical, Aloysius and a colleague, Father Augustine, became actively involved in the final stages of the Rising. They sent a message to Lieutenant-Colonel Taylor of the Staffordshires that Father Mathew Hall was a hospital, but he replied that he would treat its occupants as rebels and outlaws. The two priests now feared a massacre and approached Taylor themselves in North King Street but he listened to their pleas with a silent, icy contempt before turning and striding away. After an hour's hiatus during which they waited anxiously, the priests saw and approached Taylor again and learned that a ceasefire had been arranged. When Volunteers in a nearby house opened fire Taylor threatened severe reprisals until the priests managed to persuade the rebels to stop firing while they made contact with Pearse in the morning and got confirmation of the ceasefire. By accident they had now become intermediaries, but first they hurried back to Father Mathew Hall to evacuate the wounded to the Richmond Hospital.

Easter Saturday was a busy day for Aloysius and Augustine, as they first met Pearse and Connolly at the Castle and then shuttled between rebel garrisons and the British authorities. They helped to arrange the surrender of MacDonagh at Jacob's, Ceannt at the South Dublin Union and Colbert at Marrowbone Lane. Another Capuchin, Father Columbus of Church Street, carried the white flag when Nurse O'Farrell went to see Daly at the Four Courts with the surrender order. Aloysius later had the harrowing experience of being one of the priests who comforted those rebel leaders sentenced to death and also attended their executions. Another priest who was heavily involved in the Rising was Father John Flanagan of the Catholic pro-cathedral, which was situated about 200 yards from the GPO.[196] He had been summoned by Pearse to the General Post Office on Easter Monday night and heard confessions from the garrison until 11.30 p.m. Over the next few days as the Cathedral became increasingly isolated and the fighting intensified Flanagan attended several wounded men lying in the streets. On Easter Wednesday morning, as he celebrated Mass with a congregation which consisted of a few women, the bombardment of Liberty Hall began: 'The passage of the shells over the church was a rude accompaniment to the Holy Sacrifice.' Later, after a visit to Jervis Street Hospital, he discovered the cathedral and sacristy were full of refugees from neighbouring houses, and as night fell the fires that had been smouldering near the cathedral broke out again:

> A steady west wind swept sparks across the church roof. The Brigade, we were told in response to a call, would not be allowed out and further fires might be expected before the week closed. We therefore spent the night preparing for the removal of books, registers and sacred vessels, feeling that if the fire spread along Cathedral Street, nothing would have saved the church. Luckily the wind died down towards daybreak.

Flanagan celebrated Thursday Mass to the accompaniment of gunfire and a non-existent congregation because he had closed the church. At 10.30 a.m. his doorbell rang and he was again summoned to the GPO to attend a dying Volunteer. He was not to return to the cathedral until the end of the week and everything that he had endured hitherto was nothing compared to the ordeal which lay ahead. Flanagan had now been sucked into the tumultuous final stages of events at the heart of the Rising. His guide took him on a very circuitous route along Marlborough Street, Parnell Street and Moore Street. During the journey Flanagan anointed an old friend who had been shot just beside him and watched as he was lifted on to a handcart and carried to Jervis Street Hospital where he died two days later. After running across Henry Street he and his guide scrambled through the walls of houses into the General Post Office, where his ministrations to the wounded and dying kept him busy for the rest of the day.

The last day inside the rebel headquarters was dreadful for Flanagan: 'Friday dawned to the increasing rattle of rifle and machine gun. Early in the day I succeeded in getting through the *Freeman's Journal* office into Middle Abbey Street where I prepared for death a poor bedridden man whose house soon became his funeral pyre.' By Friday evening, Flanagan was haggard and fatigued and watched transfixed as the inferno spread within the building. It was time for him to flee with the Red Cross party, who carried the wounded on blankets as they came under fire from an armoured car and military barricades at the end of Moore Lane and Moore Street. They worked their way through houses, evading the bullets by creeping on their hands and knees beneath the windows. After crossing a roof and climbing up a ladder they got into the bar of the Coliseum Theatre, where the withering British gunfire and shrapnel even prevented an attempt to hang out a Red Cross flag. There was a considerable danger that the fires would spread to the Coliseum from the General Post Office and so Flanagan's party continued into Prince's Street and then Middle Abbey Street. Here they had to vault a barricade of burning paper as a battle raged between Volunteers in the houses and a military barricade at the dispensary entrance to Jervis Street Hospital. Fortunately their Red Cross flag was visible in the light of the fires from O'Connell Street and firing stopped to allow Flanagan's party to make its way to the corner of Liffey Street. Here it encountered a suspicious British officer but eventually Flanagan was allowed to come forward and have his identity confirmed by two medical students.

> It was within an hour of midnight when the good Nuns and Nurses in the hospital received us all – weary and well-nigh exhausted. Next day, Saturday, the male members of our Red Cross party were marched off to the Castle, the ladies being permitted to return home. The wounded all recovered, and neither they nor anyone concerned are likely to forget the experiences of that terrible night.

Dublin priests had demonstrated immense bravery in the face of considerable danger from gunfire, flames and collapsing buildings. Far from evading these dangers, they often sought them out to help others, risking their lives for wounded civilians, rebels and soldiers. Many were emotionally drained by the blood on pavements, the sight of screaming refugees, the sound of a last dying breath. Priests comforted many people, whether in a church hall, a rebel garrison, a hospital ward or the cell of a condemned man. They also provided shelter and food for those civilians who had been forced out of their houses. They undoubtedly saved lives by rescuing the wounded off the streets and getting them to hospital or, as in the case of Flanagan, Aloysius and Augustine, transferring them from rebel garrisons. The courage, endurance and humanity of the priests evoked widespread and, in some cases, grudging admiration. They had risked their lives for and dispensed their services to rebel, soldier and civilian alike. Flanagan, for instance, unhesitatingly answered the requests of the military prisoners in the GPO, including one who had suffered a nervous breakdown.

Amidst the fighting many people sought to continue normal life as best they could, a determination which led to many incongruous incidents The Dublin Spring Show, a major agricultural event held at Ballsbridge, continued while the battle of Mount Street Bridge raged not far away. Mrs Arthur Mitchell, who lived in the normally quiet South Dublin suburb, finally risked going out briefly on Wednesday to the bottom of her street to see where the firing was coming from.[197] She saw what she thought were dead and wounded bodies lying in the street but found it hard to grasp that a real battle was taking place so near to her home, especially as all around ordinary civilians were behaving as if nothing untoward was occurring: 'Whole families: Father, Mother, swarms of kids, pram with the baby and dog on a string which was a common sight.' The *Irish Times*, which managed to continue publication on 25, 26 and 27 April, also attempted to sustain the illusion of normality by allocating its main coverage for Easter Wednesday to the Dublin Spring Show. Since the schools were already closed for the Easter vacation many young people became spectators of the fighting or played games as firing took place nearby or just sat on the pavements relaxing in the sunshine. Mrs Augustine Henry recorded how her friend Nettie went out under crossfire to bring in her terrier or water the plants in her garden 'to the cheery accompaniment of whizzing bullets'.[198] At Trinity College four female students travelled through back streets to sit their French examination. Since no examiners were available these were conducted by the provost himself, after which he, the party and three professors adjourned for a lunch which was taken as shooting raged outside. Also in the college grounds was Lieutenant Luce, defending his *alma mater* and the recipient of a note from Dr Roberts, the senior lecturer, who in a truly magnificent gesture of indifference, kindly invited him to conduct a viva voce in logic. In view of other pressing engagements Luce regretfully had to decline.[199]

It is generally believed that initially Dubliners were almost unanimously hostile to the Rising and the rebels, and this was supposedly only transformed by their horror at the subsequent executions. That there was considerable civilian anger at the Volunteers is undoubtedly true. More than one insurgent was chased by an angry mob or had his home or business attacked and Volunteers marching to prison recounted depressing experiences. On the stretch from Dublin Castle to Richmond Barracks Mallin's column was surrounded by civilians hurling abuse, waving Union Jacks and inciting soldiers to mete out summary justice. Here, Frank Robbins feared that if military protection had been withdrawn there would have been no need for any courts martial. Major Wheeler, the British officer who took Mallin's surrender, was so concerned about the hostile crowd following the prisoners down Grafton Street that he ordered pickets to keep it back at bayonet point.[200] Patrick Rankin who fought in the GPO never forgot waiting interminably at the Rotunda after the surrender and his captors' hostility. The only friendliness he experienced was that of an old lady on her way to church who cried, 'God bless you, boys'. After that he encountered only blind hatred, especially approaching Richmond Barracks:

> Dublin's worst was let loose, the women being the worst. They looked like a few who were around during the French Revolution. One of my companions answered one of the women and a sergeant broke through our ranks and struck him on the breast with his rifle saying, 'You speak again I will kill you.' The women were allowed to follow the men to the barracks shouting to the soldier, 'Use your rifles on the German so and sos.'[201]

When Ceannt's garrison reached Kilmainham Cross in the gathering dusk it was greeted by an angry, jeering, cursing crowd of men, women and children that made Robert Holland despair. These onlookers shouted:

> Shoot the Sinn Fein —s. My name was called out by some boys and girls I had gone to school with and Peadar Doyle was subjected to some very rude remarks. The British troops saved us from manhandling. This was the first time I ever appreciated the British troops as they undoubtedly saved us from being manhandled that evening and I was very glad as I walked in at the gate of Richmond Barracks. I had played with some of that mob in my childhood days.[202]

But the accepted historical interpretation has to be modified in the light of various factors. First, even as the Rising was taking place, many Dubliners felt some ambivalence towards the rebels. It was an emotion which was captured well by Michael Ceannt, who did not share his brother's republican politics. He witnessed Volunteers occupying railway bridges and private houses in the Phibsborough area on Easter Monday afternoon and wrote that when a commandeered car whizzed past with three young armed rebels 'most of the spectators, including myself, thought it was a terrible mad business'. But their expression also indicated to Ceannt that they were thinking: 'Lord, if we thought they had the least chance wouldn't we all be in it.' In the days that followed he was certain that there was a shift of opinion in favour of the rebels. He felt this was due in large part to a perception that it was an unfair fight because of the overwhelming preponderance of British military power and the army's 'excessive' use of big guns and incendiaries to drive the rebels out.[203]

Secondly, the routes to captivity taken by the defeated rebels must be borne in mind. That taken by Mallin's column on its way to Richmond Barracks, for instance, was approximately 2 miles long and went via Dame Street, High Street, Thomas and James's streets, the ancient backbone of Dublin. On Thomas Street, incidentally, it passed the spot where Robert Emmet was publicly beheaded in 1803. This was an old working-class area and one can conjecture that some of the most virulent hostility came from the minority Protestant artisan class, who were strongly loyalist; but this was also the kind of district from which the Royal Dublin Fusiliers and other Irish regiments in the British army drew many of their Catholic recruits. Furthermore, it is hardly surprising that the vituperation heightened as the prisoners approached Richmond Barracks because soldiers' dependants lived in the areas as well as civilians who were economically dependent on the base. When Ceannt's 4th Battalion column of prisoners arrived at Richmond Mrs Mulhall emerged from her drapery shop to cheer them into the barracks. She was immediately arrested and lodged in Kilmainham with the Cumann Na mBan women. As such others might have felt that a display of outrage was expedient to impress the military authorities. But even at the gates of Richmond Barracks some people dared to shout expressions of support; Frank Robbins noted that 'a very small section of those assembled did spread a ray of hope amongst us by raising their voices in support'.[204]

Thirdly, the local population's response to the rebels was undoubtedly extremely friendly and supportive in some locations. After the South Dublin Union and Marrowbone Lane garrisons surrendered Ceannt's men were heartened by civilian reactions. Peadar Doyle recalled being 'met with marked enthusiasm by a great crowd of people. All along the route we were greeted with great jubilation, particularly in the poorer districts'.[205] Major de Courcy Wheeler, the British officer who accompanied MacDonagh to the South Dublin Union and Marrowbone Lane with Pearse's surrender order, recalled their car making its way through immense crowds in one of the poorest parts of the city. He felt no hostility from inhabitants, who were clearly delighted that the fighting was over, but nevertheless 'it was perfectly plain that all their admiration was for the heroes who had surrendered'.[206] When de Valera's 3rd Battalion departed from Boland's bakery after surrendering it did so to an ovation from crowds lining the pavements in Grand Canal Street and Hogan Place. Here, women unsuccessfully begged Volunteers to take refuge in their houses and men offered to hide weapons. Given such a sympathetic reception de Valera was consumed with regret.[207]

A detailed examination of one garrison area reveals complex civilian attitudes towards the rebels. In the Four Courts there was certainly resentment against Daly's battalion – fuelled by mounting deaths, injuries and considerable material destruction and social dislocation. During Easter Week, Richmond Hospital admitted fifteen persons dead on arrival and over 200 wounded, while Jervis Street Hospital dealt with forty-five fatalities and 550 injured. A woman in the Four Courts recalled how after the surrender, 'some of the Church Street priests came in and lambasted us with abuse all night for doing what we did. They disapproved highly of the Rebellion, of the damage to the city and the people who were killed and whose homes were burned. We took it all. We didn't say anything.'[208] Hostility in Church Street on Easter Monday forced Liam Archer to fix his bayonet while Jerry Golden was greeted by a fusillade of rotten fruit.[209] Later that day when strengthening the barricade at Church Street Bridge, Sean Kennedy recalled that 'separation women, tried to pull it down ... During the melee, one ... using her fingernails scratched me badly down the face'.[210] Even during Daly's moment of triumph, when his men captured the Linenhall Barracks, one Volunteer remembered that as the DMP men were being led out of the building, 'the women of the neighbourhood implored us not to shoot the prisoners ... We told them we left that kind of work to the enemy'. Later, when the premises were in flames he noticed 'the threatening attitudes of occupants of houses who thought we were trying to burn them out'.[211] On Wednesday Patrick Stephenson and Sean McLoughlin were nearing the corner of Bridge Street when:

> one of a group of women standing in a doorway called out 'There is two of them. God's curse on ye, tis out in Flanders ye should be, ye b—s, fighting the b—y Germans, By — if I lay me hands on ye I'll tear ye asunder.' As if we were deaf we ignored her threats and imprecations and hurried past, but took the precaution of having our revolvers at the ready in case of attack.[212]

Sean Harling described how after a young Volunteer died, 'a priest came up from Church Street chapel and he kicked up murder with Holohan. He said it was a bloody shame to have children like that out and insisted that Holohan pull us home.'[213] A friar at Dominick Street priory ordered a group of women out on Easter Monday when they tried to establish a first-aid post. Patricia Keating recalled a scolding from a Franciscan priest in the Four Courts: '"Girls, girls, girls", he said, "you don't know what you've done; you have blown up the whole of Dublin". We thought we were heroines, but when he had finished with us we thought we were criminals.'[214]

Many families in the area had relatives serving in the British army. Liam Archer, recalled:

> The people were very hostile and one buxom woman dressed in her holiday attire of snow-white apron and heavy shawl took a flying leap from the pathway when she saw us approaching and landing in the middle of the narrow street beat her broad bosom with her clenched fist and shouted at me, I having a fixed bayonet, 'Put it through me now for the sake of my son who is in France.'[215]

Local opposition to the insurgents can be gauged from a prisoner list compiled by Daly's headquarters which recorded civilians, men and women who had been detained as spies.

Nevertheless, public attitudes to Daly's battalion were not uniformly hostile in an area that the police believed was increasingly militant just prior to the Rising. Some soldiers sensed a strong antipathy as 'crowds of men and women greeted us with raised fists and curses'.[216] One of the lancers attacked on Easter Monday recorded considerable abuse by women and young people even before being ambushed on the quays. Undoubtedly Daly's men received significant sympathy and active support around the Four Courts. Soon after evading the distressed soldier's mother, Archer captured what he believed was a plainclothes policeman and as he was marching him up Church Street he was approached by a young lady who wanted to know if Archer was going to shoot his prisoner. When Archer said that he might, the delighted woman said that in that case she was coming with him. Although the captive turned out to be only a police clerk and was quickly released, Archer's female companion joined up with the Cumann na mBan working for the insurgents.[217] On Wednesday evening Dublin Castle was informed by a cleaner living in North Brunswick Street that people in Richmond Hospital were 'signalling to Sinn Feiners the movements of the military, some of whom are in people's gardens. She thinks some of the people are students but there is no doubt that they were giving the Sinn Feiners all the help they can.'[218] Helped by some hospital staff, every rebel casualty in the Richmond evaded arrest. Having shot himself in the foot, Archer was in a ward with other Volunteers when about a week after surrendering they were visited by two policemen. As they spoke to another patient a house surgeon, Michael Bourke, warned Archer that although police were looking for him he had told them that Archer had been discharged. He also claimed, falsely, that Eamon Martin, who was in the ward, had been fatally injured by a bullet through a lung and should be left alone to die.[219] Sir Thomas Myles, the Richmond's medical head, was a nationalist who smuggled in arms at Kilcoole using his own yacht and despite regarding the Rising as rash he cared for the wounded without distinction.

One of Daly's men, John Shouldice, was convinced that 'we gradually got the sympathy or, if not, the respect of the great majority of the people when they saw for themselves that we were conducting the Rising in a fair and clean manner and with such small numbers against the might of England'.[220] At noon on Tuesday John Clarke witnessed an incident at the quays that deeply impressed him and contributed to his growing identification with the insurgents. After a British soldier had been fired on 'the Volunteers from the Courts pinked him again. One of the priests [Father Begley] was on the spot. By simply raising his hand, the Volunteers allowed the wounded man to be removed.'[221] Liam Archer believed that after initial hostility civilian attitudes changed completely because Daly's battalion distributed bread daily to civilians and local institutions such as St John's Convent.[222] There was a considerable shortage around the Four Courts and on Easter Tuesday a large mob attempted to force its way into the still functioning Monks' bakery, forcing Daly to post armed guards to protect it. Indeed, 'one of the [Volunteers'] first activities was to regulate hundreds of people clamouring for bread'.[223] Jervis Street Hospital treated many civilians wounded while searching for food.

Some members of the religious communities actively supported the insurgents, including the nuns of St John's Convent who made food for Daly's outposts, provided accommodation and promptly reported British troop movements.[224] The Capuchin friars from the Franciscan priory in Church Street instilled amongst Volunteers the most profound feelings of gratitude and appreciation, especially for Fathers Augustine, Albert and Sebastian. They allowed Daly to use Father Mathew Hall as his battalion headquarters for most of the week, though it also functioned as a prison, a canteen, the main first-aid post and an armoury. Some neighbourhood priests also attended the garrison to provide encouragement, hear confession and give absolution. Some priests clearly sympathised with the rebels despite having to express their support somewhat guardedly. When Archer and a Volunteer officer intended using seats from the Franciscan friary to block a passage some upset priests accused them of sacrilege:

> But the superior – I think Fr Dominick – said to them, 'Let us go quietly away and we will not see or know what he does – he has a job to do.' They departed leaving us to our own devices. However, Hegarty thought better of the move and we did not remove the benches.[225]

The shopkeeper John Clarke's admiration for the rebels mounted during Easter Week – long before the executions and apparently without knowing about alleged military atrocities in North King Street.[226] Indeed, Clarke felt some sympathy, even gratitude, towards troops whom he regarded as friendly and necessary protectors. Furthermore, as a small shop owner in a deprived area, he was acutely sensitive to residents' loss of earnings. Yet despite everything, once the Rising had collapsed, he wrote disconsolately about 'the last attempt for poor old Ireland. What noble fellows. The cream of the land. None of your corner-boy class.' An incident that he witnessed just after hearing about the surrender is suggestive of a wider support:

> We ran around to the Four Courts, where we saw an officer of the Volunteers coming up the quays escorted by soldiers. The Volunteer was bareheaded but in uniform. Reaching [the] corner, [the] escort halted and he proceeded along the quays towards Church Street. As he looked back a number of times some thought he was going to be shot. Women screamed. Some men thought as women did.[227]

Although the Volunteer wasn't shot the response was a portent of possible future reaction in the event of executions. Also, though there had been extensive damage throughout the area of Daly's command, the Four Courts itself, both in structure and content, survived largely intact. The courts soon resumed business and though many public record office documents were tossed about, few had been seriously damaged. Only a few bundles of wills were missing after Volunteers threw them on to adjoining streets whose residents kept them as souvenirs.

Civilian attitudes to the Irish administration were much less ambivalent than towards the Volunteers. Many people believed that Birrell and Friend's absence in London on Easter Monday epitomised a regime riddled with incompetence and ignorance. Unionists who had despised Birrell for years now felt fully vindicated. Miss Mahaffy, daughter of Trinity College's provost, was scornful and contemptuous about 'a vain worthless man, a failure not only in all his various offices but in his profession and every walk of life, except as a talker; we must all despise him.'[228] She also poured opprobrium on the lord lieutenant whom she contrasted with a rebel leadership that had at least the courage to share with its rank and file the dangers of the GPO. She described Wimborne as having 'cowered in the safety of the Vice-regal Lodge, unconsidered by soldiers and civilians; doubtless the laughing stock of the Sinn Feiners'.[229] Another Unionist remarked on how:

the common danger draws everyone together, ninety nine out of a hundred people cursing Birrell saying he should be shot. All loyal citizens are glad to hear that the military are dealing firmly with the matter and some express surprise that the authorities allow the military to suppress the rebellion with anything but blank cartridges.[230]

Even as Birrell and Friend hurried back to Ireland they can have been in little doubt that their professional life expectancy had been dramatically reduced. On 3 May 1916 a doleful Birrell telegrammed Nathan, 'Prime Minister thinks you must share my fate', and Nathan resigned that day.[231]

During the Rising Dublin suffered both materially and in human terms. The British army caused most physical damage with artillery shells and by using how-itzers to fire incendiary bombs to create a conflagration before defenders could use extinguishing apparatus. Composed of thermite and white phosphorous, these incendiaries ignited on impact and kindled combustible objects with the resulting fire engulfing an entire building by travelling upwards along unprotected openings or burning through floors. Smoke and volatile vapours would reach the upper chambers and explode. Fire would then pass to adjoining buildings as far as 50ft away and once secondary fires combined they produced immense infernos that defeated fire-fighting equipment. Shells, incendiaries and incendiary bullets were employed so widely because they were the most effective and (in terms of manpower) cheapest method of driving Volunteers out of occupied buildings in the O'Connell Street area where almost every fire occurred. Insurgents also employed incendiary warfare, although in an amateurish, even primitive form. At the Four Courts one of Daly's men fashioned a piece of ash into a bow and an arrow, to which he attached a petrol-soaked rag and fired at the nearby medical mission. British lancers were sheltering in this building but they were not burnt out because the arrow passed through a window but failed to ignite the flooring. With nothing available to make more arrows three Volunteers tried dashing across the roadway, intending to smash in windows, pile up straw and set the building alight but were forced to turn back by intense enemy gunfire.[232]

The rebels also used fire to relieve British pressure. On Easter Wednesday Ned Daly ordered that the Linenhall Barracks, where his men had just captured a large number of men of the Army Pay Corps, be set on fire in order to prevent its reoccupation by the encircling British forces. The blaze was one of the most dramatic of Easter Week and lit up the streets around the Four Courts throughout the night. It became even more spectacular the next day when it reached a druggist's in Bolton Street and barrels of oil were tossed in the air and exploded, sending a cloud of choking smoke over the surrounding area. The fire turned night into day and subsided finally only on Easter Friday. Some fires were also started by looters, such as at Lawrence's toy shop in O'Connell Street which was set alight by rockets and other fireworks, and the Trueform shoe shop in Linenhall Street.

To many people the fires, from a distance, were very beautiful. Lieutenant Jameson wrote that they 'were the most gorgeous thing I've ever seen',[233] while a civilian wrote that they were 'a wonderful and awful sight'.[234] An observer of the fire at the Dublin Bread Company wrote that:

The flames kissing the ball on the dome's summit are singularly impressive. Standing high above the lower plane of flame and smoke, it is thrown into relief by a background of clouds. A scene of greater splendour I have never before witnessed, not even in the realms of cinematography. It is only outdone by the avalanche of flame and smoke that crashes to the ground when the dome collapses at 5 o'clock.[235]

To those living nearer its epicentre the conflagration's aesthetic qualities were irrelevant compared to escaping with their lives. By Easter Thursday afternoon flames had reached houses on Eden quay and incinerated the bedridden, and while some men, women and children fled to sanctuary in the Custom House, other petrified residents refused to leave. Eventually a soldier crept from Butt Bridge to the burning block and encouraged some residents to take flight, including young women who fell on their knees and kissed his hand while another soldier with a megaphone bellowed, 'Come out! Come out!'[236]

Many Dubliners thought the fires made O'Connell Street resemble the Western Front: the *Irish Times* compared it to Ypres while the lord mayor called the city 'a Louvain by the Liffey'.[237] Captain Purcell, the Dublin Fire Brigade's chief officer, estimated that 179 buildings had been fired with £1 million-worth of property and over £750,000 of stock destroyed in O'Connell Street – where 27,000 square yards had been affected on the east side and 34,000 square yards on the west. Principally affected on the east side were the Imperial Hotel and the Dublin Bread Company, while on the west the GPO, the Hotel Metropole, Eason's, the *Freeman's Journal* office and Bewley's were worst hit. In Abbey Street, Wynn's Hotel and the Royal Hibernian Academy, which contained the work of Ireland's famous artists, were both devastated. Outside this central area the Linenhall Barracks was the only large building seriously affected. Both sides clearly shot at or intimidated the fire brigade if they considered its presence disadvantageous, as on Easter Monday after the attempt to blow up the Magazine Fort when armed Volunteers stopped a fire engine, placed a loaded revolver to the driver's head and ordered him back to his station. Eventually the situation in O'Connell Street became so dangerous for Purcell's men that he withdrew them from the city streets in the same way that the DMP's chief commissioner had acted on the first day of the Rising.[238]

Refined Dublin society lamented the sheer injustice of those places destroyed and those left undamaged. Mrs Henry was mortified to see O'Connell Street 'a desolate wreckage. Everything on the right hand side from O'Connell Bridge to past the Pillar is in ruins. The GPO had just been newly done up. The cleanest and best buildings are destroyed. The miles of slums are intact.'[239] One of Douglas Hyde's friends, a Red Cross driver, had been allowed to pass through Westmoreland Street and as far as Nelson's Pillar in O'Connell Street:

His way of expressing it was that when you turned round the Bank of Ireland you would not know where you were. You might be in some foreign city in France or Germany. The only familiar thing was Nelson's Pillar. Every single house in Lower O'Connell Street, beginning with Hopkin's the jewellers, right out to Earl Street was burnt down and in ruins. It was nearly the same on the left side of the street. The Post Office was only shell. The houses in Henry Street leading from O'Connell

Street were also down. What struck him most was the aspect of Clery's. The front wall was standing without any back or roof or sides, balancing itself as he expressed it like a juggler balancing something on the end of a stick and threatening to fall at any moment.[240]

On 4 May 1916 Nathan suffered the final insult of a chirpy letter from George Bernard Shaw:

> Why didn't the artillery knock down half Dublin whilst it had the chance? Think of the unsanitary areas, the slums, the glorious chance of making a clean sweep of them! Only 179 houses, and probably at least nine of them quite decent ones. I'd have laid at least 17,900 of them flat and made a decent town of it.[241]

There was also human damage with official figures of 450 dead, 2,614 wounded and nine missing, almost all in Dublin. Military losses were 116 dead, 368 wounded and nine missing, while sixteen policemen were killed and twenty-nine wounded. The figures don't distinguish between Volunteers and civilians for whom the combined figure was 318 dead and 2,217 wounded. However, a roll of honour compiled later records sixty-four rebels as having died out of a grand total of 1,558 insurgents.

The burial system broke down during the Rising as funeral parlours and cemeteries closed down. It often proved impossible to remove bodies from private houses and hospitals, and the results were sometimes distressing. One young Volunteer, Gerald Keogh, who had been sent from the General Post Office by Pearse to summon fifty Volunteers from Larkfield, was shot dead as he passed Trinity College. The motley crew of defenders brought his body inside where it lay for three days in an empty room. Eventually its physical decay became so unpleasant that the corpse had to be buried in the college grounds. When Jimmie Rooney, a friend of Douglas Hyde, died on Easter Monday another friend went into town to try to make arrangements for the funeral without knowing anything about a rising having started.[242] In Cuffe Street a man was shot dead in front of him and he turned back. Then Rooney's nurse tried out of uniform but was stopped by a British soldier despite her protests that she was attached to St Vincent's Hospital and had papers proving her identity: "'I don't care" said the soldier. "I'm an HEnglishman [sic] and I does what I'm told not like the Hirishman[sic]."' Although she eventually got through there were no coffins available, having all been bought up or commandeered. When one was finally secured the funeral procession was turned back. It could only resume ten days later and even then with just the nurse and a solicitor's clerk accompanying the coffin, which soldiers opened at Glasnevin cemetery to ensure that a body was inside. This became standard practice during the Rising when, as a Volunteer recalled, 'it was nothing unusual to see a funeral with one coach and one mourner. Coffins were frequently held up and opened, sometimes they were found to contain only the regulation "stuff". Sometimes other things.'[243]

Uncoffined interment was the fate of many who were shot or had died naturally, including infants. They were buried in backyards, patches of garden and other out-of-the-way places, though after the Rising many were dug up again and given a proper burial. There were 169 temporary burials, military and civilian, in the Castle garden that had been more accustomed to fashionable ladies strolling under parasols. Those interred consisted of people killed during Easter Week and others who had died in the Castle hospital. Many years later the remains of five soldiers – all officers – were exhumed; the skull of one had a large hole in the middle of the forehead where a sniper's bullet had got him. They were re-interred at the British military cemetery in Blackhorse Avenue where lie many casualties of the Rising.[244] The staff at Glasnevin cemetery worked day and night to bury people by the score and of more than 200 who were buried over 150 had been shot dead.

Dublin's animals suffered alongside the human population, sharing its terror of the sounds of rifle and machine-gun fire; exploding grenades and artillery shells; the sight of great fires with their intense heat and dangers; the hunger and thirst. De Valera was an animal lover and he ordered cats and dogs to be freed from a nearby pets' home when it was discovered that the owners had abandoned them.[245] Mrs Salkey, who lived in Merrion Square, recorded her concern: 'My poor Olivia, my little cat is very dejected as she hates the guns and she can't get milk, poor little thing.'[246] Not every combatant, though, shared her concern for tabbies, especially those Volunteers who couldn't sleep because of catfights and constant meowing. In Northumberland Road James Doyle was annoyed when at midnight 'a lot of cats started to fight outside in the garden and this seemed to get on my nerves'.[247] At Boland's Andrew MacDonnell was guarding the railway line when 'as dawn broke I could see cats of all shapes and sizes on the railway and on the streets below'.[248] Many domestic pets roamed the streets searching for owners who had abandoned them or they were confined alone and distressed in houses from which the owners had fled. Like innocent civilians they risked being cut down by stray bullets. Min Ryan was involved in one such incident: 'It was in front of the College of Surgeons that I saw the dog being shot. It ran out in front of me and suddenly it lay on the ground. It could have been myself if I had walked on another bit. I went home then.'[249] Horse transport was the most common method of delivering bread, milk, coal and other commodities in the capital and so the disruption of normal life affected hundreds of horses. Kept either singly or in pairs in sheds behind domestic premises or in larger numbers in stables attached to large factories, their abandonment meant for them at least deprivation of food and water or, at worst, being trapped and burned to death. At Boland's de Valera made sure that the factory horses were fed and watered and when the fodder supply gave out he had them released into the streets.[250] Jacob's caretaker warned MacDonagh about fourteen unattended horses stabled a little distance away from the factory itself. Initially MacDonagh agreed to move barricades every time the animals had to be fed and watered but withdrew his consent when his men became exposed to enemy snipers. Eventually he relented, allowed the horses to be tended whenever they were in danger. Terror gripped horses stabled in Prince's Street as fires raged in the early morning hours of Easter Friday. Released just in time, they bolted up O'Connell Street.[251] But at least they survived, unlike the cavalry horses cut down by Volunteer gunfire at the GPO and Four Courts. Throughout Easter Week Douglas Hyde was distressed to see a horse shot dead on Monday continue to lie unattended in the road outside Stephen's Green because people wouldn't approach the body because of the danger of gunfire. Only on Monday 1 May was it finally removed. The rotting carcasses of horses remain one of the Rising's most disturbing and indelible images.

9

The Rising outside Dublin

MacNeill's countermand order and the confusion that it created meant that the Rising in the provinces never came close to being the nationwide insurrection that the Military Council had intended.

The Volunteers of Cork, for instance, didn't mobilise and resentment at this inactivity led to their officers resigning en masse after the Rising. In Limerick on Easter Tuesday Commandant Colivet convened a staff meeting that voted by a majority of ten to six to take no action. There was some activity in Galway, where 1,000 Volunteers mobilised on Easter Monday, but after some police stations had been raided and captured a general sense of demoralisation set in. An officers' conference on Easter Thursday rejected a proposal to disband and this decision was confirmed at another conference on the following day. However, by now, they were being pursued by a thousand British troops and when a local priest brought news that the Rising in Dublin was collapsing the officers finally agreed, early on Saturday morning, that continued resistance was impossible.[1]

The Volunteers of Enniscorthy did rise on Easter Wednesday after receiving an order from Connolly to sever the railway line from Rosslare and prevent British troop reinforcements from reaching Dublin. But although they occupied the town of Enniscorthy, the Volunteers lacked the men and weaponry even to capture the police barracks. Instead, there was a desultory exchange of fire between the police station and the rebel headquarters in the Athenaeum Club beside the Castle. When news arrived of the surrender in Dublin on Saturday 29 April, a local priest and a group of businessmen visited the Enniscorthy rebels and appealed to them to accept the inevitable. But the insurgents would only surrender if they received a direct order from Pearse and so the local British army commander authorised two Volunteer officers to travel to Dublin to meet their leader in Arbour Hill prison. In front of the guard Pearse ordered them to lay down their arms but when the soldier took this order outside to have it inspected by his superior officers, Pearse whispered to them to hide their weapons because 'They will be needed later'.

The only serious encounter outside the capital occurred north of the city, where the North County Dublin Volunteers were organised as a 5th (Fingal) Battalion. This had consistently under-performed and at best mustered only 120 men. A few weeks before the Rising its commandant, Dr Dick Hayes, exchanged positions with his more influential adjutant, 31-year-old Thomas Ashe. Ashe was the local IRB centre in close contact with the Supreme Council and he also met up with Connolly during his frequent trips to Dublin. Muscular and athletic with gold curling hair, Ashe was well over 6ft tall with a commanding presence that acquired a theatrical aspect through a full moustache kept waxed in sharp points at the end. Originally from Kerry, he had taught since 1911 at Lusk National School, a position that he used to recruit members for a plethora of nationalist organisations, including the Gaelic League, IRB and Irish Volunteers. Just how much talent and depth lay behind Ashe's impressive exterior would be revealed as he came under the pressures of command during Easter Week.

After an almost complete mobilisation on Easter Sunday only about fifty men reappeared the following day. Ashe's strategy – similar to that adopted in the capital – was to occupy, fortify and defend a fixed position and send out cycle units to destroy important railway targets. But his preparatory work had been poor and even as the battalion assembled in Finglas at noon, one officer, Joe Lawless, heard Ashe speculating about the existence of an underground telephone cable following the Dublin road.[2] His choice of garrison area was uninspired – a camp situated in farmland just south of the village and overlooking the capital's northern suburbs. Although Finglas' houses, walls and gardens constituted a series of defensive lines to the north, the southern and eastern sides consisted of open countryside across which an enemy could advance rapidly. A small shed provided the only cover and was to be used as sleeping accommodation. As his battalion strengthened the camp's defences Ashe dispatched Lawless and other Volunteers to blow up the Great Northern Railway Bridge, situated across the estuary at Rogerstown. However, no reconnaissance had been carried out beforehand on this large structure and Lawless quickly realised that they lacked the resources to destroy it. Explosives did rip up railway track and sleepers but the bridge remained intact. Unable to find a space in the sleeping quarters, Lawless ended the day curled up in a blanket beside a ditch as rain fell. At midnight he saw Ashe waving off a cycle unit in pitch darkness and drizzle with their headlights switched off:

> The object was to destroy the railway at Ashtown and thereby check the free entry of troop trains from the Curragh to the city but the inevitable happened in the conditions in which we were travelling. Not very familiar with the road at the time the party got lost and finally returned to camp with its mission unaccomplished.[3]

On Easter Tuesday Connolly further depleted Ashe's resources by summoning forty men to reinforce the GPO, but Ashe could only spare twenty. Connolly also instructed him to launch diversionary raids in his area to relieve pressure on the city Volunteers as well as to capture arms and disrupt military and police movements. At 11 a.m. Ashe's Rising was transformed when Richard Mulcahy, a lieutenant in the 3rd Battalion, entered the camp.[4] Clarke and MacDermott had made him part of a unit responsible for severing communication cables at Howth Junction on Easter Monday. Afterwards Mulcahy couldn't get back into Dublin, but on hearing that Ashe's battalion had mobilised he made his way across country to Finglas. Ashe knew Mulcahy because they were both Irish speakers from the west and members of the Gaelic

League's Keating branch. He immediately made Mulcahy his second-in-command. Lawless was delighted at the appointment, having like many others become frustrated by the 'queer unreality of our situation'.[5] The Irish Volunteers in Dublin were at war, there was constant gunfire in the city and barricades had disrupted communications, while at the same time Ashe's camp were calmly awaiting breakfast and the most eye-catching activity consisted of cows grazing in nearby fields.

'It soon became apparent to everyone that his was the mind necessary to plan and direct operations; cool, clear-headed and practical and with a personality and tact that enabled him virtually to control the situation without in any way undermining Ashe's prestige as the commander.' Lawless regarded Ashe as 'courageous and high principled, something of a poet, painter and dreamer but perhaps in military matters somewhat unpractical'.[6]

At dusk on Easter Tuesday Ashe and Mulcahy decided to abandon the vulnerable camp and transfer to a derelict farmyard north of Finglas. It was a depressing journey as the column set off in the rain and darkness, and men at the front lost touch with those at the rear. Some Volunteers wanted to light their lamps but were ordered to put them out and the situation became worse as they encountered traffic on its way back to Dublin from the Fairyhouse races. Mulcahy recalled that 'gradually a certain amount of malaise and confusion developed'.[7] On Wednesday morning, at Mulcahy's instigation, the force was reorganised into four sections, each comprising eleven men and one officer with Ashe and the remaining officers constituting a headquarters staff. They included Dr Hayes and Frank Lawless, Joe's father, who was quartermaster. Mulcahy's innovation had kick-started 5th Battalion's campaign; by readying it for mobile warfare, a hit-and-run campaign against rural police stations, he had almost accidentally created the first Volunteer flying column.

On Wednesday the battalion camped about 3 miles out of Swords. At 11 a.m., while one section remained behind guarding the camp, the others cycled into Swords from different directions. Assuming by now that the Rising was confined to Dublin, the village's police station hadn't been put in a state of readiness and indeed a sergeant was lounging against the front door, hands in pockets. When the Volunteers stormed the building Ashe demanded surrender and the six policemen raised their hands immediately. Volunteers then collected rifles, revolvers and ammunition, disconnected telephone and telegraphic equipment, trashed furniture, walls and steel shutters with sledgehammers and riddled the exterior with bullets. When two bakery vans suddenly appeared they seized the entire supply of fresh bread and one of the vehicles. Ashe's men then moved on to Donabate, whose RIC station surrendered after the briefest resistance. After returning to camp the battalion travelled in darkness the 12 miles to Garristown and launched a midnight attack on its police station. However, by now word was out and the Volunteers were met by one unarmed sergeant: his colleagues had evacuated the barracks, taking their weapons with them.

By Thursday morning 5th Battalion's campaign risked petering out. The number of weapons being seized had started to diminish and if other police stations were evacuated it would soon be chasing phantoms. Nor had they yet experienced real battle: the only casualty so far had been a policeman grazed on the hand by a single bullet. Demolishing police stations challenged their image of themselves as soldiers of the Republic and threatened to turn them into a wrecking crew. Joe Lawless recognised the danger, describing how after Donabate, 'In high humour now we set to work with a will to cut away at telegraph wires, smashed up instruments and generally the unique sensation of an orgy of destruction was elevated to the plane of a necessary duty'.[8]

Amidst an undercurrent of dissent and rumour Ashe experienced his first crisis of command. From the start some members had been complaining that MacNeill hadn't authorised the Rising and an officers' conference attempted to quell the dissent by convening a whole force meeting. After addressing it Ashe, somewhat ineptly, invited anyone with reservations to express them publicly. When one man attacked an 'illegal war' and accused Ashe of leading them in a foolish enterprise he provoked considerable hostility. Lawless feared an outbreak of fighting and 5th Battalion's whole campaign teetered on the brink of disintegration. For the first but not the last time, Mulcahy intervened decisively to rescue Ashe. He ordered half a dozen dissenters to leave and released two young teenagers and an old man, thereby ensuring that everyone left was both willing and able to fight effectively.[9]

When three sections of forty men set out on Friday morning their target was the Midland Great Western Railway near Batterstown, about 10 miles away. They had been told that British troops and artillery from Athlone would be travelling through here by train on their way to Dublin. The Volunteers route would take them through the village of Ashbourne in Co. Meath. This was only a couple of miles away from their camp but surprisingly they hadn't checked during the night whether its RIC barracks – which Ashe and Mulcahy intended to attack – had been evacuated. The barracks, a two-storey building with married sergeants' quarters, was situated about half a mile north of the village on the main road from Dublin to Slane. Between it and the road was a high bank of earth with thorn hedges on the other side, while fields at the back were skirted by dykes, banks and hedges, excellent cover for any attacking party. As news of Ashe and his men spread, the station's usual strength of one sergeant and four men was augmented by reinforcements from Navan, Slane and Dunboyne who barricaded the building and prepared to defend it.

The battle of Ashbourne began when Volunteer scouts encountered three fully armed policemen cycling round a corner of the main road. Two constables threw down their rifles, bayonets and revolvers and raised their hands in surrender. But their officer, Sergeant Brady, recognised one man, drew his revolver and shouted: 'Golden, I'll get you before I die.' Jerry Golden tried to shoot him but a cartridge jammed in his rifle breach. He then charged with his bayonet which Sergeant Brady evaded and it stuck in a ditch. Brady grabbed the rifle muzzle and wrestled Golden down on top of him while trying to draw his own revolver. Fortunately for Golden, another Volunteer helped him overpower and capture Brady. One constable had fled during the melee but was cornered in a house and found under a bed holding his rosary beads. Deciding that he no longer posed any danger, the Volunteers departed.[10]

Ashe and Mulcahy dispatched men behind the police station before having some men take Brady under a white flag to facilitate surrender – with a Volunteer's rifle aimed at his spine. Although Brady twice warned the garrison that it would be annihilated if it didn't capitulate, the officer in charge refused – whereupon Brady leapt through a gap in the hedge and escaped. Ashe now ordered one section to advance near the front of the station. As Joe Lawless and others crouched in a ditch Ashe:

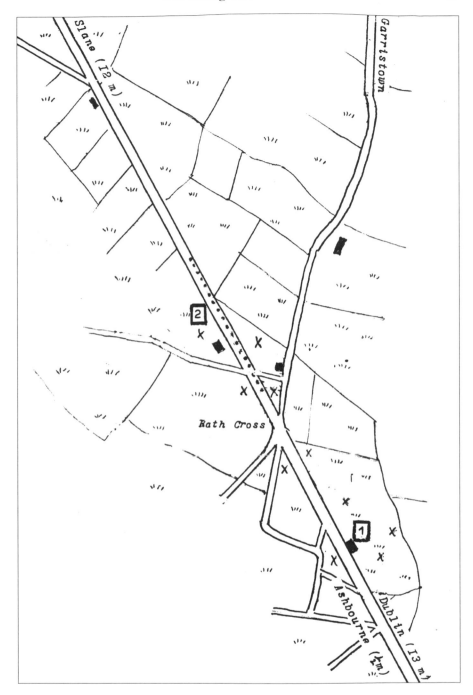

Battle of Ashbourne

1. Police barracks
2. Line of police vehicles
    X = Volunteer positions (approx.)

climbed up on the bank in full view of the police and proceeded to make a more formal demand pointing out that he had the place surrounded and that he would if necessary have the barracks destroyed. Perhaps this was a rather flamboyant gesture on Ashe's part but one that had to be admired even by those who thought it a rash act at the tine. He was undoubtedly a fine figure in his uniform and he spoke with an authoritative assurance in his voice that no doubt inhibited the defenders from firing on him for a time: but an anti-climax was reached when at the end of his speech no move was made to comply with the demand and the next minute some shots came in his direction from the loop-holed steel shutters. Those who were close behind him in the ditch and who all the time had been mighty sceptical of the wisdom of his presenting himself as a free target, now grabbed him by the legs and forced him to return to the cover of the ditch while others opened fire on the door and windows of the barracks.[11]

Ashe now ordered an attack. However, there were no rear windows through which to fire. By contrast, shooting at the front was continuous, with policemen replying through loopholes in the iron-shuttered windows. Mulcahy ordered two grenades thrown against the lower windows, but the first one rebounded from an iron shutter and fell on the ground, blowing a small hole in the wall. The second grenade cracked the wall and broke the defenders' resistance. When they shouted 'We surrender', the Volunteers ceased firing and the battle was apparently over. But just as Ashe and Mulcahy were about to enter the barrack yard and take the surrender they heard the hooting of motorcars and saw a motorised column of policemen approaching. Their arrival encouraged the station garrison to change its mind about capitulation.

These reinforcements had been mobilised at Slane to hunt down the Volunteers who had been raiding police stations. The convoy consisted of fifteen cars and fifty-five policemen led by a chief inspector and a district inspector Smith. When an old man told him that rebels were in the area, Smith tried to bring the column to a halt. He ordered one man to speed to the front and stop the lead cars but they didn't hear his warning whistle and he couldn't get ahead until the whole column stumbled into the battle at Ashbourne.[12] Their arrival completely threw Ashe because they had managed to evade two Volunteer scouts who were distracted by events at the barracks until the very last moment. The scouts and some Volunteers at the barracks fired shots and halted the motorcade. Initially the police held the initiative. They had the element of surprise, they outnumbered the Volunteers and they held the high ground from which they could observe the enemy. Shaken, Ashe ordered a retreat, but before the order could be delivered to the men Mulcahy intervened decisively and turned the tide in the Volunteers' favour. He persuaded Ashe to rescind the retreat, having realised that the police reinforcements were as taken aback as their opponents by the situation and did not have accurate information about the Volunteers' positions and strength. Exuding a quiet confidence Mulcahy assured the men that the police hadn't a chance of success and that they were going to attack and rout them. Joe Lawless thought it significant 'that Ashe who was nominally the officer in charge appeared to place himself in Mulcahy's hands'.[13]

Mulcahy instructed the men behind the barracks to attack the new arrivals on their left flank while the rest prevented the police spreading out to envelop those

Volunteers positioned at rain gullies. Ten Volunteers threw themselves into the gullies while others mounted the bank on the other side and opened fire on the enemy cars 200 yards away. Their concentrated fire was extremely effective. Jerry Golden saw:

> an RIC man step from the leading car with his rifle in his hands and just as he stepped from the running-board Mick McAllister, who was lying along the ditch on the other side of the road, stepped out into the middle of the road, raised his rifle and fired. The policeman fell into a cutting in the ditch on our side of the road and lay with his head and shoulders above the bank, with the result that we thought he was firing at us, as his rifle was held in his hands and pointing down the road towards us. But after we had each taken a shot at him and saw that there was no reply from his rifle we concluded he was dead.[14]

For half an hour the police took cover where they could – including under vehicles – until the Volunteers attacking the rear of the station returned to the main attack. It was now nearly one o'clock. As Mulcahy led a group manoeuvring for position District Inspector Smith shot one man dead. Smith had established a grimly unpopular reputation locally but he was undoubtedly extremely brave. Standing on a bank, waving a revolver at his men and accusing them of cowardice he tried to get them to stand up and fight the approaching enemy. As Frank Lawless closed on him Smith fired a shot that killed another Volunteer. Lawless fired simultaneously, hitting Smith in the forehead, smashing his skull. Joe Lawless saw Smith:

> lying feet on bank and head near the edge of the road and although his brain matter splattered the grass beside him, he yet lived, his breath coming in great gasps at long intervals in the minute or so I watched him. Then he was still and the muscles of his face relaxed.[15]

This pressure succeeded in driving the policemen down towards the crossroads. It was at 4 p.m. that Mulcahy decided to deliver the *coup de grâce* by leading half a dozen men in a bayonet charge at the enemy position. This daring stratagem broke the nerve of the defenders, some of whom fled to a labourer's cottage about 50 yards away. As they huddled together, attempting to force their way in, the pursuing Volunteers fired on them. After another ten minutes their resistance crumbled completely and they shouted: 'We surrender.' They then threw away their weapons and marched out with their hands above their heads, some waving white handkerchiefs. Between 4.30 and 5 p.m. Ashe ordered that firing cease. After five and a half hours the battle of Ashbourne was over.

As the police convoy was rounded up the station garrison also filed out. District Inspector Fitzgerald, wearing a white crowned yachtsman's hat, marched up to Ashe and said: 'Allow me to present you with my revolver, Commandant.' Ashe was puzzled and asked why Fitzgerald's men hadn't attacked the Volunteers in the rear to relieve the pressure on their besieged comrades. When the district inspector replied, 'I had already surrendered and would not break my word', Ashe was too gracious to point out that he had already done so or that, perhaps, it was safer inside the barracks. Four wounded policemen died as their injuries were being dressed and an officer succumbed to his injuries next day. While only two Volunteers were killed at Ashbourne, RIC fatalities are disputed. Volunteer Frank Lawless estimated eight to eleven killed and some police drivers, while Jerry Golden believed he counted fifteen.[16] There were also some civilian casualties. Albert Keep, the Marchioness of Conyngham's chauffeur, had been commandeered along with his car to carry policemen to the scene where he was fatally wounded. A taxi caught up in the shooting was carrying John Carroll, the son of the chief of the fire brigade at Kingstown. He was killed along with the driver, Jeremiah Hogan.[17]

The booty consisted of ninety-five Lee Enfield rifles, about 3,000 rounds of ammunition and some revolvers. Before dismissing the seventy-five police prisoners Ashe warned them never again to take up arms against the Republic or he would have them shot out of hand. He then ordered them to carry their wounded to the cars so that they could return to Slane. The conclusion of the day's grim events was not without its comic aspect. Ashe told those police who hadn't been wounded that they could march back to their homes. When one constable expressed concern about being attacked during the journey, Paddy Houlihan facetiously suggested that the police should show the white feather. Somewhat surprisingly, the constable missed the allusion so Houlihan told him that they should place white handkerchiefs on top of their helmets. Even more surprisingly, they gratefully complied and Houlihan's last sight was of white handkerchiefs at head height fading into the distance.[18]

Many myths have grown up around the battle of Ashbourne, which is often perceived as a daring Volunteer ambush against a much larger enemy force, succeeding through careful planning, tactical superiority and the leadership quality of the rebel commandant. In fact none of these factors was present. The impression of a large enemy force grew out of the victors' oversight in not counting its size and subsequent estimates by participants vary widely. Volunteer Frank Lawless believed that there were fifteen police in the barracks, but his estimate of the police reinforcements ranged from fifty to seventy and from seventy to ninety. Jerry Golden was convinced that there were twenty-one in the barracks and at least 108 in the motorised column. In fact, the true figure for the reinforcements was fifty-five and, while they did initially outnumber Ashe's men, the Volunteer reinforcements brought his force to forty-eight. Since the garrison in the barracks played no further part in the battle there was eventually a rough equality between the two sides. Nor did the Volunteers display tactical superiority. Ashe's lookouts performed very poorly and were taken by surprise, creating a potentially disastrous situation. Only the fact that the enemy was equally surprised and confused about the overall situation gave the Finglas men the opportunity to retrieve the situation. Nor was Ashe's crisis leadership particularly impressive. He proved unable to react speedily and flexibly in a fluid situation. Far from his seeking opportunities to seize the initiative, his initial response was to break off the engagement and start a retreat that might have developed into a disaster. The real victor of Ashbourne was undoubtedly Mulcahy, who kept his nerve, recognised the enemy's uncertainty and disorientation, was determined to take the battle to them and rallied his commandant and the rank and file. Once he had restored a sense of discipline the greater fighting spirit of the Volunteers did the rest.

After the battle Ashe's men moved on to camp overnight at Borranstown, where they were joined by some men who hadn't turned out on Monday as well as others who had never even been Volunteers. On Saturday they transferred to Killsallagher where that night they learnt that a cavalry column of 15th Lancers was on its way to attack them. At dawn on Sunday morning they anticipated another victorious battle but instead at 11 a.m. a picket brought two policemen to the camp under a flag of truce. To the battalion's consternation they were carrying a copy of Pearse's surrender order. Pearse's distinctive back-sloping signature was well known and that on the document certainly seemed to be his. But to many of Ashe's men, isolated from events in the capital and still gripped by the euphoria of victory, it seemed that this had to be British duplicity, possibly a forgery. Michael McAllister recalled that 'there were groans and catcalls and some of them shouted that it was a trick and that even if the Dublin men surrendered why should they do so'.[19] To dispel any doubts about the authenticity of the order the police emissaries agreed to drive Mulcahy to Arbour Hill where he could meet Pearse.

Within the hour Mulcahy was standing to attention before his commander-in-chief.[20] When he entered the cell Pearse was in uniform and lying on a plank on the floor beside a table on which lay a glass of water and a couple of biscuits. When a soldier snarled 'Get up' Pearse complied looking, Mulcahy thought, 'perfectly detached'. Surrounded by British officers listening to every word of their conversation, Pearse confirmed his surrender order and indicated that it applied to the whole of Ireland. In a barely coded reference to the Fingal battalion, Mulcahy inquired whether it would serve any purpose 'if a small band of men who had given a good account of themselves during the week were to hold out any longer?' And Pearse replied 'No'. Afterwards Mulcahy was driven to British military headquarters at Parkgate and ushered into a room to meet Major-General Friend, who although superseded by Maxwell, had clearly not yet been completely jettisoned. Ironically, it was this same room that Mulcahy was to occupy six years later as commander-in-chief of the Irish army. Mulcahy remembered Friend as a gentlemanly character who was standing in front of a fire and, surrounded by half a dozen senior officers, described vividly the overwhelming forces that the British had concentrated in the capital. When Mulcahy inquired what steps Ashe's men should take if they decided to surrender 'a young pup of an officer burst out sneeringly "Oh let them surrender to the nearest police authority."' Friend immediately slapped him down by remarking sharply: 'Unfortunately the District Inspector has been killed and the County Inspector is seriously wounded.' Instead Friend agreed to supply a cavalry unit to escort the Fingal battalion into captivity. A Volunteer recalled that during the couple of hours that Mulcahy was away 'a spirit of utter dejection settled over our camp and men spoke hardy at all'.[21] Then Mulcahy returned with his bleak news: 'It's all up boys': the Dublin Volunteers had surrendered unconditionally and the enemy expected them to lay down their arms.

Michael McAllister recalled that 'We were like the near relatives at a funeral'.[22] Distraught Volunteers broke down in tears and threw their rifles away. Others insisted defiantly on fighting on even after an officers' conference agreed to capitulate. Once more the battalion's disintegration appeared imminent; again Mulcahy rescued a faltering Ashe. He reasserted discipline by appealing to the men's loyalty, declaring that as soldiers they couldn't desert their officers at such a critical time. This allowed Ashe to play out his ceremonial role by handing his revolver over to the police hostage, replicating the British surrender to him on the previous day. The

Volunteers then piled their rifles high along with revolvers, bandoliers, ammunition and pouches. Now they waited a long time for the arrival of a cavalry escort that only hours earlier they had intended decimating. Subdued and depressed, they reflected on a rapid descent from victory to defeat – surrounded all the while, incongruously, by open countryside into which they could have easily fled. A dozen men couldn't resist the temptation, including everyone who had joined up after the Ashbourne battle.[23] Joe Lawless and two comrades were on the point of leaving as well – to fight on in the Wicklow Hills – when his father reminded him about his word of honour to surrender. The disconsolate trio threw away their revolvers and bicycles and lay down on the grass. When Michael McAllister said other men were considering escaping Mulcahy warned him that if he was one he should leave alone: 'Ashe said nothing.'[24]

During the wait many Volunteers lost their appetite. Joe Lawless thought it 'was really an indication of the depth of our feelings that nobody troubled about getting any sort of meal all day long'.[25] Some men threw their weapons and ammunition into a nearby pond. Eventually at about nine o'clock an RIC head constable and a plainclothes sergeant arrived to count the surrendered arms and note the Volunteers' names and addresses, all the while nervously attempting to engage them in small talk. Amidst palpable tension 'men gazing longingly at the rifles took one up now and then to have the last feel of it as it were, which seemed to make the policemen more nervous, though they did not say anything or try to forbid the handling of the arms'.[26]

Eventually the column formed ranks and with the British escort on both sides set off into captivity. As Joe Lawless dismally trudged the 5 miles to Swords a British officer continually berated him about how the Rising had seriously inconvenienced him. He:

> went into all the gory details of what he would like to do to us if he had his way: 'Here I am' said he 'having come safely through two blankety years in the blankety trenches of France, come here for a blankety rest and then run the chance of getting a blankety bullet from a lot of blank-blank-blanks like you' and so on ad nauseam.[27]

Even worse, there was nothing to distract him from this litany of complaints: 'There was not a soul to be seen along the way and when we arrived in Swords it was dusk and the town was equally deserted except for some activity about the police barracks.'[28] In front of the bullet-riddled barracks stood British army lorries into which Volunteers climbed and soon afterwards the vehicles set off for Richmond Barracks.

The battle of Ashbourne soon acquired a significance that went far beyond the number of combatants involved or the casualty list of dead and wounded. The type of warfare that the Volunteers conducted in North County Dublin contrasted significantly with that in the capital: indeed, it was one of movement that focused on overwhelming isolated police barracks and acquiring their weapons and ammunition. It was a precursor of the method adopted by the Irish Volunteers soon afterwards during the War of Independence. The campaign also transformed Ashe into an iconic figure, propelling him rapidly to the very top of the republican movement. With a remarkable absence of embarrassment he harvested the sole glory of victory, soon becoming President of the IRB's Supreme Council. His death in late September 1917 while being force-fed on hunger strike made Ashe a revolutionary martyr, a symbol of undying military and political resistance. The funeral procession to Glasnevin cemetery five days later – 'the most formidable act of defiance to British authority since the Rising'[29] – brought Dublin to a standstill. Whatever his undoubted courage and commitment, within eighteen months Ashe had assumed a status almost completely divorced from his actual talent and achievements.

However, those who had fought at Ashbourne knew about Mulcahy's decisive contribution to victory, a knowledge that soon helped him become first Dublin brigadier of the Irish Volunteers and then, in March 1918, chief of staff. Mulcahy's reserved personality, his preference for working behind the scenes and his distaste for personal aggrandisement meant that he felt no resentment at his lack of public adulation. Furthermore, at Ashbourne he had stumbled upon his ideal working relationship, one in which he co-operated harmoniously with a more dashing public figure while doing the vital organising. After Ashe's death his charismatic protégé Michael Collins succeeded him as President of the Supreme Council and later became the Irish Volunteers' Director of Intelligence. Collins was infinitely more talented than his mentor, something that Mulcahy, his superior, recognised with an astonishing lack of ego. Always focused on the big picture and the greater good Mulcahy protected Collins and promoted his ascent within the republican movement. The Ashe-Mulcahy partnership at Ashbourne then was a forerunner of that between Collins and Mulcahy – one that decisively influenced the course and outcome of the War of Independence.[30]

10

Suppression, Courts Martial and Executions

The Rising caught Dublin Castle completely by surprise, with both Chief Secretary Birrell and the army GOC Major-General Sir Lovick Friend away in London, leaving only Under-Secretary Nathan in charge. Nathan's military resources were seriously depleted because after discounting headquarters, training and administrative staff the Irish garrison consisted of only 2,400 troops scattered over nine barracks in Dublin and throughout the rest of Ireland. Even more seriously, at noon on Easter Monday just 400 were available for immediate duty against about 1,000 rebels. Dublin Castle itself was virtually unguarded. Within about an hour two policemen were dead and the DMP chief commissioner, Edgeworth-Johnstone, began taking his unarmed constables off the streets. There were just under 200 policemen on duty when the Rising began; they had all been withdrawn by three o'clock in the afternoon. Nevertheless, after an initial shock the British responded speedily and intelligently by summoning reinforcements from across the country and started gathering intelligence on rebel strength and dispositions. Troops rapidly secured important locations, including the Magazine Fort, Kingsbridge and Broadstone railway stations and the Vice-Regal Lodge in Phoenix Park, although the telephone exchange in Crown Alley lay unprotected until late afternoon. Trinity College was defended until noon on Tuesday by its Officer Training Corps and army officers who happened to be in the city on leave.[1]

Just after lunch on Monday soldiers from the Royal, Portobello and Richmond Barracks began arriving at the Castle and by evening its garrison had swollen to 300 men. Volunteers from the Four Courts, the Mendicity, the South Dublin Union as well as units situated at Portobello Bridge and in Camden Street attacked British army reinforcements moving into the capital. By 5.20 p.m., 1,600 troops from the Curragh had arrived at Kingsbridge station to protect the docks and secure Amiens Street railway station and the Custom House. Soon considerable reinforcements were preparing to converge on Dublin from Belfast and Athlone, while just before returning by warship, Friend had arranged to rush 10,000 soldiers to Ireland from their camp at St Albans in England.[2]

On Tuesday afternoon Brigadier-General William Lowe and a further 1,000 troops from the Curragh arrived at Kingsbridge station and, in Friend's absence, Lowe took command of British forces in Dublin. Soldiers had already occupied the Shelbourne

Hotel which dominated much of Stephen's Green and soon forced Mallin's garrison to evacuate the park in favour of the College of Surgeons. By 5.30 p.m., with an estimated 4,000 soldiers available and more arriving all the time, Lowe was able to make remarkable progress. By midnight the British had established, without significant losses, a 'protected line' of posts from Kingsbridge station in the west of the city through Dublin Castle and Trinity College to the Custom House on the docks in the east. This line split rebel forces in two and enabled advancing troops to begin extending their operations north and south. Meanwhile, the British placed a partial military cordon around the northern side of the city, while recapturing the City Hall meant that the danger to the Castle had passed. Just after lunch on Tuesday Viceroy Wimborne advised Birrell in London that no decisive action would occur until troops arrived from England, but after that drastic measures would be considered to crush the rebellion.[3]

Later on Easter Tuesday reinforcements from England disembarked at Kingstown and next day the Sherwoods were blooded at Mount Street Bridge where they suffered heavy casualties. Despite this temporary setback, British forces continued capturing isolated rebel positions around Dublin Castle, including the Mendicity Institution, and shelled Liberty Hall which they believed, mistakenly, was still in rebel hands. On Wednesday evening Nathan informed Birrell that although 'no considerable advance' had occurred in Dublin that day, troops would soon envelop and begin attacking O'Connell Street.[4] Soon afterwards he advised Asquith that although 'house-to-house fighting is necessarily slow' as troops had to overcome considerable opposition, he understood the 'necessity for disposing of the Dublin situation as quickly as possible'.[5]

By Easter Thursday the British had a firm grip on the city, having identified the most important rebel garrisons and built up vastly superior troop levels. By teatime, soon after Friend temporarily resumed command, an inner cordon had been established around the GPO, isolating the nerve centre of the Rising. By 2.30 a.m. on Friday, when Major-General Sir John Maxwell arrived in Dublin to replace Friend, British forces were on the brink of suppressing the rebellion. Friend's absence from Dublin on Easter Monday had been a lethal error of judgement, especially as he had received prior intelligence about a possible insurrection. His successor was a Scot in his mid-fifties whose patron, Field-Marshal Kitchener, had facilitated his steady if unspectacular rise in the British army. Although he had served briefly in Ireland over a decade earlier, most of Maxwell's career had been spent in Africa, an experience that had made him a fervent believer in the British Empire and its unity. During the first two years of the war he had been GOC in Egypt before being eased out to make way for General Archibald Murray, a former Chief of the Imperial General Staff. Recalled to England in March 1916, Maxwell had checked into a nursing home for a detailed medical examination and had just been passed fit when news arrived of the Rising. His replacement of the discredited Friend is often depicted as part of a deliberate British government policy to install a modern Cromwell who would crush the rebellion and govern Ireland with an iron fist, but in fact Maxwell owed his appointment to Asquith's desire not to offend Irish sensitivities. The prime minister had originally favoured General Sir Ian Hamilton but he had been in command at Gallipoli during the Dardanelles expedition when many Irish soldiers had died.[6] Faced with

Redmond's opposition to Hamilton, Asquith backed down and told Kitchener on Easter Wednesday, 26 April, that he preferred sending 'a competent man who so far as Ireland is concerned has no past record'.[7]

By the merest coincidence Maxwell had just informed Kitchener that he was medically fit for duty and looking for a posting. The field marshal in turn successfully lobbied Sir John Robertson, Chief of the Imperial General Staff, for Maxwell's appointment as Irish GOC with full authority to put down the Rising, restore order and punish the rebels.[8] So right from the start Maxwell was charged with applying a military solution to what was essentially a political problem. However, he was deemed to possess both the required military expertise and the necessary political skills. During his service in the Middle East, Maxwell had acquired 'unrivalled experience of civil work under war conditions',[9] while Kitchener respected 'his fearlessness as to assuming responsibility, his strong common sense, his imperturbable good humour'.[10] Maxwell appeared then to be a safe pair of hands, a character assessment that is often the prelude to disaster.

After being confirmed in his post on Easter Thursday, 27 April, he travelled immediately to Ireland. Next day he wrote to his wife:

> We arrived at 2 a.m. From the sea, it looked as if the entire city of Dublin was in flames, but when we got to North Wall it was not quite so bad as that, yet a great deal of the part north of the Liffey was burning. Bullets were flying about, the crackle of musketry and machine-gun fire breaking out every other minute. We were met by three motor cars and drove up to the Royal Hospital. The town is piquetted with soldiers and most of the rebels are in a ring fence and we are gradually closing in on them. I think after tomorrow it will be clearer, but a lot of men will be knocked over. These infernal rebels have got a lot of rifles and apparently a fair supply of ammunition. It is strange coming back to Dublin and living in the Royal Hospital. Since I began this letter a good deal has happened; I think the signs are that the rebels have had enough of it. I will know for certain tonight.[11]

Maxwell had between 18,000 and 20,000 troops at his disposal with substantially more due within forty-eight hours. After consulting senior officers he decided to further isolate any 'infectious patches'[12] and began by ordering Lowe to close in on O'Connell Street. The artillery bombardment of the GPO was intensified and soon it had forced the rebels out of their headquarters. Simultaneously, the British began creating a military cordon around the Four Courts and added another along the line of the Grand Canal, bringing about a complete encirclement of the inner city. But the most effective weapon in hastening the Rising's end was incendiary warfare. Once Pearse had surrendered, his order to the other garrisons to follow suit brought about the rebellion's rapid collapse on 29 and 30 April. By Sunday, Maxwell was confident that he had 'practically crushed' the Rising with 'rebels surrendering freely'. Despite fearing one or two Volunteer garrisons making a last stand, he was sufficiently confident to suspend further troop reinforcements from England and although sniping continued in the capital until 4 May he announced the city was 'reverting to the normal condition'.[13]

During the Rising's suppression Maxwell insisted that 'all surrenders must be absolutely unconditional' – a hard-line attitude that the Irish administration supported unwaveringly.[14] Nathan had rejected out of hand the lord mayor's suggestion of a deputation of citizens mediating with the rebels.[15] Likewise, on 28 April, Campbell, the Irish attorney-general, stressed to Nathan that it was 'vital that no terms other than unconditional surrender should be offered to or accepted from anyone who has taken part in armed rebellion'.[16] Lowe's message to Pearse on Saturday 29 April was unambiguous: 'I am prepared to receive you ... provided that you surrender unconditionally.'[17] Later that afternoon at military HQ Maxwell also warned Pearse that any surrender had to be 'unconditional, arms must be laid down and all come into the open'.[18]

Maxwell never deviated from this uncompromising position. On Sunday morning, 30 April, he and Birrell learnt that the officer commanding the Queenstown garrison was agreeable to rebels in Tralee handing their arms over to some responsible person. The commander was also ready to guarantee no action against anyone apart from those in recent communication with Germany, stating that unless the civil authorities objected he would return surrendered weapons at the end of the war. Just over two hours later Maxwell wired back reiterating that no terms or guarantees should be offered to people in arms and that all surrenders were to be unconditional.[19]

Maxwell's response was partly prompted by a widespread assumption that the Germans had been deeply implicated in the Rising. Lord French believed that Berlin had hoped to prevent British reinforcements being sent to France, while a Cabinet paper argued that German assistance to the rebels was intended to divert attention away from their army's failure to capture Verdun.[20] The Germans had also hoped to dent enemy morale and sow divisions within the British army on the Western Front because, coinciding with the Rising, they launched a series of devastating gas attacks that wiped out a battalion of Dublin Fusiliers. The Germans also erected a placard in sight of Irish soldiers, announcing: 'Irishmen, heavy uproar in Ireland. English guns are firing at your wives and children.'[21]

One Irish military historian believes that by crushing in under a week a serious rebellion in a built-up area against well dug-in defenders with superior local knowledge, the British had achieved an impressive military victory.[22] Although the relatively few insurgents had lacked machine guns and artillery, the British had won despite using many young and inadequately trained troops ignorant of Dublin's topography and – initially – the rebels' strength, weaponry and locations. Three-quarters of the Sherwood Foresters at Mount Street Bridge had under three months' service and lacked any training in street-fighting; one soldier claimed they had 'never fired a service rifle before ... they were not even able to load them'.[23] Many had been hastily thrown together in scratch units and led by officers whom they had never seen before. About two dozen regiments were represented in Portobello Barracks by men who had simply been in Dublin on Easter leave and couldn't get back to their own depots.[24]

Naturally, British commanders made errors in Dublin during Easter Week. By attempting to place a cordon around the Four Courts without first securing adequate intelligence about rebel dispositions in the area, they must have increased army casualties. So did launching premature and persistent Sherwood Forester attacks on Clanwilliam House before properly identifying rebel strength and locations, especially when two alternative routes into the city lay open and undefended only a few hundred yards away. According to one observer 'the telephones were working, and

any DMP man could have acted as guide and saved the massacre'.[25] However, the
political imperative of ending the rebellion quickly led British military headquarters
into continually pressing commanders on the ground for action and quick results.
Irish Command had explicitly instructed Maconchy, the Sherwoods' commanding
officer, that:

> The objective of the force is to clear the country of rebels between the area of
> Stillorgan, Donnybrook and Dublin roads. To effect this, every road and lane in
> that area must be traversed by patrols and the head of the columns will in no case
> advance beyond any house from which fire has been opened, until all the inhabit-
> ants of such houses have been destroyed or captured. Any man found in such a
> house bearing arms or not may be considered as a rebel.[26]

From the Rising's early stages power gravitated increasingly away from the Castle
towards the military authorities. Acting probably on his own initiative, Viceroy
Wimborne declared martial law in Dublin city and county on Easter Tuesday evening,
25 April, initially lasting for a month. Subsequently the Cabinet became increasingly
alarmed by unsubstantiated reports of risings in Galway, Clare, Cork and Wexford,
and attacks on police barracks and large columns marching on Athlone, Arklow and
possibly Dublin. Accordingly, on 26 April martial law was extended to the whole of
Ireland, initially also for a month. The next day Asquith informed parliament that
General Maxwell was leaving for Ireland immediately with full plenary powers and
authority over the Irish administration.[27] Kitchener told Maxwell privately that the
government wanted him to 'take all such measures as may ... be necessary for the
prompt suppression of the insurrection' and that he had a free hand militarily to take
any measures that he believed were necessary.[28]

Maxwell's relations with the Irish administration were strained from the outset.
After meeting Birrell and Wimborne for the first time on 28 April, he noted: 'They
do not altogether appreciate going under my orders but I told them I did not mean to
interfere unless it was necessary and I hoped they would do all I asked them to do.'[29]
Soon afterwards Birrell, Nathan and the Irish legal advisors registered their strong
disapproval of their loss of power to the military authorities by telegramming Asquith:

> All of us are strongly of opinion that for the moment the imminent proclamation of
> martial law for the whole of Ireland most inadvisable. First, all useful powers already
> exist under DORA ... and recent proclamation abolishing civil trial. Secondly, we
> anticipate grave possibility of bad effects produced if martial law is extended to the
> very large areas which at present show no sign of disturbance.[30]

Their intervention prompted a lengthy Cabinet discussion during which Lloyd
George expressed fears that Ireland might be 'set ablaze by the unconsidered actions
of some subordinate officer'.[31] But his colleagues were more anxious about the consequences of inaction and of appearing to undermine the military authorities and they
confirmed extending martial law. They did, however, place restrictions on Maxwell's
authority to delegate his powers to subordinate officers and Asquith instructed him
to employ extreme measures only in an emergency.[32] In practice, Maxwell's powers

proved to be ill-defined and less powerful than those for which he had hoped. He could not interfere in civil matters, and complained that 'even the RIC and the police are not directly under my orders'.[33] From the outset, he sensed that the government wasn't really committed to martial law, a lack of rigour that only heightened a soldierly distrust of politicians that was characteristic of the British officer class.[34] Maxwell perceived himself as an innocent who had been catapulted into a nest of vipers, though soon after arriving in Dublin he had the pleasure of predicting accurately that he didn't 'think that Birrell will bother Ireland much more'.[35] By 1 May 1916, the chief secretary had gone amidst Unionist cheering the demise of someone whom they had long regarded as an arch-appeaser. Birrell's farewell present to Nathan was a telegram stating that the 'P.M. thinks you must share my fate'.[36] The under-Secretary resigned immediately.

In their correspondence serving soldiers strongly condemned the Rising and favoured harshly repressive measures, though they were also deeply cynical about whether a political will actually existed to enforce such a policy. On 27 April a British officer wrote that:

> The daily papers made me pace with rage ... Is there no one in England with any guts at all. This little Irish affair will wake them up. I suppose they will shamble and slither and compromise through it ... If they don't hang or shoot that d—d swine Casement, not one of them ever deserve to be spoken to again by any decent man. Lord, what a pack of invertebrate monkeys they are.

On 2 May, he noted: 'I wish they would send us to kill some of them [the rebels].'[37] Another soldier who had served in Dublin observed that: 'I do not for a moment believe that with a firm and determined government resolved to win the war we should have been treated to this humiliating affair in Ireland.' He predicted sarcastically that Casement would either be acquitted or reprieved and released to resume his political career while the rebels would be bribed to keep the peace in future. He wrote: 'They well know that the fate that they justly deserve will not be meted out to them.'[38]

Though Maxwell largely shared these views, his own attitudes were more complex than those of the stereotypical pro-Unionist bigot that he is often depicted as being. He certainly believed that for many years British governments had appeased agitators in Ireland and failed to enforce the law firmly and impartially, an abdication of responsibility that had led directly to the current disaster. Birrell was simply the last in a long line of compromisers who had created the conditions in which revolutionaries had thrived. While conceding that the chief secretary wasn't 'as bad as he was often made out to be, like so many politicians he does not put into effect what he preaches'.[39] Nor did Maxwell equate political disaffection in Ireland solely with nationalism because he also condemned the militant Ulster Unionist campaign against Home Rule before the war and Asquith's timid response to it:

> It is the government as a whole that are to blame. Ever since they winked at Ulster breaking the law they have been in difficulties and have hoped and hoped that something would turn up ... Wait and see. Well, we waited and now see the result, viz rebellion and loss of life.[40]

But neither in the aftermath of the Rising did Maxwell favour blind, unthinking repression. One Irish public servant regarded him as 'a clever man, broadminded and open to argument'.[41] Maxwell's private papers reveal rather enlightened social opinions, such as his distress at the poverty and squalor of Dublin slums which he regarded as an indictment of British rule in Ireland. He also condemned absentee landlords for stoking discontent. But Maxwell lacked empathy with Ireland, a sense of mission and an intellectual curiosity to really understand the deep-rooted problems of English rule. Dublin was 'cold and cheerless', Ireland 'difficult and tiresome', and its people 'like small children, easy to lead or mislead, never tired of looking back'. His job was that of a soldier, restoring law and order and crushing a militant nationalism that had been 'worked for what it's worth by Germany' and poisonous elements in America.[42] Unfortunately for Maxwell, the British government had given him an impossible task with utterly conflicting demands: that he rapidly pacify the country without alienating public opinion. This would have been beyond even a political genius and it was the Cabinet's continuing ludicrous expectations of him that lay behind Maxwell's mounting frustrations in Ireland.

From the outset, though, Maxwell was determined to respond positively to moderate Irish opinion without at the same time seeming to reward rebellion with concessions. Revolutionary nationalism would be crushed and its leaders punished quickly and severely, especially after the considerable loss of life and destruction of property brought about by the insurrection.[43] Furthermore, his belief that Germany always threatened the British Empire was confirmed by Berlin's support for the rebels and that just at a time when it seemed the Allies might lose the war 'we have narrowly missed a most serious rebellion'.[44] Maxwell's analysis was supported by Sir Neville Chamberlain, the RIC's inspector-general, who argued that if the arms shipment had been landed, Volunteers outside Dublin wouldn't have held back.[45] As the British Empire stood with its back to the wall, Maxwell dismissed any suggestion of clemency for the rebels, especially as 'Dublin is still smouldering and the blood of the victims of this mad rebellion is hardly dry'.[46] Preventing a repetition meant deterring an Irish extremism with which it was impossible to reason or placate.

On Saturday 29 April, Maxwell informed French that he was incarcerating rebels at Richmond Barracks and while he proposed interning less dangerous suspects in Great Britain he would deal with the leaders himself.[47] It was an onerous burden because the number of prisoners kept growing as fugitive rebels were arrested at street cordons or by detectives monitoring ferry passengers at the four designated ports from which they could leave Ireland. Some nationalists even welcomed arrest because imprisonment turned them into political martyrs.

On Sunday 30 April, Maxwell reported that he was 'sorting out' the prisoners in Richmond Barracks.[48] First to arrive there were the GPO garrison and Daly's men who had been marched from the Rotunda. As they entered Richmond the leading British officer dismounted and handed his horse over to an old groom. The barracks square was packed with troops, off-duty soldiers, women and a few children, most of them getting their first sight of men who had convulsed Dublin for a week. Some Volunteers feared that these spectators would soon be watching their summary executions. However, despite some obvious hostility, especially from Royal Irish Regiment soldiers with broad Belfast accents, most 'showed no animosity to us as it seemed to be all part of their day's work and their relations with us were quite impersonal'.[49] One white-moustached officer even broke ranks and pushed his way through to repeatedly offer prisoners a cup of water. After standing for a couple of hours exhausted, men began falling down before the authorities began processing Volunteers through an archway at which searchers seized any apparently incriminating documents and photographs.[50] Military officers and G-men diverted leading suspects into the gymnasium, a wooden building with a glass roof, which rapidly filled up, especially as men from other surrendered garrisons began arriving. One prisoner described it as 'a large oblong building without any furniture except a vaulting horse and a wooden box'.[51]

Charles Saurin watched as:

a flock of G men appeared and swooped upon us. Willie Pearse was sitting near us and a big stout red-faced G man asked him his name. Apparently he considered him important when he saw the officer's uniform and the yellow staff tabs on his tunic lapels. When he got the name he must have felt he had a prize and he ordered Willie Pearse over to the other side.[52]

Detectives separated Clarke, MacDermott, MacDonagh, Ceannt, MacBride, Colbert and other prime suspects from rank-and-file prisoners. Eventually about twenty were sitting on the floor with their backs to the wall, except for Ceannt who defiantly 'strode up and down in front of them, arms folded, looking very much like a caged lion'.[53] There was an undercurrent of fear. One group of Volunteers shielded a small comrade as he pushed through a crack in the floorboards rounds of ammunition that searchers had somehow missed.[54]

Processing the prisoners was 'exhausting, humiliating and cruel', but at last they were each issued a blanket with which to keep warm and escorted into rooms devoid of furniture and beds.[55] In the rooms there were large iron tubs or buckets that they could use as latrines, though one room was so small that half its occupants tightened together to allow others to sleep. In another room some men actually slept standing up. Approaching the windows risked antagonising armed guards positioned in the square below and on every landing. Food and drink rations were sparse and unappetising. They consisted of a daily tin of bully beef, some hard tasteless biscuits that took a long time to digest and a drink from a bucket of tea in mugs coated in red paint that melted with the heat.[56] Eventually conditions improved with hunks of bread being issued while some guards became friendlier and even began slipping prisoners cigarettes. Others remained hostile, toying with inmates by urging them to enjoy their last meal on earth. One British sergeant announced loudly that he was fed up after hours of digging graves and was hoping for some recreation the following day as a member of a firing squad.[57] But such psychological torture usually failed to elicit the desired response. Having survived a week of tension and danger and the initial fear of summary execution, most Volunteers adopted a devil-may-care attitude, determined not to crumble. This defiant unity baffled and infuriated their gaolers and Andrew MacDonnell remembered with pleasure how 'the more cheerful we were, the more rattled became the guards, so we were very cheerful (even if it had to be forced.)'[58] At every opportunity they also demonstrated a continuing loyalty to their leaders. Once, when Joe Lawless crossed the barrack square he saw:

> P. H. Pearse accompanied by a guard of two or three soldiers walking around in a circle as if on exercise. He was in his uniform, wearing a slouch hat and a military greatcoat and looked solemnly at us as we passed. Feeling that something was called for on the occasion, and as my right hand was in a sling, I made a rather awkward left hand salute to him as we passed. Others apparently did likewise because a harsh and peremptory order from our escort commander immediately followed to look to our front and double ahead.[59]

Gerald Doyle remembered sitting beside Ceannt, Colbert, Willie Pearse and MacBride on the grass outside the court martial rooms when suddenly:

> Pearse came out of the building and faced us on the green. All at once all prisoners sprang to their feet and stood to attention. He smiled across at us, saluted and moved off under an escort of officers. I can see the picture of him as he moved away in his great green overcoat and hat.[60]

Prisoners ensured that MacDermott – who had been deprived of his walking stick at the Rotunda – always had someone to lean on when he walked about the prison.

Contemplating their likely fate, some men believed that they would be shipped to France and used as cannon fodder against the Germans while others thought they would either be transported to the colonies like convicts of old or executed by firing squads. Some, like Con Colbert, just wanted to die. He was still disorientated by the sudden collapse of the Rising and was exhibiting all the symptoms of post-traumatic shock as his will to live drained away. A Marrowbone Lane comrade recalled him saying that:

> from his point of view he would prefer to be executed and said 'We are all ready to meet our God. We had hopes of coming out alive. Now that we are defeated, outside that barrack wall the people whom we have tried to emancipate have demonstrated nothing but hate and contempt for us. We would be better off dead as life would be a torture. We can thank the Mother of God for her kindness in her intercession for us that we have had the time to prepare ourselves to meet our Redeemer.'[61]

Then the court martial selection procedure began with Volunteers ordered to sit in rows of ten, facing a half wood and half glass partition behind which they could see themselves being scrutinised by G-men. In a short time these entered the gymnasium, 'like a flock of carrion crows'. Over a period of two hours they identified those thought to have played the most prominent role in the Rising. These were ordered to one side and their names entered on a numbered list; it was lengthy – about 200 Volunteers were identified – and included prominent rebels such as MacDermott, Ceannt, Colbert and Major John MacBride.[62] British army officers, detectives and Dublin Metropolitan policemen held captive during the Rising now roamed the barracks also trying to identify leading Volunteers. But some whom the Volunteers had treated considerately gave their captors a free pass. Detective Hefferman had been made prisoner near the Four Courts and Volunteer Maurice Collins, who knew him well, ensured that Hefferman wasn't harmed. Now at Richmond Hefferman stood in front of Collins, scrutinised him, said nothing and moved on.[63] Some decisions seemed arbitrary or based on a whim. Willie Pearse was selected for court martial because he was the brother of a signatory to the Proclamation and had served alongside Patrick in the GPO. Yet John MacDonagh, who had been at Jacob's with Thomas, was deemed of no interest and directed to leave the gymnasium. On his way out a detective did detain him and told Superintendent Quinn of the DMP that he had caught Commandant MacDonagh's brother. Yet Quinn 'made little of this discovery of his subordinate and I passed through. At the door I turned and saw Tom for the last time. He waved his hand to me in the old cheery manner.'[64] A DMP constable, held captive at Jacob's, claimed: 'We pretended we never saw the men before.'[65] Maxwell had tentatively suggested that those amongst them who volunteered 'should be allowed to expiate their crime by serving the Empire as soldiers'.[66] But in the event they were transported immediately to internment camps in England. One recalled that at the North Wall, 'we were embarked on a cattle boat in filthy conditions, and tightly crammed, almost everyone vomiting under the conditions'.[67] With newcomers arriving every day the Richmond authorities decided to release or deport less prominent Volunteers and treat anyone under 19 as naïve dupes led astray by unscrupulous superiors. On 12 May a large group of teenagers assembled before a senior British officer who gave them a pep talk about gullible young men like themselves being easy prey for sinister elements, but after expressing confidence that they would sin no more he had them escorted to the prison gates and sent on their way.[68] A few years later, one of them, Vinnie Byrne, joined Michael Collins' assassination squad.

Meanwhile, as normality returned to the capital, British military platoons in the provinces concentrated on disaffected areas such as Limerick, Cork, Kilkenny, Athlone and Waterford. Their primary purpose was to complete the country's pacification by apprehending not just rebel bands still at large but anyone whom local police and intelligence personnel from Dublin regarded as dangerous. The large number of troops and heavy weaponry employed were also intended to psychologically disarm the civilian population who in some places became alarmed, mistaking smoke from the field kitchens as emanating from 'poison gas machines'.[69]

In the early morning of 2 May a clearing-up party of eight policemen went to Bawnard House, Castle Lyons in Co. Cork intending to arrest Thomas and David Kent, two prominent republicans living there with their 84-year-old mother and two brothers, Richard and William. When Head Constable Rowe knocked loudly on the back door and demanded that everyone come out a voice from inside replied: 'We will not surrender, we will leave some of you dead.'[70] As Rowe stepped back, three shots rang out, one striking him just above the ear and almost blowing off his head. In the ensuing, hour-long gun battle David Kent was gravely injured before the family offered to surrender provided a priest was summoned for a family member who was supposedly dying. The occupants then threw out most of their weapons but the police didn't move in until 100 soldiers arrived from Fermoy, 4 miles away. When the Kents finally emerged Richard made a dash for freedom and was immediately shot through the back and fatally wounded. On 4 May both Thomas and William Kent were court-martialled at Cork Detention Barracks.[71]

Lowe gauged the mopping-up operations a complete success, claiming that swift arrests and punishment of rebels had cowed their supporters while the soldiers' presence had reassured civilians throughout Ireland.[72] Although few weapons had been located, a total of 3,430 men and 79 women were arrested after the Rising. This was a considerable number in relation to the scale of the outbreak, and worried the British government because of its likely adverse impact on Irish public opinion. The Cabinet was also concerned that the blanket detention of so many people was legally dubious and 1,424 men were quickly released after inquiry.[73] William Wylie, who was soon to act as crown prosecutor at a number of courts martial, was appointed to decide which women in Kilmainham Gaol (apart from Markievicz) should be kept in custody. After encountering behaviour that ranged from truculence to tearfulness Wylie concluded that, apart from a handful, the women hadn't really understood what they had been fighting for and had had only been driven to participate in the Rising by poverty or a craving for excitement. A perplexed Maxwell was delighted by their apparent lack of real ideological zeal because he had been at a loss about what to do with 'all these silly little girls'.[74] Given cover by Wylie to treat them like naughty schoolchildren he could now send all but seven home; five were interned at Aylesbury prison in England to which another two were deported. The prison authorities couldn't resist one more of the pregnant pauses with which they unnerved prisoners when delivering news. Annie O'Brien recalled an officer lining them up and reading out a list of names until 'after a period of awful suspense he announced that the persons whose names he had called were to be released'.[75] An appeals procedure soon released 1,272 of 1,836 men who were interned in England on the premise that rebel leaders had duped them into participating in the Rising, most of the rest were freed at Christmas 1916, with a final batch amnestied in July 1917. By September 1916 the RIC was concerned that very dangerous individuals had been freed but the British government had avoided the perilous course of having to justify in court the legality of internment.[76]

Meanwhile, 186 men and a single woman, Countess Markievicz were tried by court martial.[77] All but four trials took place in Dublin – those of Thomas and William Kent were held in Cork, and another two in Enniscorthy. Such trials were not a new experience for Irishmen during the First World War; out of 2,912 traceable death sentences that British courts martial imposed on military personnel, 221 involved Irish soldiers. Despite constituting only 2 per cent of the British army, Irishmen received 8 per cent of all death sentences, a disparity that one historian argues originated in the British officer class' belief that Irishmen 'needed firm, perhaps even harsh, handling' – a perception that the Easter Rising had only reinforced.[78]

The fifteen men eventually executed were tried by field general court martial, in which evidence was heard by a panel of three officer judges, none of whom were required to have been legally trained. Any death sentence had to be unanimous and even then Maxwell had to confirm it. Consequently, before the accused knew their fate, there was an unavoidable delay that could last from a few hours to several days.

The authority to court-martial Irish civilians derived from the government's wartime emergency powers – the Defence of the Realm Acts. Initially, Maxwell had intended using 'military courts' that would be convened under martial law, but he was reluctantly dissuaded. The rules of procedure envisaged scrupulously fair trials in which the defendant's interests were paramount, but a comprehensive study of First World War military trial records has concluded that 'few of the executed men received the most elemental form of justice'.[79] Controversially, Maxwell decided unilaterally to conduct the Irish trials in secret on the grounds that the rebellion was still being quelled. Embarrassingly, Crown law officers later ruled that this procedure had been illegal. In mid-1916, Asquith – over Maxwell's strong objections – promised to publish the full text of trial proceedings, a promise on which he had to renege because of the inadequate nature of much of the evidence that was used to convict those men who were subsequently executed.[80]

Two senior officers, neither legally trained, presided over ten of the fourteen Dublin trials. Brigadier-General Blackader and Colonel Ernest Maconchy (born in Longford) had also commanded troops brought over from England to suppress the Rising, a conflict of interest that the Military Manual specifically prohibited. The chief prosecution counsel, William Wylie, was the son of an Ulster Presbyterian minister and had been born in Dublin where, as a lieutenant in Trinity College's OTC, he had helped suppress the Rising. Even so, Wylie strongly opposed speedy, secret trials and until overruled by the Irish Attorney General at least wanted to allow defendants access to defence counsel. Nonetheless, after MacDonagh's trial on 2 May, Wylie managed to ensure that future defendants could call witnesses in their defence. John MacBride did so and in court warmly thanked Wylie for his consideration.[81]

Because it could accommodate large numbers of prisoners all but two courts martial that resulted in execution were held at Richmond Barracks. It also had the advantage of being situated close to Maxwell's residence at the Royal Hospital, Kilmainham. The two exceptions were Thomas Kent in Cork Detention Barracks and James Connolly who was tried in Dublin Castle's Red Cross Hospital while propped up in bed. After what Maxwell called an 'unavoidable delay', the courts martial began on Tuesday afternoon, 2 May.[82] Thirty cases were ready for consideration including those of Pearse, Clarke and MacDonagh, which had been held over from the previous day. The proceedings began in two adjacent and rather sweltering courts. One defendant described 'a very small room, with quite a lot of office furniture and the witnesses had to sidle in and out'.[83] Some provision was made for the prisoners' spiritual needs; a local priest heard confessions in the barrack gym. The trials of those men who were later executed took place between 2 and 9 May, but in some cases the official records either don't give a precise date or mention more than one. As far as can be deduced the sequence was: Patrick Pearse, MacDonagh and Clarke, 2 May; Daly, Willie Pearse, O'Hanrahan and Plunkett, 3 May; MacBride, Kent, Colbert and Heuston, 4 May; Ceannt, 3–4 May; Mallin, 5 May; Connolly and MacDermott, 9 May.[84]

The court president was responsible for the accuracy and completeness of the official record of proceedings. Afterwards he transmitted them to Maxwell who had the final authority to confirm or commute the sentence. Some defendants noticed the president taking notes in longhand during their trial before writing out a final summary of the case. These were not absolutely full and complete because defendants' questions to prosecution witnesses were not recorded. Maconchy himself admitted that 'in many cases I refused to put down what they [the defendants] said as it only made their case worse'.[85] But the records themselves appear entirely accurate and, though brief, so also were the proceedings themselves; most, if not all, trials seem to have lasted no more than ten or fifteen minutes.

The first leaders who were tried had little or no notice of the charge against them but other defendants attended preliminary meetings with investigating officers at Richmond Barracks to hear of their forthcoming trial, learn about the charge and the depositions of prosecution witnesses. They were also told some of their legal rights. But the accused were not permitted legal or any other kind of assistance inside the court, and apparently the military authorities frustrated any attempts to consult solicitors. Nonetheless, some – including Ceannt and MacBride – did so successfully.[86] All faced the same central charge of armed rebellion and waging war against the Crown with the purpose of assisting an enemy. Connolly, MacDermott and Mallin faced a further charge of attempting to cause disaffection among the civil population, though somewhat surprisingly none was to be convicted of this lesser offence.[87] Except for Willie Pearse, every defendant pleaded not guilty. Like many other defendants, Ned Daly was incensed at being accused of assisting an enemy, telling his sister that everything he did was solely 'for Ireland, his own land'.[88] Clarke considered that this phrase alone fully justified him pleading not guilty. When one person attempted to plead guilty to just the first part of the charge about participating in an armed rebellion this was ruled inadmissible on legal grounds.[89]

The fifteen men faced broadly similar evidence though the military authorities worried that it might be insufficient to ensure convictions. The Military Manual stated that a charge had to be proven, yet Maxwell's own legal advisor admitted later that apart from the Proclamation they 'knew very little of the prime movers of the Rebellion'.[90] The prosecution relied overwhelmingly on British officers identifying the accused as having participated in the fighting and surrendering with arms in their hands. Often these officers had been held captive by the Volunteers and one testified at five of the fourteen trials in Dublin. They would identify the accused, describe their rank, actions, whether he had fired at Crown forces and if he had carried weapons at the surrender or led out a body of men. Police officers, and in McDermott's case a prison warder, also described any past involvement in extreme nationalism such as participating in route marches, visiting Liberty Hall or frequenting Irish Volunteer headquarters. Uniquely, Thomas Kent's trial in Cork heard three RIC members who had been involved in the gun battle at his home and also two military officers who supervised his family's surrender.[91]

Documentary evidence was either gathered during searches of occupied buildings or seized from Volunteers after the surrender. It included a dispatch designating MacBride 'Commandant', Connolly's note ordering Heuston to 'seize the Mendicity at all costs'[92] and a letter that Patrick Pearse tried to send to his mother on 1 May. Rather surprisingly, the Proclamation was hardly referred to at all except during Ceannt and Plunkett's trials. When Blackader inquired why this was so, Wylie responded that 'a document with certain names at the end of it was not proof of any of the alleged signatures, unless I could get the original and prove the accused's signature to it'.[93]

The whole court martial process was deeply flawed. It was established and implemented in considerable haste: three or four men would be tried together in a remarkably short time, the evidence given and the intelligence material cited was frequently circumstantial, misleading and sometimes completely inaccurate. Garrison locations were confused with one another: Volunteers from the South Dublin Union were accused of occupying Jacob's while one man who had fought in the Four Courts was held to have been in the GPO. The fifteen rebel leaders responded variously to prosecution evidence. Connolly alone challenged the court's authority. All but two – Colbert and Clarke – made statements. Three, MacBride, Ceannt and Mallin, called witnesses in their own defence. Apart from Colbert and Willie Pearse, all of them cross-examined prosecution witnesses, invariably forcing them to concede that, if held captive, they had been well treated.[94]

Ceannt put up the most energetic and skilled defence against prosecution evidence that was particularly unconvincing. An army officer, the only prosecution witness, testified that Ceannt had led a rebel column into St Patrick's Park after the surrender and had described himself as 'Commandant'. He strongly implied that Ceannt, commandant at the South Dublin Union, had been active in Jacob's Factory as well as claiming, dubiously, that he had been armed. Ceannt was well prepared for his trial. Having received legal advice at Richmond Barracks he was 'determined to make a fight for his life', and encouraged others to do the same. One member of his battalion describes Ceannt coaching him and other prisoners on rebutting the cases against them.[95] According to a legal expert Ceannt cross-examined the army officer 'very cleverly' and tried to shake his credibility with three defence witnesses who denied his presence in Jacob's. He also denied assisting the enemy, arguing that no supporting evidence had been produced. Ceannt concluded his closely argued statement by claiming that there was 'reasonable doubt and the benefit of the doubt should be given to the accused'.[96] Ceannt's aggressive cross-examination and his effective overall performance impressed Wylie, who described him as a 'brave man [who] showed no sign whatever of nervousness before the court. I would say, in fact, that he was the most dignified of the accused.'[97] His judges were less impressed, seemingly regarding Ceannt as an irritant who was using delaying tactics when they needed to rapidly expedite a large backlog of cases. Fearing a public perception that the court martial authorities were more concerned with administrative efficiency than impartial justice, the government reversed its promise to publish trial proceedings. A particularly embarrassing case would have been that of Ceannt who had wanted but was unable to call MacDonagh as a defence witness: 'Thomas MacDonagh was not available as he was shot this morning.'[98]

It has been said that John MacBride's experience of capture and trial 'brought out the best of this sad figure'.[99] Before his court martial, MacBride had heard at least some prosecution evidence, been made aware of his rights and granted access to legal advice. However, a fellow prisoner who was deeply impressed by MacBride's bearing and demeanour thought he didn't seem particularly interested in his own case. In court, two army officers testified that when surrendering in St Patrick's Park he had given his name as 'Major John MacBride', but though armed he wasn't in uniform. A document found on him indicated that MacDonagh had appointed him 'commandant'. MacBride then related the unexpected chain of events that had led him to Jacob's on Easter Monday. Unaware of an intended Rising, he left home in the morning to meet his brother, at whose wedding he was to be best man. But on the way he encountered a column of Volunteers at Stephen's Green where MacDonagh told him that a rebellion was underway and invited him to participate: 'I knew there was no chance of success and I never advised or influenced any other person to join. [At Jacob's] I was appointed second in command and I felt it my duty to occupy that position.' He 'could have escaped from Jacob's Factory after the surrender had I desired, but I considered it a dishonourable thing to do'.[100] MacBride also called his landlady, Mrs Fred Allan, who confirmed that he left home intending to have lunch with his brother at the Wicklow Hotel. Blackader was impressed by MacBride's dignity, describing him as 'the one who stands out … the most soldierly' of the defendants, adding: 'I will never think of him without taking my hat off to a brave man.'[101] Leaving the courtroom, MacBride drew his finger across his heart, indicating that he expected to be shot.[102]

Some rebel leaders, however, remained virtually silent throughout. Con Colbert didn't even bother to cross-examine a woeful prosecution witness who didn't know which garrison he had fought at let alone his role in the Rising. Nor did he call any witnesses in his defence. When invited to make a statement he merely responded: 'I have nothing to say.'[103] Similarly, Thomas Clarke intervened only once in his trial – cross-examining the sole prosecution witness and forcing him to admit that he had been well treated in the GPO. Later, he told his wife that he had made 'no statement from the dock or anything like that', and with some justification described the proceedings as a 'farce'.[104] None of the G-men who had been monitoring his activities for years were called to testify. Wylie confirmed Clarke's icy contempt for his accusers, describing him as 'calm and brave throughout. He struck me as a particularly kindly man, who could not injure anyone'. Clarke's serenity impressed another Volunteer who saw him looking just as he always did behind his shop counter 'with the same clothes, the same look, quiet, silent, with the suspicion of a smile. Tom was very satisfied with himself and the situation.'[105]

At Plunkett's trial three prosecution witnesses testified about his role in the GPO and his past revolutionary record. Their evidence was mostly circumstantial and, in one instance, factually inaccurate. Perhaps constrained by ill-health, Plunkett declared he had nothing to say in his defence, merely denying a DMP sergeant's claim that the Proclamation had been issued by the Volunteers.[106] It is unclear exactly what MacDermott said at his trial. Six witnesses were called, perhaps reflecting the mounting pressures on Maxwell over the executions, and much of their testimony related to his past involvement in revolutionary nationalism. MacDermott cross-examined four of them and then made a brief statement, but the official text of proceedings does not appear to have fully recorded it. Afterwards, MacDermott expressed his astonishment at the prosecution's evidence; it contained, he said, 'not a word of inside information', and nothing from 'the results of their shadowing'.[107] Throughout he seemed fatalistic about the outcome. Before his hearing, he borrowed a soldier's razor, joking, 'I have to make a nice corpse, you know'. He also told a fellow prisoner, Maurice Collins, 'The next time you and I will meet will be in Heaven'.[108] Going to heaven was a prospect that MacDermott faced not only with equanimity but one that he now embraced as essential to the republican cause. Afterwards he met Denis McCullough, who had been arrested in Belfast and was lodged in Richmond Barracks opposite MacDermott's cell. McCullough recalled: 'I met him on the landing being brought out after his court-martial. He embraced me, said his number was up and bade me goodbye.'[109]

Others defendants made brief statements from the dock. MacDonagh merely stated: 'I did everything I could to assist the officers in the matter of the surrender, telling them where the arms and ammunition were after the surrender was decided on.'[110] Fearing that this might be misinterpreted as a plea for mercy, he wrote to his wife a few hours before his execution, insisting that: 'I made no appeal, no recantation, no apology for my acts. In what I said I merely claimed that I acted honourably … in all that I set myself to do.'[111] In June 1916, 10,000 copies of a speech purporting to be that made by MacDonagh in court were snapped up in Dublin but the contents were entirely bogus.[112]

Willie Pearse was tried alongside three other Volunteers. A British military officer who had been held captive in the GPO identified him as a rebel but didn't know Willie's rank. A legend developed that he had condemned himself by exaggerating his own role in the Rising but in fact he stated simply and honestly: 'I had no authority or say in the arrangements for the starting of the rebellion. I was throughout only a personal attaché to my brother, Patrick Pearse. I had no direct command.'[113] Willie's sole distinction was that he alone pleaded guilty to the charges. Apparently Maxwell had some reservations about confirming his execution. Before doing so he asked to know his age: Willie Pearse was 33 years old.[114]

It is clear from the official record that both Daly and Mallin made determined attempts to evade the bullets of a firing squad, though each adopted very different strategies to achieve this goal. Having cross-examined both prosecution witnesses, Daly testified that he was pleading not guilty because he had 'no dealings with any outside forces'. Furthermore, while not denying that he had been commandant at the Four Courts he depicted himself as having been taken completely by surprise when the Rising commenced. Once it had started he only participated through an overriding sense of loyalty. Daly insisted that he 'had no knowledge of the insurrection until Monday morning, April 24. The officers, including myself, when we heard the news, held a meeting, and decided that the whole thing was foolish but that being under orders we had no option but to obey.'[115]

In contrast, Mallin's statement, almost every word of which was untrue, portrayed himself as a simple foot soldier, silk weaver, band and drill instructor in the Citizen Army, who had simply followed his superior's orders. He stated:

I had no command in the Citizen Army. I was never taken into the confidence of James Connolly. I was under the impression that we were going out for manoeuvres on Sunday, but something altered the arrangement and the manoeuvres were postponed till Monday. I had verbal instruction from James Connolly to take 36 men to St Stephen's Green and to report to the Volunteer officer there. Shortly after my arrival at St Stephen's Green, the firing started and the Countess of Markievicz [sic] ordered me to take command of the men. As I had been so long associated with them, I felt I could not leave them and from that time I joined the rebellion. I made it my business to save all the officers and civilians who were brought into Stephen's Green. I gave explicit orders to the men to make no offensive movement. I prevented them attacking the Shelbourne Hotel.[116]

Mallin cross-examined one of three prosecution witnesses, and called in his defence Lawrence Kettle, whom he had held prisoner in the College of Surgeons. Kettle confirmed that he had been treated with every possible consideration but damagingly he also asserted that 'Mallin appeared to be in command'.[117]

Mallin's testimony concerning Markievicz precisely inverted the relationship which had actually existed between them during the Rising. It was also potentially lethal to her; it literally placed in the firing line someone who had served him loyally throughout Easter Week. In view of the grim predicament in which Mallin now found himself it is perfectly understandable that he would have manoeuvred desperately to save his life. Perhaps he also believed that if the court accepted his evidence, it would never execute a woman in his place. Nevertheless, it was a tremendous gamble with a comrade's life and hardly a chivalrous one.

Sean Heuston also fought tenaciously for his life. He challenged the prosecuting counsel's documentary evidence, claiming that: 'the message in the notebook produced saying "I hope we will be able to do better next time" is not mine. The order from Connolly addressed to "Captain Houston" is not addressed to me as my name is "Heuston"' (the order had stated: 'Seize the Mendicity at all costs').[118] He also protested about not receiving the charges against him until very early that morning when he was hauled out of bed and had them read to him. Heuston believed that he was about to be shot. He was then transferred to Richmond Barracks for an immediate court martial which he described as a fraud from start to finish: 'We were condemned beforehand, and it was only a question of fixing the sentences'.[119]

At his trial in Cork, Thomas Kent forcefully denied being involved in the gun battle at his home near Fermoy. Surprisingly, the charge – that he had taken part in armed rebellion for the purpose of assisting the enemy – was identical to that faced by those on trial in Dublin. Maxwell's own legal advisor observed: 'The difficulty is that no rebellion took place in Cork and the case appears to be one of ordinary murder.'[120] Five witnesses graphically described events at Bawnard House but said nothing that directly implicated Kent in Head Constable Rowe's death. Kent himself denied firing or even holding a weapon but he couldn't explain who had fired the fatal shots from inside the house. Six weeks later, his brother David was convicted of the same offence, though his death sentence was commuted to five years' penal servitude. As one legal expert has sardonically observed regarding the trials, 'timing was everything'.[121]

The remaining defendants made impressive statements. Michael O'Hanrahan's behaviour after the surrender combined courage with high emotion. In Richmond Barracks he and his brother Henry had been seen 'crying together locked in each other's arms'. He told Henry that 'we may go under and have to suffer the penalty but in my opinion Ireland is saved'.[122] In court, O'Hanrahan stated simply and boldly: 'As a soldier of the Republican Army, acting under orders of that Republic duly constituted, I acted under orders of my superiors.'[123]

Fittingly, two of those 'superiors', James Connolly and Patrick Pearse, made the most substantial declarations after listening to prosecution witnesses. At Connolly's trial two military officers held as prisoners in the GPO throughout the Rising, testified that he had been in a position of command and complained about their treatment. Major de Courcy Wheeler recounted witnessing Connolly's acceptance of Pearse's surrender order. Two of Connolly's dispatches were also produced as evidence. After completing his cross-examination, Connolly read a prepared, handwritten statement, a copy of which he gave to his daughter, Nora, just before his execution. It resoundingly demonstrated that, despite his injuries and intense emotional strain, there had been no diminution in his intellectual vigour:

> I do not wish to make any defence except against charges of wanton cruelty to prisoners [one witness alleged that he had been tied up in a telephone box for three hours]. These trifling allegations that have been made in that direction, if they record facts that really happened, deal only with the almost unavoidable incidents of a hurried uprising and overthrowing of long established authorities and nowhere show evidence of a set purpose to wantonly injure unarmed prisoners. We went out to break the connection between this Country and the British Empire and to establish an Irish Republic. We believe that the call we thus issued to the people of Ireland was a nobler call in a holier cause than any call issued to them during this war having any connection with the war. We succeeded in proving that Irishmen are ready to die endeavouring to win for Ireland their national rights which the British government had been asking them to die to win for Belgium. As long as that remains the case the cause of Irish freedom is safe. Believing that the British government has no right in Ireland and never had any right in Ireland and never can have any right in Ireland, the presence in any one generation of even a respectable minority of Irishmen ready to die to affirm that truth makes that government for ever a usurpation and a crime against human progress. I personally thank God that I have lived to see the day when thousands of Irishmen and boys and hundreds of Irish women and girls were equally ready to affirm that truth and seal it with their lives if necessary.[124]

On the morning of 2 May, Pearse was escorted from Arbour Hill Detention Barracks to Richmond Barracks for his trial. There, a policeman testified that he had seen Pearse commanding Volunteers during the Rising, an army officer described him surrendering to General Lowe, and a prison guard at Arbour Hill claimed that on 1 May he saw Pearse writing to his mother a letter that the military authorities had confiscated – something that he must have anticipated but about which he obviously didn't care. In the letter margin, someone – perhaps Maxwell – underlined Pearse's sentence: 'I understand that the German expedition which I was counting on actually set sail but was defeated by the British.'[125] Maxwell's legal advisor regarded this as especially significant because 'the prosecution would have been in difficulty without this postscript'.[126] The letter also made clear that while believing he would be executed his mother would still have Willie. Pearse didn't call any defence witnesses but, standing in his Volunteer uniform, he stated that:

> My sole object in surrendering unconditionally was to save the slaughter of the civilian population; and to save the lives of our followers, <u>who had been led into this thing by us</u>. It is my hope that the British government who has shown its strength will also be magnanimous and spare the lives and give an amnesty to my followers as I am one of the persons <u>chiefly responsible</u>, have acted as Commander in Chief and President of the Provisional Government. I am prepared to take the consequences

of my act, but I should like my followers to have an amnesty. I went down on my knees as a child and told God that I would work all my life to gain the freedom of Ireland. I have divined it my duty as an Irishman to fight for the freedom of my Country. <u>I admit I have organised men to fight against Britain. I admit having opened negotiations with Germany. We have kept our word with her and as far as I can see she did her part to help us. She sent a ship with arms. Germany has not sent us gold</u>.[127]

The military authorities had underlined those parts of his speech which they believed were especially incriminating.

Although William Wylie described it as a 'Robert Emmet type' speech,[128] it was really Wolfe Tone's statement at his own trial that inspired Pearse. Like Tone, Pearse fully accepted his responsibility for the insurrection and by consciously overstating his role throughout the trial he may have been giving vent to his yearning for self-sacrifice. Desmond Ryan, one of his pupils, believed that 'Pearse's ideal insurrection would have had one signatory to the Proclamation and one casualty'.[129] However, his fearlessness and eloquence deeply impressed Blackader, who presided at Pearse's court martial. Occasionally Blackader dined with the Countess of Fingall who regarded him as a 'charming, sympathetic person, half French, very emotional, and terribly affected by the work he had to do'. At one meal he told her, in relation to Pearse:

I have just done one of the hardest tasks I have ever had to do. I have had to con-demn to death one of the finest characters I have ever come across. There must be something very wrong in the state of things that makes a man like that a rebel. I don't wonder that his pupils adored him.[130]

However, Brigadier Maconchy, who presided over the trials of Mallin, Plunkett, Heuston and Willie Pearse, was less impressed by the defendants' demeanour:

We tried a very large number. There could be no doubt, on the evidence before us, of the only sentence permissible but of course it rested with the confirming officer to decide as to the carrying out of the sentence and it is possible that referral was also made to the Cabinet in London. We could only recommend certain cases for mercy. When called on for their defence they generally only convicted themselves out of their own mouths … During the trial of one of the ringleaders, his whole attitude seemed so strange to me that I asked him if he would mind telling me, quite apart from his trial, what he was fighting for. He drew himself up and said, 'I was fighting to defend the rights of the people of Ireland.' I then asked him if anyone was attacking these rights and he said, 'No, but they might have been.' This seemed a strange excuse for shooting down innocent citizens in the streets, but I presume that is the fashion in all rebellions against constitutional authority.[131]

The court martial proceedings continued apace throughout most of May with the largest number, thirty-six, held on 4 May, when Markievicz was tried. Well known to and cordially detested by the authorities through her involvement in the Fianna, Cumann na mBan, the Suffragettes and Citizen Army, she had also played a leading role in the Rising. Newspapers had prominently reported her exploits as Mallin's second-in-command at St Stephen's Green. At her trial, prosecution counsel called two witnesses – a pageboy at the Shelbourne Hotel and Captain de Courcy Wheeler who had taken the surrender of Mallin's garrison. Wylie later asserted that Markievicz 'did not impress me and the court' and described her performance a repellent and undignified spectacle. She had been expected to 'make a scene and throw things' at the judge and counsel. In fact, Wylie adds:

> I saw the general getting out his revolver and putting it on the table beside him. But he need not have troubled for she curled up completely: 'I am only a woman,' she cried, 'and you cannot shoot a woman, you must not shoot a woman.' She never stopping moaning the whole time she was in the courtroom ... She crumpled up ... I think we all felt slightly disgusted, [at a person who] had been preaching to a lot of silly boys, death and glory, die for your Country etc., and yet she was literally crawling. I won't say anymore; it revolts me still.[132]

However, the official record shows that throughout she acted bravely and with characteristic defiance. De Courcy Wheeler stated that she had readily volunteered her rank when surrendering and had declined his offer of motor transport to Richmond Barracks to allow her to avoid a hostile crowd at the Green. Markievicz pleaded not guilty to the charge of armed rebellion and assisting the enemy, though she admitted attempting to cause disaffection among the civilian population. Speaking in her own defence, she retracted nothing, stating simply: 'I went out to fight for Ireland's freedom and it does not matter what happens to me. I did what I thought was right and I stand by it.'[133] She hadn't relented in the slightest from her preliminary investigation in which she declared emotionally, 'We dreamed of an Irish republic and we thought we had a fighting chance', before breaking down and sobbing.[134]

Wylie's apparently inaccurate depiction of Markievicz's behaviour at her trial is difficult to interpret. His memoirs are consistently self-serving in their attempts to mitigate his own role in prosecuting the Rising leaders and, written from memory twenty years later, they are occasionally factually inaccurate and harshly judgmental. Wylie may have been irritated by Markievicz self-assurance and boldness which he may have interpreted as contempt of court. Perhaps his attitude also reflected a deep-rooted sexual prejudice on his part – though there is no other evidence of this elsewhere in his text. Most likely, his unflattering account derived from a belief that the countess had abused her privileged social position to create anarchy by misleading and inflaming less educated and prosperous elements and in so doing had betrayed both her religion and Protestant ascendancy class. Her verdict was unique: 'Guilty. Death by being shot. The court recommends the prisoner to mercy solely and only on account of her sex.'[135]

Of the 186 men and 1 woman court-martialled, 11 were acquitted and 176 convicted; of these the official courts martial registers contain details of eighty-eight sentences of 'death by being shot' (though these records may be incomplete, and understate the number). The final decision to confirm or commute a sentence was Maxwell's and he was under considerable pressure to exact severe retribution. The pro-Union *Irish Times* demanded that 'Sedition must be rooted out of Ireland once and for all' and the *Irish Independent*, representing Catholic business interests, urged that 'the worst of the ringleaders be singled out and dealt with'.[136] Maxwell was later castigated for supposedly lacking wisdom and foresight and becoming 'the man who lost Ireland'.[137] However, he never doubted the necessity of executing the rebel leaders and told his wife that 'some must suffer for their crimes'.[138] On 9 May, he warned Asquith that he had to:

> inflict the most severe sentences on the known organizers of this detestable Rising. It is hoped that these examples will be sufficient to act as a deterrent to intriguers and to bring home to them that the murder of His Majesty's subjects or other acts calculated to imperil the safety of the realm will not be tolerated.[139]

In June 1916, Maxwell insisted that 'every trial was absolutely fair to the prisoner. The judges inclined towards leniency but, where the facts called for stern measures, these were taken.'[140] But wartime courts martial pit the state's determination to maintain order against the individual's right to justice, an unequal contest that invariably ends with a legitimising veneer on a pre-determined verdict. Some defendants were scathing about the conduct of proceedings. One recalled that the only evidence against Ceannt's quartermaster, William Cosgrave, was from 'a policeman who saw him in uniform one hour before the rebellion. Result – found guilty; sentence – death.'[141] The most withering account is that of Ned Daly's vice-commandant Piaras Beaslai. At a preliminary meeting – 'the frame-up' – he was confronted with two British officers whom Daly's men had held captive during the Rising but whom he had never seen before. Lieutenant Halpin claimed inaccurately that Beaslai had been in the Four Courts, though unarmed, when in fact he had spent almost the entire week in Church Street. Lieutenant Lindsay admitted to the investigating officer that he had never laid eyes on Beaslai, evidence that hardly guaranteed a conviction. When the investigating officer asked if he intended offering any defence at his court martial, Beaslai silently avoided giving his captors an opportunity to assemble rebuttal evidence – even though he hadn't yet been told the charge against which he was supposed to be defending himself. Nor was he informed if he was allowed access to legal counsel or had the right to call witnesses, and only later that day did Beaslai receive a typed copy of the charge that he would face at his court martial the following morning.

Although Beaslai regarded his trial as a farce it was no laughing matter because the three trial officers seemed to be making up rules as they went along, while detectives lounged at the back of the court throughout even though they were being called as witnesses. Then to Beaslai's incredulity Halpin and Lindsay's testimony completely smoothed away the flaws and inconsistencies in their previous day's evidence. Clearly overnight, coached by the prosecution, they had strolled together down memory lane and refreshed their fading recollections of the previous week. Now they were both certain: Beaslai had been in the Four Courts, armed and dangerous. Even for a hardened journalist like Beaslai this travesty was hard to take as he watched two British officers perjure themselves blind under the gaze of a defendant whom they knew understood exactly what they were doing.[142]

Even Wylie himself admitted that the trials were 'drumhead courts martial in the early stages'[143] and significantly, when Maxwell sought to justify the death sentences to Asquith, much of his evidence came from intelligence sources rather than that produced in court.

By 10 May Maxwell had confirmed fifteen verdicts of death by firing squad, though his rationale in some cases was puzzling. There were the seven signatories to the Proclamation, three of the four Volunteer garrison commandants in Dublin (Ceannt and MacDonagh had also signed the Proclamation), and the commanding officers at two significant outposts, Mallin at Stephen's Green and Colbert, de facto, at Marrowbone Lane. Colbert's execution mystified many Volunteers, especially as his nominal superior Captain Seamus Murphy escaped with his life. Rumours circulated in republican circles that Murphy had saved his own skin by setting Colbert up to take the fall, but Aine Ceannt strongly rejected them. Undoubtedly the process seemed haphazard. One commandant, de Valera, escaped the death penalty along with his entire Boland's bakery garrison even though British forces had suffered their heaviest losses in his command area at Mount Street Bridge. Three men who served at Jacob's were executed despite it being virtually inactive throughout Easter Week. Thomas Kent was executed in Cork after two policemen were killed and yet no Volunteer involved at Ashbourne was shot after a battle in which the RIC suffered much greater casualties.

Undoubtedly the timing of a prisoner's trial strongly affected his chances of avoiding execution. MacNeill admitted using every available excuse to delay his trial and so did David Kent, anticipating that mounting public horror at the shootings would compel the British government to stop.[144] The last cases after the Rising (including MacNeill's and Kent's) were held by general court martial, in which defendants had full legal support and courts were open to the public. An earlier use of these procedures would have benefited some of those executed in 1916, especially where the evidence was inconclusive. The executions of Willie Pearse, O'Hanrahan, MacBride and Heuston are particularly difficult to justify since other Volunteers had played much more prominent roles during Easter Week.

Apart from Thomas Kent, all the condemned men were shot at Kilmainham, to which they had been transferred after their trials at Richmond Barracks. This 'Irish Bastille' was historically associated with defeated Irish rebels such as Henry Joy McCracken in 1798 and Robert Emmet in 1803, but it had been closed in 1911. After the outbreak of war it was reopened as a military prison only for its inmates to hurriedly make way for male and female rebel prisoners near the end of the Rising.

Kilmainham was ill-equipped to handle the influx that occurred after the Rising both in terms of space and facilities. Ceannt's brother Michael graphically described procuring a lantern and walking 'down the dark corridors into the bowels of this hellish abode, wary of the raised gratings on the floor and up to the iron grill and door of one of the endless cells. Great God, to think poor Ned is locked and barred in that saddened tomb!'[145] Jack Plunkett believed the prison was 'lamentably lacking in the most basic amenities'.[146] Visitors recalled an almost total absence of cell furniture with prisoners sleeping on sacks or ground sheets and using buckets as latrines. Candles or naked gas flames emitted an eerie light, while the walls that had once been whitewashed were now grey and grimy. However, while conditions were undoubtedly primitive and the prison authorities unsympathetic, Kilmainham had never been designed to cope with such large numbers and its reopening for civilian use was regarded as a temporary emergency measure. The British fully expected the prison to rapidly disgorge its new inmates – either back into civilian life, to Britain as deportees or into eternity.

Executions took place in two different yards, neither of which was overlooked by windows. Maxwell's legal advisor believed that the firing squads' 'noise must have been terrific. It frightened the people living near who thought it was artillery.' It was certainly audible to prisoners, though apparently not at Maxwell's quarters a quarter of a mile away, in the Royal Hospital, Kilmainham.[147] The execution procedures were hastily improvised. Those condemned to death were to be segregated and if they wished could have relatives, friends or chaplains brought by motorcar to see them. Visitors were to leave before 3.30 a.m. the next day, at which time the first firing party paraded. The firing squads consisted of an officer and twelve men who had already marched from Richmond Barracks in the darkness before halting at Kilmainham behind a projecting wall in the execution yard. There the officer loaded rifles behind the marksmen's backs, inserting a blank cartridge into one weapon and so confirming the cinematic cliché that firing squad members should never know for certain who had fired the fatal shots. The officer was to have his men standing to attention and holding their rifles until the first condemned man was brought out at 3.45 a.m. He would then march his party from behind the projecting wall into the execution yard to a distance of twelve paces from where the prisoner would be standing with his back to the wall. After the execution the soldiers again grounded their arms. Whilst 'facing away', each rifle's breach was emptied, the weapon cleaned and cartridges collected, again to ensure that each man remained ignorant as to whether he personally had fired a fatal shot.[148]

Accounts of the condemned men's final minutes are not entirely consistent but it seems that as they reached a long corridor which ran down to the execution yard they were blindfolded, their hands were tied behind their backs and a white piece of cloth was pinned just above their hearts. This procedure was probably regarded as the most efficient because it prevented a condemned man from entering the execution yard unrestrained, seeing the firing party, panicking and putting up strong physical resistance. Instead, they were to be guided to the end of the corridor and through the door into the stonebreakers' yard. The firing party was arranged in two rows of six with the front row kneeling and the back row standing. There are varying descriptions of the executions themselves. Father Augustine stated that at MacBride's there was 'a silent signal, a loud volley and the body collapses in a heap'.[149] Major Harold Heathcote, who was in charge of one firing party, recounted waving his hand to bring the firing party to readiness as the prisoner was marched into the yard. When the prisoner had reached a point immediately opposite the firing party the priest gave him absolution and then moved away. He then waved his hand and after the firing party got into firing position he yelled 'Fire!' before the prisoner realised his end was so close: 'The prisoners fell straight backwards exactly where they had stood without moving their feet'.[150] Another officer, however, asserts that he gave every order verbally: 'Ready, Present, Fire', 'On the word "Fire", steady pressure on the trigger, just like on the range … [The rifles] went off in a single volley. The rebel dropped on the ground like an empty sack.'[151]

Arrangements for interring corpses were decided at the very top because, from the outset, Maxwell was determined that the bodies of executed men would not be released to their families. He feared that 'Irish sentimentality will turn those graves into martyrs' shrines to which annual processions etc will be made'.[152] Instead, after an execution a medical officer certified the person as dead and had a name label pinned to their breast. The body would then be removed immediately to an ambulance, which, when full, was to drive to Arbour Hill Barracks where they were all to be put in a grave alongside one another, covered in quicklime and the grave filled. One officer with the party was to note the identity of each body placed in the grave and a priest was to attend the funeral service: '[Hence] the executed rebels are to be buried in quicklime, without coffins.'[153] Such secrecy was bound to create rumours even more horrifying than the truth, including one of a 50ft-long grave ready to accommodate 200 to 300 bodies. Eoin MacNeill claimed that he was 'paraded in front of the men' digging the grave in order 'to frighten him into writing a confession'.[154]

The execution process itself generated substantial paper work but, although the various official forms appear brutally cold and formal, the officers who completed them were not. Many believed that the shootings were a grim, distasteful necessity. Father Aloysius regarded Captain Stanley, who signed a number of death certificates, as 'a kind-hearted and Christian man' who 'admired the courage of the men, and was anxious to do any service he could for them'.[155] Nora Connolly described Stanley as a 'very very kind' man whom her father held in high regard.[156] Twenty years later Stanley was still haunted by memories of executed men being 'cut to ribbons' as they 'died like lions'. The experience had ripped him apart until he 'got so sick of the slaughter that I asked to be changed'.[157]

Once Maxwell had confirmed death sentences, officers were dispatched to Kilmainham to inform the condemned men. They were allowed to write last letters to family and friends, receive visits, hand over mementoes and have priests attend to their spiritual needs. Kilmainham's governor, Major Lennon, signed most, if not all, of the dreaded letters summoning prisoners' relatives. He was a Dubliner who had served in the RIC before enlisting in the Royal Dublin Fusiliers. An injury in April 1916 had rendered him unfit for service and he returned home just before the Rising, when he reported for duty and was sent to Kilmainham.[158]

For the families of condemned men even a summons to the gaol was traumatic. On 7 May Major Lennon sent for Ceannt's brother Michael who said that he 'never in my whole life experienced my heart sinking right down to my boots till that night. I knew it was all up with poor Ned.'[159] Relatives regarded the cell conditions as deeply depressing. Daly's family found him sleeping on the floor beside a dog biscuit while O'Hanrahan had only eaten some bully beef ten hours before his sisters arrived – without even a drink of water. To Kathleen Clarke a damp smell pervaded the entire prison with seemingly the only light coming from candles stuck in jam jars.[160]

While execution arrangements were being finalised and circulated to those officers who would have to implement them, the first court martial verdicts were being pronounced. Maxwell confirmed the death sentences on Patrick Pearse, Thomas MacDonagh and Thomas Clarke. Verdicts were never announced in court but always read out later to prisoners in their cells. For some this was a moment of unutterable terror but not always. John McGallogly had been court-martialled on Wednesday 3 May, along with Willie Pearse, Sean McGarry and J.J. Walsh, in a trial lasting only fifteen minutes. Afterwards they were marched to Kilmainham:

Sometime later I was awakened by three redcaps opening the door to announce my sentence. One of them said, 'You have been tried and found guilty and sentenced to death. Do you understand?' I said, 'Yes.' He paused a second or two and then continued 'Out of considerations of mercy the sentence has been commuted to penal servitude for ten years. Do you understand?' I said, 'Yes.' He told the others to give me a shake and I was duly shaken. Then he asked did I want anything to eat and in the same sullen tone as before I answered, 'Yes.' They gave me three biscuits. I wondered afterwards why he ordered the others to shake me. It may have been that my lack of reaction to the death sentence caused him to think I was half asleep. I was wide awake but actually I was always sceptical of everything they said and always on guard against any show of feeling other than sullenness. At any rate it did not keep me awake because I heard no sound of the executions that took place the following morning although my cell was not far removed from the yard in which they were carried out. When we assembled next day J.J. Walsh said 'There are some missing.' The sergeant in charge replied 'You may thank your lucky stars you are not missing too.'[161]

After their trials Piaras Beaslai accompanied Clarke, Pearse and Plunkett to Richmond's big empty gymnasium where:

Pearse sat down on the floor apparently deep in thought. He did not once address any of us. Clarke seemed in a mood of quiet deep satisfaction that he had lived to see what he had seen. He said confidently as he had said on the Sunday in the same place, 'This insurrection will have a great effect on the country. It will be a different Ireland.' As for MacDonagh he chatted freely and seemed in the highest spirits.

Finally, towards nightfall they were all marched to Kilmainham where a little sergeant with a cockney accent showed Beaslai into a bare cell. At daybreak shooting awakened him: 'I had been hearing sounds of that kind day and night for a week. I thought the shots were fired by some of our men who had not surrendered (as a matter of fact some odd snipers kept busy for a few days after the surrender).' Beaslai fell asleep again until a British officer entered and read out his surprisingly lenient sentence of three years' penal servitude:

As soon as the officer was gone the little sergeant ran into the cell and shook hands with me. I asked him why and he answered 'I thought you were going to be shot. I did honest.' I looked surprised. He then cried, 'Didn't you hear the shooting at daybreak. I'll say no more.' He then left the cell and left me wondering.[162]

The volleys of shots about which Beaslai wondered were from Pearse, Clarke and MacDonagh's firing squads. In his final hours Pearse received Holy Communion from Father Aloysius who told him that Connolly had received Holy Communion. A delighted Pearse exclaimed: 'Thank God. It is one thing I was anxious about.'[163] Aloysius retained an abiding memory of glimpsing Pearse through a peephole, illuminated by candlelight, clasping a large 'mission cross' and kneeling, lost in prayer. It became one of the Rising's most celebrated images.[164] Before his execution,

Pearse wrote a poem, an expanded version of his speech in court, and completed his correspondence. Through his writings and his positions as president and commander-in-chief during Easter Week, he became the incarnation of the Rising. In a final, brief farewell letter he thanked Willie for his contribution to St Enda's, ending emotionally, 'No-one can ever have had so true a brother as you'.[165] Alongside MacDermott and Colbert, Pearse was one of the only condemned men not to receive family visitors. He had hoped to see his mother one last time and in a letter he told her that:

I have just received Holy Communion. I am happy except for the great grief of parting from you. This is the death I should have asked for if God had given me the choice of all deaths – to die a soldier's death for Ireland and for freedom.

We have done right. People will say hard things of us now, but later on they will praise us. Do not grieve for all this, but think of it as a sacrifice which God asked of me and of you.

Good-bye again, dear, dear Mother. May God bless you for your great love for me and for your great faith, and may He remember all that you have so bravely suffered. I hope soon to see Papa, and in a little while we shall all be together again.

Wow-Wow [Pearse's sister Margaret], Willie, Mary Brigid and Mother, good-bye. I have not words to tell my love of you, and how my heart yearns to you all. I will call to you in my heart at the last moment.[166]

Clarke had asked to see Kathleen before his execution. She went but at Kilmainham she was met by a priest whom Tom had ejected for trying to get him to apologise for the rebellion. As unbending as her husband, she instantly rebuffed him when he asked her to change Tom's mind. Inside the cell Kathleen found Clarke lying on the floor 'in a most exalted state of mind'.[167] Over twenty years before he had first entered a British prison hurling defiance and nothing had changed since. Unforgiving to the end, Tom denounced MacNeill as weak and treacherous and instructed her to make sure that the man suffered permanent political oblivion. Kathleen's worst fears were realised when he told her about his imminent execution and those of Pearse and Plunkett. That the love of her life would never see the sun rise again was almost impossible to bear and she cried out: 'I don't know how I am going to live without you. I wish the British would put a bullet in me too.' But he insisted that he was dying happy and satisfied, especially as he would never have to endure another hellish incarceration. And while he was certain that the Irish people would have to go through their own particular hell he believed they would never rest until full freedom was achieved. They talked a while about their three boys and Tom begged her not to let his death darken their lives though he wanted them to follow in his revolutionary footsteps. But he went to his grave without knowing a secret that Kathleen had been withholding from him since a few weeks before the Rising, when she discovered that she was pregnant. She hadn't told her husband because of the immense pressure that he was under and now she feared overwhelming him with the revelation that he was leaving a new baby behind:

Throughout our interview a soldier had stood at the door of the cell, holding a candle. Our time together had seemed so short when he said, 'Time up', and we had to part. I had to stand there at the cell door of what seemed to me to be my husband's tomb. The sound of that door closing has haunted me ever since.

Some weeks afterwards Kathleen awoke during the night in terrible pain and asked Mrs Sean McGarry to fetch a doctor: 'The doctor and Mrs McGarry arrived in a short time, and later a nurse. My baby was dead and I hoped soon to be.'[168]

Aware that Ned Daly was also condemned to die, Clarke had asked for a final meeting with his beloved brother-in-law though it still hadn't taken place by 2 a.m. when Clarke's firing squad was going through its final preparations. In his final minutes Clarke impressed everyone. He even requested, unsuccessfully, to be shot without a blindfold.

A policeman on duty at Kilmainham, Michael Soughly, suddenly noticed Daly and a large party of British officers hastening through the prison gates. But they were too late because soon afterwards a volley of shots rang out, followed by two more in the next twenty minutes. Even so, Daly asked to see Clarke's body which, like those of Pearse and MacDonagh, had been taken to a nearby stonebreaker's shed. There, in the early morning light, Soughly witnessed probably the most poignant scene of the entire Rising, as Daly entered, stood to attention and saluted Clarke's remains before removing his cap and kneeling in prayer. After donning his cap again, he saluted, turned round and went back to his escort. Clarke had been a member of 1st Battalion with Daly, his commanding officer and so was entitled to this soldier's farewell.[169]

Unable to say goodbye, MacDonagh wrote to his wife and children during the final hours. His sister, Francesca, did visit him, flinging her rosary around his neck as she departed. A priest described MacDonagh as happy without a trace of fear or anxiety and whistling as he entered the execution yard.[170]

The executions took place between 3.30 and 4.00 a.m. on 3 May, when daylight savings had not yet been introduced, and it was as bright then as at 5.00 or 5.30 a.m. today. Pearse, Clarke and MacDonagh were blindfolded and their hands bound behind their backs. 59th Division provided the firing squad, its official history conceding that: 'All met their fate bravely.'[171] Soon afterwards the staff officers withdrew and the bodies, wrapped in army blankets, were removed in a horse-drawn army wagon to Arbour Hill for burial.

But the arrangements didn't run entirely smoothly. On the previous night Brigadier Maconchy, officer commanding, insisted on getting his detailed instructions signed when only one firing party was used and its members 'displayed considerable nervousness when the third man was brought out to be executed'.[172] Subsequently, different firing parties shot each condemned man and after firing they immediately turned their backs on the corpse and marched away. However, sometimes these precautions against psychological strain were completely unnecessary as the firing party resolutely declined to don the mantle of solemnity normally deemed appropriate on such occasions. A.A. Dickson was an officer in charge of one execution squad from 7th Sherwood Foresters which had suffered terrible casualties at Mount Street Bridge. He found his marksmen lusting for vengeance and 'with memories of our losses, seemed to have no qualms as to doing the job'. Indeed their gripes were about having 'to dirty all these rifles; why can't we do him in with a bit of bayonet practice?' Although Dickson wasn't as hostile to the condemned men he still didn't feel:

much else except that it was just another job that had to be done; though I was glad there was no doubt the rifles had done their work and there was no need for me to do what that old Major had told me, about the officer going back and finishing the job off with his revolver.[173]

In another respect, execution procedures were not fully adhered to. Cars dispatched to convey two Capuchin priests along with Pearse's mother and MacDonagh's wife to the prison returned without the women after coming under heavy sniping from Volunteer hold-outs. The unfamiliarity of many British officers with Dublin's topography hindered their delivery of official letters and the collection of family and friends in time to see a condemned man. Later, Dublin Metropolitan policemen attached to Kilmainham began assisting military drivers after they reluctantly changed their mind about having nothing to do with the executions.[174]

On 3 May fifteen rebels were sentenced to death, of whom Maxwell confirmed the verdicts on Willie Pearse, Ned Daly, Michael O'Hanrahan and Joseph Plunkett. About 11 p.m. they were told that they would be shot at dawn. A priest attended each man just prior to his execution. Willie Pearse hadn't been able to see Patrick before the latter's execution and, in an eerie replication of Daly's experience with Clarke, he was approaching Kilmainham when he heard a volley of shots. During his final hours Willie's mother and sister visited the gaol and told him of their intense pride in both him and Patrick and that the family supported everything they had done. When they 'bade him farewell, we left him gazing after us with one longing, sad look till the cell door closed'.[175]

Daly, who had fought hard and unsuccessfully for his life, was now reconciled to losing it and acted with courage and dignity during his final hours. Five British officers escorted his three sisters, Madge, Laura and Kathleen, to Daly's cell. There, a soldier holding a candle assured Kathleen Clarke that Tom had indeed been executed – he was a member of the firing party that shot him. Daly 'jumped up from the floor where he had been lying without covering. He was in his uniform and looked about eighteen years of age, his figure so slim and boyish.'[176] As 'cool as ever' Daly spoke about his battalion with unconditional admiration – 'such heroes never lived' – and reiterated his pride in dying for Ireland.[177] After only fifteen minutes the officers outside shouted 'Time up' and rebuffed pleas for a longer stay. Kathleen recalled that she:

> had only time to kiss Ned good-bye. He whispered to me, 'Have you got Tom's body?' I said, 'No, but I have made a request for it, and have told Madge to make the same request for yours.' I thought it strange that he should ask that question. He got no time to say more.[178]

Daly, the youngest of the fifteen executed men, was shot while standing on the very same spot that Tom Clarke had occupied only twenty-four hours earlier. Appropriately, though coincidentally, Daly was buried alongside his brother-in-law at Arbour Hill.

On the evening of 3 May Michael O'Hanrahan was transferred to Kilmainham where he was informed that he would be executed at dawn. In the early hours a police officer delivered to his home a letter stating, inexplicably, that Michael wanted to see his family 'before his departure to England'.[179] With no apparent urgency, his sisters, Eileen and Cis, left their mother behind with sister Maire, only to encounter Daly's three sisters at Kilmainham just after they had said farewell to their own brother. Aware that 'they had not the faintest idea he had been sentenced to death', Kathleen Clarke, in her direct but well-meaning way, exclaimed 'Eileen he is being sent into the next world. This is a final good-bye. She screamed. I had given her an awful shock.'[180] Somehow, controlling their emotions the sisters were ushered into Michael's cell which had 'nothing in it. No light even, but an old bag thrown in the corner and a bucket. No bed, chair, no table, a place in which you would not put a dog.'[181] They told Michael that they knew why they had been called but he seemed unafraid of death and solely concerned about them, his mother and beloved brother Henry after he had gone. Six soldiers and two officers watched to ensure that they only talked abut personal matters and interjected when Eileen mentioned the women of 1798 and that Pearse, Clarke and MacDonagh were gone. At her protest the soldiers got a table, chair and candle for Michael to write letters and a will on prison notepaper, leaving everything he had – his books – to them. When they left and the cell door closed behind them Eileen fainted.

Just hours before his death Plunkett married Grace Gifford, to whom he had become engaged in December 1915. He had deflected her suggestion of an Easter wedding by warning that 'we may be running a revolution then'. Later he suggested Easter Sunday so that they could enter the Rising together, but a friend bungled arrangements and a priest failed to read the banns. After the surrender Plunkett wrote to Grace proposing a proxy marriage so that she would inherit his possessions. After the first three executions she had a premonition that Joseph would also be shot and hurriedly secured the requisite papers from a priest, acquired a ring, made arrangements with the military authorities and went to Kilmainham. In the prison chapel she waited before the altar until Plunkett arrived, escorted by soldiers – two of whom acted as witnesses. He was calm and unafraid and after his handcuffs were removed, the chaplain conducted a wedding ceremony by candlelight. Afterwards the newly-weds were denied a private conversation; Plunkett's handcuffs were replaced and he was led away. That evening Grace was allowed a last brief visit during which the guard announced, 'Ten minutes', and stood with a watch. But Grace's conversation had already run out. She later complained bitterly that 'Min Ryan was with Sean MacDermott for ages and ages'.[182] Just before his execution Plunkett was reportedly in high spirits, telling a priest, moments before standing in front of the firing squad: 'Father, I am very happy. I am dying for the glory of God and the honour of Ireland.'[183]

All four men were executed between 4.00 a.m. and 4.30 a.m. on 4 May and their bodies taken to Arbour Hill for their mass burial against an east-facing wall, alongside the three leaders who had been interred the previous morning.

Major John MacBride was executed at 3.47 a.m. on 5 May, having gone to his death with the same stylish indifference that he had displayed ever since the surrender. At Jacob's he had spurned advice to slip away, regarding escape as a futile exercise that would only return him to drab normality. Death held no terrors for MacBride, unlike the prospect of an anonymous gin-soaked end in a Dublin tenement. The Rising had presented him with one last shot at redemption and he seized it eagerly. Now, like his comrades, he could go out on his feet like a soldier cut down by enemy fire. Father

Augustine, who was with MacBride at the end, said 'he knew no fear'[184] and even requested, unsuccessfully, not to be blindfolded or have his hands bound. Tom Kettle, who was nearby, overheard him say to the riflemen: 'Fire away, I've been looking down the barrels of rifles all my life.' Kettle described this as 'a lie, but a magnificent lie. He had been looking down the necks of porter bottles all his life.'[185] On learning about MacBride's execution, his estranged wife Maud Gonne, who was living with their son in Paris, reportedly donned mourning clothes. Later she wrote that 'he made a fine, heroic end which has atoned for all. It was a death he had always desired.'[186]

Sean Heuston, Michael Mallin, Con Colbert and Eamonn Ceannt were executed between 3.45 a.m. and 4.05 a.m. on Monday 8 May. They had been transferred to Kilmainham after their trials, probably on the evening of 5 May, passing Mallin's house in Inchicore, where he saw his dog at the front door, 'the only one of my household that I could cast my longing eyes on'.[187] He had wanted to call out to his pet but was afraid that the soldiers would shoot it. On Sunday the four condemned men attended church in Kilmainham and from upper windows nearby Colbert's girl friend Annie O'Brien watched them kneeling in the front row receiving Holy Communion:

> That affected us all and I began to cry. When the Volunteer prisoners were leaving the Church these four were the last to leave and they looked up at us and we waved down to Con Colbert who waved his hand in reply, shaking his head up and down as if in farewell. They evidently knew what their fate would be.[188]

That evening they learnt that Maxwell had confirmed their death sentences and Capuchin priests attended them in adjacent cells on the ground floor of the central compound.[189] Heuston immediately summoned family members and wrote several letters, including one begging his sister Mary, a Galway nun, not to blame him for what he had done. Another informed a work colleague that soon he would have 'said farewell to this Vale of Tears and have departed for what I trust will prove a much better world. Thank God, I have no vain regrets. It's better to be a corpse than a coward.'[190] His brother Michael, who was a priest, stayed for about an hour and found Sean troubled but proud and courageous and entirely lacking in self-pity. His overwhelming concern was for his mother, to whom he bequeathed his April salary and some Volunteer money. When she visited Kilmainham Heuston reassured her that he was happy to die, a remark that caused the young British soldier guarding him to break into tears. Repeatedly he implored his family to pray for him and after they left wrote to his estranged father, urging him 'from the jaws of death to assist my mother'.[191] The priest attending him recorded Heuston's final words as: 'Father, sure you won't forget to anoint me.'[192]

Mallin's last letter to his family was a curious mixture of resignation, acceptance and hope. While denying that Volunteer lives had been lost in vain he also criticised the Rising's planning and condemned its leaders' failure to devise any alternative strategy. Near the end his pregnant wife Agnes, their children and his brother, Thomas, visited him. Twelve-year-old Seamus recalled that at Kilmainham:

> there was a big dark hall; policemen and soldiers all around us. There was hardly a word spoken, and when there was, it was very hushed. We were led through a low

doorway on the left hand side, each door exactly like the other. I noticed a light, like a yellow candle-flame, behind a half-opened door and I heard mumbling as if the Rosary was being said.[193]

They found Mallin in a miserable state, unshaven, wrapped in a blanket and staring at them with fixed, glassy eyes. Agnes had anticipated that at worst her husband would be imprisoned for twenty years and collapsed when Mallin told her that he was to be executed. In a rather disturbing attempt to control his family from beyond the grave, he instructed her to remain a widow for the rest of her life. Two of their four children were to join the Church while the others should follow in his revolutionary footsteps. If their unborn child was a boy it was to be christened Michael after himself while a girl was to be called Mary after the mother of Jesus. Although Mallin had demonstrated considerable magnanimity when surrendering and during his trial he now seemed overwhelmed with bitterness. He declared that while Ireland was a great country its people were rotten:

> The first Irishman to join the British army was a bastard. The British army is made up of these, and gaolbirds, and wasters. Some join through drink, and some through lack of work. I will show my guards how an Irishman can die for his own country in his own country. I can die praying. If these men are sent to France they will die cursing. They will die lying on the ground moaning, and not able to see their mothers and their sweethearts.[194]

Mallin also instructed his brother to burn a woollen picture that he had made of the flags and drums of the Royal Irish Fusiliers, with whom he had been a drummer for twelve years. As he said his final farewells, visitors in an adjoining cell could hear Mallin's family weeping loudly.

Colbert had retreated into his own private world, maintaining emotional control only by avoiding highly charged scenes with family and friends. He wrote to a sister that meeting her 'would grieve us both too much'.[195] He also sent a letter to his girlfriend Annie O'Brien, a fellow prisoner who had served alongside him at Marrowbone Lane. Perhaps haunted by thoughts of what might have been, Colbert had asked for a long letter to be delivered to her the night before his execution. But when his British guard insisted that it would have to be censored Colbert substituted a much shorter and less personal message.[196]

Eamonn Ceannt also faced death with courage and dignity, but with some regrets. In an address to the Irish nation on 7 May, he advised future revolutionaries 'never to treat with the enemy, never to surrender at his mercy, but to fight to a finish'.[197] He told his wife Aine emphatically that the Rising was the biggest thing since ''98' and in his last letter to her asserted that 'I die a noble death for Ireland's freedom'.[198] But his family had been reluctant to face up to an execution, especially when a newspaper reported that Eamonn had received a prison sentence. However, once an official summons to Kilmainham was delivered on 7 May, Ceannt's brother Michael knew that there was no hope. To his surprise Ceannt had never looked so well, standing calmly in a Volunteer uniform with his moustache trimmed and a tanned, healthy face. Two sentries in the cell allowed Eamonn to spend most of the time talking to his wife and even to kiss her. Ceannt mentioned that a priest, Father McCarthy, had hinted at a reprieve while sympathetic soldiers had passed remarks such as 'It's a Long Way to Tipperary'. But it was apparent to Michael that his brother, speaking in a matter-of-fact but strained manner, knew that his situation was hopeless. Ceannt was mainly concerned now with keeping his mother's spirits up. When the family finally had to leave he kissed Aine once again; she still did not know of the death sentence. Michael later recalled:

> After we left the cell and before the sentry shut the door I looked back at poor Ned and that picture I shall bear with me to the end. He stood sideways, right side towards me, the candle showing him up clearly from the external darkness, looking down at the little table where he had been writing, wrapped in thought, silent, a pucker at the base of his forehead, just at the nose. My heart welled up with infinite pity for him.[199]

Before the door was closed Michael cried out, '*Beannacht de Leat*' (God's blessing with you), to which Ceannt replied, '*Go soirbhidh Dia duit*' (May God favour you).

In the early morning hours a prisoner on the same landing as the four condemned men saw through his peephole two soldiers with fixed bayonets standing at ease. Suddenly three British officers appeared at the head of the stairs and began descending:

> Next behind them came Con Colbert and Eamonn Ceannt and as Con took the second or third step down he turned back and looked at Eamonn Ceannt. I cannot say, however, whether he spoke to Eamonn or not. Next came Sean Heuston and J.J. Mallin and I immediately knew what the decision in their cases had been. I then started to pray for them.[200]

At the bottom a British soldier fitted a piece of paper on the breast of Colbert who calmly suggested pinning it nearer his heart. Then, surprisingly, the soldier shook Colbert's hand before binding and blindfolding him. According to Father Augustine, 'some minutes later, my arm still linked in his, and accompanied by another priest, we entered the dark corridor leading to the yard and, his lips moving in prayer, the brave lad went forth to die'.[201] Annie O'Brien actually heard the volley of shots 'that killed Colbert but didn't discover until later who it was had been executed.'[202]

Father Augustine arrived just before Ceannt was led out into the execution yard and told him: 'When you fall, Eamonn, I'll run out and anoint you.' Ceannt replied: 'Oh, Oh. That will be a grand consolation, Father.'[203] Ceannt sat on a soapbox where he was bound and blindfolded and complied with an officer's request to stretch out his legs. Augustine recorded that after being shot 'poor Ceannt tumbled over from the soap-box, I stooped to take the crucifix which he was bearing in his hands, and I saw that it was spattered with blood.'[204] At daybreak next morning Aine was still unaware that she was now a widow and begged a priest at Church Street to tell her what was going to happen to her husband. The priest replied quietly that 'he has gone to Heaven'.[205]

At about 3.20 a.m. Father Albert discovered Heuston on his knees in prayer, clutching his rosary beads while on the table a small candle flickered beside his final letters to family and friends. Albert knelt beside him and even after the candle burned out they prayed in darkness for a quarter of an hour. Afterwards Heuston said that he was looking forward to being reunited soon with Pearse and the other executed leaders. He asked the priest to 'remember me to the boys of the Fianna'.[206] At about 3.45 a.m. a soldier entered the cell and told them that time was up. In the corridor leading to the execution yards Heuston was blindfolded and his hands bound, though he could still kneel to kiss a small crucifix that Albert was holding. Flanked by the priest and a British soldier he recited prayers when entering the yard. Waiting for him was a group of armed soldiers, some standing while others sat or knelt. An officer directed Colbert and Augustine to a corner, a short distance from the wall. There an officer directed Colbert to sit down on a soapbox. The priest recalled that 'He was perfectly calm and said with me for the last time, My Jesus, mercy. I scarcely had moved away a few yards when a volley went off.'[207]

Thomas Kent faced the firing squad at Cork Detention Barracks on 9 May, clasping a rosary in his bound hands. He had requested that no Irishman shoot him and his firing squad consisted of soldiers from the Scottish Borderers.[208] After Maxwell confirmed their sentences on 10 May, MacDermott and Connolly were the last rebel leaders to be executed at Kilmainham. Despite some optimism after a pause in the shootings, MacDermott himself was in no doubt that 'we'll be shot',[209] and on 11 May Asquith told the House of Commons that in his case 'the extreme penalty must be paid'.[210] MacDermott was in transcendently high spirits to the very end, hopeful about Ireland's future and fully convinced of the Rising's legitimacy. On 11 May he wrote that 'we die that the Irish nation may live. Our blood will re-baptise and reinvigorate the old land. Knowing this it is superfluous to say how happy I feel.'[211] Likewise, he reassured his family: 'I feel happiness the like of which I have never experienced in my life before', and, referring to his comrades, commented that they were 'as good men as ever trod God's earth'. Min Ryan, who saw him in his final hours, reported that MacDermott 'talked to us in a way that was in no way sad about everything under the sun. We had a good laugh. It was ridiculous in a way because there was no sign of mourning. He handed over mementoes – buttons, his signet ring, an old yellow muffler.'[212]

But MacDermott had some regrets. Like Clarke, he just couldn't forgive MacNeill whose countermand had prevented a really serious rebellion. And though asserting that he was going to be shot and wouldn't have it any other way, he retained some hope of a reprieve that would send him to prison or even allow him one day to 'have another go'.[213] After a delay to his execution, MacDermott said, 'It's only going to be postponed but you never know. Life is sweet.'[214] Harshly critical of the Catholic Church's historic opposition to republicanism, his own religious practice had lapsed only to return at the end when he declared that 'I die … in perfect peace with Almighty God'.[215] In a last letter he told his brothers and sisters that he was 'to die the death of a soldier' and join his mother and father:

> as well as my dear friends who have been shot during the week. They died like heroes and with God's help I will act throughout as heroically as they did. I only wish you could see me now. I am just as calm and collected as if I were talking to you all or taking a walk.

He urged them not to 'worry or lament my fate. No, you ought to envy me. The cause for which I die has been rebaptised during the past week by the blood of as good men as ever trod God's earth, and should I not feel proud to be numbered amongst them.'[216] In MacDermott's final hours he met with Min Ryan and her sister Phyllis who sat beside him on the plank bed. Sean related unemotionally many events of the Rising, especially those after the evacuation from the GPO. However, 'he did not wish to dwell on these matters. He preferred to talk of all sorts of casual matters, asking about different people we knew, referring to various happy events of the past and enjoying little jokes and jests almost as naturally as if we were in Bewley's.'[217] Using a penknife that the guard had rather reluctantly loaned him, MacDermott cut buttons off his clothes or scratched names on coins as keepsakes for friends.

Sean MacDermott was executed at 3.45 a.m. on Friday 12 May. Min Ryan recalled that 'a gentle rain began to fall. I remember feeling that at last there was some harmony with nature.'[218]

Soon afterwards, in the early hours of 12 May, Connolly also faced the firing squad. During a visit on the previous afternoon Father Aloysius had found him feverish after a bad night's sleep. The priest agreed to return next day to hear his confession and give him Holy Communion. Connolly's fate was still unclear and before leaving Aloysius obliquely inquired whether there was a 'danger of anything happening that night'.[219] The authorities assured him that was unlikely. Later that afternoon a British officer arrived to inform Connolly that he had been sentenced to death but that the date of his execution had not yet been set. Another officer came a few hours later when Connolly was asleep and his nurse didn't want to disturb him but the officer insisted as he brought an urgent message. Connolly was then awakened and told he would be shot the following morning and that he could send for relatives.[220]

When Aloysius received a message that he was needed at the Castle he knew in his heart the reason and a military vehicle collected him at one o'clock in the morning. At about the same time Connolly's wife, and his daughter Nora, were brought to the Castle's Red Cross hospital. Nora vividly recalled an eerie journey through deserted streets and an acrid burning smell in O'Connell Street:

> When we were shown in Papa said: 'Well, Lily, I suppose you know what this means?' She said: 'Oh, no, Jim. Oh no!' and he said: 'Yes, lovie,' and then Mama broke down sobbing, with her head on the bed. Papa said, 'I fell asleep for the first time tonight and they wakened me up at eleven and told me I was to die at dawn.' Mama said: 'Oh no!' again, and then crying bitterly, 'But your beautiful life, Jim, your beautiful life!' and he said: 'Wasn't it a full life, Lily, and isn't this a good end?' And she still cried and he said: 'Look, Lily, please don't cry. You will unman me.'[221]

Connolly's isolation meant he was unaware of the other leaders' fate and he fell silent on learning about their executions. He had been convinced that he would be first to face a firing squad but eventually remarked, 'Well, I am glad that I am going with them'. When Nora told him that newspapers were speculating about an end to the executions, Connolly replied: 'England's promises, Nora, you and I know what they mean.'[222]

Father Aloysius heard Connolly's confession and gave him Holy Communion. Just before leaving for Kilmainham he suggested that Connolly forgive the firing squad as they were ordinary soldiers obeying orders. Connolly replied, 'I do, Father. I respect every man who does his duty.'[223] Along with another Capuchin, the priest accompanied Connolly as he was carried on a stretcher down to the ambulance car and then driven to the execution yard at Kilmainham. The policeman Michael Soughly recalled that on the day before the firing parties and staff officers had withdrawn a mantle of gloom no longer hung over the prison. Its staff and the police were delighted because seemingly their grim work was finished and they returned to their barracks. About half an hour later they were astounded when a firing party with staff officers returned to the prison. Soon afterwards they saw a horse-drawn vehicle galloping along the old Kilmainham road and entering the prison. In the distance they saw a man standing in his pyjamas, surrounded by soldiers who were supporting him with their bodies. It was Connolly.[224]

Afterwards, the officer in charge of the firing squad thought a medical officer must have drugged Connolly heavily during the journey from the Castle. Connolly was blindfolded while still in the ambulance but his hands weren't tied as he was removed in a stretcher at Kilmainham and taken to the execution yard, where a chair was already in place. The officer in command then told Connolly he was going to lift him so that he could stand on his uninjured leg. Connolly was then pressed up against the chair inquiring, 'What is this?' 'It is a chair for you to sit on Mr Connolly.'[225] Connolly then sat down on the chair and held its arms tightly with his head held very high. Two members of the firing party were already primed to aim at his head and he died without any movement, the volley shattering the back of the chair.

A small group of Capuchin priests from the Franciscan friary in Church Street had played a central role in the process of trial and execution, and although Fathers Augustine, Albert, Aloysius, Columbus, Sebastian and Eugene had witnessed horrors during the Rising, for them the worst was yet to come. Having helped the various rebel garrisons to surrender, they all ended Sunday 30 April, hungry and exhausted and by the time Aloysius returned to Church Street, 'weary and weak' from Ceannt's surrender at St Patrick's Park, 'nothing had crossed our lips since morning and we were glad to get a cup of tea at 7 p.m.'[226] Yet for weeks afterwards they had to make full use of a British pass that allowed them to travel day and night through a city in which snipers still operated. The days became a blur of meetings with condemned men, male and female prisoners, families and friends, British army officers, politicians and civil servants, nationalist leaders and archbishops and bishops of the Roman Catholic Church. Their ability to interact with both sides was derived from the great respect in which they were held because, although emotionally sympathetic to the rebels, the fathers kept a promise to act only as priests and not politically. Their scrupulous behaviour generated trust in people like Connolly, who 'had seen and heard of the brave conduct of the priests during the week and I believe that they are the best friends of the workers'.[227]

For those men condemned to death the Capuchins became a rock to which they clung in the days and even hours between receiving confirmation of sentence and their execution. As they heard confessions in the cells, gave Holy Communion and absolution and joined in the prayers, the priests ensured that nobody disintegrated emotionally by keeping the minds of condemned men off their imminent death while at the same time preparing them for eternity. Often they were the last voices that the condemned men heard: on Friday morning, 5 May, Augustine whispered comforting words into MacBride's ear just before he was shot. The Capuchins were, of course, no strangers to death but nothing could have prepared them for the manner in which it befell fifteen men at Kilmainham. Accompanying them from their cells to the execution yards, they too walked through the valley of the shadow of death but unlike the blindfolded prisoners they could see everything. The sights, sounds and smells burned themselves into the priests' consciousness but they saw it through to the bitter end. Thirty years later Aloysius was still haunted by the memory of standing behind the firing squad and looking down their rifle barrels as Connolly's body slumped forward in his chair after being shot. Following an execution the Capuchins always anointed the bodies and in some cases took crucifixes that were still clasped in the hands of the dead.[228]

As they worked night and day, the Capuchins' pastoral care became physically and emotionally draining yet somehow they didn't buckle under the cumulative strain. Presumably a combination of professional training, experience, collective solidarity and will power saw them through. Sometimes they had to race against the clock to reach Kilmainham to minister to men on the brink of facing a firing squad. The usual procedure required one or more of the fathers to go to a house on the North Circular Road, where senior British army officers lodged, and be told about any executions scheduled for the following morning. Normally this allowed them sufficient time to prepare but sometimes the arrangements broke down, placing them under intense pressure. Shortly before 3 a.m. on Thursday 4 May, a soldier knocked on the abbey's Bow Street gate, having lost time by initially trying the Church Street entrance. After he warned them that there was no time to lose, Fathers Augustine, Albert, Columbus and Sebastian hurried to Kilmainham where the governor revealed that Plunkett, Daly, O'Hanrahan and Willie Pearse were about to be shot. There wasn't much time but he had secured a slight postponement so that they met the condemned men, though when Augustine reached Willie Pearse his hands were already tied behind his back.[229]

To families of prisoners the Capuchin fathers became bringers of life and death. To others they carried news that their men or women were still alive. At Captain Stanley's request Father Aloysius comforted republican casualties in the Castle hospital and told families and friends about their survival; these included an exhausted Citizen Army member captured up a chimney who was worried about his sick wife. However, Aloysius also brought bad news to Mrs Pearse and Mrs MacDonagh:

> I told Mrs Pearse that I believed Willie would be spared; that I could not conceive of them executing her second son: 'No,' she said: 'I believe they will put him to death, too. I can't imagine Willie living without Pat. They were inseparable. It was lovely to see the way they bade good night to each other every night. Willie would never be happy to live without Pat.'

Indeed she had a strong conviction from the day when they said good-bye and walked out of St Enda's that she would never see them alive again.[230]

Hours after witnessing O'Hanrahan's execution Augustine visited his brother Henry in his cell at Kilmainham:

He asked if I had seen his brother and I answered yes: 'Where is he, Father' was the next question and when I replied haltingly, with my heart stirred within me, that he was well he suspected something and I then said I'd tell him all and I felt sure he would be man enough to bear it. When I mentioned the first scene he leant his head against his right arm which was pressed against the wall and burst into tears and sobs. It was perfectly natural, of course and with a few cheery words he quickly pulled himself together.[231]

Sometimes an executed man's relatives couldn't bring themselves to inform other family members. Eileen O'Hanrahan recalled that she and her sister:

went to Church Street to try and see Father Augustine so that he would come and tell Mother that Micheal was executed. The minute he saw us he knew what we wanted. He brought us into the sitting-room of the monastery. We told him what we wanted him to do. He came back with us. He told us not to come in with him. We did not come in for some time and when we did we found him in the sitting-room with Mother and Maire. Mother was crying.

She remained forever grateful to the Capuchins: 'These priests were wonderful. They saved the reason of many people whose sons and brothers were executed.'[232]

The Capuchin Fathers also acted as go-betweens, ferrying information and messages back and forth between prisoners and the outside world. Father Augustine wrote later about how Arthur Griffith's request was written on his heart: '"Could you possibly call on my wife, Father", he inquired. "Of course I can," I replied. "Well then," he said, "will you please tell her that should anything happen to me, I shall die thinking of her." As if it were just yesterday I still see him kneeling there at my knees.'[233] O'Hanrahan's last wish was for Augustine to console his mother and sisters. The father comforted the sisters at Church Street and arranged to visit their mother and tell her about Michael's death. The Capuchins also conveyed presents for prisoners. MacBride emptied his pockets of silver and coppers and requested Augustine to give it to the poor, while he wanted his rosary to go to his mother. Sometimes they retrieved mementoes for families. The morning after MacDonagh's execution Aloysius collected the rosary that Sister Francesca had thrown around her brother at their final meeting. They received lapsed Catholics back into the Church. When Aloysius attended Pearse he pleased him by mentioning that earlier that morning he had given Holy Communion to Connolly.[234]

The Capuchins tried to use their privileged access to the British military and political authorities as leverage to extract more lenient treatment for the prisoners. On 1 May Aloysius met Maxwell, who expressed his gratitude for the work of priests whose mediation had prevented considerable bloodshed, but he sensed correctly the lack of empathy in a general who clearly regarded them as a useful tool in pacifying Ireland and punishing the rebel leaders. He found Lowe and Stanley much friendlier and more appreciative, especially as they acted to alleviate the prisoners' misery. Lowe agreed to withdraw guards while the fathers heard confession.[235]

When prisoners requested prayer books Aloysius sent these into the Castle hospital where Stanley distributed them. The Capuchins also attempted to mobilise the support of Redmond's Home Rulers to use their influence with the British government to have Maxwell restrained. On Sunday 7 May, Aloysius met Redmond's deputy John Dillon and urged him to press for an end to the executions:

> Dillon said that although he disagreed entirely with the policy of the men and believed that they had put back the Home Rule Movement, still he admired their courage and respected their convictions. He said that he had always had an admiration for Patrick Pearse. He said that he would do everything in his power to put an end to the executions.[236]

Dillon was as good as his word. He sent a telegram to Redmond and after a speech in the House of Commons four days later, he secured Asquith's promise to temporarily suspend the executions.

In Kilmainham Father Albert, a gentle retiring man, became adored by the female prisoners, many of whom were depressed by the hostility of the prison chaplain, Father Ryan, who openly disapproved of the Rising and refused even to pass on messages to their mothers. Annie O'Brien recalled the warmth of Albert, who 'showed his sympathy so that we cried on his shoulder and he consoled us, gave us his blessing and heard our confessions'.[237] He also brought them news of the executed men whom he had attended, as well as events in the outside world. He carried messages to their families and often returned with the replies on the same day.

The Capuchins forged emotional bonds with the condemned men for whose courage and dignity they felt an admiration that they expressed in the warmest and sometimes most extravagant terms. Through their accounts to families and friends as well as homilies, lectures, published articles and masses for the souls of the departed, they contributed significantly to an emerging cult that endowed the executed with an almost saint-like status. The Capuchins became keepers of their memories.

Meanwhile, Maxwell came under increasing political pressure to halt the executions. Initially Asquith had been content to allow the army to restore order and when the trials began Maxwell had been hopeful that 'politicians will not interfere until I report normal conditions prevail'.[238] He was adamant that insurgents who had 'been playing at rebellion for months … deserve no pity'. But as early as 9 May he complained to his wife 'now that the rebellion is over … the government is getting very cold feet and afraid. They are at me every moment not to overdo the death sentences. I never intended to but some must suffer.'[239]

In fact, from the outset Asquith's government had deep reservations about martial law and on 28 April had instructed Maxwell to avoid using extreme measures except in an emergency. After the first three executions the prime minister was a 'little surprised and perturbed by the drastic action of shooting so many rebel leaders', he was also concerned that a speedy judicial process might alienate British public opinion and precipitate renewed disorder in Ireland.[240] After confirming the execution of eight rebels on 5 May, Maxwell gave an assessment of the Irish situation to the Cabinet. He disclosed that he had commuted Markievicz's death sentence to penal servitude for life – Asquith had already ordered him not to execute any women. Maxwell was now told that he was generally free to act as he saw fit but that only ringleaders and proven murderers should be executed and in a timely but not hasty manner.[241] Two days later

Asquith went further and expressed a hope that the executions were finished apart from exceptional circumstances. On 10 May, when Maxwell confirmed Connolly and MacDermott's death sentences, Asquith personally suspended their executions for a day and travelled to Dublin. Yet Kitchener told Maxwell to have both men shot unless Asquith told him otherwise. Clearly no further stay of execution occurred. It would have been difficult to argue that Connolly and MacDermott were not ring-leaders and indeed Maxwell regarded them as 'the worst of the lot'.[242] While in Dublin, Asquith stipulated that only those guilty of charges like murder should be executed and Maxwell agreed to confirm no more death sentences without reference to him.[243]

Over preceding days Maxwell had responded vigorously to mounting Cabinet unease. On 9 May he gave Asquith a list of army and police casualties during the Rising, significantly longer than those suffered by the insurgents. On 10 May he justi-fied confirming death sentences by reiterating his belief in the gravity of the rebellion and its connection to Germany.[244] Next day he submitted a memorandum to Asquith entitled 'Short history of rebels on whom it has been necessary to inflict the supreme penalty'.[245] Weaving together courts martial evidence and Special Branch intelligence, it argued that the case against every executed man was overwhelming. An accompa-nying note to Kitchener asserted that he did 'not consider that in any of these cases there were any extenuating circumstances. I weighed everything before I confirmed the courts. I have done nothing vindictive.'[246] Indeed, he told his wife that the weight of responsibility on him had been a 'horrible onus'.[247]

From the outset it was certain that any executions after the Rising would include the Proclamation's seven signatories. In Pearse's case the memorandum added that he had 'taken a part in the Volunteer movement from its inception and risen to its upper echelons before acting as Commandant-General of the Army of the Irish Republic and President of the Provisional Government during the Rising'. Pearse's letter to his mother on 1 May was deemed to prove that he had communicated with Germany and that 'his object had been to defeat England'. Clarke was described as 'one of the most prominent leaders in Dublin', who 'exercised a great influence over the younger members of the organization with which he was connected'. The memorandum asserted that Plunkett had misused his good education and 'exercised a great influ-ence for evil' within the Irish Volunteers. MacDonagh had been a prominent Irish Volunteer officer who had commanded the rebel garrison at Jacob's, as well as declar-ing himself 'Commandant General and member of the Provisional Government of the Irish Republic'. Connolly was listed as a prominent leader of the Citizen Army and during Easter Week had made his headquarters at the GPO, where he 'held the rank of Commandant General of the Dublin division of the rebel army'. MacDermott was 'one of the most prominent of the leaders of the Irish Volunteers' and during the rebellion he had issued mobilisation orders and dispatches before surrendering with a body of rebels in O'Connell Street. Ceannt was labelled an extremist, identified with every pro-German movement and as having occupied high office in the Volunteers. The memorandum corrected prosecution evidence about his location at Ceannt's trial by asserting that he 'held the rank of Commandant and was in command at the South Dublin Union', where 'British troops suffered heavily'.[248]

Maxwell declared that the remaining condemned men, apart from Kent, had com-manded insurgents who had shot down troops, police and civilians. Daly had been

'Commandant at the Four Courts, where heavy fighting took place and casualties occurred', and was 'one of the most prominent extremists'. Moreover, 'he admitted being at the meeting of officers which decided to carry out the orders of the Executive Council and commence the armed rebellion'. Despite Mallin's denials in court, Maxwell described him as 'second-in-command' of the Citizen Army and in charge at Stephen's Green and the College of Surgeons, where there had been heavy military and civilian casualties. He also claimed that Mallin had led the surrender of over 100 armed rebels. Maxwell alleged that Colbert was one of the 'most active' revolutionaries and a 'close associate' of the rebel leadership, who as a captain had taken a 'prominent part in the organisation of the rebel army'. Maxwell was seemingly unaware of Colbert's position as de facto commander at Marrowbone Lane.[249]

Considerable controversy has always existed over the other executions but Maxwell's memorandum reveals his reasons for authorising them. O'Hanrahan was employed at Irish Volunteer headquarters as one of the organisation's 'most active members, a constant associate with the leaders of the rebellion'. He was also 'an officer in the rebel army' who had been armed and in uniform when arrested. Most importantly he had supposedly been active in an area of intense fighting and high British casualties when, in fact, he had served at Jacob's, which had been virtually inactive during the Rising. Only by subsuming the factory into a wider area of conflict could Maxwell's statement have been remotely valid. Maxwell recorded correctly that Willie Pearse was the brother of Patrick, the President of the Irish Republic, and had served as a Volunteer officer in the GPO before surrendering with rebels in O'Connell Street. But Maxwell also claimed, completely inaccurately, that Willie had been a Volunteer commandant.

MacBride's military record counted heavily against him since his Irish Brigade had fought alongside the Boers in South Africa. Maxwell also claimed that captured documents revealed him in close communication with rebel leaders by sending and receiving dispatches and that, at his trial, he admitted being in 'command of [a] portion of the rebel forces'. But the GOC also alleged, incorrectly, that MacBride had been 'active' in the Irish Volunteers, which he had never even joined. Similarly inaccurate was the claim that during the Rising he was a 'Commandant in the rebel army': MacDonagh had commanded at Jacob's. In Heuston's case, Maxwell commented that he had 'been in command at the Mendicity Institute' and, that though his small garrison had surrendered as early as Easter Wednesday, it had inflicted substantial British casualties.

Maxwell regarded Kent as falling into a unique category – murder – slaying Head Constable Rowe 'in the most deliberate manner'. Although Kent's actions were militarily insignificant it was almost certainly the fact that the gun battle at Bawnard House had occurred after the rebels surrendered that was decisive. His execution probably served two purposes: warning the population that now that the rebellion had been crushed no further resistance would be tolerated, and punishment for a perceived infraction of the rules of warfare.[250]

Maxwell's criteria for confirming death sentences were whether a defendant had: signed the Proclamation; been involved in extreme nationalist organisations; held high rank in the rebel forces during the Rising; the intensity of fighting and number of British casualties in his garrison area; and the role that he had played there. On this basis de Valera was clearly fortunate to escape a firing squad. Though not a signatory to the Proclamation, nor a member of the inner leadership, he had held high Volunteer rank – commandant at Boland's Mill – and at Mount Street Bridge his garrison had inflicted almost half the British casualties of the entire Rising.

Representations by the United States Consul in Dublin claimed that de Valera was an American citizen, and this may have helped his case. But if they were indeed made, their impact must have been diminished by the fact that at the time his national identity was unclear. A Home Office investigation in July and August 1916 concluded that his status was ambiguous. If his Spanish father had become an American citizen, then so was his son and if not, then de Valera was a Spaniard. Maxwell's legal advisor actually considered that the issue of American citizenship was irrelevant to de Valera having escaped execution. A more important factor was that his trial occurred just as Asquith became committed to executing men only in the most exceptional circumstances. De Valera was fortunate to have been court-martialled as late as 8 May.[251]

Just before de Valera's trial, William Wylie spoke to Maxwell who asked him if the defendant was likely to 'make trouble in the future'. Wylie replied, 'I wouldn't think so, Sir. I don't think he's important enough. From what I can hear he's not one of the leaders.' Wylie believed that on his reply 'a considerable part of subsequent Irish history depended. If I had answered differently … he would certainly have gone the way of the others.'[252] De Valera received a death sentence but Maxwell commuted it to penal servitude for life.

On 23 May, Maxwell noted with evident relief: 'I have got some very tiresome courts-martial on hand but I have nearly got through with the rebels.'[253] The most significant remaining case was that of MacNeill. On 2 May he had offered to discuss with Maxwell preventing further conflict between Crown forces and the Volunteers, but on arrival at British military headquarters MacNeill was promptly arrested and taken to Arbour Hill. The GOC was clearly uncertain about how to deal with MacNeill, telling Lord French on 4 May: 'I am a little perplexed what to do with this man … He is no doubt one of the most prominent in the movement, though I believe he did try and stop the actual rebellion taking place when it did. The priests and politicians will try and save him.'[254] MacNeill was eventually tried by general court martial because, in Maxwell's opinion, his case presented 'more difficult questions of law and the admissibility of evidence' than the others.[255] As a result, MacNeill was able to appoint his own counsel for a trial that lasted from 22 to 24 May. MacNeill was accused of causing disaffection amongst the civilian population in his role of President of the Volunteers and through his public speeches and obstructing British military recruitment. He pleaded not guilty and insisted that he had tried to prevent the Rising with his countermand order. Instead, he placed the responsibility for the rebellion on the British government by arguing that its supposed decision to suppress the Volunteers had precipitated an armed response from the rebel leadership. Afterwards MacNeill complimented the fairness of Wylie, who was acting as prosecution counsel, but not for the first time he had misread his man. Wylie believed that 'the man who loads the rifles cannot clean his hands from the blood guiltiness of the discharge'[256] and would gladly have arranged a reunion between MacNeill and his former Executive colleagues. Many years later he said:

I felt that [MacNeill], while avoiding the results of his teaching, had done more than anyone else to mislead the youth of the country and had made the revolution possible … I did prosecute really hard, but failed to prove any connection between MacNeill and Germany, so failed to get enough evidence to justify the death penalty.[257]

MacNeill was sentenced to penal servitude for life.

Overall, in seventy-three of the eighty-eight cases (83 per cent) in which the courts had imposed the death sentence, Maxwell commuted the verdict to terms of penal servitude. These ranged from life, in six cases, down to three years in thirty cases. Nevertheless, in fifteen cases (17 per cent) he confirmed the 'supreme penalty'; higher than the 10 per cent average for British military courts during the First World War. One can only speculate what might have happened without the pressure to desist that the government exerted on the GOC. Maxwell did tell his wife that he had never intended to 'overdo' the death sentences and on 29 April he had indicated to Pearse that 'clemency' might be shown to the rank and file. Initially, he had anticipated holding only seventy courts martial but he ended up authorising almost 200. From the outset he overturned most death sentences. By 3 May, he had confirmed seven out of twenty-seven (26 per cent); by 5 May, thirteen out of sixty-eight (19 per cent); and by 9 May, fifteen out of seventy-nine (just below 19 per cent). Thereafter, every case was commuted to penal servitude and the proportion executed consistently fell. This was probably largely because the Dublin rebels were tried first, and amongst them were the assumed 'ringleaders'. But it may have been due in part to external pressure. Asquith's intervention may have prevented some additional death sentences being imposed. Maxwell had regarded Markievicz as 'blood guilty and dangerous … a woman who has forfeited the privileges of her sex'. Lord French concurred. On 3 May, the day before her trial, he wrote to Maxwell saying: 'personally I agree with you – she ought to be shot.'[258]

Characteristically, Asquith actually appears to have applied only limited pressure on Maxwell. On 27 April he had stated that the 'paramount duty of government is to restore order … to stamp out rebellion'.[259] He staunchly defended Maxwell's later confirmations of the death penalty in the cases of Kent, MacDermott and Connolly, and was satisfied that the GOC had acted with discretion and humanity. When Asquith came to Ireland on 12 May, largely to investigate the impact of the executions and imprisonments, he even seemed to envisage the possibility of further shootings. With evident relief he declared that on the whole 'there have been fewer bad blunders than one might have expected with the soldiery for a whole week in exclusive charge'.[260] Executing fourteen rebels in Dublin was, after all, hardly excessive given, as Maxwell said, the scale of a rising during a great European war. Its leaders had anticipated such an outcome and, in some cases, had actively sought death. Though criticising aspects of Asquith's approach, Maxwell conceded that he 'has not interfered with me, but … has helped me very much.'[261] When it was decided in October 1916 to replace Maxwell as GOC, the Cabinet was anxious to offer him an appointment that demonstrated it 'fully appreciated his services'.[262]

Those whose death sentences had been commuted were transferred to England to serve their time with the internees. One recalled that during the train journey from Holyhead to Portland Prison in the Isle of Wight 'at all the stations we passed we were booed by the people'.[263] Meanwhile in Ireland, public sympathy for the rebels was already increasing. Quite possibly even without the death sentences and mass imprisonments, public attitudes would have changed because even during Easter Week they had shown growing sympathy towards the rebels. Tim Healy traced the origins of this change to the treatment of prisoners at the Rotunda on the night of 29–30 April, claiming that it had 'left a memory as bitter as that enkindled by the executions'.[264]

By 29 May a British soldier in Ireland noted that 'People are already sympathising with the rebels and have forgotten the poor soldiers who have lost their lives through the wicked folly of the people. I am sorry the authorities put a stop to the shooting of prisoners found guilty.'[265] Two weeks later the inspector-general of the RIC reported a reaction against the courts martial, mass arrests and deportations, and that many who had initially condemned the Rising now believed that unnecessary severity had been employed to repress it. Extreme nationalists were 'by no means cowed', and he noted that 'in some quarters it is sought to brand the Sinn Fein rebellion as a Roman Catholic Rising'.[266] This was largely successful and in the process Clarke's anti-clericalism and MacDermott's bitterness towards Church influence were largely ignored. By September 1916 Chief Secretary Duke estimated that 'three-quarters of the population' were 'sore and embittered'.[267]

RIC county inspectors recorded the symptoms of this changing tide of opinion: a growing number of memorial masses for the dead; huge sales of their photos and publications about them; songs and ballads celebrating their actions; increasing numbers of young men marching, military-style, at GAA football matches; the shouting of pro-rebel slogans; rising arms thefts; a hardening public attitude towards the police; and growing opposition to conscription. Government attempts to mollify Irish opinion after the Rising had been counter-productive. Releasing prisoners early was widely interpreted as proof they had been arrested 'without just cause'.[268] Asquith's visit to Ireland and subsequent attempt to achieve a settlement based on Home Rule were regarded as vindicating the rebels' actions, while Maxwell himself said it seemed that 'out of rebellion more had been got than by constitutional methods'.[269]

By late May, Maxwell recognised that, despite his best efforts, 'a revulsion of feeling [had] set in' and, in June, he predicted that 'if there was a general election there is a danger that Mr Redmond's party would be replaced by others less amenable to reason'.[270] He believed that initially the punishments he meted out had been favourably received, but subsequent misrepresentations had created a perception that:

Ireland is groaning under the tyranny of martial law. It is all eyewash for so far they have not felt it. But all the cranks and faddists scream before they are hurt. The dearly bought liberty of the subject is well in the limelight just now. Every rebel that was killed in Dublin they now say was murdered by soldiers in cold blood ... The Irish are beginning to think that all ... should be let off ... [and] the tendency of course is to make martyrs of all those who have been executed.[271]

Maxwell particularly resented some Catholic clergy, who were 'really intensely disloyal', and their 'infernal requiem masses' for the dead leaders.[272] But he also ridiculed Irish Nationalist MPs, especially John Dillon, for making political capital out of events, the press for magnifying every incident that could be used to attack the British government, and teachers engaged in an on-going 'conspiracy to get at the boys in schools and inculcate revolutionary ideas'.[273]

For Maxwell, the changing content of the rebel prisoners' censored correspondence provided a depressing barometer of the shifting climate of Irish opinion. He informed Asquith in mid-June that it 'showed a decided turn for the worse, for whereas in the first blush of captivity their letters were more or less apologetic and humble, now the tone is defiant and shows that they are not in the least repentant. In fact they think they are very gallant fellows.'[274] He was well aware of, and indeed had foreseen, his own growing unpopularity: in the two months after the Rising he received twenty-five letters containing death threats. In June, he wrote: 'I am getting dead sick of this job. I will be the best hated man wherever there are Irish.'[275] A month later he observed wearily that 'Yes! Some of the Irish call me very nasty names. Bloody Butcher! and such like but my skin is thick.' On 20 July he vented his frustration: 'Oh! these Irish are a truly wonderful people. It is difficult to take them seriously; they are likened to spoiled children.' By now Maxwell believed Asquith was 'giving in all along the line', and he expressed concern that he himself might be 'chucked over any day'.[276] In late May, the prime minster had written to him, stressing that there should be 'no incidents … I hope that the visits and searches are now practically over and that you may find it possible to go slowly for the next week or so'.[277]

Despite its increasing sensitivity to Irish opinion in Ireland, the Cabinet decided to execute Casement as well. On 27 April 1916, ministers had agreed to try him by a judge and jury instead of a court martial. And two months later, on 29 June, the High Court of Justice in London convicted Casement of high treason and sentenced him to death. Home Secretary Herbert Samuel canvassed the entire Cabinet about clemency but although some members wanted him confined as a criminal lunatic, expert opinion declared him 'abnormal but not certifiably insane'.[278] Indeed, leading officials regarded Casement as not only 'perfectly sane', but even 'more peculiarly hostile and malevolent' than those already executed, and 'worse in personal character'.[279] Despite this rather damning testimonial, Asquith would still have preferred a reprieve based on medical evidence but, without it, he didn't feel able to treat Casement more leniently than those men whom Maxwell had executed in Ireland. The Cabinet therefore decided against mercy and Casement was hanged at Pentonville prison on 3 August, just after ministers decided to postpone dealing with the Irish question until after the war.[280]

In his letter of 1 May to his mother Pearse had stated: 'You must not grieve for all this. We have pursued Ireland's honour and our own. Our deeds last week were the most splendid in Ireland's history. People will say hard things of me now but we shall be remembered by posterity and blessed by unborn generations.'[281] Opinion in nationalist Ireland changed more quickly than he had foreseen.

The Rising had exerted a tremendous imaginative power over contemporaries who knew instinctively that something momentous had occurred and their old world was gone for ever. Photographs and film of the burnt out General Post Office rapidly assumed an iconic status, insinuating themselves into the minds of Irish men and women and these images would never go away. Whatever the future held it was going to be very different, something that Yeats enunciated in his great poem 'Easter 1916', which ended with the lines:

All changed, changed utterly
A terrible beauty is born.

Opinion had already shifted measurably by the time W.J. Lynas, a 27-year-old soldier from Belfast's dockland, wrote home to his wife from the Western Front on 15 July. With a pride and passion that was comparable to Pearse when he complimented 'the gallantry of our boys', Lynas said of the 36th Division at the Somme:

> They did not disgrace the name of Ulster. Our boys mounted the top and made a name for Ulster that will never die in the annals of history. No doubt Belfast today and the rest of Ulster is in deep mourning for the dear ones ... doing their duty for King and Country.[282]

At Easter 1916 the republican tradition was rejuvenated by the Rising and some weeks later the pride and conviction of northern Unionists was reinforced by the UVF's sacrifice at the Somme. More than any other, these two political movements were to shape Ireland's political destiny in the decades to come.

Notes

The following abbreviations are used in these notes:

BMH WS   Bureau of Military History Witness Statement
CAB   Cabinet Papers
CO   Colonial Office Records
IWM   Imperial War Museum, London
NAI   National Archives of Ireland
NLI   National Library of Ireland
PRO   Public Record Office, Kew, London
WO   War Office Records

1 The Planning of the Easter Rising. Part One

1   For this process see Bulmer Hobson, *Ireland: Yesterday and Tomorrow*, pp. 1–13.
2   Marnie Hay, *Bulmer Hobson and the Nationalist Movement in Twentieth-Century Ireland*, p. 55.
3   Hobson, *Ireland: Yesterday and Tomorrow*, p. 3.
4   Hay, *Bulmer Hobson*, p. 104.
5   The best sources for Tom Clarke's early life are his autobiography: Tom Clarke, *Glimpses of an Irish Felon's Prison Life*; Louis le Roux, *Tom Clarke and the Irish Freedom Movement*.
6   Clarke, *Glimpses of an Irish Felon*, p. 11.
7   Ibid., p. 27.
8   P.S. O'Hegarty in his introduction to Clarke, *Glimpses of an Irish Felon*, p. 6.
9   Ibid., p. 7.
10   Kathleen Clarke, *Revolutionary Woman: An Autobiography, 1878–1972*, p. 67.
11   Ibid., p. 30.
12   Francis Jones, *History of the Sinn Fein Movement and the Irish Rebellion of 1916* (P.J. Kennedy, New York, 1917) pp. 143–4.
13   Letter of P. Martin, 31 March 1960, in papers collected by Dr Pat McCartan for a proposed life of Clarke. NLI, MS 31696.

14 For MacDermott see especially Gerard MacAtasney, *Gerard Sean MacDiarmada; The Mind of the Revolution* (Drumlin Publications, Manorhamilton, 2004).

15 Min Ryan, BMH WS 399.

16 Hobson, *Ireland: Yesterday and Tomorrow*, p. 43; Hay, *Bulmer Hobson*, pp. 109–13.

17 Donagh MacDonagh, 'Irish Leaders of our Time: Eoin MacNeill', *An Cosantoir*, (December 1945). For MacNeill see especially Michael Tierney, *Eoin MacNeill: Scholar and Man of Action, 1867–1945* (Clarendon Press, Oxford, 1980).

18 Liam Ó Briain, BMH WS 3.

19 Eamon Martin, BMH WS 591.

20 Ibid.

21 Sean McGarry, BMH WS 368.

22 Ibid.

23 Hobson, *Ireland: Yesterday and Tomorrow*, pp. 52–3.

24 Ibid., p. 52.

25 Gearoid O'Sullivan, BMH, Collected Documents.

26 Garret FitzGerald, *Irish Times*, 14 November 1998.

27 Pearse to John Devoy, 12 August 1914, NLI MS 31696.

28 For the growth and structure of the Irish Volunteers see F.X. Martin, *The Irish Volunteers, 1913–1915* (James Duffy, Dublin, 1963).

29 For Ceannt see William Henry, *Supreme Sacrifice: The Story of Eamonn Ceannt 1881–1916* (Mercier Press, Cork, 2005).

30 Statement by Michael Ceannt in the Ceannt-Brennan papers, List 97, NLI.

31 Ibid.

32 Ibid.

33 Statement by A.J. Monks in the Ceannt-Brennan papers, List 97, NLI.

34 Austin Clarke, *A Penny in the Clouds: More Memories of Ireland and England* (Routledge and Kegan Paul, London, 1968) p. 26.

35 P. Brennan, 'J.M. Plunkett, The Military Tactician', *An Cosantoir*, (Nov., 1987).

36 For Pearse see Ruth Dudley Edwards, *Patrick Pearse: The Triumph of Failure*.

37 John Ryan, 'Eoin MacNeill 1867–1945', *Studies: An Irish Quarterly Review*, 34, (December, 1945).

38 Douglas Hyde in supplementary notes to his Easter Rising diary, Manuscripts Department, Trinity College, Dublin. Hereafter Hyde, notes to diary.

39 Maeve McGarry, BMH WS 826.

40 Dudley Edwards, *Patrick Pearse*, pp. 153–4.

41 Hyde, notes to diary.

42 Ibid.

43 Maire Nic Shiubhlaigh, *The Splendid Years* (James Duffy, Dublin, 1955) pp. 147–8.

44 F.X. Martin, *Leaders and Men of the Easter Rising* (Methuen, London, 1967) p. 247.

45 Diarmuid Lynch, *The IRB and the 1916 Insurrection* (Mercier Press, Cork, 1957) pp. 25, 112 & 130–2.

46 For background see B.L. Reid, *The Lives of Roger Casement* (Yale University Press, New Haven, 1978); R. Sawyer, *Casement, the Flawed Hero* (Routledge and Kegan Paul, London, 1984); B. Inglis, *Roger Casement* (Hodder and Stoughton, London, 1973); Crime Branch Special file on Casement, PRO, CO 904/195. For Casement's German mission in general see Reinhard Doerries, 'Die Mission Sir Roger Casements im Deutschen Reich 1914–1916', *Historische Zeitschrift* (1976), pp. 586–625.

47 A copy of the Ireland Report is in the Casement Papers, NLI MS 130855(5).
    When I first located this document and realised its historical importance
    I was thrilled by the discovery. Until, that is, I learnt that a number of
    German historians had already been working productively in this field and
    had got there before me. There are two publications which are of crucial
    importance. The first is a book by Hans-Dieter Kluge, *Irland in der deutschen
    Geschichtswissenschaft, Politik und Propaganda* (P. Lang, Frankfurt am Main, 1985).
    This is complemented by an article by Andreas Kratz entitled 'Die Mission
    Joseph Mary Plunketts im Deutschen Reich und ihre Bedeutung für den
    Osteraufstand 1916', *Historische Mitteilungen* (1995), pp. 202–20. Unfortunately
    neither work has been translated into English. Even so the lack of impact that
    the researches of Kluge and Kratz have made on Irish historians is puzzling
    and regrettable (M.T.F.).

48 Sean Fitzgibbon dictated his account to Michael J. Lennon in a five-part
    series, 'The Easter Rising from the Inside'. The quotation is from Part I in
    the *Irish Times*, 18 April 1949.

49 Lynch, *The IRB*, pp. 29–30.

50 Colonel J.J. O'Connell, typescript of his history of the Irish Volunteers,
    Bulmer Hobson Papers, NLI MS 13168.

51 PRO WO904/99.

52 Florence O'Donoghue, 'Plans for the 1916 Rising', *University Review* (March,
    1963), p. 10.

53 Diarmuid Lynch, Recollections and Comments on the IRB, in documents
    sent to the Bureau of Military History, NLI MS 11128. Hereafter, Lynch,
    Recollections and Comments on the IRB.

54 For the various other meeting places see Aine Ceannt, BMH WS 264,
    Dublin; William O'Brien Papers, NLI MS 13978; Clarke, *Revolutionary Woman*,
    pp. 75–8; le Roux, *Tom Clarke*, p. 190.

55 Lynch, Recollections and Comments on the IRB.

56 Daly's account is given in a lengthy memorandum describing his involvement
    in the Irish Volunteers. He presented it to the Allen Library when he had
    later risen to the rank of major-general in the Irish Army. Hereafter, Daly,
    Irish Volunteers.

57 Lynch, *The IRB*, pp. 73 & 101–2.

58 William O'Brien, *Irish Press*, 25 January 1936; Lynch, *The IRB*, p. 73.

59 Piaras Beaslai, *Irish Independent*, 15 January 1953.

60 Annie Mannion, Assistant Matron, South Dublin Union. BMH WS 297.

61 Joseph O'Connor, 'Boland's Mill Area', *Capuchin Annual* (1966), p. 240.

62 R.M. Fox, *The History of the Irish Citizen Army* (James Duffy, Dublin, 1943), p.

63 Simon Donnelly, in a memorandum entitled 'THOU SHALT NOT PASS –
    Ireland's Challenge to the British forces at Mount Street Bridge, Easter Week,
    1916', University College, Dublin. Hereafter, Donnelly, Easter Week, 1916.

64 Clarke, *Revolutionary Woman*, p. 43.

2 The Planning of the Easter Rising: Part Two

1 Right Rev. MGR Peter Browne, BMH WS 739.

2 Diarmuid Lynch, BMH WS 4.

3 Min Ryan, WS 399.

4   Recounted by Cathal O'Shannon, December 1950, NLI MS 338718/H.
    For good studies of Connolly see Austen Morgan, *James Connolly: A Political
    Biography* (Manchester University Press, Manchester, 1988); Donal Nevin,
    James Connolly (Gill & Macmillan Ltd, Dublin, 2005).

5   Recounted by Cathal O'Shannon, 15 June 1932, NLI MS 338718/H.

6   Sean McGarry, BMH WS 368.

7   Recounted by Cathal O'Shannon, 15 June 1932, NLI MS 338718/H.

8   Lynch, BMH WS 4.

9   There are accounts of the meeting by MacNeill in NLI MS 13174(15); F.X.
    Martin, 'Select Documents: Eoin MacNeill on the 1916 Rising', *Irish Historical
    Studies*, xii, 47 (March, 1961), pp. 245–6; Hobson, NLI MS 13171 and 13174.

10 James A. Gubbins and A.J. O'Halloran, 'Limerick's Projected Role in Easter
    Week, 1916', in Colonel J.M. McCarthy (ed.), *Limerick's Fighting Story* (Anvil
    Books, Tralee, ND), pp. 31–2. See also A. Cotton, 'Kerry's Place in the
    General Plan, 1916', in *Kerry's Fighting Story 1916–1921* (The Kerryman, Tralee,
    ND), p. 51.

11 For Dublin Castle see William Oman, Account of his service in the Citizen
    Army, the Allen Library, Dublin. Hereafter, Oman, Citizen Army. For Trinity
    College see Joseph O'Connor, NLI MS 13735.

12 The message was sent to Casement in Berlin from Plunkett's father in Berne.
    See endnote 13.

13 Count Plunkett, acting as a courier for the Military Council, had dispatched a
    message to Casement giving the date of the Rising and stipulating that it was
    'imperative' that German officers should arrive with the arms shipment to assist
    the Volunteers and that a German submarine would be required in Dublin
    harbour. The incredulous Germans rejected both demands out of hand.

14 For details of the plans for the Rising in the west see Gubbins and
    O'Halloran, 'Limerick's Projected Role', in McCarthy, *Limerick's Fighting
    Story*, pp. 31–40. See also Cotton, 'Kerry's Place', in *Kerry's Fighting Story*, pp.
    46–53.

15 Denis McCullough, 'The Events in Belfast', in *Capuchin Annual* (1966), pp.
    381–4.

16 Martin, 'Select Documents', pp. 246–7.

17 Fitzgibbon, 'The Easter Rising from the Inside', Part I.

18 Hobson, typescript memorandum on the History of the Irish Volunteers sent
    to the Bureau of Military History, NLI MS 13170.

19 Hobson, History of the Irish Volunteers, NLI MS 121799.

20 Martin, 'Select Documents', p. 255. Martin dates the incident as happening on
    Sunday 5 September 1915.

21 Ibid., p. 256.

22 Liam Ó Briain, BMH WS 3.

23 Pearse to Devoy, 12 August 1914, NLI 31696.

24 John MacDonagh, WS 219.

25 NLI MS 13171 and 13174.

26 For The O'Rahilly, see his son's biography, Aodogán O'Rahilly, *Winding the
    Clock: O'Rahilly and the 1916 Rising* (Lilliput Press, Dublin, 1991).

27 The talk was given by Pearse in Dublin on 6 February 1916 to C Company
    of the 2nd Battalion. It was published in the journal *Irish Volunteer*.

28 O'Connor, 'Boland's Mill Area', p. 241.

29 Oscar Traynor, in a biographical account written shortly before his death at the request of President de Valera, de Valera Papers, Archives Department, University College, Dublin, P150/1527. Hereafter, Traynor, Biographical Account.

30 Helena Moloney, transcripts of interviews for a 1966 BBC programme on the Easter Rising, NLI MS 15015.

31 Lynch, Recollections and Comments on the IRB.

32 Hobson, NLI MS 13171 and 13174.

33 Account by Peadar Bracken of his experiences in the Irish Volunteers at Easter 1916, in the Allen Library, Dublin. Hereafter, Bracken, Easter Week, 1916.

34 Leon Ó Broin, *Dublin Castle and the 1916 Rising: the Story of Sir Matthew Nathan* (Helican, Dublin, 1966), p. 12.

35 Nathan Papers, the Bodleian, Oxford, MS 472.

36 Ibid., MS 478.

37 Ibid.

38 Ibid., MS 466.

39 PRO CO904/23/3.

40 Ibid.

41 Hobson, NLI MS 28904.

42 Desmond Fitzgerald, *The Memoirs of Desmond Fitzgerald, 1913–1916*, p. 116.

43 Denis McCullough, BMH WS 914.

44 Nancy Wyse Power, BMH WS 541.

45 Frank Robbins, BMH WS 585.

46 Aine Ceannt, BMH WS264.

47 MacNeill in a detailed memorandum on the events of Holy Week, reproduced in Martin, 'Select Documents'.

48 Fitzgerald, *Memoirs*, p. 118.

49 Matthew Connolly, BMH WS 1746.

50 For the release of information see Lynch, Recollections and Comments on the IRB; account by Frank Robbins, NLI MS 10915. For de Valera's use of bodyguards see O'Connor, 'Boland's Mill Area', p. 239.

51 Aine Ceannt, BMH WS 264.

52 From an article by Min Ryan in the possession of her son Risteard Mulcahy who generously allowed me to examine and use it.

53 Clarke, *Revolutionary Woman*, p. 60.

54 Ibid.

55 Ibid., p. 70.

56 For MacDonagh see Brian Barton, *The Secret Court Martial Records of the Easter Rising* (The History Press, Stroud, 2010); Donagh MacDonagh, 'Irish Leaders of our Time: Thomas MacDonagh', *An Cosantoir*, (October, 1945).

57 Clarke, *A Penny in the Clouds*, p. 25.

58 This has been persuasively argued in Marcus Bourke 'Thomas MacDonagh's Role in the Plans for the Easter Rising', *Irish Sword*, 8 (1967–68).

59 Martin, 'Select Documents', p. 254.

60. Michael Staines, BMH WS 284.

61 PRO CO 904/23/3.

62 O'Broin, *Dublin Castle and the 1916 Rising*, p. 149.

63 Fitzgibbon, 'The Easter Rising from the Inside', Part II, *Irish Times*, 19 April 1949.

64 Hobson, NLI MS 17613; Hobson, Account of Events in Dublin in the days preceding Easter Week 1916, NLI MS 17613.

65 Hobson, NLI 13171 and 13174.

66 MacNeill Memorandum in Martin, 'Select Documents'.

67 Mrs Bulmer Hobson (Claire Gregan), BMH WS 385.

68 Hobson Memorandum and Mrs Bulmer Hobson (Claire Gregan), BMH WS 685.

69 For this meeting see Tierney, *Eoin MacNeill*, pp. 199–203; MacNeill Memorandum in Martin, 'Select Documents'.

70 Martin, *Leaders and Men*, p. 246.

71 MacNeill Memorandum in Martin, 'Select Documents'.

72 Ibid.; Fitzgibbon, 'The Easter Rising from the Inside', Part III, *Irish Times*, 20 April 1949.

73 There is a contradiction here between the recollections of MacNeill and Hobson. MacNeill asserted that he did go to Volunteer headquarters, saw Hobson and told him the countermanding orders were of no avail, NLI MS 13174(15); Hobson was equally certain that they never met, NLI MS 13170. Hobson's memory was always sharper than MacNeill's and if a meeting had taken place its content would surely have been memorable, yet MacNeill provided no further details of the alleged meeting. MacNeill did go to Volunteer headquarters but a witness recorded him irritated at Hobson's absence. See endnote 75.

74 Hobson, *Ireland: Yesterday and Tomorrow*, pp. 76–7.

75 Kitty O'Doherty, BMH WS 355.

76 Hobson, NLI 28904.

77 Mrs Bulmer Hobson (Claire Gregan), BMH WS 685.

78 Fitzgibbon, 'The Easter Rising from the Inside', Part IV, *Irish Times*, 21 April 1949.

79 Mrs Bulmer Hobson (Claire Gregan), BMH WS 685.

80 Aine Ceannt, BMH WS 264.

81 Diarmuid Lynch, WS 4.

82 Stafford to HQ Irish Command, 22 April 1916, Nathan Papers, MS 4765. For a painstakingly researched account of the voyage of the *Aud*, see John de Courcy Ireland, *The Sea and the Easter Rising* (Maritime Institute of Ireland, Dublin, 1966) pp. 9–26.

83 See endnote 13.

84 O'Donoghue, 'Plans for the 1916 Rising', p. 13.

85 Mortimer O'Leary in an account that he deposited in the Allen Library.

86 Fionan Lynch, BMH 192.

87 Martin, 'Select Documents', p. 249.

88 Mannix Joyce, 'The Story of Limerick and Kerry in 1916', *Capuchin Annual* (1966), p. 352.

89 William O'Brien, BMH WS 1766.

90 Joyce, 'The Story of Limerick and Kerry'.

91 Le Roux, *Tom Clarke*, p. 52.

92 For details of the safe houses used see Clarke, *Revolutionary Woman*, p. 74; Michael O'Reilly, BMH WS 886; Seanus O'Sullivan, BMH WS 393; Aine Ceannt, BMH WS 264; Margaret O'Kelly, BMH WS 925.

93 Letter in possession of Risteard Mulcahy.
94 William O'Brien, BMH WS 1766.
95 Fitzgibbon, 'The Easter Rising from the Inside', Part II.
96 Ibid.
97 Colm O'Loughlin, BMH WS 751.
98 Fitzgibbon, 'The Easter Rising from the Inside', Part II.
99 For this meeting see especially Tierney, *Eoin MacNeill*, pp. 208–12; Seamus O'Kelly, BMH WS 471.
100 Min Ryan, BMH WS 399.
101 Richard Mulcahy Tapes.
102 Seamus Daly, BMH WS 360.
103 MacNeill Memorandum in Martin, 'Select Documents'.
104 John MacDonagh, BMH WS 219.
105 Paudin O'Keefe, Richard Mulcahy Tapes.
106 For The O'Rahilly's journey to the west see O'Rahilly, *Winding the Clock*, pp. 199–200.
107 Le Roux, *Tom Clarke*, p. 204.
108 Details of the frantic efforts to round up the members of the Military Council can be found in Aine Ceannt, BMH WS 264; le Roux, *Tom Clarke*, pp. 205–6; Eilis ni Chorra, 'A Rebel Remembers', in *Capuchin Annual* (1966), pp. 292–300.
109 Aine Ceannt, BMH WS 264.
110 Seamus O'Kelly, BMH WS 471.
111 Aine Ceannt, BMH WS 264.
112 Sean McGarry, WS 368.
113 Joyce, 'The Story of Limerick and Kerry', p. 353.
114 Fionan Lynch, BMH WS 182.
115 Helena Moloney, BMH WS 391.
116 Nancy Wyse Power, BMH WS 541.
117 William O'Brien, Notes on the Citizen Army, Florence O'Donoghue Papers, NLI MS 15673(1).
118 Mrs Bulmer Hobson (Claire Gregan), BMH WS 385.
119 Ibid.
120 Seamus O'Sullivan, BMH WS 393.
121 Kathleen Clarke records her husband's shock in Clarke, *Revolutionary Woman*, pp. 76–7.
122 Le Roux, *Tom Clarke*, pp. 212–3.
123 Staines, BMH WS 284.
124 Liam Tannam, BMH WS 242.
125 Ibid.
126 For a good account by one of the audience see Margaret Skinnider, *Irish Press*, 9 April 1966.
127 Sean McGarry, WS 368.
128 Beaslai, *Irish Independent*, 16 January 1953.
129 Clarke, *Revolutionary Woman*, p. 75.
130 NLI MS 13174(15).
131 Father Eugene Nevin, BMH WS 1605.
132 Ibid.

133 John Keegan, BMH WS 217.
134 NLI MS 41711; O'Connor, 'Boland's Mill Area', pp. 241–2.
135 Dudley Edwards, *Patrick Pearse*, p. 274.
136 Fitzgibbon, 'The Easter Rising from the Inside', Part II.
137 MacNeill Memorandum in Martin, 'Select Documents'; MacNeill papers LA/G/371, UCD archives.
138 Martin, 'Select Documents'.
139 MacDonagh, BMH WS 219.
140 Fitzgerald, *Memoirs*, p. 128.
141 Aine Ceannt, BMH WS 264.
142 Clarke, *Revolutionary Woman*, p. 77.
143 Nathan Papers, MS 466.
144 Ibid., MS 449.
145 On the following see a memo by Nathan, Nathan Papers, MS 476; Ó Broin, *Dublin Castle and the 1916 Rising*, pp. 83–4.
146 Ibid., pp. 86–7.
147 Dorothy Stopford, Diary, April to May 1916, NLI MS 16063.
148 IWM, 71/11/2.

3 The First Morning of the Rising and St Stephen's Green

1 For Nathan's activities on Easter Monday morning see Ó Broin, *Dublin Castle and the 1916 Rising*, pp. 87–92.
2 For accounts of the events of Easter Monday morning at Liberty Hall see Oman, Citizen Army; Nora Connolly O'Brien, *Portrait of a Rebel Father* ('Talbot Press, Dublin and Cork, 1935) pp. 297–300; Frank Robbins, *Under the Starry Plough: Recollections of the Irish Citizen Army* (Academy Press, Dublin, 1977) pp. 83–4. For Ceannt see Lily O'Brennan, 'The Dawning of the Day', in *Capuchin Annual* (1936) pp. 157–9. For the Pearse brothers see Margaret O'Kelly, BMH WS 925.
3 Oman, Citizen Army.
4 Connolly O'Brien, *Portrait of a Rebel Father*, pp. 298–9.
5 O'Rahilly, *Winding the Clock*, p. 206.
6 Oman, Citizen Army.
7 Ibid.
8 Ibid.
9 Price in his evidence on 25 May 1916 to the Royal Commission on the Rebellion in Ireland, Minutes of Evidence CMD 8279; Keith Jeffery, *The GPO and the Easter Rising* (Irish Academic Press, Dublin, 2006), p. 40.
10 Ibid.
11 Fox, *The History of the Irish Citizen Army*, pp. 149–50.
12 Matthew Connolly, BMH WS 1746.
13 Ibid.
14 Kathleen Lynn, BMH WS 357.
15 Helena Moloney, BMH WS 391.
16 Ibid.
17 Jeffery, *The GPO and the Easter Rising*, p. 44.
18 Ibid., p. 42.

19 Helena Moloney, BMH WS 391.

20 Kathleen Lynn, BMH WS 357.

21 Matthew Connolly, BMH WS.

22 Ibid.

23 Helena Moloney, BMH WS 391.

24 For the Magazine Fort operation see Paddy Daly and Eamon Martin, BMH 592.

25 Eamon Martin, BMH 592.

26 James O'Shea, BMH WS 733.

27 Frank Robbins, BMH WS.585.

28 Robbins, *Under the Starry Plough*, p. 70. For brief account of Mallin's life, see Barton, *The Secret Court Martial Records*, pp. 272–85.

29 Fox, *The History of the Irish Citizen Army*, pp. 92–3.

30 Frank Robbins, BMH WS 585.

31 Ibid.

32 O'Shea, BMH WS 733.

33 Account by Margaret Skinnider, *Irish Press*, 9 April 1966; Margaret Skinnider, *Doing My Bit for Ireland* (Century Co., New York, 1917), passim; Mallin's evidence at his court martial, PRO WO71/353; 'St Stephen's Green', *The Catholic Bulletin* (1918), pp. 502–4.

34 Robbins, *Under the Starry Plough*, p. 85.

35 Captain E. Gerard, BMH WS 348.

36 O'Shea, BMH WS 733.

37 Ibid.

38 Ibid.

39 In list of 'persons killed or wounded by rebels' by Sergeant Michael Mannion, 27 July 1916, PRO WO35/69; Skinnider, *Irish Press*, 9 April 1966; account by Belfast solicitor in *Belfast Telegraph*, 1 May 1916.

40 Account by St John Ervine, in Jeffery, *The GPO and the Easter Rising*, p. 173.

41 Frank Robbins, BMH WS 585.

42 Ann Matthews, *Renegades, Irish Republican Women 1900–1922* (Mercier Press, Dublin, 2010), p. 129.

43 William O'Brien, BMH WS 1766.

44 Skinnider, *Irish Press*, 9 April 1966; Crime Branch Special files on Markievicz, PRO CO904/209 and PRO WO35/207.

45 Diary kept by Douglas Hyde during Easter Rising, 24 April 1916, now in Trinity College, Dublin, MS 10343/7. Hereafter Douglas Hyde, Diary of Easter Week.

46 Cal McCarthy, *Cumann na mBan and the Irish Revolution* (The Collins Press, Cork, 2007), p. 59.

47 Liam Ó Briain, 'The St Stephen's Green Area', in *Capuchin Annual* (1966), p. 224; Nora O'Daly, 'The Women of Easter Week: Cumann na mBan in St Stephen's Green, and in the College of Surgeons', *An tOglac* (3 April 1926).

48 Account by Frank Robbins, NLI MS 10915.

49 Elizabeth Bowen, *The Shelbourne, a Centre in Dublin Life for more than a Century* (Harrap, London, 1951), pp. 151–5.

50 James Stephens, *The Insurrection in Dublin* (Colin Smyth, Gerrards Cross, 1978), p. 9.

51 Robbins, *Under the Starry Plough*, p. 97.

52 Breda Grace, 'I Don't Forget', de Valera Papers, University College, Dublin, MSS 94/385.

53 Robbins, *Under the Starry Plough*, p. 94.

54 Stephens, *Insurrection in Dublin*, p. 19.

55 Jeffery, *The GPO and the Easter Rising*, pp. 175–6; Maurice Headlam, *Irish Reminiscences* (Robert Hall, London, 1947), p. 167.

56 Stephens, *Insurrection in Dublin*, p. 18.

57 Account by J. William, G. Smith, in NLI MS 24952; account by Powell, assistant manager, Shelbourne Hotel, May 1916, in PRO WO35/69.

58 INA CSORP 5620/13272.

59 Jeffery, *The GPO and the Easter Rising*, p. 70.

60 See contemporary reports of incidents made to police and lists of casualty statistics at Dublin hospitals in list compiled by Sergeant M. Mannion, 29 May 1916, in ibid.; Smith, NLI MS 24952.

61 Robbins, *Under the Starry Plough*, pp. 107–8; list by Mannion of killed and wounded, 29 July 1916, in PRO WO35/69; *Irish Times*, 4 May 1916.

62 Robbins, *Under the Starry Plough*, p. 88.

63 Ibid., p. 88.

64 Ó Briain, 'Stephen's Green Area', p. 222.

65 Skinnider, *Irish Press*, 9 April 1966; O'Daly, 'The Women of Easter Week', pp. 3–6; Ó Briain, 'Stephen's Green Area', pp. 225–6.

66 Douglas Hyde, Diary of Easter Week.

67 OC, 'The Story of a Machine-gun Section', *Irish Life, Record of the Rebellion of 1916* (Dublin, 1916), p. 22; P.J. O'Connor's account, the midnight march, in NLI MS 10915.

68 OC, 'Story of Machine-gun Section', p. 24; O'Briain. 'Stephen's Green Area'.

69 Stephens, *Insurrection in Dublin*, p. 26.

70 Account by Mary Louisa Norway, in Jeffery, *The GPO and the Easter Rising*, p. 69.

71 Account by St John Ervine, in ibid., pp. 177–8.

72 Account by Mary Louisa Norway, in ibid., p. 72.

73 Fox, *The History of the Irish Citizen Army*, p. 158; Stephens, *Insurrection in Dublin* – Stephens noted four dead and one gravely injured; Robbins, *Under the Starry Plough*, pp. 103–6; Ray Bateson *They Died by Pearse's Side*, (Irish Graves Publications, Dublin, 2010) – the definitive account of insurgent casualties, four fatalities are listed as having taken place in the Green on Tuesday morning – John Adams, James Fox, Philip Clarke and James Corcoran.

74 O'Daly, 'The Women of Easter Week'.

75 Robbins, *Under the Starry Plough*, p. 103; Ó Briain, 'Stephen's Green Area', pp. 288–9.

76 OC, 'Story of a Machine-gun Section', pp. 24–5.

77 William O'Brien, BMH WS 1766.

78 Rose Hackett, BMH WS 546.

79 Bowen, *The Shelbourne*, pp. 156–61.

80 Dr J.C. Ridgeway, BMH WS 1431.

81 Robbins, *Under the Starry Plough*, p. 100.

82 O'Daly, 'The Women of Easter Week'.

83 See reference to Kathleen Clarke's letter to *Sunday Press*, April 1963, in note headed 'Occupation of Stephen's Green' in Florence O'Donoghue Papers, NLI MS 31299(2).

84 William O'Brien, BMH WS 1766.

85 Robbins, *Under the Starry Plough*, p. 101.

86 Ó Briain, 'Stephen's Green Area', p. 227; Skinnider, *Irish Press*, 9 April 1966.

87 Jeffery, *The GPO and the Easter Rising*, p. 180.

88 Frank Robbins, BMH WS 585.

89 Robbins, *Under the Starry Plough*, p. 93.

90 Skinnider, *Doing My Bit for Ireland*, pp. 115–6.

91 Rose Hackett, BMH WS 546.

92 Skinnider, *Irish Press*, 9 April 1966; O'Daly, 'The Women of Easter Week'.

93 Harry Nicholls, BMH WS 296.

94 Robbins, *Under the Starry Plough*, p. 114.

95 James O'Shea, BMH WS 733.

96 Fox, *The History of the Irish Citizen Army*, p. 160; military situation reports for 27–28 April, in PRO WO35/69; account in *Irish Independent*, 11 May 1916.

97 Robbins, *Under the Starry Plough*, pp. 115–6; Skinnider, *Irish Press*, 9 April 1966; OC, 'Story of a Machine-gun Section', p. 24; Ó Briain, 'Stephen's Green Area', p. 231.

98 Skinnider, *Doing My Bit for Ireland*, pp. 143 & 150; Robbins, BMH WS 585; Sinead McCoole, *Guns and Shiffen; Women Revolutionaries and Kilmainham Gaol* (Stationery Office, Dublin, 1997), p. 17.

99 'Women in the Fight, a Memoir by Countess Markievicz', in Roger McHugh, *Dublin, 1916* (Arlington Books, Dublin, 1966), p. 124.

100 Skinnider, *Irish Press*, 9 April 1966; Skinnider, *Doing My Bit for Ireland*, passim.

101 Douglas Hyde, Diary of Easter Week. Oman, Citizen Army.

102 Oman, Citizen Army.

103 O'Briain, 'Stephen's Green Area', p. 233; O'Daly, 'The Women of Easter Week'.

104 Smith, NLI MS 24952.

105 Stephens, *Insurrection in Dublin*, p. 50.

106 Douglas Hyde, Diary of Easter Week.

107 Jeffery, *The GPO and the Easter Rising*, p. 182.

108 James O'Shea, BMH WS 733; Frank Robbins, BMH WS 585. Just two insurgent fatalities were sustained in the College of Surgeons: James McCormack and Daniel Murray. In addition, Fred Ryan died of gunshot wounds in the attempt to burn down the Hotel Russell. See Bateson, *They Died by Pearse's Side*, pp. 66–83.

109 Robbins, *Under the Starry Plough*, pp. 117–8. Between the outbreak of war and 15 April 1916, a total of 17,536 men had enlisted from Dublin in the British army. See also *On the Rebellion in Ireland*, report of Royal Commission, Command Paper 8279, p. 125.

110 Stephens, *Insurrection in Dublin*, pp. 53 & 59.

111 Ó Briain, 'Stephen's Green Area', p. 231.

112 Ibid., p. 233; the diaries of Diarmuid Coffey and his mother record a doctor stating that there were cases of nervous breakdown in the college, NLI MS 21193.

113 Diary of John Clarke, NLI MS 10485.

114 Douglas Hyde, Diary of Easter Week.

115 Piaras MacLochlainn, *Last Words: Letters and Statements of the Leaders Executed after the Rising at Easter 1916* (Stationery Office, Dublin, 1990), p. 186.

116 Robbins, *Under the Starry Plough*, p. 120; Ó Briain, 'Stephen's Green Area', p. 234.

117 Major H.E. de Courcy Wheeler's account of surrender in *Irish Life, Record of the Rebellion of 1916*, pp. 26–32; Elizabeth O'Farrell, 'The Surrender', *Capuchin Annual* (1917), pp. 329–30.

118 Rose Hackett, BMH WS 546.

119 Frank Robbins, BMH WS 585.

120 James O'Shea, BMH WS 733.

121 Robbins, *Under the Starry Plough*, p. 121.

122 Mary Donnelly, 'With the Citizen Army in St Stephen's Green', *An Poblacht*, 19 April 1930.

123 James O'Shea, BMH WS 733.

124 Ó Briain, 'Stephen's Green Area', p. 236; Skinnider, *Doing My Bit for Ireland*, p. 155; Oman, Citizen Army; Markievicz told her sister the rebels in the college could have held out for days, in McHugh, *Dublin, 1916*, p. 310.

125 Ó Briain, 'Stephen's Green Area', p. 236.

126 Ibid., p. 234; de Courcy Wheeler, in *Irish Life*, p. 32.

127 Harry Nicholls, BMH WS 296.

128 De Courcy Wheeler, in *Irish Life*, p. 32; Oman, Citizen Army.

129 Comment attributed to Kettle, in Coffey, Diary; he also stated he was well treated by rebels, in Douglas Hyde, Diary of Easter Week.

130 Mr Purser, who worked there, and his wife stated that the rebels 'never even misarranged a bottle or did any damage whatever in the College' in ibid., 2 May.

131 Ó Briain, 'Stephen's Green Area', p. 236.

132 De Courcy Wheeler, account in NLI MS 15000; Oman, Citizen Army, recalls: 'the mob attempted to attack us. The British officer displayed great courage.'; O'Daly, 'The Women of Easter Week', states: 'I carried a Red Cross flag as some extraordinary stories were afloat, to account for the presence of women among the garrison'.

133 Ibid.

134 Robbins, *Under the Starry Plough*, pp. 127–8.

135 Ibid., p. 128.

136 Skinnider, *Irish Press*, 9 April 1966; Douglas Hyde, Diary of Easter Week; notes on Markievicz in PRO WO35/207; Johnson's diary, 27 April 1916, in J.A. Gaughan, *Thomas Johnson, 1872–1963: First Leader of the Labour Party in Dail Eireann* (Kingdom Books, Mount Merrion, 1980), p. 51.

137 Account by A.A. Dickson, Sherwood Foresters, IWM 11650 01/49/1.

138 'Momentous days; occasional diaries of Frances Taylor', entry for 30 April 1916, in *Dublin Historical Record*, Vol. XLVII (1994), pp. 80–1.

4 Boland's Bakery

1 For de Valera's life and career his official biography remains the best starting point, Lord Longford and Thomas P. O'Neill, *Eamon de Valera* (Gill and Macmillan, Dublin, 1970).

2   Ibid., p. 50.

3   Joseph O'Connor, BMH WS 142.

4   Ibid.

5   Donnelly, Easter Week, 1916.

6   Joseph O'Connor, BMH WS 142.

7   O'Connor, 'Boland's Mill Area', p. 242. The poor turn-out is also noted in Donnelly, Easter Week, 1916.

8   Donnelly, Easter Week, 1916.

9   George Lyons, 'Occupation of Ringsend Area in 1916', *An tOglac*, (10 April 1926). Lyons' marvellous three-part account in *An tOglac*, (10, 17 and 24 April 1926) of the fighting at Boland's bakery and Mount Street Bridge is perhaps the best by any participant in the Rising. It is remarkable for its descriptive power, frankness, honesty and fairness. Hereafter Lyons, 'Ringsend Area'.

10 Donnelly, Easter Week, 1916.

11 Joseph O'Connor, BMH WS 142.

12 Ibid.,

13 Donnelly, Easter Week, 1916.

14 Joseph O'Connor, BMH WS 142.

15 Lyons, 'Ringsend Area', 10 April 1926.

16 Donnelly, Easter Week, 1916.

17 Lyons, 'Ringsend Area', 10 April 1926.

18 Donnelly, Easter Week, 1916.

19 Joseph O'Connor, BMH WS 142.

20 James Doyle, BMH WS 309.

21 Ibid.

22 Seamus Kavanagh, BMH WS 208.

23 William Christian, BMI WS 646.

24 For the Volunteer Training Corps see PRO WO141/6; account by one of its members, Henry Hanna, Trinity College, Dublin, MS 10066/192. The relatives of those members killed fought a campaign for financial compensation until the government conceded that the men had been killed while on military duty.

25 Ibid.

26 Seamus Kavanagh, BMH WS 208.

27 William Christian, BMI WS 646; James Doyle, BMH WS 309.

28 Ibid.

29 Donnelly, Easter Week, 1916.

30 James Doyle, BMH WS 309.

31 Ibid.

32 Lyons, 'Ringsend Area', 10 April 1926.

33 Ibid.

34 Donnelly, Easter Week, 1916.

35 O'Connor, 'Boland's Mill Area', p. 244.

36 William Christian, BMI WS 646.

37 An unpublished manuscript, the *Memoirs of Brigadier E.W.S.K. Maconchy, 1860–1920*, now in the British Army Museum, London. Hereafter Maconchy, *Memoirs*.

38 Grace, 'I Don't Forget'.

39 Tom Walsh, 'The Epic of Mount Street Bridge', in *Irish Press, Commemoration Supplement* (April 1966).

40 Account by Mrs Ismena Rohde, NLI MS 15415.

41 From a contemporary newspaper account by an English visitor, J.F. Cronin 'Dublin Rebellion: Prestonian's Thrilling Experiences' in McHugh, *Dublin, 1916*, pp. 85–6.

42 Walsh, 'The Epic of Mount Street Bridge'.

43 Maconchy, *Memoirs*.

44 *The Catholic Bulletin* (December 1917).

45 Ibid.

46 Ibid.

47 James and Thomas Walsh, BMH WS 198.

48 Walsh, 'The Epic of Mount Street Bridge'.

49 James and Thomas Walsh, BMH WS 198.

50 These are the official figures but Maconchy, *Memoirs*, gives significantly smaller casualties: five officers dead and twelve wounded, twenty-five other ranks dead and 118 wounded. Whether the discrepancy is due to faulty memory on Maconchy's part is unclear.

51 O'Connor, 'Boland's Mill Area', p. 240.

52 'Easter Week Diary of Miss Lilly Stokes', in McHugh, *Dublin, 1916*, p. 69.

53 Lyons, 'Ringsend Area', 17 April 1926.

54 Donnelly, Easter Week, 1916.

55 Lyons, 'Ringsend Area', 17 April 1926.

56 Seamus Kavanagh, BMH WS 208.

57 O'Connor, 'Boland's Mill Area', p. 249.

58 Joseph O'Byrne, BMH WS 163.

59 Lyons, 'Ringsend Area', 24 April 1926.

60 Joseph O'Byrne, BMH WS 163.

61 Joseph O'Connor, BMH WS 142.

62 Donnelly, Easter Week, 1916.

63 Sam Erwin, Richard Mulcahy Tapes.

64 Ibid.

65 Lyons, 'Ringsend Area', 24 April 1926.

66 Donnelly, Easter Week, 1916.

67 Lyons, 'Ringsend Area', 24 April 1926.

68 Ibid.

69 Donnelly, Easter Week, 1916.

70 Lyons, 'Ringsend Area', 24 April 1926.

71 Ibid.

72 Ibid. For the surrender see also O'Connor, 'Boland's Mill Area', pp. 250–2; Donnelly, Easter Week, 1916.

73 Donnelly, Easter Week, 1916.

74 Lyons, 'Ringsend Area', 24 April 1926.

5 Jacob's Factory and the South Dublin Union

1 Ignatius Callender, 'A Diary of Easter Week', *Dublin Brigade Review*, National Assocation of Old IRA, Dublin, (1939).

2 For the hostile reaction to the occupation of Jacob's see the account by

Michael Walker, a member of E Company, 2nd Battalion, in the Allen Library, Dublin. Hereafter, Walker, Jacob's Factory; Peadar Kearney, 'Reminiscences of Easter Week', in the library of Trinity College, Dublin, MS 3560. Hereafter, Kearney, 'Reminiscences'.

3 Bill Stapleton, BMH WS 822.
4 Ibid.
5 Ibid.
6 Thomas Pugh, BMH WS 397.
7 John MacDonagh, BMH WS 219.
8 See an account of the occupation of Jacob's in Seamas O Maitui, *W&R Jacob: Celebrating 150 Years of Irish Biscuit Making* (Woodfield Press, 2001). This account is available on the website of the National Archives, Dublin.
9 John MacDonagh, BMH WS 219.
10 Seosamh de Brun, BMH WS 312.
11 Ibid.
12 Ibid.
13 'Jacob's and Stephen's Green Area', *The Catholic Bulletin* (September 1918).
14 Kearney, 'Reminiscences'.
15 Ibid.
16 Seosamh de Brun, BMH WS 312.
17 Ibid.
18 Ibid.
19 Kearney, 'Reminiscences'.
20 Oman, Citizen Army.
21 John MacDonagh, BMH WS 219.
22 Ibid.
23 Kearney, 'Reminiscences'.
24 Walker, Jacob's Factory.
25 Kearney, 'Reminiscences'.
26 Shiubhlaigh, *The Splendid Years*, p. 13.
27 Seosamh de Brun, BMH WS 312.
28 Ibid.
29 O Maitui, *W&R Jacob*.
30 Rev. Father Aloysius, OFM Cap., *Memories of Easter Week, 1916*, in the Allen Library, Dublin.
31 Shiubhlaigh, *The Splendid Years*, p. 184.
32 Sean Price, BMH WS 204.
33 Bill Stapleton, BMH WS 822.
34 Ibid.
35 Eamon Price, BMH WS 995.
36 Ibid.
37 Ibid.
38 Ibid.
39 Shiubhlaigh, *The Splendid Years*, p. 184.
40 Min Ryan, BMH WS 399.
41 Ibid.
42 Eamon Price, BMH WS 995.
43 Shiubhlaigh, *The Splendid Years*, p. 184.

44 The first quotation is from Shiubhlaigh, *The Splendid Years*, the second from Walker, Jacob's Factory.
45 Kearney, 'Reminiscences'.
46 Ibid.
47 Ibid.
48 Ibid.
49 Sean Murphy, BMH WS 204.
50 Ibid.; Walker, Jacob's Factory; Padraig O'Ceallaigh, 'Jacob's Factory Area', *Capuchin Annual* (1966), p. 217.
51 Mick McDonnell, BMH WS.
52 Aloysius, Memories of Easter Week.
53 O Maitui, *W&R Jacob*.
54 Ibid.
55 Aloysius, Memories of Easter Week.
56 Walker, Jacob's Factory; Aloysius, Memories of Easter Week.
57 Lily Brennan, Marrowbone Lane, NLI MS 41479/1.
58 Ibid.
59 Aine Ceannt, BMH WS 264.
60 Ronan Ceannt in filmed reminiscence, www.youtube.com.
61 James Coughlan, BMH WS 304.
62 Thomas King Moylan, *A Dubliner's Diary 1914 to 1918*, NLI MS 9620.
63 There is a good description of the topography of the South Dublin Union in Joseph Doolan of A Company, 4th Battalion, NLI MS 10915. Hereafter, Volunteer, South Dublin Union Area; a four-part account in *The Catholic Bulletin* (March–June, 1918).
64 James Coughlan, BMH WS 304.
65 Memoirs of Dan McCarthy, NLI MS 36149.
66 Volunteer, South Dublin Union Area.
67 Volunteer, South Dublin Union Area, p. 211.
68 Peadar Doyle, Reminiscences of Five Year's Service of an Irish Volunteer. Deposited in the Allen Library, Dublin. Hereafter Doyle, Reminiscences.
69 Volunteer, South Dublin Union Area
70 Memoirs of Dan McCarthy, NLI MS 36149.
71 Volunteer, South Dublin Union Area, p. 211.
72 *The Catholic Bulletin* (June 1918); Doyle, Reminiscences.
73 *The Catholic Bulletin* (May 1918); Volunteer, South Dublin Union Area, p. 209.
74 Henry Murray, BMH WS 300.
75 Volunteer, South Dublin Union Area, NLI 41479/1.
76 Joseph Doolan, NLI MA 10905.
77 James Coughlan, BMH WS 304.
78 Volunteer, South Dublin Union Area, NLI MS41479/1.
79 James Coughlan, BMH WS 304.
80 Ibid.
81 Patrick Smyth, BMH WS 552.
82 Sean McGlynn in a statement on 24 May 1936, Ceannt-Brennan papers.
83 James Coughlan, BMH WS 304.
84 Ibid.
85 Ibid.

86   Volunteer, South Dublin Union Area, NLI 41479/1.
87   Ibid.
88   Ibid.
89   James Coughlan, BMH WS 304.
90   Volunteer, South Dublin Union Area, NLI 41479/1.
91   Joseph Doolan, NLI MA 10905.
92   Despite his wounds, Brugha embarked on a political career and played a significant role in the events of 1916 to 1922.
93   Volunteer, South Dublin Union Area, NLI 41479/1.
94   For the surrender process at the South Dublin Union see ibid.; the accounts by Michael J. Kelly and 'L.C.', both in the Ceannt-Brennan papers.
95   James Coughlan, BMH WS 304.
96   Henry Murray, BMH WS 300.
97   Volunteer, South Dublin Union Area, NLI MS 41479/1; Doyle, Reminiscences.
98   Patrick Smyth, BMH WS 552.
99   Volunteer, South Dublin Union Area, NLI 41479/1.
100 Annie Mannion, assistant matron at the South Dublin Union, BMH WS 297.
101 Tommy McCarthy, BMH WS.
102 Patrick Egan, BMH WS 397 has a good description of Roe's layout.
103 Tommy McCarthy, BMH WS.
104 Patrick Egan, BMH WS 397.
105 James Coughlan, BMH WS 304.
106 Tommy McCarthy, BMH WS; J O'Grady, BMH WS.
107 Ibid.
108 Ibid.
109 Patrick Egan, BMH WS 397.
110 Tommy McCarthy, BMH WS.
111 Ibid.
112 Patrick Egan, BMH WS 397.
113 Ibid.
114 Ibid.
115 Lawrence O'Brien, BMH WS.
116 Tommy McCarthy, BMH WS.
117 Volunteer, South Dublin Union Area, NLI MS 41479/1.
118 Robert Holland, Lieutenant, 4th Battalion in an account of the Marrowbone Lane occupation that is deposited in the Allen Library, Dublin. Hereafter, Holland, Marrowbone Lane.
119 Lily Brennan, Marrowbone Lane, NLI MS 41479/1.
120 Ibid.
121 Holland, Marrowbone Lane.
122 Ibid.
123 Ibid.
124 Ibid.
125 Ibid.; Henry Murray, BMH WS 300; Seamus Kenny, BMH WS 158.
126 Holland, Marrowbone Lane.
127 Ibid.
128 Ibid.

129 Ibid.
130 Ibid.
131 Ibid.
132 Seamus Kenny, BMH WS 158.
133 Thomas Doyle, BMH WS 185.
134 Holland, Marrowbone Lane.
135 Lily Brennan, Marrowbone Lane, NLI MS 41479/1.
136 Seamus Kenny, BMH WS 158.
137 Lily Brennan, Marrowbone Lane, NLI MS 41479/1.
138 Annie O'Brien, BMH WS 805.
139 Lily Brennan, Marrowbone Lane, NLI MS 41479/1.
140 Henry Murray, BMH WS 300.
141 Lily Brennan, Marrowbone Lane, NLI MS 41479/1.
142 Ibid.
143 Henry Murray, BMH WS 300.
144 Holland, Marrowbone Lane.
145 Ibid.
146 Annie O'Brien, BMH WS 805.
147 Holland, Marrowbone Lane.
148 Ibid.
149 Ibid.
150 Annie O'Brien, BMH WS 805.
151 Holland, Marrowbone Lane.

6 The Four Courts and the Mendicity Institution

1 John J. Reynolds, 'The Four Courts and North King Street Area in 1916', *An tOglac*, 15 May, 22 May and 29 May 1926.
2 *Pictorial Review of 1916: An Historically Accurate Account of Events which occurred in Easter Week* (Parkgate Press, Dublin, 1966), p. 30.
3 Anon., A Company, 1st Battalion, Irish Republican Army, Historical sketch of the unit during the years 1913–1916, 1917–1923, in the Allen Library, Dublin. Hereafter Anon., A Company; *History of A Company*, Archives Department, University College, Dublin LA 9; Seamus O'Sullivan, BMH WS 393.
4 Patrick Stephenson, 'The Epic of the Mendicity', Allen Library, Dublin. For brief account of Daly's life, see Barton, *The Secret Court Martial Records*, pp. 160–71.
5 Jerry Golden, BMH WS 521.
6 Seamus O'Sullivan, BMH WS 393; Ignatius Callender, BMH WS 923; Piaras Beaslai, 'Edward Daly's Command, Easter Week, 1916', in McCarthy, *Limerick's Fighting Story*, pp. 139–46; T.P. Kilfeather, 'Commandant Edward Daly', in McCarthy, *Limerick's Fighting Story*, pp. 137–9.
7 Piaras Beaslai, BMH WS 261.
8 Beaslai, 'Edward Daly's Command', in McCarthy, *Limerick's Fighting Story*, pp. 139–41; Patrick Holohan, 'The Four Courts Area', in *Capuchin Annual* (1966), pp. 181–3; references to Daly in a book by his sister, Kathleen Clarke, *Revolutionary Woman*; Thomas Smart, BMH WS 255; Sean Prendergast, BMH WS 755; Seamus O'Sullivan, BMH WS 393.

9   Stephenson, 'Epic of the Mendicity'; Richard Balfe, BMH WS 251; Michael
     Heuston, BMH CD 309/1,2. For brief account of Heuston's life, see Barton,
     The Secret Court Martial Records, pp. 241-61.
10 Stephenson, 'Epic of the Mendicity'.
11 Ibid., Sean McLoughlin, BMH WS 290.
12 D.A. Chart, *The Story of Dublin* (Dent, London, 1907), p. 272; James J.
     Brennan, 'The Mendicity Institution Area', *Capuchin Annual* (1966), pp.
     189–90.
13 Stephenson, 'Epic of the Mendicity'.
14 Sean McLoughlin, BMH WS 290.
15 Account by A.C. Hannant, IWM 7500 75/92/1; Ignatius Callender, BMH
     WS 923; Sean O'Sullivan, BMH WS 393; Sean Kennedy, BMH WS 842.
16 Diary of John Clarke, NLI MS 10485. Hereafter Clarke, Diary; account by A.
     Hannant; for Heuston, see NLI MS 15382 and 10076; Matt Connolly, 'Dublin
     City Hall Area', in *Capuchin Annual* (1966), p. 196; Sean Kennedy, BMH WS
     842; Michael O'Flanagan, BMH WS 800.
17 Reynolds, 'The Four Courts'; Clarke, Diary; Anon., A Company.
18 John Shouldice, BMH WS 162; Nicholas Laffan, BMH WS 251.
19 See description in *Irish Times*, 5 May 1916.
20 Aine Heron, BMH WS 293; Pauline Keating, BMH WS 432; Phyllis Morkan,
     BMH WS 210; Eilis Ui Chonaill, BMH WS 568.
21 Stephenson, 'Epic of the Mendicity'.
22 Heuston court-martial, evidence by officers from Royal Dublin Fusiliers, in
     PRO WO71/351; Brennan, 'Mendicity Institution Area'; John M. Heuston
     OP, *Headquarters Battalion, Easter Week, 1916* (Nationalist Printers, Carlow,
     1966), passim.
23 Stephenson, 'Epic of the Mendicity'; Richard Balfe, BMH WS 251.
24 Stephenson, 'Epic of the Mendicity'.
25 Ibid.; Heuston's court martial records in NA WO 71/351.
26 Father Augustine, BMH WS 920; Sean Prendergast, BMH WS 755; Sean
     Kennedy, BMH WS 842; diary of Patrick Francis O'Neill, *An Cosantoir*,
     April–May 2006, pp. 31–2; *War History of the 6th Battalion South Staffordshire
     Regiment* (Heinemann, London, 1921), p. 149; Reynolds, 'The Four Courts';
     Holohan, 'Four Courts Area', p. 183.
27 Nicholas Laffan, BMH WS 251; Liam Archer, 'Events at Easter Week, 1916',
     Mulcahy Papers, Archives Department, University College, Dublin, P7/D/23;
     'A Letter by Professor George O'Neill, SJ, Easter Tuesday, April 25 1916', in
     McHugh, *Dublin, 1916*, pp. 184–5.
28 Father Augustine, BMH WS 920.
29 Aine Heron, BMH WS 293; Eilis Ui Chonaill, BMH WSD 568; Sean
     Prendergast, BMH WS 755; Liam Archer, BMH WS 819; John Shouldice,
     BMH WS 162; Pauline Keating, BMH WS 432.
30 Clarke, Diary.
31 Beaslai, 'Edward Daly's Command', in McCarthy, *Limerick's Fighting Story*, p.
     147; Liam Archer, BMH WS 819; John Shouldice, BMH WS 162.
32 See account by Paddy Holohan in NLI MS 10915.
33 Ibid.; Reynolds, 'The Four Courts'; military situation reports for 25/26 April
     in PRO WO35/69; Clarke, *A Penny in the Clouds*, p. 34.

34 John Shouldice, BMH WS 162; Thomas Smart, BMH WS 255; Sean O'Sullivan, BMH WS 393.

35 Ignatius Callender, BMH WS 923.

36 Sean Coady, 'Remembering St John's Convent', *Capuchin Annual* (1966), p. 279.

37 Richard Balfe, BMH WS 251.

38 Stephenson, 'Epic of the Mendicity'.

39 Sean McLoughlin, BMH WS 290; James Crenigan, BMH WS 148; Brennan, 'Mendicity Institution Area', pp. 190–1; notes made by Heuston, used in evidence in court-martial, PRO WO71/351.

40 Evidence given by Lieutenant A.P. Lindsay at Daly's court-martial, in PRO WO71/344.

41 Brighid Thornton quoted in K. Griffith and E. O'Grady (eds), *Curious Journey, an Oral History of Ireland's Unfinished Revolution* (Hutchinson, London, 1982), p. 70.

42 Reynolds, 'The Four Courts'; Holohan, 'Four Courts Area', pp. 184–5.

43 Reynolds, 'The Four Courts'.

44 Sean Prendergast, BMH WS 755; MacLochlainn, *Last Words*, p. 181.

45 Lord E.M.D.P. Dunsany, *Patches of Sunlight* (W. Heinemann, London), p. 279.

46 Quoted in *Pictorial Review of 1916*, p. 32.

47 Lindsay stated in his court-martial evidence that Daly told him that he 'intended to make a counter-attack as the position was hopeless … he said he could not surrender without orders from his superiors', PRO WO71/344.

48 Liam Archer, BMH WS 819; Ignatius Callender, BMH WS 923; Sean Prendergast, BMH WS 755.

49 Ignatius Callender, BMH WS 923.

50 Ibid.

51 Stephenson, 'Epic of the Mendicity'.

52 Archer, 'Events at Easter Week'.

53 Daly, Irish Volunteers.

54 See description given to police, May 1916, by Lieutenant Mills, PRO WO35/69.

55 Michael Heuston, BMH WS 309.

56 Sean McLoughlin, BMH WS 2990; Stephenson, 'Epic of the Mendicity'; Richard Balfe, BMH WS 251.

57 Brennan, 'Mendicity Institution Area'.

58 Ibid.; evidence of prosecution witnesses, PRO WO71/351.

59 Michael Heuston, BMH CD 309/1, 2.

60 Ibid.; Brennan, 'Mendicity Institution Area'.

61 Ibid.; James Crenigan, BMH WS 148. Apart from Heuston, Peter Wilson was the only insurgent fatality at the Mendicity Institution, see Bateson, *They Died by Pearse's Side,* pp. 109–115.

62 Stephenson, 'Epic of the Mendicity'.

63 Brennan, 'Mendicity Institution Area'.

64 Sean McLoughlin, BMH WS 290.

65 McLoughlin made his way to the GPO where his exploits are described in Chapter 7.

66 Christine O'Gorman, 29 May 1929, list of those who 'received first aid in Father Mathew Hall', 26–9 April, NAI D/T S6023; Beaslai, 'Edward Daly's Command', in McCarthy, *Limerick's Fighting Story*, p. 143.

67 See the eye-witness account by John J. O'Leary published by the *Dublin Saturday Post* after the Rising in a composite edition for 29 April, 6 May and 13 May 1916.

68 Clarke, Diary.

69 Message from Jervis Street Hospital to Nathan, 11.25 a.m., 28 April, in the Nathan Papers, MS 476; list of casualties in Dublin hospitals during Easter Week, 29 May 1916, by Sergeant Michael Mannion in PRO WO35/69.

70 Eilis Ui Chonail, 'A Cumann na mBan recalls Easter Week', in *Capuchin Annual* (1966), pp. 271–8; comments by Thornton in Griffith and O'Grady, *Curious Journey*, passim.

71 Ignatius Callender, BMH WS 923; McLoughlin, BMH WS 290.

72 Father Augustine, BMH WS 920; Thomas Smart, BMH WS 255; Sean Kennedy, BMH WS 842. Thomas Allen was the only insurgent fatality at the Four Courts. Ten died in the course of the fighting in the Church Street garrison area during Easter Week, see Bateson, *They Died by Pearse's Side*, pp. 84–108.

73 Con O'Donovan, BMH WS 1750.

74 G.I. Edmunds, *2/6 Battalion, Sherwood Foresters, 1914–18: its Part in the Defeat of the Irish Rebellion, 1916* (Wilfred Edmonds, Chesterfield, 1960); Reynolds, 'The Four Courts'.

75 Father Augustine, BMH WS 920.

76 Reynolds, 'The Four Courts'.

77 Ibid.

78 Account by A. Hannant, IWM; Edmunds, *2/6 Battalion, Sherwood Foresters*.

79 Sean Prendergast, BMH WS 755; Thomas Smart, BMH WS 251.

80 *1916 Rebellion Handbook*, introduction by Declan Kiberd (Mourne River Press, Dublin, 1998), p. 25.

81 *History of the 6th South Staffs*, pp. 149–50.

82 Ibid.; Holohan, 'Four Courts Area', p. 185.

83 Ibid.; Reynolds, 'The Four Courts'.

84 Ibid.

85 John Shouldice, BMH WS 162; Michael O'Flanagan, BMH WS 800.

86 Ibid.

87 Reynolds, 'The Four Courts'; *History of A Company*, Dublin LA 9.

88 Ibid.; Report of telephone call at 10.10 a.m., 28 April, in Nathan Papers, MS 476.

89 Bridget Thornton, BMH WS 259; Father Augustine, BMH WS 920.

90 O'Gorman, list of casualties at Father Mathew Hall, in NAI D/T S6023; account by D. Coffey, NLI MS 21193.

91 Heuston court martial records, NA WO 71/345; Daly told Lindsay he 'did not expect anyone who took part ... would come back alive ... The object was to save the lives of as many people as possible in the building', PRO WO71/344; Reynolds, 'The Four Courts'.

92 Beaslai, *Irish Independent*, 20 January 1953.

93 Ibid.

94 Ibid.

95 Ibid.; O'Farrell, 'The Surrender', in McHugh, *Dublin, 1916*, p. 211; account of final action and surrender also in Major H. de Courcy Wheeler, NLI MS 15000.

96 Ibid.

97 Michael O'Flanagan, BMH WS 800.

98 Beaslai, *Irish Independent*, 20 January 1953.

99 Ibid.

100 Ibid.

101 Ibid.

102 John Shouldice, BMH WS 162; Michael O'Flanagan, BMH WS 800; Thomas Smart, BMH WS 255; Sean Prendergast, BMH WS 755.

103 Thomas Smart, BMH WS 255.

104 Thornton in Griffith and O'Grady, *Curious Journey*, p. 75.

104 Beaslai, *Irish Independent*, 20 January 1953; Beaslai, 'Edward Daly's Command', in McCarthy, *Limerick's Fighting Story* p. 146.

105 Beaslai, *Irish Independent*, 20 January 1953.

106 Ibid.

107 Beaslai, 'Edward Daly's Command' in McCarthy, *Limerick's Fighting Story*, p. 146.

108 Beaslai, *Irish Independent*, 20 January 1953.

109 Holohan, 'Four Courts Area', pp. 187–8; Coady, 'St John's Convent', p. 279. See graphic accounts of the surrender in this area in Sean Duffy, BMH WS 618; Nicholas Laffan, BMH WS 251.

110 *History of 6th South Staffs*, pp. 151–2; Ui Chonail, 'A Cumann na mBan recalls', pp. 275–6.

111 Major-General P.J. Hally, 'The Easter Rising in Dublin; the Military Aspect, Part I', *The Irish Sword*, Vol. 7, (1966), p. 324.

7 The General Post Office

1 Dudley Edwards, *Patrick Pearse*, pp. 277 & 359.

2 Lynch, 'Report of Operations', *The IRB*, p. 157.

3 W.J. Brennan-Whitmore, *Dublin Burning* (Gill and Macmillan, Dublin, 1996), p. 37.

4 Lynch, 'Report of Operations', *The IRB*, p. 157.

5 From a diary of events in the GPO which was reconstructed during his subsequent internment by Dick Humphries, NLI MS 18829. Hereafter, Humphries, GPO Diary.

6 Mr Norway in Jeffery, *The GPO and the Easter Rising*, p. 45.

7 Michael Staines, BMH WS 284.

8 Catherine Byrne, BMH WS 848.

9 Michael Staines, BMH WS 284; M.W. Reilly, 'The Defence of the GPO', *An tOglac*, (23 January 1926).

10 Michael Staines, BMH WS 284.

11 For a good account of the Proclamation see Liam de Paor, *On the Easter Proclamation and other Declarations* (Four Courts Press, Dublin, 1997).

12 Corporal Liam Byrne, 'Wireless and 1916', *An Cosantoir* (April 1991).

13 For the fighting at Hopkins & Hopkins see Cormac Turner, 'The Defence of Messrs Hopkins and Hopkins, O'Connell Street, Dublin', in *An tOglac*, (5 June 1926). For the fighting at Kelly's see Bracken, Easter Week, 1916.

14 Bracken, Easter Week.

15 Liam Ó Briain, *Ciumhni Cinn*, Sairseal agus Dill, (Dublin, 1974), pp. 70 & 73.

16 Father Eugene Nevin, WS 1605.

17 Tierney, *Eoin MacNeill*, p. 220.

18 Lynch, Recollections and Comments on the IRB.

19 Humphries, GPO Diary.

20 Frank Thornton in the Humphries Papers, Archives Department, University College, Dublin, P67/45.

21 Tannam, BMH WS 242.

22 Ibid.

23 BMH WS 497.

24 Michael Staines, BMH WS 284.

25 Sean T. O'Kelly, Easter Week experiences, *Irish Press*, (6–9 August 1961).

26 Joe Good, *Enchanted by Dreams: The Journals of a Revolutionary* (Brandon Books, Dingle, 1996).

27 Brennan-Whitmore, *Dublin Burning*, pp. 52–3.

28 Good, *Enchanted by Dreams*, p. 30.

29 Martin Conlon WS.

30 O'Kelly, Easter Week Experiences.

31 NLI MS 13170.

32 Humphries, GPO Diary.

33 Michael Staines, BMH WS 284; Reilly, 'The Defence of the GPO'.

34 Joe Sweeney in a deposition made in 1934 describing his experiences in the GPO, Personal Narratives of the Rising of 1916, NLI MS 10915.

35 Michael Staines, BMH WS 284; Reilly, 'The Defence of the GPO'.

36 Thornton, statement of Easter Rising experiences.

37 For the occupation of the Metropole Hotel see Commandant Charles Saurin, 'Hotel Metropole Garrison', *An tOglac*, (13 & 20 March 1926).

38 Traynor, Biographical Account.

39 Bracken, Easter Week.

40 Ibid.

41 Humphries, GPO Diary.

42 Bracken, Easter Week.

43 Humphries, GPO Diary.

44 Traynor, Biographical Account.

45 Ibid.

46 Humphries, GPO Diary.

47 Michael Staines, BMH WS 284; Reilly, 'The Defence of the GPO'.

48 Ryan, 'General Post Office Area'.

49 Ibid.

50 Fitzgerald, *Memoirs*, p. 148.

51 Lynch, 'Report of Operations', *The IRB*, p. 172.

52 O'Rahilly, *Winding the Clock*, p. 215.

53 Michael Staines, BMH WS 284; Reilly, 'The Defence of the GPO'.

54 Thornton, statement of Easter Rising experiences.

55   Saurin, 'Hotel Metropole Garrison'.
56   Good, *Enchanted by Dreams*, p. 45.
57   Humphries, GPO Diary.
58   Molly Reynolds, BMH WS 195.
59   Good, *Enchanted by Dreams*, p. 50.
60   Humphries, GPO Diary.
61   Ibid.
62   Commandant P. Colgan, 'Maynooth Volunteers and 1916', *An tOglac*, (8 May 1926).
63   Humphries, GPO Diary.
64   Ibid.
65   Saurin, 'Hotel Metropole Garrison'.
66   Humphries, GPO Diary.
67   Traynor, Biographical Account.
68   Humphries, GPO Diary.
69   Michael Staines, BM HWS 284; Reilly, 'The Defence of the GPO'.
70   Humphries, GPO Diary.
71   Ibid.
72   Sean MacEntee, *Episode at Easter* (Gill and Macmillan, Dublin, 1966), p. 157.
73   Joyce, 'The Story of Limerick and Kerry', p. 362.
74   Traynor, Biographical Account.
75   MacEntee, *Episode at Easter*, p. 154.
76   Traynor, Biographical Account; Saurin, 'Hotel Metropole Garrison'.
77   Ryan, 'General Post Office Area'.
78   Lynch, 'Report of Operations', *The IRB*, p. 175.
79   McLoughlin, BMH WS 290.
80   Good, *Enchanted by Dreams*, p. 50.
81   Joyce, 'The Story of Limerick and Kerry', p. 363.
82   Thornton, statement of Easter Rising experiences.
83   Humphries, GPO Diary.
84   Accounts by Jack Plunkett of events 1914–22, NLI MS 11397.
85   MacEntee, *Episode at Easter*, p. 158.
86   Ibid.
87   Thomas Devine, BMH WS 428.
88   McLoughlin, BMH WS 290.
89   Good, *Enchanted by Dreams*, p. 53.
90   Lynch, 'Report of Operations', *The IRB*, p. 175.
91   McLoughlin, BMH WS 290.
92   Lynch, 'Report of Operations', *The IRB*, p. 175.
93   McLoughlin, BMH WS 290.
94   Tannam, BMH WS 242.
95   Eamon Bulfin, BMH WS497.
96   O'Rahilly, *Winding the Clock*, p. 220.
97   Sean MacEntee, 'Easter Week in the GPO', *The Irish Digest* (May 1944).
98   Devine, BMH WS 428.
99   Ibid.
100 Ibid.
101 Lynch, Roll of Honour, Florence O'Donoghue Papers, NLI MS 31409.

102 Michael Staines, BMH WS 284; Reilly, 'The Defence of the GPO'.

103 Liam Tannam, BMH WS 242.

104 Ibid.

105 Michael Staines, BMH WS 284; Reilly, 'The Defence of the GPO'.

106 Lynch, 'Report of Operations', *The IRB*, p. 179.

107 McLoughlin, BMH WS 290.

108 Eamon Bulfin, BMH WS497.

109 McLoughlin, BMH WS 290.

110 Ibid.

111 Charles Saurin, BMH WS 288.

112 Liam Tannam, BMH WS 242.

113 Michael Staines, BMH WS 284.

114 Seamus Scully, 'Moore Street 1916'.

115 Bracken, Easter Week.

116 Good, *Enchanted by Dreams*, pp. 53–4.

117 Scully, 'Moore Street 1916'.

118 O'Farrell, 'The Surrender'.

119 McLoughlin, BMH WS 290.

120 Lynch, BMH WS 4.

121 Traynor, Biographical Account.

122 Seamus Scully, 'Moore Street'.

123 Charles Saurin, BMH WS 288.

124 Eamon Bulfin, BMH WS 497.

125 Traynor, Biographical Account.

126 Charles Saurin, BMH WS 288.

127 McLoughlin, BMH WS 290.

128 Ibid.

129 Ibid.

130 Ibid.

131 Seamus Scully, 'Moore Street'.

132 Good, *Enchanted by Dreams*, p. 64; Clarke later told his wife that he alone had voted against surrender, Clarke, *Revolutionary Woman*, p. 93.

133 Ryan, 'The General Post Office Area'.

134 Traynor, Biographical Account.

135 Nurse Julia Grenan, 'Story of the Surrender', *The Catholic Bulletin* (June 1917).

136 O'Farrell, 'The Surrender'.

137 R.M. Fox, *Green Banners: The Story of the Irish Struggle* (London, 1938), p. 296.

138 O'Farrell, 'The Surrender'.

139 For Connolly's surrender see Tannam, BMH WS 242; Michael Staines, BMH WS 284; Diarmuid Lynch, BMH WS 4.

140 Tannam, BMH WS 242.

141 Plunkett, Events 1914–22.

142 Ryan, 'The General Post Office Area'.

143 Good, *Enchanted by Dreams*, p. 66.

144 Plunkett, Events 1914–22.

145 Charles Saurin, BMH WS 288.

146 Eamon Bulfin, BMH WS 497.

147 Charles Saurin, BMH WS 288.

148 Patrick Caldwell, BMH WS 638.
149 Charles Saurin, BMH WS 288.
150 Beaslai, *Irish Independent*, 20 January 1953.
151 McLoughlin, BMH WS 290.
152 Frank Henderson, BMH WS 249.
153 Volunteer Joseph Sweeney in Griffith and O'Grady, *Curious Journey*, p. 79.
154 Grenan, 'Story of the Surrender'.
155 Charles Saurin, BMH WS 288.
156 Ibid.
157 Ibid.
158 Grenan, 'Story of the Surrender'.

8 A City at War

1 O'Daly, 'The Women of Easter Week'.
2 Lyons, 'Ringsend Area'.
3 Donnelly, Easter Week, 1916.
4 *History of A Company*, Dublin LA 9.
5 Douglas Hyde, Diary of Easter Week.
6 Stephenson, 'Epic of the Mendicity'.
7 For Peadar Healy see Holohan, 'Four Courts Area'; Christina Doyle Collection, NLI MS 5816–17.
8 Papers of Reverend Patrick J. Doyle, P.P., NLI MS 13561(12).
9 Ó Briain, 'Stephen's Green Area'.
10 Captain E. Gerrard, BMH WS 348.
11 *History of the 6th South Staffs*, p. 145.
12 Good, *Enchanted by Dreams*, p. 30.
13 Ó Briain, 'Stephen's Green Area'.
14 Holohan, 'Four Courts Area'.
15 Walsh, 'The Epic of Mount Street Bridge'.
16 Good, *Enchanted by Dreams*, p. 31.
17 Griffith and O'Grady, *Curious Journey*, pp. 58–9.
18 Lieutenant Jameson's letters to his family have been presented to the Imperial War Museum, London.
19 For Begley's desertion see O'Connor, 'Boland's Mill Area'. For MacCarthy see Holland, Marrowbone Lane.
20 Donnelly, Easter Week, 1916.
21 Jameson, Letters.
22 A memoir by Patrick Rankin of his participation in the occupation of the GPO, NLI MS 22251.
23 The pleas of the two young Volunteers, Byrne and Rowe, to be allowed to remain were rejected by Malone, in Grace, 'I Don't Forget'.
24 Lyons, 'Ringsend Area'.
25 Frances Downey, diary for 22–7 April 1916, Trinity College, Dublin, MS 10066/193. Hereafter, Downey, Diary.
26 Griffith and O'Grady, *Curious Journey*, p. 57.
27 William Christian, BMH 646.
28 Andrew MacDonnell, BMH WS.

29 Sean Harling, BMH WS.
30 Jameson, Letters.
31 Ibid.
32 Jimmy O'Shea, BMH WS 733.
33 Robbins, NLI MS 10915; Robbins, *Under the Starry Plough*, pp. 111–2.
34 Archer, Events.
35 Fintan Murphy, BMH WS 370.
36 Saurin, 'Hotel Metropole Garrison'.
37 Connolly, 'Dublin City Hall Area'.
38 Liam Tannam, BMH WS 242.
39 Ibid.
40 *The Catholic Bulletin* (September 1916).
41 Griffith and O'Grady, *Curious Journey*, p. 79.
42 Holland, Marrowbone Lane.
43 Douglas Hyde, Diary of Easter Week.
44 A Sister of Mercy at the Mater Hospital, BMH WS 463.
45 O' Daly, 'The Women of Easter Week'.
46 O'Gorman, list of those who 'received first aid in Father Mathew Hall' in Easter Week, NAI D/T S6023.
47 Connolly, 'Dublin City Hall Area'.
48 Michael O'Flanagan, BMH WS 800.
49 Ó Briain, 'Stephen's Green Area'.
50 Good, *Enchanted by Dreams*, p. 44.
51 Rose Hackett, BMH WS 546.
52 Griffith and O'Grady, *Curious Journey*, p. 66.
53 Liam Tannam, BMH WS 242.
54 Traynor, Biographical Account.
55 Charles Saurin, BMH WS.
56 Harry Colley, BMH WS 1687.
57 Good, *Enchanted by Dreams*, pp. 58–9; Saurin, 'Hotel Metropole Garrison'; Traynor, Biographical Account.
58 Good, *Enchanted by Dreams*, pp. 39–40.
59 Clarke, *A Penny in the Clouds*, pp. 34–5.
60 Ó Briain, 'Stephen's Green Area'.
61 Walsh, 'The Epic of Mount Street Bridge'.
62 Account by James A. Glen, Trinity College, Dublin, MS 4456. In 1966 Nelson's Pillar was bombed and partially demolished by republicans, because of safety fears the demolition was completed by army engineers.
63 For the different flags see Lynch, NLI MS 31409.
64 Sweeney, Personal Narratives of the Rising.
65 Humphries, GPO Diary; Fitzgerald, *Memoirs*, p. 134.
66 Stephenson, 'Epic of the Mendicity'.
67 Sweeney, Personal Narratives of the Rising.
68 Jameson, Letters. Jameson was to find out for himself the conditions on the Western Front where he was transferred soon after the Easter Rising. He was killed in the summer of 1916.
69 Good, *Enchanted by Dreams*, pp. 42–3.
70 Beaslai, *Irish Independent*, 20 January 1953.

71 Douglas Hyde, Diary of Easter Week; Ó Briain, 'Stephen's Green Area'.

72 The ruse is described in Lyons, 'Ringsend Area'; Donnelly, Easter Week, 1916.

73 Turner, 'Hopkins and Hopkins'.

74 O Maitui, *W&R Jacob.*

75 Seamus Pounch, BMH WS 288.

76 Seosamh de Brun, BMH WS 312.

77 Patrick Egan, BMHWS 397.

78 Andrew MacDonnell, BMH WS.

79 Nathan Papers, MS 477.

80 Lord Dunsany, 'Recollections of 1916', *Irish Digest* (April 1939).

81 Holohan, 'Four Courts Area', p. 184; Griffith and O'Grady, *Curious Journey*, p. 70.

82 Min Ryan, BMH WS 399.

83 Ibid.

84 O'Rahilly, *Winding the Clock*, p. 214.

85 *Irish Times*, 9 May 1916.

86 Dunsany, 'Recollections of 1916'.

87 Holohan, 'Four Courts Area'.

88 O'Rahilly, *Winding the Clock*, p. 213.

89 William Christian, BMH WS 646.

90 Patrick Kelly, BMH WS 781.

91 Nathan Papers, MS 477.

92 File on unarmed victims, PRO WO 35/69.

93 Father Flanagan, 'The General Post Office Area', *Catholic Bulletin* (August 1918).

94 Lyons, 'Ringsend Area'.

95 Lynch, 'Report on Operations', *The IRB*, pp. 178–9.

96 Rankin, GPO. For the bag of ammunition left in Lansdowne Road see Denis Johnston, Diary of his experiences during the Easter Rising, Trinity College, Dublin, MS 10066/179.

97 Maconchy, *Memoirs.*

98 Elsie Mahaffy, Diary, Trinity College, Dublin, MS 2074.

99 Jameson, Letters.

100 Mrs A.H. Norway, *The Sinn Fein Rebellion as I saw it* (Smith, Elder, London, 1916) p. 48.

101 Catherine Byrne, BMH WS 848.

102 Douglas Hyde, Diary of Easter Week.

103 Kearney, 'Reminiscences'.

104 Stephenson, 'Epic of the Mendicity'.

105 Ibid.

106 Johnston, Diary.

107 Douglas Hyde, Diary of Easter Week.

108 Charles Saurin, BMH WS 288.

109 Walsh, 'The Epic of Mount Street Bridge'.

110 Coffey, Diary, NLI MS 21193.

111 Catherine Byrne, BMH WS 848.

112 Stephenson, 'Epic of the Mendicity'.

113 Douglas Hyde, Diary of Easter Week.

114 Stephenson, 'Epic of the Mendicity'.

115 Douglas Hyde, Diary of Easter Week.

116 Mrs Salkey's 1916 Journal, NLI, MS 44622.

117 Douglas Hyde, Diary of Easter Week.

118 Matthew Connolly, BMH WS 1746.

119 Joseph O'Connor, BMH WS 157.

120 Sean Kennedy, BMH WS 842.

121 NLI MS 31710.

122 Douglas Hyde, Diary of Easter Week.

123 William O'Brien, BMH 1766.

124 Ibid.

125 Douglas Hyde, Diary of Easter Week.

126 Ibid.

127 Griffith and O'Grady, *Curious Journey*, p. 72.

128 Clarke, *A Penny in the Clouds*, p. 33.

129 Humphries, GPO Diary.

130 Walter Starkie, *Scholars and Gypsies* (John Murray, London, 1963), p. 148. In 1916 Starkie was a student at Trinity College, Dublin, where he subsequently became Professor of Spanish.

131 E.U. Bradbridge, *The 59th Division 1915–1918* (Wilfred Edmunds, Chesterfield, 1928), p. 37.

132 Lieutenant-Colonel W.C. Oates, *The Sherwood Foresters in the Great War 1914–1919* (T. Forman and Sons, Nottingham, 1920), p. 42.

133 NLI MS 24952.

134 Diary of Mrs Augustine Henry (she was married to a British army officer) for the period October 1915 to June 1916, NLI MS 7984.

135 Captain E. Gerrard, BMH WS 348.

136 Douglas Hyde, Diary of Easter Week, 24 April 1916.

137 File on unarmed victims, PRO WO35/69.

138 Ibid.

139 Ibid.

140 Andrew MacDonnell, BMH WS.

141 David Fitzgerald, National Archives, Dublin.

142 Arthur Mitchell, BMH WS.

143 Downey, Diary, April 1916.

144 Nathan Papers, MS 477.

145 Brennan, 'Mendicity Institution Area', p. 191.

146 Nathan Papers, MS 476.

147 Henry, Diary.

148 Griffith and O'Grady, *Curious Journey*, p. 66.

149 Robert Hogan and Michael O'Neill, *Joseph Holloway's Irish Theatre* (Dixon, California, 1967), p. 182.

150 Jameson, Letters.

151 Nathan Papers, MS 476.

152 Reynolds, *A Fragment of 1916 History*, pp. 7–8.

153 Ibid., pp. 26–7.

154 PRO WO35/67/3.

155 Edmunds, *2/6 Battalion, Sherwood Foresters, 1914–18*, p. 45.

156   Sir Edward Troup, Undated memorandum (*c.* May 1916), PRO WO 141/21.
157   Maxwell to his wife Louise, 18 May 1916, Sir John Maxwell Papers, CO583, Princeton University Library, Box 6/9.
158   Maxwell in an undated letter to Kitchener, Maxwell Papers, Box 30/107.
159   PRO WO904/215.
160   File on the Sheehy-Skeffington affair, PRO WO30/67.
161   Ibid.
162   Ibid.
163   Ibid.
164   Ibid.
165   4 June 1916, Maxwell Papers.
166   File on the Sheehy-Skeffington affair, PRO WO30/67.
167   Ibid.
168   Ibid.
169   Rose McNamara, BMH WS 482; Seamus Kenny, BMH WS 158.
170   Jimmy O'Shea, BMH WS 733.
171   William Whelan, BMH WS 369.
172   NLI MS 15415.
173   Account by Nellie O'Brien of her experiences during Easter Week, Trinity College, Dublin, MS 10343/1.
174   Michael Kent, Diary, NLI MS 15292.
175   Jeffery, *The GPO and the Easter Rising*, p. 137.
176   Fox, *The History of the Irish Citizen Army*, pp. 172–4.
177   Gaughan, *Thomas Johnson*, p. 48 – the book contains Johnson's diary of Easter Week.
178   Starkie, *Scholars and Gypsies*, p. 144.
179   Ibid.
180   Good, *Enchanted by Dreams*, p. 35.
181   Seamus Scully, Moore Street, 1916. NLI.
182   NLI MS 31710.
183   Eamon Bulfin, BMH WS 497.
184   Stopford, Diary.
185   Henry, Diary.
186   Ibid.
187   Lyons, 'Ringsend Area'.
188   *Irish Times*, 9 May 1916.
189   For the various measures to alleviate the food shortage see Nathan Papers, MS 476; *Irish Times*, 2 May 1916; record of the activities of the Society of St Vincent de Paul, NLI MS 13737.
190   NLI MS 24952.
191   Ibid.
192   Lyons, 'Ringsend Area'.
193   O'Leary, *Dublin Saturday Post* (compendium for 29 April, 6 and 13 May).
194   Ibid.
195   Aloysius, Memories of Easter Week.
196   Flanagan, 'The General Post Office Area'. All the quotations in the subsequent account of Flanagan's experiences are from this source.
197   Mrs A. Mitchell, NLI MS 24553.

198 Henry, Diary.
199 Lieutenant A.A. Luce, 12th Royal Irish Rifles, Recollections of Easter 1916, Trinity College, Dublin, MS 4874.
200 Major H.E. de Courcy Wheeler, Army Field Message Book, recording of events connected with the surrender of the insurgents in Dublin, 29 April to 1 May 1916, NLI microfilm, n5670, p5892.
201 Rankin, GPO.
202 Holland, Marrowbone Lane.
203 Kent, Diary.
204 Robbins, *Under the Starry Plough*, p. 127.
205 Doyle, description of the South Dublin Union.
206 De Courcy Wheeler, Army Field Message Book.
207 Lyons, 'Ringsend Area'.
208 Thornton in Griffith and O'Grady, *Curious Journey*, p. 77; Sergeant Michael Mannion 'list of persons killed or wounded' brought to Dublin hospitals, 29 May 1916, PRO WO 35/69.
209 Griffith and O'Grady, *Curious Journey*, pp. 69–70.
210 Sean Kennedy, BMH WS 842.
211 Con O'Donovan, BMH WS 1750; Nicholas Laffin, BMH WS 251.
212 Stephenson, 'Epic of the Mendicity'.
213 Griffith and O'Grady, *Curious Journey*, pp. 69–70.
214 Pauline Keating, BMH WS 432.
215 Archer, Events.
216 Account by J.W. Rowarth, IWM 80/40/1; Christine O'Gorman, list of those who 'received first aid in Father Mathew Hall' in Easter Week, 29 May 1929, refers to three arrested as spies, NAI SD/T S6023. The police recorded growing militancy in the North King Street area for two to three months before the Rising, see the report by Major-General Sandbach, 25 May 1916, in PRO WO35/67.
217 Archer, Events; statement by Hannant on the experience of the lancers in IWM.
218 Nathan Papers, MS 467.
219 Archer, Events; Ui Chonaill, 'A Cumann na mBan recalls', p. 276.
220 John Shouldice, BMH WS.
221 Clarke, Diary.
222 Liam Archer, BMH WS 819.
223 John Shouldice, BMH WS 162.
224 Coady, 'St John's Convent', p. 279; Adrian and Sally Warwick-Haller, *Letters from Dublin, Easter 1916: Alfred Fannin's Diary of the Rising* (Irish Academic Press, Blackrock, 1995), pp. 32–3.
225 Archer, Events.
226 Clarke, Diary.
227 Ibid.
228 Mahaffy, Diary.
229 Ibid.
230 Mrs Salkey's 1916 Journal, NLI, MS 44622.
231 Birrell to Nathan, 3 May 1916, Nathan Papers, MS 477.
232 Daly, Irish Volunteers.

233 Jameson, Letters.

234 Stopford, Diary.

235 O'Leary, *Dublin Saturday Post*.

236 Ibid.

237 Report of a meeting between the Home Secretary and a Dublin deputation headed by the Lord Mayor after the Rising, J. Brennan Papers, NLI MS 26178.

238 Mahaffy, Diary.

239 Henry, Diary.

240 Douglas Hyde, Diary of Easter Week.

241 Nathan Papers, MS 477.

242 Douglas Hyde, Diary of Easter Week.

243 In an account by D Grimble, a GPO employee in 1916. NLI, MS 41611/1.

244 Terry de Valera, Memoir. p. 318.

245 Ibid.

246 Mrs Salkey's 1916 Journal, NLI MS 44622.

247 James Doyle, BMH WS.

248 Andrew MacDonnell, BMH WS.

249 Min Ryan, BMH WS.

250 O'Connor, 'Boland's Mill Area', p. 240.

251 Fintan Murphy, BMH 370.

9 The Rising Outside Dublin

1 For the Rising outside Dublin see Joyce, 'The Story of Limerick and Kerry'; Seumas O'Dubhghaill, 'Activities in Enniscorthy'; Mattie Nielan, 'The Rising in Galway'; Liam Ruiseal, 'The Position in Cork': all published in *Capuchin Annual* (1966). There is also a good account by Colonel Joe Lawless, 'The Fight at Ashbourne', *Capuchin Annual* (1966), pp. 307–16.

2 Joe Lawless, BMH WS 1043.

3 Ibid.

4 Mulcahy told the story of his involvement with Ashe's battalion in the Richard Mulcahy Tapes 004M18.

5 Joe Lawless, BMH WS 1043.

6 Ibid.

7 Mulcahy in the Richard Mulcahy Tapes 004M18.

8 Joe Lawless, BMH WS 1043.

9 Ibid; Mulcahy in the Richard Mulcahy Tapes 004M18.

10 Mulcahy in the Richard Mulcahy Tapes.

11 Joe Lawless, BMH WS 1043.

12 A memorandum from Sergeant O'Connell, the RIC officer who had gone ahead with the warning. (Mulcahy Papers, UCD).

13 Joe Lawless, BMH WS 1043.

14 Golden, *The Story of the Fight*.

15 Joe Lawless, BMH WS 1043.

16 Jerry Golden, *The Story of the Fight at Rath Cross Roads or The Battle of Ashbourne*, Allen Library, Dublin.

17 PRO WO 35/69.

18 Paddy Houlihan, The Battle of Ashbourne, NLI MS 18098.

19 Michael McAllister, BMH WS.

20 The description of the meeting is based on Mulcahy's own account in the Richard Mulcahy Tapes 004M18.

21 Joe Lawless, BMH WS 1043.

22 Michael McAllister, BMH WS.

23 Joe Lawless, BMH WS 1043.

24 Michael McAllister, BMH WS.

25 Joe Lawless, BMH WS 1043.

26 Ibid.

27 Ibid.

28 Ibid.

29 Florence O'Donoghue, 'Reorganisation of the Irish Volunteers 1916–1917' (1967), p. 383.

30 For the Mulcahy-Collins partnership see Risteard Mulcahy, *My Father, the General: Richard Mulcahy and the Military History of the Revolution* (Liberties Press, Dublin, 2009); Michael T. Foy, *Michael Collins's Intelligence War: The Struggle Between the British and the IRA 1919–1921* (The History Press, Stroud, 2006).

10 Suppression, Courts martial and Executions

1 This discussion of military aspects of the Rising is based mainly on the following: situation reports, PRO WO35/69; *On the Rebellion in Ireland*, report of Royal Commission (HMSO, London, 1916), Command Papers 8279, 8311; Hally, 'The Easter Rising in Dublin', Part 1 Vol. 7 (1966) pp. 213–6, & Part 2 Vol. 8 (1967) pp. 48–57; O'Neill, 'The Battle of Dublin, 1916', pp. 211–22; 'General Maxwell's Reports' *An tOglac*, (19 June 1926); undated report for chief secretary, 'The Sinn Fein or Irish Volunteers and the Rebellion', NAI DFA/IFS, Box 6, No 134, Part 5.

2 Ibid., pp. 31–2; Hally, 'The Easter Rising in Dublin', Part 2, pp. 48–51.

3 Wimborne to Birrell, at 12.58 p.m., 25 April 1916, Asquith Papers, MS 41–3, Bodleian Library, Oxford.

4 Report by Nathan, at 5.15 p.m., 26 April 1916, in PRO WO35/69.

5 Report at 10.55 p.m., 26 April, in ibid.

6 Ó Broin, *Dublin Castle and the 1916 Rising*, pp. 114–6; Sir George Arthur, *General Sir John Maxwell* (London, 1932), pp. 245–8 & passim.

7 Asquith to Kitchener, 26 April 1916, Kitchener Papers PRO 30/57/55; Asquith to King George V, 27 April, in PRO CAB37/146; Cabinet discussion in PRO CAB41/37.

8 Maxwell to Kitchener, 21 April, and Kitchener to Robertson, 26 April, in PRO 30/57/55; Arthur, *Maxwell*, pp. 247–8.

9 David Foxton, *Revolutionary Lawyers: Sinn Fein and the Courts in Ireland and Britain, 1916–1923* (Four Courts Press, Dublin, 2008), p. 67.

10 Arthur, *Maxwell*, p. 247.

11 Maxwell to his wife, 27 April 1916, Maxwell Papers, Box 6/9.

12 Arthur, *Maxwell*, p. 249.

13 See reports, 30 April and 2 May, in PRO WO35/69, and letter to wife, 30 April, Maxwell Papers, Box 6/9.

14 Report, 2 May, PRO WO35/69.

15 See comment dated 27 April 1916, in Nathan Papers, MS 476.

16 Ibid.

17 Notes to Pearse by Brigadier General Lowe, 29 April 1916, Kilmainham Museum, Dublin.

18 Maxwell to French, 29 April 1916; undated but almost certainly contemporary notes of meeting with Pearse: both in UCD P150/512.

19 The wire was sent at 9.15 a.m. and the reply at 11.30 a.m., 30 April, Nathan Papers, MS 477.

20 PRO CAB37/147, Paper No 34 forwarded by Esme Howard; ÓBroin, *Dublin Castle and the 1916 Rising*, p. 114.

21 Michael Ridge correspondence, Exhibitions Department, Imperial War Museum North, Manchester.

22 Hally, 'The Easter Rising in Dublin', Part 2, p. 51.

23 Captain E. Gerrard, BMH WS348; Oates, *The Sherwood Foresters*, p. 39.

24 Account by Lieutenant Henry Douglas. Sherwood Foresters, NLI MS 4796.

25 William Wylie, unpublished memoirs (in typescript), PRO30/89/2.

26 Instructions issued on 25 April to troops arriving at Kingstown on 26 April, in PRO WO35/69.

27 Asquith to King George V, 27 April, in PRO CAB37/146.

28 Arthur, *Maxwell*, p. 247.

29 Maxwell to his wife, 28 April 1916, Maxwell Papers, Box 6/9.

30 PRO CAB42/12, appendix 83A1.

31 Ibid., and supporting papers in PRO CAB37/146.

32 Ibid.

33 Arthur, *Maxwell*, pp. 272, 275.

34 Foxton, *Revolutionary Lawyers*, p. 66.

35 To his wife, early May, Maxwell Papers, Box 6/9; Ó Broin, *Dublin Castle and the 1916 Rising*, pp. 120–4; Foxton, *Revolutionary Lawyers*, p. 66.

36 In Nathan Papers, 3 May, MS 476.

37 Letters dated 27 April and 2 May, by Captain H. Peel, in IWM P391.

38 Letter by A.L. Franklin, IWM 93/25/1.

39 To his wife, 4 May, Maxwell Papers, Box 6/9.

40 Ibid.

41 Leon Ó Broin, *WE Wylie and the Irish Revolution, 1916–21* (Gill and Macmillan, Dublin, 1989), p. 29.

42 Maxwell to his wife, 20 May, 11 June, 20 July, 31 July, in Maxwell Papers, Box 6/9; Arthur, *Maxwell*, p. 265.

43 Arthur, *Maxwell*, p. 269; Maxwell Papers, passim, Boxes 1–6.

44 Maxwell memorandum, dated 13 May, Asquith Papers, MS 41–3.

45 Inspector General's Confidential Report for 1 April–31 May, dated 15 June 1916, in PRO CO904/99.

46 Arthur, *Maxwell*, p. 264.

47 Maxwell to French, 29 April 1916, UCD P150/512.

48 Ibid.; Maxwell to French, 30 April 1916.

49 Joe Lawless, BMH WS 1043.

50 Ibid; Fearghal McGarry, *The Rising, Ireland Easter 1916* (Oxford University Press, Oxford, 2010), p. 258.

51 William O'Brien, BMH WS 1766.

52 Charles Saurin, BMH WS 288.

53 Joe Lawless, BMH WS 1043.

54 Ibid.

55 Ibid.

56 Ibid.

57 Charles Saurin, BMH WS 288.

58 Andrew MacDonnell, BMH WS.

59 Joe Lawless, BMH WS 1043.

60 Gerald Doyle, BMH WS.

61 Robert Holland, Account of fighting at Marrowbone Lane, Allen Library, Dublin.

62 Ibid.; reports by Major-General S. MacSuibhne and P.J. O'Mara in NLI MS10915; account by Jack Plunkett, NLI MS 11397.

63 Maurice Collins, BMH WS 550.

64 John MacDonagh, BMH WS 219.

65 Constable P.J. Bermingham, BMH WS697; Piaras Beslai, in Ryan, *The Rising*, p. 258.

66 Maxwell to Kitchener, 2 May 1916, UCD P150/512.

67 Liam Tannam, BMH WS242.

68 Andrew MacDonnell, BMH WS.

69 Comment by Lieutenant-Colonel J.N. Galloway in IWM 87/45/1; Lieutenant-Colonel J.P.W. Jamie, MC, *The 177th Brigade 1914–18* (W. Thornley, Leicester, 1931), p. 14; Lieutenant W. Meakin, *The Fifth North Staffs and the North Midland Territorials, 1914–19* (Hughes and Harber, Longton, 1920), p. 73.

70 See proceedings of Kent's court-martial in PRO WO71/356; Barton, *The Secret Court Martial Records*, pp. 288–91.

71 Constable Frank King, BMH WS635; William Kent, BMH WS75; PRO WO71/356.

72 Lowe to Maxwell, 13, 27 May 1916, Asquith Papers, MS43.

73 Foxton, *Revolutionary Lawyers*, p. 104.

74 Wylie, memoirs.

75 Annie O'Brien, BMH WS 895.

76 Report for the chief secretary, 'The Sinn Fein or Irish Volunteers', in NAI DFA/IFS, Box 6, No 134, Part 5.

77 Judge Advocate General's Office to Sir Reginald Brade, Secretary, Army Council, 28 October 1916, PRO WO141/27.

78 Gerard Oram, *Worthless Men: Race, Eugenics and the Death Penalty in the British Army during the First World War*, pp. 69, 72–3; Gerard Oram, *Death Sentences passed by Military Courts of the British Army, 1914–24*, pp. 13–6.

79 Foxton, *Revolutionary Lawyers*, p. 104; *Manual of Military Law* (Stationary Office, London, 1914); Adrian Hardiman, '"Shot in Cold Blood" Military Law and Irish Perceptions in the Suppression of the 1916 Rebellion' in Gabriel Doherty and Dermot Keogh (eds), *1916, The Long Revolution* (Cork, Mercer Press, 2007), pp. 244–5.

80 Maxwell to Asquith, 13 May 1916, Asquith Papers, MS43.

81 Barton, *The Secret Court Martial Records*, pp. 41–5; Ó Broin, *WE Wylie*, p. 23; *Manual of Military Law*, passim.

82 Maxwell memorandum, 3 May 1916, in PRO WO35/69. Dr R.F. Tobin (St Vincent's Hospital) and Dr P.J. O'Farrell declared Connolly to be 'fit to undergo his trial ... His mind, memory and understanding [were] entirely unimpaired', PRO WO71/354; reports 2 & 3 May, PRO WO35/69.

83 Account by Jack Plunkett, NLI MS 11397.

84 Official reports of court martial proceedings of rebel leaders, PRO WO71/344–58; lists of the names of those court-martialled are given in PRO WO213/8.

85 Maconchy, *Memoirs*, p. 456; *Manual of Military Law*, p. 37; Jack Plunkett, BMH WS488; Jack Plunkett, NLI MS11397.

86 W.T. Cosgrave, BMH WS268; Barton, *The Secret Court Martial Records*, p. 46.

87 Official reports of court martial proceedings of rebel leaders, PRO WO71/344–58.

88 MacLochlainn, *Last Words*, p. 171.

89 See account by Maurice Brennan, NLI MS 10915; Sean McGarry's comments on Clarke, BMH WS 368.

90 Alfred Bucknill, BMH WS1019; *Manual of Military Law*, pp. 56–7.

91 PRO WO71/356.

92 PRO WO71/350; PRO WO71/351.

93 Wylie, memoirs.

94 W.T. Cosgrave, BMH WS268; John Shouldice, BMH WS162; official reports of court martial proceedings of rebel leaders, PRO WO71/344–58.

95 W.T. Cosgrave, BMH WS268; account by Patrick Doyle in the Allen Library, Dublin.

96 PRO WO71/348; Hardiman, 'Shot in Cold Blood', in Doherty and Keogh, *1916*, p. 246.

97 Wylie, memoirs.

98 Memorandum by Sir Reginald Brade, Secretary, Army Council, early January 1917, PRO WO141/27.

99 Donal McCracken, *McBride's Brigade*, p. 163.

100 PRO WO71/347; W.T. Cosgrave, BMH WS268.

101 Wylie, memoirs; MacLochlainn, *Last Words*, p. 100; Father Leonard, *Memories of Easter Week*.

102 William O'Brien, BMH WS 1766.

103 PRO WO71/352.

104 PRO WO71/347; MacLochlainn, *Last Words*, p. 44.

105 Wylie, memoirs.

106 PRO WO71/349.

107 MacAtasney, *Gerard Sean MacDiarmada*, p. 124; PRO WO71/344.

108 Maurice Collins, BMH WS 550; MacAtasney, *Gerard Sean MacDiarmada*, p. 133.

109 Denis McCullough, BMH WS915.

110 PRO WO71/346.

111 MacLochlainn, *Last Words*, p. 62.

112 Ibid., pp. 54–60.

113 PRO WO71/358.

114 Ibid.

115 PRO WO71/344.

116 PRO WO71/353.

117 Ibid.
118 PRO WO71/351.
119 Michael Heuston, BMH WS309.
120 Alfred Bucknill, BMH WS1019.
121 Foxton, *Revolutionary Lawyers*, p. 86; PRO WO71/356.
122 MacLochlainn, *Last Words*, p. 83; Father M O'Flanaghan, foreword to *Michael O'Hanrahan, Irish Heroines; being a lecture written during the winter preceding Easter Week* (The O'Hanrahans, Dublin, 1917).
123 PRO WO71/357.
124 PRO WO71/354.
125 PRO WO71/345.
126 Alfred Bucknill, BMH WS1019.
127 PRO WO71/345.
128 Ó Broin, *WE Wylie*, p. 21.
129 Desmond Ryan, *Irish Press*, 25 April 1961.
130 Countess of Fingall, *Seventy Years Young: Memories of Elizabeth, Countess of Fingall* (Lilliput, Dublin, 1991), p. 376.
131 Maconchy, *Memoirs*.
132 Wylie, memoirs; Barton, *The Secret Court Martial Records*, pp. 94–100.
133 Official record of trial, 4 May 1916, PRO HO144/1580/316818.
134 Alfred Bucknill, BMH WS1019.
135 PRO HO144/1580/316818.
136 Griffith and O'Grady, *Curious Journey*, p. 248; Eoin Neeson, *Birth of a Republic* (Prestige Books, Dublin, 1998), pp. 175–6.
137 Hally, 'The Easter Rising in Dublin', Part 2, p. 53.
138 Maxwell to his wife, 9 May, Maxwell Papers, Box 6/9.
139 Maxwell to Asquith, 9 May, Asquith Papers, MS 41–3.
140 Press cutting, June 1916, in de Valera Papers, UCD P150/512.
141 W.T. Cosgrave, BMH WS268.
142 Beaslai, *Irish Independent*, 21 January 1953.
143 William Wylie, BMH WS864.
144 Foxton, *Revolutionary Lawyers*, p. 86.
145 Account by Michael Kent, 8 May 1916, NLI MS15292; Michael Soughly, BMH WS189; Pat Cooke, *A History of Kilmainham Gaol, 1796–1924* (Stationary Office, Dublin, 1995), passim. The gaol was used for executions during the Irish civil war – on 17 November 1922, James Fisher, Peter Cassidy, John Gaffney and Fichafe Twohig were shot there and on 8 January 1923, Terence Brady, Leo Dowling, Sylvester Heaney, Anthony O'Reilly and Lawrence Sheehy.
146 Account by Jack Plunkett, NLI MS11397.
147 Alfred Bucknill, BMH WS1019.
148 Minute circulated by Brigadier J.R. Young, 2 May 1916, PRO WO35/67/2; account by A.A. Dickson, Sherwood Foresters, IWM 11650 01/49/1.
149 MacLochlainn, *Last Words*, pp. 103, 115–6.
150 Robert Barton, BMH WS264/1/3.
151 Account by A.A. Dickson, Sherwood Foresters, IWM 11650 01/49/1
152 O'Broin, *Dublin Castle and the 1916 Rising*, p. 139; Maxwell to Bonham Carter, 20 May 1916, UCD P150/512.

153 Minute by Young, PRO WO35/67/2.

154 Quoted in Peter Paul Galligan, BMH WS170.

155 Aloysius, Memories of Easter Week.

156 Nora O'Brien Connolly, BMH WS286.

157 Quoted in Captain E. Gerrard, BMH WS348.

158 See file on Major W.S. Lennon, PRO WO339/13484.

159 Account by Michael Kent, NLI MS15292.

160 Clarke, *Revolutionary Woman*, p. 92; MacLochlainn, *Last Words*, p. 84.

161 John McGallogly, BMH WS 244.

162 Beaslai, *Irish Independent*, 21 January 1953.

163 Aloysius, Memories of Easter Week.

164 Father Leonard, *Rebirth of a Nation*.

165 MacLochlainn, *Last Words*, p. 31.

166 Ibid., p. 33.

167 Clarke, *Revolutionary Woman*, p. 95.

168 Ibid., p. 127.

169 Michael Soughly, BMH WS189.

170 Aloysius, Memories of Easter Week; Alfred Bucknill, BMH WS1019.

171 Bradbridge, *The 59th Division 1915–1918*, p. 43.

172 Michael Soughly, BMH WS189; Maconchy, *Memoirs*, p. 456.

173 Account by A.A. Dickson Sherwood Foresters, IWM 11650 01/49/1

174 Account by Father Aloysius, in MacLochlainn, *Last Words*, pp. 214–5; Michael Soughly, BMH WS189.

175 MacLochlainn, *Last Words*, p. 79.

176 Clarke, *Revolutionary Woman*, p. 118.

177 Father Leonard, *Memories of Easter Week*; Madge Daly, BMH WS209; MacLochlainn, *Last Words*, pp. 68–74; note by A. Lee, dated 4 May 1916, in PRO WO35/67/1.

178 Clarke, *Revolutionary Woman*, p. 118.

179 MacLochlainn, *Last Words*, pp. 83–5.

180 Clarke, *Revolutionary Woman*, p. 119.

181 Eileen O'Hanrahan, BMH WS 270.

182 Grace Plunkett, NLI MS 21598–9; Grace Plunkett BMH WS257; Diarmuid Lynch NLI MS11128.

183 MacLochlainn, *Last Words*, pp. 96 & 105.

184 Father Augustine, BMH WS920; Father Leonard, *Memories of Easter Week*.

185 J.B. Lyons, *The Enigma of Tom Kettle: Irish Patriot, Essayist, Poet, British Soldier, 1880–1916* (Glendale Press, Dublin, 1983), p. 294.

186 Crime Branch Special Report on Maud Gonne, dated 28 September 1916, in PRO CO904/208; Jordan, p. 127.

187 Thomas Malllin, BMH WS382; MacLochlainn, *Last Words*, p. 122.

188 Annie O'Brien, BMH WS 805.

189 MacLochlainn, *Last Words*, passim.

190 Heuston to Walsh, NLI MS8497; letter to Mary, *Capuchin Annual*, 1966, p. 306.

191 Heuston Papers, Kilmainham Museum; Michael Heuston, BMH WS309; MacLochlainn, *Last Words*, p. 112.

192 MacLochlainn, *Last Words*, pp. 115–6.

193 Ibid., pp. 122–6.

194 Thomas Mallin, BMH WS382.

195 MacLochlainn, *Last Words*, p. 146.

196 Annie O'Brien, BMH WS 805.

197 MacLochlainn, *Last Words*, p. 136.

198 Lily O'Brennan, BMH WS264; MacLochlainn, *Last Words*, pp. 140–1.

199 Diary by Michael Kent, NLI MS15292.

200 Doyle, Reminiscences.

201 MacLochlainn, *Last Words*, pp. 152–3; Father Augustine, BMH WS920.

202 Annie O'Brien, BMH WS 805.

203 Diary of Michael Kent, NLI MS15292.

204 MacLochlainn, *Last Words*, p. 143; Father Augustine, BMH WS920.

205 Aine Ceannt, BMH WS264.

206 Father Albert, 'How Sean Heuston died', *Capuchin Annual*, (1966), pp. 305–6.

207 Father Augustine in a letter detailing the death of Colbert, *Capuchin Annual*, (1966), p. 304.

208 MacLochlainn, *Last Words*, p. 156; William Kent, BMH WS75.

209 MacLochlainn, *Last Words*, p. 167.

210 Parliamentary Debates, Commons, 11 May 1916, Vol. LXXXII, col. 955.

211 MacLochlainn, *Last Words*, p. 171.

212 Ibid., p. 172; Min Ryan, BMH WS416.

213 Min Ryan, BMH WS416 244; account by Frank Thornton, UCD P67/45.

214 Father Patrick Browne, BMH WS729.

215 MacAtasney, *Gerard Sean MacDiarmada*, p. 142.

216 MacLochlainn, *Last Words*, p. 168–9.

217 Min Ryan, BMH WS416.

218 From an article by Min Ryan in the possession of her son Risteard Mulcahy who generously allowed me to examine and use it.

219 Aloysius, Memories of Easter Week.

220 William O'Brien, BMH WS1766.

221 Nora O'Brien Connolly, BMH WS286; MacLochlainn, *Last Words*, p. 191.

222 Account by Nora and Lily Connolly, NLI MS 13947.

223 Aloysius, Memories of Easter Week.

224 Michael Soughly, BMH WS189.

225 William O'Brien, BMH WS1766; Robert Barton, BMH WS264/1/3.

226 Aloysius, 'Personal Recollections', pp. 280–91.

227 Ibid.

228 Ibid.

229 Ibid.

230 Ibid.

231 Father Augustine, BMH WS.

232 Eileen O'Hanrahan, BMH WS 270.

233 Father Augustine, BMH WS.

234 Aloysius, Memories of Easter Week.

235 Aloysius, 'Personal Recollections'.

236 Ibid.

237 Annie O'Brien, BMH WS 805.

238 Maxwell to Kitchener, 2 May 1916, UCD P150/512.

239 Maxwell to his wife, 9 May 1916, Maxwell Papers, Box 6/9.

240   French to Maxwell, 3 May 1916, UCD P150/512; PRO CAB42/12/16315.

241   Asquith to King George V, 6 May 1916, PRO CAB41/37/19.

242   Maxwell to his wife, 12 May 1916, Maxwell Papers, Box 6/9; Charles
      Townshend, *Easter 1916; The Irish Rebellion* (Penguin Books, London, 2006),
      pp. 279–80; Barton, *The Secret Court Martial Records*, pp. 86–9; Robert Kee,
      The Green Flag; a History of Irish Nationalism (Weidenfield and Nicolson,
      London, 1972), p. 577.

243   Alfred Bucknill, BMH WS1019; Maxwell to Bonham Carter, 20 May 1916,
      UCD P150/512; Barton, *The Secret Court Martial Records*, pp. 89–90.

244   Maxwell to French, 9 May 1916, UCD P150/512; Maxwell to Asquith, 10
      May 1916, Asquith Papers, MS43.

245   Maxwell memorandum, 11 May 1916, entitled 'Brief history of rebels on
      whom it has been necessary to inflict the supreme penalty', Asquith Papers,
      MS43. Hereafter Maxwell, memorandum.

246   Maxwell to Kitchener, 11 May 1916, UCD P150/512.

247   Maxwell to his wife, 4 June 1916, Maxwell Papers, Box 2/6; Foxton,
      Revolutionary Lawyers, p. 75.

248   Maxwell, memorandum. The quotations and references that follow are from
      this document.

249   Ibid.; Townshend, *Easter 1916*, p. 283.

250   Maxwell, memorandum.

251   Edward Bell to J.F. Moylan, 1 July 1916, and Moylan's reply, 12 August 1916,
      PRO HO144/10309/79275; Barton, *The Secret Court Martial Records*, pp. 91–4;
      Alfred Bucknill, BMH WS1019.

252   Wylie, memoirs.

253   Maxwell to his wife, 23 May 1916, Maxwell Papers, Box 6/9.

254   Maxwell to French, 4 May 1916, UCD P150/512; Tierney, *Eoin MacNeill*, p. 222.

255   Tierney, *Eoin MacNeill*, p. 227.

256   Wylie, memoirs; Tierney, *Eoin MacNeill*, pp. 233 & 239.

257   Wylie, memoirs.

258   French to Maxwell, 3 May 1916, UCD P150/512.

259   Parliamentary Debates, Commons, 27 April 1916, Vol. LXXXII, col. 2511; 11
      May 1916, Vol. LXXXII, cols 954, 955, 959.

260   Roy Jenkins, *Asquith* (Collins, London, 1964), p. 398.

261   Arthur, *Maxwell*, p.258; Maxwell to Bonham Carter, 20 May 1916, UCD
      P150/512.

262   Cabinet conclusions, 26 October 1916, PRO CAB41/37.

263   Account by Maurice Brennan, NLI MS10915.

264   Ó Broin, *WE Wylie*, p. 10.

265   Percy A. Bick to P.M. Yearsley, 29 May 1916, in IWM 27/11/2.

266   Inspector-General's Confidential Report for 1 April–31 May 1916, dated 15
      June, and another dated 10 August 1916, PRO CO904/23.

267   Cabinet conclusions, 19 September, 11 October 1916, PRO CAB41/37;
      McGarry, *The Rising*, p. 273.

268   County Inspectors' Reports, PRO CAB904/99, 100.

269   Maxwell to his wife, 11 June 1916, Maxwell Papers, Box 6/9.

270   Arthur, *Maxwell*, p. 268 & p. 275; Maxwell to his wife, 30 May, Maxwell
      Papers, Box 6/9; O'Broin, *Dublin Castle and the 1916 rising*, p. 143.

271 Arthur, *Maxwell*, p. 268; Maxwell to his wife, 30 May, Maxwell Papers, Box 6/9.

272 Maxwell to his wife, 30 May, 19 June, Maxwell Papers, Box 6/9.

273 Maxwell to his wife 16, 30 May, 19 June, 27 July 1916, Maxwell Papers, Box 6/9; Arthur, *Maxwell*, pp. 261, 266, 268–9; Maxwell to French, 16 May 1916, UCD P150/512.

274 Maxwell to Asquith, 15 June, Maxwell Papers, Box 2/8.

275 Maxwell to his wife, 1 June, Maxwell Papers, Box 6/9; Foxton, *Revolutionary Lawyers*, p. 44.

276 Maxwell to his wife, 1, 23 June, and 5, 20 July, Maxwell Papers, Box 6/9.

277 Asquith to Maxwell, 27 May, Maxwell Papers, Box 2/8.

278 Asquith to King George V, 26 July, in PRO CAB41/37.

279 Memoranda by E. Blackwell, 15 July 1916, in PRO HO144/1636/311643/52; memoranda by C.E. Trump, 17 July 1916, in PRO HO144/1636/311643/53.

280 Asquith's correspondence with King George V, late July–early August, PRO CAB41/37; Jenkins, *Asquith*, pp. 403–4.

281 PRO WO71/345.

282 Lynas to his wife, 15 July 1916, IWM 89/7/1.

Bibliography

A complete guide to the sources is to be found in the endnotes. The following comprises only the major collections and some useful secondary accounts of the Easter Rising or specific aspects of the event.

Primary Sources
Bureau of Military Archives, Dublin

Rev. Fr Aloysius, OFM Cap.
Liam Archer
Rev. Fr Augustine, OFM Cap.
J. Austin
Richard Balfe
Piaras Beaslai
P.J. Bermingham
Rt Rev. Mgr Peter Browne
Eamon Bulfin
Seosamh de Brun
James Burke
Catherine Byrne
Sean Byrne
Ignatius Callender
Aine Ceannt
William Christian
Sean Cody
Harry Colley
Martin Conlon
Matthew Connolly
Richard Connolly
Liam Cosgrave

James Coughlan
Michael Crèmen
James Crenigan
Francis Daly
Madge Daly
Paddy Daly
Seamus Daly
Thomas Devine
Geraldine Dillon
Joseph Doolan
Eamonn Dore
C. Doyle
James Doyle
Thomas Doyle
Louise Gavan Duffy
Patrick Egan
Peter Folan
James Foran
Frank Gaskin
Captain E. Gerrard
Jerry Golden
Joseph Gleeson

Rose Hackett
Richard Hayes
Frank Henderson
Aine Heron
Michael Heuston
Archie Heron
Mrs Bulmer Hobson (Claire Gregan)
Robert Holland
Julia Hughes
Seamus Kavanagh
Paulin Keating
John Keegan
Luke Kennedy
Sean Kennedy
James Kenny
Seamus Kenny
William Kent
Martin King
Michael Knightley
Nicholas Laffin
Joe Lawless
Diarmuid Lynch
Fionan Lynch
Kathleen Lynn
Bridget Lyons
George Lyons
Dan McCarthy
John MacDonagh
Bernard McAllister
Michael McAllister
Thomas McCarthy
Liam Manahan
Thomas Mallin
Annie Mannion
Eamon Martin
Tommy McCarthy
Denis McCullough
Andrew McDonnell
Mick McDonnell
John McGallgolly
Maeve McGarry
Milo McGarry
Sean McGarry
Sean McLoughlin
Rose McNamara
Agnes MacNeill
Tommy Meldon
Arthur Mitchell

Helena Moloney
Phyllis Morken
Mrs Richard Mulcahy (Min Ryan)
Fintan Murphy
Gregory Murphy
Seamus Murphy
Sean Murphy
William Murphy
Joseph Murray
Henry Murray
Eugene Nevin
Harry Nicholls
Liam Ó Briain
Annie O'Brien
Lawrence O'Brien
William O'Brien
Maire O'Brolchain
Joseph O'Byrne
Liam O'Carroll
Liam O'Carroll
Mortimer O'Connell
Joseph O'Connor
Con O'Donovan
Sean O'Duffy
Michael O'Flanagan
Liam O'Flaitheartaigh
Charles O'Grady
Eily O'Hanrahan
Sean O'Keefe
Kitty O'Kelly
Margaret O'Kelly
Seamus O'Kelly
Colm O'Loughlin
William Oman
Aine O'Rahilly
Michael O'Reilly
James O'Shea
Seamus O'Sullivan
Marie Perolz
Jack Plunkett
Seamus Pounch
Sean Prendergast
Eamon Price
Sean Price
Molly Reynolds
J. Ridgeway
Frank Robbins
Charles Saurin

Joseph Schollen
Jack Shouldice
T. Slater
Thomas Smart
Patrick Smyth
Michael Soughley
Michael Staines
Bill Stapleton
John J. Styles
Liam Tannam

Bridget Thornton
Eilis Ui Chonaill
Nancy Wyse-Power
James Walsh
Thomas Walsh
Patrick Ward
William Whelan
Michael Wilson
Thomas Young

Collected Documents

National Archives, Dublin
Chief Secretary's Official Registered Correspondence

National Library of Ireland
Ceannt-Brennan papers
Roger Casement papers
John Clarke diary
Augustine Henry diary
Bulmer Hobson papers
Dick Humphries diary
Diarmuid Lynch papers
Eoin MacNeill papers
William O'Brien papers
Florence O'Donoghue papers
Seamus Scully account. *Moore Street, 1916*
Dorothy Stopford diary

Trinity College Dublin
Douglas Hyde diary; Elsie Mahaffy diary
Peadar Kearney papers

Allen Library, Edmund Rice House, North Richmond Street, Dublin
Depositions by Father Aloysius, Peadar Bracken, Paddy Daly, Peadar Doyle, Jerry
Golden, Robert Holland, William Oman Patrick Stephenson and Michael Walker

University College, Dublin
Eoin MacNeill papers
Depositions by Liam Archer, Simon Donnelly, Frank Thornton and Oscar Traynor

Public Record Office, London
Kitchener papers
Cabinet papers
Colonial Office papers
War Office papers

Imperial War Museum
P.A. Bick papers
A.A. Dickson memoirs
A. Hannant papers
A.M. Jameson papers

British Army Museum, London
Memoirs of Brigadier E.W.S.K. Maconchy, 1860–1920

Bodleian Library, Oxford
Asquith papers
Nathan papers

Princeton University
Sir John Maxwell papers

Tapes
Richard Mulcahy tapes. I am grateful to Risteard Mulcahy for his generosity in providing us with his father's tapes which are an invaluable asset to Irish historians.

Secondary Sources

Books
Arthur, Sir George, *General Sir John Maxwell* (Murray, London, 1932)
Barton, Brian, *The Secret Court Martial Records of the Easter Rising* (The History Press, Stroud, 2010)
Bateson, Ray, *They Died By Pearse's Side* (Irish Graves Publications, Dublin, 2010)
Caulfield, Max, *The Easter Rebellion* (New English Library, London, 1965)
Clarke, Kathleen, *Revolutionary Woman: An Autobiography, 1878–1972* (The O'Brien Press Ltd, Dublin, 1991)
Connell Jnr, Joseph, *Dublin in Rebellion; a Directory, 1913–23* (The Lilliput Press, Dublin, 2006)
Cooke, Pat, *A History of Kilmainham Gaol, 1796–1924* (Stationary Office, Dublin, 1995)
Dangerfield, George, *The Damnable Question: A Study in Anglo-Irish Relations* (Constable, London, 1977)
Devine, Francis and O'Riordan, Manus, *James Connolly, Liberty Hall and the 1916 Rising* (Irish Labour History Society, Dublin, 2006)
Doherty, Gabriel and Keogh, Dermot, *1916, The Long Revolution* (Mercier Press, Cork, 2007)
Duff, Charles, *Six Days to Shake an Empire* (Dent, London, 1966)
Dunsany, Lord, *Patches of Sunlight* (William Heinemann Ltd, London, 1938)
Foster, R.F., *Modern Ireland 1600–1972* (Penguin, London, 1989)
Fox, R.M., *The History of the Irish Citizen Army* (James Duffy, Dublin, 1943)
Foxton, David, *Revolutionary Lawyers, Sinn Fein and the Crown Courts in Ireland and Britain 1916–23* (Four Courts Press, Dublin, 2008)

Hay, Marnie, *Bulmer Hobson and the Nationalist Movement in Twentieth-Century Ireland* (Manchester University Press, Manchester, 2009)

Hegarty, Shane and O'Toole, Fintan, *The Irish Times Book of the Easter Rising* (Gill & Macmillan Ltd, Dublin, 2006)

Henry, William Henry, *Supreme Sacrifice: The Story of Eamonn Ceannt 1881–1916* (Mercier Press, Cork, 2005)

Hobson, Bulmer, *Ireland: Yesterday and Tomorrow* (Anvil Books, Tralee, 1968)

Holt, Edgar, *Protest in Arms 1916–1923* (Putnam, London, 1960)

Jeffery, Keith, *The GPO and the Easter Rising* (Irish Academic Press, Dublin, 2006)

Kluge, Hans-Dieter, *Irland in der deutschen Geschichtswissenschaft, Politik und Propaganda* (P. Lang, Frankfurt am Main, 1985)

Lyons, F.S.L., *Ireland since the Famine* (Fontana, London, 1986)

Lynch, Diarmuid, *The I.R.B. and the 1916 Insurrection* (Mercier Press, Cork, 1957)

MacAtasney, *Gerard Sean MacDiarmada; The Mind of the Revolution* (Drumlin Publications, Manorhamilton, 2004)

MacLochlainn, Piaras F., *Last Words: Letters and Statements of the Leaders Executed after the Rising at Easter 1916* (Stationery Office, Dublin, 1990)

McCarthy, Cal, *Cumann na mBan and the Irish Revolution* (Cork, The Collins Press, 2007)

McCracken, Donal, *MacBride's Brigade; Irish Commanders In the Anglo-Boer War* (Four Courts Press, Dublin, 1997)

McGarry, Fearghal, *The Rising Ireland: Easter 1916* (Oxford University Press, Oxford, 2010)

McHugh, R., *Dublin, 1916* (Arlington Books, Dublin, 1966)

Manual of Military Law (London, Stationery Office, 1914)

Martin, F.X., *The Irish Volunteers, 1913–1915* (James Duffy, Dublin, 1963)

———, *The Easter Rising and University College, Dublin* (Browne & Nolan, Dublin, 1966)

———, *Leaders and Men of the Easter Rising* (Methuen, London, 1967)

Matthews, Ann, *Renegades; Irish Republican Women, 1900–1922* (Cork, Mercier Press, 2010)

Morgan, Austen, *James Connolly: A Political Biography* (Manchester University Press, Manchester, 1988)

Nevin, Donal, *James Connolly* (Gill & Macmillan Ltd, Dublin, 2005)

Ó Broin, Leon, *Dublin Castle and the 1916 Rising: the Story of Sir Matthew Nathan* (Helican, Dublin, 1966)

———, *W E Wylie and the Irish Revolution, 1916–1921* (Gill and Macmillan, Dublin, 1989)

O'Donnell, Ruan, *The Impact of the 1916 Rising: Among the Nations* (Irish Academic Press, Dublin, 2008)

Ó Dubhghaill, M., *Insurrection Fires at Eastertide* (The Mercier Press, Cork, 1966)

O'Rahilly, Aodogán, *Winding the Clock: O'Rahilly and the 1916 Rising* (Lilliput Press, Dublin, 1991)

Oram, Gerard, *Death Sentences passed by Military Courts of the British Army, 1914–24* (Boutle, London, 1998)

———, *Worthless Men; Race, Eugenics and the Death Penalty in the British Army during the First World War* (Boutle, London, 1998)

Reid, B.L., *The Lives of Roger Casement* (Yale University Press, New Haven, 1978)

Le Roux, Louis, *Tom Clarke and the Irish Freedom Movement* (Talbot Press, Dublin, 1936)

Robbins, Frank, *Under the Starry Plough; Recollections of the Irish Citizen Army* (Dublin, The Academy Press, 1977)

Ryan, Annie, *Witnesses; Inside the Easter Rising* (Liberties Press, Dublin, 2005)

Ryan, Desmond, *The Rising: The Complete Story of Easter Week* (Golden Eagle Books, Dublin, 1949)

Stephens, James, *The Insurrection in Dublin* (Colin Smyth, Gerrards Cross, 1978)

Taillon, Ruth, *The Women of 1916* (Beyond the Pale Publications, Belfast, 1996)

Thompson, William, *The Imagination of an Insurrection: Dublin, Easter 1916* (Oxford University Press, 1967)

Tierney, Michael, *Eoin MacNeill: Scholar and Man of Action, 1867–1945* (Clarendon Press, Oxford, 1980)

Townshend, Charles, *Easter 1916; The Irish Rebellion* (Penguin Books, London, 2005)

Warwick-Haller, Adrian and Sally (eds), *Letters from Dublin, Easter 1916: Alfred Fannin's Diary of the Rising* (Irish Academic Press, Dublin, 1995)

Wills, Clair, *Dublin 1916: The Siege of the GPO* (Profile, London, 2009)

Articles

Doerries, Reinhard, 'Die Mission Sir Roger Casements im Deutschen Reich 1914–1916', in *Historische Zeitschrift* (1976)

Hardiman, Adrian, '"Shot in Cold Blood" Military Law and Irish Perceptions in the Suppression of the 1916 Rebellion' in *1916, The Long Revolution*, eds Gabriel Doherty and Dermot Keogh (Cork, Mercer Press, 2007)

Jenkins, Robin, '"Old Black". The life of Major General C.G. Blackadder, 1869–1921', in *Transactions of Leicestershire Archaeological and Historical Society*, No 80 (2006)

Kratz, Andreas, 'Die Mission Joseph Mary Plunketts im Deutschen Reich und ihre Bedeutung für den Osteraufstand 1916', in *Historische Mitteilungen* (1995)

MacDonagh, Donagh, 'Irish Leaders of our Time: Sean MacDiarmada', in *An Cosantoir* (March 1945)

———, 'Irish Leaders of our Time: Thomas MacDonagh', in *An Cosantoir* (October 1945)

———, 'Irish Leaders of our Time: Joseph Plunkett', in *An Cosantoir* (November 1945)

———, 'Irish Leaders of our Time: Eoin MacNeill', in *An Cosantoir* (December 1945)

Martin, F.X., 'Select Documents: Eoin MacNeill on the 1916 Rising', in *Irish Historical Studies*, Vol. xii, No 47 (March 1961)

———, 'Myth, Fact and Mystery', in *Studia Hibernica*, No 7 (1967)

———, 'The 1916 Rising – A Coup d'Etat or a "Bloody Protest"?', in *Studia Hibernica*, No 8 (1968)

O'Donoghue, Florence, 'Plans for the 1916 Rising', in *University Review* (March 1963)

The commemorative issue of the *Capuchin Annual* (1966) contains many interesting articles on the Easter Rising.

Index